THE WPA OKLAHOMA SLAVE NARRATIVES

D1594445

THE PRINTED PAGE IS EVERYMAN'S UNIVERSITY.

THE WPA
OKLAHOMA SLAVE
NARRATIVES

Edited by T. Lindsay Baker
and Julie P. Baker

UNIVERSITY OF OKLAHOMA PRESS : NORMAN AND LONDON

ALSO BY T. LINDSAY BAKER

The First Polish Americans: Silesian Settlements in Texas (College Station, Tex., 1979)
The Polish Texans (San Antonio, Tex., 1982)
The Early History of Panna Maria, Texas (Lubbock, 1975)
A Field Guide to American Windmills (Norman, 1985)
Building the Lone Star: An Illustrated Guide to Historic Sites (College Station, Tex., 1986)
Ghost Towns of Texas (Norman, 1986)
Adobe Walls: The History and Archeology of the 1874 Trading Post (with Billy R. Harrison) (College Station, Tex., 1986)
Lighthouses of Texas (College Station, Tex., 1991)
Blades in the Sky: Windmilling through the Eyes of B. H. "Tex" Burdick (Lubbock, 1992)

This book is published with the generous assistance of the Wallace C. Thompson Endowment Fund, University of Oklahoma Foundation.

Library of Congress Cataloging-in-Publication Data

The WPA Oklahoma slave narratives / edited by T. Lindsay Baker and Julie P. Baker.
    p. cm.
    Includes bibliographical references (p.) and index.
    ISBN 0-8061-2792-9 (cloth : alk. paper)
    ISBN 0-8061-2859-3 (paper : alk. paper)
    1. Slaves—Southern States—Biography. 2. Afro-Americans—Oklahoma—Interviews. 3. Oklahoma—Biography. 4. Afro-Americans—Oklahoma—History—Sources. I. Baker, T. Lindsay. II. Baker, Julie P. (Julie Philips), 1943– . III. United States. Work Projects Administration.
E444.W82 1996
305.5'67'092273—dc20
[B]   95-16222
                                              CIP

Book designed by Bill Cason

   The paper in this book meets the guidelines for permanence and durability of the Committee on Production Guidelines for Book Longevity of the Council on Library Resources, Inc. ∞

In memory of Eva Strayhorn and Charley Williams,
masters of the African American art of storytelling

CONTENTS

ILLUSTRATIONS

PREFACE

"We have a whole box full of Oklahoma freedmen's narratives that nobody has ever done very much with. Do you want to see them?" That question from an archivist with an underused collection prompted this project to compile and publish remembrances of Oklahoma blacks who had been born into slavery.

The two of us, who were not looking for any new projects, were at the Archives and Manuscripts Division of the Oklahoma Historical Society in spring 1990 researching another topic. When archivist William D. Welge suggested that we might find specific data we were seeking in the ex-slave narratives he held, we took a look. Inside the storage box we made a once-in-a-lifetime discovery: the surviving papers and literary remains of the Oklahoma Federal Writers' Project effort of more than half a century ago to locate and interview elderly Oklahomans who had lived as slaves.

In the box were old yellowed file folders, some of them identified with names and others blank, each containing equally yellowed typescripts and sometimes manuscripts. On the often brittle pages were the remembrances of a time when men, women, and children were sold like horses and mules, when African Americans in the South lacked even the most basic rights as humans. Jumbled together were interview notes, identified and unidentified typescripts, letters, memoranda, and scribbled notes that at the time made little sense. Many of the items were still held together with rusty straight pins. It was apparent that very few researchers had handled these materials.

That very day we began photocopying the contents of the box, continuing on another research trip until we had reproduced every shred of paper, approximately twelve hundred pages of typescript and manuscript materials. Here were the guts of the 1937–39 Oklahoma Slave Narrative Project. The big question after we had photocopied the many pages remained "What do we really have here?" The material was obviously of more than passing interest, but how significant was it? The answer came a few months later.

In August 1990 we traveled to Washington, D.C., for research in the National Archives and the Library of Congress on yet another topic. During this time we visited the Manuscript Division of the Library of Congress, the repository for the "official" slave narrative collection generated by field work in several states by the 1930s Federal

Writers' Project. There we sought to ascertain exactly what Oklahoma materials had survived in Washington. As expected, we found the big grayish-green volumes containing the ribbon-copy typescripts of the roughly two thousand interviews that had been forwarded to project headquarters in the years 1937–39. Along with the official slave narratives, we also located a nearly complete carbon copy set of the final drafts of the narratives, supplementary materials sent from Oklahoma City, and appraisal sheets that had been prepared by Benjamin A. Botkin, folklore director for the project, evaluating the individual interviews. The major discovery at the Library of Congress, however, was confirmation of our suspicion that the Oklahoma Historical Society held interviews that had never been sent to Washington—fifty-five of them.

After we had learned that the Oklahoma City and the Washington collections each held interviews not in the other's holdings, we began work preparing this volume to publish for the first time all of the known Federal Writers' Project Oklahoma slave narratives. Special acknowledgment must be given to the University of Oklahoma Press, which from the outset proposed that the volume present all of the known WPA Oklahoma slave narratives unabridged and in their entirety. From the outset of manuscript preparation, the publisher has viewed this as a major (and expensive) scholarly publishing project, and editor John N. Drayton and his staff have offered continuous encouragement and support.

Archivists and librarians at both the Oklahoma Historical Society and the Library of Congress went to great lengths to make the raw materials available. Were it not for the suggestion of William D. Welge, Archivist at the Oklahoma Historical Society, that the Oklahoma narratives might provide a source of documentation on regional history, we would never have known about their existence. Bob Blackburn, Assistant Director of the society, worked throughout the editorial process to facilitate research and to provide permission for reproducing materials. In addition to Welge and his staff in the Archives and Manuscripts Division, special assistance came from Edward C. Shoemaker in the Library Resources Division, together with his staff and his ever helpful volunteers, and from Delbert Amen and his colleagues in the Newspaper Division. At the Library of Congress, the reference staff in the Manuscript Division did all in their capacity to make materials available, to facilitate the reproduction of pertinent items, and to make research by out-of-town scholars as efficient as possible.

Numerous librarians and archivists have contributed time and assistance to the preparation of this study. At the libraries of Baylor University special help came from Barbara D. Cantrell, Interlibrary
Loans Librarian; Janet E. Sheets, Reference Librarian; and John Wilson, Documents Librarian. At the Texas Collection, the special regional collection in the Baylor University Libraries, Director Kent
Keeth, Archivist Ellen K. Brown, and Librarian Michael Toon all
moved mountains to make pertinent reference materials available.

In Oklahoma repositories, special thanks go to Gary L. Harring-
ton, Head and Preservation Officer for the Oklahoma State Archives;
all the staff in the Western History Collections of the University of
Oklahoma; the staff in Special Collections at the University of Tulsa
Library; and the reference staff at the University of Oklahoma General Libraries. Special thanks go to Dr. Jimmie Lee Franklin, historian of the blacks in Oklahoma, for encouragement and insights
shared in personal consultation at the Southern Historical Association annual meeting.

Numerous librarians and archivists around the United States
contributed information used in the preparation of the study.
Among these individuals are Robert L. Schaadt and Darlene Mott at
the Sam Houston Regional Library and Research Center, Liberty,
Texas; David E. Montgomery at the Tyrrell Historical Library in
Beaumont, Texas; Roberta Allen, Director of Reference and Archives,
Danville Public Library, Danville, Illinois; Ann Alley, Archivist,
Tennessee State Library and Archives, Nashville, Tennessee; Carol
Caplan, Nashville Room, Public Library of Nashville and Davidson
County, Nashville, Tennessee; Jerry C. Cashion, Research Supervisor,
and Donna K. Flowers, Special Projects Archivist, Division of
Archives and History, North Carolina Department of Cultural Re-
sources, Raleigh, North Carolina; Judy Bolton, Public Services,
Louisiana and Lower Mississippi Valley Collection, Hill Memorial
Library, Louisiana State University, Baton Rouge, Louisiana; and
Kathryn M. Harris, Reference and Technical Services, Illinois State
Library, Springfield, Illinois. The General Reference Branch at the
National Archives and Records Administration, Washington, D.C.,
provided important copies of pertinent manuscript materials relating to the informants' remembrances, while the Fort Worth regional
branch of the National Archives made available manuscript records
of the Dawes Commission.

A number of individuals have made special contributions to the
preparation of this study of the Oklahoma slave narratives. William W.

Gwaltney, Superintendent of the Booker T. Washington National Monument, over a period of years shared significant insights into the feelings of the informants. Dr. Alwyn Barr at Texas Tech University assisted in helping us understand the general context of the informants' remembrances and in suggesting sources for corroborating content in the narratives. Dr. Stuart Sprague of Morehead State University gave important direction to locating the compiled military services records of informants and individuals mentioned in their remembrances. Calvin B. Smith, Chair of the Department of Museum Studies at Baylor University, not only allowed editor T. Lindsay Baker to have work schedule flexibility to undertake research in both Oklahoma and Washington, D.C., but also provided constant encouragement.

This study was supported in part by funds from the Baylor University Research Committee. This assistance facilitated several trips to conduct research in the University of Oklahoma Libraries at Norman, Oklahoma, and in the Oklahoma Historical Society and the Oklahoma Division of Libraries in Oklahoma City.

Special thanks go to several individuals who reviewed portions of the manuscript before its publication. These good friends and colleagues were Dr. Bob Blackburn and William D. Welge, both at the Oklahoma Historical Society, and Debra A. Reid, Theresa O. Grose, and David O. Lintz, all colleagues on the staff of the Strecker Museum at Baylor University. Responsibility for all errors lies with the editors.

THE WPA OKLAHOMA SLAVE NARRATIVES

INTRODUCTION

Lucinda Davis, blind and eighty-nine years old, wearing a gingham dress and holding her cane, sat barefooted on the porch of her daughter's house at 710 North Lansing in Tulsa. Behind her chair, rags poked through holes in the screen door kept flies out of the house. Having spent all of her life in the country, Mrs. Davis was annoyed by the city noises and by grandchildren who did not mind.

Charles Willis also sat on his front porch, but he was 115 miles away, at 714 N.E. 4th in Oklahoma City, sucking on lemon-drop candies. Hard of hearing and losing his eyesight, he visited with Oklahoma Writers' Project reporter Ida Belle Hunter. After telling her about his memories of slavery on a Mississippi plantation, he unexpectedly asked, "How old are you? Would you marry a man 90 years old?" chuckling, "I would like to marry a nice gal wid a job." Then he asked his daughter to bring him a drink of water and to help him off the porch and into the house.

Octogenarian Lizzie Farmer was living in servants' quarters behind a home "in the better residential district" of McAlester, Oklahoma. Writers' Project reporter Jessie R. Ervin found her there, physically unable to "work in white folks' kitchens" any more, but spending part of each day "doing little extra jobs for her friends" and praying for those in need. Mrs. Farmer reminisced with the white field worker about her life as a vaudeville dancer. As Ervin jotted down notes, the elderly woman explained that in one routine she danced wearing unbuttoned hightop shoes: "My partner would stoop to button them for me. I would get my pistol out of my shirtwaist and shoot him down, without losing a step."

Who were these elderly Oklahomans? They were African Americans who had been born into slavery and who in the mid-1930s shared the stories of their lives with field workers from the Oklahoma Writers' Project. Over a three-year period, former slaves were identified and interviewed by project personnel who sought them out and recorded their stories on notepads. As a consequence of this early oral-history project, we have a remarkable record today of the lives of pioneers who helped to shape society in Oklahoma.[1]

The Oklahoma slave narratives take the form of autobiographical accounts of the lives of black Oklahomans. For the most part the stories were prepared as the Oklahoma portion of a project undertaken in seventeen states to record the remembrances of African Americans who had been born into slavery. The narratives in reality consist of notes from interviews which were edited into a more-or-less standard format and presented as if they had not been prompted by the field reporters' questions. Once the interview transcripts were placed into this regular form, and sometimes reorganized to make them more understandable, the final typewritten drafts were forwarded to national project headquarters in Washington, D.C. There twenty-three hundred interviews with former slaves from several states, including seventy-five oral histories from blacks in Oklahoma, have been available to scholars for more than half a century.[2] Not all the interviews, however, were sent to Washington. In the case of Oklahoma, fifty-five additional interviews were recorded but for one reason or another were never forwarded, perhaps because they contained material at the time considered racially sensitive. These latter interviews today may comprise some of the most interesting.

In reading the slave narratives, one must be aware of several factors involved in their creation. Clearly the texts came from individuals who had lived as slaves and subsequently as freedmen and -women. They genuinely understood the experience of slavery from the inside, and many of them had conveyed it orally to their younger family members. By the time these individuals were interviewed in the mid-1930s, however, they were necessarily in their seventies, eighties, nineties, or even older. Over the years some of their memories had dimmed, while others remained as bright as if the events had just occurred. For many of the interviewees, the remembrances of slavery were those of childhood, lacking the harshness inherent in the memories of older respondents who had experienced slavery as adults.

The reporters sent to the field to collect the narratives were both black and white, and the responses elicited by white field workers likely differed considerably from those gathered by African American reporters. The 1930s rules of racial etiquette were carefully followed. Elderly informants dared not offend local white people or presumed agents of the federal government, so at times they told the field reporters what they wanted to hear. Many of the interviewees began with an almost obligatory statement about how good their masters had been, before they proceeded to describe abuses and cruelty. Some apparently did have humane masters; other owners, however, were seemingly psychopathic. Readers of the slave narratives must approach them with the same caution applied to any other primary historical evidence.[3]

Although the individuals interviewed in the Oklahoma Slave Narrative Project lived within the state at the time they shared their remembrances with field workers, they did not necessarily live there while in bondage. Twenty-eight of the 130 informants were actually in servitude in present-day Oklahoma as slaves of American Indians who were members of the Creek, Cherokee, Chickasaw, or Choctaw nation. The remaining 102 narratives came from people who were held in bondage in other states and who later moved to Oklahoma, many of them soon after the opening of the territory to settlement by non-Indians. Consequently the Oklahoma slave narratives constitute a source for the history not only of the Sooner State, but also for locations as diverse as South Carolina and Illinois, Texas and Virginia. Irrespective of their birthplaces, however, the people whose memories are preserved in these interviews clearly represented those who had built Oklahoma into the state that it had become.

One of the most intriguing aspects of the Oklahoma slave narratives is that some of them record a detailed inside view of slavery among the so-called Five Tribes. The Cherokees, Creeks, Chickasaws, and Choctaws all had taken from the Euro-Americans the practice of black slavery, while the Seminoles chose to adopt blacks into their bands. When the federal government expelled these groups from their traditional homes in the southeastern United States, they took with them their black slaves. The Indians had a reputation for showing more humanity to their slaves than the whites, although these narratives illustrate a wide range of relations between the groups. The enculturation of the blacks into the tribes was so great that some slaves knew only Indian languages until after emancipation. Lucinda Davis of Tulsa, for example, told her interviewer, "I didn't know nothing but Creek talk long after de Civil War," adding that when she did hear English spoken it sounded to her like a "whole lot of wild shoat in de cedar brake scared at something."

Indian Territory in the eastern half of present-day Oklahoma was divided in sympathies during the Civil War, with members of Indian tribes fighting on both sides during the conflict. Some of the more conservative individuals among the tribes viewed the holding of black slaves as an undesirable accommodation to the Euro-American culture, and consequently they tended to support the Union. After the Confederate surrender at Appomattox in 1865, the Five Tribes were forced to negotiate new treaties with the victorious United States government, which insisted that they make their former slaves full legal members of the tribes. This took place for the Cherokees,

Creeks, Choctaws, and Seminoles, but the Chickasaws refused to accept their former slaves as full tribal members. To this day there are many African Americans who receive full benefits of membership in four of the Five Tribes.[4]

The Oklahoma Slave Narrative Project was part of a much larger effort undertaken by the United States government during the Great Depression to provide jobs for otherwise unemployed writers. Known as the Federal Writers' Project, this program operated beneath the administrative umbrella of the Works Progress Administration, a New Deal–era agency created to provide economic relief to the unemployed while at the same time benefiting the country as a whole. Instituted in the summer of 1935, the Federal Writers' Project had as its major goal the preparation of a guidebook for each of the states. In time a number of additional projects were added. A state writers' project was begun in each of the states, and unemployed writers with varied backgrounds were hired to begin work on the guidebooks.

From the earliest days of the state projects, field reporters interviewed elderly residents about their early life experiences, a part of the field research necessary for the state guides. African Americans were among the respondents interviewed, and the quality of the black history materials forwarded to Washington prompted administrators there to consider a coordinated effort to locate and interview elderly blacks as a distinct endeavor. Although it remained subordinate to the major goal of preparing state guides, a special Slave Narrative Project was initiated in seventeen southern and border states. In the spring of 1937 field workers from Oklahoma to Florida began searching for and interviewing elderly African Americans born into slavery.

Once the reporters had interviewed the informants, their notes typically were placed in preliminary, intermediate, and final drafts in order to meet national project guidelines. During this process the notes were edited to read as if the interviews had not been prompted by field workers' questions. Editors also attempted to incorporate a standardized African American dialect into each of the narratives to provide greater literary consistency. Upon completion of final drafts, project personnel forwarded them to a central clearinghouse in Washington. Work progressed through 1937 and into early 1938, when the attention of most state and national project administrators was diverted by new programs and by the need to complete work on the state guides. Interviewing of former slaves decreased to a trickle, although a few additional narratives were compiled through 1938 and until the end of the Writers' Project in 1939.[5]

At the close of the Federal Writers' Project, approximately twenty-three hundred typewritten slave narratives were transferred to the Writers' Unit at the Library of Congress. They lay dormant for a number of months, until Benjamin A. Botkin, who had succeeded John A. Lomax as director of folklore for the Federal Writers' Project, began processing them for permanent housing in the Library of Congress, ensuring their preservation for future generations. Eventually the ribbon-copy typescripts of the narratives, bound in large grayish-green volumes, as well as associated supplementary materials, reached the Manuscript Division of the Library of Congress, where they are housed today.[6]

The Oklahoma interviews play an important role in the overall Slave Narrative Project because of their superior quality. Although the seventy-five Oklahoma interviews sent from Oklahoma City represent just 3.2 percent of the total number of narratives forwarded to Washington, they have been considered among the best of all. In published anthologies drawn from the WPA narratives at the Library of Congress, the proportion of interviews from the Oklahoma informants has been far greater than their comparatively modest number would suggest.[7]

An office for the Oklahoma headquarters of the Federal Writers' Project opened in Oklahoma City in November 1935 with William Cunningham as its director. Shortly thereafter Cunningham began hiring employees to undertake his major assignment, the preparation of a manuscript for the Oklahoma state guidebook. To accomplish this task and other, related responsibilities, he balanced the need to hire qualified employees with Works Progress Administration mandates requiring him to employ certain percentages of personnel directly from unemployment rolls. The need to produce quality writing and research often conflicted with the demand to provide jobs for the chronically unemployable. The administrators of the Oklahoma Writers' Project attempted to achieve both ends, but it was almost in spite of the clear incompetence of some employees. Cunningham himself wrote, "We have considered it the main function of the project to put people to work and so of course have a great deal of dead wood." Even so, reporters went into the field to gather materials for writers, who in turn took the raw data and prepared text for the guide, for the slave narratives, and for other projects. Despite its difficulties and the occasional criticism that the Oklahoma Writers' Project had become a hotbed of subversive leftist activity, its personnel proceeded to undertake and complete its assignments until the close of the national Writers' Project in 1939. A short-lived second Writers' Program appeared and then disappeared in the years 1939–41.[8]

Only limited information is available on personnel assigned to the Oklahoma Slave Narrative Project. The reporters who went into the field to interview elderly blacks at the peak of the project in 1937–38 included three African Americans (Willie Allen, Ida Belle Hunter, and Bertha P. Tipton), one American Indian (Ethel Wolfe Garrison), and six whites (Mrs. Jessie R. Ervin, Robert Vinson Lackey, L. P. Livingston, J. S. Thomas, Craig Vollmer, and Lura J. Wilson). Among these individuals, the only one identified as a historian, in this case an amateur, is Robert Vinson Lackey, who wrote for the journal *Chronicles of Oklahoma* and was the author of at least one historical monograph.[9]

Records of the Oklahoma Slave Narrative Project preserved in the Oklahoma Historical Society are sketchy at best, but one letter in particular sheds light on how reporters dealt with decisions in the field during the interviewing process. In October or November 1937, Jessie R. Ervin wrote to state headquarters to report on her work. Regarding a recently completed interview with Mary Frances Webb, she noted, "I could have made it longer perhaps, if I had been sure it was acceptable. . . . My interviews are short but I find them such a repetition that I do not write all they tell me." She went on to describe herself as a "rank amateur" at the typewriter, adding, "It is real labor for me and I am ashamed of every article that I send but . . . I have been sending them on."[10]

The narratives themselves have certain textual characteristics. Reporters in the Oklahoma project tailored their interviews to a standard set of questions devised at the start of the project by John A. Lomax, director of the Folklore Division for the Federal Writers' Project. This division administered the national Slave Narrative Project. The use of Lomax's list of questions helped reporters to seek more substantive information than merely where a person lived, the names of his or her family members, or the identity of the master. Thus the field workers queried informants on such topics as foodways, how they had learned about their freedom, and health, medicine, and folk cures. Readers of the narratives often are struck by the informants' obvious answers to reporters' queries, even though the texts are edited so that the actual questions do not appear.[11]

The national project office provided guidance on the rendering of

African American dialect. Although in actual practice standardized dialect was not used in all the narratives, project personnel received guidelines on how to present speech in a uniform manner for the sake of literary consistency. Greater emphasis was always placed on correct recording of idioms than on pronunciation, but even so, "this" was generally rendered "dis" and "that" was spelled "dat," no matter whether the informant spoke in standard or in dialect English.[12]

The actual texts constituting the Oklahoma slave narratives vary considerably. The most typical collection of materials from an interviewee consists of a preliminary or intermediate draft coupled with a final draft edited in the standard format requested from Washington headquarters, all prepared on 8½- by 11-inch typing paper. The slave narrative collection in the Manuscript Division of the Library of Congress is composed only of final drafts. The ribbon-copy typescripts from Oklahoma are bound together in volume 13 of the "official" slave narratives, while carbon copies and content appraisal sheets for most of the interviews are filed separately but as part of the overall Slave Narrative Project collection. In only one instance was a preliminary draft found in the Library of Congress carbon copies, apparently sent in error by an Oklahoma City staff member.[13]

The Slave Narrative Project materials preserved in the Archives and Manuscripts Division of the Oklahoma Historical Society in Oklahoma City are much more varied in volume, content, and physical appearance. Most of the interviews are organized in file folders identified with the names of informants, although a file of unidentified fragments contains pieces from numerous narratives. The individual files may contain handwritten field notes, preliminary drafts (either typewritten or handwritten), intermediate typewritten drafts, and typewritten final drafts, all generally on 8½- by 11-inch typing paper. They may also contain notes and office memoranda associated with the interviews. For example, 3- by 5-inch cards bear handwritten notations of the dates when individual final drafts were forwarded to Washington or notes from administrators concerning topics from the standard questionnaire which were not covered. Carbon copies, often fuzzy, of the final drafts are found in the Oklahoma Historical Society files. Only two sets of apparently original handwritten field notes are preserved in Oklahoma City (those for the interviews of reporter Ethel Wolfe Garrison with William W. Watson and Robert Williams in spring 1938). Preliminary and intermediate drafts generally bear the pencil or ink handwritten changes entered by the Oklahoma Writers' Project editors. These notations demonstrate how the actual interview material was modified, massaged, and shaped to fit the forms the editors interpreted as national project standards. Notably, both the Library of Congress and the Oklahoma Historical Society contain interviews not represented in the other's holdings.[14]

Also preserved in the Oklahoma Historical Society are significant nonnarrative materials relating directly or indirectly to the Slave Narrative Project. Correspondence files, for example, include carbon copies of most of the cover letters which accompanied narratives forwarded to Washington and which provide evidence to estimate dates of interviews if such information is otherwise unavailable. Also preserved are a handful of interoffice memoranda dealing specifically with informants and their interviews. The files likewise contain a substantial amount of material for a projected but never completed Writers' Project book manuscript called "The Negro in Oklahoma." The separate Federal Writers' Project Collection in the Archives and Manuscripts Division of the Oklahoma Historical Society, however, disappointingly deals almost entirely with the short-lived 1939–41 Writers' Program and contains little data relating to the earlier slave narrative effort.[15]

For decades the Federal Writers' Project slave narratives collected in the 1930s were virtually ignored. The single exception to this seeming abandonment was Benjamin A. Botkin's book *Lay My Burden Down,* which grew out of his effort to organize the narratives for long-term preservation in the Library of Congress. Consisting of selected extracts from the narratives organized around broad themes, it was published by the University of Chicago Press in 1945. Botkin selected thirty-seven extracts from Oklahoma narratives, including five complete or nearly complete interview texts. The work had the eventual effect of directing the attention of the scholarly community to the slave narratives as significant sources on American history.

In 1970, after a quarter century, Norman R. Yetman compiled another work based entirely on the WPA slave narratives. His book, *Voices from Slavery: Selections from the Slave Narratives Collection of the Library of Congress,* consisted of an introduction and complete texts from just over a hundred of the 1930s narratives. Sixteen narratives came from Oklahoma interviewees, even though the Oklahoma informants constituted only 3.2 percent of the total represented in the Library of Congress slave narrative collection. This was a major tribute to the quality of the Oklahoma narratives.[16]

The next major project stemming from the WPA slave narratives was a multiyear, forty-one-volume effort by George P. Rawick for

the Greenwood Press. Rawick began in 1972 by preparing an intro-
ductory volume and then publishing page-by-page photographic reproductions of the slave narratives preserved in bound volumes in the
Library of Congress as well as other slave-narrative materials recorded
by field workers from Fisk University in the 1920s and 1930s.[17]

Then in two separate supplement series in 1977 and 1979, Rawick attempted to publish remaining slave narratives compiled by
Federal Writers' Project personnel which had not been forwarded to
Washington and which were scattered in repositories across the
country. This effort included one volume composed exclusively of
Oklahoma narratives, as well as one individual narrative in an additional volume. Rather than being photographic reproductions of the
original typescripts as in the earlier volumes, all the narratives in the
two supplement series were retyped and published in that form.
Rawick noted in his introduction to the first supplement series that
all the Oklahoma materials had been provided to him by Dr. Norman R. Yetman, who with his "assistants and children did the finding and copying of the new Oklahoma narratives." The Oklahoma
materials consisted of a number of the WPA Oklahoma slave narratives that had not been sent to Washington as well as a selection from
the interviews with former slaves undertaken by field workers from
the Indian-Pioneer Project headed by Grant Foreman at the Oklahoma Historical Society in the 1930s. Also included were two Oklahoma interviews from the Federal Theater Project. For reasons unknown, the effort by Yetman and his assistants to locate unpublished
WPA Oklahoma slave narratives was only partially successful. Narratives at the Oklahoma Historical Society for thirteen individuals
interviewed by personnel from the Oklahoma Slave Narrative Project but never sent to Washington were missed and are published for
the first time in this collection.[18]

After Rawick had completed his publication of the WPA slave
narratives from the Library of Congress holdings but while he was
working on his supplement series, the Scholarly Press issued its own
seventeen-volume edition of the same narratives from the Library of
Congress. Published in 1976, the series included one volume com-
bining the Oklahoma and Mississippi narratives preserved in Washington. Both this edition and the one compiled by Rawick, however,
were marketed only for academic audiences.[19]

Selected interviews from the WPA Oklahoma Slave Narrative
Project soon began to receive attention elsewhere. In addition to
being used as primary source material in secondary studies,[20] textual

material drawn from eight WPA Oklahoma slave narratives was published in 1971 by Kaye M. Teall in a resource book for teachers in the Oklahoma City public schools. Then in 1977 R. Halliburton, Jr., published transcripts from ten WPA Oklahoma slave narratives, some of them the same as those chosen by Teall, as an appendix to his study of slavery among the Cherokee Indians.[21] Finally, in 1988 James Mellon compiled a book for general readers composed of extracts from the national WPA slave narratives in the Library of Congress, drawing much of his material from the Oklahoma interviews.[22]

It is important to note that none of these publications included all of the WPA Oklahoma slave narratives and many presented only a few. The present volume is the first to include all of the known WPA slave narratives contained in both the Washington and Oklahoma City collections.[23]

In preparing this work, we have, with the exception of examples noted, worked from the final edited drafts of the narratives when they exist. These final drafts are the most readable of the various drafts available, having considerably greater literary consistency than the often disorganized and variably written preliminary and intermediate drafts. This is particularly true of the texts recorded primarily in dialect. In the interests of readability, the narratives have been very lightly edited in two respects: misspellings not intended to suggest dialect or the interviewees' pronunciation have been silently corrected, and punctuation has occasionally been supplied to prevent misreading. Any other editorial additions or clarifications are shown in brackets. Information enclosed in parentheses in the narratives represents comments by field workers or the WPA editors. Documentation is provided for every known surviving historical handwritten or typewritten draft of each of the narratives in the Oklahoma project so that future researchers may trace the evolution of texts during the WPA editorial process. Additionally, all substantive differences among the various drafts are recorded in annotations.

Many scholars have considered the Oklahoma slave narratives to be important sources on the American experience, but what can they tell us today? Perhaps they open a window to a lost world that at the time was only imperfectly recorded. The elderly blacks, sitting on their ramshackle porches and visiting with eager field workers in the 1930s, could speak from their own personal experience of living in preindustrial America when masters and their subject people wrested the necessities of life from a stubborn land, racing annually against the seasons to plant, cultivate, and harvest.

The Oklahoma informants shared with their WPA interviewers their feelings about having their teeth examined and muscles felt while standing on the auction block, of being inherited by the master's relatives, and of being tied to a tree and whipped for leaving a soapy streak in the master's laundered shirt. Field worker J. S. Thomas wrote that Sam Jordan's emotions were so disturbed during his interview in Oklahoma City that he "cried most sadly" as he described his mother's whipping by an overseer. "I seen him one day strip my mother's clothes down to her waist and made her own blood brother hold her while he beat her," he remembered with tears in his eyes, telling Thomas, "I don't want nobody to ask me bout it."

Some informants also spoke unhesitatingly of resistance to the institution of slavery which made them little more than brute animals in some masters' eyes. Nancy Rogers Bean told her interviewer about one of her aunts, who, as she was being auctioned, "grabbed a hatchet, laid her hand on a log and chopped it off," whereupon she picked it up and "throwed the bleeding hand right in her master's face." Not all the slaves could resist the masters indefinitely. Annie Young's aunt tried to fend off her master's sexual advances by running off into the woods, but he sicked his hounds on her trail. "He catched her and hit her in de head wid something like de stick de police carry," she remembered, "and he made her have him." Not knowing what else to do, the frightened girl then fled to her mistress, related what had happened, and asked her what to do. The mistress, herself distraught by her husband's infidelity, advised her to "go ahead and be wid him 'cause he's gonna kill you" if she did not. Young concluded the narrative: "And he had dem two women and she had some chillun nearly white, and master and dey all worked in de fields side by side."

The Oklahoma slave narratives are a window—a window on a past about which we know a great deal and about which we know very little. Through the memories of people like Nancy Rogers Bean, Annie Young, and their contemporaries, we can see and hear slavery from the inside—through the eyes and ears of those who were bought and sold, who danced and cried, and who survived to tell of the almost feudal world of dirt-floored cabins, white columns, and bullwhips.

1. For an overview of the WPA Oklahoma Slave Narrative Project, see Monroe Billington, "Black Slavery in Indian Territory: The Ex-Slave Narratives," *Chronicles of Oklahoma* 60 (Spring 1982): 56–65.

2. Norman R. Yetman, "The Background of the Slave Narrative Collection," *American Quarterly* 19 (Fall 1967): 534–53.

3. John W. Blassingame, "Using the Testimony of Ex-Slaves: Approaches and Prob-

lems," *Journal of Southern History* 41 (November 1975): 473–92; Paul D. Escott, "The Art and Science of Reading WPA Slave Narratives," in *The Slave's Narrative,* 40–48; C. Vann Woodward, "History from Slave Sources," *American Historical Review* 79 (April 1974): 470–81.

4. There is a substantial literature on the role of African Americans in the Five Tribes. Among the works of scholarship on the subject are the following: Annie Heloise Abel, *The American Indian as Slaveholder and Secessionist: An Omitted Chapter in the Diplomatic History of the Southern Confederacy*; J. B. Davis, "Slavery in the Cherokee Nation," *Chronicles of Oklahoma* 11 (December 1933): 1056–72; Janet Halliburton, "Black Slavery in the Creek Nation," *Chronicles of Oklahoma* 56 (Fall 1978): 298–314; R. Halliburton, Jr., "Origins of Black Slavery among the Cherokees," *Chronicles of Oklahoma* 52 (Winter 1974–75): 483–96; R. Halliburton, Jr., *Red over Black: Black Slavery among the Cherokee Indians*; Neeley Belle Jackson, "Political and Economic History of the Negro in Indian Territory" (Master's thesis, University of Oklahoma, 1960); Parthena Louise James, "Reconstruction in the Chickasaw Nation: The Freedman Problem," *Chronicles of Oklahoma* 45 (Spring 1967): 44–57; Wyatt F. Jeltz, "The Relations of Negroes and Choctaw and Chickasaw Indians," *Journal of Negro History* 33 (January 1948): 24–37; J. H. Johnson, "Documentary Evidence of the Relations of Negroes and Indians," *Journal of Negro History* 14 (January 1929): 21–43; Daniel F. Littlefield, Jr., *Africans and Creeks: From the Colonial Period to the Civil War*; Daniel F. Littlefield, Jr., *Africans and Seminoles from Removal to Emancipation*; Daniel F. Littlefield, Jr., *The Cherokee Freedmen from Emancipation to American Citizenship*; Daniel F. Littlefield, Jr., *The Chickasaw Freedmen: A People without a Country*; William G. McLoughlin, "Red Indians, Black Slavery and White Racism: America's Slaveholding Indians," *American Quarterly* 26 (October 1974): 367–85; Theda Perdue, "Cherokee Planters, Black Slaves, and African Colonization," *Chronicles of Oklahoma* 60 (Fall 1982): 322–31; Theda Perdue, *Slavery and the Evolution of Cherokee Society, 1540–1866*; Sigmund Sameth, "Creek Negroes: A Study in Race Relations" (Master's thesis, University of Oklahoma, 1940); Angela Y. Walton-Raji, *Black Indian Genealogy Research: African-American Ancestors among the Five Civilized Tribes*; Hanna R. Warren, "Reconstruction in the Cherokee Nation," *Chronicles of Oklahoma* 45 (Summer 1967): 180–89; William S. Willis, "Divide and Rule: Red, White, and Black in the Southeast," *Journal of Negro History* 48 (July 1963): 157–76; Walt Wilson, "Freedmen in Indian Territory during Reconstruction," *Chronicles of Oklahoma* 49 (Summer 1971): 230–44.

5. Mary Ann Slater, "Politics and Art: The Controversial Birth of the Oklahoma Writers' Project," *Chronicles of Oklahoma* 68 (Spring 1990): 72–89; Yetman, "Background," 534–53. For overviews of the Federal Writers' Project, see Jere Mangione, *The Dream and the Deal: The Federal Writers' Project, 1935-1943*, and Monty Noam Penkower, *The Federal Writers' Project: A Study in Government Patronage of the Arts,* 140–47.

6. B. A. Botkin, *Lay My Burden Down: A Folk History of Slavery,* vii–xiv; B. A. Botkin, "The Slave as His Own Interpreter," *Library of Congress Quarterly Journal of Current Acquisitions* 2 (July/September 1944): 37–63; Yetman, "Background," 552–53.

7. Benjamin A. Botkin selected over 11 percent of his narratives and extracts from the Oklahoma interviews when he prepared a book based on the WPA collection, *Lay My Burden Down: A Folk History of Slavery,* in the 1940s. His judgment was con-

firmed in 1970 when the historian Norman R. Yetman identified narratives from Oklahoma, North Carolina, and Texas as far superior to those in the other states' collections. Fifteen percent of the narratives he identified as "the finest" in the entire Library of Congress collection came from Oklahoma. When James Mellon assembled his 1988 book, *Bullwhip Days*, compiled from the WPA narratives, he corroborated the importance of the Oklahoma material. His study consisted of 29 narratives published in their entirety as well as more than 350 brief extracts from the narratives. Ten percent of his full narratives were drawn from the Oklahoma interviews, as were more than 4 percent of his brief extracts. Botkin, *Lay My Burden Down*, 271–85; Norman R. Yetman, *Voices from Slavery: Selections from the Slave Narratives Collection of the Library of Congress;* James Mellon, *Bullwhip Days: The Slaves Remember*.

8. Slater, "Politics and Art," 72–89; Lawrence Thompson, "Works Office Aid Goes East as Reds Rally," *Daily Oklahoman* (Oklahoma City, Okla.), 27 May 1938, 12.

9. The names of field workers from the project are drawn from notations on the preliminary and intermediate drafts of the narratives in the Slave Narrative Collection, Archives and Manuscripts Division, Oklahoma Historical Society, Oklahoma City, Oklahoma (hereafter cited as OHS Slave Narratives). Identification of Willie Allen, Ida Belle Hunter, and Bertha P. Tipton as African Americans is based on city directory information as well as on internal evidence in the narratives, while the identification of Ethel Wolfe Garrison as an American Indian comes from 1937 correspondence from her supervisor, Robert Vinson Lackey. R[obert] Vinson Lackey, Tulsa, [Oklahoma], to Ned P. DeWitt, Oklahoma City, [Oklahoma], 18 and 31 October 1937, "WPA Note[s] on Interviews, Oklahoma Federal Writers' Project—Ex-Slave Narratives" file, Slave Narrative Collection, Archives and Manuscripts Division, Oklahoma Historical Society (hereafter cited as WPA Notes on Interviews); *Polk's Oklahoma City (Oklahoma County, Okla.) Directory, 1937, 368, 803, 933; Polk's Oklahoma City (Oklahoma County, Okla.) City Directory, 1938, 31, 363, 932; Polk's Oklahoma City (Oklahoma County, Okla.) Directory, 1939, 357, 717, 929; Polk's Oklahoma City (Oklahoma County, Okla.) Directory, 1940, 718, 932, 1216.*

For Robert Vinson Lackey's writings and historical research activities, see Vinson Lackey, *The Chouteaus and the Founding of Salina, Oklahoma's First White Settlement, 1796;* Vinson Lackey, "New Springplace," *Chronicles of Oklahoma* 17 (June 1939): 178–83; Vinson Lackey, "Northeast Oklahoma's 'Mystery House' May Be Sam Houston's 'Wigwam on the Neosho,'" *Tulsa Tribune*, 18 August 1937, 24; "Minutes of the Meeting of the Board of Directors of the Oklahoma Historical Society," *Chronicles of Oklahoma* 18 (March 1940): 87–91. Before his employment by the Federal Writers' Project, Lackey had served as the conventions-publicity secretary for the Tulsa Chamber of Commerce. After the close of the project, he worked as a writer and artist, as well as being a supervisor for the Douglas Aircraft Company. *Polk's Tulsa (Tulsa County, Okla.) City Directory, 1935, 339; Polk's Tulsa (Tulsa County, Okla.) City Directory, 1940, 341; Polk's Tulsa (Tulsa County, Okla.) City Directory, 1944, 320; Polk's Tulsa (Tulsa County, Okla.) City Directory, 1947, 398; Polk's Tulsa (Tulsa County, Okla.) City Directory, 1954, 525.*

10. [Mrs. Jessie R. Ervin, probably McAlester, Oklahoma] to Ned P. DeWitt, Oklahoma City, Oklahoma, [October or November 1937], WPA Notes on Interviews.

11. Botkin, *Lay My Burden Down*, xi. For the actual questions used by Slave Narrative Project personnel in the field, see U.S., Works Progress Administration, Federal

Writers' Project, Slave Narratives, Alabama, box A917, 1:xx–xii, xxxi–xxxii, Manuscript Division, Library of Congress, Washington, D.C.; also available reprinted in George P. Rawick, ed., *The American Slave: A Composite Autobiography,* series I, 1:173–76.

12. Sterling A. Brown, "On Dialect Usage," in *The Slave's Narrative,* 37–39; "Oklahoma Writers' Project Negro Dialect Corrections," typescript, 3 lvs., n.d., WPA Notes on Interviews; Federal Writers' Project, Slave Narratives, Alabama, 1:xvii, xxviii–xxx; John Edgar Wideman, "Charles Chesnutt and the WPA Narratives: The Oral and Literate Roots of Afro-American Literature," in *The Slave's Narrative,* 59–78.

13. For the final ribbon-copy typescripts in the Library of Congress, see U.S., Works Progress Administration, Federal Writers' Project, Slave Narratives, Oklahoma, vol. 13, box A927, Manuscript Division, Library of Congress (hereafter cited as LC Slave Narratives). For the carbon copies see U.S., Works Progress Administration, Federal Writers' Project, Slave Narratives, Oklahoma, Carbon Copies, boxes A905–A906, Manuscript Division, Library of Congress (hereafter cited as LC Slave Narratives Carbon Copies). For Benjamin A. Botkin's appraisal sheets evaluating the Oklahoma narratives, see U.S., Works Progress Administration, Federal Writers' Project, Slave Narratives, WPA Writers' Program Records Appraisal Sheets, "Appraisal Sheets, A–Y" file, box A905, Manuscript Division, Library of Congress.

14. All of the materials preserved by the Oklahoma Historical Society relating to the Slave Narrative Project are in the OHS Slave Narratives.

15. For the files of correspondence, memoranda, and assorted documents relating to the Oklahoma Slave Narrative Project, see WPA Notes on Interviews. The disappointing files of the Federal Writers' Project for Oklahoma may be found in the Federal Writers' Project Collection, Archives and Manuscripts Division, Oklahoma Historical Society.

16. For Yetman's own survey of the historiography of slavery as related to the use of the WPA slave narratives as source material, see Norman R. Yetman, "Ex-Slave Interviews and the Historiography of Slavery," *American Quarterly* 36 (Summer 1984): 181–210.

17. Rawick, *The American Slave: A Composite Autobiography,* series I and II. The Oklahoma slave narratives preserved in the Library of Congress are found with those from Mississippi in series I, vol. 7.

18. Rawick, *The American Slave: A Composite Autobiography,* supplement series I, vols. 1–12; supplement series II, vols. 1–10. The Oklahoma narratives are found in supplement series I, 12:1–401, and supplement series II, 1:371–74. For Rawick's comments on Norman R. Yetman's services in providing the Oklahoma materials, see supplement series I, 12:xiii–xiv, xliii, lvii–lx.

The narratives missed by Rawick and Yetman and published here include those with Carrie E. Davis, Eliza Elsey, John Field, Millie Garnes, Nannie Gordon, Sonny Greer, Martha Ann Ratliff, Alice Rawlings, Joe Ray, Sam Rhodes, Charley Ross, George Simon, and Charlotte Johnson White.

The interviews from the Indian-Pioneer Papers published by Rawick but not included in this study are those with Jane Battiest, Irena Blocker, Charley Moore Brown, Daniel Webster Burton, Ed Butler, Jack Campbell, Jefferson L. Cole, Edmond Flint, B. C. Franklin, Richard Franklin, Eliza Hardrick, John Harrison, Moses Lonian, Rose Mercer, Elsie Pryor, C. G. Samuel, Ned Thompson, Agnes Walker, Lee Weldon, and

Eliza Whitmire. These as well as other interviews with former slaves by Indian-Pioneer Project personnel are available in microform editions of the entire collection from both the Oklahoma Historical Society and the Western History Department of the University of Oklahoma Libraries, Norman, Oklahoma.

19. *Slave Narratives: A Folk History of Slavery in the United States, from Interviews with Former Slaves.* The Oklahoma and Mississippi narratives are found in vol. 6.

20. The first major secondary study to employ the WPA slave narratives as an important source was Eugene D. Genovese's book *Roll, Jordan, Roll: The World the Slaves Made,* published in 1974. In the intervening twenty years, many scholars have used the WPA slave narratives. For examples employing Oklahoma narratives, see Daniel F. Littlefield's multiple studies of African Americans among the Five Tribes, cited above, as well as Paul D. Escott, *Slavery Remembered: A Record of Twentieth-Century Slave Narratives*; and John C. Neilson, "Indian Masters, Black Slaves: An Oral History of the Civil War in Oklahoma," *Panhandle-Plains Historical Review* 65 (1992): 42–54.

21. Halliburton, *Red over Black,* 145–80; Kaye M. Teall, *Black History in Oklahoma: A Resource Book,* 32–37.

22. Mellon, *Bullwhip Days.*

23. Two interviews with whites were included, either intentionally or inadvertently, in the Oklahoma Slave Narrative Project but have not been included for publication in this work. These two interviews are "Martha Cunningham (White), Age 81 Yrs., Oklahoma City, Oklahoma," available in ribbon-copy typescript in the LC Slave Narratives and in carbon copy in U.S., Works Progress Administration, Federal Writers' Project, Slave Narratives, Oklahoma, "Non-Slave Narratives" file, box A906, Manuscript Division, Library of Congress (hereafter cited as LC Slave Narratives "Non-Slave Narratives") and in the OHS Slave Narratives; and "Interview with Charles W. Ervin, White-Pioneer, Ervin, Choctaw Co., Okla.," in ribbon-copy typescript in the OHS Slave Narratives, and "Charles W. Ervin, White-Pioneer, Ervin, Okla.," in ribbon-copy typescript in LC Slave Narratives "Non-Slave Narratives" and in carbon copy in the OHS Slave Narratives.

ISAAC ADAMS[1]

Age 87 yrs. *Tulsa, Okla.*

I was born in Louisiana, way before the War. I think it was about ten years before, because I can remember everything so well about the start of the War, and I believe I was about ten years old.

My Mammy belonged to Mr. Sack P. Gee. I don't know what his real given name was, but maybe it was Saxon. Anyways we all called him Master Sack.

He was a kind of youngish man, and was mighty rich. I think he was born in England. Anyway his pappy was from England, and I think he went back before I was born.

Master Sack had a big plantation ten miles north of Arcadia, Louisiana, and his land run ten miles along both sides. He would leave in a buggy and be gone all day and still not get all over it.

There was all kinds of land on it, and he raised cane and oats and wheat and lots of corn and cotton. His cotton fields was the biggest anywheres in that part, and when chopping and picking times come he would get negroes from other people to help out. I never was no good at picking, but I was a terror with a hoe!

I was the only child my Mammy had. She was just a young girl, and my Master did not own her very long. He got her from Mr. Addison Hilliard,[2] where my pappy belonged. I think she was going to have me when he got her; anyways I come along pretty soon, and my mammy never was very well afterwards. Maybe Master Sack sent her over to my pappy. I don't know.

Mammy was the house girl at Mr. Sack's because she wasn't very strong, and when I was four or five years old she died. I was big enough to do little things for Mr. Sack and his daughter, so they kept me at the mansion, and I helped the house boys. Time I was nine or ten Mr. Sack's daughter was getting to be a young woman—fifteen or sixteen years old—and that was old enough to be married off in them days. They had a lot of company just before the War, and they had a whole bunch of house negroes around all the time.

Old Mistress died when I was a baby, so I don't remember anything about her, but young Mistress was a winder! She would ride horseback nearly all the time, and I had to go along with her when I got big enough. She never did go around the quarters, so I don't know nothing much about the negroes Mr. Sack had for the fields. They all looked pretty clean and healthy, though, when they would come up to the Big House. He fed them all good and they all liked him.

He had so much different kinds of land that they could raise anything they wanted, and he had more mules and horses and cattle than anybody around there. Some of the boys worked with his fillies all the time, and he went off to New Orleans ever once in a while with his race horses. He took his daughter but they never took me.

Some of his land was in pasture but most of it was all open fields, with just miles and miles of cotton rows. There was a pretty good strip along one side he called the "old" fields. That's what they called the land that was wore out and turned back. It was all growed up in young trees, and that's where he kept his horses most of the time.

The first I knowed about the War coming on was when Mr. Sack had a whole bunch of whitefolks at the Big House at a function. They didn't talk about anything else all evening and then the next time they come nearly all their menfolks wasn't there—just the womenfolks. It wasn't very long till Mr. Sack went off to Houma[3] with some other men, and pretty soon we knew he was in the War. I don't remember ever seeing him come home. I don't think he did until it was nearly all over.

Next thing we knowed they was Confederate soldiers riding by pretty nearly every day in big droves. Sometimes they would come and buy corn and wheat and hogs, but they never did take any anyhow, like the Yankees done later on. They would pay with billets, Young Missy called them, and she didn't send them to git them cashed but saved them a long time, and then she got them cashed, but you couldn't buy anything with the money she got for them.

That Confederate money she got wasn't no good. I was in Arcadia with her at a store, and she had to pay seventy-five cents for a can of sardines for me to eat with some bread I had, and before the War you could get a can like that for two cents. Things was even higher then than later on, but that's the only time I saw her buy anything.

When the Yankees got down in that country the most of the big men paid for all the corn and meat and things they got, but some of the little bunches of them would ride up and take hogs and things like that and just ride off. They wasn't anybody at our place but the womenfolks and the negroes. Some of Mr. Sack's women kinfolks stayed there with Young Mistress.

Along at the last the negroes on our place didn't put in much stuff—just what they would need, and could hide from the Yankees, because they would get it all took away from them if the Yankees found out they had plenty of corn and oats.

The Yankees was mighty nice about their manners, though. They camped all around our place for a while. There was three camps of them close by at one time, but they never did come and use any of our houses or cabins. There was lots of poor whites and Cajuns that lived down below us, between us and the Gulf, and the Yankees just moved into their houses and cabins and used them to camp in.

The negroes at our place and all of them around there didn't try to get away or leave when the Yankees come in. They wasn't no place to go, anyway, so they all stayed on. But they didn't do very much work. Just enough to take care of themselves and their whitefolks.

Master Sack come home before the War was quite over. I think he had been sick, because he looked thin and old and worried. All the negroes picked up and worked mighty hard after he come home, too.

One day he went into Arcadia and come home and told us the War was over and we was all free. The negroes didn't know what to make of it, and they didn't know where to go, so he told all that wanted to stay on that they could just go on like they had been and pay him shares.

About half of his negroes stayed on, and he marked off land for them to farm and made arrangements with them to let them use their cabins, and let them have mules and tools. They paid him out of their shares, and some of them finally bought the mules and some of the land. But about half went off and tried to do better somewheres else.

I didn't stay with him because I was jest a boy and he didn't need me at the house anyway.

Late in the War my Pappy belonged to a man named Sander or Zander. Might have been Alexander, but the negroes called him Mr. Sander. When pappy got free he come and asked me to go with him, and I went along and lived with him. He had a share-cropped deal with Mr. Sander and I helped him work his patch. That place was just a little east of Houma,[4] a few miles.

When my Pappy was born his parents belonged to a Mr. Adams, so he took Adams for his last name, and I did too, because I was his son. I don't know where Mr. Adams lived, but I don't think my Pappy was born in Louisiana. Alabama, maybe. I think his parents come off the boat, because he was very black—even blacker than I am.

I lived there with my Pappy until I was about eighteen and then I married and moved around all over Louisiana from time to time. My wife give me twelve boys and five girls, but all my children are dead now but five. My wife died in 1920 and I come up here to Tulsa to live. One of my daughters takes care and looks out for me now.

I seen the old Sack P. Gee place about twenty years ago, and it was all cut up in little places and all run down. Never would have known it was one time a big plantation ten miles long.

I seen places going to rack and ruin all around—all the places I lived at in Louisiana—but I'm glad I wasn't there to see Master Sack's place go down. He was a good man and done right by all his negroes.

Yes, Lord, my feets have been in mighty nigh every parish in Louisiana, and I seen some mighty pretty places, but I'll never forget how that old Gee plantation looked when I was a boy.

¹ Isaac Adams was interviewed by WPA field worker Robert Vinson Lackey in Tulsa, Oklahoma, in autumn 1937. From his notes Lackey prepared a preliminary draft of Adams's remembrances at least by 3 November 1937 as the typescript "Interview with Isaac Adams, 87 Years Old, Latimer St. and Frankfort, Tulsa, Oklahoma, (Ex-Slave)," now in the Slave Narrative Collection in the Archives and Manuscripts Division of the Oklahoma Historical Society, Oklahoma City, Oklahoma (hereafter cited as the OHS Slave Narratives). Within a few days the Adams narrative was retyped into standard project format as "Isaac Adams, Age 87 Yrs., Tulsa, Okla." This version, published here, was sent to project national headquarters in Washington, D.C., on 18 November 1937 and is available in ribbon copy in U.S., Works Progress Administration, Federal Writers' Project, Slave Narratives, Oklahoma, vol. 13, in box A927, Manuscript Division, Library of Congress, Washington, D.C. (hereafter cited as LC Slave Narratives). Carbon copies are also available in the OHS Slave Narratives and as item 350022 in U.S., Works Progress Administration, Federal Writers' Project, Slave Narratives, Oklahoma, boxes A905–A906, Manuscript Division, Library of Congress, Washington, D.C. (hereafter cited as LC Slave Narratives Carbon Copies). Ron Stephens, [Oklahoma City, Oklahoma], to Henry G. Alsberg, Washington, D.C., 18 November 1937, "WPA Note[s] on Interviews, Oklahoma Federal Writers' Project—Ex-Slave Narratives" file, Slave Narrative Collection, Archives and Manuscripts Division, Oklahoma Historical Society (hereafter cited as WPA Notes on Interviews). A mid-1930s Tulsa city directory confirms the "Latimer St. and Frankfort" address for Isaac Adams noted in the preliminary draft of his remembrances, locating his home at 443½ East Latimer in Tulsa. *Polk's Tulsa (Tulsa County, Okla.) City Directory, 1935,* 83, 667.

² A typewritten note clipped to the earlier draft of this narrative in the OHS Slave Narratives reads: "I am quite sure that this Addison Hilliard is truly *Audubon* Hilliard who had a plantation right there and they were the only Hilliards about there. I am quite friends with his sister and several of his nieces. It makes little matter only it is

easy to see how a darkey or anyone else as for that matter might misunderstand the unusual name. Roberts."
   3 An editorial mark on the preliminary draft of this narrative queries, "Should this
be Homer?" The WPA editor probably was correct, for Homer is comparatively close
to Arcadia in northern Louisiana, whereas Houma is in the southern portion of the
state.
   4 Perhaps another garbled reference to Homer, Louisiana.

ALICE ALEXANDER[1]

Age 88 yrs.   *Oklahoma City, Okla.*

I was 88 years old the 15th of March. I was born in 1849, at Jackson
Parish, Louisiana. My mother's name was Mary Marlow, and father's
Henry Marlow.
   I can't remember much 'bout slavery 'cause I was awful small, but
I can remember that my mother's master, Colonel Threff, died, and
my mother, her husband, and us three chillun was handed down to
Colonel Threff's poor kin folks. Colonel Threff owned about two or
three hundred head of niggers, and all of 'em was tributed to his poor
kin. Ooh wee! he sho' had jest a lot of them too! Master Joe Threff,
one of his poor kin, took my mother, her husband, and three of us
chillun from Louisiana to the Mississippi Line.
   Down there we lived in a one-room log hut, and slept on home-
made rail bed steads with cotton, and sometimes straw, mostly straw
summers and cotton winners. I worked round the house and looked
after de smaller chillun—I mean my mother's chillun. Mostly[2] we
ate yeller meal corn bread and sorghum molasses. I ate possums when
we could get 'em,[3] but jest couldn't stand rabbit meat. Didn't know
there was any Christmas or holidays in dem days.[4]
   I can't 'membuh nothing 'bout no churches in slavery. I was a sinner and loved to dance. I remembuh I was on the floor one night
dancing and I had four daughters on the floor with me and my son
was playing de music—that got me! I jest stopped and said I wouldn't
cut another step and I haven't.[5] I'm a member of the Baptist Church
and been for 25 or 30 years. I jined 'cause I wanted to be good 'cause
I was an awful sinner.
   We had a overseer back on Colonel Threff's plantation[6] and my
mother said he was the meanest man on earth. He'd jest go out in de
fields and beat dem niggers, and my mother told me one day he come
out in de field beating her sister and she jumped on him and nearly
beat him half to death and old Master come up jest in time to see it

all and fired dat overseer. Said he didn't want no man working fer him dat a woman could whip.[7]

After de war set us free[8] my pappy moved us away and I stayed round down there till I got to be a grown woman and married. You know I had a pretty fine wedding 'cause my pappy had worked hard and commenced to be prosperous. He had cattle, hogs, chickens and all those things like that.[9]

A college of dem niggers got together and packed up to leave Louisiana. Me and my husband went with them.[10] We had covered wagons, and let me tell you I walked nearly all the way from Louisiana to Oklahoma. We left in March but didn't git here till May. We came in search of education. I got a pretty fair education down there but didn't take care of it. We come to Oklahoma looking for de same thing then that darkies go North looking fer now. But we got disappointed.[11] What little I learned I quit taking care of it and seeing after it and lost it all.

I love to fish. I've worked hard in my days. Washed and ironed for 30 years, and paid for dis home that way. Yes sir, dis is my home. My mother died right here in dis house. She was 111 yeahs old. She is been dead 'bout 20 yeahs.[12]

I have three daughters here married, Sussie Pruitt,[13] Bertie Shannon, and Irene Freeman. Irene lost her husband, and he's dead now.[14]

[1] WPA field worker Ida Belle Hunter, one of the three African American reporters working on the Oklahoma Slave Narrative Project, interviewed eighty-eight-year-old Alice Alexander in Oklahoma City during the spring or early summer of 1937. On 8 June 1937 she produced a preliminary draft of the notes as the typescript "Interview with Alice Alexander, Ex-Slave, Aged 88 Years, 409 East Grand Avenue, Oklahoma City, Oklahoma," now preserved in the OHS Slave Narratives. In the next weeks WPA personnel edited and revised the text into the standard project format, deleting some heavy dialect and including some content changes indicated in notes below. This later draft, forwarded to Washington on 2 September 1937 and published here, is available as "Alice Alexander, Age 88 Yrs., Oklahoma City, Okla." in ribbon copy in the LC Slave Narratives and in carbon copy in the LC Slave Narratives Carbon Copies and in two identical copies in the OHS Slave Narratives. The later version contains three sentences not found in the earlier typescript, suggesting that the informant may have been re-interviewed, a suspicion that is further reinforced by a slip of paper clipped to the earlier draft noting, "Re-interview material very scarce. I[da] B[elle] H[unter]." A contemporary city directory shows Alice Alexander living at 407½ East Grand Avenue, almost the same address given in the preliminary draft of the narrative. *Polk's Oklahoma City (Oklahoma County, Okla.) Directory, 1937,* 27, 854; Ron Stephens, [Oklahoma City, Oklahoma], to George Cronyn, Washington, D.C., 2 September 1937, WPA Notes on Interviews.

2 "Mostly" added in the later version of the text.

3 "When we could get 'em" added in later version.

4 The preliminary draft of the narrative reads, "Diden no any Crismus was in dem days."

5 "And I haven't" added in later version.

6 "Back on Colonel Threff's plantation" added in later version.

7 At this point the later version of the narrative omits the following three sentences found in the preliminary draft: "Remembuh jest a little 'bout de war. De soljers had on blue clothes. Membuh lot of talk 'bout 4th of August."

8 "After de war set us free" added in later version.

9 The preliminary draft reads "an' all dat."

10 This sentence added in the later version.

11 The preliminary draft includes the following two sentences omitted in the later version: "Never did go to school till aftah the surrender. Commence going to school in Memphis."

12 The preceding three sentences are not found in the preliminary draft of this narrative.

13 The preliminary draft at this point reads, "You know Sussie Pruitt, don'tcha?"

14 The words "and he's dead now" were added to the later version.

SAM ANDERSON[1]

Age 98 yrs.   *Oklahoma City, Okla.*

Lemme see, I guess I is about ninety. I was born in de Robian family in 1839. I wasn't sold. I was transferred to Master Pruitt when he marry Master Robian's daughter, and when I was old enough to work I was transferred to Master Sam Anderson. Amite County, Mississippi, was where I was born, but I was raised in Pike County.[2]

Lemme see, my oldest brother was called Bud, and he belong to de Robian family in Texas. Den I had another brother and a baby brother, and one sister. My mother was Clara Robian, my father named Daniel Robian.[3] Master Robian had eleven children, six boys and five girls. He had heaps of money; bring it home in a sack and throw it over de fence and mistress couldn't pick it up.[4]

We slaves live in de quarters. Beds made out of wood with shuck and moss mattress. We always put de moss in hot water so it don't grow.[5] I wore a shirt until I was ten years old. Shirts was made of old lowell or maybe weaved.[6] They was split up de sides so dey would sail out behind when you ran, but dey had buttons so you could button 'em up in winter. Nothing different on Sunday only clean clothes, but after we gets large we wear pants and shirts.[7] Wears shoes when we gets about ten or twelve years old.[8]

We all eats at Master's house. Greens, peas, and such as was raised on de farm, with biscuits once a month. I was always gladdest when dey cooked biscuits and fresh meats, and sometimes we go hunting at nights and catch possums and rabbits.

Can't tell how much land Master had, but dey was a heap of slaves. Some of the older men would plant a patch of cotton for theirselves when dey had time, and maybe get sixty dollars for it, but I never made any money. My Uncle Dollie worked for years and save up five hundred dollars and paid it to Master for his wife, Aunt Onie. His master had him to build them a house out from de quarters as he set her free, but Uncle Dollie was still a slave. After slavery he bought eighty acres of land and lived there till death.[9]

De overseer have a darky to ring bell or blow horn at four o'clock to get up by mornings.[10] Slaves was whipped when dey didn't work suitable; whip 'em with a long red and blue bull whip with lead on one end. Sometime when dey would try to keep from being whipped, de overseer would get other white men to help him. One slave named Mose was tied down to a stake, and when de overseer start to whip him he pulls up de stake and makes for 'im, and his master knock him in de head with an ax. Later and shortly dey put him up for sale and sell him for twelve hundred dollars.[11] My brother used to run away all de time, and dey couldn't catch or track him with de dogs. One day he run off and Master set two sets of dogs after him, but dey still couldn't catch him.[12]

Master didn't allow church on de plantation, but they was two preachers dat he would let preach under a tree on Sunday.[13] Doctor Hart was our doctor. He doctor us with blackmass and calomel pills, and turpentine. When we have de itch we bathe in boiled pork-root water.[14]

I believe white folks trying to get out of work was what caused slavery. Dey get rich off us without working. Didn't like Booker T. Washington. He teach de Negroes to serve de white folks.[15]

Abraham Lincoln was a good man, but they turned in and killed him. Jefferson Davis was butting against Lincoln.

[1] Slave Narrative Project field worker J. S. Thomas interviewed Sam Anderson in Oklahoma City on 3 July 1937, producing a preliminary draft of Anderson's narrative as "Ex-Slave Story, Reference: Personal Interview of Sam Anderson, 501 N. Missouri, Oklahoma City, Oklahoma, (Old Folks Home)," in the OHS Slave Narratives. The location of the interview, 501 North Missouri, was the C. L. Bryant Orphanage and Old Folks Home, and the Sam Anderson narrative is the only one in the Oklahoma collection known to be based on an interview undertaken at this institution. At some date after the interview, project editors substantially revised the narrative into a more read-

able form as the two subsequent typescripts, "Sam Anderson" and "Sam Anderson, Age 98 Yrs., Oklahoma City, Okla.," which have identical content and both of which are available in the OHS Slave Narratives. The differences between the preliminary and the later versions are described in the following notes. There was come confusion about the interviewee's age; in the title of the typescript it was originally given as 90, but that figure was scratched out and replaced in handwriting with 98. The Sam Anderson narrative was never forwarded to Washington. *Polk's Oklahoma City Directory, 1937,* 36, 882; *Oklahoma City, Oklahoma, Negro City Directory, 1941–1942,* 221.

2 At this point the preliminary version includes the following sentences: "He says, 'I's 90 years old' and when you question him and go back and ask him, 'how old are you?' he will say, lemmesee I's born 1839, then laugh 'ha, ha, ha, ha.' He never forget this year, 1839, yet he does not remember the number of brothers and sisters he has so well."

3 The preliminary version has the following two additional sentences: "'I married two times and has two boys and one girl. See there wuz some that died,' says he when you ask if that was all."

4 The preliminary version adds the following sentence: "Me Moster lived in a log house of 5 rooms, with dirt chimney first, then brick chimney."

5 The preliminary version of the narrative explains more fully: "He said, 'had to put moss in hot water to kill it so it wouldn't grow in mattress.' He says, 'You put moss in mattress, it grow, have [to] boil it and kill him. Man he grow.'" For nineteenth-century instructions on the preparation of Spanish moss for use in Louisiana-style mattresses, see Mary Austin Holley, *Texas,* 124–25.

6 The preliminary version reads "and even weaved."

7 The preliminary draft adds here "made with dem old looms."

8 "When I married I had coat, pants and shirt to marry in," adds the preliminary version.

9 The preliminary version of the narrative continues, "hence this land fell to his son-in-law who gave a deed [of] trust to Conaway, a railroad man who later took it for the money he had loaned him."

10 The preliminary draft adds concerning the overseers, "Me Mosters overseer, at first, was a good man, but others, he said pretty rough."

11 The preliminary version adds at this point: "When they auctioned him off there were three bidders or bids, viz., $1,000, $1150.00 and $1200.00 respectively by 3 different men."

12 "He says, 'He didn't know why,'" adds the preliminary draft.

13 The preliminary version adds, "and even white people would visit their churches."

14 The preliminary narrative adds the following two sentences: "Christmas lasted a week with me boss and the settlement would give balls all night dancing, by fiddle and banjo. When death on plantation, they all would stop work and bury the dead."

The "blackmass" mentioned by the interviewee as a medicine may refer to blue mass, a commonly used preparation mentioned by a number of other informants. His "pork-root water" was almost certainly an infusion of poke root.

15 The preliminary version reads as follows: "Didn't like Booker T. Washington, he helped white people to keep negroes trained to serve as slaves to white people as servants."

FRANCES BANKS[1]

I was born on a farm near Doaksville, east of Hugo, Okla., befo' de Civil War. My parents belonged to an Indian fam'ly, an we moved to Boggy Depot[2] when I was jest a little child. After de Rebellion we stayed on wid de fam'ly and I lived near de fam'ly of Governor Allen Wright[3] for sixty years. I nussed all his chillun and den later, 'long come dey's chillun and I nussed dem, and I'se even nussed de great gran'chillun.

After de War I was what you call a freedman. De Indians had to give all dey slaves forty acres of land.[4] I'se allus lived on dis land which jines dat of Ole Master's and I'se never stayed away from it long at a time. I'se allus been willing to go an nuss de sick an 'flicted, but I allus come back home for a while.

I makes dis liniment of my own p'escription, and it's good for nearly everything dat ails you.[5] A while back a man an a boy got snake-bit, an I put dis liniment on 'em and day was well in no time a'tall.

I has no real record of my being bawn but I think[6] I'se allus had good health and can do most any kind of work I wants to. My grandfather, Uncle Wallace, was a slave of the Wright fam'ly when dey lived near Doaksville, and he and my grandmother would pass de time by singing while dey toiled away in de cotton fields. Grandfather was a sweet singer. He made up songs and sung 'em. He made up "Swing Low Sweet Chariot" and "Steal away to Jesus." He made up lots more'n dem, but a Mr. Reid, a white man, liked dem ones de best and he could play music and he helped grandfather to keep dese two songs. I loves to hear 'em.[7]

I don't 'member much 'bout slavery days, 'cepting us chillun had a right good time playing. We ain' never had no jobs to speak of, cause Old Master wanted all his young slaves to grow up strong and natchel like, and none of us never done no hard work till we was plumb grown and matured. Ole Master was allus good and kind to us. I'se allus lived 'round white folks. I guess I'se de lone sentinel 'round here now. I'se 'bout all dat's left of de old days. Ever'body have gone and left me. I loves my home here cause dese hills and valleys never change. I loves to hear de Bible read too. I never did learn to read though some day I'se gwine to be wid my old friends and if our skins here are black, dey won't be no colors in Heaven. Our souls will all be white.

[1] At some date probably in autumn 1938, WPA field worker Mrs. Jessie R. Ervin interviewed Mrs. Frances Banks at Boggy Depot, Oklahoma. From her notes a preliminary draft of Banks's narrative was typed as "Interview with Frances Banks (Ex-Slave,

Aged 82, Boggy Depot, Oklahoma)," available in the OHS Slave Narratives. On 20 October 1938 this text was revised into the typescript "Frances Banks," published here and also available in the OHS Slave Narratives. Responding to questions about the informant and her life experiences, Ervin on 8 November 1938 wrote to James M. Thompson, director of the Oklahoma Writers' Project, "I called Judge Allen Wright and he says that she [Frances Banks] spoke the truth and that she is really a granddaughter of Uncle Wallace Willis." The Frances Banks narrative was never sent on to Washington. Jessie Ervin, McAlester, Oklahoma, to James M. Thompson, Oklahoma City, Oklahoma, 8 November 1938, WPA Notes on Interviews.

    2 For background on this location, see Muriel H. Wright, "Old Boggy Depot," *Chronicles of Oklahoma* 5 (March 1927): 3–17.

    3 For background on Allen Wright, principal chief of the Choctaw Nation, 1866–70, see John Bartlett Meserve, "Chief Allen Wright," *Chronicles of Oklahoma* 19 (December 1941): 314–21.

    4 Frances Banks, with her name spelled Francis Banks, was legally enrolled as a Choctaw freedwoman by the Dawes Commission on 25 June 1904. U.S., Department of the Interior, Office of Indian Affairs, Dawes Commission, Choctaw Freedmen Census Cards, no. 1414 (Francis Banks), microcopy M1186, reel 12, National Archives and Records Administration, Fort Worth, Texas; U.S., Department of the Interior, Office of Indian Affairs, Dawes Commission, Choctaw Freedmen Enrollment Application Testimony, file 1414 (Francis Banks), microcopy M1301, reel 74, National Archives and Records Administration, Fort Worth, Texas. For background on the lives of freedmen in post–Civil War Indian Territory, see Thomas F. Andrews, "Freedmen in Indian Territory: A Post–Civil War Dilemma," *Journal of the West* 4 (July 1965): 367–76; Berlin B. Chapman, "Freedmen and the Oklahoma Lands," *Southwestern Social Science Quarterly* 29 (September 1948): 150–59; Angie Debo, *The Rise and Fall of the Choctaw Republic,* 89–90, 99–109, 133, 201, 215, 218, 249–50, 255, 259, 262, 275–78; Parthena Louise James, "Reconstruction in the Chickasaw Nation: The Freedmen Problem," *Chronicles of Oklahoma* 45 (Spring 1967): 44–57; Wyatt P. Jeltz, "The Relations of Negroes and Choctaw and Chickasaw Indians," *Journal of Negro History* 33 (January 1948): 24–37; Lewis Anthony Kensell, "Phases of Reconstruction in the Choctaw Nation, 1865–1870," *Chronicles of Oklahoma,* 47 (Summer 1969): 138–53; Daniel F. Littlefield, Jr., *The Cherokee Freedmen from Emancipation to American Citizenship;* Daniel F. Littlefield, Jr., *The Chickasaw Freedmen: A People without a Country;* Hanna R. Warren, "Reconstruction in the Cherokee Nation," *Chronicles of Oklahoma* 45 (Summer 1967): 180–89; Walt Wilson, "Freedmen in Indian Territory during Reconstruction," *Chronicles of Oklahoma* 49 (Summer 1971): 230–44.

    5 The preliminary draft of this narrative has the following sentences scratched out in pencil: "'Aunt Frances' spent much of her time in the home of Dr. W. N. Wright, a leading physician, and learned what she knows of medicine and nursing from him. She has had plenty of opportunity to practice this in the farming community in which she lives. She showed me a bottle of liniment, a formula of her own which she always carries with her. 'I makes dis liniment an' it is good for nearly everything.'" Above these scratched-out lines are the following manuscript notes: "I spent lots of time at Dr. W. N. Wright's house, and learned about nursing from him. I makes a liniment now, and it is good for nearly everything."

⁶ "I'm about sixty-two &" included at this point in the preliminary version.

⁷ According to Oklahoma sources, Wallace Willis sang these songs to the Reverend Alexander Reid, superintendent of the Spencer Academy for Indians in the Choctaw Nation from 1849 to 1861, and it was Reid who made the two spirituals known in the outside world. "Swing Low: Federal Theater of Oklahoma, Works Progress Administration," in "Fed. Theatre" vertical file, box 9, Federal Writers' Project Collection, Archives and Manuscripts Division, Oklahoma Historical Society (hereafter cited as Federal Writers' Project Collection). Other theories also have been proposed for the writing of these spirituals. Mark Fisher Miles, *Negro Slave Songs in the United States*, 145.

PHOEBE BANKS[1]

Age 78   *Muskogee, Oklahoma*

In 1860, there was a little Creek Indian town of Sodom on the north bank of the Arkansas River, in a section the Indians called Chocka Bottoms, where Mose Perryman had a big farm or ranch for a long time before the Civil War. That same year, on October 17, I was born on the Perryman place, which was northwest of where I live now in Muskogee; only in them days Fort Gibson and Okmulgee was the biggest towns around and Muskogee hadn't shaped up yet.

My mother belonged to Mose Perryman when I was born; he was one of the best known Creeks in the whole nation, and one of his younger brothers, Legus Perryman, was made the big chief of the Creeks (1887) a long time after the slaves was freed.[2] Mother's name was Eldee; my father's name was William McIntosh, because he belonged to a Creek Indian family by that name. Everybody say the McIntoshes was leaders in the Creek doings away back there in Alabama long before they come out here.

With me, there was twelve children in our family: Daniel, Stroy, Scott, Segal, Neil, Joe, Phillip, Mollie, Harriett, Sally and Queenie.

The Perryman slave cabins was all alike—just two-room log cabins, with a fireplace where mother do the cooking for us children at night after she get through working in the Master's house.

Mother was the house girl—cooking, waiting on the table, cleaning the house, spinning the yarn, knitting some of the winter clothes, taking care of the mistress girl, washing the clothes—yes, she was always busy and worked mighty hard all the time, while them Indians wouldn't hardly do nothing for themselves.

On the McIntosh plantation, my daddy said there was a big number of slaves and lots of slave children. The slave men work in the fields, chopping cotton, raising corn, cutting rails for the fences, building log cabins and fireplaces. One time when father was cutting down a tree it fell on him and after that he was only strong enough to rub down the horses and do light work around the yard. He got to be a good horse trainer and long time after slavery he helped to train horses for the Free Fairs around the country, and I suppose the first money he ever earned was made that way.[3]

Lots of[4] the slave owners didn't want their slaves to learn reading and writing, but the Perrymans didn't care; they even helped the younger slaves with that stuff. Mother said her master didn't care much what the slaves do; he was so lazy he didn't care for nothing.

They tell me about the War times, and that's all I remember of it. Before the War is over some of the Perryman slaves and some from the McIntosh place fix up to run away from their masters.

My father and my uncle, Jacob Perryman, was some of the fixers. Some of the Creek Indians had already lost a few slaves who slip off to the North, and they take what was left down into Texas so's they couldn't get away. Some of the other Creeks was friendly to the North and was fixing to get away up there; that's the ones my daddy and uncle was fixing to join, for they was afraid their masters would take up and move to Texas before they could get away.

They call the old Creek, who was leaving for the North, "Old Gouge" (Opoethleyohola).[5] All our family join up with him, and there was lots of Creek Indians and slaves in the outfit when they made a break for the North.[6] The runaways was riding ponies stolen from their masters.

When they get into the hilly country farther north in the country that belong to the Cherokee Indians, they make camp on a big creek and there the Rebel Indian soldiers catch up, but they was fought back.

Then long before morning lighten the sky, the men hurry and sling the camp kettles across the pack horses, tie the littlest children to the horses' backs and get on the move farther into the mountains. They kept moving fast as they could, but the wagons made it mighty slow in the brush and the lowland swamps, so just about the time they ready to ford another creek the Indian soldiers catch up and the fighting begin all over again.

The Creek Indians and the slaves with them try to fight off them soldiers like they did before, but they get scattered around and separated so's they lose the battle. Lost their horses and wagons, and the soldiers killed lots of the Creeks and Negroes, and some of the slaves was captured and took back to their masters.

Dead all over the hills when we get away; some of the Negroes shot and wounded so bad the blood run down the saddle skirts, and some fall off their horses miles from the battle ground, and lay still on the ground. Daddy and Uncle Jacob keep our family together somehow and head across the line into Kansas. We all get to Fort Scott where there was a big army camp; daddy work in the blacksmith shop and Uncle Jacob join with the Northern soldiers to fight against the South. He come through the war and live to tell me about the fighting he been in.

He went with the soldiers down around Fort Gibson where they fight the Indians who stayed with the South. Uncle Jacob say he killed many a man during the war, and showed me the musket and sword he used to fight with; said he didn't shoot the women and children—just whack their heads off with the sword, and almost could I see the blood dripping from the point! It made me scared at his stories.

The captain of this company want his men to be brave and not get scared, so before the fighting start he put out a tub of white liquor (corn whiskey) and steam them up so's they'd be mean enough to whip their grannie! The soldiers do lots of riding and the saddlesores get so bad they grease their body every night with snake oil so's they could keep going on.

Uncle Jacob said the biggest battle was at Honey Springs (1863).[7] That was down near Elk Creek, close by Checotah, below Rentiesville.[8] He said it was the most terrible fighting he seen, but the Union soldiers whipped and went back into Fort Gibson. The Rebels was chased all over the country and couldn't find each other for a long time, the way he tell it.

After the war our family come back here and settle at Fort Gibson, but it ain't like the place my mother told me about. There was big houses and buildings of brick setting on the high land above the river when I first see it, not like she know it when the Perrymans come here years ago.

She heard the Indians talk about the old fort (1824), the one that rot down long before the Civil War. And she seen it herself when she go with the Master for trading with the stores. She said it was made by Matthew Arbuckle and his soldiers, and she talk about Company's B, C, D, K, and the Seventh Infantry who was there and made the Osage Indians stop fighting the Creeks and Cherokees. She talk of it, but that old place all gone when I first see the Fort.

Then I hear about how after the Arbuckle soldiers leave the old log fort, the Cherokee Indians take over the land and start up the town of Keetoowah. The folks who move in there make the place so wild and rascally the Cherokees give up trying to make a good town and it kinder blow away. My husband was Tom Banks, but the boy I got ain't my own son, but I found him on my doorstep when he's about three weeks old and raise him like he is my own blood. He went to school at the manual training school at Tullahassee[9] and the education he got get him a teacher job at Taft (Okla), where he is now.

[1] Mrs. Phoebe Banks was interviewed in Muskogee, Oklahoma, by WPA field worker Ethel Wolfe Garrison during the winter of 1937–38. Garrison's initial draft of the Phoebe Banks narrative, now lost, was rewritten by her coworker Craig Vollmer on 13 January 1938 as the typescript "Interview with Phoebe Banks, Slave Born, Age 78, 1008 Oak Street, Muskogee, Oklahoma" in the OHS Slave Narratives. This draft then was revised into standard project format on 19 October 1938 as "Phoebe Banks, Age 78, Muskogee, Oklahoma." This latter version, which is published here and which differs only slightly from the intermediate draft, was forwarded to national project headquarters in Washington. The ribbon copy is available in the LC Slave Narratives, and a carbon copy is available as item 350075 in the LC Slave Narratives Carbon Copies.

[2] Legus Choteau Perryman served as principal chief of the Creek Nation from 1887 to 1895. John Bartlett Meserve, "The Perrymans," *Chronicles of Oklahoma*, 15 (June 1937): 177–80; H. F. O'Beirne and E. S. O'Beirne, *The Indian Territory: Its Chiefs, Legislators and Leading Men*, 105–7.

[3] At this point the preliminary version of the narrative includes the following paragraph: "Lots of the supplies was freighted up the Arkansas river by the steamboats; sometimes daddy take me down to the river when he go to help unload the freight, but I don't remember the names on them boats."

[4] The preliminary draft here states "Some of the slave owners."

[5] For an account of Creek Chief Opothleyohola's life, see John Bartlett Meserve, "Chief Opothleyahola," *Chronicles of Oklahoma* 9 (December 1931): 439–53.

[6] For background on the exodus of Creeks and their slaves for Kansas in the autumn of 1861, see Dean Banks, "Civil War Refugees from Indian Territory in the North," *Chronicles of Oklahoma* 41 (Autumn 1963): 286–89; Edwin C. Bearss, "The Civil War Comes to Indian Territory, 1861: The Flight of Opothleyohola," *Journal of the West* 11 (January 1972): 9–42; Carter Blue Clark, "Opothleyahola and the Creeks during the Civil War," in *Indian Leaders: Oklahoma's First Statesmen*, ed. H. Glenn Jordan and Thomas M. Holm, 49–63; Edmund J. Danziger, "The Office of Indian Affairs and the Problem of Civil War Indian Refugees in Kansas," *Kansas Historical Quarterly*, 35 (Autumn 1969): 260–63; Daniel F. Littlefield, Jr., *Africans and Creeks: From the Colonial Period to the Civil War*, pp. 236–37.

[7] For overviews of the 17 July 1863 Battle of Honey Springs, see Charles R. Freeman, "The Battle of Honey Springs," *Chronicles of Oklahoma* 13 (June 1935): 154–68; Lary C. Rampp and Donald L. Rampp, *The Civil War in the Indian Territory*, 21–28.

[8] A reference to the all-black community of Rentiesville, Oklahoma. For background on this freedmen's town, see "Rentiesville," typescript, n.d., "Blacks" vertical file, Federal Writers' Project Collection.

[9] For accounts of the Tullahassee mission and school, see Althea Bass, *The Story of*

Tullahassee; Virginia E. Lauderdale, "Tullahassee Mission," *Chronicles of Oklahoma* 26 (Autumn 1948): 285–300.

SINA BANKS[1]

Age 86   *McAlester, Oklahoma*

And must I be to judgment brought,
And answer in that day,
Yes, every secret of my heart
And every word I say.

I'm going home, I'm going home
I'm going home to die no more.
To die no more, to die no more
I'm going home to die no more.

I learned those two old songs when I was just a little child going along with my mother to white folks church. Brother Green and Brother Ayers was the preachers. Our Old Master made all his slaves go to church. The women washed and ironed on Friday and mended, cleaned the house and baked on Saturday and on Sunday there wasn't much to do. Everyone black and white went to church. Old Master, John Holleman, was a real old man when the war broke out. His wife, Miss Nancy, was just a little younger than he was. They was the best and kindest people in the world. They saw that none of their slaves was ever whipped, kept us in plenty of good food and we was always clean.

My uncle Caleb ran the farm for Old Master. He was head overseer and all the men and women took orders from him with never a word. Old Master owned twenty-five slaves. Mother and her eight children, Aunt Patsy and her seven children, Hannah Scott and her four children and my two uncles and Aunt Patsy's husband, Uncle Dock Thomas.

Mother had five grown children, three boys and two girls. Aunt Patsy had six grown, two boys and three girls. Hannah had three grown boys. This group gave Old Master plenty of good work hands. He needed them as he had a big farm and they raised lots of corn, rye, wheat, hemp, flax and fruit. He had lots of hogs and mules and he kept lots of milk cows and there was always plenty of food for everybody.

He had a big orchard with apples, peaches and plums. We never could use all of them and there was always apples left on the trees to freeze and I was glad for I sure did like frozen apples. When apple-picking time came uncle and the boys would put hay on the ground and pile the apples in a heap on this hay. They then would pile more hay and dirt on till the apples were covered. When the weather got colder uncle would walk around and look at the sky and say, "Boys we are in for a spell of bad weather and we must cover the apples and vegetables deeper." They kept potatoes, cabbage, collards, and turnips in heaps this way. Parsnips were left in the ground and it was a job to dig them out of the frozen ground. I've done it lots of times, but I hated that job.

Our home was in Marion County, Missouri, near Palmyra. I was born there and was about ten years old when the war broke out. My father and mother settled about four miles from the old place after the war and we used to go there to visit real often. We lived four years about forty miles away and we went back to see the white folks once a year every year we was there. Father and mother was so dissatisfied away from their white folks that we went back to live and never moved away again.

I remember very well when the war started. An old woman came to our house one night about dark and wanted to stay all night and Old Master let her stay. She had a little bundle tied up in a handkerchief and was walking. I suppose she told them where she was going and why she was walking but I never knew. She left the next day about nine o'clock and my mother was out behind the cabins making soap. She stopped to talk to her and I remember hearing her say, "We are going to have a war—maybe soon, and if we do you colored folks will be free." She went on her way but I couldn't keep from thinking about what she said. I asked mother about it but she told me to forget it, that we would always be slaves and that we might as well forget about anything else.

I remember the men scouting around trying to keep from going to war. When things finally settled down and the white men went off to war and left the colored men to look after the farms and to take care of the women and children. They done it and would have shed the last drop of their blood to protect them if it had been necessary. Uncle and the boys worked hard and raised plenty of corn and other food and we never did suffer for anything. Old Master was too old to go to war and he never done no work. He just set in the yard in the shade or in the house in the chimney corner according to the time of the year.

Us children didn't do no work either to speak of. We mostly just run and kicked our heels, like young colts, on the bluegrass lawn. Old Master would make us pull up the weeds that come up in the yard.

The house was a big two story one with a long porch across the front downstairs and one across the front upstairs also. I think there was about eight or nine rooms. The house set on a hill and there was a lot of big shade trees in the yard close to the house. We had a regular flower garden with every kind of flower in it. Old Master's old maid daughter, Miss Nellie, took care of the flowers.

Old Master let all his slaves know that the harder they worked and the more they raised the more they and their families would have to eat and wear. He always divided with them and none of them minded the hard work and never let nothing go to waste.

He never let any of his women work in the field as he always said that they had plenty to do to look after the work at the house, spinning, weaving, sewing, cooking, mending and looking after the white folks and the children. Everybody was always busy. All the women did the spinning and weaving but they divided the rest of the work. All the food was cooked at the big house. They had big pots that hung over the fire on racks and big ovens with lids to bake bread and cakes. They had a big cook stove but hardly ever used it as they had rather cook on the fireplace. Two of the women done the cooking and two others dished it up and served the white folks and the others took part of it to their cabins for they men and children. Everybody et at the same time, and the same kind of food.

We was all perfectly happy and knowed we was well off. My father belonged to John Sykes and lived about five miles from us. He could come home often. He was crippled up with rheumatism and couldn't do much work as he walked with two canes. He stayed at the house and sort of looked after the children and done odd jobs and he raised a patch of broomcorn. His master let him make it up into brooms and sell them and keep the money. He would buy things for mother to use in our cabin. It was a nice big one and was purty well furnished as father got us some chairs, and a bedstead and trundle-bed. Mother kept our house spic and span.

When the women had plenty of cloth woven they would go to work and make it up into clothes. The men were looked after first. Mother done all the cutting. She would take her lapboard in her lap and cut out pants, coats, shirts and underwear. Another job the women had was to make hats for the men. They would plait wheat and rye straw and weave it into hats. They would line the hats with green material so it would shade their eyes.

The sheep were sheared in May. The wool was washed, picked apart and combed and taken to the factory to be made into rolls. It was then spun into thread and woven into cloth. Weaving was hard

work. The whole body was in constant motion as there was five pedals to be operated and in throwing the shuttle through you had to use
both feet and hands.

They made cloth from hemp and flax, too. From flax they made
sheets, tablecloths, towels and clothing. A coarse cloth was made from
hemp and this was made into summer work clothes as it was very cool.

Flax grew about two feet high and hemp about three high. The
hands would go through and cut it down and let it lay there till it rot-
ted. It was then gathered up and placed in the brakes. A brake was a
frame on a stand with a slatted floor about three feet long and three or
four feet high. The flax was laid across these slats and a lever pressed
down to break the chaff from the coarse thread like skin. The chaff fell
to the ground and the skins were placed in piles to be run through the
hackles. Hackles was comb-like things made of wood with teeth like
a comb or brush. The flax was combed through three or four hackles
each one a little finer than the other. This product was called tow.
This made coarse linen. Finer tow made finer linen for dresses.

When the war was finally declared some of the men in the country enlisted, especially the ones that owned slaves. Some few began
to scout around and try to keep from going and some deserted the
army and come home. They had to scout around, too, I can tell you.
I remember that they shot ten deserters down at Palmyra.

Old Master died just at[2] the beginning of the war. He left a will
saying just what he wanted done with all his property and slaves. He
give mother and Uncle Caleb and three or four of the grown men and
women to Miss Nellie and he also left her the farm. She was to take
care of Old Miss as long as she lived. All the rest of us children was
scattered out among his married children. Master Judson was killed
in the war right at the beginning and his property was also divided
up among his brothers and sisters. My grown sister and I went to the
same place. Master David was our young master's name. He wasn't
so very young as he had two grown sons. His wife was the meanest
woman that God ever made. I thought at first that she was crazy but
I found that she was just mean. She would go off and stay a week at
a time and none of us would know where she was and then she would
come riding home and how we did hate to see her. She would cuss
everything and everybody but nobody paid her any mind. Her husband and boys never said a word to her but come and went just like
she wasn't on the place.

My sister done all the cooking and as they were short handed in
the field she had to help in the field, too. She would put the meat for

the vegetables on to boil and she would mark on the floor to show me where the sun would be when it was ten o'clock and I would put the vegetables in to boil with the meat. She would come in and put the bread on and finish up the dinner. It was a lonesome job just sitting there waiting for the sun to tell me it was ten o'clock and then to wait for my sister to come so one day I decided to try my hand at cooking bread. I made up some bread and baked a little to see if it was all right and then I found it was and I went ahead and baked the rest. Sister was sure surprised when she come in and found that I had dinner ready. She was tired and it made her happy to think she had a real helper. The next day I decided to make a dessert so I made some egg custards. I made enough for all to have some and the boys was sure glad to have dessert for dinner.

One of the things Old Master said in his will was that none of his colored folks was to be struck a lick. If we was, we was to go back to the old home place and live with Miss Nellie. We wasn't afraid we would ever be whipped and I guess I was right spoiled. Young Master's wife used to try to whip me but I wouldn't give her no chance as I stayed out of her way. When I would get the dinner dishes cleaned up there wasn't anything for me to do till time to get[3] supper so I would go down to the river about three hundred yards from the house and fish all afternoon. I would have good luck and I fed them so much fish they got tired of it.

Young Master's boys liked to dress up and go to see the girls. They wore boots and they would get me to black them for them. I'd make them pay me and I wouldn't take no pennies either. They always paid me in nickels. I had a double handful of nickels to take home to my mother when I went back to live when the war was over. I didn't have to spend any of it as they bought everything I wanted. When they started to town they would ask me what I wanted and whatever I asked for they got. Some times I'd ask for ribbon and then I'd ask for candy, cookies, brown sugar or just anything I could think of and they always brought it. I didn't have such a good time after the boys had to go to the war. Young Master went before they did.

Young Master's married daughter come and begged them to let me go home with her and stay awhile. Her husband was in the war and there wasn't anybody there but one colored woman, Aunt Callie, and her little girl, smaller than I was. I went back with her and stayed about six months.

The Union soldiers came there often. They'd make out like they was hunting guns but they was hunting men that might be there.

One day I happened to look out and saw some soldiers coming. The man was at home and I told him and he just barely had time to get away before they got there. They come in without knocking and told Young Miss that they was looking for guns and they looked in the drawers and under the beds and closets. Finally they said, "Little girl where is your Master?" I told them that I didn't know. They went on directly and I guess Young Miss's husband went back to his regiment. The first time I went there he hadn't enlisted. I stayed about two months that time. He had three men then and he sure was hard on them. He made them work like dogs and was always beating them for everything. One day I took their food to them and while they was eating they told me that they was going to run off the next day which was Sunday. I didn't say a word about it, of course, and the next morning we got up and after the chores were done we went to church. Me and Aunt Callie and her little girl went to visit a family after church and didn't come home till kind of late in the evening. The men was there that morning but they didn't show up that night before we went to bed. The next morning their master jumped up and called them. They always got right up and went to feeding and master would go back to sleep till breakfast. He waked up again and didn't hear no sound so he called me and told me to go and wake them up. I got up and went to their cabin and come back and told him that they wasn't there and that their beds was still made up.

He sure rolled out of there and got busy hunting them but he didn't catch them as they got away to the Union soldiers and joined the army. Pretty soon he had to go, too, so he had to give up hunting for them.

One night about three o'clock we heard the tramp of horses' feet and of course we was scared most to death. Young Miss had had Aunt Callie and me to bring our bed and put it on the floor in the hall just outside her room so we wouldn't any of us be so scared. We just laid there and waited to see who it was. They rode up into the yard and hallooed. We put on our dresses and went down to see what they wanted.

There was about thirty men on horses and they told her they wanted a wagon and team and a load of corn. They was Union soldiers. She told them that her teams was in the pasture. They said they would go get them and two men went down and the only team they could catch was the carriage team. They opened the gate and I guess they thought it was feeding time and they walked right into the stall. When Young Miss saw what team they had she began to cry and told them that they had the only team she could drive and they told her they would bring it back, that it might be quite a while but that they would see that she got them back. They loaded the corn and drove off. Three months later she got a message that her team was about twenty miles from there and that she could get it if she would come after it. She sent a boy after them and got them back all right.

One of my brothers ran off and went to the army. It wasn't because he wasn't treated good but he just got with some other men and they persuaded him off. Union soldiers would come up to where a nigger was plowing and say to him, "Ain't you tired following that mule up and down that row? Come on and go with me and you won't have to work so hard any more." Maybe they would tie up the mule and go on with him; if they didn't go right then they would run off later.

My brother's young master came over to my mothers and he said, "Sallie, where is young Caleb?" Mother say, "Why you ought to know. How you think I would know when he don't live here no more?" They never did see him any more till after the war was over and he come back home. He said he sure was glad he went.

I went back to my Young Master's as my Young Miss's husband got killed and she took Aunt Callie and went back home to stay till the war was over. My sister was married and her husband had run away and joined the Union soldiers, too.

Sister learned me how to spin and weave and to sew. I was getting to be a purty big girl by this time. The war closed and my sister's husband come and got her and Young Miss went back and took Aunt Callie and that left me the only colored one left. Young Master told me, "You is free now, just as free as I am, and it is my duty to take you back to your mother, but if you will stay with me and help me till I get my crop in I will take you home. I need some one to cook and keep the house for me." I told him I would stay and I did. They was good to me and I worked hard to help him.

I was going home on Tuesday and on Sunday I was going over to Reverend Lowther's to spend the day. They had the purtiest farm you ever saw. The house was on a hill and the lawn was as smooth as velvet. None of his slaves left him. They had nice warm, well-built houses and he had a big farm so he made a trade with them to stay and work his farm for him. He couldn't work as he weighed about three-hundred pounds. I liked to go there and play with the colored children. We could roll down the hill and play on the grass and do purty much as we pleased.

As I went over the stile I thought I saw somebody I knew. When I got to the house I found my brother had come after me. I went home then and lived with my mother and father from then on. Father came and took all of us and we went out in the woods and built us a house and cleared a lot of land and we got along fine. His Master gave him some food and a hog, a cow and a mule. Miss Nellie gave mother a purty good start, too, so we got along all right. Miss Nellie had a sale and sold all the things she had and went to live with one of her sisters. Her mother died during the war and she didn't want to live there by herself. She gave me this tea cup when she made the sale. It was one her mother first bought after she went to housekeeping so it is no telling how old it is. I've kept it with me all these years. Don't you think it looks odd not having a handle on it?

Lots of colored folks when they set free would go around and say, "I don't have to work; I'm free," and they would roam around the country and eat with the ones that was working and trying to make a living. That would make me mad but mother would say, "Don't you say anything for you don't know what you will come to before you die." I told her that just as long as these old hands would work for me I'd not quit working and I'd not sponge off of anybody and I never has. I cooked for Mrs. Priscilla Baird for thirty years. She was president of Engleside College and of Hardin College and I cooked for her at both places. I came to McAlester with the Hailey girls one summer to take care of their mother that was sick and went back and cooked at the college that winter. Next summer I came home with them again and I just stayed as Mrs. Baird's health was bad and she decided to quit teaching.

I've never believed in ghosts, voo-doo or charms. I've seen people wear a string of buttons that people give them and called it a charm string but I think that is just a sort of custom and don't put no faith in it.

I learned a long time ago to do as I was told. One day my mother was in the loom house and my sister and I was playing around the yard and keeping an eye on the baby that was asleep. Mother had a lot of good things to eat, in a chest, and sister told me that let's us get some of the brown sugar that she had in the chest. I told her all right so we got into it and et all we wanted and even made up some sweetened water and drank that. We didn't know that when you opened up brown sugar that it would smell up the whole house. When mother came in she looked around but didn't say nothing but went to the bed and picked up the baby and sat down and nursed and she put it back on the bed and said to me, "Sina, what you been doing with that sugar?" I told her that I hadn't had no sugar. She didn't have to go out to get a switch as she always had one sticking up in the house. She switched us good and told us we didn't have no right to bother things that didn't belong to us. We never did bother anything else that didn't belong to us again.

There was an apple tree that grew in the garden. It had green looking apples with red specks on them. They smelled like spice and I wondered how they tasted. They told us not to bother them as they used all of them to make preserves out of. I never tasted one of those apples as they told me not to bother them. I learned my lesson with the sugar.

I don't git out much now. I sits here and think of the days that are gone and the life that is to come. I think of the old songs I used to sing and they comfort me.

> Jesus my God, I know his name, His name is all my trust,
> He would not put my soul to shame, or let my hopes be lost.
> Firm is His throne, His promise, and thus my soul is secure.

[1] Mrs. Jessie R. Ervin, WPA Slave Narrative Project field worker based in McAlester, Oklahoma, interviewed Mrs. Sina Banks there on 15 December 1937. From her notes Ervin prepared the typescript "Interview with Sina Banks, Age 86, 909 E. Chickasaw, McAlester, Oklahoma," now preserved in the OHS Slave Narratives. From that draft project personnel produced an almost identical final version entitled "Sina Banks, Age 86, McAlester, Oklahoma," published here and also available in the OHS Slave Narratives. For reasons not known, this narrative was never forwarded to Washington.

[2] The preliminary version of the typescript reads "before."

[3]. The passage "the dinner dishes . . . time to get" appears in the preliminary draft of the interview but was omitted, apparently inadvertently, from the final version.

MOLLIE BARBER[1]

Age 79   *Muskogee, Okla.*

Two year before de War broke out I was born, four mile north of Helena, Arkansas, on de old plantation of Nat Turner who was stomped to death by a bull 'bout 15-year ago—I read about it in de Arkansas papers.

My father was Reuben Turner; before dat he was a Slade and maybe some other names too, for he was sold lots of times. When de War come 'long he went off to de North, fought in de War, and never come back.

Mammy was Satira Turner, and she was taken from her folks in Missouri and sold when she was a child. She was sold two–three times[2] in her life, once at Jefferson, Texas, to a Master King who live someplace dey called Black Jack. During de War she was run, with some other slaves, from Missouri to Mississippi, Holly Springs she thought it was, den over into Arkansas, down to Texas, back to Arkansas, and all 'round.

My birth month is de lucky month of July, on de last day of it, Mammy told me.[3] I always been lucky too, wid plenty to eat, plenty to wear, and a good clean house to live in. Dat's about de luck folks can figure on anyways.

Dere was but one more child dan me; his name is Lucius, living down 'round Sulphur Springs, Texas, de last time I hear.

De Old Master's wife was Emma Turner, and Ann Turner was deir daughter. Dey wouldn't let any of de slaves learn reading and such, and dey had a white overseer to run things. He picked out de biggest slave man on de place and made him de "whip-man." When de overseer or de Master figured a slave was due a beating, dey call in de whip man and he lay on de lash.

My mammy work 'round de house and in de fields too; seem lak she done 'bout ever'thing. Before he run off to de North, father would haul de cotton and grain to Helena for Master, and at night he work some more to make "out money," which de Old Master keep part of and let my father keep de rest. Made boots and shoes, mostly.

Money makes me 'member 'bout dat 'Federate money. It got so dead dey give it to de chillen to make doll dresses wid; dat money was real no 'count stuff—wid a wagon-load of it, you was still poor!

Sometimes de white masters would sell de slaves, put 'em on de block and bid you off, de way mammy told me 'bout it. When de slave was put on de block de white folks gather 'round and de bidding would start. De owner talk about de sale dis-a-way:

"I got dis 'ere Negro woman, wid sound teeth; she a good cook, and can have some good little Negroes. What I offered for her?"

Den some man in de crowd say, "Fifty dollars; I give fifty!" De owner say: "We start at dat. Fifty dollar. . . . . Waiting for de next bid!" And 'fore de bidding off is done, dat woman bring in maybe one thousand dollars.

Dat's de way de Turners done; ever'time dey need some money, off dey sell a slave, jest like now dey sell cows and hogs at de auction places.

'Nother time, mammy said, one of de slave women was bid off for six-hundred dollars single; dat mean widout her chillen. De woman went 'round her new Master's house crying all de day, and he asks her: "Ain't I bein' a good Master? Don't you like me fo' a master?"

"You is a good Master," de woman told him, "but I is crying 'bout my babies. I got six pair o' twins, some of dem not yet six-month old, and I don't like bein' sold f'om chillen!"

What my mother say is—her new Master went back and brought[4] ever' child of hers and keep dem all together till dey was free.

Freedom come a year before my mammy knew 'bout it, and she learn 'bout it accidental-like. She was cooking de Christmas dinner for her Mistress, and she went out in de yard for something when a colored man come by. Dey got to talking and he told her 'bout de Freedom—dat she was free jest like all de folks dat had been slaves. She run back in de house, grab up what little clothes she had, make a bundle and leave dat place wid de dinner 'most ready. Bless her old black heart! She was glad to be free!

Most of our masters was white—Caucasians, dey call theyselves—but somewhere in de selling and trading we had some Creek Indian folks and dey give us 60-acre[5] of land.

I married "Doc" Barber at Helena, Arkansas, but he been dead a long time now. My son, Sam, lives part time wid me, but work keeps him 'way most de time.

De colored Methodist church is where I go, and I try to live right. I know if I live for Jesus he will show me de Way.

[1] Mrs. Mollie Barber, known in Muskogee as a restaurant operator, was interviewed by WPA field worker Ethel Wolfe Garrison during the winter of 1937–38. Later, on 19 January 1938, Garrison's coworker Craig Vollmer edited her initial draft, which has not survived, into an intermediate version entitled "Interview with Mollie Barber, Slave Born, Age 79, 1602 N. 5th Street, Muskogee, Oklahoma," preserved in the OHS Slave Narratives. A note appended to this intermediate draft indicates that it was forwarded to typists on 19 October 1938. The next draft, dated the next day, 20 October, is virtually the same except for some standardization of dialect renderings for readability. This later version, published here, is available in ribbon-copy typescript in the OHS Slave Narratives as "Mollie Barber, Age 79, Muskogee, Okla." The Barber narrative was never sent to Washington and survives only in the OHS Slave Narratives. *Polk's Muskogee (Oklahoma) City Directory, 1932,* 47, 235, 261.
[2] The preliminary version of the narrative states "two or three times."
[3] The preliminary version of the narrative states "mother said."
[4] The preliminary version of the narrative reads "bought."
[5] The preliminary draft states "160-acre."

JOE BEAN[1]

Age 89   *Hulbert, Oklahoma*

During the time they come to fighting in the Civil War I was about twelve year old; that make me about 89 year old now, and the year about 1849, when I was born on the Dick Bean plantation over at Lincoln, Arkansas, about 20-mile southwest of Fayetteville.

My father was name Joe Bean; mother was name Cosby Bean and when she died about 15-year back she was 112 year old. She was a Cherokee Indian slave; come here from Georgia when the Indians did, but I don't know her master's name, I mean the Indian master. Some time old Master Bean buy her, that's all I know about it.

Our old slave family was a big one, most of them is now dead, but I remember the names, all except two of the little children who died early, having no names. Dere was Anderson, Mary, Sarah, Cinda, Martha, Rochelle, and Christie; some of the girls still living.

The master was Dick Bean, the mistress was Nancy Bean; dey both dead now, the master going first someday before the war closed, while his young son, Dick the Second, was fighting for the South. He come through the war safe enough and live to raise his own son, Dick the Third (I always calls him), who lets me live in this one-room log cabin on his farm, God Bless his soul!

The old master's house in Arkansas was a big six-room, two-story place of pine planks, wid a porch all around the house. Not far from the big house was a rock building used for the looms; in dere dey made cloth and thread and dey make it for anybody what come dere with cotton or wool. I helped throw the thread in the loom, and I get the dye stuff; the walnut bark for black, the post oak bark that mix in with the copperas for yellow, the log wood mix in with alum for the red-brown colors.

I remember the old slave cabins, all just alike, setting in a row, with a box-elder tree growing in the middle of the yard. The cabins was only one room, without windows, facing the south, with a fireplace in one end. Six of dem cabins fill up the yard, near as I get to it now.

The flooring was rough plank, 'cept round the fireplace where the stones reach out, and where we eat from the wooden dishes on the floor. Lots of good eats for the old master didn't hide out the vegetables and the meats, dey always handy in the smokehouse and wide open for the slaves when dey needs it. The beds was made of posts put together wid wooden pegs, corded rope for the springs covered with cowhide first and then a homespun tick filled wid grass straw. Cover dat wid a homespun quilt and you got the bed.

During the slave times Master Bean had two horses, a bay trotter and a brown single-footer, mighty fine travelers dem riding horses. We ride on the squirrel hunts, me on the bay, master close behind on the brown, waiting for me to sight up a squirrel. Dem was the best days of all.

But dem days go when the fighting starts and we starts to moving around. The first move was to Dardanelle (Arkansas), away over from Fort Smith close by the Arkansas River, on a place where lived the old master's married daughter, Eliza. Dat's where master died.

He stayed shut up in the house a long time 'fore he died. Dat worry me, thought maybe he already died. Worry me, too, because I always used to put on the master's shoes and tie 'em for him, and bring drinks of spring water to cool him after a long ride, and then I figures to find out is he living or not.

They won't let nobody in the room, just break me up because I was near crazy to be with him when he's sick and need me. So I go around the house and rolls me up a barrel to the window of his room, and there he was laying on the bed by the window and I knock on the glass so he'll turn and see me.

"Joe, Joe, come here!" I hear him like it was yesterday. "Take a bucket to the spring and get Master Dick a fresh drink."

They let me take the water to him, and I recollect that was about the last thing I get to do for good old Master Bean.

When he first get sick he was worried about the Federals coming and taking his money. He had gold and silver around the house, heaps of it. He stack it on the floor in long rows to count it before he sack it up getting ready to hide it from the soldiers of the stealing bands that rove around the country.

The money was buried by the master and an old slave who was the most trusted one on the place. Folks heard about the money being buried and after master died some white man get hold of the old slave and try to make it tell where it was buried. The man heated an old axe and burned the old slave's feet, but he never told. Not until young Master Dick come back from the war.

Young master was full of grieving when he find his daddy dead and the money gone. The old slave ask him, "What you worry so for, Master Dick?"

Master Dick just set there on the porch, face buried in his hands. "Everything lost in the war," the young master groaned. "My daddy is gone, the money is all gone, don't know what me and mama will do."

"Hush! Young Master Dick, I show you where the money hid. I show you that, but I can't bring back your old daddy; I can't bring back the old master."

After freedom, some of the slaves kept on with old mistress and young Dick, working for good wages.

Right after the war I come to Fort Gibson. Camped in a tent-house made of elm bark. A Creek Indian drifter moved out and we moved in. Lived about one-half mile from the garrison. Been around here ever since. Once I lived in Jesse James' cave at McBride switch they calls it nowadays; another time I live on a patch of ground where folks say "Cherokee Bill" (Crawford Goldsby, hanged in 1896, by order of Judge Parker's court at Fort Smith), had a battle with officers on Fourteen-Mile Creek.[2]

When I get to thinking about slave days I always remember of the slaves that run away. Master Bean had a white overseer, but he didn't allow for no whippings, 'cept maybe he cuff a young one around if he done something real mean, or maybe sometimes he sell one for the same reason. Whippings, like some of them rich owners did, No! The old master's hide get all turned around if somebody hit a Negro. He'd let nobody chunk 'em around.

But the ones that run away, well, they get the dogs after 'em. Blood-hounds they call 'em, and if a slave be gone two days say, the dogs was used to track, and the masters would say, "If we don't catch them on this farm catch 'em on the next!"

One time I saw a slave whipped on another plantation. He was a new slave, what I mean, they had just bought him and the overseer said the whipping was "just to break him in!" First they beat him with a whip, then with a strap, after tieing him to a log. Peeled off his shirt and laid on with the whip, and then pour salt and pepper water over him so's his back would sting and burn.

I see them use blood-hounds a long time after the war. That's when the store safe was robbed at Melvin (Oklahoma), not far from where I live. Went to town when I heard about it, and they brought the dogs in to trail the robber. Them blood hounds look like fat cur dogs to me, but they starts out trailing and pretty quick they's barking and howling at a colored man's house.

Somebody yelled, "We got him!" But when they all get to where the dogs are they found them all fighting over the pickings of the scrap bucket! And the robber is still free.

A black wool suit and a white poplin shirt, that's my wedding clothes. Got them from the store at Fort Gibson. I married Louisa Alberty; she was a free. Worked for Reverend Dunkin, she did, who was our preacher at the wedding. Married Mary Rogers the next time.

There was lots of children, can't remember all the names. Minnie, Linda, John, Jack, Tom, Potum, lots more than that, can't remember.

I belong to the colored Baptist church because I want a good resting place when I go; if they is such a place as Hell it don't seem like such a good resting place to me.

1. WPA Oklahoma Slave Narrative Project field worker Ethel Wolfe Garrison interviewed Joe Bean in Hulbert, Oklahoma, sometime during the winter of 1937–38. Her coworker Craig Vollmer then edited Wolfe's now lost initial notes on 17 January 1938 into an intermediate draft of Bean's reminiscences. Entitled "Interview with Joe Bean, Slave Born, Age 89, Hulbert, Oklahoma," this typescript is found in the OHS Slave Narratives. According to a note clipped to this draft, it was sent in edited form to a typist on 19 October 1938. The almost identical subsequent typewritten draft, published here, may be found in the OHS Slave Narratives as "Joe Bean, Age 89, Hulbert, Oklahoma." For reasons not known, the Joe Bean narrative was never sent to project headquarters in Washington.

2. For biographical data on Crawford Goldsby, alias Cherokee Bill, see Paul I. Wellman, A Dynasty of Western Outlaws, 242–53, 263–70.

NANCY ROGERS BEAN[1]

Age about 82   *Hulbert, Okla.*

I'm getting old and it's easy to forget most of the happenings of slave days; anyway I was too little to know much about them, for my mammy told me I was born about six years before the War. My folks was on their way to Fort Gibson, and on the trip I was born at Boggy Depot, down in southern Oklahoma.

There was a lot of us children; I got their names somewheres here. Yes, there was George, Sarah, Emma, Stella, Sylvia, Lucinda, Rose, Dan, Pamp, Jeff, Austin, Jessie, Isaac and Andrew; we all lived in a one-room log cabin on Master Rogers' place not far from the old military road near Chouteau. Mammy was raised around the Cherokee town of Tahlequah.

I got my name from the Rogers, but I was loaned around to their relatives most of the time. I helped around the house for Bill Mc-Cracken, then I was with Cornelius and Carline[2] Wright, and when I was freed my Mistress was a Mrs. O'Neal, wife of a officer at Fort Gibson. She treated me the best of all and gave me the first doll I ever had. It was a rag doll with charcoal eyes and red thread worked in for the mouth. She allowed me one hour every day to play with it. When the War ended Mistress O'Neal wanted to take me with her to Richmond, Virginia, but my people wouldn't let me go. I wanted to stay with her, she was so good, and she promised to come back for me when I get older, but she never did.

All the time I was at the fort I hear the bugles and see the soldiers marching around, but never did I see any battles. The fighting must have been too far away.

Master Rogers kept all our family together, but my folks have told me about how the slaves was sold. One of my aunts was a mean, fighting woman. She was to be sold and when the bidding started she grabbed a hatchet, laid her hand on a log and chopped it off. Then she throwed the bleeding hand right in her master's face. Not long ago I hear she is still living in the country around Nowata, Oklahoma.

Sometimes I would try to get mean, but always I got me a whipping for it. When I was a little girl, moving around from one family to another, I done housework, ironing, peeling potatoes and helping the main cook. I went barefoot most of my life, but the master would get his shoes from the Government at Fort Gibson.

I wore cotton dresses, and the Mistress wore long dresses, with different colors for Sunday clothes, but us slaves didn't know much about Sunday in a religious way. The Master had a brother who used to preach to the Negroes on the sly. One time he was caught and the Master whipped him something awful.

Years ago I married Joe Bean. Our children died as babies. Twenty year ago Joe Bean and I separated for good and all.

The good Lord knows I'm glad slavery is over. Now I can stay peaceful in one place—that's all I aim to do.

[1] During the winter of 1937–38, project field worker Ethel Wolfe Garrison interviewed Nancy Rogers Bean at her home about four miles west of Hulbert, Oklahoma. Garrison's now lost field notes were revised into an intermediate draft by her coworker Craig Vollmer on 4 January 1938, and that text survives as the typescript "Interview with Nancy Rogers Bean, Ex-Slave, Age about 82, Living 4-Miles West of Hulbert, Okla." in the OHS Slave Narratives. This intermediate draft was subsequently lightly edited and on 19 October 1938 a final version was prepared as "Nancy Rogers Bean, Age about 82, Hulbert, Okla.," the text forwarded to Federal Writers' Project headquarters in Washington and published here. The ribbon copy is preserved in the LC Slave Narratives, while carbon copies may be found as item 350079 in the LC Slave Narratives Carbon Copies and in the OHS Slave Narratives.

[2] The preliminary draft spells the name "Caroline."

PRINCE BEE[1]

Age 85 Yrs.   *Red Bird, Okla.*

I don't know how old I was when I found myself standing on the top-pen part of a high stump with a lot of white folks walking around looking at the little scared boy that was me. Pretty soon the old master, (that's my first master) Saul Nudville, he say to me that I'm now belonging to Major Bee and for me to get down off the auction block.

I do that. Major Bee he comes over and right away I know I'm going to like him. Then when I get to the Major's plantation and see his oldest daughter Mary and all her brothers and sisters, and see how kind she is to all them and to all the colored children, why, I just keeps right on liking 'em more all the time.

They was about nine white children on the place and Mary had to watch out for them 'cause the mother was dead.

That Mary gal seen to it that we children got the best food on the place, the fattest possum and the hottest fish. When the possum was all browned, and the sweet 'taters swimming in the good mellow gravy, then she call us for to eat. Um-um-h! That was tasty eating!

And from the garden come the vegetables like okra and corn and onions that Mary would mix all up in the soup pot with lean meats. That would rest kinder easy on the stomach too, 'specially if they was a bit of red squirrel meats in with the stew!

Major Bee say it wasn't good for me to learn reading and writing. Reckoned it would ruin me. But they sent me to Sunday School. Sometimes. Wasn't many of the slaves know how to read the Bible either, but they all got the religion anyhow. I believed in it then and I still do.

That religion I got in them way back days is still with me. And it ain't this pie crust religion such as the folks are getting these days. The old time religion had some filling between the crusts, wasn't so many empty words like they is today.

They was haunts in them way back days, too. How's I know? 'Cause I stayed right with the haunts one whole night when I get caught in a norther when the Major sends me to another plantation for to bring back some cows he's bargained for. That was a cold night and a frightful one.

The blizzard overtook me and it was dark on the way. I come to an old gin house that everybody said was the hauntinest place in all the county. But I went in account of the cold and then when the noises started I was just too scared to move, so there I stood in the corner, all the time till morning come.

There was nobody I could see, but I could hear peoples' feet a-tromping and stomping around the room and they go up and down the stairway like they was running a race.

Sometimes the noises would be right by my side and I would feel like a hot wind passing around me, and lights would flash all over the room. Nobody could I see. When daylight come I went through that door without looking back and headed for the plantation, forgetting all about the cows that Major Bee sent me for to get.

When I tells them about the thing, Mary she won't let the old Major scold, and she fixes me up with some warm foods and I is all right again. But I stays me away from that gin place, even in the daylight, account of the haunts.

When the War come along the Major got kinder mean with some of the slaves, but not with me. I never did try to run off, but some of 'em did. One of my brothers tried and got caught.

The old Master whipped him till the blood spurted all over his body, the bull whip cutting in deeper all the time. He finish up the whipping with a wet coarse towel and the end got my brother in the eye. He was blinded in the one eye but the other eye is good enough he can see they ain't no use trying to run away no more.

After the War they was more whippings. This time it was the night riders—them Klan folks didn't fool with mean Negroes. The mean Negroes was whipped and some of them shot when they do something the Klan folks didn't like, and when they come a-riding up in the night, all covered with white spreads, they was something bound to happen.

Them way back days is gone and I is mighty glad. The Negroes of today needs another leader like Booker Washington. Get the young folks to working, that's what they need, and get some filling in their pie crust religion so's when they meet the Lord their souls won't be empty like their pocketbooks today!

[1] Prince Bee was interviewed at Red Bird, Oklahoma, by Oklahoma Slave Narrative Project field worker Craig Vollmer on 3 August 1937. From his interview notes, Vollmer prepared a preliminary draft of Bee's narrative as the typescript "Interview with Prince Bee (Red Bird, Okla.)," now preserved in the OHS Slave Narratives. Within just a few days project editors slightly revised the text into standard form as "Prince Bee, Age 85 Yrs., Red Bird, Okla." Published here, this WPA final draft is available in ribbon copy in the LC Slave Narratives and in carbon copy as item 350104 in the LC Slave Narratives Carbon Copies and in the OHS Slave Narratives. The final draft was forwarded to Washington on 13 August 1937. Stephens to Cronyn, 13 August 1937, WPA Notes on Interviews.

The heading on the earlier draft of this narrative contains the following information not in the later version: "*Note*: This person is an ex-slave, born in Woodville County, Miss. Birthdate: Unknown, probably about 1852. Parents: Clem and Caroline Bee. Grandparents: Caesar Coon and Jennie Linehart. Plantation: Major Bee."

ELIZA BELL[1]

Age 87   *Muskogee, Oklahoma*

I seen many a trouble hour since I was born in dem long gone days
away back in March 1851, just at the time of year when old Master
Joe Wiley took the shoes off his slaves, sending the slaves to work
barefoot and putting the shoes away in the storage waiting for winter to come again before dey'd be give out to the feets dat fit 'em
easiest.

The Wiley plantation was in the timbered lands of Pontiac
County, Mississippi.[2] Dat's where my mother and father lived when
I was born and dey stayed with the Old Master, or one of his married
daughters until after the war was over and the slaves set free.

Frebry Wiley was mother's name. She come from the Alabama
country, while my father was from Georgia and from what he said
dere was no place like Georgia. Always talking about it when he had
a chance to talk, but I'se so old now can't remember all the things he
talked about. His name was Dennis Wiley.

Also I remembers about my grandmother, but not her name. She
was plenty troubled when Mary, the Master's daughter, married and
got ready to move to Fort Smith. Dat was away over in Arkansas and
granny was mighty sad at her leaving. On the day Miss Mary went
away, granny said to her: "Miss Mary, you done married, but please
don't move away. I'se got a feeling that we ain't going to never see
you no more."

Of course the white folks didn't pay no mind to the old colored
lady and Miss Mary just laughed at her like it was something funny.
But after awhile I reckon dey done believe old granny knew something was going to be wrong.

The master said one morning he was going to visit with Miss
Mary. He called the overseers to him, dere was two or three of dem
to look after all the slaves, and told dem what he wanted done on the
place while he's gone. Den he started out on his saddle horse.

I was setting in the house close by Mistress Mary Wiley when
Master come back. He didn't say nothing, just walked into the house
and humped hisself down in a chair. He covered his face with hands
that couldn't hide de grief.

The mistress went over and asked him what's the matter. The
master didn't look at her, just answered "Mary's dead!"

Den long months after all the children was playing the yard. The
mistress and her two girls, Emma and Lucy, was in the yard too,

when somebody pointed to the front-yard gate and called, "look yonder! Look, Mistress, at the gate!"

Everybody stopped, looking to see who is coming to visit. The Mistress said, "It's Mary!" Dere she was, standing by the gate post, something bright shining around her head, and the folks knewed dey was seeing a ghost. Reckon everybody was too scared to say anything and whatever it was dat looked like Miss Mary didn't say nothing either. The form just kinder melted through the gate and run to the house. Den we heard music from the house, just like when Miss Mary was at home, always playing the piano. But the house was empty.

Aunt Betty (the cook) run to call Master Joe and we all followed him into the house, but the music stopped when we got to the porch and wasn't heard no more. The master and mistress led the way to the parlor, nobody dere. Den us all went 'round to the different rooms, but never saw nobody so we went back to the front yard only dere was nothing more we could see. I am an old granny woman myself now, but I can still see her now just like when she come back from the dead.

Old master owned a heap of colored people. They all had two room cabins built of logs, but the back room was just a shed that everybody called the lean-to. That was the kitchen and after working until dark and sometimes later, I remember lots of times carrying a pine torch for my pappy to see by, the grown-ups come to the cabins and get ready the vittles. Everybody eat just about the same things, vegetables seasoned with fat and lean pork, some corn bread and buttermilk. All the slave families had a garden spot for they ownself, take out what they need whenever they need it. The master was always good to the slaves, never kick unless they don't eat enough!

In dem days a bedstead was what the white folks slept in. The slaves had a bed frame made of split logs (my pappy split lots of logs for the master), set in the corner of the front room. The slats was sometimes rope and sometimes planks, piled up with straw for a mattress and covered with an old quilt or maybe a cow hide.

In the fields dey used oxen for plowing and when the cotton was ready for the market the old master would tell my pappy off to take it to town. The oxen was hitched to the wagon and they'd poke down the road slow as a terrapin crawling in the shade.

In times before the war my mother and Aunt Betty would help the mistress weave cloth at night. They made all the work clothes for the field hands—good coarse, heavy stuff for winter and light weight for the hot days.

The first time I was in the master's big house was with mother when she went to the loom room. The master's house was a big frame building. Eight rooms it was, with a hall in between the rooms. The parlor—where Miss Mary played the piano after she died—was the biggest room. The bedrooms was cool and fixed up like the mistress wanted them, with big cherry-wood beds that always made me tired and sleepy ever time I see 'em.

I never saw the war nor heard much about it. Young Bill Wiley, son of the master, went to the war and stayed until it was over. My Uncle Dick (Wiley) went with him, just to take care of him during the fighting and neither of 'em got hurt all the time they was gone.

One day the Yankees come to the master's house while I was setting on the end step of the porch. They wore blue coats brighted up with brass buttons. Soon as I saw them buttons I wanted one, but while one of the soldiers was talking to the mistress on the porch, old Aunt Betty took me by the ear and pulled me into the house—(she said they might start to shooting!)—before I could ask for one of them brass buttons. So I never got one.

About that time the line riders (patrollers) was busy all 'round the country. Looking for Negroes and seeing did they have a pass. If they did it was alright, but if the slave was out without one somebody sure to get flogged mighty hard when they get caught.

Everybody was glad when young Master Billie come back from the war, but when he told us the slaves was free nobody knew what to do about it. Just like turning chickens out of a coop to scratch and nothing there to scratch for!

Our family stayed with the old master long time after that. Father worked on the farm and made lots of crops for the master who give him part of the crop to sell or else sell it and give us the money.

After a pretty good crop year my father fixed up to leave for Texas. The old master give him a horse and a cow when we left and with a wagon we moved to Verona (Texas). Hitched the horse and cow to the wagon and when we got to farming at Verona them two animals pulled the plow on the first crop.

That's where I was married, at Verona. To Jim Bell who's been dead 50 years or more. A white preacher married us and we stayed with my folks to help farm, for my older brother had died and father needed us to help on the farm.

After I got married and had several children (don't know how many, "but seven lived to grown-up"), I got my first schooling. Just barely learned to read through the second reader and write my name.

I am glad slavery is over and I remember the folks talking about Lincoln, the man who was born in a log cabin and who freed the slaves. That was the right thing to do.

That's what God wants everybody to do. Treat everybody right and believe everything that's right, that's what God wants us to do, and to keep the Sabbath holy.

Religion, that was another thing the old master didn't mind us having. Oak Hill Church. There was the first church I went to and it was in slave times. Nothing like the fine churches we got now. Just a little one room log house, with a dirt floor, but it was a place to worship the Lord and nobody worried about what there was to walk on. Just the dirt, but it was God's earth, the same earth that Jesus walked on and we was all glad to be there.

Come Sunday morning and the old master would have one of the boys bring out a horse. Always it was a black mare, and he would let mother ride it to the church meeting, with me on behind holding tight. It was five miles from the farm, down through the timber. I remember the old master calling when we go through the gate: "Don't lose your pass, Frebry, the patrollers get you, 'stead of the devil!"

But the line riders didn't get us because we was careful with the pass, and we live right so's the devil don't get us when we die. I reckon that would please the old master if he knew.

---

[1] Ethel Wolfe Garrison, one of the most active of the field workers for the Oklahoma Slave Narrative Project, interviewed Mrs. Eliza Bell in Muskogee, Oklahoma, probably in late winter 1938. Although Garrison's preliminary notes are now lost, an intermediate draft of Eliza Bell's remembrances was prepared by Garrison's coworker Craig Vollmer on 8 March 1938. This intermediate draft is available as the typescript "Interview with Eliza Bell, Slave Born, Age 87, 711 Indianapolis St., Muskogee, Oklahoma" in the OHS Slave Narratives. A virtually identical but neater typescript of the Bell narrative then was prepared at a later date probably in 1938 and is available as "Eliza Bell, Age 87, Muskogee, Oklahoma," also in the OHS Slave Narratives. This slightly more readable version is published here. For reasons not known, Eliza Bell's interview was never sent to Washington.

[2] This is probably a reference to Pontotoc County, Mississippi.

AN AUTOGIOGRAPHY[1]

By William L. Bethel (Age 92 Years)   129–31 S. Klein, Oklahoma City

Many requests have been made of me to write something of the story of my life. Until recently I have never given much consideration to these requests, for the reason that I have never thought that I had done enough in the world to warrant anything in the way of an autobiography and I hope that my life work, by reason of my present age, lies more in the future than in the past.

I was born a slave on the fourth day of May 1844, Clemmonsville, North Carolina, Forsyth County. My master's name was Josiah Bethel and the mistress's name was Eliza Bethel, and their only daughter was named Mary Bethel. Finally Mary became of age and married a man by the name of Professor Gannaway, who was a Professor of Trinity College at Trinity, North Carolina. After Mr. Gannaway was married to Mary Bethel he moved from Germanton, North Carolina, where we were living, taking my mother and the rest of our family with him to Trinity College, leaving my grandmother and me with Josiah and Eliza Bethel. I was quite a pet of the mistress, and every morning and night my master would put his hand on my head and pray.

Josiah Bethel was a Methodist Preacher and of course we had to move often. We moved from Germanton, North Carolina to Greensboro, where I spent my childhood days and we lived there until the Civil War. At the age of about 18 years I went to Bristow, Virginia, enlisted in the Army, and then I went to Richmond, where we went over breast works. One of our favorite songs was: "Look over in the Valley, don't you see it lighten, looks like we are going to have a storm, but altho you are mistaken, 'tis the darky soldiers' buttons shining on the uniform." After surrender we went to Raleigh, North Carolina, where we were mustered out. I then moved to Greensboro and began working for Judge Lain, on a farm, and I worked for him 12 months and went to school at night. My meals consisted of fat meat and corn bread.

In the year of 1867, I went to Robinson County[2] to cut turpentine boxes, and while there I met a man by the name of W. E. Harley, and we organized a school and hired a white man to tutor. The school grew so large that we were required to assist the teacher.

I left Robinson County in the year of 1870 and went back to Greensboro, North Carolina and worked in a hotel and continued my scholastic attainments. My teacher's names were Jake Nocho and Reverend Crestfield.

In 1872, I married Mrs. Fannie Elizabeth Martin, purchased a home and one acre of land, built a frame cabin, at which place (Greensboro, North Carolina) my first child was born, Carrie Lee Bethel, (now Carrie Lee Lanier) and to the date of this writing she is living at Winston Salem, North Carolina. The next year, in 1873, I entered Lincoln University, in Chester County, Pennsylvania and worked in a club for my board for Dr. Golder, who is now the President of Livingston College, Saul's Borough,[3] North Carolina. After working there for some time, I purchased the Club where I worked. In the year of 1876, my second child was born, William H. Bethel, who is now living at Buffalo, New York. I was graduated from Lincoln University in the year of 1882. During the same year on the 12th day of April 1882, I was licensed to preach. After receiving my certificate of licensure I went on a mission trip to Spartanburg and Welford, South Carolina and organized a church and school, and also served several other churches in Greenville County, South Carolina. In 1884 my wife died, and I then went to Winston Salem, and organized a Presbyterian Church and served a church at Germanton, North Carolina, and also purchased some property while there. I then moved to Mt. Airy and served a church, at Streat, Virginia; I served a church at Sanford, North Carolina, and organized a church at Jonesboro, and also several other churches. I lost my health at Sanford, North Carolina and then returned to Winston Salem, North Carolina, where I married Nanie L. Brown, who is now my present wife.

In 1901 I moved to Oklahoma Territory, leaving a portion of my children in Lincoln University. The first place I lived after reaching Oklahoma Territory was Kingfisher. We then moved to Anadarko, where I purchased a home and organized a Presbyterian Church and Sunday School, and also organizing Presbyterian Churches all over the Oklahoma Territory.

I came to Oklahoma City in 1904 and purchased the premises where I now reside at 129–31 South Klein Street.[4] I also organized a church in the said city, and in the year of 1907 I received three Enabling Acts. 1st. An Enabling Act from the Presbyterians of Oklahoma to organize the Bethany Presbyterian Church in Oklahoma City. 2nd. An Enabling Act from the Synod of Indian Territory to organize a Presbytery of Rental at Oklahoma City.[5] 3rd. An Enabling Act from the General Assembly at Columbus, Ohio, where I was a Commissioner from the Presbytery of Rental to organize the Synod of Canadian. At the general assembly, Des Moines, Iowa, I was called on to give the Benediction.

However, it is impossible to remember every and all the incidents that happened from the days of my childhood until now, but I have given the most important things, that is, the things that I think would be inspiring to some one else.

I am the father of six children, and I put forth every effort possible to educate them, and I will now attempt to write what they are doing and their whereabouts. I have already mentioned heretofore where two of them are, and I might add that my children were graduated and received their degrees at Lincoln University, where I finished. Reverend Martin L. Bethel is now teaching at Tuskegee Institute, Alabama. Doctor Isaac N. R. Bethel lives at Detroit Michigan, Mrs. Bessie E. Smith (nee Bethel) is teaching in the grade schools of Oklahoma City, and Dr. Allen Paul Bethel, druggist, also lives in Oklahoma City.[6]

I am now the Honorable retired and Pastor Emeritus of the Bethany Presbyterian Church.

Give the Black Man a Chance By William L. Bethel. "God created man, male and female, after his own image, in knowledge, righteousness, and holiness, with dominion over the creatures."

Gen. 1:27—So God created man in his own image in the image of God created he him, male and female created he them.

Col. 3:10—And have put on the new man, which is renewed in knowledge after the image of him that created him.

Eph. 4:24—And that ye put on the new man which after God, created in righteousness and true holiness.

Gen. 1:28—And said unto them have dominion over the fish of the sea, and over the fowl of the air, and over every living thing that moveth upon the earth.

"Give the Black Man a Chance"
Fleecy locks and black complexion
Cannot forfeit nature's claim:
Skins may differ but affection
Dwells in white and black the same.

Deem our nation brutes no longer,
Till some reason ye shall find
Worthier of regard and stronger
Than the colour of our kind.

Slaves of old, whose sordid dealings
Tarnish all your boasted powers,
Prove that you have human feelings,
Ere you proudly question ours!

Shall we, whose souls are lighted
With wisdom from on high,

Shall we to men benighted,
The lamp of life deny?

Do unto others as you would have them do to you.
To love God with all your heart, with all your strength and mind,
makes a fine nation, community, fine family, fine Christian, the
brotherhood of man and the fatherhood of God.

Rev. William L. Bethel, Pastor Emeritus.

[1] The narrative of the Reverend William Leonidas Bethel exists only as a typescript in the OHS Slave Narratives titled "An Autobiography by William L. Bethel
(Age 92 Years), 129–31 S. Klein, Oklahoma City." Internal evidence suggests that
this narrative was written by the Reverend Bethel ca. 1936 rather than having been
conveyed by him orally to an interviewer. The undated text has appended an additional page, reprinted here, which consists of selected Bible texts, a poem or song entitled "Give the Black Man a Chance," and admonitions regarding religious faith and
patriotism.

For further background on Bethel's life and activities, see *Lincoln University College and
Theological Seminary Biographical Catalogue, 1918*, p. 19; *Minutes of the Synod of Canadian of
the Presbyterian Church in the United States of America*, p. 3; Edgar Sutton Robinson, ed., *The
Ministerial Directory of the Ministers in "The Presbyterian Church in the United States" (Southern), and in "The Presbyterian Church in the United States of America" (Northern)*, p. 171.

[2] Apparently a reference to Robeson County, North Carolina.

[3] An apparent reference to Salisbury, North Carolina, the location of Livingston
College.

[4] The 1937 Oklahoma City directory shows the Reverend and Mrs. William L.
Bethel residing at 538 Northeast Third. *Polk's Oklahoma City Directory, 1937*, 72.

[5] The Bethany Presbyterian Church was located at 429 Northeast Third in Oklahoma City. *Polk's Oklahoma City Directory, 1937*, 72; *Oklahoma City Negro City Directory*,
xxxv, 214. The correct name of Bethel's presbytery was Rendall.

[6] Allen Paul Bethel's business operated as the Bethel Drug Store at 700 Northeast
Third in Oklahoma City. *Polk's Oklahoma City Directory, 1937*, 72; *Oklahoma City Negro
City Directory*, 14.

STORY OF EX SLAVE L. B. BARNER[1]

Personal Interview   *509 N. Durland*

I's born in Palestine Texas. I don't know how old I is. I was 9 years
old when freedom cried out.

My father was name Kater Barner after master Mat Swanson and
my mother's name Amy Swanson. My father wouldn't work and just
scouted through the woods. One day they decided to catch him and
he ran into the woods and when they had ran him down he killed 18
white men or patrollers.

I have 2 brothers he says, "me and my brother" and one sister.

As a child I played in the quarters during the day and did a little work for my mistress such as churning and many nights after staying at my mistress' house later at nights I would sleep across the foot of her bed at her feet. My mother plowed a brown mule and that mule had so much sense all you had to do was turn that mule out and he would go to the field and back up to the right plow and wait untill my mother got there to hitch him up.

As a slave I ate at my master's house and I waited on the table and fanned the flies. In hot weather we wore a long shirt but in winter we wore jean[2] pants and shoes made on the plantation.

My master and mistress was good to their slaves. He never whipped his slaves unless he caught one of them in a lie as they gave them no trouble and worked hard. They had one child girl name Julia. Their house was a 3 room house on the plantation. The overseer was a Negro who would tell them each morning what to do and as my master had so many hogs and cattle Uncle John the overseer would send the work hands to the field and he would go look up the hogs and cattle as they ran wild in the woods and feed them corn, etc.

My master owned a large amount of land and between 400 and 500 slaves including children. At 4 o'clock the Negro overseer would awake the slaves for their breakfast as they cooked for themselves. One Negro lady (Aunt Claridy) stayed in the quarters and cook for the 150 or more Negro slave children and also worked around for the mistress during the other part of the day.

On Saturdays and Sundays the slaves would have church in the quarters. There were 3 or 4 preachers among them but preacher John Swanson was thought the favorite and best.

The patrollers traveled from plantation to plantation during the nights with dogs, guns and bull whips. They would sick the hounds on the slaves and when they would climb a tree they would, if slave was mean, climb tree and knock him out and the dogs would sometime tear him up before they could get them off him, or else if he would come down at their demand they would whip him so that he would be unable to work and that is how the master would know they were caught out at nights.

On Christmas and New Year's our master would buy barrels of whiskey at the end of the harvests and on these two holidays call the slaves up to the big house and give them all they could drink untill some would become drunk.

The slaves also would carry plenty pepper with them to rub on the bottom of their feet at nights when they slipped off so that the dogs couldn't scent them. The pepper would go up the dogs' nose so that they could not track them.

When a slave got sick Dr. Link would come to them and give them calomel and pills. The slaves would keep asafetida around the children's neck to keep them from having the whooping-cough, etc.

Just before the war started some of the Negro slaves went to build breast works and returned and the next day war broke out.

When master notified or told his slaves that they were free he told them "you are free now just like I am and as you have no places to go you can remain in the quarters untill you see fit to go."

My wife was name Lizzie Billinger and have 4 girls and 2 boys and 11 grandchildren.

"I think Abraham Lincoln much of a man. My pick."

"Now that slavery is over I don't care to go in it any more. I would fight first."

¹ Three distinct narratives exist for the memories of Lewis Bonner, also called L. B. Barner, of Oklahoma City. A roughly contemporary city directory (*Oklahoma City Negro City Directory*, 18) clearly identifies him by the name Lewis Bonner. The first two of the narratives are clearly distinct from each other, each containing information not in the other, and both are presented in this volume. The third version, not published here, is an incomplete but duplicatory composite of elements from the first two narratives.

The first of the narratives comes from an interview conducted by J. S. Thomas on 15 July 1937, which is preserved in the handwritten manuscript "Story of Ex Slave L. B. Barner, 509 N. Durland, Personal Interview," published here, and in the almost identical typescript "L. B. Barner, Age (about) 80, Oklahoma City, Okla.," both available only in the OHS Slave Narratives.

² The term "jean," used repeatedly by informants in the slave narratives in describing clothing, should not be confused with twentieth-century denim used in manufacturing blue jeans. Jean in the mid-nineteenth century was a woven fabric generally twilled and usually made with cotton warp and wool weft, although it could be made entirely from cotton or entirely from wool. *AF Encyclopedia of Textiles*, 556; George S. Cole, *A Complete Dictionary of Dry Goods and History of Silk, Cotton, Linen, Wool and Other Fibrous Substances*, 210; Isabel B. Wingate, ed., *Fairchild's Dictionary of Textiles*, 304.

LEWIS BONNER¹

Age 87 Yrs.   *507 N. Durland, Oklahoma City, Oklahoma*

I was born 7 miles north of Palestine, Texas on Matt Swanson's place in 1850, but I kin not remember the date. My mistress was name Celia Swanson. My mistress was so good to me till I jest loved her.

My family and all slaves on our place was treated good. Mighty few floggings went on round and about. Master was the overseer over

his darkies and didn't use no other'n. I waited table and churned in
the Big House.

I ate at the table with my mistress and her family and nothing was
evah said. We ate bacon, greens, Irish potatoes and such as we git
now. Aunt Chaddy was the cook and nurse for all the chillun on the
place.

We used to hear slaves on de other places hollering from whippings, but master never whipped his niggers 'less they lied. Sometimes slaves from other places would run off and come to our place.
Master would take them back and tell the slave-holders how to treat
them so dey wouldn't run off again.

Mistress had a little stool for me in the big house, and if I got
sleepy, she put me on the foot of her bed and I stayed there till morning, got up, washed my face and hands and got ready to wait on the
table.

There was four or five hundred slaves on our place. One morning
during slavery, my father killed 18 white men and ran away. They
said he was lazy and whipped him, and he just killed all of 'em he
could, which was 18 of 'em. He stayed away 3 years without being
found. He come back and killed 7 before they could kill him. When
he was on the place he jest made bluing.

My mother worked in the field and weaved cloth. Shirts dat she
made lasted 12 months, even if wore and washed and ironed every
day. Pants could not be ripped with two men pulling on dem with
all their might. You talking 'bout clothes, them was some clothes
then. Clothes made now jest don't come up to them near abouts.

Doing of slavery, we had the best church, lots better than today. I
am a Baptist from head to foot, yes sir, yes sir. Jest couldn't be nothing else. In the first place, I wouldn't even try.

I knows when the war started and ceaseted. I tell you it was some
war. When it was all over, the Yankees came thoo' singing, "You may
die poor but you won't die a slave."

When the War was over, master told us that we could go out and
take care of the crops already planted and plant the ones that need
planting 'cause we knowed all 'bout the place and we would go
halvers. We stayed on 3 years after slavery. We got a little money, but
we got room and board and didn't have to work too hard. It was
enough difference to tell you was no slaves any more.

After slavery and when I was old enough I got married. I married
a gal that was a daughter of her master. He wanted to own her, but
she sho' didn't return it. He kept up with her till he died and sent

her money jest all the time. Before he died, he put her name in his will and told his oldest son to be sure and keep up with her. The son was sure true to his promise, for till she died, she was forever hearing from him or he would visit us, even after we moved to Oklahoma from Texas.[2]

Our chillun and grandchillun will git her part since she is gone. She was sure a good wife and for no reason did I take the second look at no woman. That was love, which don't live no more in our hearts.

I make a few pennies selling fish worms and doing a little yard work and raising vegetables. Not much money in circulation. When I gets my old age pension, it will make things a little mite better. I guess the time will be soon.

Tain't nothing but bad treatment that makes people die young and I ain't had none.

[1] The second narrative of Lewis Bonner presented here is available as the text "Lewis Bonner, Age 87 Yrs., 507 N. Durland, Oklahoma City, Oklahoma" in ribbon-copy typescript in the LC Slave Narratives and in carbon copy as item 350051 in the LC Slave Narratives Carbon Copies. Another distinct ribbon-copy typescript with the same title and virtually identical text is found in the OHS Slave Narratives; it bears a handwritten notation, "By Allen," referring to project field worker Willie Allen. The third Bonner narrative, "Lewis Bonner, Age 87 Years, Oklahoma City, Oklahoma," in the OHS Slave Narratives—the composite drawn from the two identified distinct interview texts and not published here—bears a clipped note that identifies as Ida Belle Hunter an additional field worker who collaborated with Willie Allen on the second narrative at some date before 19 August 1937. The second narrative was forwarded to Washington on 2 September 1937 and forms part of the official slave narrative collection in the Library of Congress. Stephens to Cronyn, 2 September 1937, WPA Notes on Interviews.

[2] At this point the composite interview in the OHS Slave Narratives contains the following sentence found in neither of the other two versions: "When our grandchillun would visit us, they would call my wife 'Old White Woman,' and sho made her feel bad."

FRANCIS BRIDGES[1]

Age 73 Yrs.   *Oklahoma City, Okla.*

I was born in Red River County, Texas in 1864, and that makes me 73 years old. I had myself 75, and I went to my white folks and they counted it up and told me I was 73, but I always felt like I was older than that.

My husband's name is Henry Bridges. We was raised up children together and married. I had five sisters. My brother died here in Oklahoma about two years ago. He was a Fisher. Mary Russell, my sister, she lives in Parish, Texas; Willie Ann Poke, she lives in Greenville, Texas; Winnie Jackson lives in Adonia, Texas, and Mattie White, my other sister, lives in Long Oak, Texas, White Hunt County.[2]

Our master was named Master Travis Wright, and we all ate nearly the same thing. Such things as barbecued rabbits, coon, possums baked with sweet potatoes and all such as that. I used to hang round the kitchen. The cook, Mama Winnie Long, used to feed all us little niggers on the flo', jest like little pigs, in tin cups and wooden spoons. We ate fish too, and I like to go fishing right this very day.

We lived right in old Master Wright's yard. His house sat way up on a high hill. It was jest a little old log hut we lived in, a little old shack around the yard. They was a lot of little shacks in the yard, I can't tell jest how many, but it was quite a number of 'em. We slept in old-fashion beds that we called "corded beds," 'cause they had ropes crossed to hold the mattresses for slats. Some of 'em had beds nailed to the wall.

Master Travis Wright had one son named Sam Wright, and after old Master Travis Wright died, young Master Sam Wright come to be my mother's master. He jest died a few years ago.

My mother say dey had a nigger driver and he'd whip 'em all but his daughter. I never seen no slaves whipped, but my mother say dey had to whip her Uncle Charles Mills once for tell a story. She say he bored a hole in de wall of de store 'til he bored de hole in old Master's whiskey barrel, and he caught two jugs of whiskey and buried it in de banks of de river. When old Master found out de whiskey was gone, he tried to make Uncle Charley 'fess up, and Uncle Charley wouldn't so he brung him in and hung him and barely let his toes touch. After Uncle Charley thought he was going to kill him, he told where de whiskey was.

We didn't go to church before freedom, land no! 'cause the closest church was so far—it was 30 miles off. But I'm a member of the Baptist Church and I've been a member for some 40-odd years. I was past 40 when I heerd of a Methodist Church. My favorite song is "Companion." I didn't get to go to school till after slavery.

I 'member more after de War. I 'member my mother said dey had patrollers, and if de slaves would get passes from de Master to go to de dances and didn't git back before ten o'clock dey'd beat 'em half to death.

I used to hear 'em talking 'bout Ku Klux Klan coming to the well to get water. They'd draw up a bucket of water and pour the water in they false stomachs. They false stomachs was tied on 'em with a big leather buckle. They'd jest pour de water in there to scare 'em and say, "This is the first drink of water I've had since I left Hell." They'd say all sech things to scare the cullud folks.

I heerd my mother say they sold slaves on what they called an auction block. Jest like if a slave had any portly fine looking children they'd sell them chillun jest like selling cattle. I didn't see this, jest heerd it.

After freedom, when I was old enough to work in the field, we lived on Mr. Martin's plantation. We worked awful hard in the fields. Lawd yes'm! I've heard 'bout shucking up de corn, but give me dem cotton pickings. Dey'd pick out all de crop of cotton in one day. The women would cook and de men'd pick the cotton, I mean on dem big cotton pickings. Some would work for they meals. Then after dey'd gather all de crops, dey's give big dances, drink whiskey, and jest cut up sumpin terrible. We didn't know anything 'bout holidays.

I've heard my husband talk 'bout "Raw head an' bloody bones." Said whenever dey mothers wanted to scare 'em to make 'em be good dey'd tell 'em dat a man was outside de door and asked her if she'd hold his head while he fixed his back bone. I don't believe in voodooing, and I don't believe in hants. I used to believe in both of 'em when I was young.

I married Jake Bridges. We had an ordinary wedding. The preacher married us and we had a license. We have two sons grown living here. My husband told me that in slavery if your Master told you to live with your brother, you had to live with him. My father's mother and dad was first cousins.

I can 'member my husband telling me he was hauling lumber from Jefferson where the saw mill was and it was cold that night, and when they got halfway back it snowed, and he stopped with an old cullud family, and he said way in the night, a knock come at de door—woke 'em up, and it was an old cullud man, and he said dis old man commence inquiring, trying to find out who dey people was and dey told him best dey could remember, and bless de Lawd, 'fore dey finished talking dey found out dis old cullud man and de other cullud woman an' man dat was married was all brothers and sisters, and he told his brother it was a shame he had married his sister and dey had nine chillun. My husband sho' told me dis.

I've heerd 'em say dey old master raised chillun by those cullud women. Why, there was one white man in Texas had a cullud woman, but didn't have no chillun by her, and had this cullud woman and her old mistress there on the same place. So, when old Mistress died he wouldn't let this cullud woman leave, and he gave her a swell home right there on the place, and she is still there I guess. They say she say sometime, she didn't want no Negro man smutting her sheets up.

I think Abraham Lincoln was a good man, and I have read a whole lots 'bout him, but I don't know much 'bout Jeff Davis. I think Booker T. Washington is a fine man, but I ain't heerd so much about him.

[1] Mrs. Francis Bridges was interviewed in Oklahoma City by an unidentified field worker from the WPA Oklahoma Slave Narrative Project probably sometime during the summer of 1937. A preliminary draft of her remembrances was prepared as the typescript "Francis Bridges, Age 73 Years, 314 N.E. 2nd., Oklahoma City, Oklahoma. Home Address: Greenville, Texas," now preserved in the OHS Slave Narratives. The street address for the interview was that of Allen Matthews, possibly a relative. At some later date also probably in summer 1937, project personnel lightly edited the preliminary draft to place it in standard form as the text "Francis Bridges, Age 73 Yrs., Oklahoma City, Okla.," published here and available in ribbon-copy typescript in the LC Slave Narratives and in carbon copy as item 350089 in the LC Slave Narratives Carbon Copies and in the OHS Slave Narratives. The final draft of the Francis Bridges narrative was forwarded to Washington on 16 August 1937. Stephens to Cronyn, 16 August 1937, WPA Notes on Interviews; *Polk's Oklahoma City Directory, 1937*, 920.

[2] "Parish, Texas"; "Adonia, Texas"; and "Long Oak, Texas, White Hunt County" apparently refer to Paris, Texas; Ladonia, Texas; and Lone Oak, Hunt County, Texas, respectively.

JOHN BROWN[1]

Age (about) 87 Yrs.   *West Tulsa, Okla.*

Most of the folks have themselves a regular birthday but this old colored man just pick out any of the days during the year—one day about as good as another.

I been around a long time but I don't know when I got here. That's the truth. Nearest I figured it the year was 1850—the month don't make no difference nohow.

But I know the borning was down in Taloga County, Alabama,[2] near the county seat town. Miss Abby was with my Mammy that day. She was the wife of Master John Brown. She was with all the slave women every time a baby was born, or when a plague of misery hit the folks she knew what to do and what kind of medicine to chase off the aches and pains. God bless her! She sure loved us Negroes.

Most of the time there was more'n three hundred slaves on the plantation. The oldest ones come right from Africa. My Grandmother was one of them. A savage in Africa—a slave in America. Mammy told it to me. Over there all the natives dressed naked and lived on fruits and nuts. Never see many white mens.

One day a big ship stopped off the shore and the natives hid in the brush along the beach. Grandmother was there. The ship men sent a little boat to the shore and scattered bright things and trinkets on the beach. The natives were curious. Grandmother said everybody made a rush for them things soon as the boat left. The trinkets was fewer than the peoples. Next day the white folks scatter some more. There was another scramble. The natives was feeling less scared, and the next day some of them walked up the gangplank to get things off the plank and off the deck.

The deck was covered with things like they'd found on the beach. Two–three hundred natives on the ship when they feel it move. They rush to the side but the plank was gone. Just dropped in the water when the ship moved away.

Folks on the beach started crying and shouting. The ones on the boat was wild with fear. Grandmother was one of them who got fooled, and she say the last thing seen of that place was the natives running up and down the beach waving their arms and shouting like they was mad. The boat men come up from below where they had been hiding and drive the slaves down in the bottom and keep them quiet with the whips and clubs.

The slaves was landed at Charleston. The town folks was mighty mad 'cause the blacks was driven through the streets without any clothes, and drove off the boat men after the slaves was sold on the market. Most of that load was sold to the Brown plantation in Alabama. Grandmother was one of the bunch.

The Browns taught them to work. Made clothes for them. For a long time the natives didn't like the clothes and try to shake them off. There was three Brown boys—John, Charley and Henry. Nephews of old Lady Hyatt who was the real owner of the plantation, but the boys run the place. The old lady she lived in the town. Come out in the spring and fall to see how is the plantation doing.

She was a fine woman. The Brown boys and their wives was just as good. Wouldn't let nobody mistreat the slaves. Whippings was few and nobody get the whip 'less he need it bad. They teach the young ones how to read and write; say it was good for the Negroes to know about such things.

Sunday was a great day around the plantation. The fields was forgotten, the light chores was hurried through and everybody got ready for the church meeting.

It was out of the doors, in the yard fronting the big log [house] where the Browns all lived. Master John's wife would start the meeting with a prayer and then would come the singing. The old timey songs.

The white folks on the next plantation would lick their slaves for trying to do like we did. No praying there, and no singing.

The Master gave out the week's supply on Saturday. Plenty of hams, lean bacon, flour, corn meal, coffee and more'n enough for the week. Nobody go hungry on that place! During the growing season all the slaves have a garden spot all their own. Three thousand acres on that place—plenty of room for gardens and field crops.

Even during the war goods was plentiful. One time the Yankee soldiers visit the place. The white folks gone and I talks with them. Asks me lots of questions—got any meats—got any potatoes—got any this—some of that—but I just shake my head and they don't look around.

The old cook fixes them up though. She fry all the eggs on the place, skillet the ham and pan the biscuits! Them soldiers fill up and leave the house friendly as anybody I ever see!

The Browns wasn't bothered with the Ku Klux Klan either. The Negroes minded their own business just like before they was free.

I stayed on the plantation 'til the last Brown die. Then I come to Oklahoma and works on the railroad 'til I was too old to hustle the grips and packages. Now I just sits thinking how much better off would I be on the old plantation.

Homesick! Just homesick for that Alabama farm like it was in them good old times!

[1] Slave Narrative Project field worker L. P. Livingston interviewed John Brown in West Tulsa probably sometime during the summer of 1937. Livingston's initial draft of Brown's remembrances, now lost, was revised by project employee Craig Vollmer on 10 August 1937 as the typescript "Interview with John Brown, West Tulsa, Okla." in the OHS Slave Narratives. Almost immediately this intermediate draft was revised into final WPA form as the text "John Brown, Age (about) 87 Yrs., West Tulsa, Okla.," published here. This final draft is available in ribbon-copy typescript in the LC Slave Narratives and in carbon copy as item 350102 in the LC Slave Narratives Carbon Copies and in the OHS Slave Narratives. The final version was forwarded to Federal Writers' Project national headquarters on 12 August 1937. Stephens to Cronyn, 12 August 1937, WPA Notes on Interviews.

[2] Apparently a reference to Talladega County, Alabama.

STORY FROM EX-SLAVE [ROBERT H. BURNS][1]
Reference (A) Personal Interview, Robert Burns   *530 Mass. Street*

I's born Agefield,[2] Tennessee, south of Nashville. I's born de last of March 1856. Me father was name A[n]thony Owens and mother's name Catherine Owens. They wuz Tennessee born. During slavery I's a child. Never worked, just played around. Our beds was made of straw. Me grand parents belonged to moster Montgomery Bell. He was so rich he set free about 75 of his slaves and sent dem to Liberia. He also set de remainder of about 225 Negroes free dat he kept.

After his death his son-in-law enslaved dem again by breaking de will of his father-in-law.

During Slavery dar wuz ar white man in Mississippi doat made his living catching runaway slaves. One Negro slave one night killed 75 hounds wid ar side blade after dey had run him down and got away again and dey never did git dis slave. Anuther slave would always run away and when dey would git at him he knew of ar pond wid ar hollow tree growing a distance from the banks where he could run and jump into this pond of water and swim to this old tree and go up in its hollow and the dogs would run up to de edge of dis pond and stand dare and bark and de hunters would come dar and couldn't see nuzzin and leave.

We wore white cotton shirts and pants and shirts only during summer dat was weaved right dare on de plantation. I never seed any under-wear until I wuz bout 12 years of age. We all wore hats made from wheat straw. Dare wuz no shoes for de slaves a-tall. In winter de women would tie dar feet up in rags.

I got married me first time near Florence, Alabama. I's 25 years old. I paid $1.50 for me license and if you wanted to divorce it would cost 50 cents.

Isaac Curkendoll was me moster. His house was white ar frame building. He owned five or six farms, viz: in Tennessee, Mississippi and owned about 300 slaves on the place where I wuz. I don't know how many slaves on de other plantation, dare wuz as many as 150 Negro children in the quarters. Dare wuz so many wolves in Tennessee dat dey would at nights fight. One night dey ran a Negro slave up a tree and kept him up dare all night. Dey howled and howled and more wolves came dat it seemed to be about ar hundred. Dey dog all night at de roots of dis tree till nearly day when dey dug it down and when de tree felled it frightened de wolves and dey ran away and de slave den come home and told his moster de wolves had caused him to be out all night.

De slaves would be whipped each evening, if dey failed to pick 300 lbs. of cotton. One day de overseer tied a Negro woman to a tree and let de body part of clothing down and he sat down in a chair and whipped her for one hour.

My moster would put slave in a calaboose at nights to be whipped de next morning. He always limited de lashes to 500. After whipping dem he would rub pepper and salt on dare backs, where whipped, and lay dem before de fire until blistered and den take a cat and hold de cat and make him claw de blisters to burst them.

I had eight children by me first wife. De second time I married a half Indian and white woman. Dare wuz 11 children born to her.

Me moster wuz so mean he didn't allow any church. Four or five slaves succeeded in running away and went north to de free states. De patrollers wuz plentiful and if dey would catch you out at nights wid out a pass dey would whip um unmercifully even if you wuz caught visiting within de quarters. Sometime de slaves would be out at nights and[3] de patrollers would be looking for dem de slaves would lie down in de dark and grunt like a hog and de patrollers would go on thinking dem to be hogs.

He said, when a slave man wanted to marry, his master would never object to a big tall nigger like you as dey preferred big tall slaves as dey wuz strong and would bring more money when sold.

De white preachers who would call dem selves preaching to de slaves would only preach to de niggers about being good, obedient and work good and hard for dare moster. He would preach and tell de nigger dat dey didn't have any souls, and that niggers didn't go to heaven. Only white people had souls and went to heaven. He told dem dat niggers had no more souls than dogs, and dey couldn't go to heaven any more than could a dog.

De slaves would use rag-weed tea for bowels complaint, bone-set-weeds for chills, and Sampson-snake-root for chills. Dey wore anjil-lico roots around de neck to keep down diseases.[4]

De Slaves would all try to git dem a black cat and cook him and when done take the cooked cat to a stream of water and pour into stream and de bone dat would come to de top of de water and float up stream would be de one de slave would git to carry in his pocket for good luck to give him luck, keep moster from whipping him and many other things.

During Civil War de Yankees come to me moster's plantation and killed up me moster's chickens, hogs, cattle and told us to help our-selves.

Our Master ran off so dat de Yankees couldn't find him and when he returned he was mad and whipped de slaves because he thought dey told de Yankees where to find his hogs and cattle, etc.

We all thought Abraham Lincoln was our God, but we had to keep it a secret as our moster did not like him as he was trying to set us free. We had to pretend, to him, dat we liked Jefferson Davis, to our Master as he pretended to us dat Davis wuz de niggers' friend, and dat he, Davis, was going to set dem free and give each nigger family 40 acres and a mule.

Now dat slavery is over I wish and hope dat God would treat all dem slave owners as dey did us when they get in hell.

1 Robert H. Burns was interviewed at his home by field worker J. S. Thomas in Oklahoma City on 7 July 1937. From the interview Thomas prepared a preliminary draft of the Burns narrative entitled "Story from Ex-Slave, 530 Mass. Street, Reference (A) Personal Interview, Robert Burns." This interview is available, in both ribbon and carbon copies, only in the OHS Slave Narratives, for it was never forwarded to Washington. The ribbon copy has written in pencil by hand the words "Robert Burns Age 81 Yrs., Oklahoma City, Okla." *Polk's Oklahoma City Directory, 1937,* 117, 879.

2 This is probably phonetic spelling for Edgefield, one of the earliest suburbs of Nashville, just across the Cumberland River east of the Nashville commercial district.

3 The phrase "the slaves would be out nights and" is repeated at this point in the typescript.

4 The interviewee's "anjillico" is most likely angelico (*Ligusticum canadense*), a folk remedy, and not to be confused with angelica. John Crellin and Jane Philpott, *Herbal Medicine Past and Present,* vol. 2, *A Reference Guide to Medicinal Plants,* pp. 55–57

SALLIE CARDER[1]

Age 83 Yrs.   *Burwin, Okla.*

I was born in Jackson, Tennessee, and I'm going on 83 years. My mother was Harriett[2] Noel and father Jeff Bills, both of them named after their masters. I has one brother, J. B. Bills, but all de rest of my brothers and sisters is dead.[3]

No sir, we never had no money while I was a slave. We just didn't have nothing a-tall! We ate greens,[4] corn bread, and ash cake. De only time I ever got a biscuit would be when a misdemeanor was did, and my Mistress would give a buttered biscuit to de one who could tell her who done it.

In hot weather and cold weather dere was no difference as to what we wore. We wore dresses my mother wove for us and no shoes a-tall.

I never wore any shoes till I was grown and den dey was old brogans wid only two holes to lace, one on each side. During my wedding I wore a blue calico dress, a man's shirt tail as a head rag, and a pair of brogan shoes.

My Master lived in a three-story frame house painted white. My Mistress was very mean. Sometimes she would make de overseer whip negroes for looking too hard at her when she was talking to dem. Dey had four children, three girls and one boy.

I was a servant to my Master, and as he had de palsy I had to care for him, feed him and push him around. I don't know how many slaves but he had a good deal of 'em.

About four o'clock mornings de overseer or negro carriage driver who stayed at the Big House would ring de bell to git up and git to work. De slaves would pick a heap of cotton and work till late on moonshining nights.

Dere was a white post in front of my door with ropes to tie the slaves to whip dem. Dey used a plain strap, another one with holes in it, and one dey call de cat wid nine tails which was a number of straps plaited and de ends unplaited. Dey would whip de slaves wid a wide strap wid holes in it and de holes would make blisters. Den dey would take de cat wid nine tails and burst de blisters and den rub de sores wid turpentine and red pepper.

I never saw any slaves auctioned off but I seen dem pass our house chained together on de way to be sold, including both men and women with babies all chained to each other. Dere was no churches for slaves, but at nights dey would slip off and git in ditches and sing and pray, and when dey would sometimes be caught at it dey would be whipped. Some of de slaves would turn down big pots and put dere heads in dem and pray. My Mistress would tell me to be a good obedient slave and I would go to heaven. When slaves would attempt to run off dey would catch dem and chain dem and fetch 'em back and whip dem before dey was turned loose again.

De patrollers would go about in de quarters at nights to see if any of de slaves was out or slipped off. As we sleep on de dirt floors on pallets, de patrollers would walk all over and on us and if we even grunt dey would whip us. De only trouble between de whites and blacks on our plantation was when de overseer tied my mother to whip her and my father untied her and de overseer shot and killed him.

Negroes never was allowed to git sick, and when dey would look somewhat sick, de overseer would give dem some blue-mass pills and oil of some sort and make dem continue to work.

During de War de Yankees would pass through and kill up de chickens, and hogs, and cattle, and eat up all dey could find. De day of freedom de overseer went into de field and told de slaves dat dey was free, and de slaves replied, "free how?" and he told dem: "free to work and live for demselves." And dey said dey didn't know what to do, and so some of dem stayed on. I married Josh Forch. I am mother of four children and 35 grand children.

I like Abraham Lincoln. I think he was a good man and president. I didn't know much who Jeff Davis was. What I heard 'bout Booker T. Washington, he was a good man.

Now dat slavery is over, I don't want to be in nary 'nother slavery, and if ever nary 'nothern come up I wouldn't stay here.

[1] Mrs. Sallie Carder was interviewed at Burwin, Oklahoma, by project field worker J. S. Thomas on 8 July 1937. From his notes, Thomas prepared a preliminary draft of Carder's remembrances as the typescript "Story from Ex-Slave, Personal Interview, Sallie Carder, P.O. Box No. 27, Burwin, Oklahoma," now preserved in the OHS Slave Narratives. Later in the summer or fall project personnel edited the preliminary draft into a more standard form and prepared a final draft, "Sallie Carder, age 83 Yrs., Burwin, Okla.," which is presented here. This final draft is available in ribbon-copy typescript in the LC Slave Narratives and in carbon copy as item 350015 in the LC Slave Narratives Carbon Copies and in the OHS Slave Narratives. It was sent to project headquarters in Washington on 18 November 1937. Stephens to Alsberg, 18 November 1937, WPA Notes on Interviews.

[2] The preliminary draft spells this name the standard "Harriet."

[3] At this point the following two sentences appear in the preliminary draft but are missing from the later version: "I member me grandmother. She was name Emily Bray."

[4] The preliminary draft notes "sot greens."

BETTY FOREMAN CHESSIER[1]

Age 94 Years   *Oklahoma City, Okla.*

I was born July 11, 1843, in Raleigh, N.C. My mother was named Melinda Manley, the slave of Governor Manley of North Carolina,[2] and my father was named Arnold Foreman, slave of Bob and John Foreman, two young masters. They come over from Arkansas to visit my master and my pappy and mammy met and got married, 'though my pappy only seen my mammy in the summer when his masters come to visit our master and dey took him right back. I had three sisters and two brothers and none of dem was my whole brothers and sisters. I stayed in the Big House all the time, but my sisters and brothers was gived to the master's sons and daughters when dey got married and dey was told to send back for some more when dem died. I didn't never stay with my mammy doing of slavery. I stayed in the Big House. I slept under the dining room table with three other darkies. The flo' was well carpeted. Don't remembah my grand-mammy and grandpappy, but my master was they master.

I waited on the table, kept flies off 'n my mistress[3] and went for the mail. Never made no money, but dey did give the slaves money at Christmas time. I never had over two dresses. One was calico and one gingham. I had such underclothes as dey wore then.[4]

Master Manley and Mistress had six sons an' six darters. Dey raised dem all till dey was grown too. Dey lived in a great big house 'cross from the mansion, right in town before Master was 'lected Governor, den dey all moved in dat mansion.

Plantation folks had barbecues and "lay crop feasts" and invited the city darkies out. When I first come here I couldn't understand the folks here, 'cause dey didn't quit work on Easter Monday. That is some day in North Carolina even today. I doesn't remember any play songs, 'cause I was almost in prison. I couldn't play with any of the darkies and I doesn't remember playing in my life when I was a little girl and when I got grown I didn't want to. I wasn't hongry, I wasn't naked and I got only five licks from the white folks in my life. Dey was for being such a big forgitful girl. I saw 'em sell niggers once. The only pusson I ever seen whipped at dat whipping post was a white man.[5]

I never got no learning; dey kept us from dat, but you know some of dem darkies learnt anyhow. We had church in the heart of town or in the basement of some old building. I went to the 'piscopal church most all the time, till I got to be a Baptist.

The slaves run away to the North 'cause dey wanted to be free. Some of my family run away sometime and dey didn't catch 'em nei-ther. The patrollers sho' watched the streets. But when dey caught any of master's niggers without passes, dey jest locked him up in the guard house and master come down in the mawnin' and git 'em out, but dem patrollers better not whip one.

I know when the War commenced and ended. Master Manley sent me from the Big House to the office about a mile away. Jest as I got to the office door, three men rid up in blue uniforms and said, "Dinah, do you have any milk in there?" I was sent down to the of-fice for some beans for to cook dinner, but dem men most nigh scared me to death. They never did go in dat office, but jest rid off on horse-back about a quarter a mile and seem lak right now, Yankees fell out of the very sky, 'cause hundeds and hundeds was everywhere you could look to save your life. Old Mistress sent one of her grandchillun to tell me to come on, and one of the Yankees told dat child, "You tell your grandmother she ain't coming and never will come back there as a slave." Master was setting on the mansion porch. Dem Yankees come up on de porch, go down in cellar and didn't tech one blessed thing. Old Mistress took heart trouble, 'cause dem Yankees whipped white folks going and coming.

I laid in my bed a many night scared to death of Klu Klux Klan. Dey would come to your house and ask for a drink and no more want a drink than nothing.

After the War, I went to mammy and my step-pappy. She done married again, so I left and went to Warrington[6] and Halifax, North Carolina, jest for a little while nursing some white chillun. I stayed in Raleigh, where I was born, till 7 years ago, when I come to Oklahoma to live with my only living child.[7] I am the mother of 4 chillun and 11 grandchillun.

When I got married I jumped a broomstick. To git unmarried, all you had to do was to jump backwards over the same broomstick.

Lincoln and Booker T. Washington was two of the finest men ever lived. Don't think nothing of Jeff Davis, 'cause he was a traitor. Freedom for us was the best thing ever happened. Prayer is best thing in the world. Everybody ought to pray, 'cause prayer got us out of slavery.

[1] Ida Belle Hunter from the Oklahoma Slave Narrative Project interviewed Mrs. Betty Foreman Chessier in her home at Oklahoma City probably sometime in the spring or summer of 1937. From her notes Hunter prepared a preliminary draft of Chessier's reminiscences entitled "Interview with Betty Foreman Chessier, Ex-Slave, 624 N.E. 5th, Oklahoma City, Oklahoma, by Ida Belle Hunter," preserved today in the OHS Slave Narratives. Project personnel edited Hunter's rough draft and from it prepared a final draft in accord with project guidelines. This final draft, "Betty Foreman Chessier, Age 94 Years, Oklahoma City, Okla.," published here, is available in ribbon-copy typescript in the LC Slave Narratives and in carbon copy as item 350063 in the LC Slave Narratives Carbon Copies and in the OHS Slave Narratives. The Chessier narrative was sent to Washington on 2 September 1937. Stephens to Cronyn, 2 September 1937, WPA Notes on Interviews; *Polk's Oklahoma City Directory, 1937,* 144.

[2] Charles Manley served as governor of North Carolina from 1849 to 1851.

[3] Consistently the preliminary draft renders "mistress" as "miz."

[4] At this point the preliminary draft includes the following sentences: "I et what the white folks et an' dey diden eat no 'possums and rabbits, doe dey et fish. My choice food was soup an' still is. No gardens where I lived, cose I diden live on no plantation. I lived in town all the time. Dey all had gardens out on the plantation doe."

[5] The preliminary draft at this point includes the two sentences "Mastah had jes' 15 slaves on the place and when his chillun come home to visit ever summah dey had to bring dey own niggers. Dey brung two a piece."

[6] This may be phonetic spelling for Warrenton.

[7] The 1937 Oklahoma City directory lists Mrs. Betty Foreman Chessier as residing with Arnold and Olive Foreman at 624 Northeast Fifth. *Polk's Oklahoma City Directory, 1937,* 144, 255, 933.

INTERVIEW WITH GEORGE WASHINGTON CLARIDY[1]

Reference: A. Ex-Slave, age 84   *305 N.E. First Street,*
                                                                     Oklahoma City, Oklahoma

I was bo'n in Centerpoint, Howard County, Arkansas, October 5, 1853, so dey tell me; dat's all I know'd 'cep' what dey tell me for the truth.

Well, it's kinda surprise for someone to come around to talk to me. I never gits to talk to anybody much; folks don't care nothing bout me; dey all calls me de drunkard, gambler, horse thief and murderer. I'se been practically all dem things too. I'se been a wicked man ever since my first wife died. I confessed religion in 1863 and lived like a gentleman until de death of my wife; den I felt lak everything I had was gone so I jes started getting drunk, gambling and raising hell. I'se never fooled with any woman to mount to nothin since my wife died; I jes get drunk, gambled and forgot about de women. I've made lots o' money gambling and selling whiskey. I've seed de time when I would write a check for five thousand dollars any day. Cose I ain't got nothin' now. Jes lak I made it I let it get away from me, jes dat quick. I got in jail once bout some whiskey. I had a fellow to build me a barn right dere on dat corner, (lst and Central) and underneath dat barn I had him to build a place for me to hide my whiskey. I done good business for a long time den I decided to have me a house build so got dis same fellow dat built de barn to figger wid me on de house. Well, he knew I had plenty money so he tried to skin me, so I got a nudder fellow and he figured de house three hundred dollars cheaper. Well, I let him build it for me. Now here's what happened: dat other low down rat, jes cause I wouldn't let him skin me out o' my money he went to the sheriff's office and told him about dis place he built fo me to keep my whiskey. Well, de sheriff come out dere and began to look around fo de stuff and when he found de place, it was locked in. He told me to unlock it and he would tare de place up, pore out de whiskey, and let me go. Cose you know I was lak most Niggers would be wid a little money; I cussed him out, told him dat was my place and he better not put his damn hand on it. He didn't say a word; he jes went back got some mo fellows and dey come dere, broke dat place open and carried away seven hundred and seventy-five dollars worth of whiskey for me. Well dey put me in jail and I stayed dere one hundred and fifteen days. It cost me a lot o' money to keep from going to the penitentiary. I gave old Norman Pruitt[2] nigh five thousand dollars to git me out of it.

Ah! kid, I tell yo I am George Washington Claridy; I'se been into a little o' everything; I know de ropes. Cose dey call me a murderer, but I ain't never killed nobody. Dey jes put dat on to it case I'se such a wicked fellow. I ain't no count now. I's such a wicked fellow. I ain't no count now. I jes drag around; I don't ask nobody fo nothin.' I ain't never asked anybody for a dime in my life. I gits a little $21.50 check from de pension folks each month and I makes dat last me.

Now you want me to tell you somethin' about slavery times: sorry I got away from you in de beginning, but I jes lak to tell folks de kind o' life I've lived. Well, my father and mother was named Cats and Clarenda Claridy. Dey came from South Carolina, I don't know what place; all I know is jes South Carolina. I have two brothers and two sisters; cose one brother and one sister is jes half brother and sister to me, case after my pa went to de war and never did come back, my mother had dese two kids by another man. Now James and Ann Claridy was my whole brother and sister, and John and Arena was my half brother and sister. I don't know what their las name is case I never did know what the follow's name was my mother married the second time.

We were good livers on plantation, ole Master laked us a lot. He let us live in de best house on de plantation. It was as good as a lot o' dese little shacks you see over here now. De beds was alright; cose we slept on straw mattresses but that didn't make no diffunce to us; dey slept mighty fine.

Well, I don't recollect nothin' bout my grandmother, only a little dat my grandfather told me. Now, I know a lots bout him cose we stayed on with ole Master for six months after freedom, den we started to workin on halves for a nudder fellow down there in Arkansas. We started out hoping dat we would soon be able to buy us a farm of our own, so we began saving every dime we could git our hands on, and we did dat for eight years, den my grandpa got down wid de rheumatism. Dere was a old lady in dat country dat was a good doctor fo dat kind a stuff; so we sent for her. She came over dere and doctored on my grandpa and it seemed to have done lots o' good; so after dat, we would send for her every two or three days, and he kept on getting better and better. Now we jes kept our money in a sack hanging on de wall and every time she came, I would git de sack off of de wall, pay her and put it back. So finally, one day after Pa had got up enough to walk and thought he could make it alright from

then on, we decided we would go out and git the old lady some vegetables to take home wid her. While we were gone, I be-dog-gone if
that old lady didn't git that sack and we haven't seen or heard from
her since. We had purty near a thousand dollars in that sack too.

Well, I'll tell you how I feel bout religion. Now I jined the church
once, but I soon found out dat most o' de folks in dere didn't have religion, even de preacher. De biggest thing they want is money. Since
I'se found dat out de only thing I do is read my Bible every day and
try to treat my fellow man right; cose I tell you I don't believe in dis
here singing and shouting on Sunday and raising de devil wid yo
neighbor on Monday.

I neber did no nothing bout Abraham Lincoln, Jeff Davis and dem
fellows. I jes heard bout 'em. Cose dey was mighty big men from
what I could hear.

Well, I'll tell we lived mighty good in slavery time days, dat is,
our family did, but even at dat price, I would hate to have to go over
it again; yes sir I sho' would.

---

1 The OHS Slave Narratives contain the texts from two separate interviews undertaken by WPA field workers with George Washington Claridy of Oklahoma City. Because they are sufficiently distinct from each other, they are both published here. Neither narrative was ever forwarded to Federal Writers' Project headquarters in
Washington. The following interview, the earlier of the two, was made by Willie Allen
on 2 July 1937 and is available as the typescript "Interview with George Washington
Claridy, Reference: A. Ex- slave, age 84, 305 N.E. first Street, Oklahoma City, Oklahoma" in the OHS Slave Narratives.

For background on prohibition and bootlegging in Oklahoma, see Jimmie Lewis
Franklin, *Born Sober: Prohibition in Oklahoma, 1907–1959*; Jimmie L. Franklin, "That
Noble Experiment: A Note on Prohibition in Oklahoma," *Chronicles of Oklahoma* 43
(Spring 1965): 19–34; James Stanley Martindale, "The Bootlegger in Oklahoma City"
(master's thesis, University of Oklahoma, 1950), 1–61.

2 The name noted by field worker Willie Allen as "Norman Pruitt" must refer to
Oklahoma City attorney Moman Pruiett. *Polk's Oklahoma City Directory, 1923,* 583;
Warden's Oklahoma City Directory, 1913–1914, 523.

GEORGE WASHINGTON CLARIDY[1]

Age 84   *Center Point, Arkansas*

George Washington Claridy lives at 305 E. First Street [Oklahoma
City]. Born October 15, 1853, at Center Point, Arkansas, Howard
County. His first marriage was in 1880; professed religion 1858. Got
hurt digging a well at Ardmore 46 years ago and has been in ill
health since that time.

Four years ago he was crossing a street [when] two women driving a car and intoxicated ran over him and broke his left leg. He now uses a crutch. Did use two until recently.

He at one time owned a block of property on the corner of First and Central. After the death of his third wife his relation beat him out of this. He now lives off a pension, which is $21.00 per month.

He says he hasn't always been "down and out"; stated he was once in the wholesale liquor business in Oklahoma City, and had handled as much as $800.00 worth of whiskey in a day. He once paid a $500.00 fine and served 30 days in jail.

Has no education; says he felt he was too smart. Could have gone to school 3 or 4 weeks every year, but he thought George Washington was a smart man and he came next. The only work he ever did during the war was to keep children out of an orchard to keep them from stealing fruit and he was insulted, felt he should be given a far-better job, said "he never did see his father after the war." After the war was over his father wrote his mother and said, "You marry so and so I'm going to marry so and so," and he understood his father died in Kansas City some years ago. Says "the only lie he ever told in his life" was to keep his third wife from leaving him and he told a big one on the man she was leaving with and gained the day.

1. The second interview with George Washington Claridy was made by Lura J. Wilson on 11 October 1937. It is represented by two virtually identical texts, one handwritten, "Personal Interview with George Washington Claridy," and the other typewritten, "George Washington Claridy, Age 84, Center Point, Arkansas," both in the OHS Slave Narratives. This narrative is written entirely in the third person.

WPA administrators apparently were unsatisfied with the two Claridy narratives. A note dated 5 November 1937 and filed with the earlier Willie Allen interview states "re-interview," but then adds in different handwriting "deceased." The death of the informant and consequent inability of field workers to undertake an additional interview may explain why the Claridy material was never forwarded to Washington.

INTERVIEW WITH HENRY CLAY[1]

Ex-Slave, Aged About 100 Years　　　　*Four Miles West of Manard, Oklahoma, R.R. 1, Ft. Gibson*

I seen a lot of things in my lifetime, and I reckon the more I seen the more I got to give up my thanks for. I been in this world about a hundred years, I think, for I was a grown man and been a grown man quite a while when the Civil War come along.

I was born in North Carolina, in Jefferson county close to a little town called Rayville, on a big plantation belong to Old Master

Henry Clay. He was some akin to the Tillmans in that country and they was sure big rich.

My pappy's name was Solomon Clay and my mammy's name was Hanna. She belong to a Smalls down in South Carolina in Concordia Parish, that was some more kinfolks of the Clays I think, because when her an Pappy is freed they go and live with the Smalls until they both die. Old Master Clay already dead when the War come along, though.

I was at home with my folks until I was about fifteen years old I reckon, and then I was sold to a man name Cheet, Dyson Cheet, and he move with us to Louisiana close to Texarkana, but he hire me out to a man name Goodman Carter to work on his steamboat for a long, long time, maybe four or five years in all, so I don't know much about Old Master Dyson Cheet.

Then he give me or will me to his boy Tom Cheet and he bring me to the Creek Nation because his wife come from Mississippi and she is just part Creek Indian, so they can get a big farm out here if they want it. That was a pretty place and I always will call it home, but I been everywhere since then and I went back and took the name I was borned under because I never forget my old Master Henry Clay, and besides, Mammy and Pappy kept the name of Clay too.

Well, I had such a rambling time in my life I better start back on the old plantation in North Carolina and tell what it look like first, to give me a better start in my mind, anyway.

Mammy and Pappy and me lived in a house close to the big house back there, and Pappy was the coach boy and horse boy. The big house was two stories high with a big porch what run clean to the top, and more window blinds than I ever seen in a house since. Our little house was made of planks, heavy oak lumber, all whitewashed with lime, and we had good furniture; Old Mistress give us what she was through with. The bed was high like you could hang a curtain on, and had springs like we got today. My grandpa used to live in that house too, before I was born, and about the first thing I remember was when Old Master sell him and Grandmammy to a lady in town.

That lady lived by herself, and she knowed my grandpappy a long time and wanted to give him a good home and light work, and Mammy say she give a thousand dollars for the two of them.

Grandpappy's name was Uncle Dick Tillman and Grandmammy's name was Millie Tillman, and they belong to the Tillmans when Old Master bought them long before my pappy was borned.

Our little house was full, I'll tell you, because I had seven sisters while I was there and seven more after I left, but I never did see part of them little ones. Only the names of some of the big ones come to me; there's Chloe, Millie, Rachel, Susanna, and Hannah. That's all I remember.

We eat fish, greens, potatoes, sow belly and corn pone mostly, but sometimes in winter we get some fresh beef when they have a neighborhood killing. Everybody go to the field about seven o'clock when the big bell ring, and come in late by the same bell.

Young slaves that too little for the field work in the Mistress' garden, and we get so much for each family to take home from the garden.

Old negroes make our clothes from homespun cotton, and some mixed wool in cold weather. I had one long shirt that had five different colors in the stripes. We wear them long shirts when we was little boys, without any pants in the summer.

Old Master Clay was good to my folks, and kept on laughing at Mammy on account of so many girl babies. He just say, "Better do better next time!" And the next one was a girl, too!

She never quit work but three days on account of a baby, and when she go back in the field she carry the baby in a red blanket tied to her back. When it get hungry she just slip it around in front and feed it and go right on picking or hoeing while it have its ninny.

Old Master was awfully kind and religious. I think he would preach a little sometime or maybe teach sunday school. I never seen him whip a slave, but he had a whipping machine, to scare them with mostly. When he say to the overseer, "Drive them today," he meant we was getting behind the season and he wanted us to hurry up. But the overseer was a negro too, and he just worked harder and told us to lay into it or he'd tell on us.

Sometimes Old Master come to the field in his buggy and talk to us, and one time I seen some neighbor negroes getting a whipping in the field and I asked Old Master what for, and he say, "Hoe your row, youngun, or you might catch the like of that too."

They was about six hundred acres in the plantation, so my mammy told me one time, but I don't think it was in one piece. Then they had nearly two hundred slaves, big and little—mostly little it seems like. They all lived in the "nigger quarters" that set way off from the house. They was little one room plank cabins setting close together in a row so that you could step from one porch to the other.

When I was big enough for the field I would have to go down to the quarters in the evening and hear the rules for the next day. The overseer would get the field negroes all together and give out the rules. If he say, "Henry, tomorrow you pick cotton on the west side of the north field," or maybe, "you cut four or five good ricks of wood on the south woods lot close to the cane patch side," that would be what I do the next day as soon as that old bell ring. We never have to ask in the morning, because we already had our roles and could go to work on the bell.

That whipping machine was a funny thing. Old Master just had it to set around so the slaves could see it I think. He loaned it out to a man one time though, and the man used it. It was a big wooden wheel with a treadle to it, and when you tromp the treadle the big wheel go round. On that wheel was four or five big leather straps with holes cut in them to make blisters, and you lay the negro down on his face on a bench and tie him to it and set the machine close to him. Then when you tromp the treadle the wheel go round and flop them straps across his bare back and raise the skin. Getting a negro strapped down on that bench had him cured long before you had to tromp that treadle.

They had a little church on the plantation where we set on Sunday and heard the Mistress read out of the Bible to us and then we all sung good songs and prayed. But no school and no reading lessons before the emancipation, I'll tell you.

When I was about fourteen or fifteen I went off with Mr. Dyson Cheet to Louisiana and he started to whittle a plantation right out of the woods. All I had to do was cut down trees and grub sprouts all day every day.

I cut cord wood too, to sell to the steamboats, and pretty soon I was hired off to work on one of the boats. I guess it had a name but I don't remember it. Boss Man was Mr. Goodman Carter, and he was a good ship master. Us negro boys worked as roustabouts to load and unload and keep the fire going. The boat run from Alexandria, Louisiana, down the Red river to the Mississippi and then up to St. Louis and back to Alexandria again.

I was on that boat quite a long time, and then Old Master's boy Tom Cheet marry a part Creek woman and I go to live with them. They settle south of where Muskogee is now about two miles from the Honey Springs town. That was a good plantation, too, and they had good double log houses and lots of stock.

I lived in a cabin with a stick and mud chimney, and I had to keep putting out the fire where it set the sticks of the chimney until I daubed it all good with red clay.

Mistress had me help the children of the other slaves to make pots out of red clay because I was good at it. We made good clay pots and I have made hominy in them like the Creeks make lots of times. We would make the pots and hang them in the chimney to bake, sometimes a whole week, then pick out the ones that didn't crack.

I was a great fellow with the Master's children because I would make them clay marbles. Roll them and bake them like the pots, and the children and the grown negroes too would play "sevens" with them on Sunday.

It seem like the slaves in the Creek country had a better time than most of the negroes in Louisiana, too. They played more and had their own church and preachers.

We went to a place where the colored preacher was Reverend Seymour Perry, and we used to baptize in the Elk and sing "Oh, I wish I could find some secret place where I could find my God." They sung "When I come to die I want to be ready" and such songs as that.

The big thing on that plantation was the corn shucking. One every two weeks almost, and negroes from other plantations would come over to shuck for their masters and then we would go to another shucking the same way. The masters sold lots of corn to the army at Fort Gibson at the start of the War, and I took several loads, but before that we took it to Webbers Falls mostly.

War come along and Master go with the south side, and I went along to drive a wagon, but I got separated from Master the first thing and never seen him but once or twice in the War.

When they was going to strike a battle somewhere they would come and get us and our wagons and we would haul stuff for several days and nights to some place where they could get it. Then we would go off away from there before they had the battle so they wouldn't get us captured.

I've hauled like that all around Webbers Falls and Fort Gibson and Fort Davis and all over these rocky hills sometimes when we had to take an axe and cut a road at night, but I never seen but one battle and that was just the smoke. We was at a place close to where Braggs is now and we seen the fire when the Yankees burn up Honey Springs.

After the War all the negroes don't know what to do. My old pappy and mammy even come all the way out here in a ox wagon and then turn around and go back to North Carolina. They couldn't make a living here.

I stayed with Master until he died, and that wasn't very long, and then I married and settled down. Master been trying to get me to marry a long time, and here is how he done it.

I never did get along good with these Creek slaves out here and I always stayed around with the white folks. In fact I was afraid of these Creeks and always got off the road when I seen Creek negroes coming along. They would have red strings tied on their hats or something wild looking.

Well young Master say, "Henry, why don't you go over to Josh Brooks' house and see them folks. His daughter Maggie say to tell you to come on over to church out there. You got to make some friends out there, so you just go on over and see her. You free now."

Well, I take his good horse and Texas saddle and I ride over that-away.

Get about there and set down on a log to think about what I going to talk about. Them Creek negroes was so funny to talk to anyways. Well, I set there from in the morning to way in the evening and never go on to that house. Just turn round and go back.

Young Master say, "What that gal have to say, Henry boy?"

"Good things, Boss," I tell him. I sure lied and he knowed it, too, for he nearly died laughing.

Just the same I went on back, and pretty soon I got the gal an married her, and we got some of that Creek money and bought a house close to Honey Springs.

On the boat I learned to fiddle, and I can make an old fiddle talk. So I done pretty good playing for the white dances for a long time after the War, and they sure had some good ones. Everything from a waltz to a Schottische I played. Sometimes some white people didn't like to have me play, but young Master (I always called him that till he died) would say, "Where I go my boy can go too."

I never was sick bad in my life but once. On the old place in North Carolina Old Mistress looked after the sick and got a doctor, but out here young Mistress give the sick ones mullein, May apple, burr vine, Red Root, Life Everlasting and things like that for sickness. All the negroes wore a little bag of asafoetida around the neck to keep off disease, too.

That time I was sick I thought I seen ghosts, but I guess it was the fever. We was moving, the year after the war, and at midnight we had to break camp because I thought I seen people moving around in the woods, dogs barked out in the woods, and an old Indian with one eye come up to my pallet and when I moved the covers he disappeared.

I bin back to Africa since the War, too.[2]

Some white people come from Tennessee I think, and got up a delegation of negroes to go back and show the Africans how we are civilized. It was right about the time of statehood, for Oklahoma was a state when I got back.

They took about fifty negroes and I went along. We sailed from New Orleans on a big boat and they was negroes from every state in the bunch.

We went to the Bahama Islands and then on to Africa, and when we got to the jungle camp in Africa I seen them African negroes just like they was wild.

They had some little men with scars all over them that they said was cannibals and they would eat human meat.

In one place where we was about a month they had underground jails. Just dug a big hole and put heavy logs over it and dirt on that. Then they put the prisoners they got in their wars down in that hole and sold them off to white men that come in ships to get them.

They was still selling them, too, but not to men from America any more but from other places. The bunch I was with tried to tell them it was wrong.

In one place they ate raw meat, and we tried to offer them cooked meat and they told the black man that we had along that it was bad for the stomach, so he said.

I don't think we done any good, and still we stayed there in Africa a long time, maybe two or three years.

When we come back home I just keep on living around one place and other, in Arkansas, Louisiana, Oklahoma and two or three trips in Missouri.

We got this little place here and been here ever since, and I guess it is my last resting place.

I'm glad we are free, and don't have to work any more whether we are sick or not, like in slavery days.

I went to church always and am a good Christian, and I hope to see my Maker and both my Masters because they was both good, kind men.

Everybody should have religion, but you got to go slow and not try to change the leopard spots quick, like them people done in Africa. I don't think they done a bit of good.

Just trust in God and hoe your row and sidestep away from the
great temptation, that's what I say.

¹ The interview with Henry Clay exists in just one typescript in the OHS Slave Narrative collection, "Interview with Henry Clay, Ex-Slave, Aged About 100 Years, Four
Miles West of Manard, Oklahoma, R.R. 1, Ft. Gibson." The interview was undertaken
by Slave Narrative Project employee Ethel Wolfe Garrison and was revised by WPA editor Robert Vinson Lackey about 5 November 1937, the date on a note card attached to
the text. This narrative was never forwarded to Washington.

² The following account of the informant's trip to Africa has not been corroborated
in other sources, but there were many back-to-Africa movements in the United States
in the late nineteenth and early twentieth centuries. For perhaps the best survey of
these efforts, see Edwin S. Redkey, *Black Exodus: Black Nationalist and Back-to-Africa
Movements, 1890–1910.*

POLLY COLBERT¹

Age 83 Yrs.   *Colbert, Oklahoma*

I am now living on de forty-acre farm dat de Government give me
and it is just about three miles from my old home on Master Holmes
Colbert's plantation where I lived when I was a slave.

Lawsy me, times sure has changed since slavery times! Maybe I
notice it more since I been living here all de time, but dere's farms
'round here dat I've seen grown timber cleared off of twice during my
lifetime. Dis land was first cleared up and worked by niggers when
dey was slaves. After de War nobody worked it and it just naturally
growed up again wid all sorts of trees.² Later, white folks cleared it
up again and took grown trees off'n it and now dey are still cultivat-
ing it but it is most wore out now. Some of it won't even sprout peas.³
Dis same land used to grow corn without hardly any work but it sure
won't do it now.

I reckon it was on account of de rich land dat us⁴ niggers dat was
owned by Indians didn't have to work so hard as dey did in de old
states, but I think dat Indian masters was just naturally kinder any
way, leastways mine was.

My mother, Liza, was owned by de Colbert family and my father,
Tony, was owned by de Love family.⁵ When Master Holmes and Miss
Betty Love was married dey fathers⁶ give my father and mother to
dem for a wedding gift.⁷ I was born at Tishomingo and we moved to
de farm on Red River soon after dat and I been here ever since.⁸ I had
a sister and a brother, but I ain't seen dem since den.⁹

My mother died when I was real small, and about a year after dat
my father died. Master Holmes told us children not to cry, dat he and

Miss Betsy would take good care of us. Dey did, too. Dey took us in de house wid dem and look after us jest as good as dey could colored children. We slept in a little room close to them and she allus seen dat we was covered up good before she went to bed. I guess she got a sight of satisfaction from taking care of us 'cause she didn't have no babies to care for.

Master Holmes and Miss Betsy was real young folks but dey was purty well fixed. He owned about 100 acres of land dat was cleared and ready for de plow and a lot dat was not in cultivation. He had de woods full of hogs and cows and he owned seven or eight grown slaves and several children. I remember Uncle Shed, Uncle Lige, Aunt Chaney, Aunt Lizzie, and Aunt Suzy just as well as if it was yesterday. Master Holmes and Miss Betsy was both half-breed Choctaw Indians. Dey had both been away to school somewhere in de states and was well educated. Dey had two children but dey died when dey was little. Another little girl was born to dem after de War and she lived to be a grown woman.

Dey sure was fine young folks and provided well for us. He allus had a smokehouse full of meat, lard, sausage, dried beans, peas, corn, potatoes, turnips and collards banked up for winter. He had plenty of milk and butter for all of us, too.

Master Holmes allus say, "A hungry man caint work." And he allus saw to it that we had lots to eat.

We cooked all sorts of Indian dishes: Tom-fuller, pashofa, hickory-nut grot, Tom-budha, ash-cakes, and pound cakes besides vegetables and meat dishes.[10] Corn or corn meal was used in all de Indian dishes. We made hominy out'n de whole grains. Tom-fuller was made from beaten corn and tasted sort of like hominy.

We would take corn and beat it like in a wooden mortar wid a wooden pestle. We would husk it by fanning it and we would den put in on to cook in a big pot. While it was cooking we'd pick out a lot of hickory-nuts, tie 'em up in a cloth and beat 'em a little and drop 'em in and cook for a long time. We called dis dish hickory-nut grot. When we made pashofa we beat de corn and cook for a little while and den we add fresh pork and cook until de meat was done. Tom-budha was green corn and fresh meat cooked together and seasoned wid tongue or pepper-grass.

We cooked on de fire place wid de pots hanging over de fire on racks and den we baked bread and cakes in a oven-skillet. We didn't use soda and baking powder. We'd put salt in de meal and scald it wid boiling water and make it into pones and bake it. We'd roll de

ash cakes in wet cabbage leaves and put 'em in de hot ashes and bake
'em. We cooked potatoes and roasting ears dat way also. We sweetened our cakes wid molasses, and dey was plenty sweet too.

Dey was lots of possums and coons and squirrels and we nearly always had some one of these to eat. We'd parboil de possum or coon and
put it in a pan and bake him wid potatoes 'round him. We used de
broth to baste him and for gravy. Hit sure was fine eating dem days.

I never had much work to do. I helped 'round de house when I
wanted to and I run errands for Miss Betsy. I liked to do things for
her. When I got a little bigger my brother and I toted cool water to
de field for de hands.

Didn't none of Master Holmes' niggers work when dey was sick.
He allus saw dat dey had medicine and a doctor iffen dey needed one.
'Bout de only sickness we had was chills and fever. In de old days we
made lots of our own medicine and I still does it yet. We used polecat grease for croup and rheumatism. Dog-fennel, butterfly-root, and
life-everlasting boiled and mixed and made into a syrup will cure
pneumonia and pleurisy. Pursley-weed, called squirrel physic, boiled
into a syrup will cure chills and fever. Snake-root steeped for a long
time and mixed with whiskey will cure chills and fever also.

Our clothes was all made of homespun. De women done all de
spinning and de weaving but Miss Betsy cut out all de clothes and
helped wid de sewing. She learned to sew when she was away to
school and she learnt all her women to sew. She done all the sewing
for de children. Master Holmes bought our shoes and we all had 'em
to wear in de winter. We all went barefoot in de summer.

He kept mighty good teams and he had two fine saddle horses. He
and Miss Betsy rode 'em all de time. She would ride wid him all over
de farm and dey would go hunting a lot, too. She could shoot a gun
as good as any man.

Master Holmes sure did love his wife and children and he was so
proud of her. It nearly killed 'em both to give up de little boy and
girl. I never did hear of him taking a drink and he was kind to everybody, both black and white, and everybody liked him. Dey had lots
of company and dey never turned anybody away. We lived about four
miles from de ferry on Red River on de Texas Road and lots of travelers stopped at our house.[11]

We was 'lowed to visit de colored folks on de Eastman and Carter
plantations dat joined our farm. Eastman and Carter was both white
men dat married Indian wives. Dey was good to dey slaves, too, and
let 'em visit us.

Old Uncle Kellup (Caleb) Colbert, Uncle Billy Hogan, Rev. John Carr, Rev. Baker, Rev. Hogue, and old Father Murrow preached for de white folks all de time and us colored folks went to church wid dem. Dey had church under brush arbors and we set off to ourselves but we could take part in de singing and sometimes a colored person would get happy and pray and shout but nobody didn't think nothing 'bout dat.

De Patrollers was de law, kind of like de policeman now. Dey sure never did whip one of Master Holmes' niggers for he didn't allow it. He didn't whip 'em hisself and he sure didn't allow nobody else to either. I was afraid of de Ku Kluxers too, and I 'spects dat Master Holmes was one of de leaders iffen de truth was known. Dey sure was scary looking.

I was scared of de Yankee soldiers. Dey come by and killed some of our cattle for beef and took our meat and lard out'n de smokehouse and dey took some corn, too. Us niggers was awful mad. We didn't know anything 'bout dem fighting to free us. We didn't specially want to be free dat I knows of.

Right after de War I went over to Bloomfield Academy[12] to take care of a little girl, but I went back to Master Holmes and Miss Betsy at de end of two years to take care of de little girl dat was born to dem and I stayed with her until I was about fifteen. Master Holmes went to Washington as a delegate, for something for de Indians, and he took sick and died and dey buried him dere. Poor Miss Betsy nearly grieved herself to death. She stayed on at de farm till her little girl was grown and married. Her nigger men stayed on with her and rented land from her and dey sure raised a sight of truck. Didn't none of her old slaves ever move very far from her and most of them worked for her till dey was too old to work.

I left Miss Betsy purty soon after Master Holmes died and went back to de Academy and stayed three years. I married a man dat belonged to Master Holmes' cousin. His name was Colbert, too. I had a big wedding. Miss Betsy and a lot of white folks come and stayed for dinner. We danced all evening and after supper we started again and danced all night and de next day and de next night. We'd eat awhile and den we'd dance awhile.

My husband and I had nine children and now I've got seven grandchildren. My husband has been dead a long time.

My sister, Chaney, lives here close to me but her mind has got feeble and she can't recollect as much as I can. I live with my son and he is mighty good to me. I know I ain't long for dis world but I don't mind for I has lived a long time and I'll have a lot of friends in de other world and I won't be lonesome.

¹ Mrs. Jessie R. Ervin from the WPA interviewed Mrs. Polly Colbert at Colbert, Oklahoma, on 14 September 1937. From her interview notes she prepared a preliminary draft of Colbert's narrative as the typescript "Interview with Polly Colbert, Ex-Slave, Aged 83, Colbert, Okla.," now in the OHS Slave Narratives. This narrative was revised into the standard form for the Slave Narrative Project as the typescript "Polly Colbert, Age 83 Yrs., Colbert, Oklahoma," published here. This final draft, forwarded to Washington on 18 November 1937, is available in ribbon copy in the LC Slave Narratives and in carbon copy as item 350018 in the LC Slave Narratives Carbon Copies and in the OHS Slave Narratives. Stephens to Alsberg, 18 November 1937, WPA Notes on Interviews.

For another, contemporary although brief interview with Polly Colbert, see Polly Ann Colbert, interview by Lula Austin at Colbert, Oklahoma, 21 October 1937, Indian-Pioneer Papers, 20:182–84, Archives and Manuscripts Division, Oklahoma Historical Society (hereafter cited as Indian-Pioneer Papers).

² Here the preliminary draft states "timber."

³ This sentence does not appear in the preliminary draft.

⁴ In the preliminary draft this sentence reads, "I reckon dat was one reason us. . . . "

⁵ The following sentence appears at this point in the preliminary draft: "My grand parents was brought here by de fambly when dey come from Mississippi."

⁶ The preliminary version reads "parents."

⁷ The preliminary draft adds here, "an dey got married soon after that."

⁸ This sentence does not appear in the preliminary version of the interview.

⁹ The phrase "but I ain't seen dem since den" does not appear in the preliminary draft.

¹⁰ For background on Choctaw foodways and information on such particular food items as *ta-fula* (tom-fuller), *pishofa* (pashofa), and hickory *ta-fula* (hickory-nut grot), see T. N. Campbell, "Choctaw Subsistence: Ethnographic Notes from the Lincecum Manuscript," *Florida Anthropologist* 12 (March 1959): 9–24; Peter J. Hudson, "Choctaw Indian Dishes," *Chronicles of Oklahoma* 17 (September 1939): 333–35; Muriel H. Wright, "American Indian Corn Dishes," *Chronicles of Oklahoma* 36 (Summer 1958): 155–61.

¹¹ The ferry mentioned by Polly Colbert was operated by Benjamin Franklin Colbert and served as a major crossing on the Red River. For remembrances of Colbert's ferry and stagecoach station, see the narrative of Kiziah Love, below. The Texas Road for decades was a major trail from northeastern Indian Territory to the Red River crossing into Texas. For background on this historic route, see Grant Foreman, *Down the Texas Road: Historic Places along Highway 69 through Oklahoma*, 5–46.

¹² For background on the Bloomfield Academy, established in the 1850s in what today is southern Bryan County, Oklahoma, see Irene E. Mitchell, "Bloomfield Academy" (master's thesis, University of Oklahoma, 1953); Irene E. Mitchell and Ida Belle Renken, "The Golden Age of Bloomfield Academy in the Chickasaw Nation," *Chronicles of Oklahoma* 49 (Winter 1971–72): 412–26.

GEORGE CONRAD, JR.[1]

Age 77 Yrs. *Oklahoma City, Okla.*

I was born February 23, 1860 at Connersville, Harrison County, Kentucky. I was born and lived just 13 miles from Parish.[2] My mother's name is Rachel Conrad, born at Bourbon County, Kentucky. My father, George Conrad, was born at Bourbon County, Kentucky. My grandmother's name is Sallie Amos, and grandfather's name is Peter Amos. My grandfather, his old Master freed him and he bought my grandmother, Aunt Liza and Uncle Cy. He made the money by freighting groceries from Ohio to Maysville, Kentucky.

Our Master was named Master Joe Conrad. We sometimes called him "Mos" Joe Conrad. Master Joe Conrad stayed in a big log house with weather boarding on the outside.

I was born in a log cabin. We slept in wooden beds with rope cords for slats, and the beds had curtains[3] around them. You see my mother was the cook for the Master, and she cooked everything—chicken, roasting ears. She cooked mostly everything we have now. They didn't have stoves; they cooked in big ovens. The skillets had three legs. I can remember the first stove that we had. I guess I was about six years old.

My old Master had 900 acres of land. My father was a stiller. He made three barrels of whisky a day. Before the War whisky sold for 12½¢ and 13¢ a gallon. After the War it went up to $3 and $4 per gallon. When War broke out he had 300 barrels hid under old Master's barn.

There was 14 colored men working for old Master Joe and 7 women. I think it was on the 13th of May, all 14 of these colored men, and my father, went to the Army. When old Master Joe come to wake 'em up the next morning—I remember he called real loud, Miles, Esau, George, Frank, Arch, on down the line, and my mother told him they'd all gone to the army.[4] Old Master went to Cynthia,[5] where they had gone to enlist, and begged the officer in charge to let him see all of his boys, but the officer said "No." Some way or 'nother he got a chance to see Arch, and Arch came back with him to help raise the crops.

My mother cooked and took care of the house. Aunt Sarah took care of the children. I had two little baby brothers, Charlie and John. The old Mistress would let my mother put them in her cradle and Aunt Sarah got jealous, and killed both of the babies. When they cut one of the babies open they took out two frogs. Some say she conjured the babies. Them niggers could conjure each other but they couldn't do nothing to the whitefolks, but I don't believe in it. There's an old woman living back there now (pointing around the corner of the house where he was sitting) they said her husband put a spell on her. They call 'em two-headed Negroes.

Old Master never whipped any of his slaves, except two of my uncles—Pete Conrad and Richard Sherman, now living at Falsmouth, Kentucky.[6]

We raised corn, wheat, oats, rye and barley, in the spring. In January, February and March we'd go up to the Sugar Camp where he had a grove of maple trees. We'd make maple syrup and put up sugar in cakes. Sugar sold for $2.50 and $3 a cake. He had a regular sugar house. My old Master was rich I tell you.

Whenever a member of the white family die all the slaves would turn out, and whenever a slave would die, whitefolks and all the slaves would go. My Master had a big vault. My Mistress was buried in an iron coffin that they called a potanic coffin. I went back to see her after I was 21 years old and she look jest like she did when they buried her. All of the family was buried in them vaults, and I expect if you'd go there today they'd look the same. The slaves was buried in good handmade coffins.

I heard a lot of talk 'bout the patrollers. In them days if you went away from home and didn't have a pass they'd whip you. Sometimes they'd whip you with a long black cow whip, and then sometime they'd roast elm switches in the fire. This was called "cat-o-nine-tails," and they'd whip you with dat. We never had no jails; only punishment was just to whip you.

Now, the way the slaves travel. If a slave had been good sometimes old Master would let him ride his hoss; then, sometime they'd steal a hoss out and ride 'em and slip him back before old Master ever found it out. There was a man in them days by the name of John Brown. We called him an underground railroad man, 'cause he'd steal the slaves and carry 'em across the river in a boat. When you got on the other side you was free, 'cause you was in a free State, Ohio.

We used to sing, and I guess young folks today does too: "John Brown's Body Lies A'moulding in the Clay" and "They Hung John Brown on a Sour Apple Tree."

Our slaves all got very good attention when they got sick. They'd send and get a doctor for 'em. You see old Mistress Mary bought my mother, father and two children throwed in for $1,100 and she told Master Joe to always keep her slaves, not to sell 'em and always take good care of 'em.

When my father went to the army old Master told us he was gone to fight for us niggers' freedom. My daddy was the only one that come back out of the 13 men that enlisted, and when my daddy come back old Master give him a buggy and hoss.

When the Yanks come, I never will forget one of 'em was named John Morgan. We carried old Master down to the barn and hid him in the hay. I felt so sorry for old Master; they took all him hams, some of his whisky, and all dey could find, hogs, chickens, and jest treated him something terrible.

The whitefolks learned my father how to read and write, but I didn't learn how to read and write 'til I enlisted in the U.S. Army in 1883.[7]

They sent us here (Oklahoma Territory) to keep the immigrants from settling up Oklahoma. I went to Fort Riley the 1st day of October 1883, and stayed there three weeks. Left Fort Riley and went to Ft. Worth, Texas, and landed in Henrietta, Texas, on the 14th day of October 1883. Then, we had 65 miles to walk to Ft. Sill. We walked there in three days. I was assigned to my Company, Troop G, 9th Cavalry, and we stayed and drilled in Ft. Sill six months, when we was assigned to duty. We got orders to come to Ft. Reno, Okla., on the 6th day of January 1885 where we was ordered to Stillwater, Okla., to move five hundred immigrants under Capt. Couch.[8] We landed there on the 23rd day of January, Saturday evening, and Sunday was the 24th. We had general inspection Monday, January 25, 1885. We fell in line of battle, sixteen companies of soldiers, to move 500 immigrants to the Arkansas City, Kansas line.

We formed a line at 9:00 o'clock Monday morning and Captain Couch run up his white flag, and Colonel Hatch[9] he sent the orderly up to see what he meant by putting up the flag, so Captain Couch sent word back, "If you don't fire on me, I'll leave tomorrow." Colonel Hatch turned around to the Major and told him to turn his troops back to the camp, and detailed three camps of soldiers of the 8th Cavalry[10] to carry Captain Couch's troop of 500 immigrants to Arkansas City, Kansas. Troop L., Troop D., and Troop B. taken them back with 43 wagons and put them over the line of Kansas. Then we were ordered back to our supply camp at Camp Alice, 9 miles north of Guthrie in the Cimarron horseshoe bottom. We stayed there about three months, and Capt. Couch and his colony came back into the territory at Caldwell, Kansas June 1885.

I laid there till August 8, then we changed regiments with the 5th Cavalry to go to Nebraska. There was a breakout with the Indians at

Ft. Reno the 1st of July 1885.[11] The Indian Agency tried to make the Indians wear citizens' clothes. They had to call General [Philip H.] Sheridan from Washington, D.C., to quiet the Indians down. Now, we had to make a line in three divisions, fifteen miles apart, one non-commissioned officer to each squad, and these men was to go to Caldwell, Kansas and bring him to Ft. Reno that night. He came that night, so the next morning Colonel Brisbane[12] and General Hatch reported to General Sheridan what the trouble was. General Sheridan called all the Indian Chiefs together and asked them why they rebelled against the agency, and they told them they weren't going to wear citizens' clothes. General Sheridan called his corporals and sergeants together and told them to go behind the guard house and dig a grave for this Indian agent in order to fool the Indian Chiefs. Then, he sent a detachment of soldiers to order the Indian Chiefs away from the guard house and to put this Indian agent in the ambulance that brought him to Ft. Reno and take him back to Washington, D.C., to remain there till he returned. The next morning he called all the Indian Chiefs to the guard house and pointed down to the grave and said that, "I have killed the agent and buried him there." The Indians tore the feathers out of their hats rejoicing that they killed the agent.

On the 12th of the same July, we had general inspection with General Foresides [Forsyth?] from Washington, and we was ordered back to our supply camp to stay there till we got orders of our change. On August 8, we got orders to change to go to Nebraska, to Ft. Robinson, Ft. Nibrary, and Ft. McKinney, and we left on the 8th of August.

This is my Oklahoma history. I gave this story to the Daily Oklahoman and Times at one time and they are supposed to publish it but they haven't.

Now you see that tree up there in front of my house? That tree is 50 years old. It is called the potopic tree. That was the only tree around here in 1882. This was a bald prairie. I enlisted over there where the City Market sets now. That was our starting camp under Capt. Payne but he died.

I joined the A.M.E. Methodist Church in 1874. I love this song better than all the rest: "Am I a Soldier of the Cross?"

Abraham Lincoln was a smart man, but he would have done more if he was not killed. I don't think his work was finished. I'll tell you the truth about Booker T. Washington. He argued our people to stay out of town and stay in the country. He was a Democrat. He was a smart man, but I think a man should live wherever he choose regardless. I never stopped work whenever I'd hear he was coming to town to speak. You know they wasn't fighting for freeing the slaves; they was fighting to keep Kansas from being a slave State; so when they had the North whipped, I mean the South had 'em whipped, they called for the Negroes to go out and fight for his freedom. Don't know nothing 'bout Jeff Davis. I've handled a lots of his money. It was counterfeited after the War.

I've been married four times. I had one wife and three women. I mean the three wasn't no good. My first wife's name: Amanda Nelson. 2nd: Pokahuntas Jackson. 3rd: Nannie Shumpard. We lived together 9 years. She tried to beat me out of my home.

1 Slave Narrative Project field worker Bertha P. Tipton, one of the three African American reporters working on the project, interviewed George Conrad, Jr., in Oklahoma City on 18 June 1937. Tipton prepared a preliminary draft of Conrad's remembrances as the typescript "Interview with George Conrad, Jr., Ex-Slave Aged 77 Years, 217 So. Ellison Street, Oklahoma City, Oklahoma," now preserved in the OHS Slave Narratives. It should be noted that the informant's address on this typescript is scratched out and "27 So Klien St" is written in with pencil. At some time later in the summer or fall, project editors revised the text into a more standard format as the final draft, "George Conrad, Jr., Age 77 Yrs., Oklahoma City, Okla." This version, published here, was sent to Washington on 2 November 1937, and is available in ribbon-copy typescript in the LC Slave Narratives and in carbon copy as item 350030 in the LC Slave Narratives Carbon Copies and in the OHS Slave Narratives. Stephens to Cronyn, 2 November 1937, WPA Notes on Interviews.

2 Apparently a reference to Paris, Kentucky.

3 The preliminary draft reads "lace curtains."

4 George Conrad, the interviewee's father, volunteered and was mustered into Company D, 100th U.S. Colored Infantry, at Covington, Kentucky, on 2 June 1864. He advanced in rank from private to corporal, serving until mustered out of service at Nashville, Tennessee, on 26 December 1865. U.S., Department of War, Army, 100th Colored Infantry, Compiled Military Service Record for George Conrad, National Archives, Washington, D.C.

5 Apparently a reference to Cynthiana, Kentucky.

6 Apparently a reference to Falmouth, Kentucky.

7 George Conrad enlisted in the 9th U.S. Cavalry at Cincinnati, Ohio, on 15 September 1883, and served until he was discharged at Fort Niobrara, Nebraska, on 29 April 1887. U.S., Department of War, Army, 9th Cavalry, Compiled Military Service Record for George Conrad, National Archives, Washington, D.C.

8 For an overview of the activities of Captain William L. Couch and his illegal "boomer" settlers in Oklahoma during winter and spring 1885, see Carl Coke Rister, *Land Hunger: David L. Payne and the Oklahoma Boomers,* 189–93. African American soldiers in the U.S. Army played a significant role in helping exclude illegal settlers from the Indian Territory. W. Sherman Savage, "The Role of Negro Soldiers in Protecting

the Indian Territory from Intruders," *Journal of Negro History* 36 (January 1951): 25–34.

9 For a synopsis of the military career of General Edward Hatch, see Francis B. Heitman, *Historical Register and Dictionary of the United States Army from Its Organization, September 29, 1789, to March 2, 1903,* 1:510.

10 The preliminary draft reads "9th Cavalry."

11 For an account of this incident at Fort Reno and its background, see Peter Melton Wright, "Fort Reno, Indian Territory, 1874–1885" (master's thesis, University of Oklahoma, 1965), 93–106.

12 The "Colonel Brisbane" mentioned here is probably James S. Brisbin, who at the time was serving as lieutennant colonel in the 9th Cavalry, George Conrad's unit. Heitman, *Historical Register,* 1:246.

WILLIAM CURTIS[1]

Age 93 Yrs.   *McAlester, Oklahoma*

> "Run Nigger, run,
> De Patteroll git ye!
> Run Nigger, run,
> He's almost here!"

> Please Mr. Patteroll,
> Don't ketch me!
> Jest take dat nigger
> What's behind dat tree."[2]

Lawsy,[3] I done heard dat song all my life and it warn't no joke neither. De Patrol[4] would git ye too if he caught ye off the plantation without a pass from your Master, and he'd whup ye too. None of us dasn't leave without a pass.

We chillun sung lots of songs and we played marbles, mumble peg, and town ball. In de winter we would set around de fire and listen to our Mammy and Pappy tell ghost tales and witch tales. I don't guess dey was sho' nuff so, but we all thought dey was.

My Mammy was bought in Virginia by our Master, Hugh McKeown. He owned a big plantation in Georgia. Soon after she come to Georgia she married my pa. Old Master[5] was good to us. We lived for a while in the quarters behind the Big House, and my mammy was de house woman.

Somehow, in a trade, or maybe my pa was mortgaged, but anyway old Master let a man in Virginia have him and we never see him no more till after the War. It nigh broke our hearts when he had to leave and old Master sho' done everything he could to make it up to us.

There was four of us chillun. I didn't do no work till I was about fifteen years old. Old Master bought a tavern and mammy worked as house woman and I went to work at the stables. I drove the carriage and took keer of the team and carriage. I kept 'em shining too. I'd curry the horses till they was slick and shiny. I'd polish the harness and the carriage. Old Master and Mistress⁶ was quality and I wanted everybody to know it. They had three girls and three boys and we boys played together and went swimming together. We loved each other, I tell ye.

Old Master built us a little house jest back of de tavern and mammy raised us jest like Old Mistress did her chillun. When I didn't have to work de boys and me would go hunting. We'd kill possum, coon, squirrels and wild hogs. Old Master killed a wild hog and he give mammy her ten tiny pigs. She raised 'em and my, at the meat we had when they was butchered.

They had lots of company at de Big House, and it was de only tavern too, so they was lots of cooking to do. They would go to church on Sunday and they would spread their dinners on the ground. My, but they was feasts. We'd allus git to go as I drive the carriage and mammy looked after the food. We had our own church too, with our own preacher.

We had a spinning house where all the old women would card and spin wool in de winter and cotton in de summer. Dey made all our clothes, what few we wore. Us boys just wore long tailed shirts till we was 12 or 13 years old, sometimes older. I was 15 when I started driving the fambly carriage and I got to put on pants then.

Our suits was made out of jeans. That cloth wore like buckskin. We'd wear 'em for a year before they had to be patched.

We made our own brogan shoes too. We'd kill a beef and skin it and spread the skin out and let it dry a while. We'd put the hide in lime water to get the hair off, then we'd oil it and work it till it was soft.⁷ Next we'd take it to the bench and scrape or "plesh" it with knives. It was then put in a tight cabinet and smoked with oak wood for about 24 hours. Smoking loosened the skin. We'd then take it out and rub it to soften it. It was blacked and oiled and it was ready to be made into shoes. It took nearly a year to get a green hide made into shoes. Twan't no wonder we had to go barefooted.

Sometimes I'd work in the wood shop, dressing wagon spokes. We made spokes with a plane, by hand on a bench.

I didn't have much work to do before I was 15 except to run errands. One of my jobs was to take corn to the mill to be ground into meal. Some one would put my sack of corn on the mule's back and help me up and I'd ride to the mill and have it ground and they'd load me back on and I'd go back home.

I remember once my meal fell off and I waited and waited for somebody to come by and help me. I got tired waiting so I toted the sack to a big log and laid it acrost it. I led my mule up to the log and after working hard for a long time I managed to get it on his back. I climbed up and jest as we started off the mule jumped and I fell off and pulled the sack off with me. I couldn't do nothing but wait and finally old Master came after me. He knowed something was wrong.

Old Master was good to all of his slaves but his overseers had orders to make 'em work. He fed 'em good and took good keer of 'em and never made 'em work iffen they was sick or even felt bad. They was two things old Master jest wouldn't 'bide and dat was for a slave to be sassy or lazy. Sometimes if dey wouldn't work or slipped off de farm dey would whip 'em. He didn't whip often. Colored overseers was worse to whip than white ones, but Master allus said, "Hadn't you all rather have a nigger overseer than a white one? I don't want no white man over my niggers." I've seen the overseer whip some but I never did get no whipping. He would strip 'em to the waist and whip 'em with a long leather strop, about as wide as two fingers and fastened to a handle.

When de war broke out everything was changed. My young Masters had to go. T. H. McKeown, the oldest was a Lieutenant and was one of the first to go. It nigh broke all of our hearts. Pretty soon he sent for me to come and keep him company. Old Master let me go and I stayed in his quarters. He was stationed at Atlanta and Griffin, Georgia. I'd stay with him a week or two and I'd go home for a few days and I'd take back food and fruit. I stayed with him and waited on him till he got used to being in the army and they moved him out to fighting. I wanted to go on with him but he wouldn't let me, he told me to go back and take care of Old Master and Old Mistress. They was getting old by then. Purty soon Young Master got wounded purty bad and they sent me home. I never went back. I got a "Pass" to go home. Course, after the war nothing was right no more. Yes, we was free but we didn't know what to do. We didn't want to leave our old Master and our old home. We stayed on and after a while my pappy come home to us. Dat was de best thing about de war setting us free, he could come back to us.

We all lived on at the old plantation. Old Master and old Mistress died and young Master took charge of de farm. He couldn't a'done nothing without us niggers. He didn't know how to work. He was good to us and divided the crops with us.

I never went to school much but my white folks learned me to read and write. I could always have any of their books to read, and they had lots of 'em.

Times has changed a lot since that time. I don't know where the world is much better now that it has everything or then when we didn't have hardly nothing, but I believe there was more religion then. We always went to church and I've seen 'em baptize from in the early morning till afternoon in the Chattahoochee river. Folks don't hardly know nowadays jest what to believe they's so many religions, but they's only one God.

I was eighteen when I married. I had eight children. My wife is 86, and she lives in St. Louis, Missouri.

[1] William Curtis was interviewed in McAlester, Oklahoma, by Mrs. Jessie R. Ervin probably sometime in the first half of 1937. A preliminary version of the interview is available as the typescript "Interview with William Curtis (Ex-Slave, Aged 93 Years, East Adams St., McAlester, Oklahoma)," preserved in the OHS Slave Narratives. An edited version in standard project format, published here, is available as the typescript "William Curtis, Age 93 Yrs., McAlester, Oklahoma," in ribbon copy in the LC Slave Narratives and in carbon copy as item 350083 in the LC Slave Narratives Carbon Copies and in the OHS Slave Narratives. On 16 August 1937 this narrative was forwarded together with nine others to Washington. Stephens to Cronyn, 16 August 1937, WPA Notes on Interviews.

[2] Of all the secular songs about which informants in the Oklahoma Slave Narrative Project had memories, "Run, Nigger, Run" (also known as "The Patteroll Song") was the most frequently cited. Recorded throughout the South, it deals with the slave patrols, which consisted of white men who roamed the byways to ascertain that slaves away from their masters had valid written passes. William Francis Allen, Charles Pickard Ware, and Lucy McKim Garrison, *Slave Songs of the United States,* 89.

[3] At this point the preliminary version of the narrative adds the word "lady."

[4] "Patteroll" is the term used in the preliminary version.

[5] From this point onward the preliminary draft renders "Old Master" as "Ole Massa."

[6] From this point onward in the preliminary draft "Mistress" consistently is rendered "Missy."

[7] The preliminary version adds here "and pliant."

CARRIE E. DAVIS[1]

Age 97 Years   *Oklahoma City, Okla.*

I was born in Winnsboro, South Carolina, May 8th, 1842. De reason I 'member my age so well is 'cause it stayed in de old family Bible till I was a grown gal. De Bible got burned up or else I'd have it right now.

I am de daughter of Samuel and Amanda Williams. My father was a silversmith.[2] He worked for hisself and bought hisself. The way he done this was, he asked his Master how much he was worth and Master told him. He picked another slave-holder and let him be his guardian. The guardian recognized every check that my father paid old Master. When he was paid for, the guardian told him and then he had to mind the guardian. It was just some more slavery matter-of-course, but it wasn't so bad as the first, cause he could come & go when he wanted to. My father owned three blocks of land and brick buildings just right out from the capital.

We lived in a little shanty or shed made of sticks and bark from trees. Our beds were made from chinaberry trees. We cut dem down, tied de poles together wid de bark and put sticks across it for slats. We plaited shucks together to make our mattresses, and sometimes we pulled hay to make mattresses out of. I've had to sleep on peach-tree leaves.

I'll tell you we had a hard time, and still do! It's just a few of [us former slaves] living now, and dey do kick us around so![3] I knowed Lewis Jenkins[4] back in South Carolina, who was the son of a white woman by a nigger coachman and he up and married a white woman, who was the wife of a confederate soldier. Took her clean 'way from her husband. I can't 'member her name neither, but me and him was int'mate friends. I don't know nothing 'bout any brothers and sisters, only dem in de church.

You know we wasn't allowed to raise nothing much for ourselves and we never did have any money. Of course sometimes we would steal something from some of de white neighbors and sell it, but you know dat didn't amount to nothing much. If we was caught wid de stuff old Master would make us divide wid him, and den if de neighbor dat we stole de stuff from missed it and caught us wid it, he would tell old Master and den old Master would say I'm going to give you a hundred licks for stealing Mr. So-and-So's stuff. Now mind you brother, he didn't bother us if de neighbors didn't miss his stuff and catch us wid it.

My jobs was gathering cherries, chopping cotton, carrying mail and working as a nurse. In cotton chopping time we had to be standing on our row by five o'clock. Den old overseer would say, Work niggers, and den we'd start chopping. We didn't know nothing 'bout breakfast, only a piece of bread. We had to take dat in our hand and eat it on de way to de field. I'm telling you it was hard, mighty hard.

I saw a slave one time, his name was Townsend, and dey tell me, he has some people right here in town now (Oklahoma City). As I was going to say, Townsend killed Scott, Mr. Blakeney's overseer. Scott had whipped Townsend every morning for 'bout a month, just about nothing at all, you might say. Townsend got tired of dis so one morning when Scott went to whip him, Townsend turned things round, only he did Scott worse dan Scott ever done him. Dere just wasn't no more Scott when Townsend got through wid him. Well, dey took Townsend and carried him to de little village and made all the slaves gather 'round to look on, and Townsend's wife was dere too. They made her look right at him.[5] I don't see how she done it. She must have been praying in her heart, for it was a pitiful sight what happened. Dey tied his hands and feet to some stakes, poured turpentine all over his body and den stuck a match to it. Oh! dat was awful, it was awful! We couldn't look off, we had to look right at dat poor man. De poor fellow screamed three times and dat was all for him.[6] Another instance like that was when Mr. Abbercrumby got to be our overseer. He tied a nigger to a tree and a storm come up while they was rounding up the slaves to make dem come to the burning. He lived through all the storming and brush was up to his neck the next morning. All of us slaves was gathered up and took to the burning. He was burnt cause he said he was going to kill the overseer for whipping him so much. A nigger that was no good told on him. He was one more pitiful sight.

For food we had peas, corn, cornbread and bacon. We got our rashings on Sunday morning, and it had to last us all de week. We didn't know nothing 'bout no grease, and what grease we got had to come out of de bacon they gave us. We didn't have a garden, but some of the slaves planted gardens at night and would work dem on Sunday afternoons. We could eat fish, rabbits and possums if we caught dem at night, but we didn't do much hunting and fishing 'cause we was too tired when night came.

Dem days we had sweet 'tatoes de year 'round and de slaves had to build houses for de 'tatoes, and den cure 'em by piling dry sand and grass on them. Dat reminds me of old Mr. Osau.[7] He lived close by us. He was one of the meanest masters I knowed of. I've seen him work his slaves in de 'tato field till dey fell dead. After a slave had worked hisself to death, old Mr. Osau would make some of de slave's relatives make a box for him[8] and if it didn't fit, they broke his body up so it would fit. They was not even allowed to shed a tear for dey dead kinfolks. Dey would say, "Master, making dat box was de last thing I could do for John," or whoever it was. Oh! dat was an awful time we had den, but de good Lawd came in time.[9] Some of dem white folks dat thought right run old man Osau off for doing dem dead bodies so bad.

We had to make our clothes, and I've had to weave millions of pieces of cloth. In de summer our clothes were made of stuff dat looks like dese old gunny sacks you see now. Most of us went barefooted in de summer time. Some of de slaves wore cloth shoes in winter, but our shoes were made out of cowhides.

You know in dem days de servants went to church weddings and parties wid de white folks. Dey would walk along behind old Mistress and hold her dress to keep it from dragging. At parties the servants would take care of de wraps. De slave women could have party but de colored men was not allowed to come 'round. De white boys would go along to de party to see dat dere was no nigger men there. Now, I spose you see why de race is so mixed up cause dem white boys didn't mean no good.[10] Some of dem girls just wore chemise to dem dances, while others dressed up nice. Some just didn't have nothing to wear but chemise, dat's why. The colored boys didn't hardly ever get to dance with the girls of they own race. We had to do just what them boys said do, too. Girls who go with them now, they is just sleeping on their rights, 'cause they don't mean dem no good. Nothing to come of it but illegal children, which they don't own, not now.

I've seen slaves put on blocks and sold. Dey would have a large crowd of masters gathered 'round and dey would put de slaves on a stump or block and roll de sleeves and pants legs up and say, "Dis is good stock; got good muscles, and he's good hard-working nigger." Why, dey sold 'em just like you see 'em sell stock now. If de woman was a good breeder she would sell for big money, 'cause she could raise children.[11] They felt all over the women folks. Mr. Hughes, the official slave seller, would buy all the good looking nigger girls for him and his brother and take 'em home and put 'em in they private home, not they plantation, and raise families by them or just use 'em for they enjoyment, iffen they didn't have no children. I was put on the block seven or eight time myself.[12] The last time was when I was 10 years old. My mama was mostly Irish and she would raise cane when I would be put on the block. She say, "I'll kill myself if you sell her." Old Master said, "Iffen that nigger winch wasn't worth seven or eight hundred dollars, I'd let her kill herself." She was pink complexion, red hair, blue or green eyes and weighed 'round 200 pounds.

De slaves dat would fight, had to work with chains on. They

couldn't even get their own water, and someone would have to hold the old gourd dipper while dey drunk.[13] I 'member one time a man was killed over a ash cake 'cause all dem fighting niggers wanted it and got to fighting and killed a man. Dey just didn't recognize dat they was each other's friends. I 'member one time I was drinking out of a gourd dipper and a snake crawled out of the handle.[14]

If de slaves would work pretty good dey would give dem something good to eat[15] like 'tatoe pie and good old ham. If dey didn't work, dey would have to wear thorns in their clothes instead of pins.[16] There was no jails in dem days, and dey would lock you in a dark house and whip you when dey took you out.

We didn't have a church. Slaves would meet and shake hands over de fence. De slaves stood outside de white folks' church, and when de old preacher was through wid de services, he would come out on de steps and read de Bible to de slaves.[17] We could have church in their church sometimes when dey done got through. Old man Ashley, my uncle, was a free man. He bought hisself just like my pappy did. He was a carpenter. He bought his wife and if he had any children he bought dem too. He could come and preach in de church, if dere was four overseers dere. Dey baptized in de river, and de song dey sung most of de time was "Religion Is So Sweet." You could sing at de funeral if de Master was willing for you to, and dey would sing de same songs dey sung at church.

Some of de slaves would run off, and sometimes a good white man would slip dem off. I 'member Mr. John Brown, a good old white man, he took some slaves, put dem in his wagon, covered dem over wid hay and carried dem to New York so dey could be free. When it was found dat Mr. Brown did dis, de white folks hung him.[18] He had two or three slaves wid him when he was killed.

When we quit work in de field we had to go home, wash, and cook supper and our dinner for de next day. We didn't know nothing 'bout any hot meals only at night, 'cause den our supper was always hot.

We had Saturday night frolics. We would dance, pull candy and tell jokes. We had to be through by eleven o'clock. Den de folks who worked in de field all de time would have "dere dance." You know de folk dat worked at de Big House wasn't 'lowed to associate wid de regular field hands and in dem dances dey dared to dance wid each other.

I been in lots of corn huskings. We would have a big time, and would sing a lot. I 'member one of de songs was "Round up Sallie, Round up Corn," and when we'd get to singing dat we'd sure husk some corn. De huskers would be at one end and grinders at de other. Dey would serve gingerbread and persimmon beer, but of course de beer wasn't strong enough to make us drunk.

If some Master's folks died de slaves would be called to de house and dey would set around and cry and talk about what a good master or mistress he or she was. Of course most of the time de slaves was pretending, 'cause dey was glad for dis to happen, but you know dey had to pretend, 'cause dey was scared to do anything else.

Some of de slaves married right in de church but wouldn't be but two or three present. Dey would git some pie and cake after de wedding.[19] But this was rare. Sometimes de Master would buy husbands for women and wives for men. If a man was bought for a woman she had to live wid him and raise children.

De children played a few little games such as jumping rope, throwing horse shoes and wrestling, and dats 'bout all. We didn't know nothing 'bout de games de kids play now.

Dey wouldn't send for a doctor unless you was in a dying condition. Course every plantation had a woman doctor on it, and dey was mostly for childbirth you know.[20] Doctors was too expensive. De slaves had to take roots and herbs and make our own medicine. I 'member some of de slaves wearing charms but I never did believe in dem much, and dat's why I don't know nothing 'bout dem now.[21]

All dis happened in Montgomery, Alabama. We was moved to a plantation in dis place 'cause Master had interest in it. I was just 5 years old when this happened.

When I was 20 years old, my mother was put on the block with my two brothers. Mr. Hughes, the slave-seller, said he had a nigger winch and two bulls to go. My brother Henry shot him and he never got over it. My brother left and they never found him. It was hard to describe him after he got to manhood. He looked white. I am de darkest in my family and I am almost yellow. My mother's father was Dr. Crush, part Indian and Irish. No Negro looking people at all in my family.

When they was sending the Indians to Oklahoma, I had to stay at the train and serve coffee. I made fifty gallons. I wanted to come then, but my husband wouldn't let me. They give Oklahoma to the Indians and now they taking it. The Indians have no rights now. They just waiting for another governor to be discharged so it can be a territory one more time.

I 'member when we was told dat we was free.[22] It was the 19th of June. We danced all day and all night. De Yankees had sent old Master word to free us, but he hadn't told us 'bout it. So one day while we was laying by de corn, de Yankees come to the field and told old Master and de overseer dat if dey didn't free us dey would bust their brains out. I 'member quite well how old Master cried out and said, "Lord, ain't I going to have no more niggers to look after?" Den de old overseer came to us and said, "You are free now, just as free as you Master." Dat was a glorious day. We shouted and thanked God and dat night de plantation folk gathered from miles around and we stayed up all night dancing and singing.

Now four years before de War a large star came in de north. It was made in a kind of S-shape. At de top of de S was a large star and at de bottom was a small one, so small you couldn't hardly see it. I asked an old white woman 'bout dat star and she told me to "hush Carrie," dat represents trouble. She said something terrible is going to happen, and it did happen, 'cause dat star stayed there till we slaves was freed.

Me and my husband had a big wedding. Course I didn't know it was going to be like dat, 'cause my friends got together and surprised me.[23] I was married after freedom. After de wedding we had chicken, ham, cakes and pies. Dey didn't have weddings in dem days like we have now. My marriage took place in Montgomery, Alabama. I was married to Stephen Davis, one of Jefferson Davis' illegal children. I am a daughter-in-law of Jeff Davis. I met him during the war. Jeff Davis used to bring his one legal child, Minnie Mae, to visit us. He had nine boys in my husband's mother and one by his legal wife. Course you know in dem days de white man didn't think nothing about having a wife and a colored woman, and dey would both stay right dere wid him. White women made the colored men go with them.[24] Jeff was a mean man, I'll say dat, but he was good to me, I'll say dat for him too.

I thought Abraham [Lincoln], de old "rail splitter" as dey called him, was de best man ever lived. We mourned for him a long time after his death. We had what was known as de Lincoln Society.[25] We met and talked of what he done for us and how we all felt 'bout him and prayed for him.

I've seen Booker Washington a number of times. I used to make sheets, ironing board covers, iron holders and give dem to him for de school.[26]

I moved to Oklahoma 8 years ago after my husband died.[27] A white man come here looking for my brother Henry, who killed that white slave-seller, and I wouldn't tell him where he was. My brother is a preacher now, and he never visits me here, 'cause these folks here know him too well.

I am a member of de Tabernacle Baptist Church.[28] I love de Lawd and I think all de people should be Christians, 'cause de Lawd lifted dat heavy burden of slavery from dere heads, and dat ain't all he can do if de folks will only live by his teachings. And de main things is to treat your fellow men right, regardless of his color.

[1] Three different typescript versions of the Carrie E. Davis narrative are preserved in the OHS Slave Narratives. These documents are drawn from two separate interviews with Mrs. Davis, one of which was conducted by Willie Allen on 12 July 1937. The earliest draft of Allen's interview, "Ex-Slave Reference (A) Interview with Mr[s]. Carrie E. Davis, Age 89 Years, 820 Southeast Frisco, Oklahoma City, Okla.," has this original title scratched out in pencil and changed to "Carrie E. Davis, Age 89 Years, Oklahoma City, Okla." in handwriting. An intermediate draft, drawn from this initial interview and incorporating editorial changes marked on it, is available as the narrative "Carrie E. Davis, Age 89 Years, Oklahoma City, Oklahoma" and bears the date 19 October 1938. A final typescript, published here, is "Carrie E. Davis, Age 97 Years, Oklahoma City, Okla." It incorporates the texts represented in the two versions of the Willie Allen interview and combines them with that from a now nonexistent second interview by an unidentified field worker. A note appended to this last, combined version of the narrative states, "Combine these two! 10–19–38." The last page of the final draft was located separate from the body of the text as a loose leaf in the "Unid-Partial" file of slave narrative typescripts in the OHS Slave Narratives. This interview was never forwarded to Washington and has never before been published.

[2] The following seven sentences are found only in the last draft of the narrative.

[3] The subsequent three sentences are represented only in the last draft of the narrative.

[4] The narrative of Lewis Jenkins of Oklahoma City is included in this volume.

[5] The next two sentences appear only in the last draft of the narrative.

[6] The remainder of this paragraph appears only in the last draft of the narrative.

[7] The earliest draft of this interview spells the name Olsaw and the intermediate draft, Olsen. The next sentence appears only in the last draft of the narrative.

[8] The remainder of this sentence appears only in the last draft of the narrative.

[9] The next sentence appears only in the last draft of the narrative.

[10] The remainder of this paragraph appears only in the last draft of the narrative.

[11] The next two sentences appear only in the last version of the narrative.

[12] The earliest and intermediate drafts of the narrative read here, "I was on the block once myself."

[13] The next two sentences appear only in the last draft of the narrative.

[14] At this point the earliest draft of the narrative adds, "Yes, we traveled in wagons wid oxens hitched to it. I've seen 16 oxens to a wagon wid bout forty or fifty slaves."

[15] The remainder of this sentence appears only in the last draft of the narrative.

[16] At this point the earliest and intermediate drafts of the narrative read, "If he didn't work good dey would put thorns in his clothes."

[17] The next sentence appears only in the last version of the narrative.

18 The next sentence appears only in the last draft of the narrative.
19 The next sentence appears only in the last draft of the narrative.
20 The next sentence appears only in the last draft of the narrative.
21 The next three paragraphs appear only in the last draft of the narrative.
22 The next two sentences appear only in the last draft of the narrative. The Emancipation Proclamation was promulgated in Galveston, Texas, on 19 June 1865, a date widely commemorated by African Americans in later years as the holiday called "Juneteenth."
23 The next sentence appears only in the last draft of the narrative.
24 This section reads somewhat differently in the earlier two drafts: "Old Jeff is de father of nine children by my husband's mother. Course you know in dem days de white man didn't think nothing about having a wife and a colored woman, and dey would both stay right dere wid him. He didn't have but one child by his wife. Her name was Minnie." Jefferson Davis had four legitimate white children: Maggie; Jefferson, Jr.; Billy; and Winnie. Michael B. Ballard, *A Long Shadow: Jefferson Davis and the Final Days of the Confederacy*, 25. For specific comments on Winnie, possibly the daughter remembered by Carrie Davis, see William C. Davis, *Jefferson Davis: The Man and His Hour*, 685–86.
25 The next sentence appears only in the last draft of this narrative.
26 This sentence refers to Tuskegee Institute, Booker T. Washington's educational institution in Alabama, which was widely supported by African Americans. For background on Washington and his educational efforts, see Lewis R. Harlan, *Booker T. Washington in Perspective: Essays of Louis R. Harlan*, 3–184; Louis R. Harlan, *Booker T. Washington: The Wizard of Tuskegee*, 1901–1915.
The next paragraph appears only in the last draft of the narrative.
27 The contemporary Oklahoma City directory lists Carrie E. Davis as residing in the home of Abrom and Rachel Mosley at 820 Southeast Sixth, which was noted as formerly being called East Frisco Avenue, the location given in the preliminary draft of the narrative. *Polk's Oklahoma City Directory, 1937*, 525, 939–40.
28 Constituted in 1896, the Tabernacle Baptist Church, 515 Northeast Third, Oklahoma City, became one of the most prominent and influential of the African American institutions in Oklahoma. J. M. Gaskin, *Black Baptists in Oklahoma*, 553; Oklahoma City Negro City Directory, xxx, 215.

LUCINDA DAVIS[1]

Age (about) 89 Yrs.   *Tulsa, Okla.*

"What yo' gwine do when de meat give out?
What yo' gwine do when de meat give out?
Set in de corner wid my lips pooched out!
Lawsy!
What yo' gwine do when de meat come in?
What yo' gwine do when de meat come in?
Set in de corner wid a greasy chin!
Lawsy!"

Dat's about de only little nigger song I know, less'n it be de one about:
"Great big nigger, laying 'hind de log—
Finger on de trigger and eye on the hawg!
Click go de trigger and bang go de gun!
Here come de owner and de buck nigger run!"

And I think I learn both of dem long after I been grown, 'cause I belong to a full-blood Creek Indian and I didn't know nothing but
Creek talk long after de Civil War.[2] My mistress was part white and
knowed English talk, but she never did talk it because none of de
people talked it. I heard it sometime, but it[3] sound like whole lot of
wild shoat in de cedar brake scared at something when I do hear it.
Dat was when I was little girl in time of de War.

I don't know where I been born. Nobody never did tell me. But my
mammy and pappy git me after de War and I know den whose child
I is. De men at de Creek Agency hep 'em git me, I reckon, maybe.

First thing I remember is when I was a little girl, and I belong to
old Tuskaya-hiniha. He was big man in de Upper Creek,[4] and we
have a purty good size farm, jest a little bit to de north of de wagon
depot houses on de old road at Honey Springs. Dat place was about
twenty-five mile south of Fort Gibson, but I don't know nothing
about whar de fort is when I was a little girl at dat time. I know de
Elk River 'bout two miles north of whar we live, 'cause I been dere
many de time.

I don't know if old Master have a white name. Lots de Upper Creek
didn't have no white name. Maybe he have another Indian name, too,
because Tuskaya-hiniha mean "head man warrior" in Creek, but dat
what everybody call him and dat what de family call him too.[5]

My Mistress' name was Nancy, and she was a Lott before she marry
old man Tuskaya-hiniha. Her pappy name was Lott and he was purty
near white. Maybe so all white. Dey have two chillun, I think, but
only one stayed on de place. She was name Luwina, and her husband
was dead. His name was Walker, and Luwina bring Mr. Walker's little sister, Nancy, to live at de place too.

Luwina had a little baby boy and dat de reason old Master buy me,
to look after de little baby boy. He didn't have no name 'ause he wasn't
big enough when I was with dem, but he git a name later on, I
reckon. We all call him "Istidji." Dat mean "little man."

When I first remember, before de War, old Master had 'bout as
many slave as I got fingers, I reckon. I can think dem off on my fingers like dis, but I can't recollect de names.

Dey call all de slaves "Istilusti." Dat mean "Black man."

Old man Tuskaya-hiniha was near 'bout blind before de War, and 'bout time of de War he go plumb blind and have to set on de long seat under de bresh shelter of de house all de time. Sometime I lead him around de yard a little, but not very much. Dat about de time all de slave begin to slip out and run off.

My own pappy was name Stephany. I think he take dat name 'cause when he little his mammy call him "Istifani." Dat mean a skeleton, and he was a skinny man. He belong to de Grayson family and I think his master name George, but I don't know. Dey big people in de Creek, and with de white folks too. My mammy was Serena and she belong to some of de Gouge family. Dey was big people in de Upper Creek, and one de biggest men of the Gouge was name Hopo-ethleyoholo for his Creek name.[6] He was a big man and went to de North in de War and died up in Kansas, I think.[7] Dey say when he was a little boy he was called Hopoethli, which mean "good little boy," and when he git grown he make big speeches and dey stick on de "yoholo." Dat mean "loud whooper."

Dat de way de Creek make de name for young boys when I was a little girl. When de boy git old enough de big men in de town give him a name, and sometime later on when he git to going around wid de grown men dey stick on some more name. If he a good talker dey sometime stick on "yoholo," and iffen he make lots of jokes dey call him "Hadjo." If he is a good leader dey call him "Imala" and if he kind of mean dey sometime call him "fixigo."

My mammy and pappy belong to two masters, but dey live together on a place. Dat de way de Creek slaves do lots of times. Dey work patches and give de masters most all dey make, but dey have some for demselves. Dey didn't have to stay on de master's place and work like I hear de slaves of de white people and de Cherokee and Choctaw people say dey had to do.

Maybe my pappy and mammy run off and git free, or maybeso dey buy demselves out, but anyway dey move away some time and my mammy's master sell me to old man Tuskaya-hinihi when I was jest a little gal. All I have to do is stay at de house and mind de baby.

Master had a good log house and a bresh shelter out in front like all de houses had. Like a gallery, only it had de dirt for de flo' and bresh for de roof. Dey cook everything out in de yard in big pots, and dey eat out in de yard too.

Dat was sho' good stuff to eat, and it make you fat too! Roast de green corn on de ears in de ashes, and scrape off some and fry it!

Grind de dry corn or pound it up and make ash cake. Den bile de
greens—all kinds of greens from out in de woods—and chop up de
pork and de deer meat, or de wild turkey meat; maybe all of dem, in
de big pot at de same time! Fish too, and de big turtle dat lay out on
de bank!

Dey always have a pot full of sofki[8] settin right inside de house,
and anybody eat when dey feel hungry. Anybody come on a visit, always give 'em some of de sofki. Ef dey don't take none de old man
git mad, too![9]

When you make de sofki you pound up de corn real fine, den pour
in de water and dreen it off to get all de little skin off 'n de grain. Den
you let de grits soak and den bile it and let it stand. Sometime you
put in some pounded hickory nut meats. Dat make it real good.

I don't know whar old Master git de cloth for de clothes, less'n he
buy it. Befo' I can remember I think he had some slaves dat weave
de cloth, but when I was dar he git it at de wagon depot at Honey
Springs, I think. He go dar all de time to sell his corn, and he raise
lots of corn, too.

Dat place was on de big road, what we called de road to Texas, but
it go all de way up to de North, too. De traders stop at Honey Springs
and old Master trade corn for what he want. He git some purty
checkedy cloth one time, and everybody git a dress or a shirt made
off 'n it. I have dat dress till I git too big for it.

Everybody dress up fine when day is a funeral. Dey take me along
to mind de baby at two—three funerals, but I don't know who it is
dat die. De Creek sho' take on when somebody die![10]

Long in de night you wake up and hear a gun go off, way off yonder somewhar. Den it go again, and den again, jest as fast as dey can
ram de load in. Dat mean somebody die. When somebody die de
men go out in de yard and let de people know dat way. Den dey jest
go back in de house and let de fire go out, and don't even tech de dead
person till somebody git dar what has de right to tech de dead.

When somebody had sick dey build a fire in de house, even in de
summer, and don't let it die down till dat person git well or die.
When dey die dey let de fire go out.

In de morning everybody dress up fine and go to de house whar de
dead is and stand around in de yard outside de house and don't go in.
Pretty soon along come somebody what got a right to tech and handle de dead and dey go in. I don't know what give dem de right, but
I think dey has to go through some kind of medicine to get de right,
and I know dey has to drink de red root and purge good before dey

tech de body. When dey git de body ready dey come out and all go to de graveyard, mostly de family graveyard, right on de place or at some of the kinfolkses.

When dey git to de grave somebody shoots a gun at de north, den de west, den de south, and den de east. Iffen dey had four guns dey used 'em.

Den dey put de body down in de grave and put some extra clothes in with it and some food and a cup of coffee, maybe. Den dey takes strips of elm bark and lays over de body till it all covered up, and den throw in de dirt.

When de last dirt throwed in, everybody must clap dey hands and smile, but you sho hadn't better step on any of de new dirt around de grave, because it bring sickness right along wid you back to your own house. Dat what dey said, anyways.

Jest soon as de grave filled up dey built a little shelter over it wid poles like a pig pen and kiver it over wid elm bark to keep de rain from soaking down in de new dirt.

Den everybody go back to de house and de family go in and scatter some kind of medicine 'round de place and build a new fire. Sometimes dey feed everybody befo' dey all leave for home.

Every time dey have a funeral dey always a lot of de people say, "Didn't you hear de stikini squalling in de night?" "I hear dat stikini all de night!" De "stikini" is de screech owl, and he suppose to tell when anybody going to die right soon. I hear lots of Creek people say dey hear de screech owl close to de house, and sho' nuff somebody in de family die soon.[11]

When de big battle come at our place at Honey Springs dey jest git through having de green corn "busk." De green corn was just ripened enough to eat. It must of been along in July.[12]

Dat busk was jest a little busk. Dey wasn't enough men around to have a good one. But I seen lots of big ones. Ones whar dey had all de different kinds of "banga." Dey call all de dances some kind of banga. De chicken dance is de "Tolosabanga," and de "Istifanibanga" is de one whar dey make lak dey is skeletons and raw heads coming to git you.

De "Hadjobanga" is de crazy dance, and dat is a funny one. Dey all dance crazy and make up funny songs to go wid de dance. Everybody think up funny songs to sing and everybody whoop and laugh all de time.

But de worse one was de drunk dance. Dey jest dance ever whichaway, de men and de women together, and dey wrassle and hug and carry on awful! De good people don't dance dat one. Everybody sing about going to somebody else's house and sleeping wid dem, and shout, "We is all drunk and we don't know what we doing and we ain't doing wrong 'cause we is all drunk" and things like dat. Sometime de bad ones leave and go to de woods, too!

Dat kind of doing make de good people mad, and sometime dey have killings about it. When a man catch one his women—maybeso his wife or one of his daughters—been to de woods he catch her and beat her and cut off de rim of her ears![13]

People think maybeso dat ain't so, but I know it is!

I was combing somebody's hair one time—I ain't going tell who—and when I lift it up off'n her ears I nearly drap dead! Dar de rims cut right off'n 'em! But she was a married woman, and I think maybeso it happen when she was a young gal and got into it at one of dem drunk dances.

Dem Upper Creek took de marrying kind of light anyways. Iffen de younguns wanted to be man and wife and de old ones didn't care dey jest went ahead and dat was about all, 'cepting some presents maybe. But de Baptists changed dat a lot amongst de young ones.

I never forgit de day dat battle of de Civil War happen at Honey Springs![14] Old Master jest had de green corn all in, and us had been having a time gitting it in, too. Jest de women was all dat was left, 'cause de men slaves had all slipped off and left out. My uncle Abe done got up a bunch and gone to de North wid dem to fight, but I didn't know den whar he went. He was in dat same battle, and after de War dey called him Abe Colonel. Most all de slaves 'round dat place done gone off a long time before dat wid dey masters when dey go wid old man Gouge and a man named McDaniel.[15]

We had a big tree in de yard, and a grape vine swing in it for de little baby "Istidji," and I was swinging him real early in de morning befo' de sun up. De house set in a little patch of woods wid de field in de back, but all out on de north side was a little open space, like a kind of prairie. I was swinging de baby, and all at once I seen somebody riding dis way 'cross dat prairie—jest coming a-kiting and a-laying flat out on his hoss. When he see de house he begin to give de war whoop, "Eya-a-a-a-he-ah!"[16] When he git close to de house he holler to git out de way 'cause dey gwine to be a big fight, and old Master start rapping wid his cane and yelling to git some grub and blankets in de wagon right now!

We jest leave everything setting right whar it is, 'cepting putting out de fire and grabbing all de pots and kettles. Some de nigger women run to git de mules and de wagon and some start gitting meat and corn out of de place whar we done hid it to keep de scouters from finding it befo' now. All de time we gitting ready to travel we hear dat boy on dat horse going on down de big Texas road hollering, "Eya-a-a-he-he-hah!"

Den jest as we starting to leave here come something across dat little prairie sho' nuff! We know dey is Indians de way dey is riding, and de way dey is all strung out. Dey had a flag, and it was all red and had a big criss-cross on it dat look lak a saw horse. De man carry it and rear back on it when de wind whip it, but it flap all 'roun de horse's head and de horse pitch and rear lak he know something going to happen, sho!

'Bout dat time it turn kind of dark and begin to rain a little, and we git out to de big road and de rain come down hard. It rain so hard for a little while dat we jest have to stop de wagon and set dar, and den long come more soldiers dan I ever see befo'. Dey all white men, I think, and dey have on dat brown clothes dyed wid walnut and butternut, and old Master say dey de Confederate soldiers. Dey dragging some big guns on wheels and most de men slopping 'long in de rain on foot.

Den we hear de fighting up to de north 'long about whar de river is, and de guns sound lak hosses loping 'cross a plank bridge way off somewhar. De head men start hollering and some de hosses start rearing and de soldiers start trotting faster up de road. We can't git out on de road so we jest strike off through de prairie and make for a creek dat got high banks and a place on it we call Rocky Cliff.

We git in a big cave in dat cliff, and spend de whole day and dat night in dar, and listen to de battle going on.

Dat place was about half-a-mile from de wagon depot at Honey Springs, and a little east of it. We can hear de guns going all day, and along in de evening here come de South side making for a getaway. Dey come riding and running by whar we is, and it don't make no difference how much de head men hollers at 'em dey can't make dat bunch slow up and stop.

After while here comes de Yankees, right after 'em, and dey goes on into Honey Springs and pretty soon we see de blaze whar dey is burning de wagon depot and de houses.

De next morning we goes back to de house and find de soldiers ain't hurt nothing much. De hogs is whar dey is in de pen and de chickens come cackling 'round too. Dem soldiers going so fast dey didn't have no time to stop and take nothing, I reckon.

Den long come lots of de Yankee soldiers going back to de North, and dey looks purty wore out, but dey is laughing and joshing and going on.

Old Master pack up de wagon wid everything he can carry den, and we strike out down de big road to git out de way of any more war, if dey going be any.

Dat old Texas road jest crowded wid wagons! Everybody doing de same thing we is, and de rains done made de road so muddy and de soldiers done tromp up de mud so bad dat de wagons git stuck all de time.

De people all moving along in bunches, and every little while one bunch of wagons come up with another bunch all stuck in de mud, and dey put all de hosses and mules on together and pull 'em out, and den dey go on together awhile.

At night dey camp, and de women and what few niggers dey is have to git de supper in de big pots, and de men so tired dey eat everything up from de women and de niggers, purty nigh.

After while we come to de Canadian town. Dat whar old man Gouge been and took a whole lot de folks up north wid him, and de South soldiers got in dar ahead of us and took up all de houses to sleep in.

Dey was some of de white soldiers camped dar, and dey was singing at de camp. I couldn't understand what dey sing, and I asked a Creek man what dey say and he tell me dey sing, "I wish I was in Dixie, look away—look away."

I ask him whar dat is, and he laugh and talk to de soldiers and dey all laugh, and make me mad.

De next morning we leave dat town and git to de big river. De rain make de river rise, and I never see so much water! Jest look out dar and dar all dat water!

Dey got some boats we put de stuff on, and float de wagons and swim de mules and finally git across, but it look lak we gwine all drown.

Most de folks say dey going to Boggy Depot and around Fort Washita, but old Master strike off by hisself and go way down in de bottom somewhar to live.

I don't know whar it was, but dey been some kind of fighting all around dar, 'cause we camp in houses and cabins all de time and nobody live in any of 'em.

Look like de people all git away quick, 'cause all de stuff was in de houses, but you better scout up around de house before you go up to it. Liable to be some scouters already in it!

Dem Indian soldiers jest quit de army and lots went scouting in little bunches and took everything dey find. Iffen somebody try to stop dem dey git killed.

Sometime we find graves in de yard whar somebody jest been buried fresh, and one house had some dead people in it when old Mistress poke her head in it. We git away from dar, and no mistake!

By and by we find a little cabin and stop and stay all de time. I was de only slave by dat time. All de others done slip out and run off. We stay dar two year I reckon, 'cause we make two little crop of corn. For meat a man name Mr. Walker wid us jest went out in de woods and shoot de wild hogs. De woods was full of dem wild hogs, and lots of fish in de holes whar he could sicken 'em wid buck root and catch 'em wid his hands, all we wanted.[17]

I don't know when de War quit off, and when I git free, but I stayed wid old man Tuskaya-hiniha long time after I was free, I reckon. I was jest a little girl, and he didn't know whar to send me to, anyways.

One day three men rid up and talk to de old man awhile in English talk. Den he called me and tell me to go wid dem to find my own family. He jest laugh and slap my behind and set me up on de hoss in front of one de men and dey take me off and leave my good checkedy dress at de house!

Before long we git to dat Canadian river again, and de men tie me on de hoss so I can't fall off. Dar was all dat water, and dey ain't no boat, and dey ain't no bridge, and we jest swim de hosses. I knowed sho' I was going to be gone dat time, but we git across.

When we come to de Creek Agency dar is my pappy and my mammy to claim me, and I live wid dem in de Verdigris bottom above Fort Gibson till I was grown and dey is both dead. Den I marries Anderson Davis at Gibson Station, and we git our allotments on de Verdigris east of Tulsa—kind of south too, close to de Broken Arrow town.

I knowed old man Jim McHenry at dat Broken Arrow town. He done some preaching and was a good old man, I think.

I knowed when dey started dat Wealaka school across de river from de Broken Arrow town. Dey name it for de Wilaki town, but dat town was way down in de Upper Creek country close to whar I lived when I was a girl.

I had lots of children, but only two is alive now. My boy Anderson got in a mess and went to dat McAlester prison, but he got to be a trusty and dey let him marry a good woman dat got lots of property dar, and dey living all right now.

When my old man die I come to live here wid Josephine,[18] but I'se blind and can't see nothing and all de noises pesters me a lot in de town. And de children is all so ill mannered, too. Dey jest holler at you all de time! Dey don't mind you neither!

When I could see and had my own younguns I could jest set in de corner and tell 'em what to do, and iffen dey didn't do it right I could whack 'em on de head, 'cause dey was raised de old Creek way, and dey know de old folks know de best!

[1] Mrs. Lucinda Davis was interviewed by Slave Narrative Project field worker Robert Vinson Lackey in Tulsa probably sometime in summer 1937. From his now nonexistent notes, Lackey prepared a preliminary draft of the Lucinda Davis narrative as the typescript "Interview with Lucinda Davis, Ex-Slave, Age (about) 89 Yrs. Lives with Daughter, 710 N. Lansing, Tulsa, Okla." in the OHS Slave Narratives. Project personnel lightly edited the preliminary draft into standard project format as the typescript "Lucinda Davis, Age (about) 89 Yrs., Tulsa, Okla.," which was forwarded to Washington on 13 August 1937 and is published here. Federal Writers' Project folklore editor Benjamin A. Botkin appraised the narrative as having "full detail on persons, places, and customs treated" and observed that it was conveyed in "remarkably fine colloquial style with literary effectiveness." The final draft is available in ribbon-copy typescript in the LC Slave Narratives and in carbon copy as item 350073 in the LC Slave Narratives Carbon Copies and in the OHS Slave Narratives. Ron Stephens, [Oklahoma City, Oklahoma], to Robert V. Lackey, Tulsa, Oklahoma, 10 August 1937, and Stephens to Cronyn, 13 August 1937, both letters in WPA Notes on Interviews; B. A. B[otkin], WPA Writers' Program Records Appraisal Sheet Accession no. 350073, 13 December 1940, "Appraisal Sheets, A–Y" file, box A905, LC Slave Narratives (hereafter cited as LC Slave Narratives Appraisal Sheets).

The Lucinda Davis narrative is one of the few from the Oklahoma Slave Narrative Project to have been published in Oklahoma. Robert Vinson Lackey passed a copy of the interview text together with a photograph of Davis to journalist Ruth Sheldon, who edited the narrative for publication in the *Tulsa Tribune*, where it appeared on 18 August 1937 under the title "Tulsa Negro Woman Who Was Slave to Creek Indian Family Relates Some of Experiences."

[2] Confirming Mrs. Lucinda Davis's remembrances of bondage among the Creeks are her and her family's records of enrollment as members of the Creek Nation by the Dawes Commission on 28 March 1902. U.S., Department of the Interior, Office of Indian Affairs, Dawes Commission, Creek Freedmen Cards, no. 825 (Anderson, Lucinda, Hayman, Serena, Adam, Josephine, Belle, Minnie, Rebecca, Linnie, Anderson Jr., and Henry Davis; Willie McIntosh; David Nero), microcopy M1186, reel 67, National Archives and Records Administration, Fort Worth, Texas (cited hereafter as Creek Freedmen Census Cards).

[3] The preliminary draft at this point adds the words "seem like it."

[4] By the middle of the nineteenth century, "Upper Creeks" denoted those living on

the Canadian River in present-day Oklahoma, although the term is much older, referring in the eighteenth century to the Creeks living on the Alabama River and its tributaries, the Coosa and Tallapoosa rivers, in present-day Alabama. Angie Debo, *The Road to Disappearance: A History of the Creek Indians*, 123; J. Leitch Wright, Jr., *Creeks and Seminoles: The Destruction and Regeneration of the Muscogulge People*, 3.

5 For Creek vocabulary, see R. M. Loughridge and David M. Hodge, *English and Muskogee Dictionary Collected from Various Sources and Revised*.

6 For background on Creek chief Opothleyohola (Old Gouge), see the narrative of Phoebe Banks, above.

7 For an Oklahoma freedwoman's recollections of this exodus to Kansas in the autumn of 1861, see the narrative of Phoebe Banks, above.

8 For background on Creek foodways and *sofky* (sofki) in particular, see Muriel H. Wright, "American Indian Corn Dishes," 155–59, 163–65.

9 For a discussion of hospitality among the Creek people, see John R. Swanton, "Social Organization and Social Usages of the Indians of the Creek Confederacy," in *Forty-second Annual Report of the Bureau of American Ethnology to the Secretary of the Smithsonian Institution, 1924–1925*, 447–50.

10 For background on Creek funerary practices, see Frank G. Speck, "The Creek Indians of Taskigi Town," *American Anthropological Association Memoirs*, 2, part 2 (1907): 118–19; John R. Swanton, *The Indians of the Southeastern United States*, 724–25; John R. Swanton, "Social Organization," 388–98; Mrs. Irwin A. Watson, "Creek Indian Burial Customs Today," *Chronicles of Oklahoma* 28 (Spring 1950): 95–102.

11 The Creek people believed the screech owl to be an unfavorable spirit that either caused or announced death. John R. Swanton, "Religious Beliefs and Medical Practices of the Creek Indians," in *Forty-second Annual Report of the Bureau of American Ethnology to the Secretary of the Smithsonian Institution, 1924–1925*, 496, 549.

12 For descriptions of Creek dances, including the green corn busk, the skeleton dance, and the drunken dance, see Speck, "Creek Indians," 134–44; John R. Swanton, ed., "The Green Corn Dance," *Chronicles of Oklahoma* 10 (June 1932): 170–95; Swanton, "Religious Beliefs," 546–614.

13 For discussions of punishments for adultery among the Creek people, including cropping of hair, noses, and ears, see Swanton, *Indians of the Southeastern United States*, 732; Swanton, "Social Organization," 346–55.

14 The Battle of Honey Springs took place on 17 July 1863. For background on this Civil War fight, see the narrative of Phoebe Banks, above.

15 For background on the exodus of Creeks loyal to the United States under chief Opothleyohola (Old Gouge) in autumn 1861, see the narrative of Phoebe Banks, above.

16 At this point the preliminary draft of the narrative reads, "Jest layin out on his horse! 'Eyah-a-a-a-he-he-he-ah!' Like dat!"

17 The use of natural materials to stupefy, or "sicken," fish in pools of water was a widespread practice among the southeastern Indians, including the Creeks. The "buck root" mentioned here may refer to the root of the buckeye, which the Creeks are known to have used for this purpose. Swanton, *Indians of the Southeastern United States*, 431–44.

18 A roughly contemporary Tulsa city directory shows Lucinda Davis residing with Josephine Pressley at 808 North Lansing Avenue. *Polk's Tulsa (Tulsa County, Okla.) City Directory, 1934*, 169, 398, 600.

ANTHONY DAWSON[1]

Age 105   *1008 E. Owen St., Tulsa, Okla.2*

"Run nigger, run,
De Patteroll git you!
Run nigger, run,
De Patteroll come!

"Watch nigger, watch—
De Patteroll trick you!
Watch nigger, watch,
He got a big gun!"[3]

Dat one of the songs de slaves all knowed, and de children down on de "twenty acres"[4] used to sing it when dey playing in de moonlight 'round de cabins in de quarters. Sometime I wonder iffen de white folks didn't make dat song up so us niggers would keep in line.

None of my old Master's boys tried to git away 'cepting two, and dey met up wid evil, both of 'em.

One of dem niggers was fotching a bull-tongue from a piece of new ground way at de back of de plantation, and bringing it to my pappy to git it sharped. My pappy was de blacksmith.

Dis boy got out in de big road to walk in de soft sand, and long come a wagon wid a white overseer and five, six, niggers going somewhar. Dey stopped and told dat boy to git in and ride. Dat was de last anybody seen him.

Dat overseer and another one was cotched after awhile, and showed up to be underground railroaders. Dey would take a bunch of niggers into town for some excuse, and on de way jest pick up a extra nigger and show him whar to go to git on de "railroad system." When de runaway niggers got to de North dey had to go in de army, and dat boy from our place got killed. He was a good boy, but dey jest talked him into it. Dem railroaders was honest, and dey didn't take no presents, but de patrollers[5] was low white trash!

We all knowed dat if a patroller jest rode right by and didn't say nothing dat he was doing his honest job, but iffen he stopped his hoss and talked to a nigger he was after some kind of trade.

Dat other black boy was hoeing cotton way in de back of de field and de patroller rid up and down de big road, saying nothing to nobody.

De next day another white man was on de job, and long in de evening a man come by and axed de niggers about de fishing and hunting! Dat black boy seen he was de same man what was riding de day befo' and he knowed it was a underground trick. But he didn't see all de trick, bless God!

We found out afterwards dat he told his mammy about it. She worked at de big house and she stole something for him to give dat low white trash I reckon, 'cause de next day he played sick along in de evening and de black overlooker—he was my uncle—sent him back to de quarters.

He never did git there, but when dey started de hunt dey found him about a mile away in de woods wid his head shot off, and old Master sold his mammy to a trader right away. He never whipped his grown niggers.

Dat was de way it worked. Dey was all kinds of white folks jest like dey is now. One man in Sesesh⁶ clothes would shoot you if you tried to run away. Maybe another Sesesh would help slip you out to the underground and say "God bless you poor black devil" and some of dem dat was poor would help you if you could bring 'em sumpin you stole, lak a silver dish or spoons or a couple big hams. I couldn't blame them poor white folks, wid the men in the War and the women and children hongry. The niggers didn't belong to them nohow, and they had to live somehow. But now and then they was a devil on earth, walking in the sight of God and spreading iniquity before him. He was de low-down Sesesh dat would take what a poor runaway nigger had to give for his chance to git away, and den give him 'structions dat would lead him right into de hands of de patrollers and git him caught or shot!

Yes, dat's de way it was. Devils and good people walking in de road at de same time, and nobody could tell one from t'other.

I remember about de trickery so good 'cause I was "grown and out" at that time. When I was a little boy I was a house boy, 'cause my mammy was the house woman, but when the war broke I already been sent to the fields and mammy was still at de house.

I was born on July 25, 1832. I know, 'cause old Master keep de book on his slaves jest like on his own family. He was a good man, and old Mistress was de best woman in de world!

De plantation had more than 500 acres and most was in cotton and tobacco. But we raised corn and oats, and lots of cattle and horses, and plenty of sheep for wool.

I was born on the plantation, soon after my pappy and mammy was brought to it. I don't remember whether they was bought or come from my Mistress's father. He was mighty rich and had several hundred niggers. When she was married he give her 40 niggers. One of them was my pappy's brother. His name was John, and he was my master's overlooker.

We called a white man boss the "overseer," but a nigger was a overlooker. John could read and write and figger, and old Master didn't have no white overseer.

Master's name was Levi Dawson, and his plantation was 18 miles east of Greenville, North Carolina. It was a beautiful place, with all the fences around the Big House and along the front made out of barked poles, rider style, and all whitewashed.

The Big House set back from the big road about a quarter of a mile. It was only one story, but it had lots of rooms.

There was four rooms in a bunch on one side and four in a bunch on the other, with a wide hall in between. They was made of square adzed logs, all weatherboarded on the outside and planked up and plastered on the inside. Then they was a long gallery clean across the front with big pillars made out of bricks and plastered over. They called it the passage 'cause it didn't have no floor excepting bricks, and a buggy could drive right under it. Mostly it was used to set under and talk and play cards and drink the best whiskey old Master could buy.

Back in behind the big house was the kitchen, and the smokehouse in another place made of plank, and all was whitewashed and painted white all the time.

Old Mistress was named Miss Susie and she was born an Isley. She brought 40 niggers from her pappy as a present, and Master Levi jest had 4 or 5, but he had got all his land from his pappy. She had the niggers and he had the land. That's the way it was, and that's the way it stayed! She never let him punish one of her niggers and he never asked her about buying or selling land. Her pappy was richer than his pappy, and she was sure quality!

My pappy's name was Anthony, and mammy's name was Chanie. He was the blacksmith and fixed the wagons, but he couldn't read and figger like uncle John. Mammy was the head house woman but didn't know any letters either.

They was both black like me.[7] Old man Isley, where they come from, had lots of niggers,[8] but I don't think they was off the boat.

You can set the letters up and I can't tell them, but you can't fool me with the figgers, 'less they are mighty big numbers.

Master Levi had three sons and no daughters. The oldest son was Simeon. He was in the Sesesh army. The other two boys was too young. I can't remember their names. They was a lot younger and I was grown and out befo' they got big.[9]

Old Master was a fine Christian but he like his jewleps[10] anyways. He let us niggers have preachings and prayers, and would give us a parole to go 10 or 15 miles to a camp meeting and stay two or three days with nobody but Uncle John to stand for us. Mostly we had white preachers, but when we had a black preacher that was Heaven.

We didn't have no voodoo women nor conjure folks at our 20 acres. We all knowed about the Word and the unseen Son of God and we didn't put no stock in conjure.

Course we had luck charms and good and bad signs, but everybody got dem things even nowadays. My boy had a white officer in the Big War[11] and he tells me that man had a li'l old doll tied around his wrist on a gold chain.

We used herbs and roots for common ailments, like sassafras, and boneset and peach tree poultices and coon root tea, but when a nigger got bad sick Old Master sent for a white doctor. I remember that old doctor. He lived in Greenville and he had to come 18 miles in a buggy.

When he give some nigger medicine he would be afraid the nigger was like lots of them that believed in conjure, and he would say, "If you don't take that medicine like I tell you and I have to come back here to see you I going to break your dam black neck next time I come out here!"

When it was bad weather sometime the black boy sent after him had to carry a lantern to show him the way back. If that nigger on his mule got too fur ahead so old doctor couldn't see de light he sho' catch de devil from that old doctor and from old Master too, less'n he was one of old Missy's house niggers, and then old Master jest grumble to satisfy the doctor.

Down in the quarters we had the spinning house, where the old women card the wool and run the loom. They made double weave for the winter time, and all the white folks and slaves had good clothes and good food.

Master made us all eat all we could hold. He would come to the smokehouse and look in and say, "You niggers ain't cutting down that smoke side and that souse lak you ought to! You made dat meat and you got to help eat it up!"

Never no work on Sunday 'cepting the regular chores. The overlooker made everybody clean up and wash de children up and after the praying we had games. Antny over and marbles and "I Spy" and the likes of that. Some times de boys would go down in de woods and git a possum. I love possum and sweet taters, but de coon meat more delicate and de har don't stink up de meat.

I wasn't at the quarters much as a boy. I was at the big house with my mammy, and I had to swing the fly bresh over my old Mistress when she was sewing or eating or taking her nap. Sometimes I would keep the flies off'n old Master, and when I would get tired and let the bresh slap his neck he would kick at me and cuss me, but he never did reach me. He had a way of keeping us little niggers scared to death and never hurting nobody.

I was down in the field burning bresh when I first heard the guns in the War. De fighting was de battle at Kingston, North Carolina, and it lasted four days and nights.[12] After while bunches of Sesesh come riding by hauling wounded people in wagons, and then pretty soon big bunches of Yankees come by, but dey didn't ack like dey was trying very hard to ketch up.

Dey had de country in charge quite some time, and they had forages coming around all the time. By dat time old Master done buried his money and all de silver and de big clock, but the Yankees didn't pear to search out dat kind of stuff. All dey ask about was did anybody find a bottle of brandy!

When de War ended up most all de niggers stay with old Master and work on de shares, until de land git divided up and sold off and the young niggers git scattered to town.

I never did have no truck wid de Ku Kluckers, but I had to step mighty high to keep out'n it! De sho' nuff Kluxes never did bother around us 'cause we minded our own business and never give no trouble.

We wouldn't let no niggers come 'round our place talking 'bout delegates and voting, and we jest all stayed on the place. But dey was some low white trash and some devilish niggers made out like dey was Ku Klux ranging 'round de country stealing hosses and taking things. Old Master said dey wasn't shore enough, so I reckon he knowed who the regular ones was.

These bunches that come around robbing got into our neighborhood and old Master told me I better not have my old horse at the house, 'cause if I had him they would know nobody had been there stealing and it wouldn't do no good to hide anything 'cause they would tear up the place hunting what I had and maybe whip or kill me.

"Your old hoss ain't no good, Tony, and you better kill him to make them think you already been raided on," old Master told me, so I let him out and knocked him in the head with an axe, and then we hid all our grub and waited for the Kluckers to come most any night, but they never did come. I borried a hoss to use in the day and took him back home every night for about a year.

The niggers kept talking about being free, but they wasn't free then and they ain't now.

Putting them free jest like putting goat hair on a sheep. When it rain de goat come a running and git in de shelter, 'cause his hair won't shed the rain and he git cold, but de sheep ain't got sense enough to git in the shelter but jest stand out and let it rain on him all day.

But the good Lord fix the sheep up wid a woolly jacket that run the water off, and he don't git cold, so he don't have to have no brains.

De nigger during slavery was like de sheep. He couldn't take care of hisself but his Master looked out for him and he didn't have to use his brains. De master's protection was like de woolly coat.

But de 'mancipation come and take off de woolly coat and leave de nigger wid no protection and he cain't take care of hisself either.

When de niggers was sot free lots of them got mighty uppity, and everybody wanted to be a delegate to something or other. The Yankees told us we could go down and vote in the 'lections and our color was good enough to run for anything. Heaps of niggers believed them. You cain't fault them for that, 'cause they didn't have no better sense, but I knowed the black folks didn't have no business mixing in until they knowed more.

It was a long time after the War before I went down to vote and everything quiet by that time, but I heared people talk about the fights at the schoolhouse when they had the first election.

I jest stayed on around the old place a long time, and then I got on another piece of ground and farmed, not far from Greenville, until 1900. Then I moved to Hearne, Texas, and stayed with my son Ed until 1903 when we moved to Sapulpa in the Creek Nation. We come to Tulsa several years ago, and I been living with him ever since.

I can't move off my bed now, but one time I was strong as a young bull. I raised seven boys and seven girls.[13] My boys was named Edward, Joseph, Furney, Julius, James, and William, and my girls was Luvenia, Olivia, Chanie, Mamie, Rebecca and Susie.

I always been a deep Christian and depend on God and know his unseen Son, the King of Glory. I learned about Him when I was a little boy. Old Master was a good man, but on some of de plantations the masters wasn't good men and the niggers didn't get the Word.

I never did get no reading and writing 'cause I never did go to the schools. I thought I was too big, but they had schools and the young ones went.

But I could figger, and I was a good farmer, and now I bless the Lord for all his good works. Everybody don't know it I reckon, but we all needed each other. The blacks needed the whites, and still do.

There's a difference in the color of the skin, but the souls is all white, or all black, 'pending on the man's life and not on his skin. The old fashioned meetings is busted up into a thousand different kinds of churches and only one God to look after them. All is confusion, but I ain't going to worry my old head about 'em.

¹ Three distinct but very similar drafts of the Anthony Dawson narrative survive. There are two early typescript drafts, both of them entitled "Interview with Anthony Dawson (Ex-Slave, Aged 105, 1008 E. Owen St., Tulsa, Okla.)." One is in the OHS Slave Narratives and the other is filed with item 350071 in the LC Slave Narratives Carbon Copies. The former typescript is ten leaves long and prepared in standard pica type, whereas the latter typescript is nine leaves long and prepared in elite type. The draft at the Oklahoma Historical Society bears pencil editorial markings made in preparing the final draft. This final draft, entitled "Anthony Dawson, Age 105, 1008 E. Owen St., Tulsa, Okla." and published here, is available in ribbon copy in the LC Slave Narratives and in carbon copy as item 350071 in the LC Slave Narratives Carbon Copies and in the OHS Slave Narratives. The interview was undertaken by field worker Robert Vinson Lackey apparently in summer 1937, for Ron Stephens, Federal Writers' Project state administrator for Oklahoma, complimented him on it by letter on 10 August 1937 and forwarded it to Washington two days later. Benjamin A. Botkin, folklore editor for the Federal Writers' Project at the national level, noted that Dawson's narrative, which he described as "vigorous, colloquial, [and] expressive," gave "a complete picture of slave life with original handling of familiar material." B. A. B[otkin], WPA Writers' Program Records Appraisal Sheet Accession no. 350071, 13 December 1940, LC Slave Narratives Appraisal Sheets; Stephens to Lackey, 10 August 1937; Stephens to Cronyn, 12 and 13 August 1937; all three letters in WPA Notes on Interviews.

The Anthony Dawson narrative is one of the few from the Oklahoma Slave Narrative Project to have been published in Oklahoma. Robert Vinson Lackey passed a copy of the interview text together with a photograph of Dawson to journalist Ruth Sheldon, who edited the narrative for publication in summer 1937 in the *Tulsa Tribune*. It appeared on 12 August 1937 under the title "'Niggers Wasn't Free Then and They Ain't Now,' Says 105-Year-Old Ex-Slave in Tulsa."

² Anthony Dawson's street address apparently became garbled in transcription. Although all three versions of his narrative give his residence as 1008 East Owen Street in Tulsa, the actual address was 1008 East Queen Street. *Polk's Tulsa City Directory, 1934,* 170, 633; *Polk's Tulsa City Directory, 1935,* 195, 701.

[3] A note clipped to the carbon copy of the final draft of this narrative in the OHS Slave Narratives states, "Maybe he knows more ditties sung during that time." For more background on this particular song, see the narrative of William Curtis, above.

[4] An apparent reference to the slave quarters on the plantation.

[5] Throughout this narrative, the earlier drafts consistently spell this word "patterollers."

[6] A reference to Secessionist, or Confederate, soldiers.

[7] The two earlier drafts at this point read "and both big and husky like me."

[8] The two earlier drafts at this point read "off the boat."

[9] At this point the two earlier drafts include the following two sentences as a separate paragraph: "Old Master was too old to go at first, and later on he hid out when the conscripts come to look him up. He was the only white menfolks on the place anyway."

[10] An obvious reference to the julep, or mint julep, one of the best-known mixed alcoholic beverages of the South.

[11] A reference to World War I.

[12] This is a reference to fighting on 7–10 March 1865 at Kinston (not Kingston), North Carolina, part of the spring 1865 Carolinas Campaign by the Union Army. Hugh Talmage Lefler and Albert Ray Newsome, *The History of a Southern State: North Carolina,* 459–60; William S. Powell, *The North Carolina Gazetteer,* 265.

[13] The carbon copy of the final draft of this narrative in the OHS Slave Narratives has editorial markings changing this sentence to "I raised six boys and six girls," which agrees with the number of names given by Dawson for his children.

ALICE DOUGLASS[1]

Age 77 Yrs.   *Oklahoma City, Okla.*

I was born December 22, 1860 in Sumner County, Tennessee. My mother—I mean mammy, 'cause what did we know 'bout mother and mamma. Master and Mistress made dey chillun call all nigger women, "Black Mammy." Jest as I was saying my mammy was named Millie Elkins and my pappy was named Isaac Garrett. My sisters and brothers was Frank, Susie and Mollie. They is all in Nashville, Tennessee right now. They lived in log houses. I 'member my grandpappy and when he died. I allus slept in the Big House in a cradle wid white babies.

We all the time wore cotton dresses and we weaved our own cloth. The boys jest wore shirts. Some wore shoes, and I sho' did. I kin see 'em now as they measured my feets to git my shoes. We had doctors to wait on us iffen we got sick and ailing. We wore asafetida to keep all diseases offen us.

When a nigger man got ready to marry, he go and tell his master that they was a woman on sech and sech a farm that he'd lak to have. Iffen master give his resent, then he go and ask her master and iffen he say yes, well, they jest jump the broomstick. Mens could jest see their wives on Sadday nite.

They laid peoples 'cross barrels and whupped 'em wid bull whips till the blood come. They'd half feed 'em and niggers'd steal food and cook all night. The things we was forced to do then the whites[2] is doing of their own free will now. You gotta reap jest what you sow 'cause the Good Book says it.

They used to bid niggers off and then load 'em on wagons and take 'em to cotton farms to work. I never seen no cotton till I come heah. Peoples make big miration 'bout girls having babies at 11 years old. And you better have them whitefolks some babies iffen you didn't wanta be sold. Though a funny thing to me is, iffen a nigger woman had a baby on the boat on the way to the cotton farms, they throwed it in the river. Taking 'em to them cotton farms is jest the reason niggers is so plentiful in the South today.

I ain't got no education a'tall. In dem days you better not be caught with a newspaper, else you got a beating and your back almost cut off. When niggers got free, whitefolks killed 'em by the carload, 'cause they said it was a nigger uprising. I used to lay on the flo' with the whitefolks and hear 'em pass. Them patrollers roved trying to ketch niggers without passes to whup 'em. They was sometimes called bush whackers.

We went to white folks' church. I was a great big girl before we went to cullud church. We'd stay out and play while they worshipped.[3] We jest played marbles—girls, white chillun and all.

The Yankees come thoo' and took all the meat and everything they could find. They took horses, food and all. Mammy cooked their vittles. One come in our cabin and took a sack of dried fruit with my mammy's shoes on the top. I tried to make 'em leave mammy's shoes too but he didn't.[4]

I stayed in the house with the whitefolks till I was 19. They lak to kept me in there too long. That's why I'm selfish as I am. Within three weeks after I was out of the house, I married William Douglass.[5] Whitefolks now don't want you to tech 'em, and I slept with white chillun till I was 19. You kin cook for 'em and put your hands in they vittles and they don't say nothing, but jest you tech one!

We stayed on, on the place, three or four years and it was right then mammy give us our pappy's name. We moved from the place to one three or four miles from our master's place, and mammy cooked there a long time.

Abraham Lincoln gits too much praise. I say, shucks, give God the praise. Lincoln come thoo' Gallitan, Tennessee[6] and stopped at Hotel Tavern with his wife. They was dressed just lak tramps and nobody knowed it was him and his wife till he got to the White House and writ back and told 'em to look 'twixt the leaves in the table where he had set and they sho' nuff found out it was him.

I never mentions Jeff Davis. He ain't wuff it.

Booker T. Washington was all right in his place. He come here and told these whitefolks jest what he thought. Course he wouldn't have done that way down South. I declare to God he sho' told 'em enough. They toted him 'round on their hands. No Jim Crow here then.

I jined the church 'cause I had religion round 60 years ago. People oughta be religious sho'; what for they wanta live in sin and die and go to the Bad Man. To git to Heaven, you sho' ought to work some. I want a resting place somewhar, 'cause I ain't got none here. I am a member of Tabernacle Baptist Church, and I help build the first church in Oklahoma City.

I got three boys and three girls. I don't know none's age. I give 'em the best education I could.

[1] The interview of Ida Belle Hunter with Mrs. Alice Douglass in Oklahoma City in spring or summer 1937 is represented in two typescripts. A preliminary draft dated 18 June 1937 is available as "Interview with Alice Douglass, Ex-Slave, Aged 77, 505 N. Fonshill, Oklahoma City, Oklahoma" in the OHS Slave Narratives. The final version, entitled "Alice Douglass, Age 77 Yrs., Oklahoma City, Okla." and published here, is available in ribbon-copy typescript in the LC Slave Narratives and in carbon copy as item 350085 in the LC Slave Narratives Carbon Copies and in the OHS Slave Narratives. This interview was forwarded to Washington on 16 August 1937. Stephens to Cronyn, 16 August 1937, WPA Notes on Interviews.

The OHS Slave Narratives additionally contains a one-page typescript by Ida Belle Hunter dated 10 May 1939 and entitled "Douglas [*sic*], Alice, Exslave," which provides the following additional information abstracted from the interview:

She has a 3rd grade education and has attended WPA classes. Can hardly write her name but can read print very well. When she came to Oklahoma City, they had good school in frame building.

Back then they had prayer once a week (on Sunday). That was called family prayer. Said grace at mealtime and everybody said a verse from the Bible. Nobody got out of saying a verse, even visitor.

Some folks believed in ghosts, but she didn't.

Fruit was dried by cutting it and placing it on sheds in the sun and bringing it in at night.

They didn't have as many dances then as they do now and they didn't hug so tight, but the devil had his part just like the Christians.

There was no such thing as hours. Just worked from sun up to sun down. Men made about $9 a week. She didn't work and had no idea as to women's wages.

The biggest ailment was the smallpox. Had plenty doctors. The best home remedy for everything was asafetida worn around the neck and eat a little ever now and then.

Had quite a few white doctors here in the city and one Negro doctor (couldn't recall name) so midwives didn't do any business.
She came to Oklahoma City and helped build the first Negro church in the city.

[2] Rather than "the whites," the preliminary draft reads "they."

[3] At this point the preliminary draft includes the following two sentences: "My mammy was never whupped. She was a cook in the big house."

[4] The preliminary draft does not include "but he didn't."

[5] The contemporary city directory shows Alice Douglass as the widow of William Douglas [sic]. *Polk's Oklahoma City Directory, 1937,* 851.

Here the preliminary draft includes four sentences not presented in the later draft: "Hoodoo is nothin' unstrange or uncommon. They was sho' nuff in my home. They knowed they stuff. It's all agin you, nothin' to he'p you."

[6] An obvious reference to Gallatin, Tennessee.

DOC DANIEL DOWDY[1]

Age 81 Yrs.   *Oklahoma City, Oklahoma*

I was born June 6, 1856 in Madison County, Georgia. Father was named Joe Dowdy and mother was named Mary Dowdy. There was 9 of us boys, George, Smith, Lewis, Henry, William, myself, Newt, James and Jeff. There was one girl and she was my twin, and her name was Sarah. My mother and father come from Richmond, Va., to Georgia. Father lived on one side of the river and my mother on the other side. My father would come over ever week to visit us. Noah Meadows bought my father, and Elizabeth Davis, daughter of the old master, took my mother. They married in Noah Meadows' house.

My mother was the cook in the Big House. They'd give us pot likker with bread crumbs in it. Sometimes meat, jest sometimes, very seldom. I liked black-eyed peas and still do till now. We lived in weatherboard house. Our parents had corded-up beds with ropes and us chillun slept on the floor for most part or in a hole bored in a log. Our house had one window jest big enough to stick your head out of, and one door, and this one door faced the Big House which was your master's house. This was so that you couldn't git out 'less somebody seen you.

My job was picking up chips and keeping the calves separate so that the calves wouldn't suck the cows dry. Mostly, we had Saturday afternoons off to wash. I was show boy doing the war, me and my sister, 'cause we was twins. My mother couldn't be bought 'cause she done had 9 boys for one farm and neither my father, 'cause he was the father of 'em. I was religious and didn't play much, but I sho' did like to listen to preachings. I did used to play marbles sometimes.

We jest wore shirts and nothing else both winter and summer. They was a little heavier in winter and that's all. No shoes ever. I had none till after I was set free. I guess I was almost 12 years old then.

The overseer on our place was a large, tall black man. We had plenty poor white neighbors. They was one of our biggest troubles. They'd allus look in our window and door all the time.

I saw slaves sold. I can see that old block now. My cousin Eliza was a pretty girl, really good looking. Her master was her father. When the girls in the big house had beaux coming to see 'em, they'd ask, "Who is that pretty gal?" So they decided to git rid of her right away. The day they sold her, will allus be remembered. They stripped her to be bid off and looked at. I wasn't allowed to stand in the crowd. I was laying down under a fig brush. The man that bought Eliza was from New York. The Negroes had made up nuff money to buy her off theyself, but they wouldn't let that happen. There was a man bidding for her who was a Swedeland. He allus bid for the good looking cullud gals and bought 'em for his own use. He ask the man from New York, "Whut you gonna do with her when you git 'er?" The man from New York said, "None of your damn business, but you ain't got money nuff to buy 'er." When the man from New York had bought her, he said, "Eliza, you are free from now on." She left and went to New York with him. Mama and Eliza both cried when she was being showed off, and master told 'em to shut up before he knocked they brains out.

Iffen you didn't do nothing wrong, they whipped you now and then anyhow. I called a boy Johnny once and he took me 'hind the garden and poured it on me and made me call him master. It was from then on I started to fear the white man. I come to think of him as a bear. Sometimes fellows would be a little late making it in and they got whipped with a cow-hide. The same man whut whipped me to make me call him master, well, he whipped my mamma. He tied her to a tree and beat her unmerciful and cut her tender parts. I don't know why he tied her to that tree.

The first time you was caught trying to read or write, you was whipped with a cow-hide, the next time with a cat-o-nine tails and the third time they cut the first jint offen your forefinger. They was very severe. You most allus got 30 and 9 lashes.

They carried news from one plantation by whut they call relay. Iffen you was caught, they whipped you till you said, "Oh, pray Master!"

One day a man gitting whipped was saying "Oh pray master, Lord
have mercy!" They'd say "Keep whipping that nigger Goddamn him."
He was whipped till he said, "Oh pray Master, I gotta nuff." Then
they said, "Let him up now, 'cause he's praying to the right man."

My father was the preacher and an educated man. You know the
sermon they give him to preach?—Servant, Obey Your Master. Our
favorite baptizing hymn was On Jordan's Stormy Bank I Stand. My
favorite song is Nobody Knows the Trouble I've Seen.

Oh, them patrollers![2] They had a chief and he git 'em together and
iffen they caught you without a pass and sometimes with a pass,
they'd beat you. But iffen you had a pass, they had to answer to the
law. One old master had two slaves, brothers, on his place. They was
both preachers. Mitchell was a hardshell Baptist and Andrew was a
Missionary Baptist. One day the patroller chief was rambling thoo'
the place and found some letters writ to Mitchell and Andrew. He
went to the master and said, "Did you know you had some niggers
that could read and write?" Master said, "No, but I might have, who
did you 'spect?" The patroller answered, "Mitchell and Andrew."
The old master said, "I never knowed Andrew to tell me a lie 'bout
nothing!"

Mitchell was called first and asked could he read and write. He
was scared stiff. He said, "Naw-sir." Andrew was called and asked.
He said, "Yes-sir." He was asked iffen Mitchell could. He said, "Sho',
better'n me." The master told John Arnold, the patroller chief, not
to bother 'em. He gloried in they spunk. When the old master died,
he left all of his niggers a home apiece. We had Ku Klux Klans till
the government sent Federal officers out and put a stop to their rav-
aging and sent 'em to Sing Sing.[3]

Doing the war my father was a carpenter. His young master come
to him 'cause he was a preacher and asked him must he go to the front
and my father told him not to go 'cause he wouldn't make it. He
went on jest the same and when he come back my father had to tote
him in the house 'cause he had one leg tore off.[4] The Yankees come
thoo', ramshackled houses, leave poor horses and take fat ones and
turn the poor ones in the corn they left. They took everything they
could. They cussed niggers who dodged 'em for being fools and make
'em show 'em everything they knowed whar was.

Our old master was mighty old and him and the women folks
cried when we was freed. He told us we was free as he was.

I come to Oklahoma in 1906. I come out of that [Atlanta, Geor-
gia] riot in 1906.[5] Some fellow knocked up a colored woman or

something and we waded right in and believe me we made Atlanta a fit place to live in. It is one of the best cities in America.

I married Miss Emmaline Witt. I carried her to the preacher one of the coldest nights I ever rid. I have three chillun and don't know how many grandchillun. My chillun is one a nurse, one in Arizona for his health and the other doing first one thing and another.

I think Abraham Lincoln was the greatest human being ever been on earth 'cepting the Apostle Paul. Who any better'n a man who liberated 4,000,000 Negroes? Some said he wasn't a Christian, but he told some friends once, "I'm going to leave you and may never see you again (and he didn't) so I'm going to take the Divine Spirit with me and leave it with you."

Jeff Davis was as bloody as he could be. I don't lak him a'tall. But you know good things come from enemies. I don't even admire George Washington. White men from the south that will help the Negro is far and few between. Booker T. Washington was a great man. He made some blunders and mistakes, but he was a great man. He is the father of industrial education and you know that sho' is a great thing.

The white folks was ignorant. You know the better you prepare yourself the better you act. Iffen they had put some sense in our heads 'stead of sticks on our heads, we'ud been better off and more benefit to 'em.

I had something from within that made me fear God and taught me how to pray. People say God don't hear sinners pray, but he do. Everybody ought to be Christians so not to be lost.

I work in real estate and can do a lot of work. I don't use no crutches and no cane and walk all the time, never hardly ride. I come in at 1 and 2 o'clock a.m. and get up between 8 and 9 a.m. 'cept Sundays, I get up at 7 or 8 a.m. so I can be ready to go to Sunday School. I cook for my own self all the time too. I am a Baptist and a member of Tabernacle Baptist Church. I am a trustee in my church too.

[1] Project field worker Ida Belle Hunter interviewed Doc Daniel Dowdy at his home in Oklahoma City on 17 June 1937. From her now lost notes, Hunter prepared a preliminary draft of Dowdy's narrative as the typescript "Interview with Doc Daniel Dowdy, Ex-Slave Aged 81, 1104 N.E. 7th St., Oklahoma City, Oklahoma," preserved in the OHS Slave Narratives. This text clearly shows the pencil markings of a WPA editor. From this draft, project personnel later in the summer of 1937 prepared a revised draft of the narrative in standard format, which was forwarded to Washington on 13 August 1937 and is published here. This narrative, "Doc Daniel Dowdy, Age 81 Yrs., Oklahoma City, Oklahoma," is available in ribbon-copy typescript in the LC Slave

Narratives and in carbon copy as item 350106 in the LC Slave Narratives Carbon Copies and in the OHS Slave Narratives. In the contemporary city directory, Dowdy's first name is spelled Dock. *Polk's Oklahoma City Directory, 1937,* 213; Stephens to Cronyn, 13 August 1937, WPA Notes on Interviews.

[2] Consistently the preliminary draft spells this term "patterollers."

[3] At this point the preliminary version of the narrative includes the following two sentences missing from the later draft: "The only hants was white folks tryin' to keep the niggers f'om leavin' the farms. We used garlic and tar water to keep off all kinds of diseases."

[4] Here the preliminary draft includes the following two sentences: "Honey we come thoo the fire to make this day possible for yo'all. You sho' should love us too."

[5] The Atlanta race riot took place for four days in September 1906, resulting in the loss of both black and white lives and very substantial destruction of private property belonging to African Americans.

JOANNA DRAPER[1]

Age 83 Yrs.   *Tulsa, Okla.*

Most folks can't remember many things happened to 'em when they only eight years old, but one of my biggest tribulations come about dat time and I never will forget it! That was when I was took away from my own mammy and pappy and sent off and bound out to another man, way off two–three hundred miles away from whar I live. And dat's the last time I ever see either one of them, or any of my own kinfolks!

Whar I was born was at Hazlehurst, Mississippi. Jest a little piece east of Hazlehurst, close to the Pearl River, and that place was a kind of new plantation what my Master, Dr. Alexander, bought when he moved into Mississippi from up in Virginia a while before the War.

They said my mammy brings me down to Mississippi, and I was born jest right after she got there. My mammy's name was Margaret, and she was born under the Ramsons, back in Tennessee. She belonged to Dave Ramson, and his pappy had come to Tennessee to settle on war land, and he had knowed Dr. Alexander's people back in Virginia too. My pappy's name was Addison, and he always belonged to Dr. Alexander. Old doctor bought my mammy 'cause my pappy liked her. Old doctor live in Tennessee a little while before he go on down in Mississippi.

Old doctor's wife named Dinah, and she sho' was a good woman, but I don't remember about old doctor much. He was away all the time, it seem like.

When I is about six year old they take me into the Big House to learn to be a house woman, and they show me how to cook and clean up and take care of babies. That Big House wasn't very fine, but it was mighty big and cool, and made out of logs with a big hall, but it didn't have no long gallery like most the houses around there had.

They was lot of big trees in the yard, and most the ground was new ground 'round that place, 'cause the old Doctor jest started to done farming[2] on it when I was took away, but he had some more places not so far away, over towards the river, that was old ground and made big crops for him. I went to one of the places one time, but they wasn't nobody on 'em but niggers[3] and a white overseer. I don't know how many niggers old Doctor had, but Master John Deeson say he had about a hundred.

At old Doctor's house I didn't have to work very hard. Jest had to help the cooks and peel the potatoes and pick the guineas and chickens and do things like that. Sometime I had to watch the baby. He was a little boy, and they would bring him into the kitchen for me to watch. I had to git up way before daylight and make the fire in the kitchen fireplace and bring in some fresh water, and go get the milk what been down in the spring all night, and do things like that until breakfast ready. Old Master and old Mistress come in the big hall to eat in the summer, and I stand behind them and shoo off the flies.

Old doctor didn't have no spinning and weaving niggers 'cause he say they don't do enough work and he buy all the cloth he use for everybody's clothes. He can do that 'cause he had lots of money. He was big rich, and he keep a whole lot of hard money in the house all the time, but none of the slaves know it but me. Sometimes I would have the baby in the Mistress' room and she would go git three or four big wood boxes full of hard money for us to play with. I would make fences out of the money all across the floor, to keep the baby satisfied, and when he go to sleep I would put the money back in the boxes. I never did know how much they is, but a whole lot.

Even after the War start old Doctor have that money, and he would exchange money for people. Sometimes he would go out and be gone a long time, and come back with a lot more money he got from somewhar.

Right at the first they made him a high officer in the War and he done doctoring somewhar at a hospital most of the time. But he could go on both sides of the War, and sometime he would come in at night and bring old Mistress pretty things, and I heard him tell her he got them in the North.

One day I was fanning him and I asked him is he been to the North and he kick out at us and tell to shut up my black mouth, and it nearly scared me to death the way he look at me! Nearly every time he been gone and come in and tell Mistress he been in the North he have a lot more hard money to put away in them boxes, too!

One evening long come a man and eat supper at the house and stay all night. He was a nice mannered man, and I like to wait on him. The next morning I hear him ask old Doctor what is my name, and old Doctor start in to try to sell me to that man. The man say he can't buy me 'cause old Doctor say he want a thousand dollars, and then old Doctor say he will bind me out to him.

I run away from the house and went out to the cabin whar my mammy and pappy was, but they tell me to go on back to the Big House 'cause maybe I am just scared. But about that time old Doctor and the man come and old Doctor make me go with the man. We go in his buggy a long ways off to the South, and after he stop two or three night at people's houses and put me out to stay with the niggers he come to his own house. I ask him how far it is back home and he say about a hundred miles or more, and laugh, and ask me if I know how far that is.

I wants to know if I can go back to my mammy some time, and he say "Sho', of course you can, some of these times. You don't belong to me, Jo, I'se jest your boss and not your master."

He live in a big old rottendy house, and he ain't farming none of the land. Jest as soon as he git home he go off again, and sometimes he only come in at night for a little while.

His wife's name was Kate and his name was Mr. John. I was there about a week before I found out they name was Deeson. They had two children, a girl about my size name Joanna like me, and a little baby boy name Johnny. One day Mistress Kate[4] tell me I the only nigger they got. I been thinking maybe they had some somewhar on a plantation, but she say they ain't got no plantation and they ain't been at that place very long either.

That little girl Joanna and me kind of take up together, and she was a mighty nice mannered little girl, too. Her mammy raised her good. Her mammy was mighty sickly all the time, and that's the reason they bind me to do the work.

Mr. John was in some kind of business in the War too, but I never see him with no soldier clothes on but one time. One night he come in with them on, but the next morning he come to breakfast in jest his plain clothes again. Then he go off again.

I sho' had a hard tow at that house. It was old and rackady, and I had to scrub off the staircase and the floors all the time, and git the breakfast for Mistress Kate and the two children. Then I could have my own breakfast in the kitchen. Mistress Kate always get the supper, though.

Some days she go off with the two children and leave me at the house all day by myself, and I think maybe I run off, but I didn't know whar to go.

After I been at that place two years Mr. John come home and stay. He done some kind of trading in Jackson, Mississippi, and he would be gone three or four days at a time, but I never did know what kind of trading it was.

About the time he come home to stay I seen the first Ku Klux I ever seen one night. I was going down the road in the moonlight and I heard a hog grunting out in the bushes at the side of the road. I jest walk right on and in a little ways I hear another hog in some more bushes. This time I stop and listen, and they's another hog grunts across the road, and about that time two mens dressed up in long white shirts steps out into the road in front of me! I was so scared the goose bumps jump up all over me 'cause I didn't know what they is! They didn't say a word to me, but jest walked on past me and went on back the way I had come. Then I see two more mens step out of the woods and I run from that as fast as I can go!

I ast Miss Kate what they is and she say they Ku Klux, and I better not go walking off down the road any more. I seen them two, three times after that, though, but they was riding horses them times.

I stayed at Mr. John's place two more years, and he got so grumpy and his wife got so mean I make up my mind to run off. I bundle up my clothes in a little bundle and hide them, and then I wait until Miss Kate take the children and go off somewhere, and I light out on foot. I had me a piece of that hard money what Master Dr. Alexander had give me one time at Christmas. I had kept it all that time and nobody knowed I had it, not even Joanna. Old Doctor told me it was fifty dollars, and I thought I could live on it for a while.

I never had been away from that place, not even to another plantation, in all the four years I was with the Deesons, and I didn't know which-a-way to go, so I jest started west.

I been walking about all evening it seem like, and I come to a little town with jest a few houses. I see a nigger man and ask him whar I can git something to eat, and I say I got fifty dollars.

"What you doing wid fifty dollars, child? Where you belong at, anyhow?" He ask me, and I tell him I belong to Master John Deeson, but I is running away. I explain that I jest bound out to Mr. John, but Dr. Alexander my real master, and then that man tell me the first time I knowed it that I ain't a slave no more!

That man Deeson never did tell me, and his wife never did!

Well, dat man asked me about the fifty dollars, and then I found out that it was jest fifty cents!

I can't begin to tell about all the hard times I had working for something to eat and roaming around after that. I don't know why I never did try to git back up around Hazlehurst and hunt up my pappy and mammy, but I reckon I was jest ignorant and didn't know how to go about it. Anyways I never did see them no more.

In about three years or a little over I met Bryce Draper on a farm in Mississippi and we was married. His mammy had had harder time than I had. She had five children by a man that belong to her master, Mr. Bryce, and already named one of the boys—that my husband—Bryce after him, and then he take her in and sell her off away from all her children!

One was jest a little baby, and the master give it laudanum, but it didn't die, and he sold her off and lied and said she was a young girl and didn't have no husband, 'cause the man what bought her said he didn't want to buy no woman and take her away from a family. That new master name was Draper.

The last year of the War Mr. Draper die, and his wife already dead, and he give all his farm to his two slaves and set them free. One of them slaves was my husband's mammy.

Then right away the whites come and robbed the place of everything they could haul off, and run his mammy and the other niggers off! Then she went and found her boy, that was my husband, and he live with her until she died, jest before we is married.

We lived in Mississippi a long time, and then we hear about how they better to the Negroes up in the North, and we go up to Kansas, but they ain't no better there, and we come down to Indian Territory in the Creek Nation in 1898, jest as they getting in that Spanish [-American] War.

We leased a little farm from the Creek Nation for $15 an acre, but when they give out the allotments we had to give it up. Then we rent 100 acres from some Indians close to Wagoner, and we farm it all with my family. We had enough to do it too!

For children we had John and Joe, and Henry, and Jim and Robert and Will that was big enough to work, and then the girls big enough was Mary, Nellie, Izora, Dora, and the baby. Dora married Max Colbert. His people belonged to the Colberts that had Colbert's Crossin' on the Red River way before the War, and he was a freedman and got allotment.[5]

I lives with Dora now,[6] and we is all happy, and I don't like to talk about the days of the slavery times, 'cause they never did mean nothing to me but misery, from the time I was eight years old.

I never will forgive that white man for not telling me I was free, and not helping me to git back to my mammy and pappy! Lots of white people done that.

[1] Mrs. Joanna Draper was interviewed in Tulsa, Oklahoma, by WPA field worker Robert Vinson Lackey apparently sometime in the first half of 1937. Two typescript versions of Draper's interview have survived, the earlier being "Interview with Joanna Draper, Ex-Slave, Age 83 Yrs., 1238 North Elgin Ave., Tulsa, Oklahoma" in the OHS Slave Narratives. A later draft, incorporating editorial changes made on the former and published here, is available as the typescript "Joanna Draper, Age 83 Yrs., Tulsa, Okla.," which was forwarded to Washington on 16 August 1937. It is available in ribbon-copy typescript in the LC Slave Narratives as well as in carbon copy as item 350084 in the LC Slave Narratives Carbon Copies and in the OHS Slave Narratives. On the last-cited carbon copy, project editor Ida Belle Hunter identified specific questions that were not asked of the informant but noted, "nice interview, however." B. A. Botkin, director of folklore for the Federal Writers' Project, shared Hunter's evaluation, describing Joanna Draper's remembrances as a "full-bodied personal narrative against background of Civil War, rich in details of life of house woman and of the master." Botkin was so impressed that he included the Draper narrative in its entirety in his 1945 study *Lay My Burden Down* (98–103, 276). B. A. B[otkin], WPA Writers' Program Records Appraisal Sheet Accession no. 350084, 12 December 1940, LC Slave Narratives Appraisal Sheets; Stephens to Cronyn, 16 August 1937, WPA Notes on Interviews.

[2] The preliminary draft at this point reads "to do some farming."

[3] The preliminary draft suggests that Joanna Draper predominantly chose the term "Negroes" to denote African Americans in her interview, but the WPA editor nearly always changed the term to "niggers" in preparing the final draft.

[4] The preliminary draft consistently shows that Joanna Draper called her former mistress "Missy Kate," although the WPA editor changed all such references to "Mistress Kate" or "Miss Kate."

[5] For remembrances of slave life at Colbert's Ferry, see the narrative of Kiziah Love, below.

[6] According to the 1935 city directory, Joanna Draper resided at 915 North Frankfort Avenue in Tulsa with Mack and Andora Colbert, the Max and Dora mentioned in the interview. The preliminary draft of the narrative states that the interview took place at 1238 North Elgin Avenue, which according to the directory was the residence of James and Mittie Calbert [sic], apparently relatives of Joanna Draper. *Polk's Tulsa City Directory, 1935,* 149, 171, 207, 638, 645.

MRS. ESTHER EASTER[1]

Age 85 Yrs.   *Tulsa, Okla.*

I was born near Memphis, Tenn., on the old Ben Moore plantation, but I don't know anything about the Old South because Master Ben moves us all up into Missouri (about 14-miles east of Westport, now Kansas City), long before they started fighting about slavery.

Mary Collier was my mother's name before she was a Moore. About my father, I dunno. Mammy was sickly most of the time when I was a baby, and she was so thin and poorly when they move to Missouri the white folks afraid she going die on the way.

But she fool 'em, and she live two–three year after that. That's what good Old Master Ben tells me when I gets older.

I stay with Master Ben's married daughter, Mary, till the coming of the War. Times was good before the War, and I wasn't suffering none from slavery, except once in a while the Mistress would fan me with the stick—bet I needed it, too.

When the War come along Master he say to leave Mistress Mary and get ready to go to Texas. Jim Moore, one of the meanest men I ever see, was the son of Master Ben; he's going take us there.

Demon Jim, that's what I call him when he ain't round the place, but when he's home it was always Master Jim 'cause he was reckless with the whip. He was a Rebel officer fighting round the country and didn't take us slaves to Texas right away. So I stayed on at his place not far from Master Ben's plantation.

Master Jim's wife was a demon, just like her husband. Used the whip all the time, and every time Master Jim come home he whip me 'cause the Mistress say I been mean.

One time I tell him, you better put me in your pocket (sell me), Master Jim, else I'se going run away. He don't pay no mind, and I don't try to run away 'cause of the whips.

I done see one whipping and that enough. They wasn't no fooling about it. A runaway slave from the Jenkins plantation was brought back, and there was a public whipping, so's the slaves could see what happens when they tries to get away.

The runaway was chained to the whipping post, and I was full of misery when I see the lash cutting deep into that boy's skin. He swell up like a dead horse, but he gets over it, only he was never no count for work no more.

While Master Jim is out fighting the Yanks, the Mistress is fiddling round with a neighbor man, Mister Headsmith. I is young then, but I knows enough that Master Jim's going be mighty mad when he hears about it.

The Mistress didn't know I knows her secret, and I'm fixing to even up for some of them whippings she put off on me. That's why I tell Master Jim next time he come home.

See that crack in the wall? Master Jim say yes, and I say, it's just like the open door when the eyes are close to the wall. He peek and see into the bedroom.

That's how I find out about the Mistress and Mister Headsmith, I tells him, and I see he's getting mad.

What you mean? And Master Jim grabs me hard by the arm like I was trying to get away.

I see them in the bed.

That's all I say. The Demon's got him and Master Jim tears out of the room looking for the Mistress.

Then I hears loud talking and pretty soon the Mistress is screaming and calling for help, and if old Master Ben hadn't drop in just then and stop the fight, why, I guess she be beat almost to death, that how mad the Master was.[2]

Then Master Ben gets mad 'cause his boy Jim ain't got us down in Texas yet. Then we stay up all the night packing for the trip. Master Jim takes us, but the Mistress stay at home, and I wonder if Master Jim beat her again when he gets back.

We rides the wagons all the way, how many days, I dunno. The country was wild most of the way, and I know now that we come through the same country where I lives now, only it was to the east. (The trip was evidently made over the "Texas Road.")[3] And we keeps on riding and comes to the big river that's all brown and red looking, (Red River) and the next thing I was sold to Mrs. Vaughn at Bonham, Texas, and there I stays till after the slaves is free.

The new Mistress was a widow, no children round the place, and she treat me mighty good. She was good white folks—like old Master Ben, powerful good.

When the word get to us that the slaves is free, the Mistress says I is free to go anywheres I want. And I tell her this talk about being free sounds like foolishness to me—anyway, where can I go? She just pat me on the shoulder and say I better stay right there with her, and that's what I do for a long time. Then I hears about how the white folks down at Dallas pays big money for house girls and there I goes.

That's all I ever do after that—work at the houses till I gets too old to hobble on these tired old feets and legs, then I just sits down.

Just sits down and wishes for old Master Ben to come and get me, and take care of this old woman like he use to do when she is just a little black child on the plantation in Missouri! God Bless old Master Ben—he was good white folks!

¹ WPA field worker L. P. Livingston interviewed Mrs. Esther Easter at her home in Tulsa, Oklahoma, on 14 July 1937, and Oklahoma Writers' Project staff member Craig Vollmer prepared an edited version of the text of the interview that summer. Vollmer's preliminary draft is available as the typescript "Interview with Mrs. Esther Easter (Slave Born, 1852, Age 85) 1438 North Owasso Ave., Tulsa" in the OHS Slave Narratives. From this text project personnel prepared a final draft in standard format. This later version, "Mrs. Esther Easter, Age 85 Yrs., Tulsa, Okla.," published here, was forwarded to Washington on 2 September 1937. It is available in ribbon-copy typescript in the LC Slave Narratives and in carbon copy as item 350052 in the LC Slave Narratives Carbon Copies and in the OHS Slave Narratives. B. A. Botkin, director of folklore for the Federal Writers' Project, praised the Esther Easter interview as a "straightforward, well-rounded autobiographical portrait and narrative, giving insight into life of owners." [B. A. Botkin], WPA Writers' Program Records Appraisal Sheet Accession no. 350052, 12 December 1940, LC Slave Narratives Appraisal Sheets; *Polk's Tulsa City Directory, 1935,* 213, 690; Stephens to Cronyn, 2 September 1937, WPA Notes on Interviews.

² Esther Easter's account of the crack in the wall is one of the most frequently published stories from the Oklahoma slave narratives, having appeared in at least four separate anthologies drawn from the WPA Slave Narrative Project. Botkin, *Lay My Burden Down,* 195; James Mellon, ed., *Bullwhip Days: The Slaves Remember,* 342; George P. Rawick, ed., *The American Slave: A Composite Autobiography,* series I, 12:89–90; Norman R. Yetman, *Life under the "Peculiar Institution": Selections from the Slave Narrative Collection,* 108.

³ The preliminary draft of the narrative contains a more complete explanation: "The trip was evidently made over the old Military Trail or the 'Texas Road,' as it is commonly called today." For further comments on this route, see the narrative of Polly Colbert, above.

ELIZA ELSEY¹

Age 77   *Fort Gibson, Oklahoma*

I ain't sure how old I is, but mamma says I was born during the middle of the War, in fodder time. That means in August, 'cause that's when fodder pulling was done, and how come I was born is this way:

Old Master Tom Smith, he the one who own that big plantation, maybe 600 acres, down south in Plantersville, Grimes County, Texas, treated his slaves like animals. He take the strongest men and women, put them together in a cabin so's they raise him some more husky children. That's the kind of a child I is, and that's why I is so big and so healthy at my old age. I weighs about 250 pounds, and I'm 'most 78.

I don't know about my pappy, 'cept mamma say his name was Tom McGowan. My mamma come from North Carolina and work in the fields for old Tom Smith who raised lots of figs and cane and some kind of grapes they call "cut throats." Soon as I is born she go back to the field work, and sometime she feel so bad they whipped her for not working hard enough. She had scars on her back until she died; I see them lots of times and feel sorry that she lived in slave times.

After the War a man named Harrison Sheppard married my mamma and she change her name to Jane Smith Sheppard. They give me three half brothers; Cicero, Jim and George, and four half sisters; Alice, Nessie, Manda and Friona. They are all dead.

The only white child on the plantation was Molly, and she the daughter of Tom Smith and his wife, who lived in a big, fine white plank house, with two chimneys, double. The field hands was never allowed to come into the Master's house, and I don't know how it was fix up.

I know about the slave cabins; they was all set in a long row, and seems like they be a mile long and made of logs. There was a fire-place made of mud, and the dirt floor was rock hard from all the feets that tramp over it all the time. The cabins all alike, one room with a door, but no windows, and mamma say the room was horrible hot in the summer.

All the clothes was made of cotton cloth, even in the winter. That alright for it don't stay cold long, not down south where the sugar cane grow. When a "norther" come the slaves maybe find some old pieces of shoes or wrap up the feets in sacks; if they couldn't find nothing to wear they would work anyways, building a fire with the brush to keep warm by, but they couldn't stay by that fire too much else they get flogged by the overseer that mamma said was the worse one she ever heard of.

The Master ration out the food by the week, and should anybody eat too much they most likely starve before next ration day. Else they steals from each other, or the Master would lose a hog some night when it be darkest. Like the story my mamma told about the slave who got caught under a hog.

The colored man he got hungry, and his little girl Caroline got hungry too, so he takes her with him one night to watch out for the Master while he steal a hog. He kill the hog alright and put him on his back to carry to his cabin, but somehow he stumble in the dark and the dead hog so heavy the girl can't get him off her pappy. Caroline get scared and yell, louder all the time, till the Master come to see about the trouble. He whipped the slave for stealing and the man went hungry waiting for the next rations.

Mamma told me about another time when two men went out to kill a hog. The hogs root around and sleep under the barn, so one man was to chase them out and the other man was to knock one in the head when he scoot out from under the barn. The hogs run out the other side of the barn, but the Negro come back out the same way he went in and when he stick his head out the man waiting for a hog crack him between the eyes and lay him out. The man died and Master sold the other one to some far off plantation.

Mother always said that stealing in slave days made a birthmark on the younger generation—that's why colored boys and girls steal today.

The Master kept a doctor around most of the time to look after the slaves. He dose out castor oil and turpentine, calomel and blue-mass pills. The children had some little sacks tied around their necks; I know now it was asafetida, and it keep off the disease.

When the Negro babies cry with the stomach ache they give them hen feathers tea, and when they break out with the hives, there was nothing better than sheep wool tea.

Some of the slaves didn't believe it when they was freed, and they didn't want to leave the plantation. Whole lots of them kept on working just the same, but they was treated better. They didn't know how to sell cattle or hogs, or sugar cane, and the Master sell part of the crops and give the Negroes some of the money.

After mamma married Harrison Sheppard they move up here to Fort Gibson and I been here since then. I been married three times. First to Bill White, then to Dennis Beck and then to Robert Elsey. They all dead now, and my three children was from my first husband. Two girls and a boy; Armanda, who I lives with, Bessie and George. There is four grandchildren; Hazel Blaine, Leonard Vann, Odell Little and L. V. Little.

That all I can tell about the slave days, but I is proud we all get out of slavery and I is glad that Lincoln is the one that freed us.

¹ Mrs. Eliza Elsey was interviewed at Fort Gibson, Oklahoma, by WPA field worker Ethel Wolfe Garrison in late 1937 or early 1938. The narrative survives in a preliminary draft as edited by WPA staff member Craig Vollmer on 5 January 1938 under the title "Interview with Eliza Elsey, Ex-Slave, Age About 77, Fort Gibson, Oklahoma," and in a later version, entitled "Eliza Elsey, Age 77, Fort Gibson, Oklahoma," which was typed in standard project format on 19 October 1938 and is pub-

lished here. Both versions are preserved as ribbon-copy typescripts in the OHS Slave
Narratives. This interview was never forwarded to Washington and has not previously
been published.

ELIZA EVANS[1]

Age 87   *McAlester, Okla.*

I sho' remember de days when I was a slave and belonged to de best
old Master what ever was, Mr. John Mixon. We lived in Selma, Dallas County, Alabama.

My grandma was a refugee from Africa. You know dey was white
men who went slipping 'round and would capture or entice black
folks onto their boats and fetch them over here and sell 'em for slaves.
Well, grandma was a little girl 'bout eight or nine years old and her
parents had sent her out to get wood. Dey was going to have a feast.
Dey was going to roast a baby. Wasn't that awful! Well, they captured her and put a stick in her mouth. The stick held her mouth
wide open so she wouldn't cry out. When she got to de boat she was
so tired out she didn't do nothing.

They was a lot of more colored folks on de boat. It took about four
months to get across on de boat and Mr. John Mixon met the boat
and bought her. I think he gave five hundred dollars for her. She was
named Gigi, but Master John called her Gracie. She was so good and
they thought so much of her dat they gave her a grand wedding when
she was married. Master John told her he'd never sell none of her
chillun. He kept dat promise and he never did sell any of her grandchillun either. He thought it was wrong to separate famblys. She was
one hundred and three years old when she died. I guess her mind got
kind of feeble 'cause she wandered off and fell into a mill race and was
drowned.

Master John Mixon had two big plantations. I believe he owned
about four hundred slaves, chillun and all. He allowed us to have
church one time a month with de white folks and we had prayer
meeting every Sunday. Sometimes when de men would do something like being sassy or lazy and dey knowed dey was gonna be
whipped, dey'd slip off and hide in de woods. When dey'd slip back
to get some food dey would all pray for 'em dat Master wouldn't have
'em whipped too hard, and for fear the Patroller would hear 'em
they'd put their faces down in a dinner pot. I'd sit out and watch for
the Patroller. He was a white man who was appointed to catch runaway niggers. We all knew him. His name was Howard Campbell.

He had a big pack of dogs. The lead hound was named Venus. There was five or six in the pack, and they was vicious too.

My father was a carriage driver and he allus took the family to church. My mother went along to take care of the little chilluns. She'd take me too. They was Methodist and after they would take the sacrament we would allus go up and take it. The niggers could use the whitefolks' church in the afternoon.

De Big House was a grand place. It was a two-story house made out of logs dat had been peeled and smoothed off. There was five big rooms and a big open hall wid a wide front porch clean across de front. De porch had big posts and pretty banisters. It was painted white and had green shutters on de windows. De kitchen was back of de Big House.

De slaves quarters was about a quarter of a mile from de Big House. Their houses was made of logs and the cracks was daubed with mud. They would have two rooms. Our bedsteads was made of poplar wood and we kept them scrubbed white with sand. We used ropes woven together for slats. Our mattresses were made of cotton, grass, or even shucks. My mother had a feather bed. The chairs was made from cedar with split white oak bottoms.

Each family kept their own home and cooked and served their own meals. We used wooden trays and wooden spoons. Once a week all the cullud chillun went to the Big House to eat dinner. The table was out in de yard. My nickname was "Speck." I didn't like to eat bread and milk when I went up there and I'd just sit there. Finally they'd let me go in de house and my mother would feed me. She was the house woman and my Auntie was cook. I don't know why they had us up there unless it was so they could laugh at us.

None of old Master's young niggers never did much work. He say he want 'em to grow up strong. He gave us lots to eat. He had a store of bacon, milk, bread, beans and molasses. In summer we had vegetables. My mother could make awful good corn pone. She would take meal and put salt in it and pour boiling water over it and make into pones. She'd wrap these pones in wet cabbage or collard leaves and roll dem into hot ashes and bake dem. They sho' was good. We'd have possum and coon and fish too.

The boys never wore no britches in de summer time. Boys fifteen years old would wear long shirts with no sleeves and they went barefooted. De girls dressed in shimmys. They was a sort of dress with two seams in it and no sleeves.

Old Master had his slaves to get up about five o'clock. Dey did an ordinary day's work. He never whipped them unless they was lazy or sassy or had a fight. Sometimes his slaves would run away but they allus come back. We didn't have no truck with [underground] railroaders 'cause we like our home.

A woman cussed my mother and it made her mad and they had a fight. Old Master had them both whipped. My mother got ten licks and de other woman got twenty-five. Old Mistress sho' was mad 'cause mother got whipped. Said he wouldn't have done it if she had known it. Old Mistress taught mother how to read and write and mother taught my father. I went to school jest one day so I can't read and write now.

Weddings was big days. We'd have big dinners and dances once in a while and when somebody died they'd hold a wake. They'd sit up all night and sing and pray and talk. At midnight they'd serve sandwiches and coffee. Sometimes we'd all get together and play ring plays and dance.

Once the Yankee soldiers come. I was big enough to tote pails and piggins then. These soldiers made us chillun tote water to fill their canteens and water their horses. We toted the water on our heads.[2] Another time we heard the Yankees was coming and old Master had about fifteen hundred pounds of meat. They was hauling it off to bury it and hide it when the Yankees caught them. The soldiers ate and wasted every bit of that good meat. We didn't like them a bit.

One time some Yankee soldiers stopped and started talking to me—they asked me what my name was. "I say Liza," and they say, "Liza who?" I thought a minute and I shook my head, "Jest Liza, I ain't got no other name."

He say, "Who live up yonder in dat Big House?" I say, "Mr. John Mixon." He say, "You are Liza Mixon." He say, "Do anybody ever call you nigger?" And I say, "Yes Sir." He say, "Next time anybody call you nigger you tell 'em dat you is a Negro and your name is Miss Liza Mixon." The more I thought of that the more I liked it and I made up my mind to do jest what he told me to do.

My job was minding the calves back while the cows was being milked. One evening I was minding the calves and old Master come along. He say, "What you doin' nigger?" I say real pert like, "I ain't no nigger, I's a Negro and I'm Miss Liza Mixon." Old Master sho' was surprised and he picks up a switch and starts at me.

Law, but I was skeered! I hadn't never had no whipping so I run fast as I can to Grandma Gracie. I hid behind her and she say, "What's the matter of you child?" And I say, "Master John gwine

whip me." And she say, "What you done?" And I say, "Nothing." She
say she know better and 'bout that time Master John got there. He
say, "Gracie, dat little nigger sassed me." She say, "Lawsie child,
what does ail you?" I told them what the Yankee soldier told me to
say and Grandma Gracie took my dress and lift it over my head and
pins my hands inside, and Lawsie, how she whipped me and I dassen't
holler loud either. I jest said dat to de wrong person, didn't I?

I'se getting old now and can't work no more. I jest sits here and
thinks about old times. They was good times. We didn't want to be
freed. We hated the Yankee soldiers. Abe Lincoln was a good man,
though, wasn't he? I tries to be a good Christian 'cause I wants to go
to Heaven when I die.

¹ WPA field worker Mrs. Jessie R. Ervin's interview with Mrs. Eliza Evans of
McAlester apparently took place in spring or summer 1937, for the narrative was sent
to project headquarters on 2 September of that year. It is represented by two typescript
drafts, the preliminary one of which is entitled "Interview with Eliza Evans (Ex-Slave,
Aged 87 Years, East Adams, McAlester, Oklahoma)" and is preserved in the OHS Slave
Narratives. A later version in standard project format, forwarded to Washington and
published here, is entitled "Eliza Evans, Age 87, McAlester, Okla." and is available in
ribbon-copy typescript in the LC Slave Narratives and in carbon copy as item 350064
in the LC Slave Narratives Carbon Copies and in the OHS Slave Narratives. Stephens
to Cronyn, 2 September 1937, WPA Notes on Interviews.

² The preliminary version of the narrative here reads: "We toted water till our heads
hurt. (We toted the water on our heads.)"

AUNT LIZZIE FARMER¹

In a little two room shack that was formerly used as servants' quarters, and situated in the better residential district of McAlester, lives
an old colored woman commonly known as "Aunt Lizzie Farmer."
She is physically unable to "work in white folks' kitchens" any
longer, due to rheumatism, so whiles the time away doing little extra
jobs for her friends and neighbors and "praise'n de Lord."

Almost every evening neighbors of "Aunt Lizzie" listen in on her
devotional hour, or hours, as they often last from two to three hours.
They feel that she is sincere in her religious beliefs as she lives them.
If a neighbor or friend is ill, whether they be black or white, "Aunt
Lizzie" is the first to lend her assistance. For every good deed that
comes to her, she returns two.

"Aunt Lizzie" was born near Mount Enterprise, Texas, in 1861.
Her mother having passed away while she was only a year old, she
was sent to live with her grandparents, George A. English and fam-

ily, who were slaves of J. Booker, a plantation holder; however, her grandfather was the "mainest boss" next to Ol' Massa, over the two hundred slaves. Her grandmother Harriet English was born in Eufaula, Oklahoma, about 1827, and was one-half Creek Indian. She lived to be one hundred and three years of age. Most of her life was spent in Texas as she went there to live when she was about fourteen years of age and never returned to the place of her birth. "I remember," says "Aunt Lizzie," "that grandmother used to tell us that if we disobeyed her, she would come through the keyhole and 'witch' us. I really believed that grandma could come through the keyhole, so I stuffed it full of cotton." We were scared within an inch of our lives of grandpa because he would whip my uncles and I jes like Ol' Massa whipped the slaves, and then he used to tell us old, old slaves stories. One was bout John and Ned, slaves of Ol' Massa, way back there.

Ol' Massa had hundreds of beautiful hogs. Soon they began to disappear. He suspected John and Ned as they had absolute care of them. Then Ol' Massa's big blue barrow disappeared. He asked the boys about it but they "jes scratched their heads and acted worried too." When they would go to feed at night, Ned would sing: "Pig-o-wee. Pig-o-wee. Somebody's done been here and stole Massaa's big blue barrow. Pig-o-wee. Pig-o-wee. Somebody's done been here and stole Massa's big blue barrow. Pig-o-wee. Pig-o-wee."

One night Ol' Massa blacked up and waited for them. John came first and Ol' Massa locked him up and put on his clothes and waited for Ned. When Ned arrived he looked at Ol' Massa and said, "John is you sick, you sho looks bad?" "Bout dead," said Ol' Massa. They began their work of getting jes one more hog. Ned notices that John acted kinda funny. He didn't persuade that hog like he always did. Anyway they drove the hog down to the river where they had to cross to their hut. Ned looked at Ol' Massa's face where the charcoal had rubbed off in the heat and scramble of stealing his own hog. "John you sho' must have the leprosy. Them spots on your face done tole me what it is." "Bout dead, bout dead," said Ol' Massa.

While they were crossing the river on the little homemade ferry made by the boys, Ned began to feel kinda queer, something told him that John was really Ol' Massa. Finally he gained courage enough to ask, "Say yo ain't Ol' Massa, are you?" Ol' Massa answered, "Indeed I am, and if you and John don't return every hog you have stolen, I am going to give you five hundred licks each." Ned instantly jumped into the river and was never seen again.

Two things that I learned early besides work, was dancin' and cussin'. Took it up from my uncles, I guess. Grandpa would have killed me if he had known that I was a dancin'! I would get my clothes off and go to bed early, then I would slip around and get my best homespun dress and brass toe shoes that had been polished and set away until time to go to church. Then I would slip out with my uncles and meet my man down the road a ways. We danced until mornin', then walk home. I would walk on the brush and rocks so that my shoes would not be slick on the bottom when I got home. Grandpa would call me about four o'clock every morning. "Blackchile, black-chile, time to help yo mammy fry them flapjacks." "Gettin' my clothes on right now," I answered, when in reality I was takin' em off. Without a wink of sleep I would pick or hoe cotton until sundown that day.

When grandpa finally found out about me, I was dancin' for money. Later I did some specialty acts. One was dancin' with a tumbler of water on my head for twenty-five minutes. The other was called "Lovin' My Man." I would dance with hightop [shoes] on, and they would be unbuttoned. My partner would stoop to button them for me. I would get my pistol out of my shirtwaist and shoot him down, without losing a step. I made fifty dollars a night and a percentage of the net proceeds. Somebody brought Grandpa in the dance hall one night to see me dance. I heard him a screamin' "I'll kill her!" but I just kept a dancin' and thinkin' all the while that if he did kill me, I would die happy. I sho' loved to dance. Many times I would go off of the floor and cry and cry, cause I was so happy. I jes ate it up, and do you know what the devil had me do one time? He made me put a glass of water on my head and try to show my six little children how I used to dance. The glass fell on the floor and broke, and I was jes so clumsy. Jes' the devil's work anyway.

"Aunt Lizzie" was married the first time, at the age of fifteen years. Her husband was also a good dancer. "He worked as a contractor and I continued to dance, made mo' money than he did." He used to croon this "love melody" to his Lizzie:

> Somebody's eyes are very dark—
> Somebody's eyes are blue.
> Somebody's eyes are very dark.
> Bring my lover back to me.
>
> Bring, Oh! bring him back to me.
> Bring, my lover back to me.
> Bring, Oh! bring him back to me.

My love is like a little dove,
That flies roun' in the air.
Oh! when she's with another man
No more she thinks of me.

I wish, I wish my heart was glad
So he could feel it through and through.
Somebody's eyes are very dark.
Somebody's eyes are blue.

Bring, Oh! bring my lover back to me
Bring my lover back to me
Bring, Oh! bring her back to me.

Aunt Lizzie doesn't care for love songs and dance melodies any longer, for she has traded them off for "spirituals," and these she sings continuously.

Hold to his hand.
Hold to his hand.
Hold to his hand.
Hold to God's unchangeable hand.

Oh! brother, hold to his hand
Hold to his hand.
God's unchangeable hands.
Oh! sister, hold to God's unchangeable hands.

* * * *

I shall not be removed.
I shall not—I shall not
Shall not be removed.

Just like a tree planteth by the water
I shall not be removed.
I am on my way to glory
I shall not be removed.

Tell my lovin' mother
I shall not be removed
I shall not—I shall not
I shall not be removed.

* * * *

I came to Jesus, as I was
Feeling worried, wan and sad.
Found in him a restin' place.
And he has made me glad.

Lie down, lie down, you worried one,
With you head on my breast.
I found in him a restin' place,
And he has made me glad.

Trouble of every kind
Thank God, we always find.
Little talk with Jesus make it right,
Little talk with Jesus make it right.

Aunt Lizzie is superstitious, and believes in fortunes, however, she does not believe all fortune tellers' stories. "Some are sent by the 'Good Lowd' to warn us," she says.

"If a black and white cat passes you, good luck will come your way, but you bettah start to prayin' if a solid black cat crosses your path, cause bad luck sure catch up wid you."

Carrying an axe through the house is bad luck also. On Christmas morning, don't let a lady come into your house before a man does. If a man doesn't come in first, have a boy come into the house and go into every room and be seated. Good luck will be with you throughout the year.

Bad luck comes to the person who takes up ashes out of his stove and throws them out after sundown.

If you should happen to put your dress on wrong side out, wear it until twelve o'clock sharp, then turn it right side out and make a wish. The wish will come true.

Aunt Lizzie has had three husbands, and they were all good husbands, "cept they all alike in one way." Every morning they would yell out to me, "Get up from that bed and cook my breakfast," jes like grandpa used to yell at me. But I thinks I don't want another man, cause my seven chilluns say I am too old to cook breakfast for another one.

"Good-bye, white chile. Come back and see Auntie. Maybe I can think better for you next time. Good-bye."

[1] Two separate interviews with Mrs. Lizzie Farmer are found in the Oklahoma Slave Narratives and both are published here. The earlier one is represented by three distinct typescripts based on an interview that WPA field worker Mrs. Jessie R. Ervin con-

ducted with Lizzie Farmer in McAlester, Oklahoma, on 6 October 1936. The three typescripts, two in ribbon copy and one in carbon copy, are uniformly titled "Aunt Lizzie Farmer" and have virtually identical content. This interview was never forwarded to Washington and survives only in the OHS Slave Narratives.

LIZZIE FARMER[1]

Age 80 Years   *McAlester, Okla.*

"Cousin Lizzie!"
"What."
"I'se seventy years old."
And I say, "Whut's you telling me for?" I ain't got nothing to do with your age!

I knowed I was one year older than she was and it sorta riled me for her to talk about it. I never would tell folks my age for I knowed white folks didn't want no old woman working for 'em and I just wouldn't tell 'em how old I really was. Dat was nine years ago and I guess I'm seventy five now. I can't work much now.

I was born four years before de War.—"The one what set the cullud folks free." We lived on a big plantation in Texas. Old Master's name was John Booker and he was good to us all. My mammy died just at de close of de War and de young mistress took me and kept me and I growed up with her chillun. I thought I was quality sure nuff and I never would go to school 'cause I couldn't go 'long to de same school with de white chillun. Young mistress taught me how to knit, spin, weave, crochet, sew and embroider. I couldn't recollect my age and young Mistress told me to say, "I'se born de second year of de War dat set the cullud folks free," and the only time she ever git mad at me was when I forget to say it jest as she told me to. She take hold of me and shook me. I recollects all it, all de time.

Young mistress' name was Elizabeth Booker NcNew. I'se named after her. She finally gave me to my aunt when I was a big girl and I never lived wid white folks any more. I never saw my pappy till I was grown.

In the cullud quarters, we cooked on a fireplace in big iron pots. Our bread was baked in iron skillets with lids and we would set the skillet on de fire and put coals of fire on de lid. Bread was mighty good cooked like dat. We made our own candles. We had a candle mold and we would put a string in the center of the mold and pour melted tallow in it and let it harden. We would make eight at one time. Quality folks had brass lamps.

When we went to cook our vegetables we would put a big piece of hog jowl in de pot. We'd put in a lot of snap beans and when dey was about half done we'd put in a mess of cabbage and when it was about half done we'd put in some squash and when it was about half done we'd put in some okra. Then when it was done we would take it out a layer at a time. Go 'way! It makes me hungry to talk about it.

When we cooked possum dat was a feast. We would skin him and dress him and put him on top de house and let him freeze for two days or nights. Then we'd boil him with red pepper, and take him out and put him in a pan and slice sweet 'taters and put round him and roast him. My, dat was good eating.

It was a long time after de War 'fore all de niggers knowed dey was really free. My grandpappy was Master Booker's overseer. He wouldn't have a white man over his niggers. I saw grandpappy whip one man with a long whip. Master Booker was good and wouldn't whip 'em less'n he had to. De niggers dassent leave de farm without a pass for fear of de Ku Kluxers and patrolers.

We would have dances and play parties and have sho' nuff good times. We had "ring plays."[2] We'd all catch hands and march round, den we'd drop all hands 'cept our pardners and we'd swing round and sing:

"You steal my pardner, and I steal yours,
Miss Mary Jane.
My true lover's gone away,
Miss Mary Jane!

"Steal all round and don't slight none,
Miss Mary Jane.
He's lost out but I'se got one,
Miss Mary Jane!"

We always played at log rollin's an' cotton pickin's.

Sometimes we would have a wedding and my what a good time we'd have. Old Master's daughter, Miss Janie, got married and it took us more'n three weeks to get ready for it. De house was cleaned from top to bottom and us chillun had to run errands. Seemed like we was allers under foot, at least dat was what mammy said. I never will fergit all the good things they cooked up. Rows of pies and cakes, baked chicken and ham, my, it makes my mouth water jest thinking of it. After de wedding and de feast de white folks danced all night and us cullud folks ate all night.

When one of de cullud folks die we would allers hold a "wake." We would set up with de corpse and sing and pray and at midnight we'd all eat and den we'd sing and pray some more.

In de evening after work was done we'd sit round and de older folks would sing songs One of de favorites was:

> "Miss Ca'line gal,
> Yes Ma'am,
> Did you see dem buzzards?
> Yes Ma'am,
> Did you see dem floppin',
> How did ye' like 'em?
> Mighty well.

> "Miss Ca'line gal,
> Yes Ma'am,
> Did you see dem buzzards?
> Yes Ma'am,
> Did you see dem sailin',
> Yes Ma'am.
> How did you like 'em?
> Mighty well."

I've heerd folks talk about conjures and hoodoo charms. I have a hoss shoe over de door dat will bring good luck. I sho' do believe certain things bring bad luck. I hate to hear a scrinch (screech) owl holler at night. Whenever a scrinch owl git in dat tree at night and start to holler I gits me a stick and I say, "Confound you, I'll make yet set up dar and say 'Umph huh,'" so I goes out and time I gits dar he is gone. If you tie a knot in de corner of de bed sheet he will leave, or turn your hat wrong side out too. Dey's all good and will make a scrinch owl leave every time.

I believes in dreams and visions too. I dreamed one night dat I had tall palings all 'round my house and I went out in de yard and dere was a big black hoss and I say, "How come you is in my yard? I'll jest put you out jest lak you got in." I opened de gate but he wouldn't go out and finally he run in de door and through the house and went towards de East. Right after dat my son died. I saw dat hoss again de other night. A black hoss allus means death. Seeing it de other night mean I'se gwineter die.

I know one time a woman named May Runnels wanted to go to

church about a mile away and her old man wouldn't go with her. It made her mad and she say, "I'll be damned if I don't go." She had to go through a grave yard and when she was about half way across it a icy hand jest slap her and her mouth was twisted way 'round fer about three months. Dat was a lesson to her fer cussing.

One time there was a nigger what belonged on a adjoining farm to Master John Booker's and dey told us dis story:

"Dis nigger went down to de spring and found a terrapin and he say, 'What brung you here?' Jest imagine how he felt when it say to him, 'Teeth and tongue brung me here, and teeth and tongue will bring you here.' He run to de house and told his Master dat he found a terrapin dat could talk. Dey went back and he asked de terrapin what brung him here and it wouldn't say a word. Old Master didn't like it 'cause he went down there jest to see a common ordinary terrapin and he told de nigger he was going to git into trouble fer telling him a lie. Next day the nigger seen de terrapin and it say de same thing again. Soon after dat dis nigger was lynched right close to de place he saw de terrapin."

Master John Booker had two niggers what had a habit of slipping across de river and killing old Master's hogs and hiding de meat in de loft of de house. Master had a big blue hog and one day he missed him and he sent Ned to look fer him. Ned knowed all de time dat he had killed it and had it hid in his loft. He hunted and called "Pigooie, Pig." Somebody done stole old Master's big blue hog. Dey couldn't find it but old Master thought Ned knowed something 'bout it. One night he found out Ned was gonna kill another hog and had asked John to go with him. He borrowed John's clothes and blackened his face and met Ned at de river. Soon dey find a nice big one and Ned say, "John, I'll drive him round and you kill him." So he drove him past old Master but he didn't want to kill his own hog so he made lak he'd like to kill him but he missed him. Finally Ned got tired and said, "I'll kill him, you drive him by me." So Master John drove him by and Ned knock de hog on de head and cut his throat and dey load him on de canoe. When dey was nearly 'cross de river Old Master dip up some water and wash his face a little, then he look at Ned and he say, "Ned you look sick, I believe you've got lepersy." Ned row on little more and he jump in de river and Master had a hard time finding him again. He had the overseer whip Ned for that.

I think Lincoln was a wonderful man. Everybody was sorry when he died, but I never heerd of Jeff Davis.

¹ The later interview with Lizzie Farmer, by an unidentified WPA field worker, is entitled "Lizzie Farmer, Age 80 Years, McAlester, Okla." and is preserved as a ribbon-copy typescript in the LC Slave Narratives and in carbon copy as item 350098 in the LC Slave Narratives Carbon Copies, but is not found in the OHS Slave Narratives. Although the date of the interview is uncertain, it was forwarded to Washington on 12 August 1937. This later interview clearly employed the Slave Narrative Project list of standardized questions for informants, and with the exception of one story, which is told differently, it presents material not included in the earlier interview. Stephens to Cronyn, 12 August 1937, WPA Notes on Interviews.

² Also known as Josey parties, the ring plays and play parties described by Mrs. Lizzie Farmer were social gatherings of members of Baptist or other religious denominations who believed that dancing was evil. Singers provided music for both men and women who moved in circles or rings in a dancelike manner and who often joined in the singing. The energetic entertainment allowed lovers of music to get around the denominational prohibitions against dancing because the play party was considered to be a game and not a dance. Francis Edward Abernethy, *Singin' Texas,* 89–90.

JOHN FIELD¹

(A) John Field (Colored), General Delivery, Tahlequah, Okla. (Age 68) (Note: Parents were slaves.)

Right at the close of the Civil War, after the colored folks were freed, the rebels came in and killed a lot of the colored folks, and took a lot of them south.

The slaves were all trying to get away. They were aiming to go to Neosho, Missouri.

From what John Field's mother had told him, while she was alive, the old cabin where the slave uprising took place,² was one-fourth of a mile southeast of the Murrell house, instead of due south, according to Ed Hicks. It was such a little to the east, generally speaking, you would say south of the old place.

According to Field a large number of the slaves were living on the old Chief Ross's place.

¹ The brief narrative of John Field, never forwarded to Washington as part of the Oklahoma Slave Narrative Project, is available only in the typescript "John Field, 160 Words, 11–17–1936" in the OHS Slave Narratives. In this remembrance, published here for the first time, Field sketches experiences of slaves in the Cherokee Nation.

² This may be a reference to the 1842 uprising among Cherokee slaves sometimes called "the Great Runaway." For more information on this incident, see Carolyn Thomas Foreman, "Early History of Webbers Falls," *Chronicles of Oklahoma* 29 (Winter 1951–52): 459–60; R. Halliburton, Jr. *Red over Black: Black Slavery among the Cherokee Indians,* 82–84; Theda Perdue, *Slavery and the Evolution of Cherokee Society, 1540–1866,* 82–83. For another remembrance relating to "the Great Runaway," see the narrative of Mrs. Betty Robertson, below.

DELLA FOUNTAIN[1]

Age 69 Years   *McAlester, Oklahoma*

I was born after de War of de Rebellion but I 'member lots o' things dat my parents told me 'bout slavery.

My grandmother was captured in Africa. Traders come dere in a big boat and dey had all sorts of purty gew-gaws—red handkerchiefs, dress goods, beads, bells, and trinkets in bright colors. Dey would pull up at de shore and entice de colored folks onto de boat to see de purty things. Befo' de darkies realized it dey would be out from shore. Dat's de way she was captured. Fifteen to twenty-five would pay dem for de trip as dey all brought good prices.

I was born and raised in Louisiana, near Winnfield. My mother's Master was John Rogers and his wife was Miss Millie. Dey was awful good to deir slaves and he never whupped his grown niggers.

I 'member when I was a child dat we didn't have hardly anything to keep house wid, but we got along purty well I guess. Our furniture was home-made and we cooked on de fireplace.

We saved all our oak-wood ashes, and would put a barrel on a slanting scaffold and put sticks and shucks in de bottom of de barrel and den fill it wid de ashes. We'd pour water in it and let it drip. Dese drippings made pure lye. We used dis wid cracklings and meat scraps to make our soap.

Father took a good-sized pine log and split it open, planed it down smooth and bored holes in de bottom and drove pegs in dem for legs; dis was our battling bench. We'd spread our wet clothes on dis and rub soap on 'em and take a paddle and beat de dirt out. We got 'em clean but had to be careful not to wear 'em out wid de paddle.

We had no tubs either, so father took a hollow log and split it open and put partitions in it. He bored a hole in each section and drove a peg in it. He next cut two forked poles and drove 'em in de ground and rested de ends of de hollow log in dese forks. We'd fill de log trough wid water and rinse our clothes. We could pull out de pegs and let de water out. We had no brooms either, so we made brush brooms to sweep our floors.

Dere was lots of wild game near our home. I 'member father and two more men going out and killing six deer in jest a little while. Dey was plentiful, and so was squirrels, coon, possums, and quail. Dere was lots of bears, too. We'd be in de field working and hear de dogs, and father and de boys would go to 'em and maybe dey'd have a bear. We liked bear meat. It was dark, but awful good and sweet.

De grown folks used to have big times at log-rollings, corn-shuck-ings and quiltings. Dey'd have a big supper and a big dance at night. Us children would play ring plays, play with home-made rag dolls, or we'd take big leaves and pin 'em together wid thorns and make hats and dresses. We'd ride saplings, too. All of us would pull a sapling down and one would climb up in it near de top and git a good hold on it, and dey would turn it loose. It took a purty good holding to stay wid it, I can tell you.

All de ladies rode horseback, and dey rode side-saddles. I had a purty[2] side-saddle when I growed up. De saddle seat was flowered plush. I had a purty riding habit, too. De skirt was so long dat it al-most touched de ground.

We spun and wove all our clothes. I had to spin three broaches[3] ever night before bedtime. Mother would take bark and make dye to give us different colored dresses.

Red oak and sweet gum made purple. Bois d'arc made yellow or orange. Walnut made a purty brown. We knitted our socks and stock-ings, too.

We celebrated Christmas by having a big dance and egg-nog for ever'body.

During slavery young colored boys and girls didn't do much work but just growed up, care-free and happy. De first work boys done was to learn to hitch up de team to Master's carriage and take de young folks for a drive.

My older brothers and sisters told me lots of things dey done dur-ing slave days. My brother Joe felt mighty big after freedom and strutted about. One day he took his younger brother, Ol, wid him to where father was building a house. Dey played 'bout de house and come up to where a white man and father was talking. De white man was rolling a little ball of mud in his hands and he just pitched it over on Ol's foot. It didn't hurt him a mite, but Joe bridled up and he started to git smart, and father told him he'd break his neck if he didn't go on home and keep his mouth shet. Father finally had to whup Joe to make him know he was black. He give father and mother lots of concern, for dey was afraid the Ku Kluxers would git him. One day he was playing wid a axe and chopped off brother Ol's finger. Mother told him she was going to kill him when she caught him. He took to de woods. His three sisters and two neighbor girls run him nearly all day but couldn't catch him. Late in de evening, he come up to a white neighbor's house and she told him to go in and git under de bed and dey couldn't find him. Curtains come down to

de floor and as he was tired he decided to risk it. He hadn't much
more dan got hid when he heard de girls coming. He heard de
woman say, "He's under de bed." He knowed he was caught, and he
put up a fight, but dey took him to mother. He got a whupping, but
he was shocked dat mother didn't kill him like she said she was. He
didn't mind de whupping. He growed up to be a good man, and was
de apple of my mother's eye.

Father knowed a man that stole his Master's horse out and rode
him to a dance. For some reason de horse died. De poor man knowed
he was up against it, and he let in to begging de men to help him git
de horse on his back so he could put him back in his stable and his
Master would think he died dere. Poor fellow, he really did think he
could tote dat horse on his back. He couldn't git anybody to help
him, so he went to the woods. He was shot by a patroller 'cause he
wouldn't surrender. Dey captured him but he died.

Paul Castleberry was a white preacher. De colored would go to
church de same as de whites. He give de colored instructions on obeying Masters. He say, "while your Master is going f'om pillar to post,
looking after your intrusts, you is always doing some devilment." I
'spect dat was jest about de truth.

My sister played wid Miss Millie's little girl, Mollie. De big house
was on a high hill and at de foot of de hill, nearly a half-mile away,
was a big creek wid a big wooden bridge across it.[4] Soldiers come by
ever' few days, and you could hear deir horses when dey struck de
bridge. Sister and Mollie would run upstairs and look down de hill,
and if it was Confederate soldiers dey would run back and tell Miss
Millie and dey would start putting out de best food dey had. If dey
saw Yankee soldiers, dey would run down and tell 'em and dey'd start
hiding things.

De Yankees come through dere and took ever'body's horses. Lots
of people took deir horses and cows and hid 'em in some low place in
de deep wood.

Miss Mille had a young horse and she had 'em take him to de
wheat field and hide him. De wheat was as high as he was. De Yankees come by, and a man had stopped dere just before dey come. He
was riding an old horse, and he was wearing a long linen-duster—a
duster was a long coat dat was worn over de suit to protect it from de
dust.

Dis smart-alek hid behind de house and as de soldiers rode up he
shot at 'em. Dey started shooting at him and he started running, and
his coat was sticking straight out behind him. De soldiers surely wasn't

trying to hit him, but dey sure did scare him plenty. Miss Millie was certain dey was going to find her horse, but dey didn't.

Master John Rogers was good to all his slaves, and they all loved him and would a'died for him. One day he was sitting in his yard and Mollie come running down stairs and told him de Yankees was coming. He never say nothing, but kept sitting dere. Dat morning he had a big sack of money and he give it to my mother to hide for him. She ripped her mattress, and put it in de middle of it and sewed it up. She den made up de bed and put de covers on it. De Yankees searched de house and took de jewelry and silverware and old Master's gold mug, but dey didn't find his money.

My parents lived close to de old plantation dat they lived on when dey was slaves. De big house was still dere, but it was sure dilapidated. Ever'body was poor after de War, whites and blacks alike. I really think de colored was the best off, for they knowed all 'bout hardships and hard work and de white folks didn't.

At first some of 'em was too proud to do drudgery work, but most of 'em went right to work and build up deir homes again. Food, clothes, and in fact everything needed, was scarce.

Mother always say, "If you visit on New Year's, you'll visit all de year." We always had black-eyed peas and hog jowl for New Year's dinner, for it brought good luck.

The Nineteenth of June was Emancipation Day, and we always had a big picnic and speeches.

I knowed one woman who was a conjure woman. Lots of people went to her to git her to break a evil spell dat some one had over them. She'd brew a tea from herbs and give to 'em to drink, and it always cured 'em.

I've seen people use all kinds of roots and herbs for medicine, and I also seen 'em use all kind of things for cures. I've knowed 'em to put wood lice in a bag and tie 'em 'round a baby's neck so it'd teeth easy.

Black-haw root, sour dock, bear grass, grape root, bull nettle, sweet-gum bark and red-oak bark boiled separately and mixed, makes a good blood medicine.

[1] The interview of Mrs. Della Fountain with WPA field worker Mrs. Jessie R. Ervin at McAlester, Oklahoma, on 15 November 1937 is represented by three separate narratives. The earliest of these survives as the typescript "Interview with Della Fountain, Age 69, E. Harrison Avenue, McAlester, Okla." in the OHS Slave Narratives. An intermediate draft, available as a typescript in the same collection, is designated by the title "Della Fountain, Age 69, E. Harrison Ave., McAlester, Okla." Both of these texts are written in standard English and vary only slightly from each other. The last type-

script, a final draft edited to show standardized project dialect usage, was forwarded to Washington and is published here. It is available as the typescript "Della Fountain, Age 69 Years, McAlester, Oklahoma" in ribbon copy in the LC Slave Narratives and in carbon copy apparently misfiled ca. 1937 in the "Non-Slave Narratives" file for the Oklahoma Slave Narrative Project now preserved in box A906, Manuscript Division, Library of Congress.

2 The two earlier drafts here say "beautiful."

3 "Broach," as used here, refers to a spindle on which newly spun yarn is wound.

4 The punctuation of this sentence reflects that in the two earlier drafts of the narrative. In the final draft it appears to have been garbled. There the passage reads: "De big house was on a high hill and at de foot of de hill. Nearly a half-mile away was a big creek wid a big wooden bridge across it."

NANCY GARDNER[1]

Age 79 Yrs.   *Oklahoma City, Okla.*

Well, to tell you de truth I don't know my age, but I was born in 1858, in Franklin, Tennessee. Now, you can figger for yourself and tell how old I is. I is de daughter of Prophet and Billie Isaiah. I don't 'member much about dem as we was separated when I was seven years old. I'll never forget when me, my ma and my auntie had to leave my pa and brothers. It is jest as clear in my mind now as it was den, and dat's been about seventy years ago.

Oh God! I tell you it was awful dat day when old Jeff Davis had a bunch of us sent to Memphis to be sold. I can see old Major Clifton now. He was a big nigger trader you know. Well, dey took us on up dere to Memphis and we was sold jest like cattle. Dey sold me and ma together and dey sold pa and de boys together. Dey was sent to Mississippi and we was sent to Alabama. My pa, O how my ma was grieved to death about him! She didn't live long after dat. She didn't live long enough to be set free. Poor ma, she died a slave, but she is saved though. I know she is, and I'll be wid her some day.

It was thirty years before my pa knew if we was still living. Finally in some way he heard dat I was still alive, and he began writing me. Course I was grown and married den and me and my husband had moved to Missouri. Well, my pa started out to see me and on his way he was drowned in de Missouri River, and I never saw him alive after we was sold in Memphis.

I can't tell you much 'bout work during de slave days 'cause you see[2] I was jest a baby you might say when de War broke out. I do remember our Master's name though, it was Dr. Perkins, and he was a good Master. Ma and pa sure hated to have to leave him, he was so good to dem. He was a rich man, and had a big fine house and thousands of acres of land. He was good to his niggers too. We had a good house too, better dan some of dese houses I see folks living in now. Course Dr. Perkins' niggers had to work, but dey didn't mind 'cause he would let dem have little patches of dey own such as 'tatoes, corn, cotton and garden. Jest a little, you know. He couldn't let dem have much, there was so many on Dr. Perkins' plantation.

I don't remember seeing anybody sick in slavery time. You see I was jest a kid and dere's a lot of things I can't remember.

I am a Christian. I jined de church nigh on seventy years ago and when I say dat, I don't mean I jest jined de church. I mean I gave myself up to de Heavenly Father, and I've been gwine straight down de line for Him ever since. You know in dem days, we didn't get religion like young folks do now. Young folks today jest find de church and den call theyselves Christians, but they ain't.[3]

I remember jest as well when I was converted. One day I was thinking 'bout a sermon de preacher had preached and a voice spoke to me and said, "De Holy Ghost is over your head. Accept it!" Right den I got down on my knees and prayed to God dat I might understand dat voice, and God Almighty in a vision told me dat I should find de church. I could hardly wait for de next service so I could find it, and when I was in de water getting my baptisement, dat same voice spoke and said, "Now you have accepted don't turn back 'cause I will be wid you always!"[4] You don't know nothing 'bout dat kind of religion!

I 'member one night shortly after I jined de church I was laying in bed and dere was a vine tied 'round my waist and dat vine extended into de elements. O my God! I can see it now! I looked up dat vine and away in de elements I could see my Divine Master and he spoke to me and said, "When you get in trouble shake dis vine; I'm your Master and I will hear your cry."

I knowed old Jeff Davis good. Why I was jest as close to him as I am to dat table.[5] I've talked wid him too. I reckon I *do* know dat scoundrel! Why, he didn't want de niggers to be free! He was known as a mean old rascal all over de South.

Abraham Lincoln? Now you is talking 'bout de niggers' friend! Why dat was de best man God ever let tramp de earth! Everybody was mighty sad when poor old Abraham was 'sassinated, 'cause he did a mighty good deed for de colored race before he left dis world.

I wasn't here long during slavery, but I saw enough of it to know it was mighty hard going for most of de niggers den, and young folks[6] wouldn't stand for dat kind of treatment now. I know most of the young folks would be killed, but they jest wouldn't stand for it.[7] I would hate to have to go through wid my little share of it again.

[1] The interview of Oklahoma Writers' Project field worker Willie Allen with Mrs. Nancy Gardner at Oklahoma City on 15 July 1937 exists in two versions. A preliminary draft is available in both ribbon copy and carbon copy, both with editorial markings, in the OHS Slave Narratives as "Ex-Slave Reference (A) Interview with Mrs. Nancy Gardner, age 79, 524 N. Stonewall, Oklahoma City, Oklahoma." A final draft, entitled "Nancy Gardner, Age 79 Yrs., Oklahoma City, Okla.," forwarded to Washington on 18 November 1937 and published here, is available in ribbon-copy typescript in the LC Slave Narratives and in carbon copy as item 350020 in the LC Slave Narratives Carbon Copies. Stephens to Alsberg, 18 November 1937, WPA Notes on Interviews.

The preliminary draft of this interview includes the following note by Willie Allen: "Mrs. Gardner does not have a very clear memory about slavery, as she was only a child when the slaves were freed. She can only remember the things that were very impressive. Christianity was the main thing she was interested in talking about. In trying to recall something she would make this remark—'Oh God! help me to think.' Everytime she would put her hand to her face and make that statement. She would immediately think of what she was trying to recall."

The earlier draft notes the location of the interview as 524 North Stonewall Avenue. The 1937 Oklahoma City directory lists this as the residence of Mrs. Viney Edwards and indicates that Mrs. Nancy Gardner resided with Mrs. Eunice Miles at 181/2 South Klein Avenue. *Polk's Oklahoma City Directory, 1937,* 227, 270, 871, 907.

[2] The preliminary version adds here, "I was so little den."

[3] The preliminary draft of this interview records instances when the informant spoke directly to the field worker. In that version this sentence reads: "You know you all jes fine de church and den call yo sefs christians."

[4] At this point the preliminary version adds, "Oh! son."

[5] In the preliminary draft, this sentence ends "as I am to you" rather than "as I am to dat table."

[6] The preliminary draft adds here "lak you son."

[7] In the preliminary version this sentence reads: "Cose I know most of you would be kilt, but you jest wouldn't stand for it."

MILLIE GARNES[1]

Age 86   *McAlester, Oklahoma*

Way down below, way down below,
Gwine to see my yaller gal,
Way down below.
Way down below, way down below,
Gwine to see my yaller gal,
Way down below.

She could make the nicest hoecake
Out of Indian corn,
Make the nicest music on the old dinner horn
Dance the nicest polka,
On her heel and toe,
Gwine to see my yaller gal,
Way down below.

Dat was one of the songs us young folks used to sing at dances and other shin-digs when I was a girl. We sung lots of others, too, but I remember this one better for some reason. I guess it is because it had such a good dance tune to it. I sure did like to dance and never missed one if I could help it. Dey would have log rollings, quiltings and sech and after supper us young folks would dance and sing, sometimes all night.

I was born near Noonan,[2] Georgia and was born in slavery. Our old Master was Terry Harris and his wife was Miss Mary. They had several children. Their oldest son, Jimmie, was killed in the war and they had another grown son, Judson, and a grown daughter, Caroline. Their two little girls, Adelaide and Sallie, was about my age and we played together so much that I thought that I was white, too. I et at the same table with dem and slept on a pallet in their room. We never had a cross word and played from daylight till dark. We played with our dolls, jumped the rope and played hide and seek. Dey had boughten dolls but I had a rag doll dat Miss Mary made for me. Their dolls had pretty clothes but I thought my doll was just as nice as theirs was and we made it pretty clothes, too.

After the war my parents moved about forty miles from our white folks but we went to see dem at least twice a year. Us children was always glad to see each other and started right in playing. Father and mother visited with old Master and Miss Mary. It always seemed like we was going back home when we started back to the old plantation for a visit.

The house was built in a T-shape and had a big gallery across the front and one on each side of the back, one on the east and one the west side. Back of the house was a big well, with a well house over it. We drawed water with a windlass. Dere was a spring, too, just below the house and we had a milk house dere. We would take the milk in large crocks or jars and tie a cloth over dem and set dem in a wooden trough. The water from the spring would overflow and run through the trough and cool the milk. It was always nearly as cold as ice even in the hottest weather.

Once during the war some Yankee soldiers come to our house and said dey was hunting guns. Dey just walked in without knocking and mother had just finished baking a lot of pies and put dem out on a shelf to cool. Dey said, "Are you cooking dem pies for rebels?" She say, "No, I make dem for my white folks and the field hands."

Den he asked her if she would sell him one of the pies and she told him dat she would ask her mistress. Old Miss told her to let dem have as many as dey wanted. Mother went back and give him a pie and den he asked her for some milk. I went to the milk house and brought back a big crock full of milk covered with a rich cream and I was going to give it to mother to skim. He took the crock from my hands and he and his buddy went and set down in the shade of one of the trees in the yard. He broke the pie in two and each one took time about drinking out of the milk. When dey had finished, dey brought the crock back and paid mother for the pie and the milk. Old Miss let mother keep the money for herself.

If the soldiers come and wanted anything you had better let dem have it or dey just took what they wanted. One of our neighbors had a cellar full of cider and wine and the soldiers heard about it. One day a whole passel of dem come dere and asked for some wine. She didn't want to let dem have it but they told her dey would break the door in if she didn't let dem have the key. She finally give it to dem and dey went down and drunk all they wanted. Dey went away and about a week later come back again and said, "Kind Mistress, Whar's de key to your cellar?" She didn't say a word but give dem de the key and after they drunk what dey wanted dey went away and never bothered her any more.

Dere was a man dat lived near us dat had a fine home and lots of niggers, but he was always scouting around all the time. He never stayed at home. He rode a black pony and hid out in the woods all the time. Dat pony sure was well trained for his master could hide in the deep woods or in a canyon and dat horse wouldn't make a sound. I remember he come to our house one time and asked father if he could set by the fire till two o'clock. Father told him he could and we all went to bed but father. He set up and talked to him till he got ready to go. He left about two o'clock jest like he said.

His mother died and he went to the funeral. Some of his friends happened to see some men in the crowd that had been looking for him and dey give him the signal and he give dem the slip. Dey finally caught him and I remember they put a barrel over his head and marched him up and down the street and a gang of children run along behind him making fun of him. I never knew what he done, nor what dey finally done with him.

We had lots of money after the war. Us children played with great rolls of it. It was Confederate money and wasn't worth nothing. I've seen rolls of it as big as my arm. At first dey could use it and it just kept gitting lower and lower in worth till finally it got to where it wasn't worth nothing. My mother bought her the goods to make her a worsted dress and give two-hundred dollars for it.

My father was sold lots of times but only twice on the sale block. He was bad to run off and he was sold lots of times in the woods. He was brought to that country with a gang of slaves in chains. He was bought by some speculators and dey had a big drove dat dey was taking to Louisiana to be sold in the Delta country for the cotton fields. Father was sold to a man at Noonan, Georgia. Dis man was so mean to him that he run off. Dey hunted for him with dogs but didn't catch him so his master sold him to another man dere in the woods. He was finally captured and his new master wasn't no better to him than his old one was. He whupped him mighty hard and give him hard tasks to do. If he didn't do the work that he was 'lowanced to do he was whupped. His master said he was gonna break his nasty, mean, stubborn will or kill him trying. He run off again and this time Master Terry Harris bought him in the woods again. Dey caught him again and Master Terry told him dat he wasn't gonna lay the weight of a whup on him again if he would settle down and go to work. Master Terry was as good as his word and father didn't give no more trouble. He married my mother right after dat.

My mother belonged to the Allen family. Dey wasn't good to none of their slaves either. Mother had to work from daylight to dark. She would work in the field all day and wash for the family at night. Dey wouldn't 'low her to lose no time out in the field in the day time. She had to use the battling bench and stick to clean the clothes and dey had to be clean, too, I can tell you.

I've seen scars on her back where she had been whupped. She was whupped till she was unconscious lots of times. Dere was scars on her feet, too, where she went barefooted on frozen ground and cut her feet.

After father and mother married, Master Terry made a trade with mother's master and bought her from him unbeknownst to mother and father. Was dey both happy when he took her to his plantation to live for good! All us children was born on the Harris plantation and we never knowed any unkindness. Mother done the cooking here and never worked in the field any more except when dey was short handed.

We was allowed to go to church every Sunday evening and we could visit on joining farms when the work was all done.

When the war was over father and mother stayed a year with Master Terry and den he leased some land and cleared it up and built us a house. Father still worked for Master Terry and he paid us in meat, lard, corn and other food stuff. We never did go hungry but got along purty fair. Miss Mary give mother a start of chickens.

We finally moved about forty miles from dem and didn't git to see dem often but we sure did enjoy visiting dem though.

We had to use make-shift things to keep house with. I'd like to see you women trying to keep house on the things that we had to work with. Dey cooked on a fireplace in pots hanging on racks over the fire and baked bread and cakes in a Dutch oven, a sort of skillet with a deep lid that you piled full of live coals.

Dey either used a battling bench and stick when they washed or they rubbed the clothes clean between two rocks. We finally got us some wooden tubs and a wooden rubboard after I was about grown.

I married when I was twenty-two. I didn't have no wedding—just went and got married. We had seven children. My husband has been dead for a long time.

[1] Only one full typescript survives for the Millie Garnes narrative. WPA field worker Mrs. Jessie R. Ervin interviewed her at McAlester, Oklahoma, sometime probably in 1937 or 1938. The typescript, never forwarded to Washington, is available as "Millie Garnes, Age 86, McAlester, Oklahoma" in the OHS Slave Narratives. Four leaves (pages 2–5) of an edited typewritten draft of the Millie Garnes narrative, with virtually identical text and only dialect changes, may be found in the "Unid-Partial" file in the OHS Slave Narratives. This narrative, never before published, is presented here as preserved in the original complete typescript.

[2] This may be phonetic for Newnan.

OCTAVIA GEORGE[1]

Age 85 Yrs.   *Oklahoma City, Okla.*

I was born in Mansieur, Louisiana, Avoir Parish.[2] I am the daughter of Alfred and Clementine Joseph. I don't know much about my grandparents other than my mother told me my grandfather's name was Fransuai, and was one time a king in Africa.

Most of the slaves lived in log cabins, and the beds were homemade. The mattresses were made out of moss gathered from trees, and we used to have lots of fun gathering that moss to make those mattresses.[3]

My job was taking care of the white children up at the Big House (that is what they called the house where our master lived), and I also had to feed the little Negro children. I remember quite well how those poor little children used to have to eat. They were fed in boxes and troughs, under the house. They were fed corn meal mush and beans. When this was poured into their box they would gather around it the same as we see pigs, horses and cattle gather around troughs today.

We were never given any money, but were able to get a little money this way: our master would let us have two or three acres of land each year to plant for ourselves, and we could have what we raised on it. We could not allow our work on these two or three acres to interfere with Master's work, but we had to work our little crops on Sundays. Now remind you, all the Negroes didn't get these two or three acres, only good masters allowed their slaves to have a little crop of their own. We would take the money from our little crops and buy a few clothes and something for Christmas. The men would save enough money out of the crops to buy their Christmas whiskey. It was all right for the slaves to get drunk on Christmas and New Year's Day; no one was whipped for getting drunk on those days. We were allowed to have a garden and from this we gathered vegetables to eat; on Sundays we could have duck, fish and pork.

We didn't know anything about any clothes other than cotton; everything we wore was made of cotton, except our shoes, they were made from pieces of leather cut out of a raw cowhide.

Our Master and Mistress was good, they let us go to church with them, have our little two- or three-acre crops and any other thing that the good masters would let their slaves do. They lived in a big fine house and had a fine barn. Their barn was much better than the house we lived in. Master Depriest (our master) was a Frenchman, and had eight or nine children, and they were sure mean. They would fight us, but we were not allowed to fight our little Master or Mistress as we had to call them.

The overseer on Master's plantation was a mean old fellow, he carried his gun all the time and would ride a big fine horse and go from one bunch of slaves to the other. Some poor white folks lived close to us. They could not own slaves and they had to work for the rich plantation owners. I believe that those poor white folk are to blame for the Negroes stealing because they would get the Negroes to steal their master's corn, hogs, chickens and many other things and sell it to them for practically nothing.

We had to work plenty hard, because our Master had a large plantation. Don't know just how many acres it was, but we had to be up at 5 o'clock in the morning and would work until dark, then we would have to go home to do our night work, that is cook, milk, and feed the stock.

The slaves were punished for stealing, running off, not doing what their master told them and for talking back to their master. If any of these rules were disobeyed their feet and hands were chained together and they were put across a log or a barrel and whipped until the blood came from them.

There were no jails; the white man was the slaves' jail. If whipping didn't settle the crime the Negro committed—the next thing would be to hang him or burn him at stake.

I've seen them sell slaves. The whites would auction them off just as we do cattle and horses today. The big fine healthy slaves were worth more than those that were not quite so good. I have seen men sold from their wives and I thought that was such a crime. I knew that God would settle things someday.

Slaves would run away but most of the time they were caught. The Master would put blood hounds on their trail, and sometimes the slave would kill the blood hound and make his escape. If a slave once tried to run away and was caught, he would be whipped almost to death, and from then on if he was sent any place they would chain their meanest blood hound to him.

Funerals were very simple for slaves, they could not carry the body to the church, they would just take it to the grave yard and bury it. They were not even allowed to sing a song at the cemetery. Old Mistress used to tell us ghost stories after funerals and they would nearly scare me to death. She would tell of seeing men with no head, and see cattle that would suddenly turn to cats, and she made us believe if a fire was close to a cemetery it was coming from a ghost.

I used to hear quite a bit about voodoo, but that something I never believed in, therefore, I didn't pay any attention to it.

When a slave was sick, the master would get a good doctor for him if he was a good slave, but if he wasn't considered a good slave he would be given cheap medical care. Some of the doctors would not go to the cabin where the slaves were, and the slave would have to be carried on his bed to his master's back porch and the doctor would see him there.

When the news came that we were free, all of us were hid on the Mississippi River. We had been there for several days, and we had to catch fish with our hands and roast them for food. I remember quite well when old Master came down to there and hollered, Come on out niggers; you are free now and you can do as you please! We all went to the Big House and there we found old Miss crying and talking about how she hated to lose her good niggers.

Abraham Lincoln! Why we mourned three months for that man when he died! I wouldn't miss a morning getting my black arm band and placing it on in remembrance of Abraham, who was the best friend the Negroes ever had. Now old Jeff Davis, I didn't care a thing about him. He was a Democrat and none of them mean anything to the Negro. And if these young Negroes don't quit messing with the democratic bunch they are going to be right back where we started from. If they only knew as I know they would struggle to keep such from happening, because although I had a good master I wouldn't want to go through it again.

¹ Mrs. Octavia George was interviewed at her home in Oklahoma City by project field worker Willie Allen on 9 June 1937. From Allen's now lost initial notes he prepared a preliminary draft of the interview as the typescript "Interview with Octavia George, Ex-Slave, 709 S.E. 4th St., Oklahoma City, Okla.," preserved in the OHS Slave Narratives. This text was edited and placed into standard project format as the typescript "Octavia George, Age 85 Yrs., Oklahoma City, Okla.," sent to Washington on 14 September 1937 and published here. It is available in ribbon-copy typescript in the LC Slave Narratives and in carbon copy as item 350059 in the LC Slave Narratives Carbon Copies and in the OHS Slave Narratives. The preliminary draft of the narrative includes the following note from Willie Allen which is not included in the later version: "Mrs. George does not speak the dialect usually heard among ex-slaves, most of her words are spoken in French. A number of times I would have to have her daughter interpret her words for me. She was born and raised around French people. For this reason she never acquired the usual Negro dialect." Polk's Oklahoma City Directory, 1937, 275, 931; Stephens to Cronyn, 14 September 1937, WPA Notes on Interviews.

² This is an apparent reference to Mansura, the seat of Avoyelles Parish, Louisiana.

³ For another remembrance of Spanish moss mattresses, see the narrative of Sam Anderson, above.

INTERVIEW WITH NANNIE GORDON¹

Ex-Slave, Age 79   *1750 Dennison Street, Muskogee, Oklahoma*

I got a letter from Ann Berry a long time ago that told about my birth date. The letter come from the daughter of my old Mistress Berry. It said I was born April 23, 1859, and that makes me 79 year old now. I still got that old letter from my old town of Everglade, Kentucky. It was written April 12, 1875, and the young mistress said for any of us to come back and see her, but somehow nobody ever get the chance to go.

My father was Major Jamison, and my mother was Luretia. There was a brother named Morriman. He soldiered for the South in the Civil War and died at Paducah, Ky., about 1865 my folks told me. I had two sisters—Ann and Mary. Neither of my sisters ever had any children, but I had two girls—Clarissa and Ann; four boys name of Willie, Phil, Robert and Alec.

Master Berry's place was on the Ohio river at Berry's Ferry. He lived in a big red brick house. They said when the Georgia (Cherokee) Indians come out to this country where at I'm living now, that lots of them Indians was ferried across the river at the master's place. My father and grandfather helped to tow them over.

The master had another big place at Everglade, Ky., and there my old grandpaw was the driver of about 100 slaves. Most of the time he was there; sometimes he worked at the ferry.

Mistress Mandy Berry had two boys. Eddie and John. There was three girls, Julia, Mary and Ann. Ann is the one who write me about my birth.

Young Master Eddie was a fine looking man. Some folks called him pretty, he was so fine. He was a spy in the war. The slaves was never told nothing and I can't piece together all about the how of his doings but he was killed for being a spy for the North.

Somehow he was captured around Richmond. He was brought to Louisville where he was killed—he stood up before the firing squad. But before that the army allowed him to come by the old place and say good-bye to his folks. He was in chains.

During the slave days my mother (she was born April 6, 1820) was the cook for Master Berry. We lived in a nice clean brick servant house in the side yard. The other slaves was in the row of cabins—all them cabins was part of brick and logs.

When I was a good size girl I went to school at Paducah. Then later I went for schooling at Nashville.

When the war was over my mother cooked for some folks in Paducah. My sister Ann got a job there and saved enough money to build us all a home of our own.

My husband was Felix Gordon, a good man who kept busy with the schools and church work. He helped to build the first negro school here and got his education in some college, and was a teacher in college. He was the first pastor in the 7th street church, and then superintendent of the Sunday School for nineteen year.[2]

We always had good times in the old days but now being all crippled up there's nobody comes around any more.

That's all I know.

[1] Only one typescript has been found for the narrative of Mrs. Nannie Gordon. Ethel Wolfe Garrison interviewed her at Muskogee, Oklahoma, probably sometime in spring or early summer 1938, for the surviving typescript bears the note that it was edited and revised by project employee Craig Vollmer on 13 June 1938. The narrative is available as "Interview with Nannie Gordon, Ex-Slave, Age 79, 1750 Dennison Street, Muskogee, Oklahoma" in the OHS Slave Narratives. This interview was never forwarded to Washington and is published here for the first time.

[2] For a remembrance of an African American minister named Gordon who may have been the informant's husband, see Walter Gray, interview by James Russell Gray, Indian-Pioneer Papers, 105:454–61. A roughly contemporary Muskogee city directory gave Nannie Gordon's husband's name as F. J. Gordon; it also noted that there were two African American churches on Seventh Street in Muskogee, the Bebee Memorial Methodist Episcopal Church at 518 South Seventh and the Spencer Methodist Episcopal Church at 539 North Seventh. *Polk's Muskogee City Directory, 1932,* 94, 287.

MARY GRAYSON[1]

Age 83 Yrs. *Tulsa, Oklahoma*

I am what we colored people call a "native." That means that I didn't come into the Indian country from somewhere in the Old South, after the War, like so many negroes did, but I was born here in the old Creek Nation, and my master was a Creek Indian. That was eighty three years ago, so I am told.

My mammy belonged to white people back in Alabama when she was born—down in the southern part I think, for she told me that after she was a sizeable girl her white people moved into the eastern part of Alabama where there was a lot of Creeks. Some of them Creeks was mixed up with the whites, and some of the big men in the Creeks who come to talk to her master was almost white, it looked like. "My white folks moved around a lot when I was a little girl," she told me.

When mammy was about 10 or 12 years old some of the Creeks begun to come out to the Territory in little bunches. They wasn't the ones who was taken out here by the soldiers and contractor men— they come on ahead by themselves and most of them had plenty of money, too.[2] A Creek come to my mammy's master and bought her to bring out here, but she heard she was being sold and run off into the woods. There was an old clay pit, dug way back into a high bank, where the slaves had been getting clay to mix with hog hair scrapings to make chinking for the big log houses that they built for the master and the cabins they made for themselves. Well, my mammy run and hid way back in that old clay pit, and it was way after dark before the master and the other man found her.

The Creek man that bought her was a kind sort of a man, mammy said, and wouldn't let the master punish her. He took her away and was kind to her, but he decided she was too young to breed and he sold her to another Creek who had several slaves already, and he brought her out to the Territory.

The McIntosh men was the leaders in the bunch that come out at that time, and one of the bunch, named Jim Perryman, bought my mammy and married her to one of his "boys," but after he waited and she didn't have a baby he decided she was no good breeder and he sold her to Mose Perryman.

Mose Perryman was my master, and he was a cousin to Legus Perryman, who was a big man in the Tribe. He was a lot younger than Mose, and laughed at Mose for buying my mammy, but he got fooled, because my mammy got married to Mose's slave boy Jacob, the way the slaves was married them days, and went ahead and had ten children for Mr. Mose.[3]

Mose Perryman owned my pappy and his older brother, Hector, and one of the McIntosh men, Oona, I think his name was, owned my pappy's brother William. I can remember when I first heard about there was going to be a war. The older children would talk about it, but they didn't say it was a war all over the country. They would talk about a war going to be "back in Alabama," and I guess they had heard the Creeks talking about it that way.

When I was born we lived in the Choska bottoms,[4] and Mr. Mose Perryman had a lot of land broke in all up and down the Arkansas river along there. After the War, when I had got to be a young woman, there was quite a settlement grew up at Choska (pronounced Choe-skey) right across the river east of where Haskell now is, but when I was a child before the War all the whole bottoms was marshy kind of wilderness except where farms had been cleared out. The land was very rich, and the Creeks who got to settle there were lucky. They always had big crops. All west of us was high ground, toward Gibson station and Fort Gibson, and the land was sandy. Some of the McIntoshes lived over that way, and my Uncle William belonged to one of them.

We slaves didn't have a hard time at all before the War. I have had people who were slaves of white folks back in the old states tell me that they had to work awfully hard and their masters were cruel to them sometimes, but all the Negroes I knew who belonged to Creeks always had plenty of clothes and lots to eat and we all lived in good log cabins we built. We worked the farm and tended to the horses and cattle and hogs, and some of the older women worked around the owner's house, but each Negro family looked after a part of the fields and worked the crops like they belonged to us.

When I first heard talk about the War the slaves were allowed to go and see one another sometimes and often they were sent on errands several miles with a wagon or on a horse, but pretty soon we were all kept at home, and nobody was allowed to come around and talk to us. But we heard what was going on.

The McIntosh men got nearly everybody to side with them about the War, but we Negroes got word somehow that the Cherokees over back of Ft. Gibson was not going to be in the War, and that there were some Union people over there who would help slaves to get away, but we children didn't know anything about what we heard our parents whispering about, and they would stop if they heard us listening. Most of the Creeks who lived in our part of the country, between the Arkansas and the Verdigris, and some even south of the Arkansas, belonged to the Lower Creeks and sided with the South, but down below us along the Canadian River they were Upper Creeks and there was a good deal of talk about them going with the North. Some of the Negroes tried to get away and go down to them, but I don't know of any from our neighborhood that went to them.

Some Upper Creeks came up into the Choska bottoms talking around among the folks there about siding with the North. They were talking, they said, for old man Gouge, who was a big man among the Upper Creeks. His Indian name was Opoeth-le-ya-hola, and he got away into Kansas with a big bunch of Creeks and Seminoles during the War.[5]

Before that time, I remember one night my uncle William brought another Negro man to our cabin and talked a long time with my pappy, but pretty soon some of the Perryman Negroes told them that Mr. Mose was coming down and they went off into the woods to talk. But Mr. Mose didn't come down. When pappy came back Mammy cried quite a while, and we children could hear them arguing late at night. Then my uncle Hector slipped over to our cabin several times and talked to pappy, and mammy began to fix up grub, but she didn't give us children but a little bit of it, and told us to stay around with her at the cabin and not go playing with the other children.

Then early one morning, about daylight, old Mr. Mose came down to the cabin in his buggy, waving a shot gun and hollering at the top of his voice. I never saw a man so mad in all my life, before nor since!

He yelled in at mammy to "git them children together and git up to my house before I beat you and all of them to death!" Mammy began to cry and plead that she didn't know anything, but he acted like he was going to shoot sure enough, so we all ran to mammy and started for Mr. Mose's house as fast as we could trot.

We had to pass all the other Negro cabins on the way, and we could see that they were all empty, and it looked like everything in them had been tore up. Straw and corn shucks all over the place, where somebody had tore up the mattresses, and all the pans and kettles gone off the outside walls where they used to hang them.

At one place we saw two Negro boys loading some iron kettles on a wagon, and a little further on was some boys catching chickens in a yard, but we could see all the Negroes had left in a big hurry.

I asked mammy where everybody had gone and she said, "Up to Mr. Mose's house, where we are going. He's calling us all in."

"Will pappy be up there too?" I asked her.

"No. Your pappy and your Uncle Hector and your Uncle William and a lot of other menfolks won't be here any more.[6] They went away. That's why Mr. Mose is so mad, so if any of you younguns say anything about any strange men coming to our place I'll break your necks!" Mammy was sure scared!

We all thought sure she was going to get a big whipping, but Mr. Mose just looked at her a minute and then told her to get back to the cabin and bring all the clothes, and bed ticks and all kinds of cloth we had and come back ready to travel.

"We're going to take all you black devils to a place where there won't no more of you run away!" he yelled after us. So we got ready to leave as quick as we could. I kept crying about my pappy, but mammy would say, "Don't you worry about your pappy, he's free now. Better be worrying about us. No telling where we all will end up!" There was four or five Creek families and their Negroes all got together to leave, with all their stuff packed in buggies and wagons, and being toted by the Negroes or carried tied on horses, jack asses, mules and milk cattle. I reckon it was a funny looking sight, or it would be to a person now; the way we was all loaded down with all manner of baggage when we met at the old ford across the Arkansas that lead to the Creek Agency. The Agency stood on a high hill a few miles across the river from where we lived, but we couldn't see it from our place down in the Choska bottoms. But as soon as we got up on the upland east of the bottoms we could look across and see the hill.

When we got to a grove at the foot of the hill near the agency Mr. Mose and the other masters went up to the Agency for a while. I suppose they found out up there what everybody was supposed to do and where they was supposed to go, for when we started on it wasn't long until several more families and their slaves had joined the party and we made quite a big crowd.

The little Negro boys had to carry a little bundle apiece, but Mr. Mose didn't make the little girls carry anything and let us ride if we could find anything to ride on. My mammy had to help lead the cows part of the time, but a lot of the time she got to ride an old horse, and she would put me up behind her. It nearly scared me to death, because I had never been on a horse before, and she had to hold on to me all the time to keep me from falling off.

Of course I was too small to know what was going on then, but I could tell that all the masters and the Negroes seemed to be mighty worried and careful all the time. Of course I know now that the Creeks were all split up over the War, and nobody was able to tell who would be friendly to us or who would try to poison us or kill us, or at least rob us. There was a lot of bushwhacking all through that country by little groups of men who was just out to get all they could. They would appear like they was the enemy of anybody they run across, just to have an excuse to rob them or burn up their stuff. If you said you was with the South they would be with the North and if you claimed to be with the Yankees they would be with the South, so our party was kind of upset all the time we was passing through the country along the Canadian. That was where old Gouge had been talking against the South. I've heard my folks say that he was a wonderful speaker, too.

We all had to move along mighty slow, on account of the ones on foot, and we wouldn't get very far in one day, then we Negroes had to fix up a place to camp and get wood and cook supper for everybody. Sometimes we would come to a place to camp that somebody knew about and we would find it all tromped down by horses and the spring all filled in and ruined. I reckon old Gouge's people would tear up things when they left, or maybe some Southern bushwhackers would do it. I don't know which.

When we got down to where the North Fork runs into the Canadian we went around the place where the Creek town was.[7] There was lots of Creeks down there who was on the other side, so we passed around that place and forded across west of there. The ford was a bad one, and it took us a long time to get across. Everybody got wet and a lot of the stuff on the wagons got wet. Pretty soon we got down into the Chickasaw country, and everybody was friendly to us, but the Chickasaw people didn't treat their slaves like the Creeks did. They was more strict, like the people in Texas and other places. The Chickasaws seemed lighter color than the Creeks but they talked more in Indian among themselves and to their slaves. Our masters talked English nearly all the time except when they were talking to Creeks who didn't talk good English, and we Negroes never did learn very good Creek. I could always understand it, and can yet, a little, but I never did try to talk it much. Mammy and pappy used English to us all the time.

Mr. Mose found a place for us to stop close to Fort Washita, and got us places to stay and work. I don't know which direction we were from Fort Washita, but I know we were not very far. I don't know how many years we were down in there, but I know it was over two for we worked on crops at two different places, I remember. Then one day Mr. Mose came and told us that the War was over and that we would have to root for ourselves after that. Then he just rode away and I never saw him after that until after we had got back up into the Choska country. Mammy heard that the Negroes were going to get equal rights with the Creeks, and that she should go to the Creek Agency to draw for us, so we set out to try to get back.

We started out on foot, and would go a little ways each day, and mammy would try to get a little something to do to get us some food. Two or three times she got paid in money, so she had some money when we got back. After three or four days of walking we came across some more Negroes who had a horse, and mammy paid them to let us children ride and tie with their children for a day or two. They had their children on the horse, so two or three little ones would get on with a larger one to guide the horse and we would ride a while and get off and tie the horse and start walking on down the road. Then when the others caught up with the horse they would ride until they caught up with us. Pretty soon the old people got afraid to have us do that, so we just led the horse and some of the little ones rode it.

We had our hardest time when we would get to a river or big creek. If the water was swift the horse didn't do any good, for it would shy at the water and the little ones couldn't stay on, so we would have to just wait until someone came along in a wagon and maybe have to pay them with some of our money or some of our goods we were bringing back to haul us across. Sometimes we had to wait all day before anyone would come along in a wagon.

We were coming north all this time, up through the Seminole Nation, but when we got to Weleetka we met a Creek family of freedmen who were going to the Agency too, and mammy paid them to take us along in their wagon. When we got to the Agency mammy met a Negro who had seen pappy and knew where he was, so we sent word to him and he came and found us. He had been through most of the War in the Union army.

When he got away into the Cherokee country some of them called the "Pins"[8] helped to smuggle him on up into Missouri and over into Kansas, but he soon found that he couldn't get along and stay safe unless he went with the Army. He went with them until the War was over, and was around Gibson quite a lot. When he was there he tried to find out where we had gone but said he never could find out. He was in the battle of Honey Springs, he said, but never was hurt or sick. When we got back together we cleared a selection of land a little east of the Choska bottoms, near where Clarksville now is, and farmed until I was a great big girl.

I went to school at a little school called Blackjack school. I think it was a kind of mission school and not one of the Creek nation schools, because my first teacher was Miss Betty Weaver and she was not a Creek but a Cherokee. Then we had two white teachers, Miss King and John Kernan, and another Cherokee was in charge. His name was Ross, and he was killed one day when his horse fell off a bridge across the Verdigris, on the way from Tullahassee to Gibson Station.

When I got to be a young woman I went to Okmulgee and worked for some people near there for several years, then I married Tate Grayson. We got our freedmen's allotments on Mingo Creek, east of Tulsa, and lived there until our children were grown and Tate died, then I came to live with my daughter in Tulsa.

---

[1] The Mary Grayson narrative is available in three separate typescripts, each differing from the others only in heading, capitalization, and paragraph divisions. WPA employee Robert Vinson Lackey undertook the interview with Mrs. Mary Grayson in Tulsa, Oklahoma, probably in spring or summer of 1937, for the final draft of her narrative was mailed to Washington on 14 September 1937. The earliest draft is available as the typescript "Interview with Mary Grayson (Colored), 1841 N. Madison, Tulsa, Okla." in the OHS Slave Narratives. An intermediate version is available as "Interview with Mary Grayson, Ex-Slave, 1841 N. Madison, Tulsa, Okla.," a typescript filed with item 350056 in the LC Slave Narratives Carbon Copies. Both of these drafts indicate that the interview took place at 1841 North Madison Avenue in Tulsa, which is where the

contemporary city directory shows Mary E. Grayson resided with Robert and Jessie Ligons, operators of a grocery store at the same address. The final draft, published here, is available in ribbon-copy typescript as "Mary Grayson, Age 83 Yrs., Tulsa, Oklahoma" in the LC Slave Narratives and in carbon copy as item 350056 in the LC Slave Narratives Carbon Copies and in the OHS Slave Narratives. *Polk's Tulsa City Directory, 1935*, 258, 352, 673; Stephens to Cronyn, 14 September 1937, WPA Notes on Interviews.

Both the preliminary and intermediate drafts of this narrative contain the following note from the field worker concerning Mary Grayson's speech: "This 83-year-old ex-slave's speech contains none of the negro dialect so common among ex-slaves of white southern owners. Her pronunciation is the same as that of the average native southwesterner, with even less slurring of r's and flattening of a's."

The Mary Grayson narrative has been considered one of the finest among the Oklahoma slave narratives. In 1940 Benjamin A. Botkin, director of folklore for the Federal Writers' Project, described it as a "rare piece of autobiographical writing against [a] vivid background in time and place," adding that it had "high literary merit." B. A. B[otkin], LC Slave Narratives Appraisal Sheets, Accession no. 350056, 11 December 1940. Botkin was the first to publish this interview, in his *Lay My Burden Down* (130–35) in 1945. See also Mellon, *Bullwhip Days*, 409, 411–17.

2 This relocation of Creeks who came "on ahead by themselves" was that of the McIntosh group, which moved to present-day Oklahoma in 1828. For background on this event, see Debo, *The Road to Disappearance*, 91–96; Wright, *Creeks and Seminoles*, 242–43.

3 For background on the Perryman family, which immigrated to the Indian Territory in 1828, see Meserve, "The Perrymans."

4 "Choska bottoms" refers to the fertile floodplain on the east side of the Arkansas River in the vicinity of present-day Choska in Wagoner County, Oklahoma.

5 For an account of this incident, see the narrative of Phoebe Banks, above.

6 Twenty-year-old William McIntosh, on reaching Kansas, enlisted as a private in the 1st Kansas Colored Volunteer Infantry at Leavenworth on 15 March 1863, remaining in the army until he was mustered out of service at Pine Bluff, Arkansas, on 1 October 1865. U.S., Department of War, Army, 1st Kansas Colored Volunteer Infantry (17th U.S. Colored Infantry), Compiled Military Service Record for William McIntosh, National Archives and Records Administration, Washington, D.C.

7 The Creek town referred to here is the North Fork Town.

8 The "Pins" were members of a Cherokee secret society known as the Keetoowah (night hawks), which protested Cherokee acceptance of slavery as well as other elements of Euro-American culture. Their name came from their emblem, a pair of crossed pins worn on a shirt or coat. Morris L. Wardell, *A Political History of the Cherokee Nation, 1838–1907*, 221–22. For specific remembrances of the "Pins," see the narratives of Patsy Perryman and Morris Sheppard, below.

INTERVIEW WITH SONNY GREER[1]
Ex-Slave, Age 88   *620 North 15th Street, Muskogee, Oklahoma*

I was born in Arkansas, January 6, 1850. My father was Henry Rogers Greer and mother was Lucena Greer.[2] She was born in Mississippi and was sold several times.

The master was Hugh Rogers.[3] He had four boys—Jim, who died just about the time war started, John, Hugh and Sam. The girls were Caroline, Easter, Mary, Annie, Susie.

My wife is named Phyllis. We were married at Clarksville, Red River county, Texas, on March 4, 1874. She was eighteen and belonged to the Worthams[4] during slave days. We had no children, but I had some brothers and sisters. There was Harry and Shedrick, and Violet, Betsy, America, Jane, Ann, and Delsey.[5] They all stayed in Texas.

The master took his slaves, said there was 80 or 90, to Texas when the war got started. We was refugees. Down there we built one room log cabins for the slaves. They had no porches and the quarters was without furniture, just home made beds.

I worked in the fields raising cotton and tobacco. Start to work at daylight and quit when the sun went down. Then lots of nights work around the house. Plenty of work to do, but no money until after the war. Then I worked for the same master. He paid me fifty cents a day.

The master bought good heavy clothes for winter but in the summer we was about naked.

When a slave needed a whipping he got it. I was never whipped but lots of the negroes were. We had to have passes when going off the plantation. The patrollers would pick up the ones without a pass and they had the right to whip—just the same as if they was the master. I never saw any slave run away. But I heard about them.

Christmas time wasn't much different than any other, except if it come in the middle of the week we got the rest of the week to ourselves. Just take care of the light chores. If Christmas come on Saturday then we had to be ready for work on the next Monday.

The master told us about freedom on August 4, 1865. He called everybody to the big house. I stayed on and worked, like I said, for fifty cents a day.

We never learned to read or write. The master didn't think it was right for slaves to learn.

My mind is not so good anymore. It is hard to remember things. I can't think good. That's why I can't tell more about the slave days.

[1] WPA reporter Ethel Wolfe Garrison interviewed Sonny Greer at his home in Muskogee, Oklahoma, probably sometime in spring or early summer 1938, for on 8 June 1938 project employee Craig Vollmer edited its text, producing the only version of this interview that survives. Entitled "Interview with Sonny Greer, Ex-Slave, Age 88, 620 North 15th Street, Muskogee, Oklahoma," it is in the OHS Slave Narratives. This interview was not forwarded to Washington and has never before been published. *Polk's Muskogee City Directory, 1932,* 96, 234. For another, contemporary inter-

view with this informant, see Soney [sic] Greer, interview by James S. Buchanan at Muskogee, Oklahoma, 18 August 1937, Indian-Pioneer Papers, 63:236–38.

[2] In his interview with Buchanan, Greer related that his parents' names were Harry and Loucenda Greer. Indian-Pioneer Papers, 63:237.

[3] In his interview with Buchanan, Greer remembered his master's name as Cal Rogers. Indian-Pioneer Papers, 63:237.

[4] In his interview with Buchanan, Greer remembered his wife's owners to have been named Wartham. Indian-Pioneer Papers, 63:237.

[5] The typescript of the narrative gives the name Delsey twice in the list of brothers and sisters.

ROBERT R. GRINSTEAD[1]

Age 80 Yrs.   *Oklahoma City, Okla.*

I was born in Lawrence County, Mississippi, February 17, 1857. My father's name is Elias Grinstead, a German, and my mother's name is Ann Greenstead [sic] after that of her master. I am a son of my mother and her Master. I have four other half brothers: William (Bill) oldest, Albert, Silas, and John.

I was only eight years of age at freedom and for that reason I was too young to work and on account of[2] being the son of my Master's I received no hard treatment and did little or no work.[3] Yet, I wore the same clothing as did the rest of the slaves: a shirt of lowell for summer and shirt and trousers for winter and no shoes. I could walk through a briar patch in my bare feet without sticking one in the bottom of my feet as they were so hard and resistant.

I was the only child of my Master as he had no wife. When the War broke out he went to the War and left the plantation in charge of his overseer and his two sisters. As the overseers were hard for them to get along with they were oftener without an overseer as with one, and therefore they used one of the Negroes as overseer for the most of the time.

Across the river was another large plantation and slave owner by the name of Master Wilson. We called him Master too, for he was a close friend and neighbor to our Mistresses. There was one Negro man slave who decided to not work after Master went to the War and the white overseer was fired and the Negro overseer was acting as overseer, so my Mistress gave him a note to take across the river to Master Wilson. The note was an order to whip this Negro and as he couldn't read he didn't know what the note contained until after Master Wilson read it and gave orders to his men to tie him for his whipping. After this, the whipping was so severe that they never had any more trouble in making this Negro slave work and they never had to send him back again to Master Wilson to be whipped. The fun part of this above incidence was the Negro carried his own note and went alone to be whipped and didn't know it till the lashes was being put on him.

My Master's plantation was about 2 miles long and 1½ mile wide and he owned between 30 and 40 slaves. The Negro overseer would wake up the slaves and have them in the field before they could see how to work each morning and as they would go to work so soon their breakfast was carried to the field to them. One morning the breakfast was taken to the field and the slaves were hoeing cotton and among them was a lad about 15 years of age who could not hoe as fast as the older slaves and the breakfast was sat at the end of the rows[4] and as they would hoe out to the end they would eat, and if you would be late hoeing to the end, the first to get to the end would began eating and eat everything. So, this 15 year old lad in order to get out to eat before everything was gone did not hoe his row good and the overseer, who was white at this time, whipped him so severely that he could not eat nor work that day.

The Negroes went to church with the white people and joined their church. The church was Baptist in denomination, and they built a pen in the church in which the Negroes sat, and when they would take sacrament the Negroes would be served after the whites were through and one of the Negro group would pass it around to the others within the pen.

As there were no dances held on the plantation the Negroes would ofttimes slip off and go at nights to a nearby dance or peanut parching or rice suppers at nights after work. Some of the slaves would be allowed to make for themselves rice patches which they would gather and save for the dances. To prepare this rice for cooking after harvested they would burn a trough into a log they called mortar, and with a large wooden mallet they called pessel [pestle], and which they would pound upon the rice until hulled and ready for cooking. This rice would be boiled with just salt and water and eaten as a great feast with delight.

During slavery some of the Negro slaves would kill snakes and skin them and wear these snake skins to prevent being voodooed they said. When some of the slaves would take sick and the home remedies would fail to cure them our Mistress would allow one of the Negro men slaves to go to the white doctor and get some medicine for the patient. The doctor would ask questions as to the actions of the patient and from said description would send medicine without ever going to see the patient and his medicine would always cure the patient of his disease if consulted in time.

After the news came that brought our freedom a white union officer with 20 trained Negro soldiers visited the plantations and saw that the Negroes received their freedom. He would put on a demonstration with his Negro soldiers by having them line up and then at a command they would all rush forward and stand their guns up together on the stock end without one falling and get back into line and upon another command they would rush forward and each get his gun again without allowing one to fall and again reline up.

When I was large enough to pay attention to my color and to that of the other slaves I wondered to myself why I was not black like the rest of the slaves and concluded to myself that I would [be] when I got grown like they were, as I knew not then that I was the son of my Master.

During the War and as the men and our Master all went to the War the Negroes or a Negro would have to go to the Mistress' homes each morning and start fires and never, did I ever hear of a rape case under such close conditions as Negroes going into the bed rooms each morning of the white mistress to start fires.[5]

My first wife was name Tracy Smith. As I had been free for over 12 years. We had ordinary marriage ceremony. I have 11 grown children, 15 or 20 grandchildren and 3 great grandchildren.

I think Abraham Lincoln was a fine old gentleman and as to Jeff Davis I don't think he was what he should have been, and as to Booker T. Washington I think his idea of educating or training Negroes as servants to serve the white race appealed more to the white race than the Negroes.

My viewpoint as to slavery is that it was as much detrimental to the white race as it was to the Negroes, as one elevated one's minds too highly, and the other degraded one's mind too lowly.

[1] J. S. Thomas interviewed Robert R. Grinstead at his home in Oklahoma City on 6 July 1937. The field worker's handwritten notes in pencil are preserved as "Story from Ex-Slave Robert R. Grinstead, 614 N. Kate St., a Personal Interview" in the OHS Slave Narratives. This manuscript bears editorial markings for the addition of dialect speech, but those changes were not incorporated into the typewritten final draft of the narrative, "Robert R. Grinstead, Age 80 Yrs., Oklahoma City, Okla.," published here. This typewritten version, forwarded to Washington on 14 September 1937, is available in ribbon copy in the LC Slave Narratives, in carbon copy as item 350054 in the LC Slave Narratives Carbon Copies and the OHS Slave Narratives, and in photocopy in the OHS

Slave Narratives. *Polk's Oklahoma City Directory, 1937,* 299, 869; Stephens to Cronyn, 14 September 1937, WPA Notes on Interviews.

[2] Rather than "on account of," the manuscript version of the narrative reads here: "for that reason and to[o], by my being."

[3] The manuscript version reads here: "did no work."

[4] The words "of the rows" were added in the typewritten version.

[5] The manuscript version reads, "and never, he says, 'did I ever . . . to start fires.'"

MATTIE HARDMAN[1]

Age 78 Yrs.   *Oklahoma City, Okla.*

I was born January 2, 1859, at Gunalis, Texas.[2] My father's name was William Tensley and my mother's name Mildred Howard. They was brought from Virginia. I did have 8 brothers and sisters but all of them are dead.[3]

My Master was name William Henry Howard. Since[4] I was too young to work I nursed my sisters' children while they worked. The cooking was done all up to the general kitchen at Master's house and when slaves come from work they would send their children up to the kitchen to bring their meals to their homes in the quarters. Our Mistress would have one of the cooks to dish up vegetables and she herself would slice or serve the meat to see that it wasn't wasted, as seemingly it was thought so precious.

As my mother worked 'round[5] the Big House quite a deal I would go up to the Big House with her and play with the white children who seemed to like for me to come to play with them. One day in anger while playing I called one of the white girls, "old black dog" and they pretended they would tell their mother (my Mistress) about it. I was scared,[6] as they saw, and they promised me they would not tell if I'd promise to not do it again, and which I was so glad to do and be let off so lightly.

For summer I wore a cotton slip and for winter my mother knitted at nights after her day's work was done so I wore red flannels for underwear and thick linsey for an over-dress, and had knitted stockings and bought shoes. As my master was a doctor he made his slaves wear suitable clothes in accordance to the weather. We also wore gloves my mother knitted in winter.

My Mistress was good to all of the slaves. On Sunday morning she would make all the Negro children come to the Big House and she would stand on the front steps and read the Catechism to us who sat or stood in front on the ground.

My Master was also good. On Wednesdays and Friday nights he

would make the slaves come up to the Big House and he would read the Bible to them and he would pray. He was a doctor and very fractious and exact. He didn't allow the slaves to claim they forgot to do thus and so nor did he allow them to make the expression, "I thought so and so." He would say to them if they did: "Who told you, you could think!"

They had 10 children, 7 boys and 3 girls. Their house was a large 2-story log house painted white. My father was overseer on the plantation.

The plantation consisted of 400 acres and about 40 slaves including children. The slaves were so seldom punished until they never'd worry about being punished. They treated their slaves as though they loved them. The poor white neighbors were also good and treated the slaves good, for my Master would warn them not to bother his Negroes. My Mistress always told the slaves she wanted all of them to visit her and come to her funeral and burial when she died and named the men slaves she wanted to be her pall-bearers, all of which was carried out as she planned even though it was after freedom.

The slaves even who lived adjoining our plantation would have church at our Big House.[7] They would hold church on Sundays and Sunday nights.

As my mother worked a deal for her Mistress she had an inkling or overheard that they was going to be set free long before the day they were. She called all the slaves on the plantation together and broke to them this news after they had promised her they would not spread the news so that it would get back to our Master. So, everybody kept the news until Saturday night June 19th, when Master called all the slaves to the big gate and told them they were all free, but could stay right on in their homes if they had no places to go and which all of them did.[8] They went right out and gathered the crop just like they'd always done, and some of them remained there several years.

My first husband was name S. W. Warnley.[9] We had 4 children, 1 girl and three boys, and 3 grandchildren. I now have two grandchildren.

Now that slavery is over I sometime wish 'twas still existing for some of our lazy folks, so that so many of them wouldn't or couldn't loaf around so much lowering[10] our race, walking streets day by day and running from house to house living corruptible lives which is keeping the race down as through there be no good ones among us.

¹ WPA field worker J. S. Thomas interviewed Mrs. Mattie Hardman at her home in Oklahoma City on 9 July 1937. His notes were placed in typewritten form and forwarded to Washington with seven other Oklahoma slave narratives on 2 November 1937. The interview survives in two forms, as a handwritten manuscript entitled "Story of an Ex-Slave, Mattie Hardman, 524 N. Bath, a Personal Interview" in the OHS Slave Narratives, and in typewritten form as forwarded to Washington with the title "Mattie Hardman, Age 78 Yrs., Oklahoma City, Okla." The final edited version, presented here, is preserved in ribbon-copy typescript in the LC Slave Narratives and in carbon copy as item 350029 in the LC Slave Narratives Carbon Copies and in the OHS Slave Narratives. Benjamin A. Botkin appraised the Mattie Hardman interview as "a somewhat distorted view of slavery by one who was born two years before the War" and noted that it presented "a credulous view." [B. A. Botkin], LC Slave Narratives Appraisal Sheets, Accession no. 350029, n.d.; *Polk's Oklahoma City Directory, 1937,* 315, 827; Stephens to Cronyn, 2 November 1937, WPA Notes on Interviews.

At the end of his handwritten notes from the Mattie Hardman interview, J. S. Thomas appended the statement "She having been taught as a child slave and in after life shows a fair degree of intelligence and almost correct speech."

² This may be a misspelled reference to Gonzales, Gonzales County, Texas.

³ The manuscript version of the narrative here adds the sentence "I have 2 grandchildren."

⁴ The manuscript version reads "As."

⁵ The manuscript version reads "around."

⁶ The manuscript version reads, "I was so scared."

⁷ The manuscript version reads "at our house in which we lived."

⁸ In the manuscript version this sentence continues, "and gathered the crop and some of them remained there several years."

⁹ In the manuscript version the spelling of this name can be interpreted as "Warnly" or "Warney."

¹⁰ The manuscript version reads "lorating the race."

GEORGE W. HARMON¹

Age 83 Yrs.   *Oklahoma City, Okla.*

I was born December 25, 1854, in Lamar County, Texas. I don't know my real age, but I was 9 years old at Freedom, June 14, 1863. My father was named Charles Harmon and mother Mary Roland, after her owners. My father come from Tennessee and my mother from Virginia.

Well, my brother-in-law was named Daniel and the other one named John; my sisters were named Huldy and Polly. During slavery we had wood beds and mattresses were spun and woven for them. Some of the mattresses were stuffed with moss that had been buried to kill it so that it wouldn't grow.²

The first and only money I earned was when I cleaned and shined a pair of boots for a white man and he gave me $5.00 of Confederate money. Don't remember what I did with it.

In hot weather we wore only shirts made of home made cotton and split up each side, and if they didn't have any cloth they would take a crocus sack and cut holes in each corner for arm holes and in the center for the head and wear that. In cold weather we wore woven cloth called drilling for underwear, and a kind of cloth called hickory check for shirts and made into cloth for trousers. On Saturdays the clothes were washed to have clean for Sunday. My father was a shoemaker and we wore the coarse brogans.

When I was married, my wedding clothes were good. I married Margaret Blunt of Lamar County, Texas. My Master, Mistress and their children were very good to their slaves. They lived in a log house, two stories high.

The overseer was one of the negro slaves who was more evil and meaner than our Master. My owner owned two plantations about 300 or 400 acres. He owned one family of negroes and my mother, totaling eight in number. The slaves were whipped for any misdemeanor dislikeable. One lady was charged with stealing some home-made twisted tobacco and her owner made her lie down and whipped her until she fainted, then turned her over and hit her in the face to see if that would bring her to.

I never saw a sale of any slaves but when Lincoln was talking of freeing the negroes an agent came around and appraised all of us and said that the Government was thinking of buying us free.

In slavery an old man was said to be a conjurer, who had all kinds of snakes and insects. He took sick and died and the saying is that after he had died one night he came back and carried his box of insects and snakes out of the house and set them down and nobody could even go and get his body as these insects and snakes would come up and run them away.

The church of that day was held under brush arbors and though they could not read they would preach of better times and conditions.

I always would fight even my Master's children, and one day I had a stick and was about to hit one of Master's boys when one negro child ran and told my Master. He sent for me and told me that if I ever hit one of his children he would skin me and feed my hide to his hounds and it seemed he said, that those hounds were just waiting for him to feed them.

During slavery there was one slave who would not work only when he chose and when they would get at him to whip him, he was so fast a runner they could not catch him. He could run so fast that he named or called himself, "Bird in the Air." So my Master learned of a white fellow who made a specialty of running and had the reputation of catching any slaves who might be uncatchable. So my Master sent for this fellow and had warned this fast-running slave that he had sent for this runner to catch him whose title or reputation was heard of as "Hawk-running-son-of-a-gun," to catch the slave, "Bird-in-the-Air."

So on the day he was to arrive, "Bird-in-the-Air" awaited his arrival. When he arrived he went into Master's house to receive orders of whom to catch and after getting all details he and Master came out and went to where this slave lived and just when they reached the cabin where "Bird-in-the-Air" was, he ran out and hollowed, "Bird-in-the-Air." This white slave-catcher replied to him, "Yes and the hawk is after you!"

So the chase begun and[3] "Hawk-running-son-of-a-gun" caught him within a half an hour, and with power to hold him until Master and others on horses arrived who took him in charge and whipped him. From that day on all that was necessary in controlling "Bird-in-the-Air" was to warn him by saying, "If you don't do so-and-so I'll send again for 'Hawk-running-son-of-a-gun!'"

Lincoln was a durn fool man, but he was better'n John de Baptist; next to Christ. Don't think much of Jefferson Davis. He's durn poor trash. As to Booker T. Washington I like him better'n Douglas[4] 'cause Douglas married [a] white woman.

[1] George W. Harmon was interviewed in Oklahoma City by WPA reporter J. S. Thomas on 3 July 1937, and two typewritten drafts of Harmon's narrative are preserved at the Oklahoma Historical Society. A preliminary version is the ribbon-copy typescript "Ex-Slave—Story, Reference: Personal Interview of George W. Harmon, 5th & Massachusetts—Oklahoma City, Oklahoma," available in the OHS Slave Narratives. The address given as the location for the interview is corroborated by the contemporary city directory, which lists Harmon as residing at 528 Massachusetts Avenue. The preliminary draft was edited and retyped on 13 October 1937, with only cosmetic changes, as "George W. Harmon, Age 83 Yrs., Oklahoma City, Okla.," and this version is published here. The latter draft is available in ribbon copy and carbon copy in the OHS Slave Narratives. Oklahoma Federal Writers' Project administrators apparently intended to send a field worker back to interview George W. Harmon a second time, for a note bearing the initials of Ida Belle Hunter attached to the initial draft reads, "A re-interview will probably mean more information," and another note reads, "George Harmon More Info: 11–5–37." Project personnel seemingly did not return, and George

W. Harmon's interview was never sent to Washington. *Polk's Oklahoma City Directory, 1937,* 317, 879.

² For another remembrance of mattresses filled with Spanish moss, see the narrative of Sam Anderson, above.

³ The preliminary draft here adds "to 'Bird-in-the-Air' surprise."

⁴ A reference to Frederick Douglass, African American abolitionist, leader, and statesman.

INTERVIEW WITH PLOMER HARSHAW¹

Ex-Slave, Age 86 Years   *Route 1, Box 53, Muskogee, Oklahoma*

I was born away down in Marshall County, Mississippi on August 10, 1852, at Holly Springs. My father was Plomer Jo Vann, and my mother was Gradey Dowden. She died right after I was born and my mistress raised me like I was her own child. My mother was carried over here from Africa on a slave boat, but I don't know where my father come from.

Daniel Harshaw was my first master's name. He was a good master and the mistress was too. She told me I had a brother name of Oliver and a half brother name of Plumer. Maybe there was a sister, or another brother. Anyway she said either a sister or brother was born in 1837.

That Civil War was bad business. The master leave out of Mississippi and the white people took all the slaves to Arkansas. There was about eighty slaves and we all tried to settle at work but the war kept us running from place to place all the time.

We make several trips from Arkansas down to Wood County, Texas. We went to Texas in wagons and I reckon most of them was pulled with oxen.

In Arkansas the master fixed himself up a fine double frame house with lots of outbuildings. In them days he was wealthy. The furniture was good; high-post beds and plenty to eat. His stock was good stuff until the war broke him up.

The mistress wouldn't let any of the slaves sing about Yankee songs. They let us have church meetings but no singing about the Yankees. One slave girl got a whipping for sometimes singing about that John Brown. They tied her to a tree and the lashing bloodied up the tree all around.

There was lots of mean things done in the slave days. Both the white people and the negroes was wrong part of the time. Like the time a white man Jim Standley, one of our neighbors, put one of his slaves in chains account of not doing something right. He sent the slave to work in the fields, chain and all. That evening when the work day was over that slave slipped up to where Jim Standley was rocking his baby on the porch of his own house. The master didn't know the slave was around and never did know, for the slave man chopped him with an axe while some negroes in the yard looked on. He was dead. The slave run away, and how he got rid of them chains nobody know, they never saw that negro again.

The patrollers took up the chase but even the bloodhounds couldn't track him. One slave man was killed by a hound.

It happened on our own place. Master had a hickory club and was going to lay it on but the negro grabbed that stick and took it away from master. Then he run, out toward some bushes. But that was far as he got. The dogs leap on him and tear him to pieces. I saw it with my own eyes.

There was an old slave woman on the place in Arkansas who scared the young folks with her haunts. Me too. One time the master had a thrashing machine in the field. The old woman said to us, "Look at that big haunt! That's the biggest ghost I ever knowed about."

The master had told me what it was and I wasn't scared. "That ghost done the master lots of good," I told her, "just about thrashed out all the oats!" That made her so mad she took off her leather belt and most smother me down with it.

Every New Year all the masters around the country have what they called a "nigger show." Just an auction for to get rid of the older slaves. The ones going to be sold was stripped down to show off the muscles. Like folks buy a horse, they look at the teeth.

Down in Texas I worked in what folks said was "government service."[2] Same as slavery, I couldn't see no difference. Got whipped just the same. Worked in a loom house. Girls and men working hard all the day but nobody get any money for that. Part of the time I worked in a brickyard. The boss kept us trotting or running all the day. Nobody have time to just walk. That was work!

I didn't know what the white people meant when they said "Free." My young master was a lieutenant in the army under Col. Monroe. When the war was over my young master got me and took me back to Arkansas with him. I rode a mule out of Pine Bluff.

I been married three times and got so many grandchildren—must be nearly thirty-seven, and 15 great-grandchildren. They are all scattered, don't know where.

I belong to the Baptist Church in Muskogee.

That's all I remember of slavery.

[1] WPA field worker Ethel Wolfe Garrison interviewed Plomer Harshaw in Muskogee, Oklahoma, probably sometime in spring or early summer 1938, for on 7 June of
that year her fellow employee Craig Vollmer edited and revised her now lost notes into
the one version of Harshaw's narrative that survives. This typescript, published here, is
available as "Interview with Plomer Harshaw, Ex-Slave, Age 86 Years, Route 1, Box 53,
Muskogee, Oklahoma" in the OHS Slave Narratives. The narrative was never sent to
Washington.
   [2] For background on the impressment of slaves for government service by Confederate authorities in Texas, see Randolph B. Campbell, *An Empire for Slavery: The Peculiar Institution in Texas, 1821–1865,* 234–39.

ANNIE HAWKINS[1]

Age 90   *Colbert, Okla.*

I calls myself 90, but I don't know jest how old I really am but I was
a good sized gal when we moved from Georgia to Texas. We come on
a big boat and one night the stars fell. Talk about being scared! We
all run and hid and hollered and prayed. We thought the end of the
world had come.

   I never had no whitefolks that was good to me.[2] We all worked jest
like dogs and had about half enough to eat and got whupped for
everything. Our days was a constant misery to us. I know lots of niggers that was slaves had a good time but we never did. Seems hard
that I can't say anything good for any of 'em but I sho' can't. When I
was small my job was to tote cool water to the field to the hands. It
kept me busy going back and forth and I had to be sho' my old Mistress[3] had a cool drink when she wanted it, too. Mother and my sister and me worked in the field all day and come home[4] in time to
clear away the things and cook supper. When we was through in the
kitchen we would spin fer a long time. Mother would spin and we
would card.

   My old Master[5] was Dave Giles, the meanest man that ever lived.
He[6] didn't have many slaves, my mammy, and me, and my sister,
Uncle Bill, and Truman. He had owned my grandma but he give her
a bad whupping and she never did git over it and died. We all done
as much work as a dozen niggers—we knowed we had to.

   I seen old Master git mad at Truman and he buckled him down
across a barrel and whupped him till he cut the blood out of him and
then he rubbed salt and pepper in the raw places. It looked like Truman would die it hurt so bad. I know that don't sound reasonable
that a white man in a Christian community would do such a thing
but you can't realize how heartless he was. People didn't know about

it and we dassent tell for we knowed he'd kill us if we did. You must remember he owned us body and soul and they wasn't anything we could do about it. Old Mistress and her three girls was mean to us too.

One time me and my sister was spinning and old Mistress went to the well-house and she found a chicken snake and killed it. She brought it back and she throwed it around my sister's neck. She jest laughed and laughed about it. She thought it was a big joke.

Old Master stayed drunk all the time. I reckon that is the reason he was so fetched mean. My, how we hated him! He finally killed hisself drinking and I remember Old Mistress called us in to look at him in his coffin. We all marched by him slow like and I jest happened to look up and caught my sister's eye and we both jest natchelly laughed—Why shouldn't we? We was glad he was dead. It's a good thing we had our laugh fer old Mistress took us out and whupped us with a broomstick. She didn't make us sorry though.

Old Master and Mistress lived in a nice big house on top of a hill and us darkies lived in log cabins with log floors. Our dresses was made out of coarse cloth like cotton sacking and it sho' lasted a long time. It ort to been called mule-hide for it was about that tough.

We went to church sometimes. They had to let us do that or folks would have found out how mean they was to us. Our Master'd[7] give us a pass to show the patroller. We was glad to git the chance to git away and we always went to church.

During the War we seen lots of soldiers. Some of them was Yankees and some were Sesesh soldiers. My job every day was to take a big tray of food and set it on a stump about a quarter of a mile from our house. I done this twice a day and ever time I went back the dishes would be empty. I never did see nobody and didn't nobody tell me why I was to take the food up there but of course it was either for soldiers that was scouting 'round or it may been for some lowdown dirty bushwhacker, and again it might a been for some of old Master's folks scouting 'round to keep out of the army.

We was the happiest folks in the world when we knowed we was free. We couldn't realize it at first but how we did shout and cry for joy when we did realize it. We was afraid to leave the place at first for fear old Mistress would bring us back or the pateroller would git us. Old Mistress died soon after the War and we didn't care either. She didn't never do nothing to make us love her. We was jest as glad as when old Master died. I don't know what become of the three gals. They was about grown.

We moved away jest as far away[8] as we could and I married soon after. My husband died and I married again. I been married four times and all my husbands died. The last time I married it was to a man that belonged to a Indian man, Sam Love.[9] He was a good owner and was one of the best men that ever lived. My husband never did move far away from him and he loved him like a father. He always looked after him till he died. My husband has been dead five years.

I have had fifteen children. Four pairs of twins, and only four of them are living. The good Lawd wouldn't let me keep them. I'se lived through three wars so you see I'se no baby.

[1]. WPA field worker Jessie R. Ervin interviewed Mrs. Annie Hawkins at Colbert, Oklahoma, probably in spring or summer 1937, for her narrative was forwarded to Washington on 12 August of that year. The interview is available in two versions, the preliminary one being the typescript "Interview with Annie Hawkins, Ex-Slave, Aged 90, Colbert, Oklahoma" in the OHS Slave Narratives. An edited draft, sent to Washington and presented here, is available as the typescript "Annie Hawkins, Age 90, Colbert, Okla." in ribbon copy in the LC Slave Narratives and in carbon copy as item 350094 in the LC Slave Narratives Carbon Copies and in the OHS Slave Narratives. In appraising this interview, Federal Writers' Project folklore director B. A. Botkin described the text as "somewhat rambling, fragmentary," and this was after the WPA editor in Oklahoma had rearranged some of the sentences to give the text more coherence. Despite its organizational problems, however, Botkin chose an extract from Annie Hawkins's remembrances for inclusion in his 1945 book, *Lay My Burden Down* (164–65, 278). B. A. B[otkin], LC Slave Narratives Appraisal Sheets, Accession no. 350094, 15 December 1940; Stephens to Cronyn, 12 August 1937, WPA Notes on Interviews.

[2] The preliminary draft begins this sentence with the words "No Ma'am."

[3] The word "Mistress" is consistently given in the preliminary draft as "Miss."

[4] The word "home" is missing in the final draft, apparently omitted inadvertently by the typist.

[5] Consistently in the preliminary draft "old Master" is rendered as "Old Massa."

[6] In the preliminary draft this sentence begins "Old Massa" rather than "He."

[7] The preliminary draft begins this sentence "He'd."

[8] The word "away" was added in the revised text.

[9] For more remembrances of Sam Love, see the narrative of Kiziah Love, below.

INTERVIEW WITH LONDON LAW HEMMETT[1]

Ex-Slave, Age 89 Years   1620 Lamaroy Street, Muskogee, Oklahoma

I was born in Georgia, on the banks of the Flint (To-To) river. That was December 15, 1849. My father was John Hemmett and my mother was Celia Law. They were both from North Carolina, and was taken away from their parents before they were grown.

There was three brothers—Tom, Henderson and Billie; and five sisters name of Sarah, Ann, Jane, Martha and Jennie. Before the war we had a nice frame cabin in Georgia.

I married Julia Ann Brown who was a slave girl of General Brown. Married 67-year ago. My wife is dead now, and she was 101 year old when she died. We been together all the time and raised 13 children. Some of them is dead. The only living ones are Ann, Peggy, Maggie, Martha, Savana and a boy George.

The old master was George Law. He had two sons, John and Andy. The two near market places in Georgia was Linden and Douglasville. I remember there was a corn field right where most of Atlanta is now.

When the Civil War started the master moved to near Jefferson, Texas. That was a big cotton market place in them days. There was about fifty of us slaves with the master. We come to the Texas country and settled in the woods. Spend all day clearing out the thickets. Clean up the ground for farming.

We split the logs and built log cabins and made cabins for the slave families. The master had a two room house, hall in the middle. We had to build a barn, fence in some of the land with split rail for fences. Each slave family had their own cabin. The fireplace for cooking was made of mud and sticks. We never saw a stove like they got now. We dug a well but before we got it finished I had to carry water from a spring. I never like to tote water since then.

The master had two four wheel wagons. My father made them. The whole thing was of ash wood and put together with wooden pins, no nails or screws in them days. Everybody traveled in ox wagons. It was slow goings and took days to get anywhere. Sometimes the men would ride the oxen like they was horses. I was a big chunk of a boy and would drive the wagons to market at Jefferson.

We children never heard of money in the old days. We helped to make clothes. The older folks wore dresses and pants but the young ones just had a long tail cotton shirt.

None of the slaves on our place ever tried to run away. The Laws were good white people. The old mistress always see that everybody get plenty to eat.

The master had the slaves build a church place. It was called the Law Chapel and the master preached in it. He was Methodist. But since the Confederate War (as he calls it) I been a Baptist.

I remember about people going to War. I heard them telling about Vicksburg and Shiloh and I saw soldiers once marching along and the master said there was 17,000 in the bunch. He said they were going to Honey Springs. (That is in the "now Oklahoma").

When peace was made and the overseer called all the slaves up and Master George Law said, "You slaves are all free by law and bloodshed. Go do as you please. Make money. Take your family and build a house. Farm and raise all you can for to eat. Trust in the Lord and he will show you the way through this world of wilderness."

We was all glad to be free from slavery even though we didn't understand why we were free. It was great to have our own liberty. What earning we got was on our own and we never had money before freedom. We worked for just anybody. Traveled around and moved to the north. Not far, but we crossed the Red River and come to Checotah. There was plenty of work to do, but not much money. The best hands got seventy-five cents a day, the rest twenty-five and fifty cents. Mostly I picked cotton.

We come on to Muskogee and I use to ride the stage coach from there to Fort Gibson and it connect there for Tahlequah and on to Stilwell and Fort Smith.

The first year after the war we lived mostly on hunt game like rabbits and possums. We fire hunted at night. That's by building a big fire and waiting for the game to get curious and come up to see the light. Then we trap 'em with branches or else club 'em while they're watching the fire.

The greatest man that ever lived was Lincoln. I keep his picture on the wall. Booker Washington was the best colored educator.

[1] Ethel Wolfe Garrison interviewed London Law Hemmett in Muskogee, Oklahoma, probably sometime in the spring or early summer of 1938, because WPA employee Craig Vollmer edited and typed the text of the narrative on 7 June of that year. Only Vollmer's edited version of the interview is known to survive. It is preserved as the typescript "Interview with London Law Hemmett, Ex-Slave, Age 89 Years, 1620 Lamaroy Street, Muskogee, Oklahoma" in the OHS Slave Narratives and was never forwarded to Washington. The roughly contemporary Muskogee city directory gives the informant's name as London H. Hemmett. Ethel Wolfe Garrison apparently misinterpreted the name of the street on which he lived, for he resided at 1620 Tamaroa Street. *Polk's Muskogee City Directory, 1932,* 104, 267.

HENRY HENDERSON[1]

Age 95   *Muskogee, Oklahoma*

In the War time, when the Captain give the charge order, I would pick me out one of the enemy for my own personal fight and while I was making for him I would always say: "Bayonet to bayonet, skull to skull, if you ain't faster than I is, I get you in the rib!"—and then I would let him have it!

I use to be a fighting man and a strong Southern soldier, until the Yanks captured me and made me fight with them. I don't know what the year was, but there was some Southern Indians took in the same battle and they fought with the North too. There was whole regiments deserted from the South, but I was captured; I never figured on running away from my own people. Some of the Cherokee Indians who fought with the North were Bob Crittenden, Zeke Proctor, and Luke Six Killer. Luke's father was with the South and got killed; some of the folks said young Luke killed his own father in the war.

Some of the time I was fighting in Virginia against Lee's army, and there I saw a many a man ripped with the bayonet and fall dead on the ground. I still got the bayonet I used in the War, but the gun is gone. A white man borrowed it to take a picture of the old gun and he ain't never come back with it yet. He's a Muskogee man, but I forgot his name.

That's what I do best—forgets names. I done forgot my own mother's name and step-pappy's too. But I recollects that old Harriett Vann was my great grandmother. I was born with the Vanns and stayed with the Vanns until the war come along and I went with the soldiers. I was born June 4, 1843, on the Martin Vann place near Tullahassee. A. Vann was my father and he run a steamboat on the Arkansas River, away down into Arkansas past Van Buren.² He take a load of cotton that he gather up all the way between Fort Gibson and Van Buren to the Mississippi River where he would load it on old Ben Johnson's boat the Negroes all called the "Cotton Planter." Old Ben's boat hauled lots and lots of slaves from Louisiana in her hull on the way back for another load of cotton.

I done forgot my Cherokee that I heard when I was young. I been living around with the Creeks so long that I picked up some of their words, like "Lag-ashe" when they mean to set down or take a chair; "Hum-buc-sha" is the call for meals or come eat; "Pig-ne-dee" is the Creek way of saying good morning, and "Car-a-she" is corn bread.

The Vann family was always going to someplace new and I can't remember the different places. The slaves was all divided among the Vanns; Joe, Martin, Sena and Clarena was some of their names. Altogether the Vanns owned hundreds of slaves and thousands of land acres all over the country from Webbers Falls to Tullahassee on to the North around Bible's Prairie near Vinita.

They bought and sold slaves, raised corn and cotton and run the steamboat. They always treated their slaves good, only whipped the mean ones who wouldn't work. Master Martin Vann would tell the overseer: "Take them Negroes out for to cut up some wood, pile up the chips and keep them working good, then when Saturday night come around you all go to the corral for rations and do what you want until Monday morning, just so you stay on the farm."

The Vann home at Webbers Falls was built of logs cut by the slaves. The cracks was made solid with small chunks of burr oak, daubed over with a mix of hay and clay mud. The outside was then covered with burr oak planks maybe six inches thick to make the house warm.

When I got old enough to work around the farm, my job was to care for the sheep, until I got still older enough to work on the river boat. With them sheep I had a bobtail bull dog, a brindle colored animal, who went with me all the time. Help to bring them back to the barns at night and round up the strays if they get lost in a hollow.

In them days I wore a long-tailed shirt, hickory stripe, bed tick style. The cloth was made out of the cotton and sheep's wool right on the Vann place, and when the shirt get dirty I soak it up in board or wood tubs, then lay it out on a bench and smack the dirt out with a paddle. That was the kind of wash machine we had in the old times.

Some of the slave owners built log pens on their place for keeping a Negro should he get mean or do something wrong. They called it the bull ring. Maybe some slave man get off his own place without the master giving him a pass. A neighbor pick him up and bring him home. The master put that slave in the bull ring and lay on with the lash. When the whipping is over the master say: "Now go do that again!" Most always the man didn't do it again.

My father died about two years before the war started. I had four half brothers; Sam, Jimmie, Billie and Dave McCurtain (mixed-blood Creek Negroes), and a half sister Elmira, of the same blood. All of them dead now, just me left here to do nothing but draw my pension check.

I guess Lincoln was a good man to free the slaves, but I was getting along alright anyway. It suited me, what I got to eat and wear, and there was always plenty of both before the war.

Lincoln was alright, like I said, but right now we got the best President we ever had, that's all I got to say.

[1] Two virtually identical drafts survive from the interview of Ethel Wolfe Garrison with Henry Henderson in Muskogee, Oklahoma. The interview apparently was undertaken sometime in the winter of 1937–38, because WPA employee Craig Vollmer edited and typed the text on 16 February 1938. A preliminary draft is available as the typescript "Interview with Henry Henderson, Slave Born, Age 95, Muskogee, Okla-

homa," and the later, almost identical draft published here is available as the typescript "Henry Henderson, Age 95, Muskogee, Oklahoma," both in the OHS Slave Narratives. Henry Henderson's narrative was never forwarded to Washington.

For another, contemporary interview with this informant, see Henry Henderson, interview with Carl R. Sherwood, 26 November 1937, Indian-Pioneer Papers, 28: 395–97.

2 In his interview with Carl R. Sherwood for the Indian-Pioneer Papers Project, Henderson stated that his father was named Martin Vann. Indian-Pioneer Papers, 28:395.

For background on the steam navigation on the Arkansas River in Indian Territory, see Muriel H. Wright, "Early Navigation and Commerce along the Arkansas and Red Rivers in Oklahoma," *Chronicles of Oklahoma* 8 (March 1930): 65–88.

IDA HENRY[1]

Age 83   *Oklahoma City, Okla.*

I was born in Marshall, Texas, in 1854. Me mother was named Millie Henderson and me father Silas Hall.[2] Me mother was sold in South Carolina to Mister Hall, who brought her to Texas. Me father was born and raised by Master John Hall. Me mother's and father's family consisted of five girls and one boy. My sisters' names were: Margrette, Chalette, Lottie, Gracy and Loyo, and me brother's name was Dock Howard. I lived with me mother and father in a log house on Master Hall's plantation. We would be sorry when dark, as de patrollers would walk through de quarters and homes of de slavers all times of night wid pine torch lights to whip de niggers found away from deir home.

At nights when me mother would slip away for a visit to some of de neighbors' homes, she would raise up the old plank floor of de log cabin and make pallets on de ground and put us to bed and put the floor back down so dat we couldn't be seen or found by the patrollers on their stroll around at nights.

My grandmother Lottie would always tell us not to let Master catch you in a lie, and to always tell him de truth.

I was house girl to me Mistress and nursed, cooked, and carried de children to and from school. In summer we girls wore cotton slips and yarn dresses for winter. When I got married[3] I was dress in blue serge and was de third person to marry in it. Wedding dresses was not worn after de wedding in dem days by niggers as we was taught by our Mistress dat it was bad luck to wear de wedding dress after marriage. Therefore, 'twas handed down from one generation to the other one.

Me Mistress was sometimes good and sometimes mean. One day de cook was waiting de table and when passing around de potatoes, old Mistress felt of one and as hit wasn't soft done, she exclaimed to de cook, "What you bring these raw potatoes out here for?" and grab a fork and stuck it in her eye and put hit out. She, de cook, lived about 10 years and died.

Me Mistress was de mother of five children, Crock, Jim, Boss and two girls name, Lea and Annie.

Dere home was a large two-story white house wid de large white posts.

As me Master went to de War de old overseer tried himself in meanness over de slaves as seemingly he tried to be important. One day de slaves caught him and one held him whilst another knocked him in de head and killed him.

Master's plantation was about 300 acres and he had 'bout 160 slaves. Before de slaves killed our overseer, he would work 'em night and day. De slaves was punished when dey didn't do as much work as de overseer wanted 'em to do.

He would lock 'em in jail some nights without food and kept 'em dere all night, and after whipping 'em de next morning would only give 'em bread and water to work on till noon.

When a slave was hard to catch for punishment dey would make 'em wear ball and chains. De ball was 'bout de size of de head and made of lead.

On Sunday mornings before breakfast our Mistress would call us together, read de Bible and show us pictures of de Devil in de Bible and tell us dat if we was not good and if we would steal and tell lies dat old Satan would git us.

Close to our Master's plantation lived several families of old "poor white trash" who would steal me Master's hogs and chickens and come and tell me Mistress dat dey seen some of de slaves knock one of dere hogs in de head. Dis continued up till Master returned from de War and caught de old white trash stealing his hogs. De niggers did at times steal Master's hogs and chickens, and I would put biscuits and pieces of chicken in a sack under me dress dat hung from me waist, as I waited de table for me Mistress, and later would slip off and eat it as dey never gave de slaves none of dis sort of food.

We had church Sundays and our preacher Rev. Pat Williams would preach and our Master and family and other nearby white neighbors would ofttime attend our services. De patrollers wouldn't allow de slaves to hold night services, and one night dey caught me mother

out praying. Dey stripped her naked and tied her hands together and
wid a rope tied to de hand cuffs and threw one end of de rope over a
limb and tied de other end to de pommel of a saddle on a horse. As
me mother weighed 'bout 200, dey pulled her up so dat her toes
could barely touch de ground and whipped her. Dat same night she
ran away and stayed over a day and returned.

During de fall months dey would have corn shucking and cotton
pickings and would give a prize to de one who would pick de highest amount of cotton or shuck de largest pile of corn. De prize would
usually be a suit of clothes or something to wear and which would be
given at some later date.

We could only have dances during holidays, but dances was held
on other plantations. One night a traveler visiting me Master wanted
his boots shined. So Master gave de boots to one of de slaves to shine
and de slave put de boots on and went to a dance and danced so much
dat his feet swelled so dat when he returned he could not pull
'em off.

De next morning as de slave did not show up with de boots dey
went to look for him and found him lying down trying to pull de
boots off. He told his Master dat he had put de boots on to shine 'em
and could not pull 'em off. So master had to go to town and buy de
traveler another pair of boots. Before he could run away de slave was
beaten wid 500 lashes.[4]

De War dat brought our freedom lasted about two years. Me Master went and carried one of de slaves for a servant. When he returned
he seemed a much different man dan he was before de War. He was
kind and good and from dat day on he never whipped another slave
nor did he allow any of his slaves whipped. Dis time lasted from January to June de 19th when we was set free in de State of Texas.

Lincoln and Davis both died short of promise. I means dat dey
both died before dey carried out dere plans and promises for freeing
de slaves.[5]

<hr>

[1] Mrs. Ida Henry was interviewed in Oklahoma City by WPA field worker J. S.
Thomas on 15 July 1937. A preliminary typescript of this interview is available as "Story
from Ex-Slaves, Reference, (A) a Personal Interview, 530 N. Nebraska (Mrs. Ida Henry)"
in the OHS Slave Narratives. A later version, edited in standard project format and differing mainly in the use of dialect, is published here. It is available as the typescript "Ida
Henry, Age 83, Oklahoma City, Okla." in ribbon copy in the LC Slave Narratives and
in carbon copy as item 350026 in the LC Slave Narratives Carbon Copies and in the OHS
Slave Narratives. The Ida Henry interview was forwarded to Washington on 2 November 1937. Stephens to Cronyn, 2 November 1937, WPA Notes on Interviews.

2 Benjamin A. Botkin, in appraising the Ida Henry narrative, noted that the style was "colloquial, with one or two false attempts at dialect. (e.g., 'me mother,' p. 1)." [B. A. Botkin], LC Slave Narratives Appraisal Sheets, Accession no. 350026, [ca. 1940].

3 The Oklahoma City directory contemporary with the interview noted that the interviewee was the widow of Rollie H. Henry. *Polk's Oklahoma City Directory, 1937,* 335, 883.

4 In the preliminary version of the narrative, this sentence reads: "Before he could leave and for dis, dis slave was beaten 500 lashes."

5 In the preliminary draft, these two sentences read as follows: "When asking her, what she thought of Lincoln and Davis she replies: 'Both died short of promise.' She means that they both died before they carried out their plans and promises as to the freeing of slaves as Lincoln was assassinated before the day of freedom."

MORRIS HILLYER[1]

Age 84 Yrs. *Alderson, Okla.*

My father was Gabe Hillyer and my mother was Clarissy Hillyer, and our home was in Rome, Georgia. Our owner was Judge Hillyer. He was de last United States senator to Washington, D.C., before de War.[2]

My mother died when I was only a few days old and the only mother I ever knew was Judge Hillyer's wife, Miss Jane. Her nine children were all older than I was and when mother died Miss Jane said mother had raised her children and she would raise hers. So she took us into her house and we never lived at de quarters any more. I had two sisters, Sally and Sylvia, and we had a room in de Big House and sister Sally didn't do nothing else but look after me. I used to stand with my thumb in my mouth and hold to Miss Jane's apron while she knitted.

When Judge Hillyer was elected he sold out his farm and gave his slaves to his children. He owned about twelve or fourteen slaves at this time. He gave me and my sister Sylvia to his son, Dr. Hillyer, and my father to another of his sons who was studying law. Father stayed with him and took care of him until he graduated. Father learned to be a good carpenter while he lived with George Hillyer. George never married until after de War.

Dr. Hillyer lived on a big plantation but he practiced medicine all de time. He didn't have much time to look after de farm but he had good overseers and they sure didn't beat his slaves or mistreat 'em in any way. Dr. Hillyer married a rich girl, Miss Mary Cooley, and her father gave her fifteen slaves when she married and Judge Hillyer gave him five so he had a purty good start from de first and he knowed how to make money so he was a wealthy man when de Rebellion started.

My sister and I didn't know how to act when we was sent out there among strangers. We had to live in de quarters just like de other niggers, and we didn't especially like it. I guess I was a sort of bad boy.

There was several more boys about my age and we didn't have any work to do but just busy ourselves by getting into mischief. We'd ride de calves, chase de pigs, kill de chickens, break up hens' nests, and in fact do most everything we hadn't ought to do. Finally they put us to toting water to de field hands, minding[3] de gaps, taking de cows to pasture and as dat kept us purty busy we wasn't so bad after dat.

My happiest days was when I was with de old Judge and Miss Jane. I can sit here and think of them old times and it seems like it was just yesterday dat it all happened. He was a great hand to go to town every day and lounge around wid his cronies. I used to go with him, and my how they would argue. Sometimes they would get mad and shake their canes in each other's faces. I guess they was talking politics.

Our old master liked cats better than any man I ever saw, and he always had five or six that followed him about de place like dogs. When he went to eat they was always close to him and just as soon as he finished he would always feed them. When he was gone us boys used to throw at his cats or set de dogs on 'em. We was always careful dat no one saw us for if he had known about it he would a-whipped us and no mistake. I wouldn't a-blamed him either, for I like cats now. I think they are lots of company.

He was a typical Southern gentleman, medium sized, and wore a Van Dyke beard. He never whipped his slaves, and he didn't have a one dat wouldn't a-died for him.

Judge Hillyer had one son, William, dat wouldn't go to college. He made fun of his brothers for going to school so long, and said that he would be ashamed to go and stay five or six years. After de War he settled down and studied law in Judge Akin's office and opened a office in Athens, Georgia, and he made de best lawyer of them all.

Us boys used to go hunting with Master William. He hunted rabbits, quails, squirrels, and sometimes he would kill a deer. He hunted mostly with dogs. He never used a gun but very little. Lead was so scarce and cost so much dat he couldn't afford to waste a bullet on rabbits or snakes. He made his own bullets. The dogs would chase a rabbit into a hollow tree and we'd take a stick and twist him out. Sometimes we'd have nearly all de hide twisted off him when we'd git him out.

Old Judge Hillyer smoked a pipe with a long stem. He used to give me ten cents a day to fill it for him. He told me I had to have $36 at the end of the year, but I never made it. There was a store right close to us and I'd go down there and spend my money for lemon stick candy, ginger cakes, peanuts, and firecrackers. Old Master knowed I wouldn't save it, and he didn't care if I did spent it for it was mine to do with just as I pleased.

Every time a circus come to town I'd run off and they wouldn't see me again all day. Seemed like I just couldn't help it. I wouldn't take time to git permission to go. One time to punish me for running off he tied me up by my thumbs, and I had to stay home while de rest went. I didn't dare try to git loose and run off for I knowed I'd git my jacket tanned if I did. Old Master never laid his hand on me, but I knowed he would if I didn't do as he told me. He never told us twice to do anything either.

Coins had curious names in them days. A dime was called a thrip. Four-pen was about the same value as three cents or maybe a little more. It took three of 'em to make a thrip. There was all sorts of paper money.

Every first Tuesday slaves were brought in from Virginia and sold on de block. De auctioneer was Cap'n Dorsey. E. M. Cobb was de slave bringer. They would stand de slaves up on de block and talk about what a fine looking specimen of black manhood or womanhood dey was, tell how healthy dey was, look in their mouth and examine their teeth just like they was a horse, and talk about de kind of work they would be fit for and could do. Young healthy boys and girls brought the best prices. I guess they figured dat dey would grow to be valuable. I used to stand around and watch de sales take place but it never entered my mind to be afraid for I knowed old Judge wasn't going to sell me. I thought I was an important member of his family.

Old Judge bought every roguish nigger in the country. He'd take him home and give him the key to everything on de place and say to help hisself. Soon as he got all he wanted to eat he'd quit being a rogue. Old Judge said that was what made niggers steal—they was hungry.

They used to scare us kids by telling us dat a runaway nigger would git us. De timber was awful heavy in de river bottoms, and dey was one nigger dat run off from his master and lived for years in these bottoms. He was there all during de War and come out after de surrender. Every man in dat country owned him at some time or other. His owner sold him to a man who was sure he could catch him—he never did, so he sold him to another slave owner and so on till nearly everybody had him. He changed hands about six or seven times. They would come in droves with blood hounds and hunt for him but dey couldn't catch him for he knowed them woods too well. He'd feed de dogs and make friends with 'em and they wouldn't bother him. He lived on nuts, fruit, and wild game, and niggers would slip food to him. He'd slip into town and get whiskey and trade it to de niggers for food.

Judge Hillyer never 'lowanced his niggers and dey could always have anything on de place to eat. We had so much freedom dat other slave owners in our neighborhood didn't like for us to come among their slaves for they said we was free niggers and would make their slaves discontented.

After I went to live with Judge Hillyer's son, Dr. Hillyer, one of my jobs was to tote the girls' books to school every morning. All the plantation owners had a colored boy dat did that. After we had toted de books to de school house we'd go back down de road a piece and line up and have the "gone-bying-est" fight you ever see. We'd have regular battles. If I got licked in de morning I'd go home and rest up and I'd give somebody a good licking dat evening. I reckon I caught up with my fighting for in all my working life I have always worked with gangs of men of from one to two-hundred and I never struck a man and no man ever struck me.

Jim Williams was a patroller,[4] and how he did like to catch a nigger off de farm without a permit so he could whip him. Jim thought he was de best man in de country and could whip de best of 'em. One night John Hardin, a big husky feller, was out late. He met Jim and knowed he was in for it. Jim said, "John, I'm gonna give you a white man's chance. I'm gonna let you fight me and if you are de best man, well and good."

John say, "Master Jim, I can't fight wid you. Come on and give me my licking, and let me go on home."

But Jim wouldn't do it, and he slapped John and called him some names and told him he is a coward to fight him. All dis made John awful mad and he flew into him and give him the terriblest licking a man ever toted. He went on home but knew he would git into trouble over it.

Jim talked around over the country about what he was going to do to John but everybody told him dat he brought it all on hisself. He never did try to git another nigger to fight with him.

Yes, I guess charms keep off bad luck. I have wore 'em but money always was my best lucky piece. I've made lots of money but I never made good use of it.

I was always afraid of ghosts but I never saw one. There was a graveyard beside de road from our house to town and I always was afraid to go by it. I'd shut my eyes and run for dear life till I was past de grave yard. I had heard dat there was a headless man dat stayed there [and] on cold rainy days or foggy nights he'd hide by de fence and throw his head at you. Once a man got hit and he fell right down dead. I believed dat tale and you can imagine how I felt whenever I had to go past there by myself and on foot.

I saw lots of Ku Kluxers but I wasn't afraid of them. I knowed I hadn't done nothing and they wasn't after me. One time I met a bunch of 'em and one of 'em said, "Who is dis feller?" Another one said, "Oh, dat's Gabe's foolish boy, come on, don't bother him." I always did think dat voice sounded natural but I never did say anything about it. It sounded powerful like one of old Judge's boys. Dey rode on and didn't bother me and I never was a bit afraid of 'em any more.

I went to school one month after de War. I never learned much but I learned to read somewhere along de road dat I come over. My father come from Athens, Georgia, and took us away with him. I learned the carpenter's trade from him. He was so mean to me dat I run away when I was nineteen. I went back to Rome, Georgia, and got a job with a bridge gang and spent two years with 'em. I went then to Henderson, Kentucky, and worked for ten years. There was hundreds of colored people coming to de mines at Krebs and Alderson [Oklahoma] and I decided to come along, too. I never worked in de mines but I did all sorts of carpentering for them.[5]

I married in Atoka, Oklahoma, thirty-three years ago. I never had no children.

I've made lots of money but somehow it always got away from me. But me and my wife have our little home here and we are both still able to work a little, so I guess we are making it all right.

[1] Mrs. Jessie R. Ervin from the Oklahoma Writers' Project interviewed Morris Hillyer at Alderson, Oklahoma, on 18 October 1937. A preliminary draft of the interview is available in typescript as "Interview with Morris Hillyer, Ex-Slave, Aged 84, Alderson, Okla." in the OHS Slave Narratives. A later version, with minor editorial changes, is available as the typescript "Morris Hillyer, Age 84 Yrs., Alderson, Okla." in ribbon copy in the LC Slave Narratives and in carbon copy as item 350021 in the LC Slave Narratives Carbon Copies and in the OHS Slave Narratives. On 18 November 1937 the interview was sent to Washington, where three years later B. A. Botkin, di-

rector of folklore for the Federal Writers' Project, observed that it was "notable for slave boyhood[,] stories of runaway slave . . . and patrollers." Botkin himself published a selection from the Hillyer narrative in *Lay My Burden Down* (177–78, 279) in 1945. B. A. B[otkin], LC Slave Narratives Appraisal Sheets, Accession no. 350021, 14 December 1940; Stephens to Alsberg, 18 November 1937, WPA Notes on Interviews.

   [2] Morris Hillyer's first master was Junius Hillyer, who served as congressman from the Sixth District of Georgia from 1851 to 1855. Junius Hillyer's son George served in 1859–60 as clerk of the U.S. House of Representatives and later, from 1885 to 1887, as mayor of Atlanta. Kenneth Coleman and Charles Stephen Gurr, *Dictionary of Georgia Biography,* 1:457–60.

   [3] This appears to be a misspelling of "mending," as in mending gaps in fences.

   [4] The preliminary draft spells the word "patteroller."

   [5] For background on Oklahoma coal mining, and particularly that at Krebs and Alderson, see Gene Aldrich, "A History of the Coal Industry in Oklahoma to 1907" (Ph.D. diss., University of Oklahoma, 1952); Steve Sewell, "Amongst the Damp: The Dangerous Profession of Coal Mining in Oklahoma, 1870–1935," *Chronicles of Oklahoma* 70 (Spring 1992): 66–83; C. W. Shannon, *Coal in Oklahoma.*

HAL HUTSON[1]

Age 90 Yrs.   *Oklahoma City, Okla.*

I was born at Galveston,[2] Tennessee, October 12, 1847. There were 11 children: 7 brothers: Andrew, George, Clent, Gilbert, Frank, Mack and Horace; and 3 girls: Rosie, Marie and Nancy. We were all Hutsons. Together with my mother and father we worked for the same man whose name was Mr. Barton Brown, but who we all call Master Brown,[3] and sometimes Mr. Brown.

Master Brown had a good weather-board house, two story, with five or six rooms. They lived pretty well.[4] He had eight children. We lived in one-room log huts. There were a long string of them huts. We slept on the floor like hogs. Girls and boys slept together—jest everybody slept every whar. We never knew what biscuits were![5] We ate "seconds and shorts" (wheat ground once) for bread.[6] Ate rabbits, possums baked with taters, beans, and bean soup. No chicken, fish and the like. My favorite dish now is beans.

Master Brown owned about 36 or 40 slaves, I can't recall jest now, and about 200 acres of ground. There was very little cotton raised in Galveston—I mean jest some corn. Sometimes we would shuck corn all night. He would not let us raise gardens of our own, but didn't mind us raising corn and a few other truck vegetables to sell for a little spending change.

I learned to read, write and figger at an early age. Master Brown's boy and I were the same age you see (14 years old) and he would send me to school to protect his kids, and I would have to sit up there until school was out. So while sitting there I listened to what the white teacher was telling the kids, and caught on how to read, write and figger—but I never let on, 'cause if I was caught trying to read or figger dey would whip me something terrible. After I caught on how to figger the white kids would ask me to teach them. Master Brown would often say: "My God O'mighty, never do for that nigger to learn to figger."

We weren't allowed to count change. If we borrowed a fifty-cent piece, we would have to pay back a fifty-cent piece—not five dimes or fifty pennies or ten nickels.

We went barefooted the year round and wore long shirts split on each side. All of us niggers called all the whites "poor white trash." The overseer was nothing but poor white trash and the meanest man that ever walked on earth. He never did whip me much 'cause I was kind of a pet. I worked up to the Big House, but he sho' did whip them others. Why, one day he was beating my mother, and I was too small to say anything, so my big brother heard her crying and came running, picked up a chunk and that overseer stopped a'beating her. The white boy was holding her on the ground and he was whipping her with a long leather whip. They said they couldn't teach her no sense and she said, "I don't wanna learn no sense." The overseer's name was Charlie Clark. One day he whipped a man until he was bloody as a pig 'cause he went to the mill and stayed too long.

The patroller rode all night and iffen we were caught out later than 10:00 o'clock they would beat us, but we would git each other word by sending a man round way late at night. Always take news by night.[7] Of course the Ku Klux Klan didn't come 'til after the war. They was something like the patrollers. Never heard of no trouble between the black and whites 'cause them niggers were afraid to resist them.

My biggest job was keeping flies off'n the table up at the Big House. When time come to go in for the day we would cut up and dance. I can't remember any of the songs jest now, but we had some that we sung. We danced a whole lots and jest sung "made up" songs.[8]

Old Master would stay up to hear us come in. Of course Saturday afternoon was a holiday. We didn't work no holidays. Master gave us one week off for Christmas, and never worked us on Sunday, unless the "ox was in the ditch." When the slaves got sick we had white doctors, and we would wait on each other. Drink dock root tea, mullein tea and flaxweed tea, but we never wore charms.

I think it's a good thing that slavery's over. It ought to been over a good while ago. But its going to be slavery all over again if things don't git better.[9] But I thank God I've been a Christian for 70 years, and now is a member of Tabernacle Baptist Church and deacon of the church, and a Christian 'cause the Bible teaches me to be.

That war was a awful thing. I used to pack them soldiers water on my head, and then I worked at Fort Sill and Fort Dawson in Tennessee. Those Yankees came by nights—got behind those rebels, and took their hams, drove horses in the houses, killed their chickens and ate up the rebels' food, but the Yanks didn't bother us niggers.

When freedom came old Master called us all in from the fields and told us, "All of you niggers are free as frogs now to go wherever you choose. You are your own man now." We all continued working for him at $5.00 a month. After the crops were gathered the niggers scattered out. Some went North—and we would say when they went North that they had "crossed the water."

I never married till after the War. Married at my mother's house 'cause my wife's mother didn't let us marry at her house, so I sent Jack Perry after her on a hoss and we had a big dinner—and jest got married.

I an the father of nine children, but jest three is living. One is a dentist in Muskogee, Dr. Andrew Hutson.[10] All of the children are pretty well read. We never had school for niggers until after slavery.

I think Abraham Lincoln was a great man, but I don't know much about Jeff Davis. Booker T. Washington was a fine man.

[1] Hal Hutson of Oklahoma City was interviewed at his home by field worker Bertha P. Tipton on 17 May 1937. An intermediate draft of Tipton's interview notes is available as the typescript "Interview with Hal Hutson, Ex-Slave 90 Years of Age, 605 Northeast 2nd Street, Oklahoma City, Oklahoma" in the OHS Slave Narratives. At the end of the typescript Tipton noted: "Hal Hutson does not use much dialect. This interview was taken in shorthand and transcribed exactly as he spoke. He is a property owner." Clipped to the interview was the additional note by project employee Ida Belle Hunter, "This ex-slave is very ill and unable to be re-interviewed." An unidentified WPA employee edited the narrative, rearranging the order of several sentences to make the text more coherent. The final typescript, "Hal Hutson, Age 90 Yrs., Oklahoma City, Okla.," published here, is available in ribbon copy in the LC Slave Narratives and in carbon copy as item 350058 in the LC Slave Narratives Carbon Copies and in the OHS Slave Narratives. The narrative was sent to Washington on 14 September 1937. *Polk's Oklahoma City Directory, 1937,* 371, 920; Stephens to Cronyn, 14 September 1937, WPA Notes on Interviews.

2 The preliminary draft consistently spells this placename "Galvaton," perhaps a corruption of "Gallatin."

3 The preliminary draft reads here "Marster or Mars Brown" and consistently renders "master" as "marster."

4 These two sentences read in the preliminary draft as three sentences: "Marster Brown's house had five or six rooms. Yes, he had a good weather-board house two story. Yes, they lived well."

5 In the preliminary draft this sentence begins with a direct address to the interviewer, "Chile."

6 Seconds constitute a type of coarse flour; shorts are the part of milled grain next finer than the bran.

7 At this point the preliminary draft includes the following sentence: "The man [sic] couldn't see their wives only twice a week—Wednesday and Sunday."

8 At this point the preliminary version includes the following two sentences: "I don't believe in ghost. Never did see one—hear a lots talk about them tho."

9 The first three sentences in this paragraph appear as follows in the preliminary draft: "When asked, now that slavery is over what he thought, he replied: 'I think it is a good thing. It ought to been over a good while ago. Gonna be ag[a]in if things don't git better.'"

10 The interviewee's son is listed in a roughly contemporary city directory as Dr. Andrew H. Hudson [sic], a dentist with his office at 202 Nave Building in Muskogee. *Polk's Muskogee City Directory, 1932,* 110, 289.

WILLIAM HUTSON[1]

Age 98 Yrs.   *Tulsa, Okla.*

When a feller gets as old as me it's a heap easier to forget things than it is to remember, but I ain't never forgot that old plantation where good old Doctor Allison lived back there in Georgia long before the War that brought us slaves the freedom.

I hear the slaves talking about mean masters when I was a boy. They wasn't talking about Master Allison though, 'cause he was a good man and took part for the slaves when any trouble come up with the overseer.

The Mistress' name was Louisa (the same name as the gal I was married to later after the War), and she was just about as mean as was the old Master good. I was the house boy when I gets old enough to understand what the Master wants done and I does it just like he says, so I reckon that's why we always get along together.

The Master helped to raise my mammy. When I was born he says to her (my mammy tells me when I gets older): "Cheney," the old Master say, "that boy is going be different from these other children. I aims to see that he is. He's going be in the house all the time, he ain't going work in the fields; he's going to stay right with me all the time."

They was about twenty slaves on the plantation but I was the one old Master called for when he wanted something special for himself. I was the one he took with him on the trips to town, I was the one who fetch him the cooling drink after he look about the fields and sometimes I carry the little black bag when he goes a-doctoring folks with the misery away off [on] some other farm.

The Master hear about there going be an auction one day and he figgered maybe he needed some more slaves if they was good ones, so he took me and started out early in the morning. It wasn't very far and we got there early before the auction started. Reckon that was the first time I ever see any slaves sold.

They was a long platform made of heavy planks and all the slaves was lined up on the platform,[2] and they was stripped to the waist, men, women, and children. One or two of the women folks was bare naked. They wasn't young women neither, just middle age ones, but they was built good. Some of them was well greased and that grease covered up many a scar they'd earned for some foolishment or other.

The Master don't buy none and pretty soon we starts home. The Master was riding horseback,—he didn't ever use no buggy 'cause he said that was the way for folks to travel who was too feeble to sit in the saddle—and I rode back of him on another horse, but that horse I rides is just horse while the Master's was a real thoroughbred like maybe you see on race tracks down in the South.

That auction kept bothering me all the way back to the plantation. I kept seeing them little children standing on the flatform (platform), their mammy and pappy crying hard 'cause their young'uns is being sold. They was a lot of heartaches even [if] they was slaves and it gets me worried.

I asked the Master is he going to have an auction and he jest laugh. I ain't never sold no slaves yet and I ain't going to, he says. And I gets easier right then. I kind of hates to think about standing up on one of them platforms, kinder sorry to leave my old mammy and the Master, so I was easy in the heart when he talked like that.

The plantation house was a big frame [one] and the yard was shaded with trees all around. The Master's children—four boys and two girls—would play in the yard with me just like I was one of the family. And we'd go hunting and fishing. There was a creek not far away and they was good fishing in the stream and squirrels in the trees. Mighty lot of fun to catch them fishes but more fun when they is all fried brown and ready for to eat with a piece of hot pone. Ain't no fish ever taste that good since!

One thing I sort of ponders about. The old Master don't let us have no religion meetings and reading and writing is something I learn after the War. Some of the slaves talk about meeting 'round the country and wants to have preaching on the plantation. Master says NO. No preacher around here to tell about the Bible and religion will be just a puzzlement, the Master say, and we let it go at that. I reckon that was the only thing he was set against.

That and the Yankees. The Master went to the War and stayed 'til it was most over. He was a mighty sick man when he come back to the old place, but I was there waiting for him just like always. All the time he was away I take care around the house. That's what he say for me to do when he rides away to fight the Yankees. Lots of talk about the War but the slaves goes right on working just the same, raising cotton and tobacco.

The slaves talk a heap about Lincoln and some trys to run away to the North. Don't hear much about Jeff Davis, mostly Lincoln. He give us slaves the freedom but we was better off as we was.

The day of freedom come around just like any other day, except the Master say for me to bring up the horses, we is going to town. That's when he hears about the slaves being free. We gets to the town and the Master goes into the store. It's pretty early but the streets was filled with folks talking and I wonder what makes the Master in such a hurry when he comes out of the store.

He gets on his horse and tells me to follow fast. When we gets back to the plantation he sounds the horn calling the slaves. They come in from the fields and meet 'round back of the kitchen building that stood separate from the Master's house. They all keeps quiet while the Master talks! "You-all is free now, and all the rest of the slaves is free too. Nobody owns you now and nobody going to own you anymore!" That was good news, I reckon, but nobody know what to do about it.

The crops was mostly in and the Master wants the folks to stay 'til the crop is finished. They talk about it the rest of that day. They wasn't no celebration 'round the place, but they wasn't no work after the Master tells us we is free. Nobody leave the place though. Not 'til in the fall when the work is through. Then some of us go into the town and gets work 'cause everybody knows the Allison slaves was the right kind of folks to have around.

That was the first money I earn and then I have to learn how to spend it. That was the hardest part 'cause the prices was high and the wages was low.

Then I moves on and meets the gal that maybe I been looking for, Louisa Baker, and right away she takes to me and we is married. Ain't been no other woman but her and she's waiting for me wherever the dead waits for the living.

I reckon she won't have so long to wait now, even if I is feeling pretty spry and got good use of the feets and hands. Ninety-eight years brings a heap of wear and some of these days the old body'll need a long time rest and then I'll join her for all the time.

I is ready for the New Day a-coming!

[1] William Hutson was interviewed in Tulsa, Oklahoma, by WPA field worker Craig Vollmer on 5 August 1937. A preliminary draft of the interview is available as the typescript "Interview with William Hutson, 519 North Greenwood, Tulsa, Okla." in the OHS Slave Narratives. A virtually identical later draft, published here, is the typescript "William Hutson, Age 98 Yrs., Tulsa, Okla.," available in ribbon copy in the LC Slave Narratives and in carbon copy as item 350093 in the LC Slave Narratives Carbon Copies and in the OHS Slave Narratives. Hutson's narrative was sent to Washington on 12 August 1937. Stephens to Cronyn, 12 August 1937, WPA Notes on Interviews.

Between the title and the body of the interview, the preliminary draft contains the following information from Vollmer: "Note: This person is an ex-slave, born March 10, 1839, Dalsville, Ga., on the Dr. Allison plantation. Parents: Anthony and Cheney Hutson. Wife: Louisa Baker. Sons: (Two)—William—other name unknown."

[2] The preliminary draft includes the field worker's note: "Uncle William pronounces it 'flatform.'"

INTERVIEW WITH FRANK JACKSON[1]

Slave Born, Age 95   *3423 Spruce Street, Muskogee, Oklahoma*

The Vicksburg Siege!—that's the one most thing I remember about the Civil War. Them soldiers in gray fought the blue coated ones with guns and bayonets, but when them Yankees get under the river (Mississippi) and blow it up the fighting was over for sure! That July 4th day in 1863, when the rebels surrender Vicksburg, is the one day I won't never forget.

The time I went there was with Master Steve Jackson. All the time during the war we was helping the rebel soldiers. Lots of trips I made to Alexandria, La., with a wagon load of soldiers and when the Red River was up we crossed it on a "flat," down by the place they called Florence landing.

That flat was just a fixed-up ferry boat and on it we load the wagon, the horses and the soldiers. Some of the men had poles, some of the others had paddles, and they would push and oar the "flat" to the other side; then we would be on our way again.

The wagons was all home made. Made by white carpenters with slaves around to help them. Made all of wood, even to the wheels and axles, they was powerful heavy in themselves. Loaded up with stuff for the market it would take six yoke of oxen to budge it over the road to town.

I was with the old master all during the war and long before. From the time I was born (Sept. 6, 1843) to the day of freedom he was the only Master I ever had. And he just have one slave family, my mother, brother Billy and me. Guess my pappy belonged to some other master for I can't 'member ever seeing him and don't know his name. Now I'm so old I even forgets my mother's name.

I was born down in Choctaw County, Alabama. Master Jackson had a small farm dere when I was born. He had small farms all over the south. He traded in farms instead of slaves, I reckon.

He look around and find a likely place he figure to fix up if he can buy it. He ask the price, maybe the owner say $500 for it and try to make master think what a bargain it was. But the old master was a powerful good trader and before that man knew it almost, the deal was made. He didn't get no $500 though; he was mighty lucky if he get $200. Dey was just small farms and it didn't take much work to get dem looking worth lots more than the old master paid, so when somebody come along looking to buy a farm dere it was waiting for him! That's how the master made his money all the time.

The master's wife was Jane Jackson, the dearest old mistress who ever lived. Mistress Jane Jackson was always busy around her looms. My mother help with spinning and dying the thread. Lot of the thread was dyed red, I reckon because of the Indian mulberry (they called the tree "Aal" in those days, he says), that was easy to get.

When somebody get sick Mistress Jackson tell the master, ". . . fix some blue moss[2] and calomel, they needs some medicine." The master does it and doctors us wid dat for a while; if the misery leaves dat's all dere is to it, but if it don't he calls the regular doctor from town with his pills and stuff.

There was an old water mill near one of Master Jackson's farms, where I take corn for grinding. The grinding rocks was shaped up round and when they come together the corn was mashed up, then the millman put plugs in the end hole and tighten the rocks so's to make the meal fine.

I always took a pass to the mill with me, else the patrollers get me.

The pass say to go a certain place and get back to the farm in a certain time. If you was slow in getting back and stay over the time on the pass the patrollers get you and plenty they could do. I use the passes right, but some of the slaves tried to run away, but mostly I heard they was caught and whipped. The night riders was thick around the country, always watching for the runoffs.

There was no churches or schools for the slaves, but they could go to the white folks' church, stand outside by the door and hear the preaching. That's the way we did, and then we get back home and tell the master what the preacher said. He wanted us to know about religion, but he said schools would spoil us negroes—there wasn't a reason for us to learn reading or writing. After freedom I was too busy trying to work that I couldn't find no time for either.

Two weeks before the old master told me I was free—that's when we was living near Winnfield, La.—I married Susan Teagle, who was a slave girl on a plantation seven miles away. I got a pass to go see her when I could; sometimes the master let me stay 36 hours.

The first thing I do after that June day when I was freed, I set my feet to walking them seven miles! When I got to the plantation and find my wife I say to her: "All the slaves is free now and they can live where they want. Me, I'se staying on with Master Jackson for awhile, and you can come with me and live there. What do you say?"

I remember she was glad as me. "I'se ready!—that's what I say!" What I was most glad about was that her coming with me stopped that walking to her place!

There was thirteen children; some of them died and I can only remember three of their names. Susan, Jance and Steve, all living in Oklahoma.

All the children was raised like the old Master told us boys in slave times. He never make no rules for us, excepting to do right and always tell the truth. That's what everybody ought to do.

¹ The interview of Frank Jackson of Muskogee, Oklahoma, with WPA field worker Ethel Wolfe Garrison in late 1937 or early 1938 is available only in two incomplete typescripts, the pieces from which fit together to create a complete narrative. The earlier of the two typescripts, which was edited and retyped by WPA employee Craig Vollmer on 14 February 1938, is available as "Interview with Frank Jackson, Slave Born, Age 95, 3423 Spruce Street, Muskogee, Oklahoma," but its incomplete pages are found in two separate files. Page 1 is filed under the name of Frank Jackson in the OHS Slave Narratives, while pages 3 and 4 are unmarked and found in the "Unid-Partial" file in the OHS Slave Narratives. The later of the two drafts, for which only pages 1 and 2 survive, is available as the typescript carbon copy "Frank Jackson, Age 95,

Muskogee, Oklahoma" filed under the name of Frank Jackson in the OHS Slave Nar-
ratives. The text presented here is drawn from the more complete of the two narratives,
"Interview with Frank Jackson," with the missing paragraphs drawn from the "Frank
Jackson" typescript. This narrative was never sent to Washington.
    2 Apparently a reference to blue mass, a common remedy in the South.

MRS. ISABELLA JACKSON[1]

Age 79 Yrs.   *Tulsa, Okla.*

"Boom . . . Boom! Boom . . . Boom!" That's the way the old weaver
go all day long when my sister, Margaret, is making cloth for the
slaves down on old Doc Joe Jackson's plantation in Louisiana. The
Jackson plantation was small and there was only three or four slave
families kept on it regular. The master's house was just a common ordinary plank building made from sawed lumber that come from the
saw mill on another plantation. There wasn't many what-you-call log
cabins down there in Louisiana as I remember, mostly like the
"Doc's" house, plank.

That was near the little place of Bunkie, and it's my birthplace,
and I guess where all Mammy's children were born because she was
never sold but once and nobody but the old Doc ever did own her
after she come to his place.

He always say couldn't nobody get work out of Mammy but him.
I guess that's just his foolery 'cause if she ain't no good the Old Doc
most likely sell her to some of the white folks in Texas.

That's what they done to them mean, no account slaves—just send
them to Texas. Them folks sure knew how for to handle 'em!

There was lots of babies among the slave families and while the
older folks was working in the fields the babies were taken care of by
the cook. Not in the kitchen either.

There was a special house for the children—that's where I got my
raising. The children were fed from wooden troughs and the food was
mostly pot likker and corn pone seasoned with fat meats. The way
they'd feed 'em was just about like folks would feed the hogs, except
the food had to be good.

What I mean it was clean and it had to be cooked right or else the
cook would be punished with the whip. Every Sunday morning the
overseer come to eat with the children. That's what you'd call an inspection trip, and Who-ee-ee!—if the food wasn't right, clean and
fresh, the cook better watch out!

But I was talking about my sister, Margaret. I can still see her weaving the cloth—Boom! . . . Boom!—and she hear that all the day and get mighty tired. Sometimes she drop her head and go to sleep. The Mistress get her then sure. Rap her on the head with almost anything handy, but she hit pretty easy, just trying to scare her that's all.

The old Master though, he ain't so easy as that. The whippings was done by the master, and the overseer just tell the old Doc about the troubles, like the old Doc say:

"You just watch the slaves and see they works and works hard, but don't lay on the whip, because I is the only one who knows how to do it right!"

Maybe the old Master was sickened of whippings from the stories the slaves told about the plantation that joined ours on the north. If they ever was a living Devil that plantation was his home and the owner was it! That's what the old slaves say, and when I tell you about it see if I is right.

That man got so mean even the white folks was scared of him, 'specially if he was filled with drink. That's the way he was most of the time, just before the slaves was freed.

All the time we hear about slaves on that place getting whipped or being locked in the stock—that one of them things where your head and hands is fastened through holes in a wide board, and you stands there all the day and all the night—and sometimes we hears of them staying in the stock for three-four weeks if they trys to run away to the north.

Sometimes we hears about some slave who is shot by that man while he is wild with the drink. That's what I'm telling about now.

Don't nobody know what made the master mad at the old slave— one of the oldest on the place. Anyway, the master didn't whip him; instead of that he kills him with the gun and scares the others so bad most of 'em runs off and hides in the woods.

The drunk master just drags the old dead slave to the graveyard which is down in the corner away from the growing crops, and hunts up two of the young boys who was hiding in the barn. He takes them to dig the grave.

The master stands watching every move they make, the dead man lays there with his face to the sky, and the boys is so scared they could hardly dig. The master keeps telling them to hurry with the digging.

After while he tells them to stop and put the body in the grave. They wasn't no coffin, no box, for him. Just the old clothes that he wears in the fields.

But the grave was too short and they start digging some more, but the master stop them. He says to put back the body in the grave, and then he jumps into the grave hisself. Right on the dead he jumps and stomps till the body is mashed and twisted to fit the hole. Then the old nigger is buried.

That's the way my Mammy hears it and told it to us children. She was a Christian and I know she told the truth.

Like I said, Mammy was never sold only to Master Jackson. But she's seen them slave auctions where the men, women and children was stripped naked and lined up so's the buyers could see what kind of animals they was getting for their money.

My pappy's name was Jacob Keller and my mother was Maria. They's both dead long ago, and I'm waiting for the old ship Zion that took my mammy away, like we used to sing of in the woods!

> "It has landed my old Mammy,
> It has landed my old Mammy,
> Get on board, Get on board,
> 'Tis the Old Ship of Zion—
> "Get on board!"

The Civil War didn't reach in to the Jackson plantation, what I mean I didn't see a Yankee soldier all the time of the war nor none of them after it was over. We heard about the fighting down around New Orleans, I reckon it was, but it didn't get no closer to us than that.

Slave days were bad, even if the master was what you call good. Sometime the good masters have a bad day and the slaves would get it took out on them. But the freedom done away with all that whipping and beating.

What I know about my marriage is mostly DON'T'S. Because I don't know the year it was, nor the day, not who was the preacher, nor how old I was, nor how old was the man I married, Moses Jackson. That's the one thing I most remember—his name, and it's the most important, I guess. And the marriage was at Bunkie.

We farmed and lived down in Louisiana 'til my husband died and I moved to Oklahoma in 1921. Come to Tulsa then and it was just before the riot—bad business, that was, but I was working for a fine white family and living in the quarters, minding my own business, so I wasn't bothered at all.[2]

Three of my children live in Tulsa, one is farming somewhere in Louisiana and the other is in New Orleans. There was ten in all, but five of them died.

[1] In spring or summer 1937, WPA field worker L. P. Livingston interviewed Mrs. Isabella Jackson in Tulsa, Oklahoma. On 13 July 1937 project employee Craig Vollmer

edited the interview to create the typescript "Interview with Mrs. Isabella Jackson
(Slave Born, 1858—at Bunker [*sic*], La.), 1008 North Lansing, Tulsa," now preserved
in the OHS Slave Narratives. This narrative went next to the Oklahoma City headquarters for the Oklahoma Slave Narrative Project, where the state administrator for
the Federal Writers' project on 10 August 1937 asked Robert Vinson Lackey in the
Tulsa office to secure a new "*word for word*" interview with . . . Mrs. Isabella Jackson,"
among other informants. In the interval, however, the initial narrative was further
edited and retyped into the text "Mrs. Isabella Jackson, Age 79 Yrs., Tulsa, Okla.,"
which was sent to Washington on 12 August 1937; this narrative became part of the
official slave narrative collection now housed in the Library of Congress and is available
in ribbon copy in the LC Slave Narratives and in carbon copy as item 350096 in the LC
Slave Narratives Carbon Copies. Even though this version of the Isabella Jackson interview had already gone to Washington, personnel in the Tulsa office, who may not
have been informed, proceeded with interviewing Mrs. Jackson a second time, producing a narrative nearly double the length of the earlier drafts. This narrative was forwarded from Tulsa to Oklahoma City on 24 August 1937. Published here, it is available in the OHS Slave Narratives as "Mrs. Isabella Jackson, Age 79 Yrs., Tulsa, Okla."
(the same title as the narrative in the Library of Congress collection). *Polk's Tulsa City
Directory, 1934,* 166, 275, 600; *Polk's Tulsa City Directory, 1935,* 191, 310, 666; Stephens to Lackey, 10 August 1937; Stephens to Cronyn, 12 August 1937; Craig
Vollmer, Tulsa, [Oklahoma], to [Ned] DeWitt, [Oklahoma City, Oklahoma], 24 August 1937; all three letters in WPA Notes on Interviews.
   [2] For background on the 1921 Tulsa race riot, see the narrative of Salomon Oliver,
below.

INTERVIEW WITH LIZZIE JACKSON[1]

Ex-Slave, About 88 Years Old   *21st St., and Topeka Ave.,*
                                                                    Muskogee, Oklahoma

I was born on Master Ned Yarger's plantation on the Mississippi river.
Don't know the name of the place, just remember the river and the
boats that use to come to the landing place. That old river took the
lives of folks just like the war.

   My brother Ned was one of them. He always went down to the
landing when the boat come in. He would hear the whistle from
away off and streak out to beat the boat in.

   One day the "Miss Myrtle" was about ready to go on down stream.
She was a center wheel boat. Instead of having the big paddle wheel
on the side, that boat's wheel was in the middle. It was the only one
like it I ever saw.

   Well, all the folks that was leaving had got onto the boat and the
plank was took down, when my brother Ned took a fool notion to get
on the boat. Nobody ever knew why he wanted to do that, for he
wasn't going any place. The boat was away from the landing, but I

guess not very far. Anyway, Ned tried to jump from the bank onto the boat. He missed it. That's the last we ever saw of him and Pappy said that a big fish must of got him. Guess it must have been an alligator.

Then the master's son Ned was the next to go. He was always a sickly boy and never do any thing much around the place. Just sit and watch. But one day he went with a fishing party to boat the river. Somehow he fell out or else the boat went down and he was drowned.

It was a month later when the body was found. Nobody in the slave quarters got to see him, though. All we ever saw was something under a white sheet being toted into the big house.

My own folks was named Rose and William Caesar. Where they got that name I can't say. Maybe my pappy was a free man once and got the name, but all I ever go by was Caesar, Yarger and then Jackson.

It was a cruel world during them war days. The old master lost most everything he had during that time. He had most about one hundred slaves on his place, and slave quarters was row and rows of log huts.

Each of the cabins had a rock fireplace. But I never saw any chairs or furniture, excepting what was in the master's house or on the front porch. We had rags and benches to rest on. The beds was just planks nailed around to keep in the straw what we slept on. That's all.

The plantation was loaded with cows, hogs, sheep and goats when the war come along. Before that happened we always had plenty to eat and still during the first year after war was declared. There was lots of days there was nothing to eat except of meat rines.

Finally the war got so hot that old master up and left the place, leaving the slaves behind with young master Dave, his only son since Ned died.

The soldiers come to the plantation. They was Yankee soldiers I reckon for they burned the buildings, took what little food stuffs they could find and then sure enough we was hungry. Everybody almost starve to death. Some of the negroes did die with starvation. Everywhere was the same, not just on our place.

Young master looked after what was left of the slaves. He was a Creek Indian, a big, big man in size, and good to everybody. He took us all to a place he called Canadian creek. (That must have been a settlement on Oklahoma's Canadian river.)

There wasn't many of my own family left by that time. They was killed off with the guns and some died starved.

Master Dave took the best care of me until after the war was over. And then he come to see me right here in Muskogee a long time after

I was free. He stayed in the house all night and talked about his father who never did come back from the war. Mistress Polly, Dave's mother, was with him.

When I went to fix up the bed for Master Dave that night he said, "No, I'll just tuck-a-liser right here by the fire." And that's where he slept.

I'm glad that slave days is gone. Even if the master was good the slaves was bad off. Like the time they sold one of the women on our plantation.

That woman was one of the best workers on the place. Always happy, full of life, and could work better in the fields than lots of the men.

Then come along a slave buyer. It was about eating time and the buyer looked at the woman and talked with the master. They didn't put her on no auction block, just looked at her while she waiting for a place at the table.

Then master spoke to her. "Mary," he said, "hurry up and eat. That man done bought you and wants you to eat before he takes you with him."

Mary didn't answer. She just quit laughing and fell to the floor. Fainted. But she was took away just the same.

¹ Only one version of the Lizzie Jackson narrative is available, a typescript prepared on the back side of blank WPA stationery. Field worker Ethel Wolfe Garrison interviewed Mrs. Jackson in Muskogee, Oklahoma, probably in spring 1938, for on 23 May of that year project employee Craig Vollmer edited the interview to create the narrative surviving today. It is available as the ribbon-copy typescript "Interview with Lizzie Jackson, Ex-Slave, About 88 Years Old, 21st St., and Topeka Ave., Muskogee, Oklahoma" in the OHS Slave Narratives. This interview was never forwarded to Washington.

LEWIS JENKINS¹

Age 93 Yrs.   *Oklahoma City, Okla.*

I was born in Green County, Alabama in January 1844.

My mother was a white woman and her name was Jane Jenkins. My father was a nigger. He was a coachman on my Master's place. I was told this in 1880 by the white doctor, Lyth Smith, which brung me into the world. My Master, who was my grandfather, brung me to Texas when I was jest 7 or 8 years old. A few years later, he brung my mother down to Texas and she had with her three boys, which was her children and my brothers. They was white children and name

Jones. They first names was Tom, Joe and Lije. They parted from me and I never heered no more about 'em. I didn't even know my mother when I seen her. All my life I done jest knowed my white kinfolks and nothing 'tall about the other part of my color.

Before I was born, my mother was tucken away from her playmates and kept in the attic hid. They tuck me soon as I was born from her. When her time to be in bed was up, she'd ask the waitman[2] whar I was at. The waitman was Dr. Lyth Smith. He'd tell her I was at Ann's house. I never got a chance to nurse my mother. After she got up and come down, she wanted to see her baby. Now she goes to Ann's house and couldn't find me. After she couldn't find me there, she looked in all the houses on the place for me, her baby. Then she commenced screaming, tearing her clothes off and tearing her hair out. They sent her to the calaboose till they could git her some clothes to put on. She went distracted. She tore out towards town. The way they got her to hush, they tole her I was with my grandma. They had me hid on the road to Texas. The doctor's wife said I was the first nigger she shed a tear over. It was a destruction thing. Well, that scandalized the family and they moved to Texas, and come by and got me and tuck me to Texas. When they crossed the big river, Tom Bigby River in Alabama,[3] 3 miles wide on boat, the woman that had me in hand, was just churning me up and down in the river. They hollered at her, and I says that there's whar God tuck me in his bosom. When I was 7 or 8 years old, the white folks tuck me in charge. They was gonna make me a watchman to watch for 'em at night.[4] But when they begun this, I wasn't old enough to remember.

The first house I was sont to, was the cook's house. The cook said, "what you come down heah for?" I told her I didn't know. "Who sont you?" I said, "Old Master Jenkins." She knowed 'mediately what I was sont for, don't you see? She says to me, "Set down little rascal[5] I'll knock you in the head." Well, what could I do but set, child lak. Before long I was asleep and they tuck me out door. Next mawning I was told to go to the big house. Old Master axe "What'd you see last night?" I told him I didn't seed nothing. Now they got the cow hide an' hit me three of four licks and axe me 'at same question agin. I tole 'em I didn't seed nothing. This went on for 'bout a hour. I had to take a whipping ever mawning, 'cause I had to go to ever house and never seen nothing. The last house I went to, well, in the mawning as I was gwine back to the big house, a voice come to me and said, "See nothing, tell nothing." It meant for me not to lie and on and on as I growed for years to come, as I was big enough to plow corn, I was out in the field and a voice, that same voice too, said, "Iffen I was you, I'd leave this place, 'cause you'll come to want and won't have." All this was the causing of my conversion.

My first job was scouring floors and I mean I scoured 'em too. Next I scoured knives and forks. From 'at job I went into real work, and no play.

My master and his family jest lived in a log house. My mistress was my grandfather's wife and my grandmother, but I couldn't claim her. Her and her oldest child treated me some rough. I never had no good time till that old white woman died, and talking about somebody glad she died, I sure was. They tuck turns about treating me bad.

There was about 20 slaves on our place, children and all. Dewan, which was my uncle, was the overseer. He waked us up jest before sunrise and we worked from sun to sun. I seen 'em tie niggers hand and foot to mill posts and whip 'em with bull whips. Them was neighbors' though, not our'n. They whipped the women by pulling they dresses down to they hips and beat 'em till they was satisfied. For myself, my grandfather whipped me till his dog tuck pity on me and tried to drag me away. This is the scar on my leg whar he pulled on me. He was beating me till I said, "Oh! Pray Master." He didn't tell me till after he was through beating me though.

I seen 'em sell people what wasn't able to work from the block jest lak cattle. They would be chained togedder. They tuck mothers from children even just a week old and sell 'em. They stripped the slaves, women and all, and let the bidders look at 'em to see iffen they was scarred before they would buy 'em.

Them old white folks wouldn't learn us to read and write and wouldn't let they youngins learn us. My youngest mistress, which was my auntie 'mind you, was trying to| learn me to read and write and was caught and she got some whipping, almost a killing.

I never seen but one nigger man hung. He was crippled and had run away. I seen dis[6] wid my own eyes, no guess work. He had caught a little white girl, school girl, too, ravaged her and cut off her tongue off. Oh, that was barbous. He oughta been burnt. He didn't git his jest due at hanging.

Patterollers was sure through the country. They was out to keep down nigger and white mixing and to keep niggers from having liberty to go out 'specially at night. They didn't 'low you to come to see a gal 'less she was 18 and you was 21. The cause of this was to raise good stock. The gals couldn't marry till they was 18 neither, but dey could have children. You had to have a pass to go see your gal even. Now you got your pass from your master. Iffen you was under 15, you could go play and didn't need no pass, but all over 15 jest had to have a pass.

They would go right to bed after they et. No Saturday off, jest washday. Some Sundays old mistress let us have sugar, flour and lard.[7]

We was in a great game country and sure et our fill of coons, 'possums, rabbits, deer, turkeys and the sich and things people wouldn't notice now. Cornbread and sweet potatoes was my fav-*rite* foods. Milk and butter was best eating.

We jest wore what you call slips wid jest two sleeves slipped over our head. No buttons. We wore the same thing in winter, jest heavier. Never wore no shoes till I was old enough to chop cotton.

At weddings they wore stripes all the time. They made 'em on hand looms. They was mostly white and red stripes.

We played marbles and ring plays. We used to sing this ditty during playing:

> So many pretty gals
> So they say
> So many pretty gals
> So they say.
> Jest peep through the window Susie gal.

They used to scare me death talking 'bout ole raw head and bloody bones out in the yard. For me, that meant staying in a mighty long time and having a fit to boot.

We used onions to keep off consumption. They was a family taken the black disease and they all died but one and he was ready to die. They tuck him out to burn the house up to keep that disease from spreading. They put the nigger in a house full of onions and he got sure enough well. The doctor said the onions had cured him. We sure believed in our onions and do till today. Even the next mawning after he was put in the house and couldn't walk he axe for some milk.

That war that freed the niggers started in 1861. I had two young Masters to go. It lasted 4 years. They was figuring on taking me that very next year, and it was so fixed that the war ended. We had a big drought during the war, which made it bad on the soldiers. I never seen the Yankees only when they was passing 'long the road. One day whilst we was eating our dinner, our Master said, "All you, young and old, when you git through come out on the gallery, I got something to tell you." When we got through we all trooped out and he said,

"This is military law, but I am forced to tell you." He says, "This law says free the nigger, so now you is jest as free as me by this law. I can't make you all stay wid me 'less you want to, therefore you can go any place you want to." That was about laying-by crop time in June. It was on June 19th an' we still celebrates 'at day in Texas, 'at is "Nigger Day" down there. He say, "I'd lak for you to stay till the crops is laid by iffen you will." Iffen it hadn't been for his wife maybe we would've stayed on, but she jest kept bossing the nigger women and we jest didn't lak it and that's what brung on the scatter. I left my old Master and went wid one of my young Masters, which was my uncle.

I was sure once tickled at my young Master. I done broke in a mule for him and he got on him one night and go jine the Ku Klux band. He had to go 'bout 4 miles. He got jest 'bout one mile and they come to two trees with a real white stone in 'twixt the trees. The mule seen this and throwed my Master off and hurt him something terrible. He come back and told his wife what done happened. He said, "Damn the Ku Klux." He never went to jine 'em no more.

I never went to school in my life. Never had the opportunity, 'cause I never had no kinfolks to own me or give me advice or help me. White kinfolks jest bossed me. I was jest lak a orphan. White folks will mess you up and be so treacherous.

I married Jane Deckers. The white man jest read out of the Bible and put our names and ages in the Bible and 'at was all the ceremony we had. I got three children and four grandchildren. One do stone work, another brick work and my daughter, housework.

I think Abe Lincoln was next to Jesus Christ. The best human man ever lived. He died helping the poor nigger man. Old Jeff Davis was right in his place. He was trying to help his race. He wasn't nothing lak right. It was God's plan that ever man be free. I don't believe Davis believed in right.

I am sure glad slavery is over. I glory in it. I trust and pray it'll never be again.

I think the church is the gospel way and ever body ought to be on it. The Baptist is my dear belief, 'cause I was baptized by the spirit and then by the water, nothing but the Baptist. I belongs to the Shiloh Baptist Church, right here on the West Side.[8]

[1] Lewis Jenkins was interviewed at his home in Oklahoma City by WPA field worker Ida Belle Hunter on 15 June 1937. An early draft of the narrative based on the interview is available as the typescript "Interview with Lewis Jenkins, Ex-Slave, Aged 93, 18 So. Douglass, Oklahoma City, Oklahoma" in the OHS Slave Narratives. A note

card appended to a later draft of the narrative is dated 15 November 1937. This later version, which incorporates editorial markings written by hand on the earlier draft, is available as the typescript "Lewis Jenkins, Age 93 Yrs., Oklahoma City, Okla." in the OHS Slave Narratives and is published here. Neither draft of the narrative was ever sent to Washington. For a remembrance of Lewis Jenkins by another of the informants in the Oklahoma Slave Narrative Project, see the narrative of Carrie E. Davis, above. *Oklahoma City Negro City Directory,* 94; *Polk's Oklahoma City Directory, 1937,* 382, 845.

[2] The preliminary typescript at this point has written in pencil within parentheses the words "waiting man."

[3] An apparent reference to the Tombigbee River of northeastern Mississippi and western Alabama.

[4] In the preliminary draft the preceding two sentences read: "Now you may say, on an' on as I growed, then I was 7 or 8 years old when the white folks tuck me in charge. They was gonna make a watchman outta me to watch fer 'em at night."

[5] The preliminary version adds here the phrase "wid her fis' drawed back."

[6] The preliminary draft at this word adds the direct address "honey."

[7] The preliminary version of the narrative presents this sentence as follows: "On Sunday, old mistress let us have sugar, flour and lard, but jes' some Sundays. No other day doe."

[8] Shiloh Baptist Church was located at 1 South Brauer in Oklahoma City. *Oklahoma City Negro City Directory,* 215.

NELLIE JOHNSON[1]

I don't know how old I is, but I is a great big half grown gal when the time of the War come, and I can remember how everything look at that time, and what all the people do, too.

I'm pretty nigh to blind right now, and all I can do is set on this little old front porch and maybe try to keep the things picked up behind my grandchild and his wife, because she has to work and he is out selling wood most of the time.

But I didn't have to live in any such a house during the time I was young like they is, because I belonged to old Chief Rolley McIntosh,[2] and my pappy and mammy have a big, nice, clean log house to live in, and everything round it look better than most renters got these days.

We never did call old Master anything but the Chief or the General for that's what everybody called him in them days, and he never did act towards us like we was slaves, much anyways. He was the mikko of the Kawita town long before the War and long before I was borned, and he was the chief of the Lower Creeks even before he got to be the chief of all the Creeks.

But just at the time of the War the Lower Creeks stayed with him and the Upper Creeks, at least them that lived along to the south of where we live, all go off after that old man Gouge, and he take most of the Seminole too.[3] I hear [of] old Tuskenugge, the big man with the Seminoles, but I never did see him, nor mighty few of the Seminoles.

My mammy tells me old General ain't been living in that Kawita town very many years when I was borned. He come up there from down in the fork of the river where the Arkansas and the Verdigris run together a little while after all the last of the Creeks come out to the Territory. His brother old Chili McIntosh,[4] live down in that forks of the rivers too, but I don't think he ever move up into that Kawita town. It was in the narrow stretch where the Verdigris come close to the Arkansas. They got a pretty good sized white folks' town there now they call Coweta, but the old Creek town was different from that. The folks lived all around in that stretch between the rivers, and my old Master was the boss of all of them.

For a long time after the Civil War they had a court at the new town called Coweta court, and a school house too, but before I was born they had a mission school down the Kawita Creek from where the town now is.

Earliest I can remember about my master was when he come to the slave settlement where we live and get out of the buggy and show a preacher all around the place. That preacher named Mr. Loughridge, and he was the man had the mission down on Kawita Creek before I was born, but at that time he had a school off at some other place.[5] He git down out of the buggy and talk to all us children, and ask us how we getting along.

I didn't even know at that time that old Chief was my master, until my pappy tell me after he was gone. I think all the time he was another preacher.

My pappy's name was Jackson McIntosh, and my mammy was Hagar. I think old Chief bring them out to the Territory when he come out with his brother Chili and the rest of the Creek people. My pappy tell me that old Master's pappy was killed by the Creeks because he signed up a treaty to bring his folks out here, and old Master always hated that bunch of Creeks that done that.[6]

I think old man Gouge was one of the big men in that bunch, and he fit in the War on the Government side, after he done holler and go on so about the Government making him come out here.

Old Master have lots of land took up all around that Kawita place, and I don't know how much, but a lot more than anybody else. He have it all fenced in with good rail fence, and all the Negroes have all the horses and mules and tools they need to work it with. They all live in good log houses they built themselves, and [have] everything they need.

Old Master's land wasn't all in one big field, but a lot of little fields scattered all over the place. He just take up land what already was a kind of prairie, and the niggers don't have to clear up much woods.

We all live around on them little farms, and we didn't have to be under any overseer like the Cherokee Negroes had lots of times. We didn't have to work if they wasn't no work to do that day.

Everybody could have a little patch of his own, too, and work it between times, on Saturdays and Sundays if he wanted to. What he made on that patch belong to him, and the old Chief never bothered the slaves about anything.

Every slave can fix up his own cabin any way he want to, and pick out a good place with a spring if he can find one. Mostly the slave houses had just one big room with a stick-and-mud chimney, just like the poor people among the Creeks had. Then they had a brush shelter built out of four poles with a roof made out of brush, set out to one side of the house where they do the cooking and eating, and sometimes the sleeping too. They set there when they is done working, and lay around on corn shuck beds, because they never did use the log house much only in cold and rainy weather.

Old Chief just treat all the Negroes like they was just hired hands, and I was a big girl before I knowed very much about belonging to him.

I was one of the youngest children in my family; only Sammy and Millie was younger than I was. My big brothers was Adam, August and Nero, and my big sisters was Flora, Nancy and Rhoda. We could work a mighty big patch for our own selves when we was all at home together, and put in all the work we had to for the old Master too, but after the War the big children all get married off and took up land of they own.

Old Chief lived in a big log house made double with a hall in between, and a lot of white folks was always coming there to see him about something. He was gone off somewhere a lot of the time, too, and he just trusted the Negroes to look after his farms and stuff. We would just go on out in the fields and work the crops just like they was our own, and he never come around excepting when we had harvest time, or to tell us what he wanted planted.

Sometimes he would send a Negro to tell us to gather up some chickens or turkeys or shoats he wanted to sell off, and sometimes he would send after loads of corn and wheat to sell. I heard my pappy say old Chief and Mr. Chili McIntosh was the first ones to have any wheat in the Territory, but I don't know about that.

Along during the War the Negro men got pretty lazy and shiftless, but my pappy and my big brothers just go right on and work like they always did. My pappy always said we better off to stay on the place and work good and behave ourselves because old Master take care of us that way. But on lots of other places the men slipped off.

I never did see many soldiers during the War, and there wasn't any fighting close to where we live. It was kind of down in the bottoms, not far from the Verdigris and that Gar Creek, and the soldiers would have bad crossings if they come by our place.

We did see some whackers riding around sometimes, in little bunches of about a dozen, but they never did bother us and never did stop. Some of the Negro girls that I knowed of mixed up with the poor Creeks and Seminoles, and some got married to them after the War, but none of my family ever did mix up with them that I knows of.

Along towards the last of the War I never did see old Chief come around any more, and somebody say he went down into Texas. He never did come back that I knows of, and I think he died down there.

One day my pappy come home and tell us all that the Creek done sign up to quit the War, and that old Master send word that we all free now and can take up some land for our own selves or just stay where we is if we want to. Pappy stayed on that place where he was at until he died.

I got to be a big girl and went down to work for a Creek family close to where they got that Checotah town now. At that time it was just all a scattered settlement of Creeks and they call it Eufala town. After while I marry a man name Joe Johnson, at a little settlement they call Rentiesville. He have his freedmen's allotment close to that place, but mine is up on the Verdigris, and we move up there to live.[7]

We just had one child, named Louisa, and she married Tom Armstrong. They had three–four children but one was named Tom, and it is him I live with now.[8] My husband's been dead a long, long time now.

[1] WPA field worker Robert Vinson Lackey interviewed Mrs. Nellie Johnson in Tulsa, Oklahoma, sometime probably in summer 1937, for the preliminary draft of her narrative was edited and typed by project personnel prior to the mailing of a final draft to Washington on 13 August 1937. The preliminary draft of the interview is available

as the typescript "Interview with Nellie Johnson, Ex-Slave, Age about 90 Yrs. (Living with grandson, Tom Armstrong, 1011 East Pine St., Tulsa, Oklahoma)" in the OHS Slave Narratives. The later draft, which varies only slightly from the earlier except for uniformity in the presentation of dialect, and which is published here, is available as the typescript "Nellie Johnson" in ribbon copy in the LC Slave Narratives and in carbon copy as item 350101 in the LC Slave Narratives Carbon Copies and in the OHS Slave Narratives. Stephens to Cronyn, 13 August 1937, WPA Notes on Interviews.

[2] For a biographical sketch of Roley McIntosh, Creek leader, or mikko, see John Bartlett Meserve, "The MacIntoshes," *Chronicles of Oklahoma* 10 (September 1932): 318–20.

[3] For more on this incident, see the narrative of Phoebe Banks, above.

[4] For a biographical sketch of Chilly McIntosh, see Meserve, "The MacIntoshes," 320–21.

[5] The Reverend Robert McGill Loughridge, missionary and educator, first came to the Creek Nation in the Indian Territory representing the Presbyterian Board of Foreign Missions in 1843. In 1844 he founded a boarding school at Kowetah, but within a short time it proved to be too small to accommodate all the Creek children seeking admission. Consequently in 1849 he opened a new boarding school at Tullahassee, which operated there for many years serving both Creeks and Creek freedmen. Bass, *Story of Tullahassee,* 1–269; Lauderdale, "Tullahassee Mission," 285–300; Robert M. Loughridge, "History of Mission Work among the Creek Indians from 1832 to 1888 under the Direction of the Board of Foreign Missions, Presbyterian Church in the U.S.A.," 1–15.

[6] For background on the death of William McIntosh, who was assassinated by other Creeks in 1824 for signing a treaty ceding tribal lands to the United States government, see Angie Debo, *The Road to Disappearance,* pp. 89–90; Meserve, "The MacIntoshes," 313–18.

[7] The Dawes Commission enrolled Nellie Johnson, her daughter, and two grandchildren as freedmen members of the Creek Nation on 28 March 1902, and this formality led to their receipt of land allotments. Creek Freedmen Census Cards, no. 874 (Nellie Johnson, Louisa Manuel, Arthur Malvern, and Mattie Murrell).

[8] According to a roughly contemporary Tulsa city directory, the 1011 East Pine address for Nellie Johnson cited in the prelimininary draft of her narrative was the home of Thomas and Clara Watson, not Armstrong. *Polk's Tulsa City Directory, 1935,* 564, 696.

MRS. JOSIE JORDAN[1]

Age 75 Yrs.   *Tulsa, Oklahoma*

I was born right in the middle of the War on the Mark Lowery plantation at Sparta, in White County, Tennessee, so I don't know anything much about them slave days except what my mammy told me long years ago. 'Course I mean the Civil War, for to us colored folks they just wasn't no other war as mean as that one.

My mother she come from Virginia when a little girl, but never nobody tells me where at my pappy is from. His name was David Lowery when I was born, but I guess he had plenty other names, for like my mammy he was sold lots of times.

Salina was my mammy's name, and she belonged to a Mister Clark, who sold her and pappy to Mark Lowery 'cause she was a fighting, mule-headed woman.

It wasn't her fault 'cause she was a fighter. The Master who owned her before Mister Clark was one of them white mens who was always whipping and beating his slaves and mammy couldn't stand it no more.

That's the way she tells me about it. She just figured she would be better off dead and out of her misery as to be whipped all the time, so one day the master claimed they was something wrong with her work and started to raise his whip, but mammy fought back and when the ruckus was over the Master was laying still on the ground and folks thought he was dead, he got such a heavy beating.

Mammy says he don't die and right after that she was sold to Mister Clark I been telling you about. And mammy was full of misery for a long time after she was carried to Mark Lowery's plantation where at I was born during the War.

She had two children while belonging to Mister Clark and he wouldn't let them go with mammy and pappy. That's what caused her misery. Pappy tried to ease her mind but she jest kept a'crying for her babies, Ann and Reuban, till Master Lowery got Clark to leave them visit with her once a month.

Mammy always says that Mark Lowery was a good master. But he'd heard things about mammy before he got her and I reckon was curious to know if they was all true. Mammy says he found out might[y] quick they was.

It was mammy's second day on the plantation and Mark Lowery acted like he was going to whip her for something she'd done or hadn't, but mammy knocked him plumb through the open cellar door. He wasn't hurt, not even mad, for mammy says he climbed out the cellar a'laughing, saying he was only fooling to see if she would fight.

But mammy's troubles wasn't over then, for Mark Lowery he got hisself a new young wife (his first wife was dead), and mammy was round of the house most of the time after that.

Right away they had trouble. The Mistress was trying to make mammy hurry up with the work and she hit mammy with the broom stick.[2] Mammy's mule temper boiled up all over the kitchen and the Master had to stop the fighting.

He wouldn't whip mammy for her part in the trouble, so the Mistress she sent word to her father and brothers and they come to Mister Lowery's place.

They was going to whip mammy, they was good and mad. Master was good and mad, too, and he warned 'em home.

"Whip your own slaves." He told them. "Mine have to work and if they're beat up they can't do a day's work. Get home—I'll take care of this." And they left.

My folks didn't have no food troubles at Mark Lowery's like they did somewheres else. I remember mammy told me about one master who almost starved his slaves. Mighty stingy I reckon he was.

Some of them slaves was so poorly thin they ribs would kinder rustle against each other like corn stalks a-drying in the hot winds. But they gets even one hog-killing time, and it was funny too, mammy said.

They was seven hogs, fat and ready for fall hog-killing time. Just the day before old Master told off they was to be killed something happened to all them porkers. One of the field boys found them and come a-telling the Master: "The hogs is all died, now they won't be any meats for the winter."

When the Master gets to where the hogs is laying, they's a lot of Negroes standing round looking sorrow-eyed at the wasted meat. The Master asks: "What's the illness with 'em?"

"Malitis," they tell him, and they acts like they don't want to touch the hogs. Master says to dress them anyway for they ain't no more meat on the place.

He says to keep all the meat for the slave families, but that's because he's afraid to eat it hisself account of the hogs' got malitis.

"Don't you-all know what is Malitis?" Mammy would ask the children when she was telling of the seven fat hogs and seventy lean slaves. And she would laugh, remembering who they fooled, the old master, so's to get all them good meats.

"One of the strongest Negroes got up early in the morning," Mammy would explain, "long 'fore the rising horn called the slaves from their cabins. He skitted to the hog pen with a heavy mallet in his hand. When he tapped Mister Hog 'tween the eyes with that mallet 'malitis' set in mighty quick, but it was a uncommon 'disease,' even with hungry Negroes around all the time."

There was a public road going by the plantation and lots of Yankees rode along the road after the War was over on their way home. Sometime during the War a rebel bushwhacker, man by the name of Champ Ferguson, was captured, but what happened to him I was never told.

Some of the slaves was pretty anxious for freedom. They'd run away, or try to, to the North. Sometimes the Rebs would dress up in Yankee clothes and come around the fields talking with the slaves, telling them to run away and they would tell them there wasn't any use of working like they did—tell them anything to make them want to leave.

And what happened when the slaves would sneak away. I'll tell you. The Rebs killed him! Sometimes he'd be found shot dead a little ways in the woods, then sometimes he'd be whipped and die from the beating.

Mother told about how they tried to get my father in one of their traps. He wouldn't listen to them. Said he was going to stay with the Master, do his work right and wouldn't ever talk about running away. The Rebs cussed him for a fool Negro, but father told them it was the fools what tried to get away![3]

It was a long time after the War and we was all freed before we left old Master Lowery. Stayed right there where we was at home, working in the fields, living in the same old cabins, just like before the War. Never did have no big troubles after the war, except one time the Ku Klux Klan broke up a church meeting and whipped some of the Negroes.

The preacher was telling about the Bible days when the Klan rode up. They was all masked up and everybody crawled under the benches when they shouted: "We'll make you damn niggers wish you wasn't free!"

And they just about did. The preacher got the worst whipping, blood was running from his nose and mouth and ears, and they left him laying on the floor.

They whipped the women just like the men, but Mammy and the girls wasn't touched none and we run all the way back to the cabin. Layed down with all our clothes on and tried to sleep, but we's too scairt to close our eyes.

Mammy reckoned old Master Lowery was a-riding with the Klan that night, else we'd got a flogging too.

We first moved about a mile from Master Lowery's place and ever week we'd ask mammy if we children could go to see old Master and she'd say: "Yes, if you-all are good niggers." The old Master was always glad to see us children and he would give us candy and apples and treat us mighty fine.

In 1882, I was married to James Jordan down in Tennessee. He is dead now and three of the seven children are dead, too. All their names were, Frank, Mary Liza, Peter, Lowery, Daisy, Bennie, Hattie. The ones living are just farming around, one in Oklahoma and three in California. I moved to Guthrie in 1900, and came to Tulsa some years after that, but can't remember the exact date.

The old plantation's gone, the old Master's gone, the old slaves is gone, and I'll be going some of these days, too, for I been here a mighty long time and they ain't nobody needs me now 'cause I is too old for any good.

[1] WPA field worker L. P. Livingston interviewed Mrs. Josie Jordan in Tulsa twice during the summer of 1937. A typescript of his first interview was forwarded to Oklahoma City on 11 July 1937, and this draft was retyped in the Oklahoma City office with virtually no editorial changes and sent to Federal Writers' Project headquarters in Washington on 13 August. In the meantime, however, the Tulsa office received instructions from the head of the Oklahoma Writers' Project for a field worker to return for a second interview to obtain more information from Mrs. Jordan, recording her remembrances *"word for word."* Within only a matter of days an unidentified interviewer, probably Livingston, reinterviewed the elderly woman, preparing a revised narrative that includes several paragraphs of material found in none of the other typescripts. Even though the earlier version sent to Washington lacked some of the material included in the reinterview, Federal Writers' Project folklore editor Benjamin A. Botkin was highly impressed with Josie Jordan's narrative, noting that it represented a "vivid recreation of [her] mother's experiences." He even included Mrs. Jordan's "Malitis" story in his 1945 study, *Lay My Burden Down* (4–5, 271).

Three distinct typescripts have virtually identical texts of the earlier version of the Josie Jordan narrative. These include "Interview with Mrs. Josie Jordan, 840 East King St., Tulsa, Ex-Slave, Age 75, Born July 20, 1862," in ribbon copy in the OHS Slave Narratives; "Mrs. Josie Jordan, Age 75 Yrs., 840 East King St., Tulsa, Oklahoma," in ribbon copy in the LC Slave Narratives and in carbon copy as item 350095 in the LC Slave Narratives Carbon Copies and in the OHS Slave Narratives; and another ribbon-copy typescript with the almost identical title "Mrs. Josie Jordan, Age 75, 840 East King St., Tulsa, Okla." in the OHS Slave Narratives. Tulsa city directories indicate Josie Jordan's address to have been 640 East King Street, not 840 as shown on the interview transcripts. The latest Josie Jordan narrative, which includes several paragraphs found in none of the other versions and which is published here, is available only in the ribbon-copy typescript "Mrs. Josie Jordan, Age 75 Yrs., Tulsa, Oklahoma" in the OHS Slave Narratives.

[B. A. Botkin], LC Slave Narratives Appraisal Sheets, Accession no. 350095, 11 December 1940; *Polk's Tulsa City Directory, 1934,* 286, 599; *Polk's Tulsa City Directory, 1935,* 323, 664; Craig Vollmer, Tulsa, Oklahoma, to [William] Cunningham, [Oklahoma City, Oklahoma], 11 July 1937; Stephens to Lackey, 10 August 1937; Stephens to Cronyn, 13 August 1937; Craig Vollmer, Tulsa, [Oklahoma], to [Ned] DeWitt, [Oklahoma City, Oklahoma], 24 August 1937; all letters in WPA Notes on Interviews.

[2] The earliest draft of Mrs. Josie Jordan's narrative states "broom handle," but "handle" is struck and "stick" written in pencil above it.

[3] At this point all of the other drafts include two sentences that appear to have been

omitted inadvertently from the last version: "Mammy had me, three sisters and a brother while on the Lowery Plantation. They was Liza, Addie, Alice and Lincoln."

SAM JORDAN[1]

Age ___ Yrs.   *Oklahoma City, Okla.*

In asking him questions he would reply as following:

Born in Crenshaw County, Alabama. I don't know my age; they never told me my age.

My mother was name Polly Nichols before she married my father whose name was Henry Jordan. After they were married my father had permission to leave his Master's plantation and come over to her Master's plantation to see her twice a week, viz: Wednesdays and Saturday nights. My father was a half Cherokee Indian. I was the only child. I was not old enough to work before freedom. I played in the streets of days while my mother and father work for Master Nichols and Jordan. I had one pair of shoes a year for winter. There were no schools so us children only played during the days.

Our beds were made of striped ticking cloth with a long slit in the middle where grass or shucks was stuffed in and could be sewed[2] up, they termed, making up the beds for soft sleeping. The beds were made of wood when there was a bed.

The only food we had was furnished us from Master's smoke house.

There were no individual gardens. The cooking was done on fireplaces in pots, skillets with lids and corn cakes called Jonny cakes roasted or baked on the hearth. The plantation was 4 miles long and far in width, he said.

There were about 75 or 100 slaves on the plantation who worked as early as they could see and till 'twas too late or dark to see, and sometime on bright moon shiny nights.

The slaves were not taught to read till after freedom. At nights the slaves would at nights slip around in the quarters and even from plantation to plantation as they worked from Monday morning till Saturday nights. On Sunday mornings they would go and get their rations for the week consisting most of meal, meat, black molasses, lard, rice, a cooking of flour for Sunday, and some seasoning, as salt, soda, etc.

After freedom I courted and married a girl in Montgomery County, which joined my county. She was name Mattie Murray and my first wife.

My Master owned two large plantations joining each other and his

house sat about the middle of them. His house was a big 2-story
white house with a large yard in which a large ration house called
smoke house sat off to one side. He had 6 children, 2 boys and 4 girls.
The quarters were long, and built of logs and called Nichols quarters.

There were two overseers, one for each plantation and they both
poor and mean. They would punish by whipping with bullwhip if
the slaves failed to work to suit them.

The slaves wuz not taught at all but some of them managed to
learn to read and write by another slave. My master bought and when
the overseers found out that this Negro could read and write and was
teaching the other slaves they whipped him giving him 500 lashes
and cut off his index finger so that he could not write nor teach the
other slaves.

After freedom a teacher from the North was sent to teach the
slaves. This white lady taught our school and slaves for 2 years. Her
name was Miss Clanzy and the blue back speller was our school
book. For some reason she went back home and a man, Mr. Cot-
tridge, came in her place. Each morning he would read the Bible and
pray and then teach Bible lessons to us. He was a whale of a good
teacher.

As my Master had so many slaves, now and then one would run
away and as he also kept 5 or 6 Negro hounds in which to catch them
these hounds would run all through the quarters and through the
Negro houses hunting for runaway slaves and wouldn't bother any of
the other Negroes but would catch the runaway and if the runaway
would fight them they would jump on him and bite him so badly
they would have to get a doctor for him, and if he didn't fight them
they would just find him and stand around him and bark tremen-
dously until Master and overseers came. Sometime some of the runaways would kill hounds and get away and some of them would
smear fresh cow manure under the bottom of their feet so that the
blood hounds couldn't scent them.

In asking him did you ever see any patrollers he replied: "I seen
them but I never had any tarry with um."

When a slave took sick the overseers would go to see about them
and if serious would get a doctor who would come and give them
blue-mass pills. If one would die they would make one of the slaves
take him in a wagon and take him to the woods and dig a little hole
and put him in.

The Negro slaves were very superstitious and believed in voodooism. All of them wore a silver dime on a raw cotton thread around their ankles to keep from being voodooed.

On the day that the Yankees came to set us free, he says, "A dark cloud rose and brought darkness almost as night and the sun wasn't down." The Yankees after freedom also came to see that the Negroes attended school and the white people didn't bother them. They would put up tents in the quarters and stay around and see that the Negroes attended school each day.

As there were no land for the Negroes they continued to live in the quarters.

My first wife was name Mattie Murray. We had 12 children to live. After her death I married Magel Jordan and we had 1 child. I don't know much about my children by my first wife as they are still in Alabama. The child by my second wife is here with 2 grandchildren.[3]

In reply as to what he thinks of Abraham Lincoln he ways: "Will never git anothern." In reply as to Jeff Davis he said, "Jeff Davis was like Thomas Heffling, 'I don't know nothing good of 'em and can't say anything good 'bout um.'"[4]

Thomas Heffling, he said, was a Congressman from Georgia who went about making speeches after freedom and persuading Negroes to vote democratic tickets. I was freed by the republicans and will die a republican.

Heffling said in one of his speeches he was making to a white crowd that: "We educate Negroes to do what we tell them and if they don't we'll hang them to a limb."

In asking him about Booker T. Washington he said I think him a great man and next to Lincoln.

After freedom he said the Negroes made up this song:

> "Hung Jeff Davis in the sour apple tree,
> Hung Jeff Davis in the sour apple tree
> Hung Jeff Davis in the sour apple tree
> Now we go marching home."

Sung to the tune of the chorus of Glory, Glory Hallelujah.

I asked him: "Now that slavery is over what do you think of it," he says, "Well I can't [come] down on our Master," he replies in these words, "I can't come down on um so much perpendicular as he bought um, he ought to own um and have um."

This last question created upstir in the old man that he cried most sadly when I asked him concerning the overseer as poor white trash. He said, "You ask me dat question and I never talk to nobody 'bout dis," he said, "I seen him one day strip my mother's clothes down to her waist and made her own blood brother hold her while he beat her and that stirs my soul today and I don't want nobody to ask me bout it,[5] I don't talk 'bout it to nobody, I hate to think 'bout the dirty dogs."

[1] On 2 July 1937, WPA field worker J. S. Thomas interviewed the elderly Sam Jordan in Oklahoma City about his experiences as a slave in Alabama. Thomas's now lost notes were drafted into a handwritten narrative that subsequently was edited and placed in typewritten form. Today this interview survives only in two preliminary drafts in the OHS Slave Narratives, one the handwritten narrative "Story from Ex-Slaves, a Personal Interview, 612 North Missouri, Sam Jordan," and the other the typescript "Sam Jordan, Age Yrs., Oklahoma City, Okla.," published here. The typewritten draft has written in pencil near the title the comment "about 80 years old." This narrative was never sent to Washington.

[2] The typist was unable to read an apparently garbled word in the now lost notes and indicated its place with a blank space and a question mark in the text, to which someone later added in pencil "sewed." The manuscript version here reads "luicened" [loosened?].

[3] The contemporary Oklahoma City directory indicates Sam Jordan was residing with Estella Price, the widow of Warren P. Price, at 612 Missouri Avenue. *Polk's Oklahoma City Directory, 1937,* 398, 596, 882.

[4] James Thomas Heflin served in the U.S. House of Representatives from 1904 to 1920 and in the U.S. Senate from 1920 to 1931. One of the framers of the Alabama constitution of 1901, which disfranchised both blacks and many poor whites, he was known for decades as one of the most flamboyant demagogues in the South. David C. Roller and Robert W. Twyman, *Encyclopedia of Southern History,* 586.

[5] The words "I don't want nobody to ask me bout it" appear in the handwritten draft of the narrative but were omitted, apparently inadvertently, from the typewritten version.

"UNCLE" GEORGE G. KING[1]

Age 83 Yrs.   *Tulsa, Oklahoma*

"Prayers for sale . . . Prayers for sale . . ." Uncle George chants in sing-song fashion as he roams around Tulsa's Greenwood Negro district—pockets filled with prayer papers that are soiled and dirty with constant handling.

But they are potent, Uncle George tells those who fear the coming of some trouble, disaster or just ordinary misery, and there's a special prayer for each and every trouble—including one to keep away the bill collector when the young folks forget to make payments on the radio, the furniture, the car, or the Spring outfit purchased months ago from the credit clothier.

It's all in the Bible and the Bible is his workshop—'cause folks don't know how to pray.

He's mighty old, is Uncle George King, and he'll tell you that he was born on two-hundred acres of Hell, but the whitefolks called it Samuel Roll's plantation (six miles N.E. of Lexington, South Carolina).

Kinder small for a plantation, Uncle George explains, but plenty room for that devil overseer to lay on the lash, and plenty room for the old she-devil Mistress to whip his mammy 'til she was just a piece of living raw meat!

The old Master talked hard words, but the Mistress whipped. Lots of difference, and Uncle George ought to know, 'cause he's felt the lash layed on pretty heavy when he was no older than kindergarten children of today.

The Mistress owned the slaves and they couldn't be sold without her say-so. That's the reason George was never sold, but the Master once tried to sell him 'cause the beatings was breaking him down. Old Mistress said "No," and used it for an excuse to whip his Mammy. Uncle George remembers that, too.

They crossed her wrists and tied them with a stout cord. They made her bend over so that her arms was sticking back between her legs and fastened the arms with a stick so's she couldn't straighten up.

He saw the Mistress pull his Mammy's clothes over her head so's the lash would reach the skin. He saw the overseer lay on the whip with hide busting blows that left her laying, all a shiver, on the ground, like a wounded animal dying from the chase.

He saw the Mistress walk away, laughing, while his Mammy screamed and groaned—the old Master standing there looking sad and wretched, like he could feel the blows on Mamma's bared back and legs as much as she.

The Mistress was a great believer in the power of punishment, and Uncle George remembers the old log cabin jail built before the War, right on the plantation, where runaway slaves were stowed away till they would promise to behave themselves.

The old jail was full up during most of the War. Three runaway slaves were still chained to its floor when the Master gave word the Negroes were free.

They were Prince, Sanovey (his wife), and Henry, who were caught and whipped by the patrollers, and then brought back to the plantation for another beating before being locked in jail.

The Mistress ordered them chained, and the overseer would come every morning with the same question: "Will you niggers promise not to run-away no more?"

But they wouldn't promise. One at a time the overseer would loosen the chains, and lead them from the jail to cut them with powerful blows from the lash, then drag them back to be chained until the next day when more lickings were given 'cause they wouldn't promise.

The jail was emptied on the day Master roll called together all the men, women and children to tell them they wasn't slaves no more. Uncle George tells it this way:

"The Master he says we are all free, but it don't mean we is white. And it don't mean we is equal. Just equal for to work and earn our own living and not depend on him for no more meats and clothes."

Food was scarce before the War; it was worse after the shooting and killing was over, and Uncle George says: "There wasn't no corn bread, no bacon—just trash eating trash, like when General Sherman marched down through the country taking everything the soldiers could lug away, and burning all along the way.

"Wasn't nothing to eat after he march by. Darkies search 'round the barns, maybe find some grains of corn in the manure, and they'd parch the grains—nothing else to eat, except sometimes at night Mammy would skit out and steal scraps from the Master's house for the children.

"She had lots of hungry mouths, too. They was seven of us then, six boys and a girl, Eliza. The boys was Wesley, Simeon, Moses, Peter, William and me, George. This pappy's name was Griffin.

"But they was other pappys (Mammy told him) when Eva was born long before any of us, and Laura come next, but from a white daddy. Mammy lost them when she was sold around on the markets.

"The Klan they done lots of riding around the country. One night they come down to the old slave quarters where the cabins is all squared round each other, and called everybody outdoors. They's looking for two women.

"They picks 'em out of the crowd right quick and say they been with white men. Says their children is by white men, and they're going to get whipped so's they'll remember to stay with their own kind. The women kick and scream, but the mens grab them and roll them over a barrel and let fly with the whip."

It was a long time after the Civil War that Uncle George got his first schooling or attended regular church meetings. Like he says:

"Getting up at four o'clock in the morning, hoeing in the fields all day, doing chores when they come in from the fields, and then piddling with the weaver till nine or ten every night—it just didn't leave no time for reading and such, even if we was allowed to."

And religion, that came later too, for during the old plantation days Uncle George's white folks didn't think a Negro needed reli-gion—there wasn't a Heaven for Negroes anyhow.

Finally, though, the Master gave them right to hold meetings on the plantation, and old Peter Coon was the preacher. The overseer was there with guards to keep the Negroes from getting too much riled up when old Peter started talking about Paul or some of the things in the Old Testament. That's all he would talk about; nothing 'bout Jesus, just Paul and the Old Testament.

His Mammy went to every meeting. Like he says: "She knew them good things was good for her children and she told us about the Bible."

Like his old Mammy, Uncle George is a firm believer in the power of the word. "Prayers are Saving!" Uncle George says, "But they's lots of folks don't know how to pray."

That's why he has prayers for sale—and he knows they are never failing, "If you tack 'em up on the wall and say 'em over and over every day they's sure to be answered."

¹ George G. King was interviewed by an unidentified WPA field worker probably sometime in the spring or summer of 1937. On 10 August 1937 Ron Stephens, state administrator for the Works Progress Administration, commended Robert Vinson Lackey in the Tulsa office for the quality of recent interviews forwarded from that office, naming specifically that of King as "among the best that we have received." After editing in Oklahoma City, the text was sent to Washington on 2 September 1937. Only one version of the George G. King narrative is available, that sent to the federal capital under the title "'Uncle' George G. King, Age 83 Yrs., Tulsa, Oklahoma" and published here. The ribbon copy is in the LC Slave Narratives and carbon copies are available as item 350065 in the LC Slave Narratives Carbon Copies and in two discrete sets in the OHS Slave Narratives. Stephens to Lackey, 10 August 1937; Stephens to Cronyn, 2 September 1937; both letters in WPA Notes on Interviews.

MARTHA KING[1]

Age 85 Yrs.   *McAlester, Oklahoma*

"They hung Jeff Davis to a sour apple tree!
They hung Jeff Davis to a sour apple tree!
They hung Jeff Davis to a sour apple tree!
While we go marching on!"

Dat was de song de Yankees sang when they marched by our house. They didn't harm us in any way. I guess de War was over den 'cause a few days after dat old Master say, "Matt," and I say, "Suh?" He say, "Come here. You go tell Henry I say come out here and to bring the rest of the niggers with him." I went to the north door and I say, "Henry, Master Willis say ever one of you come out here." We all went outside and line up in front of old Master. He say, "Henry." Henry say, "Yes sah." Old Master say, "Every one of you is free—as free as I am. You all can leave or stay 'round here if you want to."

We all stayed on for a long time 'cause we didn't have no other home and didn't know how to take keer of ourselves. We was kind of scared I reckon. Finally I heard my mother was in Walker County, Alabama, and I left and went to live with her.

My mother was Harriet Davis and she was born in Virginia. I don't know who my father was. My grandmother was captured in Africa when she was a little girl. A big boat was down at the edge of a bay an' the people was all excited about it an' some of the bravest went up purty close to look at it. The men on the boat told them to come on board and they could have the pretty red handkerchiefs, red and blue beads and big rings. A lot of them went on board and the ship sailed away with them. My grandmother never saw any of her folks again.

When I was about five years old they brought my grandmother, my mother and my two aunts and two uncles to Tuscaloosa from Fayettesville, Alabama.[2] We crossed a big river on a ferry boat. They put us on the "block" and sold us. I can remember it well. A white man "cried" me off just like I was a animal or varmit or something. He said, "Here's a little nigger, who will give me a bid on her. She will make a good house gal someday." Old man Davis give him $300.00 for me. I don't know whether I was afraid or not; I don't think I cared just so I had something to eat. I was allus hungry. Miss Davis' grandmother and one of my aunts and uncles. [sic] Old man Davis bought the rest of us. Uncle Henry looked after me when he could. I could see my mother once in awhile but not often.

I had a purty easy time. I didn't have to work very hard till I was about ten years old. I started working in the field and I had to work in the weaving room too. We made all our own clothes. I spun and wove cotton and wool. Old Master bought our shoes. We made fancy cloth. We could stripe the cloth or check it or leave it plain. We also wove coverlids[3] and jeans to make men's suits out of. I could still do that if I had to.

We all went to church with the white folks. We didn't have no colored preachers. The niggers would get happy and shout all over the place. Sometimes they'd fall out doors.

The Big House was a double log, two story house, not very fine but awful comfortable. They was four big fireplace rooms downstairs and two upstairs. Then they was two sort of shed rooms. There was a big piazza across the front. The kitchen was a way off from the house, seems like it was 200 feet at least. Our quarters were close by at the back. He didn't have many slaves and they was nearly all my kin-folks. There was Aunt Emmy and Phyllis, Uncles Henry, Mitchell, Louis and Andy, and the others were Uncle Logan and Uncle Nathan. They was old Mistress' slaves when she done married.

Old Master and old Mistress had three boys, Eli, Billy and Dock. They had to go to war and old Mistress sho' did cry. She say they might get killed and she might not see 'em any more. I wonder why all dem white folks didn't think of that when they sold mothers away from they chillun. I had to be sold away from my mother. Two of her boys was badly wounded but they all come back.

Abe Lincoln done everything he could for the niggers. We lost our best friend when he got killed.

[1] Mrs. Martha King was interviewed in McAlester, Oklahoma, by an unidentified WPA field worker, possibly Mrs. Jessie R. Ervin, probably in spring or summer of 1937, for the typewritten narrative based on her interview was forwarded to Washington on 16 August 1937. The text sent to Washington is the only version of her remembrances surviving from the Oklahoma Slave Narrative Project. Published here, it is available as "Martha King, Age 85 Yrs., McAlester, Oklahoma" in ribbon-copy typescript in the LC Slave Narratives and in carbon copy as item 350081 in the LC Slave Narratives Carbon Copies. Stephens to Cronyn, 16 August 1937, WPA Notes on Interviews.

[2] "Fayettesville" probably refers to Fayette, Alabama, approximately forty-five miles north-northwest of Tuscaloosa.

[3] Coverlets, or bedspreads.

GEORGE KYE[1]

Age 110 Yrs. *Fort Gibson, Okla.*

I was born in Arkansas under Mr. Abraham Stover, on a big farm about twenty miles north of Van Buren. I was plumb grown when the Civil War come along, but I can remember back when the Chero-kee Indians was in all that part of the country.

Joe Kye was my pappy's name what he was born under back in Garrison County, Virginia, and I took that name when I was freed, but I don't know whether he took it or not because he was sold off by old Master Stover when I was a child. I never have seen him since. I think he wouldn't mind good, leastways that what my mammy say.

My mammy was named Jennie and I don't think I had any broth-ers or sisters, but they was a whole lot of children at the quarters that

I played and lived with. I didn't live with mammy because she worked all the time, and us children all stayed in one house.

It was a little one room log cabin, chinked and daubed, and you couldn't stir us with a stick. When we went to eat we had a big pan and all ate out of it. One what ate the fastest got the most.

Us children wore homespun shirts and britches and little slips and nobody but the big boys wore any britches. I wore just a shirt until I was about 12 years old, but it had a long tail down to my calves. Four or five of us boys slept in one bed, and it was made of hewed logs with rope laced acrost it and a shuck mattress. We had stew made out of pork and potatoes, and sometimes greens and pot liquor, and we had ash cake mostly, but biscuits about once a month.

In the winter time I had brass toed shoes made on the place, and a cloth cap with ear flaps.

The work I done was hoeing and plowing, and I rid a horse a lot for old Master because I was a good rider. He would send me to run chores for him, like going to the mill. He never beat his negroes but he talked mighty cross and glared at us until he would nearly scare us to death sometimes.

He told us the rules and we lived by them and didn't make trouble, but they was a neighbor man that had some mean negroes and he nearly beat them to death. We could hear them hollering in the field sometimes. They would sleep in the cotton rows, and run off, and then they would catch the cat-o-nine tails sure nuff. He would chain them up, too, and keep them tied out to trees, and when they went to the field they would be chained together in bunches sometimes after they had been cutting up.

We didn't have no place to go to church, but old Master didn't care if we had singing and praying, and we would tie our shoes on our backs and go down the road close to the white church and all set down and put our shoes on and go up close and listen to the service.

Old Master was baptized almost every Sunday and cussed us all out on Monday. I didn't join the church until after freedom, and I always was a scoundrel for dancing. My favorite preacher was old Pete Conway. He was the only ordained colored preacher we had after freedom, and he married me.

Old Master wouldn't let us take herb medicine, and he got all our medicine in Van Buren when we was sick. But I wore a buckeye on my neck just the same.

When the War come along I was a grown man, and I went off to serve because old Master was too old to go, but he had to send somebody anyways. I served as George Stover, but every time the sergeant would call out "Abe Stover," I would answer "Here."

They had me driving a mule team wagon that Old Master furnished, and I went with the Sesesh soldiers from Van Buren to Texarkana and back a dozen times or more. I was in the War two years, right up to the day of freedom. We had a battle close to Texarkana and another big one near Van Buren, but I never left Arkansas and never got a scratch.

One time in the Texarkana battle I was behind some pine trees and the bullets cut the limbs down all over me. I dug a hole with my bare hands before I hardly knowed how I done it.

One time two white soldiers named Levy and Briggs come to the wagon train and said they was hunting slaves for some purpose. Some of us black boys got scared because we heard they was going to Squire Mack and get a reward for catching runaways, so me and two more lit out of there.

They took out after us and we got to a big mound in the woods and hid. Somebody shot at me and I rolled into some bushes. He rid up and got down to look for me but I was on t'other side of his horse and he never did see me. When they was gone we went back to the wagons just as the regiment was pulling out and the officer didn't say nothing.

They was eleven negro boys served in my regiment for their masters. The first year was mighty hard because we couldn't get enough to eat. Some ate poke greens without no grease and took down and died.

How I knowed I was free, we was bad licked, I reckon. Anyways, we quit fighting and a Federal soldier come up to my wagon and say: "Whose mules?" "Abe Stover's mules," I says, and he tells me then, "Let me tell you, black boy, you are as free now as old Abe Stover his own self!" When he said that I jumped on top of one of them mules' back before I knowed anything!

I married Sarah Richardson, February 10, 1870, and had only eleven children. One son is a deacon and one grandson is a preacher. I am a good Baptist. Before I was married I said to the gal's old man, "I'll go to the mourners' bench if you'll let me have Sal," and sure nuff I joined up just a month after I got her. I am head of the Sunday School and deacon in the St. Paul Baptist church in Muskogee now.

I lived about five miles from Van Buren until about twelve years ago when they found oil and then they run all the negroes out and leased up the land.[2] They never did treat negroes good around there anyways.

I never had a hard time as a slave, but I'm glad we was set free.

Sometimes we can't figger out the best thing to do, but anyways we can lead our own life now, and I'm glad the young ones can learn and get somewhere these days.

[1] George Kye was interviewed by Ethel Wolfe Garrison at Fort Gibson, Oklahoma, probably sometime in the summer or autumn of 1937. Robert Vinson Lackey in the Tulsa office of the Oklahoma Writers' Project edited the text into the earliest surviving version, the typescript "Interview with George Kye, Ex-Slave, 110 Years Old, General Delivery, Fort Gibson, Oklahoma," preserved in the OHS Slave Narratives. An inscription in pencil on its front page notes, "4 copies 11–4–37," referring to a retyping of the text with some additional editorial changes in the Oklahoma City office, which produced the typescript published here, "George Kye, Age 110 Yrs., Fort Gibson, Okla." This final draft was forwarded to Washington on 18 November 1937 and is available in the LC Slave Narratives, while three carbon copies are available, one as item 350013 in the LC Slave Narratives Carbon Copies and in two in the OHS Slave Narratives. *Polk's Muskogee City Directory, 1932,* 317; Stephens to Alsberg, 18 November 1937, WPA Notes on Interviews.

[2] George and Sarah Kye are listed as residents of Fort Gibson in the Muskogee County directory at least as early as 1921. *Phoenix Directory of Muskogee and Muskogee County, 1921,* 548.

BEN LAWSON[1]

Age 84 Yrs.   *Oklahoma City, Okla.*

I was born in Danville, Illinois. De best I can get at my age I is 84 years old. My father dey tell me was name Dennis Lawson and died before I was born. My mother's name was Ann Lawson, who I saw once. I was given by her to my Mistress, Mrs. Jane Brazier, when a kid and she [the mother] was too. She [the mistress] raised me, she and her son, to manhood.[2] I got no brothers or sisters to my knowledge. I was de only slave dey had and dey raised me to be humble and fear dem as a slave and servant. As I was de only slave I slept in de same room wid my Mistress and her son who was grown, her husband and father being dead.

I worked on the farm doing general farm work, hoeing, plowing, harvesting the crop of wheat, corn, barley, oats, rice, peas, etc.[3] To make and harvest the crops dey would hire poor white help and as dey was grown and I was a lad, dey kept me in a strain in order to keep up wid dem for if I didn't it was just too bad for my back. So's dere would be work[4] for me to do during the bad days of winter dey built a pen under a shed and dey would lay a cloth on de ground in the pen and wid small mesh wire on top of de pen on which de wheat was laid and wid a wooden maul I would pounder out wheat all day long, even though dey could have thrashed it as dey did de biggest part[5] of it.

At meal time dey would give me what was left of de scraps off dey table in a plate, which I would eat most de time on de back porch in warm weather and in de kitchen in winter.

For summer I wore a lowell shirt and for winter I wore de same old lowell shirt only wid outing slips and a pair of brogan shoes or a pair of old shoes dat was thrown away by my Mistress' son.

Their house was a 3-room log house unpainted, wid only one bed room and a dining room and kitchen.

The plantation had 'bout 160 acres and was worked by my Mistress' son and myself plus poor white hired help, me being de only slave.

I was treated most harshly 'mongst a group of just white people and who seemed to think me de old work ox for all de hardest work. De nearest other Negro slaves were 'bout 15 or 20 miles from me.

When I was grown I ran away one night and walked and rode de rods under stage coaches to Paducah, Kentucky. I got me a job and worked as a roustabout on a boat where I learned to gamble wid dice. I fought and gambled all up and down de Mississippi River, and in de course of time I had 'bout $3,000, but I lost it.

I don't know de month or de year I was born in but I can 'member de sinking of de biggest circus show in de Mississippi River at Mobile, Alabama when I was 10 or 14 years old, I ain't sure which.[6]

There wasn't no children for me to play with and it seem like I never was a child but was just always a man. I wasn't never told dat I was free, and I didn't know nothing 'bout de War much dat brought my freedom. Dey kept all of dat away from me and I couldn't read or write so I didn't know.[7]

I've been married only once. My wife is 54 years old, and her name is Hattie Lawson.[8] We have no children. Since we married after freedom there wasn't nothing unusual at our wedding.

---

[1] Ben Lawson was interviewed in Oklahoma City by WPA field worker J. S. Thomas on 7 July 1937. From his notes, Thomas prepared a handwritten draft of Lawson's remembrances as the manuscript "Story from Ex-Slave Ben Lawson, 714 N. Wisconsin, a Personal Interview" in the OHS Slave Narratives. From this draft an intermediate typescript entitled "Ben Lawson, Age 84 Yrs., Oklahoma City, Okla.," now in the OHS Slave Narratives, was prepared, incorporating some editorial changes marked on the earlier manuscript. This intermediate draft then was edited in pencil and, on 10 September 1937, typed in ribbon copy and carbon copies into a final draft, published here, with precisely the same title as the intermediate draft. On 2 November 1937 the ribbon copy and one carbon copy of the final draft were sent to Washington, where they

are available, respectively, in the LC Slave Narratives and as item 350028 in the LC Slave Narratives Carbon Copies. A carbon copy is also available in the OHS Slave Narratives. Stephens to Cronyn, 2 November 1937, WPA Notes on Interviews.

   [2] The meaning of this sentence was garbled in the 1930s editing. In the final draft it reads: "My mother raised me, she and her son to manhood."

   [3] This sentence underwent considerable editing by WPA personnel. In the original manuscript draft it reads: "As to my work, I work on the farm doing general farm work, viz, hoeing, plowing, harvesting the crop of wheat, corn, barley, oats, rice, peas, etc."

   [4] In the manuscript draft, this sentence begins "In order to have work."

   [5] The manuscript version of the narrative here reads "greater potion."

   [6] The manuscript draft includes the following note by interviewer J. S. Thomas: "This statement of Mobile being on the Miss. river isn't a true statement as he thinks."

   [7] This sentence was edited heavily by the WPA personnel, reading as follows in the manuscript version: "'They kept all that away from me and as I could not read nor write,' he said, 'no way me could find out.'"

   [8] Ben Lawson is listed in Oklahoma City directories as living at 714 Wisconsin Avenue with his wife, Hattie. *Polk's Oklahoma City Directory, 1937,* 431, 914; *Oklahoma City Negro City Directory,* 111.

MARY LINDSAY[1]

Age 91 Yrs.   *Tulsa, Oklahoma*

My slavery days wasn't like most people tell you about, 'cause I was give to my young Mistress and sent away to Texas when I was jest a little girl, and I didn't live on a big plantation a very long time.

I got an old family Bible what say I was born on September 20, in 1846, but I don't know who put de writing in it unless it was my mammy's mistress. My mammy had de book when she die.

My mammy come out to the Indian country from Mississippi two years before I was born. She was the slave of a Chickasaw part-breed name Sobe Love. He was the kinsfolks of Mr. Benjamin Love, and Mr. Henry Love what bring two big bunches of the Chickasaws out from Mississippi to the Choctaw country when the Chickasaws sign up de treaty to leave Mississippi, and the whole Love family settle 'round on the Red River below Fort Washita. There whar I was born.[2]

My mammy say dey have a terrible hard time again the sickness when they first come out into that country, because it was low and swampy and all full of cane brakes, and everybody have the smallpox and the malaria and fever all the time. Lots of the Chickasaw families nearly died off.

Old Sobe Love marry her off to a slave named William, what belong to a full-blood Chickasaw man name Chick-a-lathe, and I was one of de children.

De children belong to the owner of the mother, and me and my brother Franklin, what we called "Bruner," was born under the name of Love and then old Master Sobe bought my pappy William, and we was all Love slaves then. My mammy had two more girls, name Hetty and Rena.

My mammy name was Mary, and I was named after her. Old Mistress' name was Lottie, and they had a daughter name Mary. Old Master Sobe was powerful rich, and he had about a hundred slaves and four or five big pieces of that bottom land broke out for farms. He had niggers all on the places, but he didn't have no overseers, jest hisself and he went around and seen that everybody behave and do they work right.

Old Master Sobe was a mighty big man in the tribe, and so was all his kinfolks, and they went to Fort Washita and to Boggy Depot all the time on business, and leave the Negroes to look after old Mistress and the young daughter. She was almost grown along about that time, when I can first remember about things.

'Cause my name was Mary, and so was my mammy's and my young Mistress' too. Old Master Sobe called me Mary-Ka-Chubbe to show which Mary he was talking about.

Miss Mary have a black woman name Vici what wait on her all the time, and do the carding and spinning and cooking 'round the house, and Vici belong to Miss Mary. I never did go 'round the Big House, but jest stayed in the quarters with my mammy and pappy and helped in the field a little.

Then one day Miss Mary run off with a man and married him, and old Master Sobe nearly went crazy! The man was name Bill Merrick, and he was a poor blacksmith and didn't have two pair of britches to his name, and old Master Sobe said he jest stole Miss Mary 'cause she was rich, and no other reason. 'Cause he was a white man and she was mostly Chickasaw Indian.

Anyways old Master Sobe wouldn't even speak to Mr. Bill, and wouldn't let him set foot on the place. He jest reared and pitched around, and threatened to shoot him if he set eyes on him, and Mr. Bill took Miss Mary and left out for Texas. He set up a blacksmith shop on the big road between Bonham and Honey Grove, and lived there until he died.

Miss Mary done took Vici along with her, and pretty soon she come back home and stay a while, and old Master Sobe kind of soften up a little bit and give her some money to git started on, and he give her me too.

Dat jest nearly broke my old mammy's and pappy's heart, to have me took away off from them, but they couldn't say nothing and I had to go along with Miss Mary back to Texas. When we git away from the Big House I jest cried and cried until I couldn't hardly see, my eyes was so swole up, but Miss Mary said she gwine to be good to me.

I ask her how come Master Sobe didn't give her some of the grown boys and she say she reckon it because he didn't want to help her husband out none, but jest wanted to help her. If he give her a man her husband have him working in the blacksmith shop, she reckon.

Master Bill Merrick was a hard worker, and he was more sober than most the men in them days, and he never tell me to do nothing. He jest let Miss Mary tell me what to do. They have a log house close to the shop, and a little patch of a field at first, but after awhile he git more land, and then Miss Mary tell me and Vici we got to help in the field too.

That sho' was hard living then! I have to git up at three o'clock sometimes so I have time to water the hosses and slop the hogs and feed the chickens and milk the cows, and then git back to the house and git the breakfast. That was during the times when Miss Mary was having and nursing her two children, and old Vici had to stay with her all the time. Master Bill never did do none of that kind of work, but he had to be in the shop sometimes until way late in the night, and sometimes before daylight, to shoe people's hosses and oxen and fix wagons.

He never did tell me to do that work, but he never done it his own self and I had to do it if anybody do it.

He was the slowest one white man I ever did see. He jest move 'round like de dead lice falling off'n him all the time, and everytime he go to say anything he talk so slow that when he say one word you could walk from here to way over there before he say de next word. He don't look sick, and he was powerful strong in his arms, but he acts like he don't feel good jest the same.

I remember when the War come. Mostly by the people passing 'long the big road, we heard about it. First they was a lot of wagons hauling farm stuff into town to sell, and then purty soon they was soldiers on the wagons, and they was coming out into the country to git the stuff and buying it right at the place they find it.

Then purty soon they commence to be little bunches of mens in soldier clothes riding up and down the road going somewhar. They seem like they was mostly young boys like, and they jest laughing and jollying and going on like they was on a picnic.

Then the soldiers come 'round and got a lot of the white men and took them off to the War even iffen they didn't want to go. Master Bill never did want to go, 'cause he had his wife and two little children, and anyways he was gitting all the work he could do fixing wagons and shoeing hosses, with all the traffic on de road at that time. Master Bill had jest two hosses, for him and his wife to ride and to work to the buggy, and he had one old yoke of oxen and some more cattle. He got some kind of paper in town and he kept it with him all the time, and when the soldiers would come to git his hosses or his cattle he would jest draw that paper on 'em and they let 'em alone.

By and by the people got so thick on the big road that they was somebody in sight all the time. They jest keep a dust kicked up all day and all night 'cepting when it rain, and they git all bogged down and be strung all up and down the road camping. They kept Master Bill in the shop all the time, fixing the things they bust trying to git the wagons out'n the mud. They was whole families of them with they children and they slaves along, and they was coming in from every place because the Yankees was gitting in their part of the country, they say.

We all git mighty scared about the Yankees coming but I don't reckon they ever git thar[3] 'cause I never seen none, and we was right on the big road and we would of seen them. They was a whole lot more soldiers in them brown looking jeans, round-about jackets and cotton britches a-faunching up and down the road on their hosses, though. Them hoss soldiers would come b'iling by, going east, all day and night, and then two–three days later on they would all come tearing by going west! Dey acted like dey didn't know whar dey gwine, but reckon dey did.

Den Master Bill git sick. I reckon he more wore out and worried than anything else, but he go down with de fever one day and it raining so hard Mistress and me and Vici can't neither one go nowhar to git no help.

We puts peach tree poultices on his head and wash him off all the time, until it quit raining so Mistress can go out on de road, and then a doctor man come from one of the bunches of soldiers and see Master Bill. He say he going be all right and jest keep him quiet, and go on.

Mistress have to tend de children and Vici have to take care of Master Bill and look after the house, and dat leave me all by myself wid all the rest of everything around the place.

I got to feed all the stock and milk the cows and work in the field too. Dat the first time I ever try to plow, and I nearly git killed, too! I got me a young yoke of oxens I broke to pull the wagon, 'cause Vici have to use the old oxens to work the field. I had to take the wagon and go 'bout ten miles west to a patch of woods Master Bill owned to git fire wood, 'cause we lived right on a flat patch of prairie, and I had to chop and haul the wood by myself. I had to git postoak to burn in the kitchen fireplace and willow for Master Bill to make charcoal out of to burn in his blacksmith fire.

Well, I hitch up them young oxen to the plow and they won't follow the row, and so I go git the old oxens. One of them old oxens didn't know me and took in after me, and I couldn't hitch 'em up. And then it begins to rain again.

After the rain was quit I git the bucket and go milk the cows, and it is time to water the hosses too, so I starts to the house with the milk and leading one of the hosses. When I gits to the gate I drops the halter across my arm and hooks the bucket of milk on my arm too, and starts to open the gate. The wind blow the gate wide open, and it slap the hoss on the flank. That was when I nearly git killed!

Out the hoss go through the gate to the yard, and down the big road, and my arm all tangled up in the halter rope and me dragging on the ground!

The first jump knock the wind out of me and I can't git loose, and that hoss drag me down the road on the run until he meet up with a passel of soldiers and they stop him.

The next thing I knowed I was laying on the back kitchen gallery, and some soldiers was pouring water on me with a bucket. My arm was broke, and I was stove up so bad that I have to lay down for a whole week, and Mistress and Vici have to do all the work.

Jest as I getting able to walk 'round here come some soldiers and say they come to git Master Bill for the War. He still in the bed sick, and so they leave a parole paper for him to stay until he git well, and then he got to go into Bonham and go with the soldiers to black-smith for them that got the cannons, the man said.

Mistress take on and cry and hold onto the man's coat and beg, but it don't do no good. She say they don't belong to Texas but they belong in the Chickasaw Nation, but he say that don't do no good, 'cause they living in Texas now.

Master Bill jest stew and fret so, one night he fever git way up and he go off into a kind of a sleep and about morning he died.

My broke arm begin to swell up and hurt me, and I git sick with it again, and Mistress git another doctor to come look at it.

He say I got bad blood from it how come I git so sick, and he git out his knife out'n his satchel and bleed me in the other arm. The next day he come back and bleed me again two times, and the next day one more time, and then I git so sick I puke and he quit bleeding me.

While I still sick Mistress pick up and go off to the Territory to her pappy and leave the children thar for Vici and me to look after. After while she come home for a day or two and go off again somewhere else. Then the next time she come home she say they been having big battles in the Territory and her pappy moved all his stuff down on the river, and she home to stay now.

We git along the best we can for a whole winter, but we nearly starve to death, and then the next spring when we getting a little patch planted Mistress go into Bonham and come back and say we all free and the War over.

She say, "You and Vici jest as free as I am, and a lot freer, I reckon, and they say I got to pay you if you work for me, but I ain't got no money to pay you. If you stay on with me and help me I will feed and home you and I can weave you some good dresses if you card and spin the cotton and wool."

Well, I stayed on, 'cause I didn't have no place to go, and I carded and spinned the cotton and wool and she make me just one dress. Vici didn't do nothing but jest wait on the children and Mistress.

Mistress go off again about a week, and when she come back I see she got some money, but she didn't give us any of it.

After a while I asked her ain't she got some money for me, and she say no, ain't she giving me a good home? Den I starts to feeling like I ain't treated right.

Every evening I git done with the work and go out in the back yard and jest stand and look off to the west towards Bonham, and wish I was at that place or some other place.

Den along come a nigger boy and say he working for a family in Bonham and he git a dollar every week. He say Mistress got some kinfolks in Bonham and some of Master Sobe Love's niggers living close to there.

So one night I jest put that new dress in a bundle and set foot right down the big road a-walking west, and don't say nothing to nobody!

It's ten miles into Bonham, and I gits in town about daylight. I keeps on being afraid, 'cause I can't git it out'n my mind I still belong to Mistress.

Purty soon some niggers tells me a nigger name Bruner Love living down west of Greenville, and I know that my brother Franklin, 'cause we all called him Bruner. I don't remember how all I gits down to Greenville, but I know I walks most the way, and I finds Bruner. Him and his wife working on a farm, and they say my sister Hetty and my sister Rena what was little is living with my mammy way back up on the Red River. My pappy done died in time of the War and I didn't know it.

Bruner taken me in a wagon and we went to my mammy, and I lived with her until she died and Hetty married. Then I married a boy name Henry Lindsay. His people was from Georgia, and he live with them way west at Cedar Mills, Texas. That was right close to Gordonville, on the Red River.

We live at Cedar Mills until three of my children was born and then we come to the Creek Nation in 1887. The last one was born here.

My oldest is named Georgia on account of her pappy. He was born in Georgia and that was in 1838, so his whitefolks got a book that say. My next child was Henry. We called him William Henry, after my pappy and his pappy. Then come Donie, and after we come here we had Madison, my youngest boy.

I lives with Henry here on this little place we got in Tulsa.[4]

When we first come here we got some land for $15 an acre from the Creek Nation, but our papers said we can only stay as long as it is the Creek Nation. Then in 1901 comes the allotments, and we found out our land belong to a Creek Indian, and we have to pay him to let us stay on it. After while he makes us move off and we lose out all around.

But my daughter Donie git a little lot, and we trade it for this place about thirty year ago, when this town was a little place.

[1] Mrs. Mary Lindsay was interviewed by WPA field worker Robert Vinson Lackey in Tulsa, Oklahoma, probably sometime in the spring or summer of 1937. On 10 August 1937 WPA state administrator Ron Stephens commended Lackey on this and several other interviews undertaken by personnel from the Tulsa office. The interview was placed in a final edited form and on 12 August 1937 sent to project headquarters in Washington. A preliminary version of the narrative is available as the typescript "Interview with Mary Lindsay, Age 91, Ex-Slave, 444 East Newton Place, Tulsa, Okla." in the OHS Slave Narratives. The later, lightly edited draft, as forwarded to Washington and published here, is available as the typescript "Mary Lindsay, Age 91 Yrs., Tulsa, Oklahoma" in ribbon copy in the LC Slave Narratives and in carbon copy as item 350092 in the LC Slave Narratives Carbon Copies and in the OHS Slave Narratives (with the last page separate in the "Unid-Partial" file). Stephens to Lackey, 10 August 1937; Stephens to Cronyn, 12 August 1937; both letters in WPA Notes on Interviews.

2 For remembrances of the Love family and of African American bondage among its members, see Robert Love, interview by Ja[me]s S. Buchanan at Muskogee, Oklahoma, 13 April 1937, Indian-Pioneer Papers, 6:323; Joe Love, "Joe Love, 705 North 3rd Avenue, Purcell, Oklahoma" [ca. 1937], Indian-Pioneer Papers, 76:39; Mrs. Alice Curry, interview by Maurice R. Anderson at Pauls Valley, Oklahoma, 17 December 1937, Indian-Pioneer Papers, 100:488–89. See also the narrative of Matilda Poe, below.

3 The final draft renders this word as "that," an apparent misreading of "thar" in the preliminary draft.

4 Roughly contemporary Tulsa city directories list Mrs. Mary Lindsay, widow of Henry Lindsay, residing at 444 Newton Place with her daughter, Mrs. Georgia Freeney, herself the widow of Wesley E. Freeney. Daughter Georgia worked as a maid for the Tulsa clothier Henry V. Holmes. *Polk's Tulsa City Directory, 1935*, 239, 295, 353, 621, 685; *Polk's Tulsa (Tulsa County, Okla.) City Directory, 1940*, 217, 358.

MRS. MATTIE LOGAN[1]

Age 79 Yrs.   *Route 5, West Tulsa, Oklahoma*

This is a mighty fitting time to be telling about the slave days, for I'm just finishing up celebrating my seventy-nine years of being around and the first part of my life was spent on the old John B. Lewis plantation down in old Mississippi.

Yes, sir! my birthday is just over. September 1 it was and the year was 1858. Borned on the John B. Lewis plantation just ten mile south of Jackson in the Mississippi country. Rankin County it was.

My mother's name was Lucinda, and father's name was Levi Miles. My mother was part Indian, for her mother was a half-blood Cherokee Indian from Virginia.

There were children a-plenty besides me. There was Sally, Julia, Hubbard, Ada, Ira, Anthony, Henry, Amanda, Mary, John, Lucinda, Daniel and me, Mattie. That was my family.

The master's family was a large one, too. Six children was born to the Master and Mistress. Her name, his first wife, was Jennie, the second and last was named Louise. The children was Rebecca, Mollie, Jennie, Susie, Silas, and Begerlan. They kind of leaned to females.

My mother belonged to Mistress Jennie who thought a heap of her, and why shouldn't she? Mother nursed all Miss Jennie's children because all of her young ones and my mammy's was born so close together it wasn't no trouble at all for mammy to raise the whole kaboodle of them. I was born about the same time as the baby Jennie. They say I nursed on one breast while that white child, Jennie, pulled away at the other!

That was a pretty good idea for the Mistress, for it didn't keep her tied to the place and she could visit around with her friends most any time she wanted 'thout having to worry if the babies would be fed or not.

Mammy was the house girl and account of that and because her family was so large, the Mistress fixed up a two room cabin right back of the Big House and that's where we lived. The cabin had a fireplace in one of the rooms, just like the rest of the slave cabins which was set in a row away from the Big House. In one room was bunk beds, just plain old two-by-fours with holes bored through the plank so's ropes could be fastened in and across for to hold the corn-shuck mattress.

My brothers and sisters was allowed to play with the Master's children, but not with the children who belonged to the field Negroes. We just played yard games like marbles and tossing a ball. I don't rightly remember much about games, for there wasn't too much fun in them days even if we did get raised with the Master's family. We wasn't allowed to learn any reading or writing. They say if they catched a slave learning them things they'd pull his finger nails off! I never saw that done, though.

Each slave cabin had a stone fireplace in the end, just like ours, and over the flames at daybreak was prepared the morning meal. That was the only meal the field negroes had to cook.

All the other meals was fixed up by an old man and woman who was too old for field trucking. The peas, the beans, the turnips, the potatoes, all seasoned up with fat meats and sometimes a ham bone, was cooked in a big iron kettle and when meal time come they all gathered around the pot for a-plenty of helpings! Corn bread and buttermilk made up the rest of the meal.

Ten or fifteen hogs was butchered every fall and the slaves would get the skins and maybe a ham bone. That was all, except what was mixed in with the stews. Flour was given out every Sunday morning and if a family run out of that before the next week, well, they was just out that's all!

The slaves got small amounts of vegetables from the plantation garden, but they didn't have any gardens of their own. Everybody took what old Master rationed out.

Once in a while we had rabbits and fish, but the best dish of all was the 'possum and sweet potatoes—baked together over red-hot coals in the fireplace. Now, that was something to eat!

The Lewis plantation was about three hundred acres, with usually fifty slaves working on the place. Master Lewis was a trader. He couldn't sell off our family, for we belonged to Mistress Jennie. Negro girls, the fat ones who was kinder pretty, was the most sold. Folks wanted them pretty bad but the Mistress said there wasn't going to be any selling of the girls who was mammy's children.

There was no overseer on our place, just the old Master who did all the bossing. He wasn't too mean, but I've seen him whip Old John. I'd run in the house to get away from the sight, but I could still hear Old John yelling, "Pray, Master! Oh! Pray, Master!", but I guess that there was more howling than there was hurting at that.

My uncle Ed Miles run away to the North and joined with Yankees during the War. He was lucky to get away, for lots of them who tried it was ketched by the patrollers. I seen some of them once. They had chains fastened around their legs, fastened short, too, just long enough to take a short step. No more running away with them chains anchoring the feets!

There wasn't any negro churches close by our plantation. All the slaves who wanted religion was allowed to join the Methodist church because that was the Mistress' church.

A doctor was called in when the slaves would get sick. He'd give pills for most all the ailments, but once in a while, like when the children would get the whooping cough, some old negro would try to cure them with home made remedies.

The whooping cough cure was by using a land turtle. Cut off his head and drain the blood into a cup. Then take a lump of sugar and dip in the blood, eat the sugar and the coughing was supposed to stop. If it did or not I don't know.

And that makes me think about another cure they use to tell about. A cure for mean overseers. And I don't mean kill, just scare him, that's all. They say the cure was tried on an overseer who worked for Silas Stien, who was a slave owner living close by the Lewis plantation.

It seems like this overseer was the meanest kind, always whipping the slaves for no reason at all, and the slaves tried to figure out a way to even up with him by chasing him off the place.

One of the slaves told how to cure him. Get a King snake and put the snake in the overseer's cabin. Slip the snake in about, no, just about, but jest exactly nine o'clock at night. Seems like the time was important, why so, I don't remember now.

That's what the slaves did. Put in the snake and out went the overseer. Never no more did he whip the slaves on that plantation because he wasn't working there no more! Where[2] he went, when he went, or how he went nobody knows, but they all say he went. That's what counted—he was gone!

The Yankees didn't come around our plantation during the war. All we heard was, "They'll kill all the slaves," and such hearing was a-plenty!

After the war some man come to the plantation and told the field negroes they was free. But he didn't know about the cabin we lived in and didn't tell my folks nothing about it. They learned about the freedom from the old Master.

That was some days after the man left the place. The Master called my mother and father into the Big House and told them they was free. Free like him. But he didn't want my folks to leave and they stayed, stayed there three year after they was free to go anywhere they wanted.

The master paid them $200 [sic] a month to work for him and that wasn't so much if you stop to figure there was two grown folks and thirteen children who could do plenty of work around the place.

But that money paid for an 80-acre farm my folks bought not far from the old plantation and they moved onto it three year after the freedom came.

I think Lincoln was a mighty good man, and I think Roosevelt is trying to carry some of the good ideas Lincoln had. Lincoln would have done a heap more if he had lived.

The young negroes who are living now are selfish and shiftless. They're not worth two cents and don't have the respect for other folks to get along right. That's what I think.

I been married three times, but no children did I have. The first man was Frank Morris, the next was Jim White, and the last was John Logan. All gone. Dead.

From Mississippi I come to Idabel, Oklahoma, in 1909, two year later [than] statehood. I moved to Muskogee in 1910, staying there while the times was good and coming to Tulsa some years ago.

I'm pretty old and can't work hard anymore, but I manage to get along. I'm glad to be free and I don't believe I could stand them slavery days now at all.

I'm my own boss, get up when I want, go to bed the same way. Nobody to say this or that about what I do.

Yes, I'm glad to be free!

¹ Mrs. Mattie Logan was interviewed by WPA field worker L. P. Livingston probably sometime in early September 1937. Livingston noted her as living at "Route 5, West Tulsa," while a roughly contemporary Tulsa city directory listed her in the South Haven community on the Oklahoma Union Railway line at the west side of the city. On 3 September 1937 project employee Craig Vollmer edited a now lost initial draft of the Mattie Logan interview into an intermediate draft. This version, the typescript "Interview with Mrs. Mattie Logan, Route 5, West Tulsa, Oklahoma," is available in ribbon copy in the OHS Slave Narratives. It bears a pencil notation that it was retyped with further editorial changes on 10 September 1937. This final version, forwarded to Washington on 14 September 1937 and published here, "Mrs. Mattie Logan, Age 79 Yrs., Route 5, West Tulsa, Oklahoma," is available in ribbon copy in the LC Slave Narratives and in carbon copy as item 350061 in the LC Slave Narratives Carbon Copies. After Mattie Logan's and several other Oklahoma narratives were received in Washington, Henry G. Alsberg, director of the Federal Writers' Project, wrote back to William Cunningham, the state director of the Federal Writers' Project for Oklahoma, that he found the interviews to be "an unusually interesting collection" and congratulated Cunningham for "the material itself and on the way it is presented." Stephens to Cronyn, 14 September 1937; Henry G. Alsberg, Washington, D.C., to William Cunningham, Oklahoma City, Oklahoma, 21 September 1937; both letters in WPA Notes on Interviews; Preston George and Sylvan R. Wood, *The Railroads of Oklahoma*, 70–71; *Polk's Tulsa City Directory, 1935*, 355, 709; *Polk's Tulsa City Directory, 1940*, 361, 790.

² The final draft of the narrative here uses "When," but "Where," found in the earlier draft, appears to have been intended.

KIZIAH LOVE¹

Age 93   *Colbert, Okla.*

Lawd help us,² I sho' remembers all about slavery times for I was a grown woman, married and had one baby, when de War done broke out.³ That was a sorry time for some poor black folks but I guess Master Frank Colbert's niggers was about as well off as the best of 'em. I can recollect things that happened way back better than I can things that happen now. Funny ain't it?

Frank Colbert, a full-blood Choctaw Indian, was my owner.⁴ He owned my mother but I don't remember much about my father. He died when I was a little youngun. My Mistress' name was Julie Colbert. She and Master Frank was de best folks that ever lived.⁵ All the niggers loved Master Frank and knowed jest what he wanted done and they tried their best to do it, too.

I married Isom Love, a slave of Sam Love, another full-blood Indian that lived on a jining farm. We lived on Master Frank's farm and Isom went back and forth to work fer his master and I worked ever day fer mine. I don't 'spect we could of done that way iffen we hadn't of had Indian masters. They let us do a lot like we pleased jest so we got our work done and didn't run off.

Old Master Frank never worked us hard and we had plenty of good food to eat. He never did like to put us under white overseers and never tried it but once. A white man come through here and stopped overnight. He looked 'round the farm and told Master Frank that he wasn't gitting half of what he ought to out of his rich land. He said he could take his bunch of hands and double his amount of corn and cotton.

Master Frank told him that he never used white overseers, that he had one nigger that bossed around some when he didn't do it hisself. He also told the white man that he had one nigger named Bill that was kind of bad, that he was a good worker but he didn't like to be bothered as he liked to do his own work in his own way. The white boss told him he wouldn't have any trouble and that he could handle him all right.

Old Master hired him and things went very well for a few days. He hadn't said anything to Bill and they had got along fine. I guess the new boss got to thinking it was time for him to take Bill in hand so one morning he told him to hitch up another team before he caught his own team to go to work.

Uncle Bill told him that he didn't have time, that he had a lot of plowing to git done that morning and besides it was customary for every man to catch his own team. Of course this made the overseer mad and he grabbed a stick and started cussing and run at Uncle Bill. Old Bill grabbed a single-tree and went meeting him. Dat white man all on a sudden turned 'round and run fer dear life and I tell you, he fairly bust old Red River wide open gitting away from there and nobody never did see hide nor hair of him 'round to this day.

Master Colbert run a stage stand and a ferry on Red River and he didn't have much time to look after his farm and his niggers. He had lots of land and lots of slaves. His house was a big log house, three rooms on one side and three on the other, and there was a big open hall between them. There was a big gallery clean across the front of the house. Behind the house was the kitchen and the smokehouse. The smokehouse was always filled with plenty of good meat and lard.[6] They would kill the polecat and dress it and take a sharp stick and run it up their back jest under the flesh. They would also run one up each leg and then turn him over on his back and put him on top of the house and let him freeze all night. The next morning they'd pull the sticks out and all the scent would be on them sticks and the cat wouldn't smell at all. They'd cook it like they did possum, bake it with taters or make dumplings.

We had plenty of salt. We got that from Grand Saline. Our coffee was made from parched meal or wheat bran. We made it from dried sweet potatoes that had been parched, too.

One of our choicest dishes was "Tom Pashofa," an Indian dish.[7] We'd take corn and beat it in a mortar with a pestle. They took out the husks with a riddle and a fanner. The riddle was a kind of a sifter. When it was beat fine enough to go through the riddle we'd put it in a pot and cook it with fresh pork or beef. We cooked our bread in a Dutch oven or in the ashes.

When we got sick we would take butterfly root and live-everlasting and boil it and make a syrup and take it for colds. Balmony and queen's delight boiled and mixed would make good blood medicine.[8]

The slaves lived in log cabins scattered back of the house. He wasn't afraid they'd run off. They didn't know as much as the slaves in the states, I reckon. But Master Frank had a half brother that was as mean as he was good. I believe he was the meanest man the sun ever shined on. His name was Buck Colbert and he claimed he was a patroller. He was sho' bad to whup niggers. He'd stop a nigger and ask him if he had a pass and even if they did he'd read it and tell them they had stayed over time and he'd beat 'em most to death. He'd say they didn't have any business off the farm and to git back there and stay there.

One time he got mad at his baby's nurse because she couldn't git the baby to stop crying and he hit her on the head with some fire-tongs and she died. His wife got sick and she sent for me to come and take care of her baby. I sho' didn't want to go and I begged so hard for them not to make me that they sent an older woman who had a baby of her own so she could nurse the baby if necessary.

In the night the baby woke up and got to crying and Master Buck called the woman and told her to git him quiet. She was sleepy and was sort of slow and this made Buck mad and he made her strip her clothes off to her waist and he began to whip her. His wife tried to git him to quit and he told her he'd beat her iffen she didn't shut up. Sick as she was she slipped off and went to Master Frank's and woke him up and got him to go and make Buck quit whipping her. He had beat her so that she was cut up so bad she couldn't nurse her own baby any more.

Master Buck kept on being bad till one day he got mad at one of his own brothers and killed him. This made another of his brothers mad and he went to his house and killed him. Everybody was glad that Buck was dead.

We had lots of visitors. They'd stop at the stage inn that we kept. One morning I was cleaning the rooms and I found a piece of money in the bed where two men had slept. I thought it was a dime and I showed it to my mammy and she told me it was a five dollar piece. I sho' was happy fer I had been wanting some hoops fer my skirts like Mistress had so Mammy said she would keep my money 'til I could send fer the hoops. My brother got my money from my mammy and I didn't git my hoops fer a long time. Miss Julie give me some later.

When me and my husband got married we built us a log cabin about half-way from Master Frank's house and Master Sam Love's house. I would go to work at Master Frank's and Isom would go to work at Mister Sam's. One day I was at home with jest my baby and a runner come by and said the Yankee soldiers was coming. I looked 'round and I knowed they would git my chickens. I had 'em in a pen right close to the house to keep the varmits from gitting 'em so I decided to take up the boards in the floor and put 'em in there as the wall logs come to the ground and they couldn't git out. By the time I got my chickens under the floor and the house locked tight the soldiers had got so close I could hear their bugles blowing so I jest fairly flew over to old Master's house. Them Yankees clumb down the chimbley and got every one of my chickens and they killed about fifteen of Master Frank's hogs. He went down to their camp and told the captain about it and he paid him for his hogs and sent me some money for my chickens.

We went to church all the time. We had both white and colored preachers. Master Frank wasn't a Christian but he would help build brush-arbors fer us to have church under and we sho' would have big meetings I'll tell you.

One day Master Frank was going through the woods close to where niggers was having church. All on a sudden he started running and beating hisself and hollering and the niggers all went to shouting and saying "Thank the Lawd, Master Frank has done come through!" Master Frank after a minute say, "Yes, through the worst of 'em." He had run into a yellow jacket's nest.

One night my old man's master sent him to Sherman, Texas. He aimed to come back that night so I stayed at home with jest my baby. It went to sleep so I set down on the steps to wait and ever minute I thought I could hear Isom coming through the woods. All a sudden I heard a scream that fairly made my hair stand up. My dog that was laying out in the yard give a low growl and come and set down right by me. He kept growling real low.

Directly, right close to the house I heard that scream again. It sounded like a woman in mortal misery. I run into the house and made the dog stay outside. I locked the door and then thought what must I do. Supposing Isom did come home now and should meet that awful thing? I heard it again. It wasn't more'n a hundred yards from the house. The dog scratched on the door but I dassent open it to let him in. I knowed by this time that it was a panther screaming. I turned my table over and put it against the opening of the fireplace. I didn't aim fer that thing to come down the chimbley and git us.

Purty soon I heard it again a little mite further away—it was going on by. I heard a gun fire. Thank God, I said, somebody else heard it and was shooting at it. I set there on the side of my bed fer the rest of the night with my baby in my arms and praying that Isom wouldn't come home. He didn't come till about nine o'clock the next morning and I was that glad to see him that I jest cried and cried.

I ain't never seen many sperits but I've seen a few. One day I was laying on my bed here by myself. My son Ed was cutting wood. I'd been awful sick and I was powerful weak. I heard somebody walking real light like they was barefooted. I said, "Who's dat?"

He catch hold of my hand and he has the littlest hand I ever seen, and he say, "You been mighty sick and I want you to come and go with me to Sherman to see a doctor."

I say, "I ain't got nobody at Sherman what knows me."

He say, "You'd better come and go with me anyway."

I jest lay there fer a minute and didn't say nothing and purty soon he say, "Have you got any water?"

I told him the water was on the porch and he got up and went outside and I set in to calling Ed. He come hurrying and I asked him why he didn't lock the door when he went out and I told him to go see if he could see the little man and find out what he wanted. He went out and looked everywhere but he couldn't find him nor he couldn't even find his tracks.[9]

I always keep a butcher-knife near me but it was between the mattress and the feather bed and I couldn't get to it. I don't guess it would have done any good though fer I guess it was jest a sperit.

The funniest thing that ever happened to me was when I was a real young gal. Master and Miss Julie was going to see one of his sisters that was sick. I went along to take care of the baby fer Miss Julie. The baby was about a year old. I had a bag of clothes and the baby to carry.

I was riding a pacing mule and it was plumb gentle. I was riding along behind Master Frank and Miss Julie and I went to sleep. I lost the bag of clothes and never missed it. Purty soon I let the baby slip out of my lap and I don't know how far I went before I nearly fell off myself and just think how I felt when I missed that baby! I turned around and went back and found the baby sitting in the trail sort of crying. He wasn't hurt a mite as he fell in the grass. I got off the mule and picked him up and had to look fer a log so I could get back on again.

Jest as I got back on Master Frank rode up. He had missed me and come back to see what was wrong. I told him that I had lost the bag of clothes but I didn't say anything about losing the baby. We never did find the clothes and I sho' kept awake the rest of the way. I wasn't going to risk losing that precious baby again! He was sho' a sweet baby though.

Jest before the War people would come through the Territory stealing niggers and selling 'em in the states. Us women dassent git fur from the house. We wouldn't even go to the spring if we happened to see a strange wagon or horsebacker. One of Master Sam Love's women was stole and sold down in Texas. After freedom she made her way back to her fambly. Master Frank sent one of my brothers to Sherman on an errand. After several days the mule come back but we never did see my brother again. We didn't know whether he run off or was stole and sold.

I was glad to be free.[10] What did I do and say? Well, I jest clapped my hands together and said, "Thank God Almighty, I'se free at last!"

I live on the forty acres that the government give me. I have been blind for nine years and don't git off my bed much. I live here with my son, Ed.[11] Isom has been dead for over forty years. I had fifteen children, but only ten of them are living.

[1] WPA field worker Mrs. Jessie R. Ervin interviewed ninety-three-year-old Mrs. Kiziah Love at Colbert, Oklahoma, probably in the spring or summer of 1937. Her field notes were placed into a preliminary typewritten form that survives as "Interview with Kiziah Love (Ex-Slave, Aged 93, Colbert, Oklahoma)" in the OHS Slave Narratives. The preliminary draft was edited in pencil and then retyped, with mostly stylistic changes, into the text "Kiziah Love, Age 93, Colbert, Okla.," forwarded to Washington on 12 August 1937 and published here. The ribbon-copy typescript of this later draft is available in the LC Slave Narratives and carbon copies may be found as item 350097 in the LC Slave Narratives Carbon Copies and in the OHS Slave Narratives. Benjamin A. Botkin, folklore editor for the Federal Writers' Project, appraised Love's remembrances as "well-rounded and well-balanced" and selected two extracts for in-

clusion in his 1945 *Lay My Burden Down* (27, 52, 273, 275). B. A. B[otkin], LC Slave Narratives Appraisal Sheets, Accession no. 350097, 17 December 1940; Stephens to Cronyn, 12 August 1937, WPA Notes on Interviews. For another, contemporary interview with this informant, see Kizzie Love, interview by Robert W. Small at Colbert, Oklahoma, 14 October 1937, Indian-Pioneer Papers, 61:420–25.

2 The preliminary draft of this interview includes the personal address "Chile."

3 The preliminary draft at this point includes the following sentence, which was marked out in pencil and not included in the later version: "What is it you want me to tell you about it?"

4 Benjamin Franklin Colbert is well known in western history as the operator of Colbert's Ferry across the Red River. He purchased a functioning ferry at the site in 1852 and continued its operation even after the construction of a railroad bridge across the river in 1872. During the time that Kiziah Love worked as a member of the Colbert household, the ferry and its stagecoach station constituted one of the prominent stops on the Butterfield Overland Mail (1858–61). Grant Foreman, "The California Overland Mail Route through Oklahoma," *Chronicles of Oklahoma* 9 (September 1931): 312–13; John Malcolm, "Colbert Ferry on Red River, Chickasaw Nation, Indian Territory," edited by W. B. Morrison, *Chronicles of Oklahoma* 16 (September 1938): 302–14; Ruth Ann Overbeck, "Colbert's Ferry," *Chronicles of Oklahoma* 57 (Summer 1979): 212–23; Muriel H. Wright, "Historic Places on the Old Stage Line from Fort Smith to Red River," *Chronicles of Oklahoma* 11 (June 1933): 812–14.

5 The preliminary draft consistently renders "mistress" as "mistis" and "master" as "marse."

6 At this point the preliminary draft includes the following four sentences omitted from the later draft: "Indian masters wasn't a bit stingy with food and clothes fer their slaves. We raised nearly all the food we et. There was abundance of wild turkey, deer, rabbits, squirrels, 'possum, 'coon and some folks even et polecats. I never did."

7 Either the interviewee or the field worker apparently garbled the name of this Choctaw food item, either *ta-fula* or *pishofa*, both of which are hominy-based. The description of hominy making which follows leaves out the soaking stage. For background on Choctaw foodways, see Campbell, "Choctaw Subsistence," 9–24; Hudson, "Choctaw Indian Dishes," 333–35; Wright, "American Indian Corn Dishes," 156–61.

8 For an overview of medicine among the Choctaw people, see Virginia R. Allen, "Medical Prctices and Health in the Choctaw Nation, 1831–1855," *Chronicles of Oklahoma* 48 (Spring 1970): 60–73.

9 "Little people" play an important role in the religion and folklore of many of the southeastern tribes of American Indians, and this dream may stem from those beliefs. Swanton, *Indians of the Southeastern United States,* 774.

10 In the preliminary draft, this sentence begins with the direct address "Yassum."

11 The Dawes Commission enrolled Kiziah Love and her family as Chickasaw freedmen in 1903, and they subsequently received land allotments as members of the Chickasaw Nation. Although Kiziah Love's master was Choctaw, he and his slaves resided in the Chickasaw Nation, so the freedmen became members of the Chickasaw and not the Choctaw Nation. U.S., Department of the Interior, Office of Indian Affairs, Dawes Commission, Chickasaw Freedmen Census Cards, no. 328 (Jack, Netty, and Kizzia Love), Microcopy M1186, reel 27, National Archives and Records Administration, Fort

Worth, Texas (cited hereafter as Chickasaw Freedmen Census Cards); Chickasaw Freedmen Census Cards, no. 1001 (Kissiah, Jack, Jake, Brit, Emma, and Jeanie Love; Texanna and Jesse McFarland); Chickasaw Freedmen Census Cards, no. 1003 (Ed and Rosa Love); U.S., Department of the Interior, Office of Indian Affairs, Dawes Commission, Chickasaw Freedmen Enrollment Application Testimony file no. 328 (Jack, Netty, and Kizzie Love), Microcopoy M1301, reel 384, National Archives and Records Administration, Fort Worth, Texas (cited hereafter as Chickasaw Freedmen Enrollment Application Testimony); Chickasaw Freedmen Enrollment Application Testimony file no. 1001 (Kissiah, Jack, Jake, Brit, Emma, and Jeanie Love; Texanna and Jesse McFarland); Chickasaw Freedmen Enrollment Application Testimony file no. 1003 (Ed and Rosa Love).

DANIEL WILLIAM LUCAS[1]

Age 94 Yrs.   *Red Bird, Okla.*

I remember them slave days well as it was yesterday, and when I get to remembering the very first thing comes back to me is the little log cabin where at I lived when I was a slave boy back 'fore the War.

Just like yesterday—I see that little old cabin standing on a bit of hill about a quarter-mile from the Master's brick mansion, and I see into the cabin and there's the old home-made bed with rope cords a-holding up the corn shuck bedding where on I use to sleep after putting in the day at hoeing cotton or following a slow time mule team down the corn rows till it got so dark the old overseer just naturally had to call it a day.

And when I see the old baker swinging in the fireplace. That cooked up the corn pone to go with the fat side meats the Master Doctor (didn't I tell you the Master was a doctor?) give us for the meals of the week day. But on a Sunday morning we always had flour bread, excepting after the War is over and then we is lucky do we get anything.

Just like yesterday—I hear the old overseer making round of the cabins every day at four, and I means in the morning, too, when the night sleep is the best, and the folkses tumbling out of the door getting ready for the fields.

All the mens dressed about the same. Just like me. Wearing the grey jeans with the blue shirt stuck in loose around the belt, brogan shoes that feels like brakes on the feet about the hot time of day when the old sun's a-grinning down like he was saying: "work, niggers, work!" And the overseer is saying the same thing, only we pays more attention to him 'cause of the whip he shakes around when the going gets kinder slow down the row.

Now I sees them getting ready for the slave auction. Many of 'em there was. The Master Doctor done owned about two hundred slaves and sometimes he sell some for to beat the bad crops.

There they'd stand on the wooden blocks, their faces greased and shiny, their arms and bodies pretty well greased too; seemed like they looked better and stronger that way, maybe some other reason, I dunno. And when the auction was over lots of the slaves would try to figger out when would the next one be and worry some afraid they'd be standing up there waiting for the buyers to punch and slap to see is they sound of limb and able to do the day's work without loafing down the rows.

There's the old white preacher who tried to tell the slaves about the Lord. He had a mighty hard job sometimes, 'cause of the teaching was hard to understand. And then—then he'd just seem to be riled with anger and lay down the law of the Lord between cusswords that all the slaves could understand. So finally I guess everybody was religionized even it was cussed into 'em right from the pulpit!

That old preacher always makes me think of haunts, 'cause every evening when I drive up the cows for milking, there's a old, old log cabin right on the way that I pass every night—and it's so haunted won't nobody pass it after the darkness covers in the daylight.

I didn't always get by 'fore then, and the sounds I hear! Like they was people inside jumping and knocking on the floor, maybe they was dancing, I dunno. But they was a light in the big room. Wasn't the moon a-shining through the windows either, 'cause sometimes I would stop at the gate and say HELLO, then out go the light and the noises would stop quick, like them haunts was a-scairt as me—and then, then I run like the old preacher's Devil is after me with all his forks.

Then along come the War. The slaves would go around from cabin to cabin telling each other about how mean and cruel was the master or the overseer, and maybe some of them would make for the North. They was the unlucky ones, 'cause lots of times they was caught.

And when the patrollers get 'em caught, they was due for a heavy licking that would last for a long time.

The slaves didn't know how to travel. The way would be marked when they'd start North, but somehow they'd get lost, 'cause they didn't know one direction from another, they was so scairt.

Just like yesterday—I remember the close of the War. Nothing exciting about it down on the plantation. Just the old overseer come around and say:

"The Yankees has whipped the Rebels and the War is over. But the Old Master don't want you to leave. He just wants you to stay right on here where at is your home. That's what the Master say is best for you to do."

That's what I do, but some of them other slaves is kinder filled up with the idea of freedom and wants to find out is it good or bad, so they leave and scatter around.

But I stays, and the Master Doctor pays me ten dollars every month, gives me board and my sleeping place just like always, and when I gets sick there he is with the herb medicine for my ailment and I is well again.

It's long after the War before I leaves the old place. And that's when I gets married in 1885. That was my first licensed wife and we is married in Holly Springs. Her name was Josephine and we has maybe eight–ten children, I dunno.

And I is thankful they ain't none of my children born slaves and have to remember all them terrible days when we was ruled by the whip—like I remember it, just like it was yesterday.

[1] Daniel William Lucas was interviewed in Red Bird, Oklahoma, by Craig Vollmer on 2 August 1937. From that interview Vollmer prepared the preliminary typescript, "Interview with Daniel William Lucas (of Red Bird, Okla.)," available in the OHS Slave Narratives. WPA personnel lightly edited the preliminary draft of the narrative, preparing the typescript published here, "Daniel William Lucas, Age 94 Yrs., Red Bird, Okla.," which was sent to Washington on 2 September 1937. This final version is available in ribbon copy in the LC Slave Narratives and in carbon copy as item 350066 in the LC Slave Narratives Carbon Copies and in the OHS Slave Narratives. Stephens to Cronyn, 2 September 1937, WPA Notes on Interviews.

The preliminary draft contains beneath its title the following background information on Daniel William Lucas: "Note: This person is an ex-slave, born in 1843, at Holly Springs, Marshall Co., Mississippi. Parents: Matt and Caroline Lucas. Grandparents: Friday and Nancy Prior. Plantation: owned by William and Jane Lucas."

BERT LUSTER[1]

Age 85 Yrs.   *Oklahoma City, Oklahoma*

I'll be jest frank,[2] I'm not for sho' when I was born, but it was in 1853. Don't know the month, but I was sho' born in 1853 in Watson County, Tennessee.[3] You see my father was owned by Master Luster and my mother was owned by Masters Joe and Bill Asterns (father and son). I can remember when Master Astern moved from Watson County, Tennessee he brought me and my mother with him to Barnum County Seat, Texas.[4] Master Astern owned about twelve slaves,

and dey was all Astern 'cept Miriah Elmore's son Jim. He owned
'bout five or six hundred acres of ground, and de slaves raised and
shucked all de corn and picked all de cotton. De whites folks lived in
a big double log house and we slaves lived in log cabins. Our white
folks fed us darkies! We ate nearly ever'thing dey ate. Dey ate turkey,
chickens, ducks, geese, fish and we killed beef, pork, rabbits and
deer. Yes, and possums too. And whenever we killed beef we tanned
the hide and dere was a white man who made shoes for de white folks
and us darkies. I tell you I'm not gonna lie, dem white folks was good
to us darkies. We didn't have no mean overseer. Master Astern and
his son jest told us niggers what to do and we did it, but 50 miles
away dem niggers had a mean overseer, and dey called him "poor
white trash," "old whooser," and sometime "old red neck," and he
would sho' beat 'em turrible iffen dey didn't do jest like he wanted
'em to.

Seem like I can hear dem "nigger hounds" barking now. You see
whenever a darky would get a permit to go off and wouldn't come
back dey would put de "nigger hounds" on his trail and run dat nigger down.

De white women wove and spin our clothes. You know dey had
looms, spins, and weavers. Us darkies would stay up all night sometime sep'rating cotton from the seed. When dem old darkies got
sleepy dey would prop their eyes open wid straws.

Sho' we wore very fine clothes for dem days. You know dey dyed
the cloth with poke berries.

We cradled de wheat on pins, caught the grain, carried it to de
mill and had it ground. Sho', I ate biscuits and cornbread too. Keep
telling you dat we ate.

We got de very best care when we got sick. Don't you let nobody
tell you dem white folks tried to kill out dem darkies 'cause when a
darkey took sick dey would send and git de very best doctors round
dat country. Dey would give us ice water when we got sick. You see
we put up ice in saw dust in winter and when a slave got sick dey give
him ice water, sometimes sage tea and chicken gruel. Dey wanted to
keep dem darkies fat so dey could get top price for 'em. I never saw
a slave sold, but my half brother's white folks let him work and buy
hisself.

I was about 14, and I milked the cows, packed water, seeded cotton, churned milk up at de Big House and jest first one chore and den
another. My mother cooked up at de Big House.

Dey was a lot of talk 'bout conjure but I didn't believe in it. Course

dem darkies could do everything to one another, and have one another scared, but dey couldn't conjure dat overseer and stop him from
beating 'em near to death. Course he didn't flog 'em till dey done
sumping.

I married my woman, Nannie Wilkerson, 58 years ago. Dat was
after slavery, and I love her, honest to God I does. Course in dem days
we didn't buy no license, we jest got permits from old Master and
jumped over a broom stick and jest got married.

I sho' did hate when the Yanks come 'cause our white folks was
good to us, and jest take us right along to church with 'em. We didn't
work on Sad'days or Christmas.

We raised gardens, truck patches and such for spending change.[5]

I sho' caught hell after dem Yanks come.[6] Befo' de war, you see de
patroller rode all nite but wouldn't bother a darkey iffen he wouldn't
run off. Why dem darkeys would run off I jest couldn't see.

Dose Yanks treated old master and mistress so mean. Dey took all
his hams, chickens, and drove his cattle out of the pasture, but didn't
bother us niggers honest.[7] Dey drove old master Astern off'n his own
plantation and we all hid in de corn field.

My mother took me to Greenville, Texas, 'cause my step-pappy
was one of dem half smart niggers round dere trying to preach and
de Ku Klux Klan beat him half to death.

Dere was some white folks who would take us to church wid
'em—dis was aftah the war now—and one night we was all sitting up
thar and one old woman with one leg was dah and when them Klans
shot in amongst us niggers and white folks aunt Mandy beat all of us
home. Yes suh.

My first two teachers was two white men, and dem Klans shot in
de hotel what dey lived in, but dey had school for us niggers jest de
same. After dat, dose Klans got so bad Uncle Sam sent soljers down
dere to keep peace.

After de soljers come and run de Klans out we worked hard dat
fall and made good crops. 'Bout three years later I came to Indian
Territory in search of educating my kids.

I landed here 46 years ago on a farm not far from now Oklahoma
City. I got to be a prosperous farmer. My bale of cotton amongst
5,000 bales won the blue ribbon at Guthrie, Oklahoma, and dat bale
of cotton and being a good democrat won for me a good job as a clerk
on the Agriculture Board at the State Capitol. All de white folks
liked me and still like me and called me "cotton king."[8]

I have jest three chillun living. Walter is parcel post clerk here at de post office downtown. Delia Jenkins, my daughter, is a housewife and Cleo Luckett, my other daughter, a common laborer.

Have been a christian 20 years. Jest got sorry for my wicked ways. I am a member of the Church of God. My wife is a member of the Church of Christ. I'm a good democrat and she is a good republican.

My fav'rite song is: "Dark Was the Nite, and Cold the Ground" and "Couldn't Hear Nobody Pray."

I'm glad slavery is over, but I don't think dem white folks was fighting to free us niggers. God freed us. Of course, Abraham Lincoln was a pretty fine man. Don't know much about Jeff Davis. Never seen him. Yes, and Booker T. Washington.[9] He was one of the Negro leaders. The first Negro to represent the Negroes in Washington. He was a great leader.

During slavery time never heerd of a cullud man commiting 'sault on a white woman. The white and cullud all went to church together too. Niggers and white shouted alike.

I remember some of the little games we played now: "Fox in the wall," "Mollie, Mollie Bride," and "Hide and go seek."

[1] Bert Luster was interviewed at his home in Oklahoma City by Bertha P. Tipton on 7 June 1937. A preliminary typescript of his remembrances is available as "Interview with Bert Luster, Ex-Slave, Aged About 85 Years, 512 North Lindsay, Oklahoma City, Oklahoma" in the OHS Slave Narratives. This text, edited in pencil and retyped as "Bert Luster, Age 85 Yrs., Oklahoma City, Oklahoma," was forwarded to Washington on 16 August 1937 and is published here. This later draft is available in ribbon-copy typescript in the LC Slave Narratives and in carbon copy as item 350082 in the LC Slave Narratives Carbon Copies and in the OHS Slave Narratives. *Oklahoma City Negro City Directory,* 118; *Polk's Oklahoma City Directory, 1937,* 438, 874; Stephens to Cronyn, 16 August 1937, WPA Notes on Interviews.

[2] In the preliminary draft this sentence begins with the direct address "Chile."

[3] This placename must have been garbled in oral transmission, for there is no Watson County in Tennessee.

[4] This placename must have been garbled in oral transmission, for the encyclopedic *Handbook of Texas* lists only one town named Barnum in the state, and that was a sawmill camp in Polk County never a county seat and not founded until the 1880s. Walter Prescott Webb, *The Handbook of Texas,* 2:112.

[5] In the preliminary draft this sentence begins with the direct address "Cos chile."

[6] In the preliminary draft this sentence begins with the direct address "Chile."

[7] In the preliminary draft this sentence ends "didn't bother us dough."

[8] Bert Luster was working as a janitor for the Oklahoma State Board of Agriculture at least as early as July 1911, becoming a shipping clerk by 1918. He retained that position for the agency until leaving its employment in June 1927. Luster's known salary began at $65.00 monthly, increasing to $90.00 in 1919. Oklahoma, State Board of Agriculture, Annual Reports for the Years Ended 30 June 1912 (p. 25), 30 June 1919

(p. 3), 30 June 1920 (p. 4), 30 June 1922 (p. 3), 30 June 1923 (p. 3), 30 June 1924 (p. 4), 30 June 1925 (unpaged), 30 June 1926 (unpaged), and 30 June 1927 (unpaged), Oklahoma Department of Agriculture Biennial, Annual, Semiannual, Quarterly, and Financial Reports, box 1, Oklahoma State Archives, Oklahoma City, Oklahoma.
    [9] In the preliminary draft this sentence begins, "Yes, you asked about."

STEPHEN MCCRAY[1]

Age 88 Yrs.   *Oklahoma City, Okla.*

I was born in Huntsville County, Alabama, right where the Scottsboro boys was in jail, in 1850.[2]
    My parents was Wash and Winnie McCray. They was the mother and father of 22 chillun. Jest five lived to be grown and the rest died at baby age. My father's mother and father was named Mandy and Peter McCray, and my mother's mother and father was Ruthie and Charlie McCray. They all had the same Master, Mister McCray, all the way thoo'.
    We live in log huts and when I left home grown, I left my folks living in the same log huts. Beds was put together with ropes and called rope beds. No springs was ever heard of by white or cullud as I knows of.
    All the work I ever done was pick up chips for my grandma to cook with. I was kept busy doing this all day.
    The big boys went out and got rabbits, possums and fish. I would sho' lak to be in old Alabama fishing, 'cause I am a fisherman. There is sho' some pretty water in Alabama and as swift as cars run here. Water so clear and blue you can see the fish way down, and dey wouldn't bite to save your life.
    Slaves had their own gardens. All got Friday and Sadday to work in garden during garden time. I liked cornbread best and I'd give a dollar to git some of the bread we had on those good old days and I ain't joking. I went in shirt tail all the time. Never had on no pants 'til I was 15 years old. No shoes, 'cept two or three winters. Never had a hat 'til I was a great big boy.
    Marriage was performed by getting permission from Master and go where the woman of your choice had prepared the bed, undress and flat-footed jump a broom-stick together into the bed.
    Master had a brick house for hisself and the overseer. They was the only ones on the place. The overseer woke up the slaves all the way from 2 o'clock till 4 o'clock of mornings. He wasn't nothing but white trash. Nothing else in the world but that. They worked till

they couldn't see how to work. I jest couldn't jedge the size of that big place, and there was a mess of slaves, not less'n three hundred.

I doesn't have no eggycation, edgecation, or ejecation, and about all I can do is spell. I jest spell till I get the pronouncements.

We had church, but iffen the white folks caught you at it, you was beat most nigh to death. We used a big pot turned down to keep our voices down. When we went to hear white preachers, he would say, "Obey your master and mistress." I am a hard shell–flint Baptist. I was baptized in Pine Bluff, Arkansas. Our baptizing song was mostly "On Jordan's Stormy Banks I Stand" and our funeral song was "Hark From The Tomb."

We had some slaves who would try to run off to the North but the white folks would catch 'em with blood hounds and beat 'em to death. Them patrollers done their work mostly at night. One night I was sleeping on cotton and the patrollers come to our house and ask for water. Happen we had plenty. They drunk a whole lot and got warm and told my father to be a good nigger and they wouldn't bother him at all. They raided till General Grant come thoo'. He sent troops out looking for Ku Klux Klanners and killed 'em jest lak killing black birds. General Grant was one of the men that caused us to set heah free today and able to talk together without being killed.

I didn't and don't believe in no conjure. No sensible person do either. We had a doctor on the place. Ever master had a doctor who waited on his slaves, but we wore asafetida or onion 'round our necks to keep off diseases. A dime was put 'round a teething baby's neck to make it tooth easy, and it sho' helped too. But today all folks done got 'bove that.

The old folks talked very little of freedom and the chillun knew nothing at all of it, and that they heard they was daresome to mention it.

Bushwhacker, nothing but poor white trash, come thoo' and killed all the little nigger chillun they could lay hands on. I was hid under the house with a big rag on my mouf many a time. Them Klu Klux after slavery sho' got enough from them soldiers to last 'em.

I was married to Kan Pry in 1884. Two chillun was born. The girl is living and the boy might be, but I don't know. My daughter works out in service.

I wish Lincoln was here now. He done more for the black face than any one in that seat. Old Jeff Davis kept slavery up till General Grant met him at the battle. Lincoln sho' snowed him under. General Grant put fire under him jest lak I'm fixing to do my pipe. Booker T. Washington was jest all right.

Every time I think of slavery and if it done the race any good, I think of the story of the coon and dog who met. The coon said to the dog: "Why is it you're so fat and I am so poor, and we is both animals?" The dog said: "I lay round Master's house and let him kick me and he gives me a piece of bread right on." Said the coon to the dog: "Better then that I stay poor." Them's my sentiment. I'm lak the coon, I don't believe in 'buse.

I used to be the most wicked man in the world but a voice converted me by saying, "Friend, friend, why is you better to everybody else than you is to your self? You are sending your soul to hell." And from that day I lived like a Christian. People here don't live right and I don't lak to 'tend church. I base my Christian life on: "Believe in me, trust my work and you shall be saved, for I am God and beside me there is no other."

---

[1] Stephen McCray was interviewed in Oklahoma City by an unidentified WPA field worker probably sometime in spring or summer of 1937, for on 16 August 1937 his typewritten narrative was forwarded from the Oklahoma Writers' Project office to Washington, where it became part of the formal slave narrative collection. The interview is available only in the form sent to Washington, "Stephen McCray, Age 88 Yrs., Oklahoma City, Okla.," published here and available in ribbon-copy typescript in the LC Slave Narratives and in carbon copy as item 350088 in the LC Slave Narratives Carbon Copies. Stephens to Cronyn, 16 August 1937, WPA Notes on Interviews.

[2] Huntsville is actually in Madison County, Alabama; there is no Huntsville County. The "Scottsboro boys" were nine young African American men accused of rape on board a freight train in Alabama in 1931. Initially eight of them were convicted and sentenced to death. In subsequent retrial and legal maneuvering, four of the defendants were freed and the others received reduced sentences. Because of the extreme youth of the defendants, the unfairness of the first legal proceedings, and the extreme initial punishments, the case became a cause célèbre in 1930s American race relations. Dan T. Carter, *Scottsboro: A Tragedy of the American South*.

HANNAH MCFARLAND[1]

Age 85 Yrs.   *Oklahoma City, Okla.*

I was born in Georgetown, South Carolina, February 29, 1853.[2] My father was name James Gainey and my mother was name Katie Gainey. There was three chillun born to my folks doing slavery. My father was a free man, but my mother was de slave of the Sampsons, some Jews. My father was de richest Negro in South Carolina doing this time. He bought all three of we chillun for $1,000 apiece, but dem Jews jest wouldn't sell mamma. Dey was mighty sweet to her. She come home ever night and stayed with us. Doing the day a Virginian nigger woman stayed with us and she sho' was mean to we chillun. She used to beat us sumpin' terrible. You know Virginia people is mean to cullud people. My father bought her from some white folks too.

We lived in town and in a good house.

It was a good deal of confusion doing the War. I waited on the Yankees. Dey captured mamma's white people's house. Dey tried to git mamma to tell dem jest whut de white folks done done to her and all she could say was dey was good to her. Shucks, dey wouldn't sell her. She jest told them she had a free husband.

My father was a blockader. He run rafts from one place to another and sho' made a lot of money. He was drowned while doing this while I was a good size child.

Dem patrollers tied you to a whipping post iffen dey caught you out after 10 o'clock. They 'tempted to do my mother that way, but my papa sho' stopped dat. I can't say I lak white people even now, 'cause dey done done so much agin us.

I was free, but I couldn't go to school, 'cause we didn't had none. I been in Oklahoma over 40 years. Have done some traveling and could go some whar else, but I jest stays here 'cause I ain't got no desire to travel.

All we ever wore to keep off diseases was asafetida, nothing else.

I done heard more 'bout conjure in Oklahoma than I ever heerd in South Carolina. All dat stuff is in Louisiana. I didn't heah nothing 'bout the Klu Klux Klan till I come to Oklahoma neither. More devilment in Oklahoma than any place I know. South got more religion too. I jest as soon be back with the Rebels.

Bushwhackers whipped you iffen you stayed out late, and sho' nuff if dey didn't lak you.

I felt sorry for Jeff Davis when the Yankees drilled him through the streets. I saw it all. I said, "Mama, Mama, look, dey got old Jeff Davis." She said, "Be quiet, dey'll lynch you." She didn't know no better! She was a old slave nigger. I showed the Yankees where the white folks hid their silver and money and jewelry, and Mamma sho' whipped me about it too. She was no fool 'bout slavery. Slavery sho' didn't he'p us none to my belief.

I didn't care much 'bout Lincoln. It was nice of him to free us, but 'course he didn't want to.

The overseer was sho' nothing but poor white trash, the kind who didn't lak niggers and dey still don't, old devils. Don't let 'em fool you; dey don't lak a nigger a'tall.

I'm a Methodist. People ought to praise God 'cause he done done so much for dese sinners. Dey was heap more religious in my early days. I jined church in 1863. I jined the Holiness so I could git baptized and the Methodist wouldn't baptize you. After my baptism, I went back to the Methodist Church. You know my pastor, Reverend Miller, is the first Methodist preacher I ever knowed that was baptized, and that baptizes everybody.

I was married in Akin, South Carolina to Andrew Pew. We had 12 chillun. Jest one boy is my only living child today.

¹ Mrs. Hannah McFarland was interviewed by an unidentified WPA field worker probably sometime in summer or autumn of 1937, for on 14 September 1937 her typewritten remembrances were sent to the Federal Writers' Project headquarters in Washington. Today only that version of her interview survives. Published here, it is available as "Hannah McFarland, Age 85 Yrs., Oklahoma City, Okla." in ribbon copy in the LC Slave Narratives and in carbon copy as item 350057 in the LC Slave Narratives Carbon Copies. Stephens to Cronyn, 14 September 1937, WPA Notes on Interviews.

² The date intended here must have been 1852, which was a leap year and which would conform with the interviewee's age of eighty-five.

REMINISCENCES OF AUNT CHANEY MCNAIR
*One-Time Slave of William Penn Adair*¹

My parents came from Georgia with the Cherokees. They came by boat I 'spect. I don't know much about 'em. Can't even remember my mother; she died when I'se so young. She belonged to Vina Ratliff. My father must have belonged to John Drew but he was sold and sent to Mississippi long before the war.

I'se born in 1852 down below Tahlequah on the Ratliff Plantation. Yes, I'se born a Ratliff. I remember the big log house of my marster and the little ones the slaves lived in.

I got into Mart McCoy's hands somehow. There was an attachment or bond or something. He was sheriff down near Dwight Mission. I couldn't tell how come; we slaves didn't know nuthin' anyhow. Then Marster Ratliff got me back again. I'se there for a while then sold to William Penn Adair. I remember the old Adair Plantation. Marster Adair had his first wife then. They lived in a double log house. There was two big rooms with an entry in between. Didn't you never see a house with an entry? Well, you go in just like this: I walk in entry, I go this way and there's the door of one room, then I go that way and there's the door of other room.

You ask why they didn't have no bigger house. Why, they couldn't have done no better. They hadn't had time. They was drove here in '35 and I lived there in '62. They hadn't had much time to build much house, but it was warm. Them two rooms had rock fireplaces, with a big rock hearth. They had big mantle-boards like. You don't see none no more. They cooked on the kitchen fireplace; baked the bread in a skillet laid in the coals. Everybody had fireplaces. I never seen no stove till I got free up in Kansas. The bedstead had curtains all around, I remember that, too. And there was a trundle bed for the children. You slide it under the big bed in the day time. Never see them no more, either.

Marster William had about ten slaves. I remember the names of five, Francis, Margaret, Tobe and Bean, not countin' myself. Francis and Margaret washed, spinned and weaved. They wove lots and lots of goods. Didn't you never see no weavin'? They carded the wool first, make roll, then they put it, the cotton, on a wheel and spin it round and round like this. They use their feet too. They made bed spreads, sheets, jeans for pants. Oh, we ain't no count now; we don't know how to do nuthin'.

We lived in the Joe Martin community. I've heard tell how mean he was. Lots of the Cherokees had slaves. There was the Adairs, William Penn, my marster, Fran, John and George Washington, the Martins, the Drews and old Dick Sanders. Most of the Cherokees was good to their slaves, but old Joe Martin wasn't. My last marster, William Penn Adair, was tall, slender man. He was pretty good looking, smart lawyer. Most of the time he was good to his slaves but he crossed up with sometimes. Mistress Sarah, his wife, she was good to us, yes, awful good to us. Them Adairs was all smart people. I used to go and visit old Aunt Suzanna McNair (she was a Bell). We liked to talk over old times. Washington Adair got shot one time. His home was just a little ways from Marster William's, all live close together. Well, he set up his gun some way and it fell, shot him right through the leg. You just talk to some of his gran' children. They tell you I'se tellin' you the truth.

Does I believe in Spirits? Sure I do. This old flesh and bones goin' back from what God make it, but our spirits never die. Sometimes the spirits of folks what's dead come back. I've heard of haunted house where there was rappin's and the like, but I never did hear any myself. Tell you what I did see, more than once. Back in Ft. Scott

where I worked there's little girl, beautiful little girl with long curls.
I wondered why God made me black and ugly and that little girl so
white. Before I left she died, I saw her lyin' in the casket. Long time
after she came to me in a dream like. I saw a little girl with curls, all
dressed in white. Seemed like she was here a minute, then she walked
out the door and was gone. She come more than once and stand right
here in that door. Sometime that little girl goin' come back all
dressed in white and take old Aunt Chaney out the door and I won't
never come back.

[1] Mrs. Chaney McNair was interviewed in Vinita, Oklahoma, by field worker Annie
L. Faulton of the WPA Federal Theater Project in Oklahoma during the week ending
8 July 1939. Although her typewritten interview was undertaken as part of another
WPA program, its text was filed with those of the Oklahoma Slave Narrative Project
at the Oklahoma Historical Society and for over half a century has been associated with
those materials and consequently is published here. The original text is available as
"Reminiscences of Aunt Chaney McNair, One-Time Slave of William Penn Adair" in
the OHS Slave Narratives. For another, roughly contemporary interview with this informant, see Chaney McNair, interview by James Carselowey at Vinita, Oklahoma, 11
May 1937, Indian-Pioneer Papers, 106:442–49.
    William Penn Adair (1830–80) was a well-known Cherokee statesman and leader,
often representing the Cherokee Nation in Washington, D.C. For a sketch of his life,
see Cherrie Adair Moore, "William Penn Adair," *Chronicles of Oklahoma* 29 (Spring
1951): 32–41.

MARSHALL MACK[1]

Age 83 Yrs.   *Oklahoma City, Okla.*

I was born September 10, 1854. I am the second child of five. My
mother was named Sylvestus Mack and my father Booker Huddleston. I do not remember my mother's master, 'cause he died before I
was born. My Mistress was named Nancy Mack. She was the mother
of six children, four boys and two girls. Three of dem boys went to
the War and one packed and went off somewhar and nobody heard
from him doing of the whole War. But soon as the War was over he
come home and he never told whar he had been.
    I never saw but one grown person flogged during slavery and dat
was my mother. The younger son of my mistress whipped her one
morning in de kitchen. His name was Jack. De slaves on Mistress'
place was treated so good, all de people round and 'bout called us
"Mack's Free Niggers." Dis was 14 miles northwest of Liberty,
county seat of Bedford County, Virginia.
    One day while de War was going on, my Mistress got a letter from

her son Jim wid jest one line. Dat was "Mother: Jack's brains spattered on my gun this morning." That was all he written.

Jack Huddleston owned my father, who was his half-brother, and he was the meanest man I ever seen. He flogged my father with tobacco sticks and my mother after these floggings (which I never seen) had to pick splinters out of his back. My father had to slip off at night to come and visit us. He lived a mile and a half from our house on the south side of the Blue Ridge Mountains, and it sho' is a rocky country. He'd oversleep hisself and git up running. We would stand in our door and hear him running over them rocks 'til he got home. He was trying to git dere before his master called him.

It was a law among the slave-holders that if you left you master's place, you had to have a pass, for if the patroller caught you without one, he would give you 9 and 30 lashes and carry you to your master, and if he was mean, you got the same again!

On the 3-foot fireplace my mother and father cooked ash cakes and my father having to run to work, had to wash his cakes off in a spring betwixt our house and his. My mother was the cook in the Big House.

All the time we would see "nigger traders" coming through the country. I have seen men and women cuffed to 60-foot chains being took to Lynchburg, Va., to the block to be sold. Now I am talking 'bout what I know,[2] for it would not mean one thing for me to lie. I ain't jest heard dis. My uncle John was a carpenter and always took Mistress' chillun to school in a two-horse surrey. On sech trips, the chillun learned my uncle to read and write. Dey slipped and done this, for it was a law among slave-holders that a slave not be caught wid a book.

One morning when I was on my way to de mill with a sack of corn, I had to go down the main pike. I saw sech a fog 'til I rid close enough to see what was gwine on. I heard someone say "close up." I was told since dat it was Hood's Raid. They took every slave that could carry a gun. It was at dis time, Negroes went into de service. Lee was whipping Grant two battles to one 'til them raids, and den Grant whipped Lee two battles to one, 'cause he had Negroes in the Union Army. Dey took Negroes and all de white people's food. Dey killed chickens and picked dem on horseback. I never will forgit that time long as I live.

Ever day I had to get the mail for three families. I carried it around in a bag and each family took his'n out. I guess I was one of the first Negro mailmen.

We had church on the place and had right good meetings. Everybody went and took part in the service. We had to have passes to go off the place to the meetings.

The children wore just one garment from this time of year (spring) till the frost fell. Mistress' daughters made dese. We sure kept healthy and fat.

I will be 83 years of age September 10, 1937 and am enjoying my second eyesight. I could not see a thing hardly for some few years, but now I can read sometimes without glasses. I keep my lawn in first class shape and work all the time. I think this is 'cause I never was treated bad during slavery.

[1] WPA field worker Ida Belle Hunter interviewed Marshall Mack at his home in Oklahoma City probably in spring of 1937. From her notes a preliminary draft of Mack's narrative was prepared at least by 27 May 1937, the date rubber-stamped on the ribbon copy of the typescript, "Interview with Marshall Mack, Ex-Slave, 501 N.E. 4th, Okla. City, Okla." This preliminary typescript is filed without further explanation with item 350053 in the LC Slave Narratives Carbon Copies. Personnel in the Oklahoma City office of the project lightly edited the preliminary draft and prepared a final version, published here, "Marshall Mack, Age 83 Yrs., Oklahoma City, Okla.," available in ribbon copy in the LC Slave Narratives and in carbon copy as item 350053 in the LC Slave Narratives Carbon Copies. This final draft was forwarded to Washington on 14 September 1937. *Oklahoma City Negro City Directory,* 119; *Polk's Oklahoma City Directory, 1937,* 457, 928; Stephens to Cronyn, 14 September 1937, WPA Notes on Interviews.

Between the heading and the body of the interview, Ida Belle Hunter added the following typewritten comment on the preliminary draft of the narrative: "Note: This ex-slave (Marshall Mack) is not to my mind a typical slave. For at times, he talks as an educated person and at other times as a very illiterate person. Thus, the variation in the copy of words used by him. I.B.H."

[2] The preliminary draft at this point includes the direct address "chile."

ALLEN V. MANNING[1]

Age 87   *Tulsa, Okla.*

I always been somewhar in the South, mostly in Texas when I was a young man, and of course us Negroes never got much of a show in court matters, but I reckon if I had of had the chance to set on a jury I would of made a mighty poor out at it.

No sir, I jest can't set in judgement on nobody, 'cause I learned when I was jest a little boy that good people and bad people—makes no difference which—jest keep on living and doing like they been taught, and I jest can't seem to blame them none for what they do iffen they been taught that way.

I was born in slavery, and I belonged to a Baptist preacher. Until I was fifteen years old I was taught that I was his own chattel-property, and he could do with me like he wanted to, but he had been taught that way too, and we both believed it. I never did hold nothing against him for being hard on Negroes sometimes, and I don't think I ever would of had any trouble even if I had of growed up and died in slavery.

The young Negroes don't know nothing 'bout that today, and lots of them are rising up and amounting to something, and all us Negroes is proud of them. You see, it's because they been taught that they got as good a show to be something as anybody, if they tries hard.

Well, this old Negro knows one thing; they getting somewheres 'cause the young whitefolks is letting them and helping them to do it, 'cause the whitefolks has been taught the same way, and I praise God it's getting to be that way, too. But it all go to show, people do like they been taught to do.

Like I say, my master was a preacher and a kind man, but he treated the Negroes jest like they treated him. He been taught that they was jest like his work hosses, and if they act like they his work hosses they git along all right. But if they don't—Oh, oh!

Like the Dixie song, I was born "on a frosty mornin'" at the plantation in Clarke County, Mississippi, in the fall of 1850 they tell me. The old place looked the same all the time I was a child, clean up to when we pull out and leave the second year of the War.

I can shet my eyes and think about it and it seem to come right up in front of me jest like it looked. From my Pappy's cabin the Big House was off to the west, close to the big road, and most of the fields stretched off to the north. They was a big patch of woods off to the east, and not much open land between us and the Chickasawhay River. Off to the southwest a few miles was the Bucatunna Creek, and the plantation was kind of in the forks between them, a little ways east of Quitman, Mississippi.

Old Master's people been living at that place a mighty long time, and most the houses and barns was old and been repaired time and time again, but it was a mighty pretty place. The Big House was built long, with a lot of rooms all in a row and a long porch, but it wasn't fine like a lot of the houses we seen as we passed by when we left that place to go to Louisiana.

Old Master didn't have any overseer hired, but him and his boys looked after the place and had a Negro called the driver. We-all shore hated that old black man, but I forget his name now. That driver never was allowed to think up nothing for the slaves to do, but jest was told to make them work hard at what the master and his boys told them to do. Whitefolks had to set them at a job and then old driver would whoopity and whoopity around, and egg them and egg them until they finish up, so they can go at something else. He worked hard hisself, though, and set a mighty hard pattern for the rest to keep up with. Like I say, he been taught he didn't know how to think, so he didn't try.

Old Mistress' name was Mary, and they had two daughters, Levia and Betty. Then they had three sons. The oldest was named Bill Junior, and he was plumb grown when I was a boy, but the other two, Jedson and Jim, was jest a little older then me.

Old Master didn't have but two or three single Negroes, but he had several families, and most of them was big ones. My own family was pretty good size, but three of the children was born free. Pappy's name was William and Mammy's was Lucy. My brother Joe was the oldest child and then come Adeline, Harriet, and Texana and Betty before the surrender, and then Henry, Mattie and Louise after it.

When the War come along old Master jest didn't know what to do. He always been taught not to raise his hand up and kill nobody—no matter how come—and he jest kept holding out against all them that was talking about fighting, and he wouldn't go and fight. He been taught that it was all right to have slaves and treat them like he want to, but he been taught it was sinful to go fight and kill to keep them, and he lived up to what he been taught.

They was some Choctaw people lived 'round there, and they flew up and went right off to the War, and Mr. Trot Hand and Mr. Joe Brown that had plantations on the big road towards Quitman both went off with their grown boys right at the start, but old Master was a preacher and he jest stayed out of it. I remember one day I was sent up to the Big House and I heard old Master and some men out at the gate 'xpounding about the War. Some of the men had on soldier clothes, and they acted like they was mad. Somebody tell me later on that they was getting up a home guard because the yankees done got down in Alabama not far away, but old Master wouldn't go in with them.

Two, three days after that, it seems like, old Master come down to the quarters and say git everything bundled up and in the wagons for a long trip. The Negroes all come in and everybody pitch in to help pack up the wagons. Then old Master look around and he can't find

Andy. Andy was one Negro that never did act like he been taught, and old Master's patience about wore out with him anyways.

We all know that Andy done run off again, but we didn't know where to. Leastwise all the Negroes tell old Master that. But old Master soon show us we done the work and he done the thinking! He jest goes ahead and keeps all the Negroes busy fixing up the wagons and bundling up the stuff to travel, and keeps us all in his sight all the time, and says nothing about Andy being gone.

Then that night he sends for a white man name Clements that got some blood hounds, and him and Mr. Clements takes time about staying awake and watching all the cabins to see nobody slips out of them. Everybody was afraid to stick their head out.

Early next morning we has all the wagons ready to drive right off, and old Master call Andy's brother up to him. He say, "You go down to that spring and wait, and when Andy come down to the spring to fill that cedar bucket you stole out'n the smokehouse for him to git water in you tell him to come on in here. Tell him I know he is hiding out way down the branch whar he can come up wading the water clean up to the cornfield and the melon patch, so the hounds won't git his scent, but I'm going to send the hounds down there if he don't come on in right now." Then we all knowed we was for the work and old Master was for the thinking, 'cause pretty soon Andy come on in. He'd been right whar old Master think he is.

About that time Mr. Sears come riding down the big road. He was a deacon in old Master's church, and he see us all packed up to leave and so he light at the big gate and walk up to whar we is. He ask old Master where we all lighting out for, and old Master say for Louisiana. We Negroes don't know where that is. Then old deacon say what old Master going to do with Andy, 'cause there stood Mr. Clements holding his bloodhounds and old Master had his cat-o-nine-tails in his hand.

Old Master say just watch him, and he tell Andy if he can make it to that big black gum tree down at the gate before the hounds git him he can stay right up in that tree and watch us all drive off. Then he tell Andy to git!

Poor Andy jest git hold of the bottom limbs when the blood hounds grab him and pull him down onto the ground. Time old Master and Mr. Clements git down there the hounds done tore off all Andy's clothes and bit him all over bad. He was rolling on the ground and holding his shirt up 'round his throat when Mr. Clements git there and pull the hounds off of him.

Then old Master light in on him with that cat-o-nine-tails, and I don't know how many lashes he give him, but he jest bloody all over and done fainted pretty soon. Old Deacon Sears stand it as long as he can and then he step up and grab old Master's arm and say, "Time to stop, Brother! I'm speaking in the name of Jesus!" Old Master quit then, but he still powerful mad. I don't think he believe Andy going to make that tree when he tell him that.

Then he turn on Andy's brother and give him a good beating too, and we all drive off and leave Andy sitting on the ground under a tree and old Deacon standing by him. I don't know what ever become of Andy, but I reckon maybe he went and live with old Deacon Sears until he was free.

When I think back and remember it, it all seems kind of strange, but it seem like old Master and old Deacon both think the same way. They kind of understand that old Master had a right to beat his Negro all he wanted to for running off, and he had a right to set the hounds on him if he did. But he shouldn't of beat him so hard after he told him he was going to let him off if he made the tree, and he ought to keep his word even if Andy was his own slave. That's the way both them white men had been taught, and that was the way they both lived.

Old Master had about five wagons on that trip down into Louisiana, but they was all full of stuff and only the old slaves and children could ride in them. I was big enough to walk most of the time, but one time I walked in the sun so long that I got sick and they put me in the wagon for most the rest of the way.

We would come to places where the people said the Yankees had been and gone, but we didn't run into any Yankees. They was most to the north of us I reckon, because we went on down to the south part of Mississippi and ferried across the big river at Baton Rouge. Then we went on to Lafayette, Louisiana, before we settled down anywhere.

All us Negroes thought that was a mighty strange place. We would hear white folks talking and we couldn't understand what they said, and lots of the Negroes talked the same way, too. It was all full of French people around Lafayette, but they had all their menfolks in the Confederate Army just the same. I seen lots of men in butternut clothes coming and going hither and yon, but they wasn't in bunches.[2] They was mostly coming home to see their folks.

Everybody was scared all the time, and two–three times when old

Master hired his Negroes out to work the man that hired them quit his place and went on west before they got the crop in. But old Master got a place and we put in a cotton crop, and I think he got some money by selling his place in Mississippi. Anyway, pretty soon after the cotton was all in he moves again and goes to a place on Simonette Lake for the winter. It ain't a bit cold in that place, and we didn't have no fire 'cepting to cook, and sometimes a little charcoal fire in some crock pots that the people left on the place when they went on out to Texas.

The next spring old Master loaded up again and we struck out for Texas, when the Yankees got too close again. But Master Bill didn't go to Texas, because the Confederates done come that winter and made him go to the army. I think they took him to New Orleans, and old Master was hopping mad, but he couldn't do anything or they would make him go too, even if he was a preacher.

I think he left out of there partly because he didn't like the people at that place. They wasn't no Baptists around anywheres, and they was all Catholics, and old Master didn't like them.

About that time it look like everybody in the world was going to Texas. When we would be going down the road we would have to walk along the side all the time to let the wagons go past, all loaded with folks going to Texas.

Pretty soon old Master say git the wagons loaded again, and this time we start out with some other people, going north. We go north a while and then turn west, and cross the Sabine River and go to Nachedoches, Texas.[3] Me and my brother Joe and my sister Adeline walked nearly all the way, but my little sister Harriet and my mammy rid in a wagon. Mammy was mighty poorly, and jest when we got to the Sabine bottoms she had another baby. Old Master didn't like it 'cause it was a girl, but he named her Texana on account of where she was born and told us children to wait on Mammy good and maybe we would get a little brother next time.

But we didn't. Old Master went with a whole bunch of wagons on out to the prairie country in Coryell County and set up a farm where we just had to break the sod and didn't have to clear off much. And the next baby Mammy had the next year was a girl. We named her Betty because Mistress jest have a baby a little while before and its name was Betty.

Old Master's place was right at the corner where Coryell and McLennan and Bosque Counties come together, and we raised mostly cotton and jest a little corn for feed. He seem like he changed a lot since we left Mississippi, and seem like he paid more attention to us and looked after us better. But most the people that already live there when we git there was mighty hard on their Negroes. They was mostly hard drinkers and hard talkers, and they work and fight jest as hard as they talk, too!

One day Old Master come out from town and tell us that we all been set free, and we can go or stay jest as we wish. All of my family stay on the place and he pay us half as shares on all we make. Pretty soon the whitefolks begin to cut down on the shares, and the renters git only a third and some less, and the Negroes begin to drift out to other places, but old Master stick to the halves a year or so after that. Then he come down to a third too.

It seems like the white people can't git over us being free, and they do everything to hold us down all the time. We don't git no schools for a long time, and I never see the inside of a school. I jest grow up on hard work. And we can't go 'round where they have the voting, unless we want to ketch a whipping some night, and we have to jest keep on bowing and scraping when we are 'round white folks like we did when we was slaves. They had us down and they kept us down. But that was the way they been taught, and I don't blame them for it none, I reckon.

When I git about thirty years old I marry Betty Sadler close to Waco, and we come up to the Creek Nation forty years ago. We come to Muskogee first, and then to Tulsa 'bout thirty seven years ago.

We had ten children but only seven are alive. Three girls and a boy live here in Tulsa and we got one boy in Muskogee and one at Frederick, Oklahoma.

I sells milk and makes my living, and I keeps so busy I don't think back on the old days much, but if anybody ask me why the Texas Negroes been kept down so much I can tell them. If they set like I did on the bank at that ferry across the Sabine, and see all that long line of covered wagons, miles and miles of them, crossing that river and going west with all they got left out of the War, it ain't hard to understand.

Them whitefolks done had everything they had tore up, or had to run away from the places they lived, and they brung their Negroes out to Texas and then right away they lost them too. They always had them Negroes, and lots of them had mighty fine places back in the old states, and then they had to go out and live in sod houses and little old boxed shotguns[4] and turn their Negroes loose. They didn't see no justice in it then, and most of them never did until they died. The folks that stayed at home and didn't straggle all over the country had their old places to live on and their old friends around them, but the Texans was different.

So I says, when they done us the way they did they was jest doing the way they was taught. I don't blame them, because anybody will do that.

Whitefolks mighty decent to me now, and I always tried to teach my children to be respectful and act like they think the whitefolks they dealing with expects them to act. That the way to git along, because some folks been taught one way and some been taught another, and folks always thinks the way they been taught.

[1] Robert Vinson Lackey interviewed Allen V. Manning in Tulsa probably sometime during the spring or summer of 1937, for on 16 August of that year a final draft of Manning's interview transcript was forwarded to Washington. A preliminary draft of the narrative bearing Lackey's name as interviewer is available in ribbon copy as "Interview with Allen V. Manning, Ex-Slave, Age 87, 1330 N. Kenosha Ave., Tulsa, Okla." in the OHS Slave Narratives. At the top of this typescript an anonymous comment reads, "The Person who edited this must ha[ve been] a dam Yankee." The final draft, lightly revised from the earlier version and as published here, is available as "Allen V. Manning, Age 87, Tulsa, Okla." in ribbon copy in the LC Slave Narratives and in carbon copy as item 350086 in the LC Slave Narratives Carbon Copies. After Manning's narrative had arrived in Washington, B. A. Botkin, folklore editor for the Federal Writers' Project, described it as "a philosophical portrait, remarkably understanding and revealing in its insight into slave-master relations," and appraised it as both "thoughtful and powerful." He was so impressed that he published virtually the entire narrative in his book *Lay My Burden Down* (93–98, 276) in 1945. B. A. B[otkin], LC Slave Narratives Appraisal Sheets, Accession no. 350086, 12 December 1940; Stephens to Cronyn, 16 August 1937, WPA Notes on Interviews.

[2] "Butternut clothes" here refers to the Confederate uniforms.

[3] Obviously a phonetic spelling for Nacogdoches, Texas.

[4] "Boxed shotguns" here refers to board-and-batten-style shotgun houses, a typically African American form of building that employed vertical lumber planks to form the walls of houses one room wide, one story tall, and several rooms deep. John Michael Vlach, "The Shotgun House: An African Architectural Legacy," in *Common Places: Readings in American Vernacular Architecture,* edited by Dell Upton and John Michael Vlach, 58–78.

BOB MAYNARD[1]

Age 79   *23 East Choctaw, Weleetka, Oklahoma*

I was born near what is now Marlin, Texas, Falls County. My father was Robert Maynard and my mother was Chanie Maynard, both born slaves. Our Master, Gerard Branum, was a very old man and wore long white whiskers. He sho' was a fine built man, and walked straight and tall like a young man.

I was too little to do much work so my job was to carry the key basket for old Mistress. I sho' was proud of that job. The basket held the keys to the pantry, the kitchen, the linen closet, and extra keys to the rooms and smokehouse. When old Mistress started out on her rounds every morning she'd call to me to get de basket and away we'd go. I'd run errands for all the house help too, so I was kept purty busy.

The "big house" was a fine one. It was a big two-story white house made of pine lumber. There was a big porch or veranda across the front and wings on the east and west. The house faced south. There was big round white posts that went clean up to the roof and there was a big porch upstairs too. I believe the house was what you'd call colonial style. There was twelve or fifteen rooms and a big wide stairway. It was a purty place, with a yard and big trees and the house that set in a walnut and pecan grove. They was graveled walks and driveways and all along by the driveway was cedars. There was a hedge close to the house and a flower garden with purty roses, holly hocks and a lot of others I don't know the name of.

Back to the right of the house was the smokehouse, kept full of meat, and further back was the big barns. Old Master kept a spanking pair of carriage horses and several fine riding horses. He kept several pairs of mules, too, to pull the plow. He had some ox teams too.

To the left and back of the "big house" was the quarters. He owned about two thousand acres of land and three hundred slaves. He kept a white overseer and the colored overlooker was my uncle. He sho' saw that the gang worked. He saw to it that the cotton was took to the gin. They used oxen to pull the wagons full of cotton. There was two gins on the plantation. Had to have two for it was slow work to gin a bale of cotton as it was run by horse power.

Old Master raised hundreds of hogs; he raised practically all the food we et. He gave the food out to each family and they done their own cooking except during harvest. The farm hands was fed at the "big house." They was called in from the farm by a big bell.

Sunday was our only day for recreation. We went to church at our own church and we could sing and shout jest as loud as we pleased and it didn't disturb nobody.

During the week after supper we would all set round the doors outside and sing or play music. The only musical instruments we had was a jug or big bottle, a skillet lid or frying pan that they'd hit with a stick or a bone. We had a flute too, made out of reed cane and it'd make good music. Sometimes we'd sing and dance so long and loud old Master'd have to make us stop and go to bed.

The Patrollers, Ku Kluxers or night riders come by sometimes at night to scare the niggers and make 'em behave. Sometimes the slaves would run off and the Patroller would catch 'em and have 'em whipped. I've seen that done lots of times. They was some wooden stocks (a sort of trough) and they'd put the darky in this and strap him down, take off his clothes and give him 25 to 50 licks, 'cording to what he had done.

I reckon old Master had everything his heart could wish for at this time. Old Mistress was a fine lady and she always went dressed up. She wore long trains on her skirts and I'd walk behind her and hold her train up when she made de rounds. She was awful good to me. I slept on the floor in her little boy's room, and she give me apples and candy just like she did him. Old Master gave ever chick and child good warm clothes for winter. We had store boughten shoes but the women made our clothes. For underwear we all wore "lowers" but no shirts.

After the war started old Master took a lot of his slaves and went to Natchez, Mississippi. He thought he'd have a better chance of keeping us there I guess, and he was afraid we'd be freed and he started running with us. I remember when General Grant blowed up Vicksburg. I had a free born Uncle and Aunt who sometimes visited in the North and they'd tell us how easy it was up there and it sho' made us all want to be free.

I think Abe Lincoln was next to de Lawd. He done all he could for de slaves; he set 'em free. People in the South knowed they'd lose their slaves when he was elected president. 'Fore the election he traveled all over the South and he come to our house and slept in old Mistress' bed. Didn't nobody know who he was. It was a custom to take strangers in and put them up for one night or longer, so he come to our house and he watched close. He seen how the niggers come in on Saturday and drawed four pounds of meat and a peck of meal for a week's rations. He also saw 'em whipped and sold. When he got back up north he writ old Master a letter and told him he was going to have to free his slaves, that everybody was going to have to, that the North was going to see to it. He also told him that he had visited at his house and if he doubted it to go in the same room he slept in and look on the bedstead at the head and he'd see where he'd writ his name. Sho' nuff, there was his name: A. Lincoln.

Didn't none of us like Jeff Davis. We all liked Robert E. Lee, but we was glad that Grant whipped him.

When the War was over, old Master called all the darkies in and lined 'em up in a row. He told 'em they was free to go and do as they pleased. It was six months before any of us left him.

Darkies could vote in Mississippi. Fred Douglas, a colored man, came to Natchez and made political speeches for General Grant.[2]

After the war they was a big steam boat line on the Mississippi River known as the Robert E. Lee Line. They sho' was fine boats too.

We used to have lots of Confederate money. Five cent pieces, two bit pieces, half dollar bills and half dimes. During the war old Master dug a long trench and buried all de silver, fine clothes, jewelry and a lot of money. I guess he dug it up, but I don't remember.

Master died three years after the War. He took it purty good, losing his niggers and all. Lots of men killed theirselves. Old Master was a good old man.

I'm getting old, I reckon. I've been married twice and am the father of 19 chillun. The oldest is 57 and my youngest is two boys, ten and twelve. I had great grandchillun older than them two boys.

[1] Bob Maynard was interviewed by an unidentified WPA field worker in Weleetka, Oklahoma, probably sometime in summer 1937, for a typescript of his narrative was sent from the Oklahoma City office of the Federal Writers' Project to Washington on 2 September 1937. Only the final draft of Maynard's narrative is known to survive. It is published here and is available as "Bob Maynard, Age 79, 23 East Choctaw, Weleetka, Oklahoma" in ribbon copy in the LC Slave Narratives and in carbon copy as item 350067 in the LC Slave Narratives Carbon Copies. Stephens to Cronyn, 2 September 1937, WPA Notes on Interviews.

[2] This sentence refers to the black abolitionist and statesman Frederick Douglass. The visit to Natchez may have been on Douglass's April 1872 trip to attend a national convention of African American citizens held in New Orleans. John W. Blassingame and John R. McKivigan, eds., *The Frederick Douglass Papers*, 4:xxiv–xxxii; Frederick Douglass, *Life and Times of Frederick Douglass Written by Himself,* 507–8; William S. McFeely, *Frederick Douglass,* 277–79.

JANE MONTGOMERY[1]

Age 80 Yrs.   *Oklahoma City, Oklahoma*

I was born March 15, 1857, in Homer, Louisiana. I claim to be 75 years old, but that's jest my way of counting. My mother was Sarah Strong and my father was Edmond Beavers. We lived in a log cabin that had jest one door. I had two sisters named Peggy and Katie.

Mammy was bought from the Strong family and my pappy was bought from Beavers by Mister Eason.

We slept on wooden slabs which was jest make-shift beds. I didn't do no work in slave times 'cause I was too little. You jest had to be good and husky to work on that place. I listened and told mammy everything I heerd. I ate right side dat old white woman on the flo'. I was a little busy-body. I don't recollect eating in our quarters on Sunday and no other time.

I don't remember no possums and rabbits being on our place, 'cause when white folks killed a chicken for their selves, dey killed one for the niggers. My pappy never ate no cornbread in all his put-together. Meat was my favorite food. I never ate no dry bread without no meat.

We wore homespun clothes. My first pair of shoes was squirrel skin. Mammy had 'em made. We wore clothes called linsey that was wool and cotton mixed.[2]

My father was the onliest overseer. It was sho' a great big old place. My master jest seen the place on Sundays. They was jest seven Niggers on our plantation. No working late at night but we had to git up at daylight. When our day's work was done, we went to bed, but sometimes they sung. Sadday was a holiday from working on the plantation. You had Sadday to wash for yourself. We didn't do nothing on Christmas and all holidays.

Mistress never whip us and iffen master would start, mistress would git a gun and make him stop. She said, "Let ever bitch whip her own chillun." I never seen no patrollers, I jest heered of 'em. They never come on our place. I guess they was scared to. The Klu Klux whipped niggers when so ever they could catch 'em. They rid at night mostly.

I am a Baptist. I belong to Cavalry Baptist Church. I was baptized in a creek. Our favorite hymn was "Dark Was the Night an' Cold the Ground." Our favorite revival hymn was "Lord I'd Come to Thee, a Sinner Undefiled." Our favorite funeral song was "Hark From the Tomb."

My family didn't believe in conjure an' all that stuff, 'though theys a heap of it was going on and still is for that matter. They had "hands" that was made up of all kinds of junk. You used 'em to make folks love you more'n they did. We used asafetida to keep off smallpox and measles. Put mole foots round a baby's neck to make him teethe easy. We used to use nine red ants tied in a sack round they neck to make 'em teethe easy and never had no trouble with 'em neither.

I think I seen a haunt once, 'cause when I looked the second time, what I seen the first time was gone.

When the War was over, mistress' son come home and he cleaned his guns on my dress tail. It sho' stunk up my dress and made me sick too. He told old mistress that niggers was free now. I went and told mammy that old Betsy's son told her the niggers was free and what did he mean. She said, "Shhhhhh!" They never did jest come out and tell us we was free. We was free in July and mammy left in September. We lived in Jordan Saline, out from Smith County.[3] Then my mother give me to my father 'cause she was married to another man. Her and my step-father moved to Gilmore, Texas.[4] They sent for me round 'bout Christmas and we lived on Sampers' farm.

We lived so far out, we couldn't go to school, 'though they was for us. We didn't own no land. Didn't nobody learn me to read and write.

Abe Lincoln was a good man. It was through Mr. Lincoln that God fit to free us. I don't know much 'bout Jeff Davis and don't care nothing 'bout him. Booker T. Washington built that school through God. He used to live in a cabin jest lak I done. He was sho' a great man.

I married Trole Kemp in 1883. I 'mind you they didn't marry in slavery, they jest took up. Master jest give a permit. I am the mother of 10 chillun and 5 grandchillun. Four of my chillun died young. Them what's living is doing different things sech as: writing policy, working on made work, housework, government clerk and hotel maid. One is in the pen.

[1] Mrs. Jane Montgomery was interviewed in Oklahoma City by an unidentified WPA field worker probably sometime in the spring or summer of 1937, for on 16 August of that year the final draft of the narrative based on her interview was sent to project headquarters in Washington. Her remembrances survive today only in that final draft typescript, published here, which is available as "Jane Montgomery, Age 80 Yrs., Oklahoma City, Oklahoma" in ribbon copy in the LC Slave Narratives and in carbon copy as item 350087 in the LC Slave Narratives Carbon Copies. Stephens to Cronyn, 16 August 1937, WPA Notes on Interviews.

[2] This is a reference to linsey-woolsey cloth, a coarse combination of either wool and linen or wool and cotton.

[3] Located just east of present-day Grand Saline, Jordan's Saline from 1848 to 1850 was the seat of Van Zandt County, the county immediately to the west of Smith County, Texas. Ed Bartholomew, *The Encyclopedia of Texas Ghost Towns,* 52; Webb, *Handbook of Texas,* 1:716.

[4] This may be a reference in phonetic spelling to Gilmer, the seat of Upshur County, Texas.

Frances Banks at Button Spring, ca. 1910. *Courtesy Archives and Manuscripts Divison of the Oklahoma Historical Society.*

Lucinda Davis in Tulsa, summer 1937. *Courtesy Manuscript Division of the Library of Congress.*

Anthony Dawson in Tulsa, summer 1937. *Courtesy Manuscript Division of the Library of Congress.*

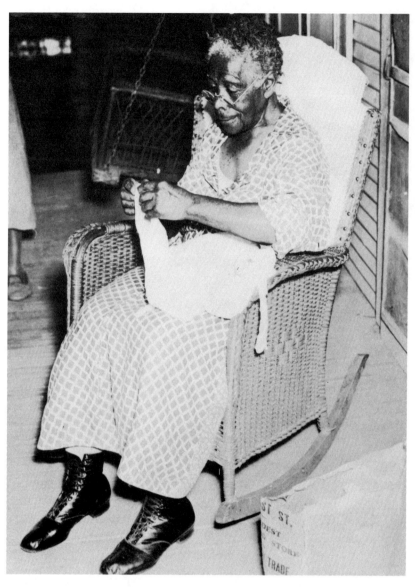

Katie Rowe in Tulsa, summer 1937. *Courtesy Manuscript Division of the Library of Congress.*

Morris Sheppard, ca. 1937. *Courtesy Archives and Manuscripts Division of the Oklahoma Historical Society.*

Morris Sheppard with members of his family, ca. 1930s. *Courtesy Archives and Manuscripts Division of the Oklahoma Historical Society.*

William W. and Betsy Ann Watson with two of their great-grandchildren, near Muskogee, ca. 1938. *Courtesy Archives and Manuscripts Division of the Oklahoma Historical Society.*

Charlotte Johnson White near Fort Gibson, ca. 1937–38. *Courtesy Archives and Manuscripts Division of the Oklahoma Historical Society.*

Charley Williams with his granddaughter in Tulsa, summer 1937. *Courtesy Manuscript Division of the Library of Congress.*

Robert and Sofa Williams at Muskogee, ca. 1934–37. *Courtesy Archives and Manuscripts Division of the Oklahoma Historical Society.*

CORNELIUS NEELY NAVE[1]

Age 70 Years   *Fort Gibson, Okla.*

I was born after the War, about 1868, and what I knows 'bout slave times is what my pappa told me, and maybe that not be very much. Two year old when my mamma die so I remember nothing of her, and most of my sisters and brothers dead too. Pappa named Charley Nave; mamma's name was Mary Vann before she marry, and her pappa was Talaka Vann, one of Joe Vann's slaves down around Webber's Falls.[2]

My father was born in Tahlequah just about where the colored church stands on depot hill. His master, Daniel Nave, was Cherokee. In the master's yard was the slave cabin, one room long, dirt floor, no windows. I think I heard 'em say mamma was born on Bull Creek; that somewhere up near Kansas, maybe near Coffeyville.

Vinita was the closest town to where I was born; when I get older seem like they call it "the junction," on account the rails cross there, but I never ride on the trains, just stay at home.

I remember that home after the war brought my pappa back home. He went to the war for three year wid the Union soldiers. But about the home—it was a double-room log house with a cooling-off space between the rooms, all covered with a roof, but no porch, and the beds was made of planks, the table of pine boards and there was never enough boxes for the chairs so the littlest children eat out of a tin pan off the floor.

That house was on the place my pappa said he bought from Billy Jones in 1865. The land was timbered and the oldest children clear the land, or start to do the work, while pappa go back to Tahlequah to get my sick mamma and the rest of the family. Because mamma was sick then he brought her sister, Sucky Pea, and her husband Charley Pea, to help around wid him.

We lived there a long time, and I was old enough to remember setting in the yard watching the river (Grand River) go by, and the Indians go by. All Indians lived around there, the real colored settlement was four mile from us, and I wasn't scared of them Indians for pappa always told me his master, Henry Nave, was his own father; that make me part Indian and the reason my hair is long, straight and black like a horse mane.

Some of them Indian families was Joe Dirt Eater, Six Killer (some of the Six Killers live a few miles SE of Afton at this time, 1938), Chewey Noi and Gus Buffington. One of the Six Killer women was mighty good to us and we called her "mammy," that a long time after my mammy die though.

Pappa got the soldier fever from being in the War; no, I don't mean like the chills and fever, but just a fever to be in the army, I guess, for he joined the regular U.S. Army after awhile, serving five years in the Tenth Cavalry at Fort Sill during the same time John Adair of Tahlequah, and John Gallagher of Muskogee, was in the army.

Coming out of the army for the last time, pappa took all the family and moved to Fort Scott, Kansas, but I guess he feel more at home wid the Indians for pretty soon we all move back, this time to a farm near Fort Gibson.

I never would hear much about the war that my father was in, but know he fought for the North. He didn't tell us children much about the War, except he said one time that he was in the battle of Honey Springs in 1863 down near Elk Creek south of Fort Gibson. That sure was a tough time for the soldiers, for father said they fought and fought before the "Seesesh" soldiers finally took off to the south and the northern troops went back to Fort Gibson. Seem like it take a powerful lot of fighting to rid the country of them Rebs.

Another time his officer give him a message; he was on his way to deliver it when the enemy spy him and cry out to stop, but father said he kept on going until he was shot in the leg. Then he hide in the bushes along the creek and got away. He got that message to the captain just the same.

When father was young he would go hunting the fox with his master, and fishing in the streams for the big fish. Sometimes they fish in the Illinois river, sometimes in the Grand, but they always fish the same way. They make pens out in the shallow water with poles every little ways from the river banks. They'd cut brush saplings, walk out into the stream ahead of the pen and chase the fish down to the riffle where they'd pick 'em up. Once they catch a catfish most as big as a man; that fish had eggs big as hen eggs, and he made a feast for twenty-five Indians on the fishing party.[3]

Florence Smith was my first wife and Ida Vann the second. All my children was from the first marriage: Thomas, Dora, Charley, Marie, Opal, William, Arthur, Margaret, Thadral and Hubbard. The last one was named for Hubbard Ross; he was related to Chief John Ross and was some kin to Daniel Nave, my father's master.

[1] WPA field worker Ethel Wolfe Garrison interviewed Cornelius Neely Nave at Fort Gibson, Oklahoma, probably sometime during the early winter of 1937–38, for on 7 January 1938 project staff member Craig Vollmer edited and revised her now lost preliminary draft of Nave's narrative. This intermediate draft is available as the typescript "Interview with Cornelius Neely Nave, Negro, Age 70 Years, Route 1, Box 114,

Fort Gibson, Okla." in the OHS Slave Narratives. The edited draft apparently sat for a number of months with no further attention, but on 19 October 1938 a new, final draft typescript was prepared. It was never forwarded to Washington, however, and survives today only as the ribbon-copy typescript "Cornelius Neely Nave, Age 70 Years, Fort Gibson, Okla." in the OHS Slave Narratives and is published here.

  [2] On the basis of his and his wife's years as as slaves among the Cherokees, Cornelius Nave successfully enrolled himself, his wife, and five of his children as freedmen members of the Cherokee Nation in 1903 and 1905. U.S., Department of the Interior, Office of Indian Affairs, Dawes Commission, Cherokee Freedmen Census Cards, no. 138 (Cornelius, Florence, Thomas G., Dora E., Charles, William, and Margaret O. Nave), Microcopy M1186, reel 47, National Archives and Records Administration, Fort Worth, Texas (cited hereafter as Cherokee Freedmen Census Cards); U.S., Department of the Interior, Office of Indian Affairs, Dawes Commission, Cherokee Freedmen Enrollment Application Testimony, file 138 (Cornelius, Florence, Thomas G., Dora E., Charles, William, and Margaret O. Nave), Microcopy M1301, reel 261, National Archives and Records Service, Fort Worth, Texas (cited hereafter as Cherokee Freedmen Enrollment Application Testimony).

  [3] The use of fish weirs was common practice among many of the southeastern tribes of Indians, including the Cherokees among whom Nave and his parents lived. Swanton, *Indians of the Southeastern United States,* 333–36.

AMANDA OLIVER[1]

Age 80 Yrs.   *Oklahoma City, Okla.*

I 'membuh what my mother say—I was born November 9, 1857, in Missouri. I was 'bout eight years old, when she was sold to a master named Harrison Davis. They said he had two farms in Missouri, but when he moved to northern Texas he brought me, my mother, Uncle George, Uncle Dick and a cullud girl they said was 15 with 'im. He owned 'bout 6 acres on de edge of town near Sherman, Texas, and my mother and 'em was all de slaves he had. They said he sold off some of de folks.

We didn't have no overseers in northern Texas, but in southern Texas dey did. Dey didn't raise cotton either; but dey raised a whole lots of corn. Sometime de men would shuck corn all night long. Whenever dey was going to shuck all night de women would piece quilts while de men shuck de corn and you could hear 'em singing and shucking corn. After de cornshucking, de cullud folks would have big dances.

Master Davis lived in a big white frame house. My mother lived in the yard in a big one-room log hut with a brick chimney. De logs was "pinted" (what dey call plastered now with lime). I don't know whether young folks know much 'bout dat sort of thing now.

I slept on de floor up at de "Big House" in de white woman's room on a quilt. I'd git up in de mornings, make fires, put on de coffee, and tend to my little brother. Jest do little odd jobs sech as that.

We ate vegetables from de garden, sech as that. My favorite dish is vegetables now.

I don't remember seeing any slaves sold. My mother said dey sold 'em on de block in Kentucky where she was raised. I don't remembuh when de War broke out, but I remembuh seeing the soldiers with de blue uniforms on. I was afraid of 'em.

Old mistress didn't tell us when we was free, but another white woman told my mother and I remembuh one day old mistress told my mother to git to that wheel and git to work, and my mother said, "I ain't gwineter, I'm just as free as you air." So dat very day my mother packed up all our belongings and moved us to town, Sherman, Texas. She worked awful hard, doing day work for 50¢ a day, and sometimes she'd work for food, clothes or whatever she could git.

I don't believe in conjuring though I heard lotta talk 'bout it. Sometimes I have pains and aches in my hands, feel like sometime dat somebody puts dey hands on me, but I think jest de way my nerves is.

I can't say much 'bout Abe Lincoln. He was a republican in favor of de cullud folk being free. Jeff Davis? Yeah, the boys usta sing a song 'bout 'im:

> Lincoln rides a fine hoss,
> Jeff Davis rides a mule.
> Lincoln is de President,
> Jeff Davis is de fool.

Booker T. Washington—I guess he is a right good man. He's for the cullud people I guess.

I been a Christian thirty some odd years. I've been here some thirty odd years. Had to come when my husband died. He died in 1902. We married in 18 I've forgot, but we went to de preacher and got married. We did more than jump over de broom stick.

In those days we went to church with de white folks. Dey had church at eleven and the cullud folks at three, but all of us had white preachers. Our church is standing right there now, at least it was de last time I was there.

I don't have a favorite song, they's so many good ones, but I like, "Bound for the Promised Land." I'm a Baptist, my mother was a Baptist, and her white folks was Baptist.

I have two daughters, Julia Goodwin and Bertha Frazier, and four grandchildren, both of 'ems been separated. Dey do housework.[2]

[1] Mrs. Amanda Oliver was interviewed in Oklahoma City by an unidentified WPA field worker sometime probably in the spring or summer of 1937, for on 12 August of that year a final draft of her remembrances was sent to the Washington headquarters of the Federal Writers' Project. Only this final draft of her narrative has been located and it is published here. It is available as the typescript "Amanda Oliver, Age 80 Yrs., Oklahoma City, Okla." in ribbon copy in the LC Slave Narratives and in carbon copy as item 350091 in the LC Slave Narratives Carbon Copies. Stephens to Cronyn, 12 August 1937, WPA Notes on Interviews.

[2] The contemporary Oklahoma City directories list Mrs. Amanda Oliver as living at 410 Northeast Fourth with her daughter, Bertha Frasier, whose occupation is noted as maid. *Oklahoma City Negro City Directory,* 119; *Polk's Oklahoma City Directory, 1937,* 261, 557, 928.

SALOMON OLIVER[1]

Age 78 Yrs.   *Tulsa, Oklahoma*

John A. Miller owned the finest plantation in Washington County, Mississippi, about 12-mile east of Greenville. I was born on this 20,000-acre plantation November 17, 1859, being one of about four hundred slave children on the place.

About three hundred negro families living in box-type cabins made it seem like a small town. Built in rows, the cabins were kept whitewashed, neat and orderly, for the Master was strict about such things. Several large barns and storage buildings were scattered around the plantation. Also, two cotton gins and two old fashioned presses, operated by horses and mules, made Miller's plantation one of the best equipped in Mississippi.

Master John was quite a character. The big plantation didn't occupy all his time. He owned a bank in Vicksburg and another in New Orleans, and only came to the plantation two or three times a year for a week or two visit.

Things happened around there mighty quick when the Master showed up. If the slaves were not being treated right—out go the white overseer. Fired! The Master was a good man and tried to hire good boss men. Master John was bad after the slave women. A yellow child show up every once in a while. Those kind always got special privileges because the Master said he didn't want his children whipped like the rest of them slaves.

My own Mammy, Mary, was the Master's own daughter! She married Salomon Oliver (who took this name of Oliver after the War), and the Master told all the slave drivers to leave her alone and not whip her. This made the overseers jealous of her and caused trouble. John Santhers was one of the white overseers who treated her bad, and after I was born and got strong enough (I was a weakling for three–four years after birth), to do light chores he would whip me just for the fun of it. It was fun for him but not for me. I hoped to whip him when I grew up. That is the one thing I won't ever forget. He died about the end of the War so that's one thing I won't ever get to do.

My mother was high-tempered and she knew about the Master's orders not to whip her. I guess sometimes she took advantage and tried to do things that maybe wasn't right. But it did her no good and one of the white men flogged her to death. She died with scars on her back!

Father use to preach to the slaves when a crowd of them could slip off into the woods. I don't remember much about the religious things, only just what Daddy told me when I was older. He was caught several times slipping off to the woods and because he was the preacher I guess they layed on the lash a little harder trying to make him give up preaching.

Ration day was Saturday. Each person was given a peck of corn meal, four pounds of wheat flour, four pounds of pork meat, quart of molasses, one pound of sugar, the same of coffee and a plug of tobacco. Potatoes and vegetables came from the family garden and each slave family was required to cultivate a separate garden.

During the Civil War a battle was fought near the Miller plantation. The Yankees under General Grant came through the country. They burned 2,000 bales of Miller cotton. When the Yankee wagons crossed Bayou Creek the bridge gave way and quite a number of soldiers and horses were seriously injured.

For many years after the War folks would find bullets in the ground. Some of the bullets were "twins" fastened together with a chain.

Master Miller settled my father upon a piece of land after the War and we stayed on it several years, doing well.

I moved to Muskogee in 1902, coming on to Tulsa in 1907, the same year Oklahoma was made a state. My six wives are all dead,—Liza, Lizzie, Ellen, Lula, Elizabeth and Henrietta.[2] Six children, too. George, Anna, Salomon, Nelson, Garfield, Cosmos—all good children. They remember the Tulsa riot and don't aim ever to come back to Oklahoma.[3]

When the riot started in 1922 (I think it was), I had a place on the corner of Pine and Owasso Streets. Two hundred of my people gathered at my place, because I was so well known everybody figured we wouldn't be molested. I was wrong. Two of my horses was shot and killed. Two of my boys, Salomon and Nelson, was wounded, one in the hip, the other in the shoulder. They wasn't bad and got well alright. Some of my people wasn't so lucky. The dead wagon hauled them away!

White men came into the negro district and gathered up the homeless. The houses were most all burned. No place to go except to the camps where armed whites kept everybody quiet. They took my clothes and all my money—$298.00—and the police couldn't do nothing about my loss when I reported it to them.

That was a terrible time, but we people are better off today than any time during the days of slavery. We have some privileges and they are worth more than all the money in the world!

[1] Salomon Oliver was interviewed in Tulsa by a now unidentified WPA field worker sometime probably in the summer of 1937. Although preliminary drafts of his narrative have not been located, the final draft, forwarded to Washington on 2 September 1937, is preserved in the Library of Congress. This narrative, published here, is available as "Salomon Oliver, Age 78 Yrs., Tulsa, Oklahoma" in ribbon copy in the LC Slave Narratives and in carbon copy as item 350069 in the LC Slave Narratives Carbon Copies. This informant's name is shown as Solomon Z. Oliver in the 1929 Tulsa city directory but is rendered as Sol Oliver in the 1935 edition. *Polk's Tulsa (Oklahoma) City Directory, 1929,* 506, 808; *Polk's Tulsa City Cirectory, 1935,* 423, 653; Stephens to Cronyn, 2 September 1937, WPA Notes on Interviews.

[2] The 1929 Tulsa city directory lists Oliver as residing at 1101 East Pine with his wife, Henrietta. *Polk's Tulsa City Directory, 1929,* 506, 808.

[3] The Tulsa race riot of June 1921 resulted in several dozen deaths and the destruction through arson of thirty-five city blocks of the African American neighborhood. For more background on this incident, see, among other sources, Scott Ellsworth, *Death in a Promised Land: The Tulsa Race Riot of 1921;* Jimmie Lewis Franklin, *Journey toward Hope: A History of Blacks in Oklahoma,* 142–49; R. Halliburton, Jr., *The Tulsa Race War of 1921;* Lee E. Williams and Lee E. Williams II, *Anatomy of Four Race Riots: Racial Conflict in Knoxville, Elaine (Arkansas), Tulsa and Chicago, 1919–1921,* 56–73.

NOAH PERRY[1]

Age 81   *Krebs, Oklahoma*

Old Dixie Land . . .
The land of cotton,
Good times there are not forgotten.

That is the truth all right for I still remember the good and the bad times we had before and just after the war of the rebellion. We had a lot harder time after the war than when we lived wid our old Master. He always looked after us in every way and we didn't have any thing to worry about. We always had plenty to eat and to wear and if we got sick he saw to it that we had plenty of attention and medicine.

I was born in slavery on the plantation of Master William Gore, near Summerville, Georgia. Master William and his wife Miss Sallie owned my mother and my brother and me. My father, Ben Perry, belonged to Squire Perry who owned a plantation about a mile from us. He came to see us often and spent every Saturday night and Sunday wid us. Sometimes he'd come in the middle of the week but as he had to be back on his master's farm so early in the morning to go to work he didn't come very often when the days was short.

Mother and father both had kind masters who never whipped them but looked after them good and give them a good home in return for the work they did for them.

Once father come over to see us. His master didn't care for him coming and he didn't get no pass from him before he left. A patroller got after him and father started running down across the orchard and the patroller right after him. Father ducked under a crooked peach tree and the patroller didn't see it in time and he hit it wid his head and it knocked him out cold. Father didn't stay to see if he got taken care of but went on home. Old Squire Perry gave orders that father was not to be meddled with any more as he didn't have to have a pass. They never did bother him any more.

Mother's rightful owner was Old Man Gore, Master William's father. He had two big plantations and he gave one to Master William and the other to his other son, Master Frank. He give each of his sons a equal number of slaves but always kept a claim on mother and us kids. He had a little house near the big house and when he was visiting Master William he stayed in this little house and mother kept house for him. He usually stayed abut six months and we'd get to live at the little house all that time. He thought about as much of me as he did his own grandchildren. Sometimes when they'd get after me to whip me he would take me to his room and keep me away from them. Sometimes he'd make me a pallet and keep me all night. They sure didn't whip me neither. I loved him a lot, too.

When he left to go stay with his son Master Frank, mother would put everything to rights and lock up and we'd go back to Master William's to stay till he come back again. Mother liked to stay with him, too, as she didn't have to work so hard there and she was her own boss.

Our white folks lived in a fine house. It was a two-story building facing the south and it had a big gallery across the front and on the east. A big wide hall went clear through the house both upstairs and down and there was rooms on each side of this hall. There was a basement with four rooms in it. The househelp lived down there.

The house set up on a hill and was painted white. You could see it for a long distance. A long winding road lead up to the house from the main big road. There was big shade trees all around the house and the barn. The quarters was below the house about three hundred yards. We had a nice house in the quarters. It was made out of logs but it was well made and had a good floor and was good and warm.

Mother was a good field hand as she was young and strong. She usually run the plow. She liked to plow and made such a good hand at it that the overseer let her plow all the time if she wanted to. She never took much foolishness off any of the other hands neither. One day one of the men got mad at me and whipped me. When she come home of course I told her about it. He went to the barn and hid when he saw her coming. She went out there and drug him out and give him a good thrashing. He never bothered us kids any more either. Mother spanked us good and proper though.

One time I was up at the big house playing with Master William's boys and we got into a fuss about something and I went home. Walter followed me and I run and got over the fence into our yard. Walter climbed on the fence to jump over and I say to him, "Don't you come in this yard, I left your house to keep from fighting and I want you to go on back home." But Walter never paid no attention to what I said and he kept on coming. I picked up a rock and throwed it and hit him right on the forehead. He fell off that fence just like he was shot off and he just lay there and sort of trembled. I just knowed I'd killed him. Lawsy, I was scared. I run down through the woods lot and hid in some buckeye bushes. I could hear Miss Sallie screaming and saying, "He's killed my Walter, he's killed my Walter." I just laid there and shook. Purty soon here come Master William looking for me. He come so close that I thought sure he could hear my heart beat but he had to give it up. I was afraid to go to the house for I thought they would kill me. Finally mother come home from the field. Master William told her about it and told her she had to whip me. She wanted to know where I was. They told her I was in the woods somewhere and she commenced calling me. I decided that if mother was at home she wouldn't let them kill me as she always had taken my part so I went to the house. She sure dusted my britches for me but I didn't mind that like I would have Master William. Walter has that scar till this day if he is still living. We played together after that just like nothing ever happened.

The war come on and times got purty scarey. Master Frank went to the army but Master William didn't. I guess he was too old.

The Yankees come along and took all the able-bodied colored men to the army. Father went as a cook and it was a many long day before we ever saw him again. Our family was all broke up after dat.

Master William took what niggers he had left and refugeed us to Macon, Georgia. Things was so bad in northern Georgia that he decided to stay there, so he took over a place and we raised rice. We stayed there about five years after the war.

Master William decided to go back and see about his old home and he loaded his household goods, tools, niggers, and everything he had onto a freight train and we went back home. The farm was awful run down and all his nigger men and young women quit him so Master William had a hard time rebuilding it. Father had come back after the war and couldn't find us so he married again. Mother and us two boys just stayed on with Master William till I was about fourteen years old. Mother married again and my father come and took me to live with him.

My stepmother had four boys of her own. One of them was grown but the other three were at home with father and her. Her oldest son was a school teacher. They had belonged to a man that taught them all to read and write and even sent the boys to school. He made an awful smart man. I went to school to him and learned all I ever learned at school. I went to another man but I was so scared of him that I couldn't learn. He felt so big that he could teach school that he beat on us kids all the time. He'd make us set on a stool and wear a dunce cap, too. I also went to school to a white teacher that come down from the north. He was smart and I could a learned from him but the Ku Kluxers made him quit teaching us so he went back home.

It was the sorriest day of my life when I went to live with my father. My stepmother just fairly hated me and she done everything she could to make my life a misery to me. She was fairly good to me if father was at home but if he was gone I had an awful time. She wouldn't let me wash my face and hands till her boys all washed. One morning I waited and waited for them to wash and I got tired so I set the pan down in the kitchen door and squatted down to wash. She come up behind me and kicked me out in the yard. Father was out feeding the pigs and he saw it and here he came to the house. I had told him how they treated me but he acted like he hated to believe me but he had to believe his eyes. He come in and cleaned out the whole bunch. This didn't stop them though for every time he left home it was the same thing over again. One day father was gone from home and I done something and she took a big hank of cotton thread and put it around my neck and hung me to a joist. I thought my time had come for I knew there wasn't anybody there that cared whether I lived or died. One of my aunts come up to the back and hollered for my stepmother. She let me down and told me if I told it she would kill me. I believed her and I didn't tell it. I knew she wanted to kill me bad enough. She took sick and died not long after that and that was the only time in my life that I ever said that I was glad that a person was dead. I said it and I sure meant it.

I went back to Master William's to live after that. He give me ten dollars a month and my board to work for him. I stayed with him till I was about twenty-five years old and I married and rented a place for myself.

Bob Perry, one of my stepmother's sons that always seemed to have it in for me worse than any of the boys, married and had two children. His wife died and he had her buried. The day of the funeral he told me, "Noah, I've always wanted to have my way and now I'm gonna do it from now on. You can just mark my words." Well sir, he left that day and none of us ever seen him again. He went off and left his children. My wife and me took his little girl and kept her till she was a grown woman. I tried my best never to be mean to her and I never told her how her grandmother and daddy used to treat me. I think that is one reason that I have always been sort of lucky was that I always tried to be better to people than they was to me.

The country there begun to be thickly settled and I hope [help] my Pappy to buy and pay for 80 acres of land. I took my family and moved to Texas. We didn't stay there but three years and we come to Oklahoma or Indian Territory as it was then.

My wife didn't like it here and I told her she could go back to her mother's if she wanted to, that I was going to stay here. We had lost our little girl and just had one child, a boy, so she took him and went back. I been living here by myself ever since. My boy would come out to see me but would go back to his mother. He was killed in France during the World War. My wife is still living.

While I lived in Texas I worked for an old lady named Aunt Patsy Caraway.[2] Every body called her Aunt Patsy. She owned a nice farm and lived by herself. Her family was all dead. She was lonesome and lots of nights my wife and I would go in to her room and set by the fire and listen to her tell of her life in the early days there. She was born in North Carolina she said and married and they come to Texas soon after that. Her husband died when their children was all young and she had to work hard to make a living for them. She was a little woman; I don't suppose she would weigh more than 115 or 120 pounds. A lot of the things she told us seemed kind of hard to believe but I guess they was true; any way I will tell you what she told me and you can take it or leave it.

She and her husband had settled on a place and started to improve it. They were doing very well and her husband took sick and after a long time he died. She had no one to help her with making a living for her children so she just worked harder. She had a few head of cattle that had a free range and she also had some hogs that had free range. She lived close to a swamp and the hogs did well on the mast. The hogs raised themselves in the woods and she always had plenty of meat, milk and butter. She also raised lots of bees and they had honey the year round. They raised corn for bread and used honey for sugar as they didn't know what it was to have coffee or sugar or flour. She usually had honey to sell and they spun and wove their clothes. By every body working they managed to keep going.

Her farm lay at the edge of a big swamp and was about fifteen or twenty miles from Beaumont, Texas. This swamp was a regular jungle and she had some of it cleared and had her farm there. She had about twenty acres cleared and in cultivation. The house set back on a hill. She said wild beasts of almost every kind ranged the swamps at the time they settled there and you could believe it, too, as it looked plenty wild then. Black bear was plentiful. They feasted on her young calves and pigs and she had a hard time with them. One day she said the dogs began to bark and run as if something terrible was around and she took her gun and kept mooching them along till finally they came to bay down in the swamp. She went on to see what they had and found a big black bear. She shot it and butchered it and brought it home. She had to make several trips on horseback and found a ready sale for it at a good price. She always made the trip to town in one day, always on horseback and carried whatever she had for sale. She said that once she even took her churn full of milk and churned it as she rode along the road. When she got to Beaumont her churning was done so she sold her butter and milk and returned home that evening with whatever produce she needed.

She said that one night she heard something out in the yard and she went out to see what it was. She went to the smokehouse door and she saw a Mexican lion[3] in the smokehouse. It gave a loud scream and run out the door past her and was so scared that it kept on running. I asked her if she wasn't afraid and she said, "Afraid, what is that? I never saw one of them things. I couldn't afford to be afraid for I was the man and the woman of the family."

I left there and come to the mines at Krebs[4] and I been here ever since. I never had no trouble till just here lately. A boy was living here with me and we got along good for he was a good boy. He was keeping company with one of my nieces.

One night I was setting here by the fire and he come running in and said, "Uncle Noah, let me have your gun, quick!" I said, "I can't let you have my gun, you might kill somebody." He said, "That's just what I want it for, so let me have it." I always kept it leaning against the wall behind the door and he grabbed it and started by me and I grabbed hold of it and told him that I couldn't let him have my gun to kill anybody, that I'd be just as guilty as he was and besides he didn't need to kill anybody. He kept jerking on the gun, a shotgun, and I kept holding on to it. He give a big jerk and it went off and shot him in the stomach and killed him right then. They arrested me and I stayed in jail for 24 days. The good Lord knows that I didn't kill him. We was good friends and besides I wouldn't a killed nobody. My lawyer says he don't think it ever will come up any more but I just worry about it all the time. I never had no trouble in my young days and it looks hard for me to have this to worry about in my old days. I bought me a Bible and I reads it a lot. I ain't never been converted but I wants to be.

[1] Noah Perry of Krebs, Oklahoma, was interviewed by a now unidentified WPA field worker probably in 1937. Perry's remembrances were placed in typewritten form as "Noah Perry, Age 81, Krebs, Oklahoma," but the narrative was never forwarded to Washington. Today it remains in ribbon-copy typescript in the OHS Slave Narratives, and that text is published here.

[2] The "Aunt Patsy" Caraway for whom Noah Perry worked was actually Martha J. Caraway (1816–1902), a native of North Carolina who was widowed and who operated her farm in Hardin County, Texas, as the head of the household. Mildred S. Wright, *Hardin County, Texas, Cemeteries,* 178; U.S. Census of 1860, Texas, Population Schedules, Hardin County, 7.

[3] "Mexican lion" here refers to a puma.

[4] For another informant's memories of living in the Krebs area, see the narrative of Morris Hillyer, above.

PATSY PERRYMAN[1]

Age 80   *Muskogee, Oklahoma*

My mother didn't know how old any of her children was; she told me I was born about three year before the war and dat the same thing she told my sister Victoria about her age, so I claim the age of eighty and hope to live long like mother who died last year (1937), 115-years old.

The Taylor place, where I was born, was in the Caney Creek settlement, near Walkingstick Spring, in the old Flint District of the Cherokee Nation. The Taylor family was Cherokees and the mistress and master always treated us mighty good. We didn't know what whippings were, only what we heard about other slaves getting beaten for trying to run away or too lazy to work.

My mother had always been with Mistress Judy Taylor and she was the only mother my mama ever had, least the only she could remember for her own mother (my grandmother) died when she was three days old. She was raised by the Indians and could talk Cherokee.

There was two boys and three girls; myself, Jude and Victoria, "Boney" (Bonaparte) and Lewis. Father belonged to some other man for a long time; he would get a pass to visit with mother and us children, then go back the next day. The Taylors bought him so that we could all be together.

My brother Lewis married a full-blood Indian woman and they got lots of Indian children on their farm in the old Cherokee country around Caney Creek. He's just like an Indian, been with them so much, talks the Cherokee language and don't notice us Negroes any more.

The last time I saw him was thirty years ago when he come to see mammy at the agency. We started out walking and pretty soon he dropped behind, leaving me to walk in front. I looked back and there he was standing in the middle of [?] with his eyes shut.

"What's the matter, brother Lewis?" I wanted to know. "Sister wants you to come on," I told him.

"I darn tired looking at Negroes!" he said, keeping his eyes shut tight, and I knew just how he felt.

That's what I use to tell Mistress Taylor when I leave my own mammy and run to the mistress, crying to stay with her, even after the peace come that set us free.

"Honey," Mistress Judy say kindly, "stay with your own mammy, she cries for you."

And I would cry some more, keeping my eyes shut all the time, for like my brother said, "I tired looking at Negroes."

The Taylor house was a beautiful place to live; it was a long double log house, weatherboarded, with a yard of clover under the big oak trees that made plenty of shade. I use to pick up leaves to keep the yard clean and sweet smelling, and go to the big spring close to the house for water.

Besides helping that way I would feed the chickens, take care of the children and sometimes I would get money for it and buy candy; once I bought a doll.

When I was little Victoria and me would go hunting for rabbits and quail birds in the snow. In the summer we catch terrapins, roast them over the fire for some good eating. Mostly we had bean bread and bean dumplings with corn bread. Making corn bread was a big job. First the corn had to soaked, then put in a mortar and pounded to meal with a pessel—"beating the meal" is what my mammy called it.

Cotton clothes for summer, wool clothes for winter, with knitted stocking and gloves made by Mammy and Mistress Taylor. For Sunday our dress was calico and our bonnets was trimmed up with corn stalks. Our shoes were home made, with brass toes and braided soles to keep the flint rocks from cutting through the leather.

The main crops were corn and cotton and if they were big ones the master would hire Negroes to come in and help with the work. There was nobody around the place but Indians and Negroes; I was a full-grown girl before I ever saw a white man.

There was no way to learn reading and writing; I was a big girl when I learn the letters and how to write, and tried to teach mammy but she didn't learn, so all the writing about allotments had to be done by me. I have written many letters to Washington when they gave the Indian lands to the native Indians and their Negroes.

Mammy said the patrollers and "Pin" Indians[2] caused a lot of trouble after the war started. The master went to war and left my mistress to look after the place. The "Pins" came to the farm one day and broke down the doors, cut feather beds open and sent the feathers flying in the wind, stole the horses, killed the sheep and done lots of mean things.

Then mistress took her slaves and went somewhere in Texas until after the war. She started back to the old home place, but wasn't going to take us with her until mammy cried so hard she couldn't stand it and told us to get ready. We drove through in an ox wagon and sometimes had to wait along the way because the streams were flooded and we couldn't ford.

We found the old house burned to the ground when we got back and the whole place was a ruin. There was no stock and no way for any of us to live. The mistress told us that we were free anyway and to go wherever we wanted to.

We went to Fort Gibson and then to Tahlequah; mammy earning our way cooking at both them places. Victoria was hired out to Judge Wolfe and that's where she was when father had her stolen. We was all worried about her for a time, until we found out she was with him.

My first husband was Charley Clark, a full-blood Creek Indian, living on the river near Yohola; the next man was a black African, but we couldn't get along so I let him go, and married Randolph Perryman, who, like Charley Clark, is dead now.[3] I never had any children.

I am glad slavery is over and I do not want to see any more wars. Lincoln freed us, but I never liked him because of the way his soldiers done in the south.

[1] Mrs. Patsy Perryman was interviewed in Muskogee, Oklahoma, by a now unidentified WPA field worker probably sometime in 1938. Her remembrances were placed in typewritten form as a narrative but for unknown reasons were never forwarded on to the Washington headquarters of the Federal Writers' Project. Her interview, published here, is available in ribbon-copy typescript as "Patsy Perryman, Age 80, Muskogee, Oklahoma" only in the OHS Slave Narratives.

[2] For additional remembrances and background on the "Pin Indians," the Cherokee secret society that opposed Cherokee ownership of slaves as well as other elements of Euro-American society, see the narratives of Mary Grayson, above, and Morris Sheppard, below.

[3] Patsy Perryman's third husband, Randolph Perryman, was enrolled as a Creek freedman by the Dawes Commission on 28 March 1902. Creek Freedmen Census Cards, no. 863 (Randolph Perryman).

PHYLLIS PETITE[1]

Age 83 Yrs.   *Fort Gibson, Okla.*

I was born in Rusk County, Texas, on a plantation about eight miles east of Belleview.[2] There wasn't no town where I was born, but they had a church.

My mammy and pappy belonged to a part Cherokee named W. P. Thompson when I was born. He had kinfolks in the Cherokee Nation, and we all moved up here to a place on Fourteen-Mile Creek close to where Hulbert now is, 'way before I was big enough to remember anything. Then, so I been told, old master Thompson sell my pappy and mammy and one of my baby brothers and me back to one of his neighbors in Texas name of John Harnage.

Mammy's name was Letitia Thompson and pappy's was Riley Thompson. My little brother was named Johnson Thompson,[3] but I had another brother sold to a Vann and he always call hisself Harry Vann. His Cherokee master lived on the Arkansas river close to Webber's Falls and I never did know him until we was both grown. My only sister was Patsy and she was borned after slavery and died at Wagoner, Oklahoma.

I can just remember when Master John Harnage took us to Texas. We went in a covered wagon with oxen and camped out all along the way. Mammy done the cooking in big wash kettles and pappy done the driving of the oxen. I would set in a wagon and listen to him pop his whip and holler.

Master John took us to his plantation and it was a big one, too. You could look from the field up to the Big House and any grown body in the yard look like a little body, it was so far away.

We negroes lived in quarters not far from the Big House and ours was a single log house with a stick and dirt chimney. We cooked over the hot coals in the fireplace.

I just played around until I was about six years old I reckon, and then they put me up at the Big House with my mammy to work. She done all the cording and spinning and weaving, and I done a whole lot of sweeping and minding the baby. The baby was only about six months old I reckon. I used to stand by the cradle and rock it all day, and when I quit I would go to sleep right by the cradle sometimes before mammy would come and get me.

The Big House had great big rooms in front, and they was fixed up nice, too. I remember when old Mistress Harnage tried me out sweeping up the front rooms. They had two or three great big pictures of some old people hanging on the wall. They was full blood Indians it look like, and I was sure scared of them pictures! I would go here and there and every which-a-way, and anywheres I go them big pictures always looking straight at me and watching me sweep! I kept my eyes right on them so I could run if they moved, and old Mistress take me back to the kitchen and say I can't sweep because I miss all the dirt.

We always have good eating, like turnip greens cooked in a kettle with hog skins and crackling grease, and skinned corn, and rabbit or possum stew. I liked big fish tolerable well too, but I was afraid of the bones in the little ones.

That skinned corn ain't like the boiled hominy we have today. To make it you boil some wood ashes, or have some drip lye from the hopper to put in the hot water. Let the corn boil in the lye water until the skin drops off and the eyes drop out and then wash that corn in fresh water about a dozen times, or just keep carrying water from the spring until you are wore out, like I did. Then you put the corn in a crock and set it in the spring, and you got good skinned corn as long as it last, all ready to warm up a little batch at a time.

Master had a big, long log kitchen setting away from the house, and we set a big table for the family first, and when they was gone we negroes at the house eat at that table too, but we don't use the china dishes.

The negro cook was Tilda Chisholm. She and my mammy didn't do no outwork. Aunt Tilda sure could make them corn-dodgers. Us children would catch her eating her dinner first out of the kettles and when we say something she say: "Go on child, I jest tasting that dinner."

In the summer we had cotton homespun clothes, and in winter it had wool mixed in. They was dyed with copperas and wild indigo.

My brother, Johnson Thompson, would get up behind old Master Harnage on his horse and go with him to hunt squirrels. Johnson would go 'round on the other side of the tree and rock the squirrels so they would go 'round on Master's side so's he could shoot them.[4] Master's old mare was named "Old Willow," and she knowed when to stop and stand real still so he could shoot.

His children was just all over the place! He had two houses full of them! I only remember Bell, Ida, Maley, Mary and Will, but they was plenty more I don't remember.

That old horn blowed 'way before daylight, and all the field negroes had to be out in the row by the time of sun up. House negroes got up too, because old Master always up to see everybody get out to work.

Old Master Harnage bought and sold slaves most all the time, and some of the new negroes always acted up and needed a licking. The worst ones got beat up good, too! They didn't have no jail to put slaves in because when the Masters got done licking them they didn't need no jail.

My husband was George Petite. He tell me his mammy was sold away from him when he was a little boy. He looked down a long lane after her just as long as he could see her, and cried after her. He went down to the big road and set down by his mammy's barefooted tracks in the sand and set there until it got dark, and then he come on back to the quarters.

I just saw one slave try to get away right in hand. They caught him with bloodhounds and brung him back in. The hounds had nearly tore him up, and he was sick a long time. I don't remember his name, but he wasn't one of the old regular negroes.

In Texas we had a church where we could go. I think it was a white church and they just let the negroes have it when they got a preacher sometimes. My mammy took me sometimes, and she loved to sing them salvation songs.

We used to carry news from one plantation to the other I reckon, 'cause mammy would tell about things going on some other plantation and I know she never been there.

Christmas morning we always got some brown sugar candy or some molasses to pull, and we children was up bright and early to get that 'lasses pull, I tell you! And in the winter we played skeeting on the ice when the water froze over. No, I don't mean skating. That's when you got iron skates, and we didn't have them things. We just get a running start and jump on the ice and skeet as far as we could go, and then you run some more.

I nearly busted my head open, and brother Johnson said: "Try it again," but after that I was scared to skeet any more.

Mammy say we was down in Texas to get away from the War, but I didn't see any war and any soldiers. But one day old Master stay after he eat breakfast and when us negroes come in to eat he say: "After today I ain't your master any more. You all as free as I am." We just stand and look and don't know what to say about it.

After while pappy got a wagon and some oxen to drive for a white man who was coming to the Cherokee Nation because he had folks here. His name was Dave Mounts and he had a boy named John.

We come with them and stopped at Fort Gibson where my own grand mammy was cooking for the soldiers at the garrison. Her name was Phyllis Brewer and I was named after her. She had a good Cherokee master. My mammy was born on his place.

We stayed with her about a week and then we moved out on Four Mile Creek to live. She died on Fourteen-Mile Creek about a year later.

When we first went to Four Mile Creek I seen negro women chopping wood and asked them who they work for and I found out they didn't know they was free yet.

After a while my pappy and mammy both died, and I was took

care of by my aunt Elsie Vann. She took my brother Johnson too, but I don't know who took Harry Vann.

I was married to George Petite,[5] and I had on a white underdress and black high-top shoes, and a large cream colored hat, and on top of all I had a blue wool dress with tassels all around the bottom of it. That dress was for me to eat the terrible supper in. That what we called the wedding supper because we eat too much of it. Just danced all night, too! I was at Mandy Foster's house in Fort Gibson, and the preacher was Reverend Barrows. I had that dress a long time, but it's gone now. I still got the little sun bonnet I wore to church in Texas.

We had six children, but all are dead but George, Tish, and Annie now.

Yes, they tell me Abraham Lincoln set me free, and I love to look at his picture on the wall in the school house at Four Mile branch where they have church. My grand mammy kind of help start that church, and I think everybody ought to belong to some church.

I want to say again my Master Harnage was Indian, but he was a good man and mighty good to us slaves, and you can see I am more than six feet high and they say I weighs over a hundred and sixty, even if my hair is snow white.

[1] Mrs. Phyllis Petite was interviewed at Fort Gibson, Oklahoma, probably sometime in summer or autumn 1937, but the identity of her interviewer is not known. The notes from the interview were edited into a preliminary draft available as the typescript "Phyllis Petite, Age 83 Yrs., Fort Gibson, Oklahoma" in the OHS Slave Narratives. This draft was further edited on 4 November 1937 into a final draft, published here, "Phyllis Petite, Age 83 Yrs., Fort Gibson, Okla.," available in ribbon copy in the LC Slave Narratives and in carbon copy as item 350010 in the LC Slave Narratives Carbon Copies and in the OHS Slave Narratives. The narrative was sent to Washington on 18 November 1937 and rubber-stamped "received" there four days later. Stephens to Alsberg, 18 November 1937, WPA Notes on Interviews.

For another, contemporary interview with this informant, see Phyllis Pettit [sic], interview by O. C. Davidson, [probably near Fort Gibson, Oklahoma], 22 February 1937, Indian-Pioneer Papers, 8:209–12. This interviewee's surname is elsewhere spelled Pettit or Petitt, but generally not Petite.

[2] This is probably the field worker's spelling for Bellview, a mid-nineteenth-century post office in Rusk County, Texas. Bartholomew, *Encyclopedia of Texas Ghost Towns,* 11.

[3] For an interview with the informant's brother, see the narrative of Johnson Thompson, below.

[4] The typist of the final draft garbled the preceding two sentences, producing a single sentence that reads: "My brother, Johnson Thompson, would get up behind old Master Harnage on his horse and go with him to hunt squirrels so they would go 'round on Master's side so's he could shoot them."

⁵ Phyllis and George Petitt [*sic*] and their children were enrolled as freedmen members of the Cherokee Nation by the Dawes Commission in 1904. Cherokee Freedmen Census Cards, no. 102 (George, Phylis [*sic*], Sophie, Annie, and Henry Petitt); Cherokee Freedmen Enrollment Application Testimony, file 102 (George, Phylis [*sic*], Sophia, Annie, and Henry Petitt).

INTERVIEW WITH MAGGIE PINKARD¹

Slave Born, Age 80   *625 South 4th St., Muskogee, Oklahoma*

I was born at Nashville, Tenn., in my grandmother's two room log cabin on the big farm place of Master Billie Robertson and his wife Annie. Folks said in the old days that Master was a millionaire and that he had thousands of acres, hundreds of slaves and plenty of sense. He was a good master and wouldn't have overseers around who was mean either.

Susan and Billie was the master's children. The boy was kinder crazy-like and my pappy, Martin Robertson, was tolled off to watch over him. Went everywhere the boy did, even when he growed up and was big enough to drive the oxen to the mills for corn grinding and all such. The girl Susan was just like her folks. Kind and good, always try to help me. She's the one who take me out side by the house and teach me out of the books. And write, too. She took me and mammy with her when she got married and moved on another big farm about three mile from the old master's plantation.

My mammy was name Annie, after her mistress. Annie Robertson. Both my parents were born slaves and my grandparents was slave born, too. I remember seeing my grandfather; he was 110 year old when he died. My brothers were Cupe, Robertson, Ed and Buddy; sisters were Ona and Julia, but I am the only child of them all who is still living.

Mammy was a house girl and all us children work around in the yard and the house. I saw the field mothers marching to the fields, but we never worked there. The field workers lived in the slave cabins down the path from the master's big house. Now that was a house!

Twelve rooms it was, with a big hall that let the breeze swept through on the hot days, and a gallery that was long and high where the folks use to sit in the evening and talk and laugh and listen to some of the young negroes singing around the place. Them was the best times the negroes ever had and I expect they'll never have no more good times as that. The parlor was a big room, fixed up with nice chairs and colored rugs scattered on the floor—most of the things was made by the slaves. The master sent off somewhere and fetched in a carpenter one time. He built some things and the master paid him to teach (show) the slaves how to do what he did with a saw and hammer.

The kitchen where old black Betty Robertson use to cook for the white folks was just like any other such place until the master went down to New Orleans one time and come back with a stove. A cook stove. Why, folks from all over the country come in to see that stove and watch Betty pan up the food stuffs. She had plenty to cook with and plenty of folks to cook for. The master killed his own beef and pork, part of it was for the slaves and part for hisself, but everybody get all they need. And there was always white folks come a-visiting, so Betty done cooked about just all the time all day long.

At night the rooms in the big house was lighted with grease lamps. The base was green copper stuff with a string to make the light after my mammy pour on the grease. She take such a lamp down to the creek at night, sometimes I go with her and hold it while she wash a few of the children's clothes.

In them days washing wasn't so easy. It ain't too easy nowadays, but then it was real work. They had no bought soap. It was homemade lye soap and I use to tote water from the spring to the ash hopper where mammy and some of the others made that soap. There wasn't any washboards. They had a big wide board. Lay the clothes on the board after they soak 'em up and with a paddle they would beat out the dirt. That was work!

When I was a child I done lots of playing. Swinging on the grape vines that trailed down from high up in the trees. And hunting for rabbits. Soon as we children fetch in the rabbit to the old cook (Betty) she would have [it] in the iron skillet almost before the rabbit knew he was caught! She was the best rabbit cook in the whole country, least we always thought so.

My mammy would weave all the cloth and make clothes. She knew how to run the loom but I don't know how. She would send out in the woods for certain kinds of roots and bark. Mix 'em up and boil, and when the color was right all the cloth was dyed and made ready for hand sewing the dresses and shirts. I learned to knit and made stockings even if I was a little girl.

The master had bells and horns to wake up the slaves. They would start their work at daybreak, soon as the bells ring and the horns blow. At noon the bells ring and the horns would blow again. The slaves come in from the fields and go to the long kitchen eating place where all the field hands eat and everybody pile in the food.

We use to hear about other masters whipping their slaves, but on the Robertson place everybody treated alright. Sometimes they would be somebody needing a going over. Then the master order him to the calaboose. That was a jail. Just a little old log cabin thing without windows, but the door was locked and nobody could get out without the overseer's keys.

The master bought slaves from the slave traders what use to travel around the country. Sometimes he go to the big markets and buy a few. He didn't sell many himself. But when the slaves got a feeling there was going to be an auction they would pray. The night before the sale they would pray in their cabins. They didn't pray loud but they prayed long and you could hear the hum of voices in all the cabins down the row.

There was an old negro woman on the place who doctored the slaves. Somebody get sick she was called in and give 'em medicine made of roots and herbs. If they got well right away she was mighty glad, but if her medicine didn't do no good the old master would call in the white doctor, Dr. Ganaway.

When the master and his wife went to visit with neighbors they always took one or two of the negro children with them. I went lots of times. Come to a gate I would get out of the buggy or wagon and open the gate.

After the war started everything was different. During the war the old master had his meats and stuff hid out. Some of it he put in the lofts of the slave cabins, some he hide out in the fields.

The Yanks finally come to our place. They went through the house and tore up the feather beds. They cut off the ears of the dogs; they killed the chickens running in the yard; they burn the master's barn and killed his cows and take off with his horses.

All the time we was hiding in the oat field, scared to death. The mistress was with us, and she told us to keep down on the ground lest we get hit with the bullets that was aimed for a chicken.

After the master lost all his things he left out for Coffee County, Tenn., where we stayed during the rest of the war. Sometime though he took a bunch of the field hands down in Louisiana somewheres.

One of the neighbors down in Coffee County made a wedding dress for my oldest sister when she married. It was a wool dress, but I don't remember what was its style. After the war they had big weddings. The parents fix up the wedding dinner. There was cakes two foot high! Pound cakes they was. Everything was pound cakes in them days. They was baked in the old time iron dutch oven.

When I married James Pinkard we had a big wedding.[2] I can't describe it, it's been so long ago. There was no children and my husband been dead a long time.

That's all I can tell about the slave times.

[1] WPA field worker Ethel Wolfe Garrison interviewed Mrs. Maggie Pinkard in Muskogee, Oklahoma, probably sometime in the late winter or spring of 1938, for on 17 March of that year agency employee Craig Vollmer revised Pinkard's narrative into the standard form for the Slave Narrative Project. Vollmer's typewritten revision, "Interview with Maggie Pinkard, Slave Born, Age 80, 625 South 4th St., Muskogee, Oklahoma," is the only version of her interview found and is published here. For reasons not known, this narrative was never forwarded to Washington; it survives in the OHS Slave Narratives.

[2] The 1932 Muskogee city directory lists the informant as residing with her husband, the Reverend James Pinkard, at 625 South Fourth in Muskogee. *Polk's Muskogee City Directory, 1932,* 157, 238.

MATILDA POE[1]

Age 80 Yrs.   *McAlester, Okla.*

I was born in Indian Territory on de plantation of Isaac Love. He was old Master,[2] and Henry Love was young Master. Isaac Love was a full blood Chickasaw Indian but his wife was a white woman.[3]

Old Master was sure good to his slaves. The young niggers never done no heavy work till dey was fully grown. Dey would carry water to de men in de field and do other light jobs 'round de place.

De Big House set way back from de road 'bout a quarter of a mile. It was a two-story log house, and the rooms was awful big and they was purty furniture in it. The furniture in de parlor was red plush and I loved to slip in and rub my hand over it, it was so soft like. The house was made of square logs and de cracks was filled out even with the edges of de logs. It was white washed and my but it was purty. They was a long gallery clean across de front of de house and big posts to support de roof. Back a ways from de house was de kitchen and nearby was de smokehouse. Old Master kept it well filled with meat, lard and molasses all de time. He seen to it that we always had plenty to eat. The old women done all de cooking in big iron pots that hung over the fire. De slaves was all served together.

The slave quarters was about two hundred yards back of de Big House. Our furniture was made of oak 'cepting de chairs, and dey was made out of hackberry. I still have a chair dat belonged to my mammy.

The boys didn't wear no britches in de summer time. Dey just wore long shirts. De girls were homespun dresses, either blue or gray.

Old Master never hired no overseer for his slaves, but he looked after 'em hisself. He punished dem hisself too. He had to go away one time and he hired a white man to oversee while he was gone. The only orders he left was to keep dem busy. Granny Lucy was awful old but he made her go to the field. She couldn't hold out to work so he ups and whips her. He beat her scandalous. He cut her back so bad she couldn't wear her dress. Old Master come home and my, he was mad when he see Granny Lucy. He told de man to leave and iffen he ever set foot on his ground again he'd shoot him, sure!

Old Master had a big plantation and a hundred or more slaves. Dey always got up at daylight and de men went out and fed de horses. When de bell rang dey was ready to eat. After breakfast dey took de teams and went out to plow. Dey come in 'bout half past 'leven and at twelve de bell rung again. Dey eat their dinner and back to plowing dey went. 'Bout five o'clock dey come in again, and den they'd talk, sing and jig dance till bedtime.

Old Master never punished his niggers 'cepting dey was sassy or lazy. He never sold his slaves neither. A owner once sold several babies to traders. Dey stopped at our plantation to stay awhile. My mammy and de other women had to take care of dem babies for two days, and teach dem to nuss a bottle or drink from a glass. Dat was awful, dem little children crying for they mothers. Sometimes dey sold de mothers away from they husbands and children.

Master wasn't a believer in church but he let us have church. My we'd have happy times singing an' shouting. They'd have church when dey had a preacher and prayer meeting when dey didn't.

Slaves didn't leave de plantation much on 'count of de Patrollers. De patroller was low white trash what jest wanted a excuse to shoot niggers. I don't think I ever saw one but I heard lots of 'em.

I don't believe in luck charms and things of the such. Iffen you is in trouble, there ain't nothing gonna save you but de Good Lawd. I heard of folks keeping all kind of things for good luck charms. When I was a child different people gave me buttons to string and we called them our charm string and wore 'em round our necks. If we was mean dey would tell us "Old Raw Head and Bloody Bones" would git us. Grand mammy told us ghost stories after supper, but I don't remember any of dem.

I never did know I was a slave, 'cause I couldn't tell I wasn't free.

I always had a good time, didn't have to work much, and allus had
something to eat and wear and that was better than it is with me
now.

When de War was over and old Master told us we was free, Mammy
she say, "Well, I'm heading for Texas." I went out and old Master ask
me to bring him a coal of fire to light his pipe. I went after it and
mammy left pretty soon. My pappy wouldn't leave old Master right
then but old Master told us we was free to go where we pleased, so
me an' pappy left and went to Texas where my mammy was. We
never saw old Master any more. We stayed a while in Texas and then
come back to de Indian Territory.

Abe Lincoln was a good man, everybody liked him. See, I've got
his picture. Jeff Davis was a good man too, he just made a mistake.
I like Mr. Roosevelt, too.

[1] Mrs. Matilda Poe was interviewed in McAlester, Oklahoma, by WPA field worker
Mrs. Jessie R. Ervin probably sometime in summer or autumn 1937, for on 18 November of that year the final draft of the Poe narrative was sent to project headquarters
in Washington. Ervin's now lost notes were transcribed into a typewritten narrative,
"Interview with Matilda Poe (Ex-Slave, Aged 80 Years, North McAlester, Oklahoma),"
available in carbon copy in the OHS Slave Narratives. This text was edited and retyped
into the final draft, "Matilda Poe, Age 80 Yrs., McAlester, Okla.," forwarded to Washington and published here. This final draft is available in ribbon copy in the LC Slave
Narratives and in carbon copy as item 350012 in the LC Slave Narratives Carbon Copies
and in the OHS Slave Narratives. Stephens to Alsberg, 18 November 1937, WPA Notes
on Interviews.

[2] "Master" consistently is rendered as "marster" in the preliminary draft.

[3] For another remembrance of the Love family and of African American bondage
among its members, see the narrative of Mary Lindsay, above. Matilda Poe and seven
of her children were enrolled by the Dawes Commission in 1902 as Chickasaw freedmen because of their bondage as slaves of the Love family within the political bounds
of the Chickasaw Nation. Chickasaw Freedmen Census Cards, no. 25 (Tildy, Eveline,
Annie, Lucinda, Daniel, Millard, Eddie, and Jimmie Poe); Chickasaw Freedmen Enrollment Application Testimony file 25 (Tildy, Eveline, Annie, Lucinda, Daniel, Millard, and Eddie Poe).

J. L. PUGH[1]

Reference: Personal Interview

J. L. Pugh, Negro, school teacher, and Baptist minister of the Gospel,
was born April 12, 1876 in Mississippi, immigrating from that state
to Oklahoma Territory in 1906. In that same year he was employed
to teach a country school in Oklahoma Territory. He then went to
Colorado where he taught in several country schools, coming back to

Oklahoma in 1910, finishing his education in 1915 at Langston University.

J. L. Pugh bears a cultured mien despite the fact that, at twenty years of age he had not finished the fifth elementary school grade.

In relating some of the events incidental to his struggle for a higher education he says:—in part—

"I stole my knowledge of common fractions from a young Negro boy. This boy was in my class. I didn't know how to find the least common denominator, so I said to him, 'Julius, let's go out on the campus and study.' He said, 'All right.' We went out and Julius began an addition of fractions in computing the common denominator. I studiously asked him, 'Now, Julius, have you got that right?' He said, 'Yes sir, because all of these numerators will go into the denominator without a remainder.' Thus I learned common fractions without his knowing that he was teaching me."

One of my class mates, E. J. Money who being in a little better financial condition than I, helped me all he could. At one time he gave me a pair of trousers that were so worn that if I stooped over carelessly when I wore them they would burst across the seat or knees, which kept me busy a goodly part of the time patching them.

In retrospect, he remarked, "It isn't the heights to which I have ascended, that counts most, but the depths from which I came."

Another reflective remark was: "One must die before he can live. I died twice, physically, also mentally in the acquisition of an education. The consequence is that the struggle for such is seen in my child. She finished her college work while scarcely twenty years of age; would have finished two years earlier if I'd had money in 1936 to keep her in school. Whatever is thoroughly worked out in the parent is an inheritance to the child."

J. L. Pugh is now employed as a teacher in a WPA educational project at Orchard Park school.[2]

[1] J. L. Pugh was interviewed in Oklahoma City by Oklahoma Writers' Project reporter N. L. Phillips on 4 May 1939. Although his interview was not part of the formal Slave Narrative Project, for half a century it has been associated with that effort as part of the larger Federal Writers' Project for Oklahoma. The interview is available as the ribbon-copy typescript "J. L. Pugh, Reference: Personal Interview" in the "Interviews" file, Federal Writers' Project Collection, Archives and Manuscripts Division, Oklahoma Historical Society, with a photocopy available in the "J. L. Pugh" folder in the vertical files of the Library Resources Division, Oklahoma Historical Society. Pugh is listed in the 1941 African American city directory of Oklahoma City as a WPA adult education teacher serving at the Calvary Baptist Church. *Oklahoma City Negro City Directory,* 229.

² Orchard Park School, part of the separate school system that operated for blacks in Oklahoma City, was located at 3 North Brauer Street. *Oklahoma City Negro City Directory*, 223; *Polk's Oklahoma City Directory, 1937*, 1219. For background on the African American segregated schools in Oklahoma City, see Mildred McCraken Crossley, "A History of the Negro Schools of Oklahoma City" (M.A. thesis, University of Oklahoma, 1939).

HENRY F. PYLES[1]

Age 81 Yrs.   *Tulsa, Okla.*

Little pinch o' pepper
Little bunch o' wool

Mumbledy—Mumbledy

Two, three Pammy Christy beans
Little piece o' rusty iron

Mumbledy—Mumbledy

Wrop it in a rag and tie it wid hair,
Two fum a hoss an' one fum a mare

Mumbledy, Mumbledy, Mumbledy

Wet it in whiskey
Boughten wid silver;
Dat make you wush² so hard your sweat pop out,
And he come to pass, sho'!

That's how the niggers say old Bab Russ used to make the hoodoo "hands" he made for the young bucks and wenches, but I don't know, 'cause I was too trusting to look inside de one he make for me, and anyways I lose it, and it no good nohow!

Old Bab Russ live about two mile from me, and I went to him one night at midnight and ask him to make me de hand. I was a young strapper about sixteen years old, and thinking about wenches pretty hard and wanting something to help me out wid the one I liked best.

Old Bab Russ charge me four bits for dat hand, and I had to give four bits more for a pint of whiskey to wet it wid, and it wasn't no good nohow!

Course dat was five–six years after de War. I wasn't quite eleven when de War close. Most all the niggers was farming on de shares and whole lots of them was still working for their old Master yet. Old Bab come in there from deep South Carolina two–three years befo', and live all by hisself. De gal I was worrying about had come wid her old pappy and mammy to pick cotton on de place, and dey was staying in one of de cabins in the "settlement," but dey didn't live there all de time.

I don't know whether I believed in conjure much or not in dem days, but anyways I tried it that once and it stirred up sech a rumpus everybody called me "Hand" after that until after I was married and had a pack of children.

Old Bab Russ was coal black, and he could talk African or some other unknown tongue, and all the young bucks and wenches was mortal 'fraid of him!

Well sir, I took dat hand he made for me and set out to try it on dat gal. She never had give me a friendly look even, and when I would speak to her polite she just hang her head and say nothing!

We was all picking cotton, and I come along up behind her and decided to use my "Hand." I had bought me a pint of whiskey to wet the hand wid, but I was scared to take [it] out of my pocket and let the other niggers see it, so I jest set down in de cotton row and taken a big mouthful. I figgered to hold it in my mouth until I catched up wid that gal and then blow it on the hand jest before I tech her on the arm and speak to her.

Well, I take me a big mouthful, but it was so hot and scaldy it jest slip right on down my throat! Then I had to take another, and when I was gitting up I kind of stumbled and it slip down, too!

Then I see all the others get way on ahead, and I took another big mouthful—the last in the bottle—and drap the bottle under a big stalk and start picking fast and holding the whiskey in my mouth this time. I missed about half the cotton I guess, but at last I catch up with de rest and git close up behind dat purty gal. Then I started to speak to her, but forgot I had de whiskey in mouth and I lost most of it down my neck and all over my chin, and then I strangled a little on the rest, so as when I went to squirt it on de "hand" I didn't have nothing left to squirt but a little spit.

That make me a little nervous right then, but anyways I step up behind dat gal and lay my hand on her arm and speak polite and start to say something, but I finish up what I start to say laying on my neck with my nose shoved up under a cotton stalk about four rows away!

De way that gal lam me across the head was a caution! We was in new ground, and she jest pick up a piece of old root and whopped me right in de neck with it!

That raise sech a laugh on me that I never say nothing to her for three–four days, but after while I gets myself wound up to go see her at her home. I didn't know how she going to act, but I jest took my foot in my hand and went on over.

Her old pappy and mammy was asleep in the back of the room on a pallet, and we set in front of the fireplace on our hunches and jest looked at the fire and punched it up a little. It wasn't cold, but de malary fog was thick all through de bottoms.

After while I could smell the whiskey soaked up in dat "hand" I had in my pocket, and I was scared she could smell it too. So I jest reached in my pocket and teched it for luck, then I reached over and teched her arm. She jerked it back so quick she knocked over the churn and spilled buttermilk all over de floor! Dat make de old folks mad, and dey grumble and holler and told de gal, "Send dat black rapscallion on out of here!" But I didn't go.

I kept on moving over closer and she kept on backing away, but after while I reach over and put my hand on her knee. All I was going to do was say something but I shore forgot what it was the next minnit, 'cause she jest whinnied lak a scared hoss and give me a big push. I was settin straddledly-legged on the floor, and that push sent me on my head in the hot ashes in the fur corner of the chimney!

Then the old man jump up and make for me and I make for the door! It was dark, all 'cepting the light from the chimney, and I fumble all up and down the door jamb before I find de latch pin. The old man shorely git me if he hadn't stumble over the eating table and whop his hand right down in de dish of fresh made butter. That make him so mad he jest stand and holler and cuss.

I git de pin loose and jerk de door open so quick and hard I knock de powder gourd down what was hanging over it, and my feet git caught in the string. The stopper gits knocked out, and when I untangle it from my feet and throw it back in de house it fall in the fireplace.

I was running all de time, but I hear dat gourd go "Blammity Blam!" and then all de yelling, but I didn't go back to see how dey git the hot coals all put out what was scattered all over de cabin!

I done drap dat "hand" and I never did see it again. Never did see the gal but two–three times after that, and we never mention about dat night. Her old pappy was too old to work, so I never did see him neither, but she must of told about it because all the young bucks called me "Hand" after that for a long time.

Old Bab kept on trying to work his conjure with the old niggers, but the young ones didn't pay him much mind 'cause they was hearing about the Gospel and de Lord Jesus Christ. We was all free then, and we could go and come without a pass, and they was always some kind of church meeting going on close enough to go to. Our niggers never did hear about de Lord Jesus until after we was free, but lots of niggers on de other plantations had masters that told them all about him, and some of dem niggers was pretty good at preaching. Then de good church people in de North was sending white preachers amongst us all the time too. Most of de young niggers was Christians by that time.

One day old Bab was hoeing in a field and got into a squabble about something with a young gal name Polly, same name as his wife. After while he git so mad he reach up with his fingers and wet them on his tongue and point straight up and say, "Now you got a trick on you! Dere's a heavy trick on you now! Iffen you don't change your mind you going to pass on before the sun go down!"

All the young niggers looked like they want to giggle but afraid to, and the old ones start begging old Bab to take the trick off, but that Polly git her dander up and take in after him with a hoe!

She knocked him down, and he jest laid there kicking his feet in the air and trying to keep her from hitting him in the head!

Well, that kind of broke up Bab's charm, so he set out to be a preacher. The Northern whites was paying some of the Negro preachers, so he tried to be one too. He didn't know nothing about de Bible but to shout loud, so the preacher board at Red Mound never would give him a paper to preach. Then he had to go back to tricking and trancing again.

One day he come in at dinner and told his wife to git him something to eat. She told him they ain't nothing but some buttermilk, and he says give me some of dat. He hollered around till she fix him a big ash cake and he ate that and she made him another and he ate that. Then he drunk the rest of de gallon of buttermilk and went out and laid down on a tobacco scaffold in de yard and nearly died.

After while he jest stiffened out and looked like he was dead, and nobody couldn't wake him up. 'Bout forty niggers gathered round and tried but it done no good. Old mammy Polly got scared and sent after the white judge, old Squire Wilson, and he tried, and then the white preacher Reverend Dennison tried and old man Gorman tried. He was a infidel, but that didn't do no good.

By that time it was getting dark, and every nigger in a square mile

was there, looking on and acting scared. Me and my partner who was
a little bit cripple but mighty smart come up to see what all the rumpus was about, and we was jest the age to do anything.

He whispered to me to let him start it off and then me finish it
while he got a head running start. I ast him what he talking about.

Then he fooled round the house and got a little ball of cotton and
soaked it in kerosene from a lamp. It was a brass lamp with a hole and
a stopper in the side of the bowl. Wonder he didn't burn his fool head
off! Then he sidle up close and stuck dat cotton 'tween old Bab's toes.
Old Bab had the biggest feet I ever see, too.

'Bout that time I lit a corn shuck in de lamp and run out in de yard
and stuck it to de cotton and jest kept right on running!

My partner had a big start but I catch up wid him and we lay
down in the bresh and listened to everybody hollering and old Bab
hollering louder than anybody. Old Bab moved away after that.

All that foolishness happen after the War, but before de War
while I was a little boy they wasn't much foolishness went on I warrant you.

I was born on de 15th of August in 1856, and belonged to Mister Addison Pyles. He lived in town, in Jackson, Tennessee, and was
a old man when de War broke. He had a nephew named Irvin T.
Pyles he raised from a baby, and Mister Irvin kept a store at de corner of de roads at our plantation. The plantation covered about 300
or 400 acres I reckon, and they had about 25 slaves counting de children.

The plantation was about 9 miles north of Red Mound, close to
Lexington, Tennessee, and about a mile and a half from Parker's
Crossroads where they had a big battle in de War.

They wasn't no white overseer on the place, except Mister Irvin,
and he stayed in de store or in town and didn't bother about the farm
work. We had a Negro overlooker who was my stepdaddy. His name
was Jordan, and he run away wid the Yankees about de middle of de
War and was in a Negro Yankee regiment. After he left we jest worked
on as usual because we was afraid not to. Several of de men got away
like that but he was de only one that got in de army.

They was a big house in de middle of de place and a settlement of
Negro cabins behind and around it. We called it de settlement, but
on other plantations where white folks lived there too they called it
de quarters. We always kept this big house clean and ready, and sometimes de white folks come out from town and stay a few days and
hunt and fish and look over de crops.

We all worked at farm work. Cotton and corn and tobacco mostly. We all laid off Sunday after noontime, but we didn't have no church nor preaching and we didn't hear anything 'bout Jesus much until after de emancipation.

I reckon old Master wasn't very religious, 'cause he never tell us 'bout the Holy Word. He jest said to behave ourselves and tell him when we wanted to marry, and not have but one wife.

We had little garden patches and cotton patches we could work on Sunday and what de stuff brung we could sell and keep the money. Old Master let us have what we made that way on Sunday. We could buy ribbons and hand soap and coal oil and such at de store. Master Irvin was always honest 'bout countin'³ de money, too.

We didn't have no carders and spinners nor no weavers on de plantation. They cost too much money to buy just for 25 niggers, and they cost a lot more than field niggers. So we got our clothes sent out to us from in town, and sometimes we was give cloth from de store to make our clothes out of.

We got de shorts and seconds from de mill when we had wheat ground, and so we had good wheat bread as well as corn pone, and de big smokehouse was on de place and we had all de meat we wanted to eat. Old Master sent out after de meat he wanted every day or so and we kept him in garden sass that way too.

We was right between de forks of Big Beaver and Little Beaver and we could go fishing without getting far off de place. We couldn't go far away without a pass, though, and they wasn't nobody on the place to write us a pass, so we couldn't go to meeting and dances and sech.

But de niggers on de other plantations could get passes to come to our place, and so we had parties sometimes there at our place. We always had them on Sundays, 'cause in the evening we would be too tired to work if we set up, and the other masters wouldn't give passes to their niggers to come over in de evening.

We had a white doctor lived at de next plantation, and old Master had a contract with old Dr. Brown to look after us. He had a beard as long as your arm. He come for all kinds of misery except bornings. Then we had a midwife who was a white woman lived down below us. They was poor people renting or living on war land. Nearly all de white folks in that country been there a long time and their old people got de land from de government for fighting in the Revolutionary War. Most all was from North Carolina—way back. I think old Master's pappy was from dere in de first place.

Old Master had two sons named Newton and Willis. Newton was

in de War and was killed, and Willis went to war later and was sick a long time and come home early. Old Master was too old to go.

There was two daughters, Mary, de oldest, married a Holmes, and Miss Laura never did marry I don't think.

My mammy's name was Jane, and she was born on de 10th day of May in 1836. I know de dates 'cause old Master kept his book on all his niggers de same as on his own family. Mammy was the nurse of all de children but I think old Master sent her to de plantation about the time I was born. I don't think I had any pappy. I think I was jest one of them things that happened sometimes in slavery days, but I know old Master didn't have nothing to do with it—I'm too black.

Mammy married a man named Jordan when I was a little baby. He was the overlooker and went off to de Yankees, when dey come for foraging through dat country de first time.

He served in de Negro regiment in de battle at Fort Piller[4] and a lot of Sesesh was killed in dat battle, so when de War was over and Jordan come back home he was a changed nigger and all de whites and a lot of de niggers hated him. All 'cepting old Master, and he never said a word out of de way to him. Jest told him to come on and work on de place as long as he wanted to.

But Jordan had a hard time, and he brung it on his self I reckon.

'Bout de first thing, he went down to Wildersville Schoolhouse, about a mile from Wildersville, to a nigger and carpet bagger convention and took me and mammy along. That was de first picnic and de first brass band I ever see. De band men was all white men and they still had on their blue soldier clothes.

Lots of de niggers there had been in the Union army too, and they had on parts of their army clothes. They took them out from under their coats and their wagon seats and put them on for de picnic.

There was a saloon over in Wildersville, and a lot of them went over there but they was scared to go in, most of them. But a colored delegate named Taylor and my pappy went in and ordered a drink. The bartender didn't pay them no mind.

Then a white man named Billy Britt walked up and throwed a glass of whiskey in Jordan's face and cussed him for being in de Yankee army. Then a white man from the North named Pearson took up the fight and him and Jordan jumped on Billy Britt, but de crowd stopped them and told pappy to git on back to whar he come from.

He got elected a delegate at de convention and went on down to Nashville and helped nominate Brownlow for governor.[5] Then he couldn't come back home for a while, but finally he did.

Old Master was uneasy about de way things was going on, and he come out to de farm and stayed in de big house a while.

One day in broad daylight he was on de gallery and down de road come 'bout 20 bushwhackers in Sesesh clothes on horses and rid up to de gate. Old Master knowed all of them, and Captain Clay Taylor, who had been de master of de nigger delegate, was at the head of them.

They had Jordan Pyles tied with a rope and walked along on de ground betwixt two horses.

"Whar you taking my nigger?" Old Master say. He run down off de gallery and out in de road.

"He ain't your nigger no more—you know that," old Captain Taylor holler back.

"He jest as much my nigger as that Taylor nigger was your nigger, and you ain't laid hands on him! Now you jest have pity on my nigger!"

"Your nigger Jordan been in de Yankee army, and he was in de battle at Fort Piller and help kill our white folks, and you know it!" Old Captain Taylor say, and argue on like that, but old Master jest take hold his bridle and shake his head.

"No, Clay," he say, "that boy maybe didn't kill Confederates, but you and him both know my two boys killed plenty Yankees, and you forgot I lost one of my boys in de War. Ain't that enough to pay for letting my nigger alone?"

And old Captain Taylor give the word to turn Jordan loose, and they rid on down de road.

That's one reason my stepdaddy never did leave old Master's place, and I stayed on dere till I was grown and had children.

The Yankees come through past our place three–four times, and one time they had a big battle jest a mile and a half away at Parker's Crossroads.[6]

I was in de field hoeing, and I remember I hadn't watered the cows we had hid way down in de woods, so I started down to water them when I first heard the shooting.

We had de stock hid down in de woods and all de corn and stuff hid too, 'cause the Yankees and the Sesesh had been riding through quite a lot, and either one take anything they needed iffen they found it.

First I hear something way off say "Br-r-rup!" Then again, and again. Then something sound like popcorn beginning to pop real slow. Then it git faster and I start for de settlement and de big house.

All Master's folks was staying at de big house then, and couldn't git back to town 'count of de soldiers, so they all put on they good clothes, with de hoop skirts and little sunshades and the lace pantaloons, and got in the buggy and go see de battle!

They rid off and it wasn't long till all the niggers was following behind. We all got to a hill 'bout a half a mile from the crossroads and stopped when we couldn't see nothing but thick smoke all over de whole place.

We could see men on horses come in and out of de smoke, going this way and that way, and then some Yankees on horses broke through de woods right close to us and scattered off down through de field. One of de white officers rid up close and yelled at us and took off his hat, but I couldn't hear nothing he said.

Then he rid on and catch up with his men. They had stopped and was turning off to one side. He looked back and waved his hat again for us to git away from thar,[7] and jest then he clapped his hand to his belly and fell off his hoss.

Our white folks turned their buggy round and made it for home and no mistake! The niggers wasn't fur behind neither!

They fit on back toward our plantation, and some of the fighting was inside it at one corner. For three–four days after that they was burying soldiers 'round there, and some of de graves was on our old place.

Long time afterwards people come and moved all them to other graveyards at Shiloh and Corinth and other places. They was about a hundred killed all around there.

After de War I married Molly Timberlake and we lived on there 'til 1902, when we come to Indian Territory at Haskell. They wasn't no Haskell there then, and I helped to build dat town, doing carpenter work and the like.

We had two boys, Bill and Jim Dick, and eight daughters, Effie,[8] Ida, Etta, Eva, Jessie, Tommie, Bennie and Timmie. Her real name is Timberlake after her mammy. They all went to school and graduates in the high schools.

My wife has been dead about ten years.

[1] Henry F. Pyles was interviewed at his home in Tulsa, Oklahoma, probably sometime in spring 1937 by WPA field worker Robert Vinson Lackey. From Lackey's notes a preliminary draft of the elderly black man's remembrances was prepared in narrative form as the typescript "Interview with Henry F. Pyles, Ex-Slave, Age 81 Yrs., 1059 N. Lansing Ave., Tulsa, Oklahoma." The ribbon copy of this early draft of the interview for reasons now not known was forwarded to the Washington headquarters of the Federal Writers' Project, where it was stamped "received" on 27 May 1937, and it is now

filed with item 350070 in the LC Slave Narratives Carbon Copies. From the preliminary version a final draft was prepared and sent to Washington on 14 September 1937. This typescript, "Henry F. Pyles, Age 81 Yrs., Tulsa, Okla.," published here, is the version now in the official slave narrative collection in the Manuscript Division of the Library of Congress, and it is available in ribbon copy in the LC Slave Narratives and in carbon copy as item 350070 in the LC Slave Narratives Carbon Copies, as well as in carbon copy in the OHS Slave Narratives (with pages 11 and 12 separated and in the "Unid-Partial" file). Benjamin A. Botkin, folklore editor for the Federal Writers' Project, was highly impressed with the Henry F. Pyles interview, appraising it as an "outstanding narrative of unusual episodes in plantation life, war, and Reconstruction." He chose two lengthy extracts for inclusion in his 1945 study, *Lay My Burden Down* (29–33, 254–55, 274, 284). B. A. B[otkin], LC Slave Narrative Appraisal Sheets, Accession no. 350070, 6 December 1940; *Polk's Tulsa City Directory, 1935,* 450; Stephens to Cronyn, 14 September 1937, WPA Notes on Interviews.

The Henry F. Pyles interview is one of the very few from the WPA Oklahoma Slave Narratives Project to have been published in Oklahoma. Robert Vinson Lackey passed a copy of the interview text to journalist Ruth Sheldon, who edited and considerably abridged it for publication in the *Tulsa Tribune,* 23 August 1937, under the title "Hoodoo 'Hand' Didn't Win Him His Gal, Just Got Him into Trouble, Ex-Slave Here Relates."

² Although the preliminary draft of the narrative here reads "wush," the final draft contains "wash," an apparent typographical error.

³ "Countin'" appears in the preliminary draft; the final draft here contains a misreading, "continuing."

⁴ The Battle of Fort Pillow, Tennessee, was one of the infamous incidents of the Civil War. In this engagement the Confederate general Nathan Bedford Forest attacked the Union position, held by both black and white federal soldiers, and succeeded in capturing it. Several score of the African American defenders who had surrendered were subsequently murdered rather than being taken prisoners of war. For background on this battle, see *Fort Pillow Massacre,* U.S., 38th Cong., 1st Sess., House Report 65; James M. McPherson, *The Negro's Civil War: How American Negroes Felt and Acted during the War for the Union,* 216–22. For an overview of the treatment of black federal troops by Confederate forces, see Brainerd Dyer, "The Treatment of Colored Union Troops by the Confederates, 1861–1865," *Journal of Negro History* 20 (July 1935): 273–86.

⁵ William Gannaway Brownlow served as the Republican governor of Tennessee from 1865 to 1869, during the Reconstruction period.

⁶ For the official reports of the fighting that took place at Parker's Crossroads, Tennessee, on 30 and 31 December 1862, see U.S., Department of War, *The War of Rebellion: A Compilation of the Official Records of the Union and Confederate Armies,* series 1, vol. 17, part 1, 551–52, 568–90.

⁷ The preliminary version here reads "thar," but the final draft says "that," an apparent typographical error.

⁸ The roughly contemporary Tulsa city directory shows Henry F. Pyles, by vocation a carpenter, living with his daughter Effie M. Hamilton, the widow of Fletcher Hamilton, at 1059 North Lansing. *Polk's Tulsa City Directory, 1935,* 268, 450, 666.

MARTHA ANN RATLIFF[1]

Age—Unknown *Oklahoma City, Okla.*

I was born in Cotton Plant, Mississippi.[2] I don't know how old I am but I suppose I'm nearly a hundred. Mother was named Celia. Her first husband was named George Moore and the second was named Jesse Ratliff. Dere was four children by Moore and none by Ratliff. I married Riley Ratliff after freedom. I got two children living and four dead. I now live wid Ella Luster,[3] and Richard Ratliff, my son, is in Perry.

My mother was de mother of four children, names as following: Frank Moore, only brother, and three sisters, Ruth Moore, George Ann Moore and Martha Ann Moore or me. During slavery my parents lived in our Master's[4] back yard as me and mother did the cooking for my Master and de slaves as dey all ate in the kitchen.

Our beds was made of wood and the mattresses wove on a loom by the slaves. In winter we wore jean underskirts made of wool and cotton top dresses. In summer we wore thin cotton goods. Master was a tailor and he would cut out de cloth himself for his slaves' clothing and de women did de sewing.

As a slave, I stayed in de house and wait on my Mistress, kept house clean and killed flies in de house with pea-fowl tails and at meal time I had to fan de flies off de table. As my Master and family would eat so long, I would sometime go to sleep fanning flies and let my fan fall and if dere was company my Mistress would whip or slap me when dey was gone.

I never earned or had any money as a slave. We got everything else dey thought we needed but money. Slaves hunted but dey never ate rabbits or possums till after freedom. There wasn't no gardens but Master's. My Master was name Master Riddle. He had two children, one boy and a girl. I can't think of de boy's name but de girl was named Atsia. They lived in a frame house but slaves lived in log houses in quarters.

The overseers were not allowed to whip or treat slaves mean, but if dey needed whipping Master would do it hisself. My Master was kind to his slaves. He said de slaves couldn't work if dey was sore from beatings. But other white Masters around, some of them was mean.

The plantation was a big one and slaves all stayed in de quarters and went to work without any bells or horns. My Master raised all his slaves after he bought his first ones.[5] Dey had to go and clean up and wash on Saturdays and go to church on Sundays. We went to the white's church and sat in the back of the church and were allowed to join and be baptized by de white preacher after de white folks was baptized. I don't know how many slaves he had but he had heap of 'em. I saw slaves auctioned or sold but my Master didn't buy or sell any. None of us was taught to read or write.

My father was a fiddler and some nights he would slip off to play for dances as well as for me. He would slip off at other times and as he never would get a pass and when patrollers would git at him, he would outrun them most of de time. They would sometime catch him and whip him. When I would sometime be with him, he would get me on his back and run.

My Master would give us a week for Christmas and the slaves would frolic and go to dances.

Cornshucking and quilting would be done at de same time. De men would shuck corn while the women do de quilting. When you wanted to get married you would have to tell your Master and if it was all right wid him he would tell you and if he objected you couldn't marry dat person.

We didn't know anything 'bout voo-dooing till after freedom. We had only de habit of wearing asafetida 'round de neck to keep from being sick.

When the news come dat we was free, Master called us together and told us dat we was free, yet most of us still stayed. He told us also dat he liked all of us and dat when he died he wanted de niggers to come to de burial which they all thought was near around.

Our Master was so good to us dat even after freedom, when he heard of some of us being sick he would come to see us and bring us something.

¹ On 25 June 1937, J. S. Thomas from the Oklahoma Federal Writers' Project interviewed the elderly Mrs. Martha Ann Ratliff in Oklahoma City. From his field notes a rough typewritten transcription was prepared under the title "Ex-Slave—Story, Reference: Martha Ann Ratliff—1333 NE 6th, Oklahoma City, Oklahoma." A complete carbon copy of this typescript is available in the OHS Slave Narratives, while the ribbon copy is available with the first page filed under the informant's name and the remaining two pages filed loosely in the "Unid-Partial" file in the OHS Slave Narratives. A note appended to the carbon copy and written by project staff member Ida Belle Hunter states, "More information necessary for complete interview." Nevertheless, the preliminary draft was edited and revised on 15 October 1937 into the typescript "Martha Ann Ratliff, Age—Unknown, Oklahoma City, Okla.," which is published here. A note by Oklahoma Federal Writers' Project employee Ned DeWitt attached to this text reads, "More info! Reinterview." No project personnel, however, are known to have returned to interview Mrs. Ratliff fur-

ther, and her memories recorded in the transcripts in the OHS Slave Narratives are her only known recorded remembrances. This interview has never before been published.

[2] In the rough draft this sentence reads, confusingly, "I's born in Cotton Plant, Mississippi, County sity, Ripley." Cotton Plant is in extreme southern Tippah County, and Ripley is its county seat.

[3] The rough draft of this narrative indicates that Mrs. Martha Ann Ratliff was interviewed at 1333 Northeast 6th in the city. The contemporary Oklahoma City directory does not list Mrs. Ratliff, but the address nearest the one noted in the interview transcript is 1335 Northeast 6th, which was the residence of Mrs. Ella Luster, the daughter mentioned by the interviewee. *Polk's Oklahoma City Directory, 1937,* 937.

[4] Throughout the rough draft "master" consistently is rendered phonetically as "moster."

[5] At this point the later draft omits the following sentence that appears in the rough draft: "My Moster was kind to us or his neggers (Negroes)."

INTERVIEW WITH ALICE RAWLINGS[1]

Ex-Slave, Age 80 Years   *812 So. 7th Street, Muskogee, Oklahoma*

My mother, Tishea Mickens, was sold to an owner in Virginia just a little while after I was born, and I didn't see her for a long time, not until old Master Major Jackson bought her back and kept her till the freedom come.

My mistress Lucy told me I was born on February 1, 1858, near Linden, Cash County, Texas.[2] My father was Jack Mickens, the hardest working slave on Major Jackson's Texas plantation. He was the blacksmith and even before the slaves was made free my father earned outside money that his master allowed him to keep. He had money when he was set free.

Father was born in Montgomery, Alabama. There was seven of us children but I forgot the names of all but my brother Albert Mickens who lives down in Texas somewheres to this day.

Major Jackson had two plantations, one in Texas and the other in Alabama. Guess he moved from that country to Texas when the war come along.

His house was a large one and it was about 10-mile from the river dock. I was born in his house. There was a big smokehouse, and plenty of hogs was killed to keep it full. He had the men kill beef and dry it out, and everybody had good things to eat all the time.

There was lots of overseers around the plantation; folks said there was about 6,000-acre of the place and it took lots of work to keep it going. It was all cleared by slaves, just land, good farm land made right from under the trees they chopped down.

A long time after slavery was over, just about the time I had three children of my own, I saw the old place again. It was still standing. We was traveling through the country and Lord! I look around and over from the road about a mile was the old house setting lonesome on a little hill. But the Major and the Mistress was no more, they gone to Heaven I know, because they was both good folks.

I heard talk about the war times. About Vicksburg. How it was a terrible fight, and how General Pemberton give up his sword to General Grant, and everybody said that was the turning point of victory for the North Yankees. My father said General Grant laid siege for 47 days in 1863, but that's all I remember.

Saturday night, according to what my paw told me, was negro night. The slaves could get passes and go to town. The white folks seems like didn't go out on that night, just leave it to the negroes and they've still got the habit of parading around the streets on Saturday nights.

The Master Major had one boy who went off to the war. Took some of his own slaves with him. They took good care of that boy because he come through the war without getting even hurt and all the negroes was happy when he come on the Texas place.

The war was over then. But slavery wasn't. No, the old master didn't tell us about freedom until after the crops was in and made. Six months after all the rest was free.

Master's place was called Elms Court and the plantation next to his was owned by a friendly planter. He talked with my father in the road one day. Before we all knew that the other slaves was freed. I guess that's how we heard about it.

The white man asked pa why don't you buy your own land? But pa told though he had saved a little money it wouldn't go far enough to buy a farm and mules and plows and such, for when it come to buying his own rations and clothes for all the children there wouldn't be much left to save for a farm.

The Major was sick when they finally told us about the freedom. His son James was back from the war and he seemed glad for us to know about [it]. So did his sister, Liza, and another girl who I done forgot her name.

One time during the war some of the Yankee soldiers come to the place. The Major knew they was coming and he locked up the house, made everybody hide out. He was hiding too. Them soldiers look around and found my mother. She was the cook. They stack their guns on the porch, feed their horses and water them and tell my mother to start cooking. She said she never cook so much before in all her life.

Some of the slaves come out from hiding places and the soldiers told them to take all the food stuffs they wanted. My father told the negroes not to touch the master stuff and just one negro stole a ham, and she was my aunt who said she just had to have some lean meat.

My uncle Amos worked in the tanyard. He got sick one evening but the overseer didn't think he was so bad off but the next morning he was dead. The master fix up a box to bury him and all the children sat around and cried.

My mother was kinder mean sometimes, and wasn't scared of overseers or nothing. One time when she was working on the master's Alabama place an overseer tried to shoot her. She grabbed the gun and run for the river. She dropped the gun in the river and the overseer got over his temper and left her alone.

There was another overseer on the place that was terrible mean. That's what my folks said about him. If a slave done something to make him mad that man would burn their nose or their ears with fire brands. I saw some of them who had their ears burned nearly off.

The slaves was allowed to go to church. Set in a corner away in the back of the building. Some of the old people could leave to stay at home for washing their clothes on Sunday. That was the only thing keep 'em out of church.

Well, I had another uncle who was a runaway. They said he was never caught. Like another slave the master bought once. He run away too. He didn't like the Major and one day he said, "I won't serve you, just put me in your pocket." He meant for the master to sell him. Then he ran for a hideout. The overseers found him in a boat hull and they near cut him to pieces. An old negro woman greased him every morning and he got well.

Then he run off again. This time he got away and wrote to the master a long time after, bragging how the master couldn't get him now because he was in a free state.

My first husband was Thomas Pepper, the second was Eliza Henry. They was just husbands by agreement but the last one, John Rawlings, I married him. Got three children—Carrie, Harrison and Joe.

I belong to the Methodist church and I think all should be religious. The Lord done helped us [out of] slavery; now it's our turn to help the Lord. That's the way I feel about it.

¹ WPA field worker Ethel Wolfe Garrison interviewed Mrs. Alice Rawlings in Muskogee, Oklahoma, probably sometime in the spring or early summer of 1938. On 9 June 1938 her coworker Craig Vollmer edited and retyped her now lost material into the narrative "Interview with Alice Rawlings, Ex-Slave, Age 80 Years, 812 So. 7th

Street, Muskogee, Oklahoma," available in the OHS Slave Narratives. This interview is published here for the first time.

² "Cash County" is obviously phonetic spelling for Cass County; Linden is the county seat.

JOE RAY¹

Age 83   *Muskogee, Oklahoma*

My folks was shipped from Africa across the waters and fetched a good price on the slave market at New Orleans where my pappy stayed for a long time helping with the fresh Negroes that come over on the slave boats.

His name was John and my mammy's name was Rhoda. She belonged to Jim Hawkins who had a plantation at Fulton, Arkansas, down in Hempstead County. When she met my pappy old master Hawkins sold her to pappy's master, name of Ray, so's dey could stay together.

Dere at Fulton I was born in 1855. I was eight year old when Vicksburg give up to the Yankees and an old slave man dere looked at the lines on my hand and said I was eight year old. My twin sister, Josephine, is still living down in Shreveport, La., and a brother Charles lives in Tampico, Mexico. Dat's where I want to go for I is afraid the Japs is coming over here and I is too feeble to dodge stray cannon balls!

Some of the slaves was moved around all over the south during the War. Me and pappy was at Vicksburg when the Rebels stuck their swords in the ground to give up. But dem Yanks had a terrible time whipping us. The Yank soldiers dug holes in the ground and put in kegs of powder. Den dey blowed up the land down by the river and almost turned the river (Mississippi) around! When the powder blasts go off lots of Rebels was killed and dere wasn't many left to give up when General Grant took the town.

I remember General Grant talking and laughing about the war. He was a fighter, dat man! I eat two–three meals at the General's place; he took me in one terrible cold night, I was almost froze.

Master Ray sold mammy, me and my twin sister and two brothers to Enoch Smith, and he was the last master we had. Some of my folks stayed with him a long time after they was free—doing washings, ironings and cooking. The boys tend to his horses and work in the fields.

The Smith plantation was called "Seven Mile Square"—it was that size and had about 350 slaves most of the time. He was a big trader. His house was made of sawed cedar logs from a close by mill, and the beds had round logs of cedar posts, with rope slats made diamond fashion. When the ropes was drawn up it made the bottom tight as a dollar bill.

The slaves lived in log huts, mostly one room, with a tar roof. Dere was no beds like the master had. Just a kind of bunk with corn shuckings stuck in a cotton bag for to lay on. After working in the fields all day, sometimes without anything to eat for dinner, the slaves come to the cabins at night, cook their supper of white salt meat and talk awhile before going to sleep. Dey had to get sleep early and get up early; nobody sleep late, even on Sunday.

Dere was two overseers on the place and dey carried a bull whip all the time. Dey didn't whip the girls; the old master pinch their ears if dey get mean and not mind. But I saw a slave man whipped until his shirt was cut to pieces! Dey whipped dem like horses, but the master didn't want dem beat to death. If dey whip dem too hard the old master shake his head and say, "Dat's too much money to kill!"

My pappy killed an overseer who tried to lash him; dey sent him off to another plantation for a while. Dat's all the punishment he got.

The auction sales brought the master lots of money. One man sold for $1,500. The slaves stand bare to the waist, men and women alike, the buyers feeling of dem to see if dey was solid and looking for scars to see if dey had been mean enough for whippings.

The old master kept his money hidden in two kegs under the stairway. I seen him putting money dere one day and he chased me out of the house. But another Negro found out about it and he stole some of it and run off to Texas. Dey said he bout a farm dere; anyway, dey never got the slave nor the money back, dat's what I know.

Alma Cinda was the mistress' name. Dere was boy name of Joe and a girl name of Athlene. Dat boy was a terror; folks said he was a cattle stealer. One year he come home and died of pneumonia.

The master give each slave family about 4-pounds of fat meats every week, with a quart of molasses, a peck of corn meal and some bran for flour. When dat run out you was just out until Saturday night come around again.

The clothes was all home spun, made of cotton, and when I was a little boy the master give me a pair of red shoes. In dem days I wore a charm for sharp luck. It was a needle with a blue velvet string through the eye, but when I do something mean that charm didn't keep the master's whip off my back!

After freedom one time I worked at the old Peabody hotel in Memphis. Lots of gamblers around dere den; dey come down the river and have some big gambling games. I done some gambling too, but not like dem white folks who paid me a dollar for a cigar after dey have a streak of big winnings.

Dem old south slave girls I love, but not dem northern girls—dere is a difference! I lived with one of them south girls name of Jennie Harris from Mississippi. She leave me for a nappy headed preacher. Den I married Mandy Drew, another Mississippi girl, who leave me for a man with two kinky heads (children). A long time later I see dat man on a river boat and I was fixing to shoot him but dere was too many laws at the boat landing so he got away.

That black-as-a-skillet Mandy give me a boy, Dick Ray, and a girl Jabo who full grown weighted about 400-pounds. Dere was four other wives, but dey're all gone now and I ain't studying nobody now, I is dat old!

Lincoln was a great man, but dis country needs a king.

Folks call me a prophet, because I tell dem things dat comes true. Now I been telling dem dat slavery is coming back and it ain't far away. Maybe dey won't believe it—but slavery is coming soon.

[1] Joe Ray was interviewed in Muskogee, Oklahoma, by WPA field worker Ethel Wolfe Garrison probably sometime in the winter of 1937–38. On 7 February 1938 project staff member Craig Vollmer revised Garrison's now lost initial rough draft of Ray's remembrances into the typescript "Interview with Joe Ray, Slave Born, Age 83, General Delivery, Muskogee, Oklahoma," available in ribbon copy in the OHS Slave Narratives. At some later date in 1938 project personnel edited the intermediate draft into a final typescript entitled "Joe Ray, Age 83, Muskogee, Oklahoma," which remains in the OHS Slave Narratives and is published here for the first time.

SAM RHODES[1]

Age 91   *Tulsa, Oklahoma*

On February 25, 1847, I was born on the plantation of Hugh Crawford in the Franklin district [county] of Georgia. Dat's where my mother, Cenie Crawford, was born too, but my daddy was born a free Negro, only dey stole him and sold him into slavery.

His name was Ned Rhodes, and he had a brother and sister, all living in Washington, D.C., when they was children. Dey all three stolen at the same time and carried to the South; sold for slaves they was, and dat how I come to be born into slavery.

My folks had 10 children besides me. I can name them right off:

Maria, Ned, Manda, Millie, Hannah, Freeman, Sarah, King, Fannie and George.

Master Crawford had a daughter name of Melinda and she marry Sam Vernon, who lived in the Pickens district [county], South Carolina. The master give our whole family to them for a wedding present and we went with them when they moved somewhere in North Carolina.

Dat plantation was in a hilly section, and it took about 20 slaves for the raising of grain, like corn and wheat, and a little cotton. Dat was hard ground to work, and we worked 10 hours a day, except on Sunday and sometimes on a Saturday we get a little time off like it was a holiday.

We lived in a log cabin just like all the rest. Chinked with clay it was, with a stone fireplace where mammy done the cooking. Dere was plenty of wild game for all of us, and whatever it was—'possum, rabbit, turkey or fish—mammy cook it up just right for our hungry bellies and mix it in with some good garden stuff from the master's garden; but best of all I liked the 'possum best, and still do. Give me dat 'possum, done baked brown with sweet potatoes steaming hot inside their yellow skins, and I is content! Mostly we had corn bread, but biscuits was pretty scattering.

Master Vernon was good to us, never whip us, and look after the work hisself. Kept us in shoes too, said nobody could work good with hurting feet; he sure was right.

He lived in a big frame house, just one story, fixed up with mighty fine furniture. The house had one large stone fireplace, dat all I remember.

Dere was some poor whites lived around us, and some not so poor, and some pretty well fixed. Dere was a slave trader live not far away, and when he sell a batch of slaves dey would pass by our place. All chained up dey was; a trace chain was locked around their necks and fastened to the wagon. The same way when he buy new slaves and bring dem back home. Mostly dey was young slaves for no one got any use for an old Negro; just like dey is today. The buyers was always on the watch for big breasted women; dey got a bigger price than for the scrawny ones.

At the corn shuckings we got news from the other plantations. One time I hear about the patrollers catch up with some boys and girls who went to a dance without a pass. The patrollers flogged dem pretty hard and took dem home.

My mammy was a kind of herb doctor and when a cold get us children she boil up pine tops and steam our heads; for measles she give sheep-shire tea to bring dem out quicker, I guess.

About the war; don't know much about it for dere was no fighting around where we live. One of my brothers went with the Rebels and we never hear from him again.

Lincoln was the best president we ever had, but Jeff Davis was just as good, only he was on the wrong side. For slavery is cruel, and it was cruel to sell the mammy and pappy away from their little babies and children like dey did Frank Verden's wife. Where she went nobody know and nobody ever hear of her again. Dat can't happen now.

Wind stuff! Dat's what dem stories about ghosts and voodoo is—all wind stuff. I never see any such thing and I never hear any such thing. Wind stuff—like when the Yankees say I was free and going to get 40-acres of good lands. Instead, I just got to stay on the same plantation and work for part of the crops and get too old to work. Dat what I get.

And I don't like the restricted suffrage business a bit. I think the Negroes should have the same privileges as the whites, and should be equal.

I married Lizzie Batton in Franklin County, Georgia. We had 10 children; Frank, John, Connie, Mary, Annie, Olive, Cordia, J.C., Florence and Maude. All except Maude is dead. She teaches school in Tulsa and I live with her.[2] Dere's seven grandchildren, doing one thing and another, living here and dere.

[1] Sam Rhodes was interviewed in Tulsa probably in the winter of 1938–39 by WPA field worker L. P. Livingston. On 5 January 1939 project staff member Craig Vollmer revised Livingston's notes into a preliminary draft, "Interview with Sam Rhodes, Ex-Slave, Age 91 Years, 1031 East Pine Street, Tulsa, Oklahoma," now in the OHS Slave Narratives. Project employee Ida Belle Hunter then reedited the text at a later date, after which a revised narrative was prepared. This final draft, "Sam Rhodes, Age 91, Tulsa, Oklahoma," preserved in the OHS Slave Narratives and presented here, has never before been published.

[2] A roughly contemporary Tulsa city directory shows Samuel Rhodes residing with Maud Rhodes, a teacher in the public schools, at 1031 East Pine Street. *Polk's Tulsa City Directory, 1935,* 461, 696.

CHANEY RICHARDSON[1]

Age 90 Years   *Fort Gibson, Okla.*

I was born in the old Caney settlement southeast of Tahlequah on the banks of Caney Creek. Off to the north we could see the big old ridge of Sugar Mountain when the sun shine on him first thing in the morning when we all getting up.

I didn't know nothing else but some kind of war until I was a grown woman, because when I first can remember my old Master, Charley Rogers, we always on the lookout for somebody or other he was lined up against in the big feud.[2]

My master and all the rest of the folks was Cherokees, and they'd been killing each other off in the feud ever since long before I was borned, and jest because old Master have a big farm and three–four families of Negroes them other Cherokees keep on pestering his stuff all the time. Us children was always afeared to go any place less'n some of the grown folks was along.

We didn't know what we was a-feared of, but we heard the Master and Mistress keep talking 'bout "another Party killing" and we stuck close to the place.

Old Mistress' name was Nancy Rogers, but I was a orphan after I was a big girl and I called her "Aunt" and "Mamma" like I did when I was little. You see my own mammy was the house woman and I was raised in the house, and I heard the little children call old mistress "mamma" and so I did too. She never did make me stop.

My pappy and mammy and us children lived in a one-room log cabin close to the creek bank and jest a little piece from old Master's house.

My pappy's name was Joe Tucker and my mammy's name was Ruth Tucker. They belonged to a man named Tucker before I was born and he sold them to Master Charley Rogers and he just let them go on by the same name if they wanted to, because last names didn't mean nothing to a slave anyways. The folks jest called my pappy "Charley Rogers' boy Joe."

I already had two sisters, Mary and Mandy, when I was born, and purty soon I had a baby brother, Louis. Mammy worked at the Big House and took me along every day. When I was a little bigger I would help hold the hank when she done the spinning and old Mistress done a lot of the weaving and some knitting. She jest set by the window and knit most all of the time.

When we weave the cloth we had a big loom out on the gallery, and Miss Nancy tell us how to do it.

Mammy eat at our own cabin, and we had lots of game meat and fish the boys get in the Caney Creek. Mammy bring down deer meat and wild turkey sometimes, that the Indian boys git on Sugar Mountain.

Then we had corn bread, dried bean bread and green stuff out'n Master's patch. Mammy make the bean bread when we git short of corn meal and nobody going to the mill right away. She take and bile the beans and mash then up in some meal and that make it go a long ways.

The slaves didn't have no garden 'cause they work in the old Master's garden and make enough for everybody to have some anyway.

When I was about 10 years old that feud got so bad the Indians was always talking about getting their horses and cattle killed and their slaves harmed. I was too little to know how bad it was until one morning my own mammy went off somewhere down the road to git some stuff to dye cloth and she didn't come back.

Lots of the young Indian bucks on both sides of the feud would ride around the woods at night, and old Master got powerful oneasy about my mammy and had all the neighbors and slaves out looking for her, but nobody find her.

It was about a week later that two Indian men rid up and ast old master wasn't his gal Ruth gone. He says yes, and they take one of the slaves along with a wagon to show where they seen her.

They find her in some bushes where she'd been getting bark to set the dyes, and she been dead all the time. Somebody done hit her in the head with a club and shot her through and through with a bullet too. She was so swole up they couldn't lift her up and jest had to make a deep hole right along side of her and roll her in it she was so bad mortified.

Old Master nearly go crazy he was so mad, and the young Cherokee men ride the woods every night for about a month, but they never catch on to who done it.

I think old Master sell the children or give them out to somebody then, because I never see my sisters and brother for a long time after the Civil War, and for me, I have to go live with a new mistress that was a Cherokee neighbor. Her name was Hannah Ross, and she raised me until I was grown.

I was her home girl, and she and me done a lot of spinning and weaving too. I helped the cook and carried water and milked. I carried the water in a home-made pegging set on my head. Them peggings was kind of buckets made out of staves set around a bottom and didn't have no handle.

I can remember weaving with Miss Hannah Ross. She would weave a strip of white and one of yellow and one of brown to make it pretty. She had a reel that would pop every time it got to a half skein so she would know to stop and fill it up again. We used copperas and some kind of bark she bought at the store to dye with. It was cotton clothes winter and summer for the slaves, too. I'll tell you.

When the Civil War come along we seen lots of white soldiers in them brown butternut suits all over the place, and about all the Indian men was in it too. Old master Charley Rogers' boy Charles went along too. Then pretty soon—it seems like about a year—a lot of the Cherokee men come back home and say they not going back to the War with that General Cooper and some of them go off to the Federal side because the captain go to the Federal side too.[3]

Somebody come along and tell me my own pappy have to go in the war and I think they say he on the Cooper side, and then after while Miss Hannah tell me he git kilt over in Arkansas.

I was so grieved all the time I don't remember much what went on, but I know pretty soon my Cherokee folks had all the stuff they had et up by the soldiers and they was jest a few wagons and mules left.

All the slaves was piled in together and some of the grown ones walking, and they took us way down across the big river and kept us in the bottoms a long time until the War was over.

We lived in a kind of a camp, but I was too little to know where they got the grub to feed us with. Most all the Negro men was off somewhere in the War.

Then one day they had to bust up the camp and some Federal soldiers go with us and we all start back home. We git to a place where all the houses is burned down and I ask what is that place. Miss Hannah say: "Skullyville, child. That's where they had part of the War."[4]

All the slaves was set out when we git to Fort Gibson, and the soldiers say we all free now. They give us grub and clothes to the Negroes at that place. It wasn't no town but a fort place and a patch of big trees.

Miss Hannah take me to her place and I work there until I was grown. I didn't git any money that I seen, but I got a good place to stay.

Pretty soon I married Ran Lovely and we lived in a double log house here at Fort Gibson. Then my second husband was Henry Richardson, but he's been dead for years, too. We had six children, but they all dead but one.[5]

I didn't want slavery to be over with, mostly because we had the War I reckon. All that trouble made me the loss of my mammy and pappy, and I was always treated good when I was a slave. When it was over I had rather be at home like I was. None of the Cherokees ever whipped us, and my mistress give me some mighty fine rules to live by to get along in this world, too.

The Cherokees didn't have no jail for Negroes and no jail for themselves either. If a man done a crime he come back to take his punishment without being locked up.

None of the Negroes ran away when I was a child that I know of. We all had plenty to eat. The Negroes didn't have no school and so I can't read and write, but they did have a school after the War, I hear. But we had a church made out of a brush arbor and we would sing good songs in Cherokee sometimes.

I always got Sunday off to play, and at night I could go git a piece of sugar or something to eat before I went to bed and Mistress didn't care.

We played bread-and-butter and the boys played hide the switch. The one found the switch got to whip the one he wanted to.

When I got sick they give me some kind of tea from weeds, and if I et too many roasting ears and swole up they biled gourds and give me the liquor off'n them to make me throw up.

I've been a good church-goer all my life until I git too feeble, and I still understand and talk Cherokee language and love to hear songs and parts of the Bible in it because it make me think about the time I was a little girl before my mammy and pappy leave me.

1 WPA field worker Ethel Wolfe Garrison interviewed Mrs. Chaney Richardson at Fort Gibson, Oklahoma, sometime probably in the summer or autumn of 1937. On 5 October of that year her coworker Robert Vinson Lackey revised her now lost interview notes into an intermediate draft entitled "Interview with Chaney Richardson (Ex-Slave, Age 90 Years), General Delivery, Fort Gibson, Oklahoma," preserved as a ribbon-copy typescript in the OHS Slave Narratives. Eight days later, on 13 October, the narrative was again edited and retyped into a final draft, "Chaney Richardson, Age 90 Years, Fort Gibson, Okla.," which was forwarded to Washington on 2 November 1937 and is published here. This final draft is available in ribbon-copy typescript in the LC Slave Narratives and in carbon copy as item 350024 in the LC Slave Narratives Carbon Copies and in the OHS Slave Narratives. Stephens to Cronyn, 2 November 1937, WPA Notes on Interviews.

2 For background on the unrest in the Cherokee Nation leading up to and during the early phases of the Civil War, see, among other sources, Halliburton, *Red over Black,* 106–33; Perdue, *Slavery and the Evolution of Cherokee Society,* 119–39; Wardell, *Political History of the Cherokee Nation,* 118–41.

3 Colonel Douglas H. Cooper, formerly a U.S. Indian agent to the Choctaws, became the commander of Confederate military forces in the Indian Territory. Muriel H. Wright, "General Douglas H. Cooper, C.S.A.," *Chronicles of Oklahoma* 32 (Summer 1954): 142–84.

The mention of Cherokee men who went "off to the Federal side" may be a reference to the disenchanted Cherokee Confederate troops under Colonel John Drew, who refused to take up arms against other Indians who offered less than staunch support for the Rebel cause. Perdue, *Slavery and the Evolution of Cherokee Society,* 134–35; Wardell, *Political History of the Cherokee Nation,* 164–65.

[4] Skullyville, the first Choctaw capital in the Indian Territory, was probably the most important town in the Choctaw Nation before the coming of the railroads. W. B. Morrison, "The Saga of Skullyville," *Chronicles of Oklahoma* 16 (June 1938): 234–40.

[5] Mrs. Chaney Richardson and her daughters, Mish Lovely Daniels and Nannie Daniels, were enrolled as Cherokee freedmen by the Dawes Commission by virtue of Mrs. Richardson's servitude in the household of a Cherokee, Charley Rogers. Cherokee Freedmen Census Cards, no. 134 (Chaney Richardson and Mish Lovely and Nannie Daniels); Cherokee Freedmen Enrollment Application Testimony file 134 (Chaney Richardson and Mish Lovely).

RED RICHARDSON[1]

Age 75 Yrs.   *Oklahoma City, Oklahoma*

I was born July 21, 1862, at Grimes County, Texas. Smith Richardson was my father's name, and Eliza Richardson was my mother's. My father came from Virginia. My mother was born in Texas.

We lived in so many places round there I can't tell jest what, but we lived in a log house most of the time. We slept on the flo' on pallets[2] on one quilt.[3] We ate cornbread, beans, vegetables, and got to drink plenty milk. We ate rabbits, fish, possums and such as that but we didn't get no chicken. I don't have no fav'rite food, I don't guess.

We wore shirts, long shirts slit up the side. I didn't know what pants was until I was 14. In Grimes County it ain't even cold these days, and I never wore no shoes. I married in a suit made of broad cloth. It had a tail on the coat.[4]

Master Ben Hadley, and Mistress Minnie Hadley, they had three sons: John, Henry and Charley. Didn't have no overseer. We had to call all white folks, poor or rich, Master and Mistress. Master Hadley owned 'bout 2,000 acres. He had a big number of slaves. They used to wake 'em up early in the mornings by ringing a large bell. They said they used to whip 'em, drive 'em, and sell 'em away from their chillun,—I'd hear my old folks talk about it. Say they wasn't no such thing as going to jail. The master stood good for anything his nigger done. If the master's nigger killed 'im another nigger, the old master stood good.

They never had no schools for the Negro chillun. I can't remember the date of the first school—it's in a book someplace[5]—but anyway I went to one of the first schools that was established for the education of Negro chillun.

You know Mr. Negro always was a church man, but he don't mean nothing. I don't have no fav'rite spiritual. All of them's good ones. Whenever they'd baptize they'd sing:

"Harp from the Tune the Domeful Sound."

Which starts like this:

> "Come live in man and view this ground
> where we must sho'ly lie."[6]

I'm a member of Tabernacle Baptist Church myself, and I think all people should be religious 'cause Jesus died for us all.

The patrollers used to run after me but I'd jump 'em. They used to have[7] a permit to go from one plantation to another. You had to go to old master and say, "I want to go to such and such a place." And if you had a permit they didn't bother you. The pateroller would stop you and say, "Where you going? You got a permit to go to such and such a place?" You'd say, yes suh, and show that pass. Den he wouldn't bother you and iffen he did old Master would git on 'em.

When 10:00 o'clock come which was bed time the slaves would go to their cabins and some of 'em would go stealing chickens, hogs, steal sweet potatoes, and cook and eat 'em. Jest git in to all kind of devilment.

Old Master would give 'em Sadday afternoon off, and they'd have them Sadday breakdowns. We played a few games such as marbles, mumble peg, and cards—jest anything to pass off the time. Heahs one of the games we'd play an' I sho did like it too:

> She is my sweetheart as I stan'.
> Come an' stan' beside me,
> Kiss her sweet an'
> Hug her near.

On Christmas they'd make egg nog, drink whiskey and kiss their girls.[8]

Wore some charms to ward off the devil, but I don't believe in such. I do believe in voodoo like this: People can put propositions up to you and fool you. Don't believe in ghost. Tried to see 'em but I never could.[9]

Old master didn't turn my father loose and tell 'em we was free. They didn't turn us loose 'til they got the second threat from President Lincoln. Good old Lincoln; they was nothing like 'im. Booker T. Washington was one of the finest Negro Educators in the world, but old Jefferson Davis was against the cullud man.[10]

I think since slavery is all over, it has been a benefit to the cullud man. He's got more freedom now.[11]

[1] Red C. Richardson was interviewed at his home in Oklahoma City by Bertha P. Tipton on 11 June 1937. From the interview a preliminary draft of Richardson's remembrances was prepared as the typescript "Interview with Red Richardson, Ex-Slave Aged 75 Years, 917 East 6th Street, Oklahoma City, Oklahoma" in the OHS Slave Narratives. An edited draft was prepared later in the summer and forwarded to Washington on 13 August 1937. This final draft, published here, is available as "Red Richardson, Age 75 Yrs., Oklahoma City, Oklahoma" in ribbon copy in the LC Slave Narratives and in carbon copy as item 350105 in the LC Slave Narratives Carbon Copies and in the OHS Slave Narratives. *Polk's Oklahoma City Directory, 1937,* 397, 619; Stephens to Cronyn, 13 August 1937, WPA Notes on Interviews.

[2] The preliminary draft at this point includes the additional words "made our pallets down an' slept on the flo'."

[3] Here the preliminary draft includes the four sentences: "My grandmother's name is Nellie Lowery. Grandfather's name is Cy Lowery. I was only three years old. Well I tell you what we et."

[4] At this point the preliminary draft includes the following sentence: "Yes, I remembuh the master's house, but I don't know that I can discribe [*sic*] it to you."

[5] The preliminary draft here states instead, "you have a history for that."

[6] The name and words to this hymn apparently were garbled by either the interviewee or the reporter, for the hymn is "Hark! From the Tomb" and the words are "Ye living men come view the ground where you must shortly lie." Abernethy, *Singin' Texas,* 112–13; W. M. Cooper, *The Sacred Harp Revised and Improved,* 162.

[7] The preliminary draft here reads "to have to have."

[8] At this point the preliminary draft includes the following two sentences, the first one struck out in pencil and the other handwritten at its side: "I sho' did luve Lizzie. This pretty little girl beside me."

[9] Here the preliminary draft includes the following three sentences: "Whenever slaves got sick they'd dig herbs an' make teas. Saspharilla [*sic*] tea. Wear asafetida to ward off whooping cough an' measles."

[10] At this point the preliminary draft includes the following family information from the informant: "I married in 1887 to Julia Lee an' ole tim' sweetheart. We had an' ole fashion weddin'. Lots of good eats. We have five chillun. 2 girl chillun. Luther R. is a barber here in my shop. Johnnie R. is in New York. Newt R. is heah working out at the packing plant."

[11] At the close of the earlier draft of the Ned Richardson narrative, the interviewer added the following note: "Remarks: Mr. Red Richardson owns and operates a shoe store with approximately $1,000.00 worth of equipment, and a Barber Shop in the 300 block East 1st Street. When asked how he learned the trade he said that while in Texas he ran a Grocery Store, and learned the shoe trade from an old Dutchman, later he left Texas and moved to Coffeyville, Kansas. While there worked in a shoe shop, and then moved to Oklahoma in 1891 and settled on 160 acres of land, later established a shop for himself. Bertha P. Tipton." The contemporary Oklahoma City directory notes that Red C. Richardson and his son, Red Richardson, Jr., operated their shoe repair shop at 311 Northeast 1st in conjunction with barber John Barnwell. *Polk's Oklahoma City Directory, 1937,* 619, 1220.

BETTY ROBERTSON[1]

Age 93 Yrs.   *Fort Gibson, Oklahoma*

I was born close to Webbers Falls, in the Canadian District of the Cherokee Nation, in the same year that my pappy was blowed up and killed in the big boat accident that killed my old Master.

I never did see my daddy excepting when I was a baby and I only know what my mammy told me about him. He come from across the water when he was a little boy, and was grown when old Master Joseph Vann bought him, so he never did learn to talk much Cherokee. My mammy was a Cherokee slave, and talked it good. My husband was a Cherokee born negro, too, and when he got mad he forgit all the English he knowed.

Old Master Joe had a mighty big farm and several families of negroes, and he was a powerful rich man. Pappy's name was Kalet Vann, and mammy's name was Sally.[2] My brothers' name was Sone and Frank. I had one brother and one sister sold when I was little and I don't remember the names. My other sisters was Polly, Ruth and Liddle. I had to work in the kitchen when I was a gal, and they was ten or twelve children smaller than me for me to look after, too. Sometime Young Master Joe and the other boys give me a piece of money and say I worked for it, and I reckon I did for I have to cook five or six times a day. Some of the Master's family was always going down to the river and back, and every time they come in I have to fix something to eat. Old Mistress had a good cookin' stove, but most Cherokees had only a big fireplace and pot hooks. We had meat, bread, rice, potatoes and plenty of fish and chicken. The spring time give us plenty of green corn and beans too. I couldn't buy anything in slavery time, so I jest give the piece of money to the Vann children. I got all the clothes I need from old Mistress, and in winter I had high top shoes with brass caps on the toe. In the summer I wear them on Sunday, too. I wore loom cloth clothes, dyed in copperas what the old negro women and the old Cherokee women made.

The slaves had a pretty easy time I think. Young Master Vann never very hard on us and he never whupped us, and old Mistress was a widow woman and a good Christian and always kind. I sure did love her. Maybe old Master Joe Vann was harder, I don't know, but that was before my time. Young Master never whip his slaves, but if they don't mind good he sell them off sometimes. He sold one of my brothers and one sister because they kept running off. They wasn't very big either, but one day two Cherokees rode up and talked a long time, then young Master came to the cabin and said they were sold because mammy couldn't make them mind him. They got on the horses behind the men and went off.

Old Master Joe had a big steam boat he called the Lucy Walker, and he run it up and down the Arkansas and the Mississippi and the Ohio river, old Mistress say. He went clean to Louisville, Kentucky, and back. My pappy was a kind of a boss of the negroes that run the boat, and they all belong to old Master Joe. Some had been in a big run-away and had been brung back, and wasn't so good, so he keep them on the boat all the time mostly. Mistress say old Master and my pappy on the boat somewhere close to Louisville and the boiler bust and tear the boat up. Some niggers say my pappy kept hollering, "Run it to the bank! Run it to the bank!" but it sunk and him and old Master died.[3]

Old Master Joe was a big man in the Cherokees, I hear, and was good to his negroes before I was born. My pappy run away one time, four or five years before I was born, mammy tell me, and at that time a whole lot of Cherokee slaves run off at once. They got over in the Creek country and stood off the Cherokee officers that went to git them, but pretty soon they give up and come home.[4] Mammy say they was lots of excitement on old Master's place and all the negroes mighty scared, but he didn't sell my pappy off. He jest kept him and he was a good negro after that. He had to work on the boat, though, and never got to come home but once in a long while.

Young Master Joe let us have singing and be baptized if we want to, but I wasn't baptized till after the War. But we couldn't learn to read or have a book, and the Cherokee folks was afraid to tell us about the letters and figgers because they have a law you go to jail and a big fine if you show a slave about the letters.

When the War come they have a big battle away west of us, but I never see any battles. Lots of soldiers around all the time though.

One day young Master come to the cabins and say we all free and can't stay there less'n we want to go on working for him just like we'd been, for our feed and clothes. Mammy got a wagon and we traveled around a few days and go to Fort Gibson. When we git to Fort Gibson they was a lot of negroes there, and they had a camp meeting and I was baptized. It was in the Grand River close to the ford, and winter time. Snow on the ground and the water was muddy and all full of pieces of ice. The place was all woods, and the Cherokees and the soldiers all come down to see the baptizing.

We settled down a little ways above Fort Gibson. Mammy had the wagon and two oxen, and we worked a good size patch there until she died, and then I git married to Cal Robertson to have somebody to take care of me. Cal Robertson was eighty-nine years old when I married him forty years ago, right on this porch. I had on my old clothes for the wedding, and I ain't had any good clothes since I was a little slave girl. Then I had clean warm clothes and I had to keep them clean, too!

I got my allotment as a Cherokee Freedman, and so did Cal, but we lived here at this place because we was too old to work the land ourselves. In slavery time the Cherokee negroes do like anybody else when they is a death—jest listen to a chapter in the Bible and all cry. We had a good song I remember. It was "Don't Call the Roll, Jesus, Because I'm Coming Home." The only song I remember from the soldiers was: "Hang Jeff Davis to a Sour Apple Tree," and I remember that because they said he used to be at Fort Gibson one time. I don't know what he done after that.

I been a good Christian ever since I was baptized, but I keep a little charm here on my neck anyways, to keep me from having the nose bleed. Its got a buckeye and a lead bullet in it. I had a silver dime on it, too, for a long time, but I took it off and got me a box of snuff. I'm glad the War's over and I am free to meet God like anybody else, and my grandchildren can learn to read and write.

[1] Project field worker Ethel Wolfe Garrison interviewed the woman identified as Mrs. Betty Robertson at Fort Gibson, Oklahoma, sometime probably in the autumn of 1937. The name of this informant may have been garbled at the time of the interview. She was enrolled as a Cherokee freedwoman by the Dawes Commission in 1904 under the name Belle Roberson and is listed in a 1921 directory as Betty Robison. Garrison apparently made at least two trips to interview the informant, for on 18 October 1937 her supervisor, Robert Vinson Lackey, wrote from Tulsa to project headquarters in Oklahoma City, "Mrs. Garrison is going to see Betty Robertson again and get all she knows." From Garrison's notes a preliminary draft of the narrative was prepared under the title "Interview with Betty Robertson, Ex-Slave, Age 93 Years, General Delivery, Ft. Gibson, Okla." and is now preserved in ribbon-copy typescript in the OHS Slave Narratives. At a later date Lackey edited and retyped the narrative into final form and sent it on 31 October 1937 to Oklahoma City along with several other slave narratives he described in his cover letter as "another bunch of slave stuff." This final draft, published here, was mailed to Washington on 18 November 1937 and is available as "Betty Robertson, Age 93 Yrs., Fort Gibson, Oklahoma" in ribbon-copy typescript in the LC Slave Narratives and in carbon copy as item 350011 in the LC Slave Narratives Carbon Copies and in the OHS Slave Narratives. Robert Vinson Lackey, Tulsa, [Oklahoma], to Ned P. DeWitt, Oklahoma City, [Oklahoma], 18 October and 31 October 1937; Stephens to Alsberg, 14 November 1937; all three letters in WPA Notes on Interviews;

Cherokee Freedmen Census Cards, no. 117 (Calvin, Belle, Bertha, Watie, Amanda, and Arthur Roberson; Minnie Ivory); Cherokee Freedmen Enrollment Application Testimony, file 117 (Calvin, Belle, Bertha, Watie, Amanda, and Arthur Roberson; Minnie Ivory); *Phoenix Directory of Muskogee, 1921,* 549; *Polk's Muskogee City Directory, 1932,* 317.

  [2] According to the census of Cherokee freedmen compiled by the Dawes Commission early in the twentieth century, the interviewee's parents were named Caleb and Sally Vann. Cherokee Freedmen Census Cards, no. 117 (Calvin, Belle, Bertha, Watie, Amanda, and Arthur Roberson; Minnie Ivory).

  [3] Joseph Vann's steamboat, the *Lucy Walker,* blew up and sank in the Ohio River in the autumn of 1844 a few miles below Albany, Indiana, with the loss of 50 of its 130 passengers, including Vann and 12 of his slaves. R. P. Vann, "Reminiscences of Mr. R. P. Vann, East of Webbers Falls, Oklahoma, September 28, 1932," edited by Grant Foreman, *Chronicles of Oklahoma* 11 (June 1933): 838–39; Marguerite McFadden, "The Saga of 'Rich Joe' Vann," *Chronicles of Oklahoma* 61 (Spring 1983): 75–76. For more on this incident, see the narrative of Lucinda Vann, below.

  [4] On the night of 15 November 1842, thirty-five Cherokee slaves belonging to Joseph Vann and others took arms from a store and fled into the Creek Nation. A hundred-man force of Cherokees apprehended the runaways and returned them to their owners. For more on this incident, see the narrative of John Field, above.

HARRIETT ROBINSON[1]

Age 95 Yrs.   *500 Block N. Fonshill, Oklahoma City, Oklahoma*

I was born September 1, 1842, in Bastrop, Texas, on Colorado River. My pappy was named Harvey Wheeler and my mammy was named Carolina Sims. My brothers and sisters was named Alex, Taylor, Mary, Cicero, Tennessee, Sarah, Jeff, Ella and Nora. We lived in cedar log houses with dirt floors and double chimneys, and doors hung on wooden hinges. One side of our beds was bored in the walls and had one leg on the other. Them white folks give each nigger family a blanket in winter.

I nussed 3 white chillun, Lulu, Helen Augusta, and Lola Sims. I done this before that War that set us free. We kids use to make extra money by toting gravel in our aprons. They'd give us dimes and silver nickels.

Our clothes was wool and cotton mixed. We had red rustic[2] shoes, soles one-half inch thick. They'd go a-whick a-whack.[3] The mens had pants wid one seam and a right-hand pocket. Boys wore shirts.

We ate hominy, mush, grits and pone bread for the most part. Many of them ate out of one tray with wooden spoons. All vittles for field hands was fixed together.

Women broke in mules, throwed 'em down and roped 'em. They'd do it better'n men. While mammy made some hominy one day both my foots was scalded and when they clipped them blisters, they just put some cotton round them and catched all dat yellow water and made me a yellow dress out of it.[4] This was 'way back yonder in slavery, before the War.

Whenever white folks had a baby born den all de old niggers had to come thoo the room and the master would be over 'hind the bed and he'd say, "Here's a new little mistress or master you got to work for." You had to say, "Yessuh Master" and bow real low or the overseer would crack you. Them was slavery days, dog days.

I remember in slavery time we had stages. Them devilish things had jest as many wrecks as cars do today.[5] One thing, we jest didn't have as many.

My mammy belonged to Master Colonel Sims and his old mean wife Julia. My pappy belonged to Master Meke Smith and his good wife Harriett. She was sho' a good woman. I was named after her. Master Sam and Master Meke was partners. Ever year them rich men would send so many wagons to New Mexico for different things. It took 6 months to go and come.

Slaves was punished by whip and starving. Decker was sho' a mean slave-holder. He lived close to us. Master Sam didn't never whip me, but Miss Julia whipped me every day in the mawning. During the war she beat us so terrible. She say, "You master's out fighting and losing blood trying to save you from them Yankees, so you kin git your'n here." Miss Julia would take me by my ears and butt my head against the wall. She wanted to whip my mother, but old Master told her, naw sir. When his father done give my mammy to Master Sam, he told him not to beat her, and iffen he got to whar he just had to, jest bring her back and place her in his yard from whar he got her.

White folks didn't 'low you to read or write. Them what did know come from Virginny. Mistress Julia used to drill her chillun in spelling any words. At every word them chillun missed, she gived me a lick 'cross the head for it. Meanest woman I ever seen in my whole life.

This skin I got now, it ain't my first skin. That was burnt off when I was a little child. Mistress used to have a fire made on the fireplace and she made me scour the brass round it and my skin jest blistered. I jest had to keep pulling it off'n me.

We didn't had no church, though my pappy was a preacher. He preached in the quarters. Our baptizing song was "On Jordan's Stormy Bank I Stand" and "Hark From The Tomb." Now all dat was before the War. We had all our funerals at the graveyard. Everybody, chillun and all, picked up a clod of dirt and throwed in on top the coffin to help fill up the grave.

Talking 'bout niggers running away, didn't my step-pappy run away? Didn't my uncle Gabe run away? The frost would jest bite they toes most nigh off too, whiles they was gone. They put Uncle Isom (my step-pappy) in jail and while's he was in there he killed a white guardman. Then they put him in the paper, "A nigger to kill," and our Master seen it and bought him. He was a double-strengthed man, he was so strong. He'd run off so help you God. They had the blood hounds after him once and he caught the hound what was leading and beat the rest of the dogs. The white folks run up on him before he knowed it and made them dogs eat his ear plumb out.[6] But don't you know he got away anyhow. One morning I was sweeping out the hall in the big house and somebody come a-knocking on the front door and I goes to the door. There was Uncle Isom wid rags all on his head. He said, "Tell old master heah I am." I goes to Master's door and says, "Master Colonel Sam, Uncle Isom said heah eh am." He say,[7] "Go 'round to the kitchen and tell black mammy to give you breakfast." When he was thoo' eating they give him 300 lashes and, bless my soul, he run off again.

When we went to a party the nigger fiddlers would play a chune dat went lak this:

> I fooled Old Mastah 7 years
> Fooled the overseer three;
> Hand me down my banjo
> And I'll tickle you bel-lee.

We had the same doctors the white folks had and we wore asafetida and garlic and onions to keep from taking all them ailments.

I 'member the battle being fit. The white folks buried all the jewelry and silver and all the gold in the Blue Ridge Mountains, in Orange, Texas.[8] Master made all us niggers come together and git ready to leave 'cause the Yankees was coming. We took a steamer. Now this was in slavery time, sho' 'nuff slavery. Then we got on a steamship and pulled out to Galveston. Then he told the captain to feed we niggers. We was on the bay, not the ocean. We left Galveston and went on trains for Houston.

One, my sister Liza, was mulatto and Master Colonel Simms' son had 3 chillun by her. We never seen her no more after her last child was born. I found out though that she was in Canada.

After the War, Master Colonel Sims went to git the mail and so he call Daniel Ivory, the overseer, and say to him, "Go round to all the quarters and tell all them niggers to come up, I got a paper to read to 'em. They're free now, so you kin git you another job, 'cause I ain't got no more niggers which is my own." Niggers come up from the cabins nappy-headed, jest lak they gwine to the field. Master Colonel Sims say, "Caroline (that's my mammy), you is free as me. Pa said bring you back and I'se gwina do jest that. So you go on and work and I'll pay you and your three oldest chillun $10.00 a monthly a head and $4.00 for Harriett," that's me, and then he turned to the rest and say, "Now all you'uns will receive $10.00 a head till the crops is laid by." Don't you know before he got half way thoo', over half them niggers was gone.

Them Klu Klux Klans come and ask for water with their false stomachs and make lak they was drinking three bucketsful. They done some terrible things, but God seen it all and marked it down.

We didn't had no law, we had "bureau." Why, in them days iffen somebody stole anything from you, they had to pay you and not the Law. Now they done turned that round and you don't git nothing.

One day whiles master was gone hunting, Mistress Julia told her brother to give Miss Harriett (me) a free whipping. She was a nigger killer. Master Colonel Sam come home and he said, "Your infernal sons o' bitches don't you know there is 300 Yankees camped out here and iffen they knowed you whipped this nigger the way you done done, they'd kill all us. Iffen they find it out, I'll kill all of you." Old rich devils, I'm here, but they is gone.[9]

God choosed Abraham Lincoln to free us. It took one of them to free us so's they couldn't say nothing.

Doing one 'lection they sung:

> Clark et the watermelon
> J. D. Giddings et the vine!
> Clark gone to Congress
> An' J. D. Giddings left behind.[10]

They hung Jeff Davis up a sour apple tree. They say he was a president, but he wasn't, he was a big senator man.

Booker T. Washington was all right in his way, I guess, but Bruce and Fred Douglass, or big mens, jest sold us back to the white folks.

I married Haywood Telford and had 13 chillun by him. My oldest daughter is the mammy of 14. All my chillun but four done gone to heaven before me.

I jined the church in Chapel Hill, Texas. I am born of the Spirit of God sho' nuff. I played with him seven years and would go right on dancing at Christmas time. Now I got religion. Everybody oughta live right, though you won't have no friends iffen you do.

Our overseer was a poor man. Had us up before day and lak-a-that. He was paid to be the head of punishment. I jest didn't like to think of them old slavery days, dogs' days.

---

[1] Mrs. Harriett Robinson was interviewed by Ida Belle Hunter in Oklahoma City on 21 June 1937. From the interview notes Hunter put together a preliminary draft of Robinson's narrative as the typescript "Interview with Harriett Robinson, Ex-Slave, Aged 95, 500 Block N. Fonshill, Oklahoma City, Oklahoma," now preserved in the OHS Slave Narratives. This draft was revised and retyped by mid-August, for on 13 August 1937 it was among ten slave narratives forwarded from the Oklahoma City office to Washington. The final draft, published here, is available as "Harriett Robinson, Age 95 Yrs., 500 Block N. Fonshill, Oklahoma City, Oklahoma" in ribbon-copy typescript in the LC Slave Narratives and in carbon copy as item 350100 in the LC Slave Narratives Carbon Copies and in the OHS Slave Narratives. Both the preliminary and final drafts in the OHS collection have the street name, Fonshill, struck and the name Lottie, in Ida Belle Hunter's handwriting, put in its place. The contemporary Oklahoma City directory confirms this editorial change, for it shows the interviewee residing at 524 Lottie Avenue with Pinkie V. and Homer Gray. After the narrative reached Washington, B. A. Botkin rated it highly as both "frank and full," and he selected four extracts from it for inclusion in his 1945 study, *Lay My Burden Down* (3, 180, 193–94, 229, 271, 279, 280, 282). [B. A. Botkin], LC Slave Narratives Appraisal Sheets, Accession no. 350100, 31 December 1940; *Polk's Oklahoma City Directory, 1937,* 292, 628, 875; Stephens to Cronyn, 13 August 1937, WPA Notes on Interviews.

[2] The preliminary draft has the word "russet" written by hand above "rustic."

[3] The preliminary draft repeats, for the effect of the sound, "a-whick a-whack."

[4] The preliminary draft has here in handwriting the interviewee's expression "Whooee!"

[5] The preliminary draft has here in handwriting the interviewee's expression "Whooee!!"

[6] In the preliminary draft the interviewee's expression "Whooee!" appears here in handwriting.

[7] The earlier draft at this point includes the additional sentence, "Well, well, Mr. Isom, thought you was dead."

[8] This sentence must have been garbled in oral transmission or transcription, for Orange, Texas, is on the gulf coastal plain scores of miles from hills, not to mention mountains.

[9] The preliminary draft has here in handscript the interviewee's expression "Whooee!!!"

[10] This rhyme was repeated during the disputed congressional election in the third district of Texas in 1871–72 between Democrat DeWitt Clinton Giddings and Republican William T. Clark. Webb, *Handbook of Texas,* 1:687.

INTERVIEW WITH CHARLEY ROSS[1]

Ex-Slave, Age 87 Years   *Gibson Station, Oklahoma*

I was born in the hill country around Arkadelphia, Arkansas, on May 13, 1851, a Friday it was, and Friday the 13th is my Lucky Day.[2]

My father's name was Strotter Adams, the same as master's. The master was a preacher and a lawyer at Arkadelphia, and when his daughter married I went with her; her husband was Charley Ross. Then one of the master's sons took my father with him. He was John Adams. All the places was close together and we wasn't separated much.

The master had children named John, Billie, Christ, Walker, Miss Cornelia, Miss Liddie, and my sisters were Jane, Martha, and my brothers were Walter and Bob.

I was too young to work much, that's in the fields I mean. I use to help take care of the stock. One time I was sitting on top of rail fence, hold of a mule. I jest kept the rope light in my hands letting the mule graze, and then somehow I went to sleep. Right on top of the fence. The master saw me and slip up back of the mule. He hit the mule and when he jumped I went off the fence. Right on the ground. Hard. And the master laughed when I sat there rubbing my eyes.

Then the young boys would ride the calves to make them gentle for driving, or what folks called "bridle wise." Most of the time we didn't ride only just long enough to get tossed off on the ground.

We had long-tailed cotton shirts in the summer and wool shirts and jackets in the winter. Once a white woman give some boys' shoes to the mistress and she gave them to me. It took time to get use to them but I was sure enough proud of them shoes. I was about nine years old before I ever had new shoes.

The master lived in a big up-to-date house like folks have now. There was three fireplaces in the house. He owned lots of slaves.

I didn't know anything about the Civil War. Except one day a smart negro told us that there was fighting and soon all the slaves would be free. And they was.

The master didn't allow dancing on the plantation but the slaves could get passes and go to dances on Saturday, but they had to get up Sunday and go to church.

The master never went to war. Maybe he was too old. Sometimes he would be gone three or four days. He said he was going to the war but he didn't go.

I've been married twice. My wife now is Rosy. She had two children when we married. Henry and Lutha Evans. My first wife had children named Bessie, Christine, and Jordan; and later on there was Norman, Winfred and Charley, Jr.

I am too sick to talk much and my time is about come.

¹ WPA field worker Ethel Wolfe Garrison interviewed Charley Ross at Gibson Station, Oklahoma, probably sometime in the spring or early summer of 1938. On 8 June of that year her coworker Craig Vollmer edited and typed her notes into the one draft now surviving of Ross's remembrances. This typescript, published here for the first time, is available as "Interview with Charley Ross, Ex-Slave, Age 87 Years, Gibson Station, Oklahoma" only in the OHS Slave Narratives. The Charley Ross narrative was never forwarded to Washington.

² In reality 13 May 1851 fell on a Tuesday, not a Friday.

KATIE ROWE¹

Age 88 Yrs.   *Tulsa, Oklahoma*

I can set on de gallery, whar de sunlight shine bright, and sew a powerful fine seam when my grandchillun wants a special purty dress for de school doings, but I ain't worth much for nothing else I reckon.

These same old eyes seen powerful lot of tribulations in my time, and when I shets 'em now I can see lots of li'l chillun jest lak my grandchillun, toting hoes bigger dan dey is, and dey poor little black hands and legs bleeding whar dey scratched by de brambledy weeds, and whar dey got whuppings 'cause dey didn't git out all de work de overseer set out for 'em.

I was one dem little slave gals my own self, and I never seen nothing but work and tribulations till I was a grown up woman, jest about.

De niggers had hard traveling on de plantation whar I was born and raised, 'cause old Master live in town and jest had de overseer on de place, but iffen he had lived out dar hisself I speck it been as bad, 'cause he was a hard driver his own self.

He git biling mad when de Yankees have dat big battle at Pea Ridge and scatter de 'Federates all down through our country all bleeding and tired up and hungry, and he jest mount on his hoss and ride out to de plantation whar we all hoeing corn.

He ride up and tell old man Saunders—dat de overseer—to bunch us all up round de lead row man—dat my own uncle Sandy—and den he tell us de law!

"You niggers been seeing de 'Federate soldiers coming by here looking purty raggedy and hurt and wore out," he say, "but dat no sign dey licked!

"Dem Yankees ain't gwine git dis fur, but iffen dey do you all ain't gwine git free by 'em, 'cause I gwine free you befo' dat. When dey git here dey going find you already free, 'cause I gwine line you up on de bank of Bois d'Arc Creek and free you wid my shotgun! Anybody miss jest one lick wid de hoe, or one step in de line, or one clap of dat bell, or one toot of de horn, and he gwine be free and talking to de debil long befo' he ever see a pair of blue britches!"

Dat de way he talk to us, and dat de way he act wid us all de time.

We live in de log quarters on de plantation, not far from Washington, Arkansas, close to Bois d'Arc Creek, in de edge of the Little River bottom.

Old Master's name was Dr. Isaac Jones, and he live in de town, whar he keep four, five house niggers, but he have about 200 on de plantation, big and little, and old man Saunders oversee 'em at de time of de War. Old Mistress' name was Betty, and she had a daughter name Betty about grown, and then they was three boys, Tom, Bryan, and Bob, and they was too young to go to de War. I never did see 'em but once or twice till after de War.

Old Master didn't go to de War, 'cause he was a doctor and de onliest one left in Washington, and purty soon he was dead anyhow.

Next fall after he ride out and tell us dat he gwine shoot us befo' he let us free he come out to see how his steam gin doing. De gin box was a little old thing 'bout as big as a bedstead, wid a long belt running through de side of de gin house out to de engine and boiler in de yard. De boiler burn cord wood, and it have a little crack in it whar de nigger ginner been trying to fix it.

Old master come out, hopping mad 'cause de gin shet down, and ast de ginner, old Brown, what de matter. Old Brown say de boiler weak and it liable to bust, but old Master jump down off'n his hoss and go 'round to de boiler and say, "Cuss fire to your black heart! Dat boiler all right! Throw on some cordwood, cuss fire to your heart!"

Old Brown start to de wood pile grumbling to hisself and old Master stoop down to look at de boiler again, and it blow right up and him standing right dar!

Old Master was blowed all to pieces, and dey jest find little bitsy chunks of his clothes and parts of him to bury.

De wood pile blow over, and old Brown land way off in de woods, but he wasn't killed.

Two wagons of cotton blowed over, and de mules run away, and all de niggers was scared nearly to death 'cause we knowed de overseer gwine be a lot worse, now dat old Master gone.

Before de War when Master was a young man de slaves didn't have it so hard, my mammy tell me. Her name was Fanny and her old mammy name was Nanny. Grandma Nanny was alive during the War yet.

How she come in de Jones family was dis way: old Mistress was jest a little girl, and her older brother bought Nanny and give her to her. I think his name was Little John, anyways we called him Master Little John. He drawed up a paper what say dat Nanny allus belong to Miss Betty and all de chillun Nanny ever have belong to her, too, and nobody can't take 'em for a debt and things like dat. When Miss Betty marry, old Master he can't sell Nanny or any of her chillun neither.

Dat paper hold good, too, and grandmammy tell me about one time it hold good and keep my own mammy on de place.

Grandmammy say mammy was jest a little gal and was playing out in de road wid three, four other little chillun when a white man and old Master rid up. The white man had a paper about some kind of a debt, and old Master say take his pick of de nigger chillun and give him back de paper.

Jest as Grandmammy go to de cabin door and hear him say dat de man git off his hoss and pick up my mammy and put her up in front of him and start to ride off down de road.

Pretty soon Mr. Little John come riding up and say something to old Master, and see grandmammy standing in de yard screaming and crying. He jest job de spur in his hoss and go kiting off down de road after dat white man.

Mammy say he ketch up wid him jest as he git to Bois d'Arc Creek and start to wade de hoss across. Mr. Little John holler to him to come back wid dat little nigger 'cause de paper don't kiver dat child, 'cause she old Mistress' own child, and when de man jest ride on, Mr. Little John throw his big old long hoss-pistol down on him and make him come back.

De man hopping mad, but he have to give over my mammy and take one de other chillun on de debt paper.

Old Master allus kind of techy 'bout old Mistress having niggers he can't trade or sell, and one day he have his whole family and some more white folks out at de plantation. He showing 'em all de quarters when we all come in from de field in de evening, and he call all de niggers up to let de folks see 'em.

He make grandmammy and mammy and me stand to one side and den he say to the other niggers, "Dese niggers belong to my wife but you belong to me, and I'm de only one you is to call Master.

"Dis is Tom, and Bryan, and Bob, and Miss Betty, and you is to call 'em dat, and don't you ever call one of 'em Young Master or Young

Mistress, cuss fire to your black hearts!" All de other white folks look kind of funny, and old Mistress look 'shamed of old Master.

My own pappy was in dat bunch, too. His name was Frank, and after de War he took de name of Frank Henderson, 'cause he was born under dat name, but I allus went by Jones, de name I was born under.

Long about de middle of de War, after old Master was killed, de soldiers begin coming 'round de place and camping. Dey was Southern soldiers and dey say dey have to take de mules and most de corn to git along on. Jest go in de barns and cribs and take anything dey want, and us niggers didn't have no sweet 'taters nor Irish 'taters to eat on when dey gone neither.

One bunch come and stay in de woods across de road from de overseer's house, and dey was all on hosses. Dey lead de hosses down to Bois d'Arc Creek every morning at daylight and late every evening to git water. When we going to de field and when we coming in we allus see dem leading big bunches of hosses.

Dey bugle do jest 'bout de time our old horn blow in de morning and when we come in dey eating supper, and we smell it and sho' git hungry!

Before old Master died he sold off a whole lot of hosses and cattle, and some niggers too. He had de sales on de plantation, and white men from around dar come to bid, and some traders come. He had a big stump whar he made de niggers stand while dey was being sold, and dem men and boys had to strip off to de waist to show dey muscle and iffen dey had any scars or hurt places, but de women and gals didn't have to strip to de waist.

De white men come up and look in de slave's mouth jest lak he was a mule or a hoss.

After old Master go, de overseer hold one sale, but mostly he jest trade wid de traders what come by. He make de niggers git on de stump, though. De traders all had big bunches of slaves and dey have 'em all strung out in a line going down de road. Some had wagons and de chillun could ride, but not many. Dey didn't chain or tie 'em 'cause dey didn't have no place dey could run to anyway.

I seen chillun sold off and de mammy not sold, and sometimes de mammy sold and a little baby kept on de place and give to another woman to raise. Dem white folks didn't care nothing 'bout how de slaves grieved when dey tore up a family.

Old man Saunders was de hardest overseer of anybody. He would git mad and give a whipping some time and de slave wouldn't even know what it was about.

My uncle Sandy was de lead row nigger, and he was a good nigger and never would tech a drap of likker. One night some de niggers git hold of some likker somehow, and dey leave de jug half full on de step of Sandy's cabin. Next morning old man Saunders come out in de field so mad he was pale.

He jest go to de lead row and tell Sandy to go wid him, and start toward de woods along Bois d'Arc Creek wid Sandy follering behind. De overseer always carry a big heavy stick, but we didn't know he was so mad, and dey jest went off in de woods.

Purty soon we hear Sandy hollering and we know old overseer pouring it on, den de overseer come back by his self and go on up to de house.

Come late evening he come and see what we done in de day's work, and go back to de quarters wid us all. When he git to mammy's cabin, whar grandmammy live too, he say to grandmammy, "I sent Sandy down in de woods to hunt a hoss, he gwine come in hungry purty soon. You better make him an extra hoe cake," and he kind of laugh and go on to his house.

Jest soon as he gone we all tell grandmammy we think he got a whipping, and sho' nuff he didn't come in.

De next day some white boys find uncle Sandy what dat overseer done killed him and throwed him in a little pond, and dey never done nothing to old man Saunders at all!

When he go to whip a nigger he make him strip to de waist, and he take a cat-o-nine tails and bring de blisters, and den bust the blisters wid a wide strap of leather fastened to a stick handle. I seen de blood running out'n many a back, all de way from de neck to de waist!

Many de time a nigger git blistered and cut up so dat we have to git a sheet and grease it wid lard and wrap 'em up in it, and dey have to wear a greasy cloth wrapped around dey body under de shirt for three–four days after dey git a big whipping!

Later on in de War de Yankees come in all around us and camp, and de overseer git sweet as honey in de comb! Nobody git a whipping all de time de Yankees dar!

Dey come and took all de meat and corn and 'taters dey want too, and dey tell us, "Why don't you poor darkeys take all de meat and molasses you want? You made it and it's your'n as much as anybody's!" But we know dey soon be gone, and den we git a whipping iffen we do. Some niggers run off and went wid de Yankees, but dey had to work jest as hard for dem, and dey didn't eat so good and often wid de soldiers.

I never forget de day we was set free!

Dat morning we all go to de cotton field early, and den a house nigger come out from old Mistress on a hoss and say she want de overseer to come into town, and he leave and go in. After while de old horn blow up at de overseer's house, and we all stop and listen, 'cause it de wrong time of day for de horn.

We start chopping again, and dar go de horn again.

De lead row nigger holler "Hold up!" And we all stop again. "We better go on in. Dat our horn," he holler at de head nigger, and de head nigger think so too, but he say he afraid we catch de devil from the overseer iffen we quit widout him dar, and de lead row man say maybe he back from town and blowing de horn hisself, so we line up and go in.

When we git to de quarters we see all de old ones and de chillun up in de overseer's yard, so we go on up dar. De overseer setting on de end of de gallery wid a paper in his hand, and when we all come up he say come and stand close to de gallery. Den he call off everybody's name and see we all dar.

Setting on de gallery in a hide-bottom chair was a man we never see before. He had on a big broad black hat lak de Yankees wore but it didn't have no yaller string on it lak most de Yankees had, and he was in store clothes dat wasn't homespun or jeans, and dey was black. His hair was plumb gray and so was his beard, and it come way down here on his chest, but he didn't look lak he was very old, 'cause his face was kind of fleshy and healthy looking. I think we all been sold off in a bunch, and I notice some kind of smiling, and I think they sho' glad of it.

De man say, "You darkies know what day dis is?" He talk kind, and smile.

We all don't know of course, and we jest stand dar and grin. Pretty soon he ask again and de head man say, No, we don't know.

"Well dis de fourth day of June, and dis is 1865, and I want you all to 'member de date, 'cause you allus going 'member de day. Today you is free, jest lak I is, and Mr. Saunders and your Mistress and all us white people," de man say.

"I come to tell you," he say, "and I wants to be sho' you all understand, 'cause you don't have to git up and go by de horn no more. You is your own bosses now, and you don't have to have no passes to go and come."

We never did have no passes, nohow, but we knowed lots of other niggers on other plantations got 'em.

"I wants to bless you and hope you always is happy, and tell you got all de right and lief dat any white people got," de man say, and den he git on his hoss and ride off.

We all jest watch him go on down de road, and den we go up to Mr. Saunders and ask him what he want us to do. He jest grunt and say do lak we dam please, he reckon, but git off dat place to do it, less'n any of us wants to stay and make de crop for half of what we make.

None of us know whar to go, so we all stay, and he split up de fields and show us which part we got to work in, and we go on lak we was, and make de crop and git it in, but dey ain't no more horn after dat day. Some de niggers lazy and don't git in de field early, and dey git it took away from 'em, but dey plead around and git it back and work better de rest of dat year.

But we all gits fooled on dat first go-out! When de crop all in we don't git half! Old Mistress sick in town, and de overseer was still on de place and he charge us half de crop for de quarters and de mules and tools and grub!

Den he leave, and we gits another white man, and he sets up a book, and give us half de next year, and take out for what we use up, but we all got something left over after dat first go-out.

Old Mistress never git well after she lose all her niggers, and one day de white boss tell us she jest drap over dead setting in her chair, and we know her heart jest broke.

Next year de chillun sell off most de place and we scatter off, and I and mammy go into Little Rock and do work in de town. Grand-mammy done dead.

I git married to John White in Little Rock, but he died and we didn't have no chillun. Den in four, five years I marry Billy Rowe. He was a Cherokee citizen and he had belonged to a Cherokee name Dave Rowe, and lived east of Tahlequah before de War. We married in Little Rock, but he had land in de Cherokee Nation, and we come to east of Tahlequah and lived till he died, and den I come to Tulsa to live wid my youngest daughter.

Billy Rowe and me had three chillun, Ellie, John, and Lula. Lula married a Thomas, and it's her I lives with.

Lots of old people lak me say dat dey was happy in slavery, and dat dey had de worst tribulations after freedom, but I knows dey didn't have no white master and overseer lak we all had on our place. Dey both dead now I reckon, and dey no use talking 'bout de dead, but I know I been gone long ago iffen dat white man Saunders didn't lose his hold on me.

It was de fourth day of June in 1865 I begins to live, and I gwine take de picture of dat old man in de big black hat and long whiskers, setting on de gallery and talking kind to us, clean into my grave wid me.

No, bless God, I ain't never seen no more black boys bleeding all up and down de back under a cat o' nine tails, and I never go by no cabin and hear no poor nigger groaning, all wrapped up in a lardy sheet no more!

I hear my chillun read about General Lee, and I know he was a good man. I didn't know nothing about him den, but I know now he wasn't fighting for dat kind of white folks.

Maybe dey dat kind still yet, but dey don't show it up no more, and I got lots of white friends too. All my chillun and grandchillun been to school, and dey git along good, and I know we living in a better world, whar dey ain't nobody "cussing fire to my black heart!"

I sho' thank de good Lawd I got to see it.

[1] Mrs. Katie Rowe was interviewed in Tulsa by Robert Vinson Lackey probably sometime in the spring or summer of 1937. From his notes Lackey prepared a preliminary typewritten draft entitled "Interview with Mathilda Rowe (Ex-Slave, Age 88, 1004 N. Lansing, Tulsa, Okla.)" that is available in the OHS Slave Narratives. Then on 14 July 1937 he wrote to the state director of the Federal Writers' Project to say that he had returned to visit further with Mrs. Rowe and learned that he had rendered her first name incorrectly—"Much to my surprise, she told me that her first name was Katie and not Mathilda"—adding that "she said she didn't know how she came to say Mathilda when I interviewed her first, unless it was because she had a baby sister named Mathilda and was probably thinking of her when she was relating the events of her own life." Lackey's preliminary draft was edited and retyped as "Katie Rowe, Age 88 Yrs., Tulsa, Oklahoma" and forwarded to Washington on 13 August 1937. This version, published here, is available in ribbon-copy typescript in the LC Slave Narratives and in carbon copy as item 350074 in the LC Slave Narratives Carbon Copies and in the OHS Slave Narratives (where the last page is misfiled with the narrative of Mary Lindsay). In Washington, Federal Writers' Project folklore editor Benjamin A. Botkin found Katie Rowe's interview to be "an exceptional narrative" that was "first-rate in social significance and literary quality." He included it in its entirety in his 1945 study, *Lay My Burden Down* (103–9, 276). B. A. B[otkin], LC Slave Narratives Appraisal Sheets, Accession no. 350074, 6 December 1940; R[obert] Vinson Lackey, Tulsa, Oklahoma, to [William] Cunningham, [Oklahoma City, Oklahoma], 14 July 1937; Stephens to Cronyn, 13 August 1937; both letters in WPA Notes on Interviews; *Polk's Tulsa City Directory, 1935,* 475, 697.

In summer 1937, Robert Vinson Lackey passed a copy of the Katie Rowe interview text together with a photograph of Rowe to journalist Ruth Sheldon, who edited and shortened the narrative for the *Tulsa Tribune,* making this one of the few of the Oklahoma slave narratives ever to have been published in Oklahoma. It appeared in the Tulsa newspaper on 30 July 1937 under the title "'I Seen Chillun Sold Off an' de Mammy Not Sold,' Former 'Slave Gel' Reminisces Here."

ANNIE GROVES SCOTT[1]

Age 93   *Muskogee, Oklahoma*

Just before the war broke out I was fifteen year old and my mistress told me I was born March 18, 1845, at a little place she called Lyonsville, South Carolina.

Ma (that's all the name she ever called her mother) was born at Charlotte, N.C., and father was born at Lyonsville, same as me, and his name was Levi Grant, which changed to Groves when he was sold by Master Grant. Dat was when I was a baby and I wants to tell you about dat on down the line. I had a brother name of Robert.

How old my folks was I never know, but I know their folks come from Africa on a slave boat. One of my uncles who was done brought here from that place, and who was a slave boatman on the Savannah river, he never learned to talk plain, mostly just jabber like the Negroes done when they first get here.

Ma told about how the white people fool the Negroes onto the slave boat; how the boatmen would build pens on the shore and put red pieces of cloth in the pens and the fool Negroes would tear the pen down almost getting themselves after the cloth and then getting caught. Den dey get 'em onto the boat and shove off on the big waters, leaving the little children crying on the shore, never to be seen no more. Dem's the Negroes who just jabber, jabber when dey was brought here; wasn't many of dem learn to read or write but some of the children like me the old mistress would teach; dat's how come me to know about words and things.

Like I said, my father was sold when I was a baby and Ma saw him sold. He had another woman and some children somewheres and the master say to him one day, I'm going to sell you at the auction tomorrow!

Ma said the next day all the slaves to be sold was brought to the auction block down by the master's barn and dere was a white man dere who lived about two-hundred miles from the Grant plantation who bought my father, paying $1,000 for him because he was a good strong worker. Dat was the last we ever see of him.

Sometimes the master go clean to New Orleans for to buy some new slaves, especially girl slaves. One time he brought back two of the prettiest ones I ever see; they had long hair, their faces was kinder bright and dey seem different than the real black girls. One of dem work in the kitchen, the other in the store-room, and dey stayed 'til the freedom come.

Squire Tom Grant of Lyonsville, South Carolina—dat's the way my master use to speak of himself. The mistress' name was Emma Grant and she was the one who really raised me because she took me into the big house when I was a baby, so I was raised among the rich folks just like their own children, Dick and Larry. Dick was the oldest and he got to be a doctor; the medicine that boy could fix up for the slaves was something! Rhubarb pills and calomel was the main medicine.

The young boy, Larry, was sent down to school at Lexington, Georgia, and he didn't come to the old plantation but once after the war started. Don't know if he was in the Confederacy army or just if he kept on at the school; after the war we all scattered so's I don't know what happen to him.

The master's house was a big one, with a hall in the middle and a long front porch where I would set and watch the slave children playing in the yard, but when the mistress see me looking like I wanted to go run with dem, she frown and say: "Don't you go out dere with dem dirty children, the Devil will get you sure!"

The master was the same way about it, too. "Stay on the porch," he say to me, times and more, "your place is here by the mistress and not out chasing with them rascals."

Dey treat me good all the time; made a pet of me is what the folks said. I slept in the same room with the mistress; there was a little bed for me that was pushed under her big bed during the day and pulled out at night. The mistress' bed had high posts what come almost to the ceiling of her room and she was mighty fussy about it being made up careful, with no wrinkles in the covers.

Along in the war times—and dem was trouble days—the master give me some of the Confederate money when I help to hide some of the keepsakes he was afraid the Yanks would get if dey come around. He give Ma enough of dat kind of money dat she trade it in before it got so worthless and had $100 all for herself. Sometimes she get a pass and go to town and always she bring back new muslin for a dress or something to wear—she spoil me just like the mistress did.

She never went to town without a pass. Afraid the patrollers get after her unless she got the word it's alright for her to be away from Master Grant's. She was more afraid than ever after what happened to my uncle Bill Grant. He schemed out to run off and got as far as the river, but the water was high and he couldn't get across of it. He hid around in the brush and pretty soon the hounds was after him, and the patrollers, too, with bull whips what they carried all the time.

Anyway, dem bloodhounds track Uncle Bill to the river and smell him out where he was hiding. They tell about if after they come back to tell Master Grant his slave is dead. "The dogs got him" one of the men say, "they got him so good he is tore to pieces!" From what dey say the dogs just eat him like dey would cow meat; dere wasn't nothing left to bury!

The master was always afraid of the Yankees coming and one day during the war he called Ma and some of the other slaves in one of the big rooms and say to them, "The damn Yanks ain't here, but dey is coming soon enough! Dey'll take everything on the place unless we hide it. Dat's what I want you all to do, hide the lard, put the meats in a hard place and all the trinkets of things dat you don't want to lose."

So dat was all done when the Yankee soldiers first come to the big house. The mistress and master was upstairs time of the coming and I was rocking on the front porch. Dat day I had on a white muslin dress, flounced up with blue and a blue hair ribbon on my curls. Dat time I was sure scared; dey got to coming around the place so regular after dat I wasn't scared no more.

The captain ride up to the porch and say, "Where is your mother?" "Down in the cornfield." I was most too scared to answer him and when he say he wants to water all dey horses, I just say, "Go ahead!" When dey leave the place and dey don't do nothing but water the horses, the captain stops by and gives me some money. "Give part of it to your mother!" And away he rides.

Dere was fighting around the country all the time after dat, but I seen no battles. Only sometimes I hear the guns going BOOM! BOOM! away off and know that pretty soon the soldiers will come running by the place going every-whichway—dey come by lots of times and I see them bleeding and wanting water to drink.

One morning I got up and went out on the porch. Dere was a man dere waiting for help. "Would your master give me some medicine?" the man say to me, and I go into the house and get Master Grant.

When the master come out he look at the man and say, "Henry! What's the matter?" When he finds out the man is shot and sick he takes him into the house and lets him stay. Henry Hill, dat was the man's name, was kin to Tom Hill, one of the plantation owners down in the country more. They say he married a sister of Master Grant after the war ended.

Before the war was over Master Grant search out all the things dat was hid and take his slaves to Elberton, Georiga. All the other slave owners do the same. Dat was the last year of the war and dat is where we was all freed.

The master got mean along about the time of freedom; some of the slaves was shot because dey wouldn't work. The master say, "If dey won't work just get rid of dem!" The overseer done what he said, but Ma and me was one of the family and nobody get mad at us for nothing we do or nothing we don't.

Somehow after the freedom Ma got a little farm and worked on it. She didn't do no more spinning for Mistress Grant and no more working in the master's garden, but she had to work harder than ever before, even though it was for her ownself. Dat's when I work too. Wore myself out after freedom and got kinder tired hearing folks yelling about Grant and Lincoln setting us free.

I married Abraham Scott, then sometime after come to Muskogee; before Statehood it was. Dere was four children; two of dem died. The living are Lizzie and Booey; the boy Booey has a good job at Atlanta. The dead are Robert Scott and John Henry Washington Scott.

I belong to the church every year since 80 years ago. Everybody ought to have religion and if anybody gets behind in their religion, just boot him back into the church—just like the overseer boot 'em along the cotton rows in slave times.

[1] Mrs. Annie Groves Scott was interviewed by a now unidentified WPA field worker in Muskogee, Oklahoma, sometime probably in 1938, but only one copy of her remembrances is known to have survived. This typescript, "Annie Groves Scott, Age 93, Muskogee, Oklahoma," which is published here, is available in ribbon copy in the OHS Slave Narratives. It was never sent to Washington. The informant is identified in a roughly contemporary city directory as Mrs. Anna Scott, widow of Abraham Scott, residing at 1021 Oak Street. *Polk's Muskogee City Directory, 1932,* 171, 253.

MORRIS SHEPPARD[1]

Age 85 Yrs.   *Fort Gibson, Okla.*

Old Master tell me I was borned in November 1852, at de old home place about five miles east of Webbers Falls, mebbe kind of northeast, not far from de east bank of de Illinois River.

Master's name was Joe Sheppard, and he was a Cherokee Indian. Tall and slim and handsome. He had black eyes and mustache but his hair was iron gray, and everybody liked him because he was so good-natured and kind.

I don't remember old Mistress' name. My mammy was a Crossland negro before she come to belong to Master Joe and marry my pappy, and I think she come wid old Mistress and belong to her. Old Mistress was small and mighty pretty too, and she was only half Cherokee. She inherit about half a dozen slaves, and say dey was her own and old Master can't sell one unless she give him leave to do it.

Dey only had two families of slaves wid about twenty in all, and dey only worked about fifty acres, so we sure did work every foot of it good. We git three or four crops of different things out of dat farm every year, and something growing on dat place winter and summer.

Pappy's name was Caesar Sheppard and Mammy's name was Easter. Dey was both raised 'round Webber's Falls somewhere. I had two brothers, Silas and George, dat belong to Mr. George Holt in Webber's Falls town. I got a pass and went to see dem sometimes, and dey was both treated mighty fine.

The Big House was a double log wid a big hall and a stone chimney but no porches, wid two rooms at each end, one top side of de other. I thought it was mighty big and fine.

Us slaves lived in log cabins dat only had one room and no windows so we kept de doors open most of de time. We had home-made wooden beds wid rope springs, and de little ones slept on trundle beds dat was home made too.

At night dem trundles was jest all over de floor, and in de morning we shove dem back under de big beds to git dem out'n de way. No nails in none of dem nor in de chairs and tables. Nails cost big money and old Master's blacksmith wouldn't make none 'cepting a few for old Master now and den, so we used wooden dowels to put things together.

They was so many of us for dat little field we never did have to work hard. Up at five o'clock and back in sometimes about de middle of de evening, long before sundown, unless they was a crop to git in before it rain or something like dat.

When crop was laid by de slaves jest work 'round at dis and dat and keep tol'able busy. I never did have much of a job, jest tending de calves mostly. We had about twenty calves and I would take dem out and graze 'em while some grown-up negro was grazing de cows so as to keep de cows' milk. I had me a good blaze-faced horse for dat.

One time old Master and another man come and took some calves off and Pappy say old Master taking dem off to sell. I didn't know what "sell" meant and I ast Pappy, "Is he going to bring 'em back when he git through selling them?" I never did see no money neither, until time of de War or a little before.

Master Joe was sure a good provider, and we always had plenty of corn pone, sow belly and greens, sweet potatoes, cow peas and cane molasses. We even had brown sugar and cane molasses most of de time before de War. Sometimes coffee, too.

De clothes wasn't no worry neither. Everything we had was made by my folks. My aunt done de carding and spinning and my mammy done de weaving and cutting and sewing, and my pappy could make cowhide shoes wid wooden pegs. Dey was for bad winter only.

Old Master bought de cotton in Ft. Smith because he didn't raise no cotton, but he had a few sheep and we had wool-mix for winter.

Everything was stripedy 'cause Mammy like to make it fancy. She dye wid copperas and walnut and wild indigo and things like dat and make pretty cloth. I wore a stripedy shirt till I was about eleven years old, and den one day while we was down in de Choctaw Country old Mistress see me and nearly fall off'n her horse! She holler, "Easter, you go right now and make dat big buck of a boy some britches!"

We never put on de shoes until about late November when de front begin to hit regular and split our feet up, and den when it git good and cold and de crop all gathered in anyways, they is nothing to do 'cepting hog killing and a lot of wood chopping, and you don't git cold doing dem two things.

De hog killing mean we gits lots of spare-ribs and chitlings, and somebody always git sick eating too much of dat fresh pork. I always pick a whole passel of muskatines[2] for old Master and he make up sour wine, and dat helps out when we git the bowel complaint from eating dat fresh pork.

If somebody bad sick he git de doctor right quick, and he don't let no negroes mess around wid no poultices and teas and sech things like cupping-horns neither!

Us Cherokee slaves seen lots of green corn shootings and de like of dat,[3] but we never had no games of our own. We was too tired when we come in to play any games. We had to have a pass to go any place to have singing or praying, and den they was always a bunch of pa-trollers around to watch everything we done. Dey would come up in a bunch of about nine men on horses and look at all our passes, and if a negro didn't have no pass dey wore him out good and made him go home. Dey didn't let us have much enjoyment.

Right after de War de Cherokees that had been wid the South kind of pestered the freedmen some, but I was so small dey never bothered me; jest de grown ones. Old Master and Mistress kept on asking me did de night riders persecute me any but dey never did.

Dey told me some of dem was bad on negroes but I never did see none of dem night riding like some say dey did.

Old Master had some kind of business in Fort Smith, I think, 'cause he used to ride in to dat town 'bout every day on his horse. He would start at de crack of daylight and not git home till way after dark. When he get home he call my uncle in and ask about what we done all day and tell him what we better do de next day. My uncle Joe was de slave boss and he tell us what de Master say do.

When dat Civil War come along I was a pretty big boy and I remember it good as anybody. Uncle Joe tell us all to lay low and work hard and nobody bother us, and he would look after us. He sure stood good with de Cherokee neighbors we had, and dey all liked him. There was Mr. Jim Collins, and Mr. Bell, and Mr. Dave Franklin, and Mr. Jim Sutton and Mr. Blackburn that lived around close to us and dey all had slaves. Dey was all wid the South, but dey was a lot of dem Pin Indians all up on de Illinois River and dey was wid de North and dey taken it out on de slave owners a lot before de War and during it too.[4]

Dey would come in de night and hamstring de horses and maybe set fire to de barn, and two of 'em named Joab Scarrel and Tom Starr killed my pappy one night just before de War broke out.

I don't know what dey done it for, only to be mean, and I guess they was drunk.

Them Pins was after Master all de time for a while at de first of de War, and he was afraid to ride into Fort Smith much. Dey come to de house one time when he was gone to Fort Smith and us children told dem he was at Honey Springs, but they knowed better and when he got home he said somebody shot at him and bushwhacked him all the way from Wilson's Rock to dem Wildhorse Mountains, but he run his horse like de devil was setting on his tail and dey never did hit him. He never seen them neither. We told him 'bout de Pins coming for him and he just laughed.

When de War come old Master seen he was going into trouble and he sold off most of de slaves. In de second year of de War he sold my mammy and my aunt dat was Uncle Joe's wife and my two brothers and my little sister. Mammy went to a mean old man named Pepper Goodman and he took her off down de river, and pretty soon Mistress tell me she died 'cause she can't stand de rough treatment.

When Mammy went old Mistress took me to de Big House to help her, and she was kind to me like I was part of her own family. I never forget when they sold off some more negroes at de same time, too, and put dem all in a pen for de trader to come and look at.

He never come until the next day, so dey had to sleep in dat pen in a pile like hogs.

It wasn't my Master done dat. He done already sold 'em to a man and it was dat man was waiting for de trader. It made my Master mad, but dey didn't belong to him no more and he couldn't say nothing.

The man put dem on a block and sold 'em to a man dat had come in on a steamboat, and he took dem off on it when de freshet come down and de boat could go back to Fort Smith. It was tied up at de dock at Webbers Falls about a week and we went down and talked to my aunt and brothers and sister. De brothers was Sam and Eli. Old Mistress cried jest like any of de rest of us when de boat pull out with dem on it.

Pretty soon all de young Cherokee menfolks all gone off to de War, and de Pins was riding 'round all de time, and it ain't safe to be in dat part around Webber's Falls, so old Master take us all to Fort Smith where they was a lot of Confederate soldiers.

We camp at dat place a while and old Mistress stay in de town wid some kinfolks. Den old Master get three wagons and ox teams and take us all way down on Red River in de Choctaw Nation.

We went by Webber's Falls and filled de wagons. We left de furniture and only took grub and tools and bedding and clothes, 'cause they wasn't very big wagons and was only single-yoke.

We went on a place in de Red River bottoms close to Shawneetown and not far from de place where all de wagons crossed over to go into Texas. We was at dat place two years and made two little crops.

One night a runaway negro come across from Texas and he had de blood hounds after him. His britches was all muddy and tore where de hounds had cut him up in de legs when he clumb a tree in de bottoms. He come to our house and Mistress said for us Negroes to give him something to eat and we did.

Then up come de man from Texas with de hounds and wid him was young Mr. Joe Van and my uncle that belong to young Joe. Dey called young Mr. Joe "Little Joe Vann" even after he was grown on account of when he was a little boy before his pappy was killed. His pappy was old Captain "Rich Joe" Vann, and he had been dead ever since long before de War. My uncle belong to old Captain Joe nearly all his life.[5]

Mistress try to get de man to tell her who de negro belong to so she can buy him, but de man say he can't sell him and he take him on back to Texas wid a chain around his two ankles. Dat was one poor negro dat never got away to de North, and I was sorry for him 'cause I know he must have had a mean master, but none of us Sheppard negroes, I mean the grown ones, tried to git away.

I never seen any fighting in de War, but I seen soldiers in the South army doing a lot of blacksmithing 'long side de road one day. Dey was fixing wagons and shoeing horses.

After de War was over, old Master tell me I am free but he will look out after me 'cause I am just a little negro and I ain't got no sense. I know he is right, too.

Well, I go ahead and make me a crop of corn all by myself and then I don't know what to do wid it. I was afraid I would get cheated out of it 'cause I can't figure and read, so I tell old Master about it and he bought it off'n me.

We never had no school in slavery and it was agin the law for anybody to even show a negro de letters and figures, so no Cherokee slave could read.

We all come back to de old place and find de negro cabins and barns burned down and de fences all gone and de field in crab grass and cockleburs. But de Big House ain't hurt 'cepting it need a new roof. De furniture is all gone, and some said de soldiers burned it up for firewood. Some officers stayed in de house for a while and tore everything up or took it off.

Master give me over to de National Freedmen's Bureau and I was bound out to a Cherokee woman name Lizzie McGee. Then one day one of my uncles name Wash Sheppard come and tried to git me to go live wid him. He say he wanted to git de family all together agin.

He had run off after he was sold and joined de North army and discharged at Fort Scott in Kansas, and he said lots of freedmen was living close to each other up by Coffeyville in the Coo-ee-scoo-ee District.

I wouldn't go, so he sent Isaac and Joe Vann dat had been two of old Captain Joe's negroes to talk to me. Isaac had been Young Joe's driver, and he told me all about how rich Master Joe was and how he would look after us negroes. Dey kept after me 'bout a year, but I didn't go anyways.

But later on I got a freedman's allotment up in dat part close to Coffeyville, and I lived in Coffeyville a while but I didn't like it in Kansas.

I lost my land trying to live honest and pay my debts. I raised eleven children just on de sweat of my hands and none of dem ever tasted anything dat was stole.

When I left Mrs. McGee's I worked about three years for Mr. Sterling Scott and Mr. Roddy Reese. Mr. Reese had a big flock of peafowls dat had belonged to Mr. Scott and I had to take care of dem.

Whitefolks, I would have to tromp seven miles to Mr. Scott's house two or three times a week to bring back some old peafowl dat had got out and gone back to de old place!

Poor old Master and Mistress only lived a few years after de War. Master went plumb blind after he move back to Webber's Falls and so he move up on de Illinois River 'bout three miles from de Arkansas, and there old Mistress take de white swelling and die and den he die pretty soon. I went to see dem lots of times and they was always glad to see me.

I would stay around about a week and help 'em, and dey would try to git me to take something but I never would. Dey didn't have much and couldn't make anymore and dem so old. Old Mistress had inherited some property from her pappy and dey had de slave money and when dey turned everything into good money after de War dat stuff only come to about six thousand dollars in good money, she told me. Dat just about lasted 'em through until dey died, I reckon.

By and by I married Nancy Hildebrand what lived on Greenleaf Creek, 'bout four miles northwest of Gore. She had belonged to Joe Hildebrand and he was kin to old Steve Hildebrand dat owned de mill on Flint Creek up in de Going Snake District. She was raised up at dat mill, but she was borned in Tennessee before dey come out to de nation. Her master was white but he had married into de Nation and so she got a freedmen's allotment too. She had some land close to Catoosa and some down on Greenleaf Creek.[6]

We was married at my home in Coffeyville, and she bore me eleven children right. We never had no church in slavery, and no schooling, and you had better not be caught wid a book in your hand even, so I never did go to church hardly any.

Wife belong to de church and all de children too, and I think all should look after saving their souls so as to drive de nail in, and den go about de earth spreading kindness and hoeing de row clean so as to clinch dat nail and make dem safe for Glory.

Of course I hear about Abraham Lincoln and he was a great man, but I was told mostly by my children when dey come home from school about him. I always think of my old Master as de one dat freed me, and anyways Abraham Lincoln and none of his North people didn't look after me and buy my crop right after I was free like old Master did. Dat was de time dat was the hardest and everything was dark and confusion.

¹ Morris Sheppard was interviewed near Fort Gibson, Oklahoma, by WPA field worker Ethel Wolfe Garrison probably sometime in the summer or autumn of 1937. From her notes a preliminary typewritten draft of Sheppard's narrative was prepared as "Interview with Morris Sheppard, Ex-Slave, Aged 85 Years. Lives with Daughter, Mrs. Emma Parker, Five Miles Northeast of Fort Gibson, Oklahoma, R.R. No. 1." It is available in carbon copy in the OHS Slave Narratives. From this draft, an edited final typescript, published here, was prepared and sent to Washington on 18 November 1937. It is available as "Morris Sheppard, Age 85 Yrs., Fort Gibson, Okla." in ribbon-copy typescript in the LC Slave Narratives and in carbon copy as item 350019 in the LC Slave Narratives Carbon Copies. *Polk's Muskogee City Directory, 1932,* 327; Stephens to Alsberg, 18 November 1937, WPA Notes on Interviews. For another, contemporary interview with this informant, see Morris S. Sheppard, interview by H. L. Rumage at Fort Gibson, Oklahoma, 22 February 1937, Indian-Pioneer Papers, 9:254–56.

² Muscadine grapes.

³ This is an apparent reference to the annual green corn dance of the Cherokees, a fertility rite in which thanks were given for the new corn crop. Swanton, *Indians of the Southeastern United States,* 769–72.

⁴ For other remembrances of encounters with the "Pin Indians," see the narratives of Mary Grayson and Patsy Perryman, above.

⁵ For background on Joseph Vann and his father, "Rich Joe" Vann, see the narrative, above, of Betty Robertson, who was a slave of both men.

⁶ Nancy Hildebrand Sheppard and her children were enrolled as Cherokee freedmen by the Dawes Commission between 1903 and 1905, giving them all rights to land allotments in the Cherokee Nation. Cherokee Freedmen Census Cards, no. 186 (Nancy, Fannie, Emma, Annie, Thomas, and Claud Sheppard); Cherokee Freedmen Enrollment Application Testimony, file 186 (Nancy, Fannie, Emma, Annie, Thomas, and Claud Sheppard). No enrollment records were found for Morris Sheppard. For background on the Hildebrand mill, see the narrative of Rachel Aldrich Ward, below.

ANDREW SIMMS[1]

Age 80   *Sapulpa, Okla.*

My parents come over on a slave ship from Africa about twenty year before I was born on the William Driver plantation down in Florida. My folks didn't know each other in Africa but my old Mammy told me she was captured by Negro slave hunters over there and brought to some coast town where the white buyers took her and carried her to America.

She was kinder a young gal then and was sold to some white folks when the boat landed here. Dunno who they was. The same thing happened to my pappy. Must have been about the same time from the way they tells it. Maybe they was on the same boat, I dunno.

They was traded around and then mammy was sold to William Driver. The plantation was down in Florida. Another white folks had a plantation close by. Mister Simms was the owner. Bill Simms— that's the name pappy kept after the War.

Somehow or other mammy and pappy meets 'round the place and the first thing happens they is in love. That's what mammy say. And the next thing happen is me. They didn't get married. The Masters say it is alright for them to have a baby. They never gets married, even after the War. Just jumped the broomstick and goes to living with somebody else I reckon.

Then when I was four year old along come the War and Master Driver takes up his slaves and leaves the Florida country and goes way out to Texas. Mammy goes along, I goes along, all the children goes along. I don't remember nothing about the trip but I hears mammy talk about it when I gets older.

Texas, that was the place, down near Fairfield. That's where I learn to do the chores. But the work was easy for the Master was kind as old Mammy herself and he never give me no hard jobs that would wear me down. All the slaves on our place was treated good. All the time. They didn't whip. The Master feeds all the slaves on good clean foods and lean meats so's they be strong and healthy.

Master Driver had four children, Mary, Julia, Frank and George. Every one of them children kind and good just [like] the old Master. They was never mean and could I find some of 'em now hard times would leave me on the run! They'd help this old man get catched up on his eating!

Makes me think of the old song we use to sing:

> Don't mind working from Sun to Sun,
> Iffen you give me my dinner—
> When the dinner time comes!

Nowadays I gets me something to eat when I can catch it. The trouble is sometimes I don't catch! But that ain't telling about the slave days.

In them times it was mostly the overseers and the drivers who was the mean ones. They caused all the misery. There was other white-folks caused troubles too. Sneak around where there was lots of the black children on the plantation and steal them. Take them poor children away off and sell them.

There wasn't any Sunday Schooling. There was no place to learn to read and write—no big brick schools like they is now. The old Master say we can teach ourselves but we can't do it. Old Elam Bowman owned the place next door to Mister Driver. If he catch his slaves toying with the pencil, why, he cut off one of their fingers. Then I reckon they lost interest in education and get their mind back on the hoe and plow like he say for them to do.

I didn't see no fighting during of the War. If they was any Yankees soldiering around the country I don't remember nothing of it.

Long time after the War is over, about 1885, I meets a gal named Angeline. We courts pretty fast and gets married. The wedding was a sure enough affair with the preacher saying the words just like the whitefolks' marriage. We is sure married.

The best thing we do after that is raise us a family. One of them old fashioned families. Big 'uns! Seventeen children does we have and twelve of them still living. Wants to know they names? I ain't never forgets a one! There was Lucy, Bill, Ebbie, Cora, Minnie, George, Frank, Kizzie, Necie, Andrew, Joe, Sammie, David, Fannie, Jacob, Bob and Myrtle.

All good children. Just like their old pappy who's tried to care for 'em just like the old Master takes care of their old daddy when he was a boy on that plantation down Texas way.

When the age comes on a man I reckon religion gets kind of meanful. Thinks about it mor'n when he's young and busy in the fields. I believes in the Bible and what it says to do. Some of the Colored folks takes to the voodoo. I don't believe in it. Neither does I believe in the fortune telling or charms. I aims to live by the Bible and leave the rabbit foots alone!

[1] Andrew Simms was interviewed near Sapulpa, Oklahoma, by WPA field worker L. P. Livingston probably sometime in spring or summer 1937. On 6 August project employee Craig Vollmer prepared a draft of the Simms narrative which is preserved today as "Interview with Andrew Simms, Route 1, Box 164, Sapulpa, Okla." in the OHS Slave Narratives. This typescript includes the following information just below its title: "NOTE: This person is an ex-slave, born in Florida, June 26, 1857. Parents: Bill Simms–Kizzie Driver." The preliminary draft was edited and retyped into a final version sent to Washington on 12 August 1937. This final draft, published here, is available as "Andrew Simms, Age 80, Sapulpa, Okla." in ribbon-copy typescript in the LC Slave Narratives and in carbon copy as item 350099 in the LC Slave Narratives Carbon Copies and in the OHS Slave Narratives. A note appended to the carbon copy in the OHS Slave Narratives in the handwriting of project employee Ida Belle Hunter states, "Since this ex-slave was so very young, he hardly knows more to tell." Stephens to Cronyn, 12 August 1937, WPA Notes on Interviews.

GEORGE SIMON[1]

Age 74   *Tulsa, Oklahoma*

I was born during of the war but too late for to know anything about it or the slave days before freedom. Only thing I know is that pappy told me I was born near the close of the war about 15-mile from Mendin, Louisiana, on the line between Claybourne and Banville parishes.[2] And my mammy died when I was a baby so I know nothing about her; don't even know my pappy name, but mammy was named Millie and some of my brothers and sisters was: Jordan, John, Joe, Andrew, Henry, Jake, Nelson, Ann, Hulda, Amy, George—that's all I can remember but there was sixteen children all together.

My pappy never told me about where he is born or about his master. Guess he didn't like his master, because when he is free somehow he just pick on the name of Simon and all us children keep that name from him.

My Uncle Henry run a little store on the Red River close by Shreveport right after the war. Pappy took me there and Uncle Henry helped raise me. He do a good job of it too, for I've always been honest and don't ever tell lies, because lies is like weeds; where one is when you get it up, a lot more comes where it was!

The young Negroes didn't have no fun the way I remember it. Soon as I could hang onto the hoe I was put to work, and I work early and I quit late; the days was long then, and never no money did I get either. One of my brothers would get the money for us working, then on Sunday before we foot it off to the church meeting he give me a half dollar to rattle against my knife, but come evening and he makes me give it back. That's all the money I see for a long time.

It ain't like the young ones do now. They go to shows all the time, spend what little they earn for that and other things worse, or if they can't earn money they steal their mammy's bread money from the hiding place.

I figures the Negro was better off during slavery than now. Then someone always look after them, plenty to eat, enough clothes and a sleeping place, with a doctor around when he needed one. Have to rustle everything now, and when they's no work and no money the Negro just got to tighten his belt a little more and trust a little more to the Lord to make everything come out alright. As for the doctor, the Negro who ain't got the money to pay just has to forget about him.

Folks talk about ghosts, but I never see one. Only time maybe I was near one was when I riding a mule through a skit of woods. The mule got scared, mighty scared, he acted, but I never see what make him take on so.

Twenty-four year ago I come to Osage Junction; two years later I moved to Tulsa and live here all the time since,[3] and in all that time two shows is all I ever see.

[1] Field worker L. P. Livingston interviewed George Simon in Tulsa probably sometime in the winter of 1937–38. From Livingston's now lost initial notes, a first draft of Simon's narrative was prepared by project employee Craig Vollmer as the typescript "Interview with George Simon, Slave Born, Age About 74, 1151 North Lansing St., Tulsa, Oklahoma," available in ribbon-copy typescript in the OHS Slave Narratives. At some later date this preliminary draft was edited and retyped into a final version, "George Simon, Age 74, Tulsa, Oklahoma," published here and available in carbon-copy typescript in the OHS Slave Narratives. This interview was never forwarded to Washington and is published here for the first time.

[2] These placenames refer to the town of Minden and the parishes of Claiborne and Bienville, Louisiana.

[3] The 1935 Tulsa city directory lists George W. Simon, a laborer, residing at 1151 North Lansing Avenue. *Polk's Tulsa City Directory, 1935,* 498, 666.

ALFRED SMITH[1]

Age (About) 80   *Oklahoma City, Okla.*

I was born in Calhoon, Georgia.[2] I don't know the date of birth, but as near as I can get at, my age is 80 years old. My mother's name is Mary Johnson and my father's name is Alexandra [*sic*] Hamilton. He was named for his first master, but was later sold to Master Smith.

I haven't seen neither of them. I don't even know how or who raised me up into the teens in age. I just remember my working here and there for what I could get. I learned to count myself, one day. I gathered some straws and went into the woods and broke them into short pieces and laid on my belly and first counted by 1 to 100, then I took them and counted by 2 to 100 and so on.

I have one sister who is older than I and I give her credit in raising me up to the teens.

I was not old enough to work in slavery and know but little concerning slavery. Since freedom I have worked in the States of Georgia, Tennessee, Illinois, Kentucky, Pennsylvania, Kansas and Oklahoma.

I remember I went in my shirt tail in summer and same for winter with home-made outing underwear and no shoes 'til I was able and old enough to buy them for myself.

I really didn't have a master but had some mighty mean employers. Even though I came along in school age a few years before freedom, I had no teaching. I have made a success in life without ever being able to read. I came to Oklahoma shortly after the run and bought 160 acres from a white man who had squatted on land in Kansas and as he could only squat on one tract he sold me his Oklahoma land for $200.[3] Since then, I have been a successful farmer to the extent of winning a gold medal at the World's Fair in France, with the best cotton,[4] and am now a retired farmer with $25,000 in cash in the banks and postoffice in Oklahoma City and a comfortable home to live in.[5] The little town of Smithville about five miles from here on 23rd Street was named for me.

My advice of success to others less fortunate than I is: "Cook small and eat all. Plan your business year ahead, if you live you'll have it and if you die you won't need it."

I think Abraham Lincoln was the best President of all of them. Booker T. Washington equals to Negroes as a leader as Lincoln for the white people.

---

[1] Alfred Smith was interviewed by a now unidentified WPA field worker probably sometime in 1937 or 1938. His remembrances are recorded in just one known typescript, "Alfred Smith, Age (About) 80, Oklahoma City, Okla.," preserved in the OHS Slave Narratives and published here. This interview was never sent to project headquarters in Washington. For another, contemporary interview with this informant, one focusing on his life in the Oklahoma Territory from 1889 on, see Alfred Smith, interview by Harry M. Dreyer at Oklahoma City, Oklahoma, [ca. 1937], Indian-Pioneer Papers, 9:450–53.

[2] This is probably a reference to Calhoun, Gordon County, Georgia.

[3] The "run" mentioned by Smith refers to the 22 April 1889 opening of the Oklahoma District, or Unassigned Lands, to non-Indian settlement. These lands were made available to firstcomers and prospective settlers flooded in to stake claims on areas of their choosing.

[4] Although a front-page article in the *Daily Oklahoman* (2 February 1901) lauded Alfred Smith, "one of the industrious colored cotton farmers of the county," for winning both "first and second prizes" for his cotton at the 1900 International Universal Exposition in Paris, France, this article apparently exaggerated his role in the world's fair competition. According to the official report of the U.S. Commissioner-General to the exposition, Smith's contribution was of samples of "Storm-proof" and "Cheatham" cotton and/or cotton seed which formed part of a collective exhibit of several hundred cotton samples collected by U.S. Department of Agriculture personnel for display at the fair. U.S. Commissioner-General to the International Universal Exposition, Paris, 1900, *Report of the Commissioner-General for the United States to the International Universal Exposition, Paris, 1900*, 3:424–25, 431; 4:331; 5:347.

[5] According to contemporary city directories, at the time of the interview Alfred

Smith resided at 1021 Northeast Seventh in Oklahoma City. *Oklahoma City Negro City Directory,* 168; *Polk's Oklahoma City Directory, 1937,* 678, 924. In his interview for the Indian-Pioneer Project, Smith attributed his comparative affluence to "accumulations and oil profits of his farm." Indian-Pioneer Papers, 9:451.

LIZA SMITH[1]

Age 91   *Muskogee, Oklahoma*

Both my mammy and pappy was brought from Africa on a slave boat and sold on de Richmond (Va.) slave market. What year dey come over I don't know. My mammy was Jane Mason, belonging to Frank Mason; pappy was Frank Smith, belonging to a master wid de same name. I mean, my pappy took his Master's name, and den after my folks married mammy took de name of Smith, but she stayed on wid de Masons and never did belong to my pappy's master. Den, after Frank Mason took all his slaves out of de Virginia country, mammy met up wid another man, Ben Humphries, and married him.

In Richmond, dat's where I was born, 'bout 1847, de Master said; and dat make me more dan 90-year old dis good year. I had two brothers named Webb and Norman, a half-brother Charley, and two half-sisters, Mealey and Ann. Me, I was born a slave and so was my son. His father, Toney, was one of de Mason slave boys; de Master said I was 'bout 13-year old when de boy was born.

Frank Mason was a young man when de War started, living wid his mother. Dey had lots of slaves, maybe a hundred, and dey always try to take good care of 'em; even after de War was over he worried 'bout trying to get us settled so's we wouldn't starve. De Master had overseer, but dere was no whuppings.

All de way from Richmond to a place dey call Waco, Texas, we traveled by ox-wagon and boats, and den de Master figures we all be better off over in Arkansas and goes to Pine Bluff.

What wid all de running 'round de slaves was kept clean and always wid plenty to eat and good clothes to wear. De Master was plenty rich man and done what his mother, Mis Betty Mason, told him when we all left de Big Mansion, way back dere in Richmond. De Mistress say, "Frank, you watch over dem Negroes cause dey's good men and women; keep dem clean!" Dat's what he done, up until we was freed, and den times was so hard nobody wanted us many Negroes around, and de work was scarce, too. Hard times! Folks don't know what hard times is.

When a Negro get sick de master would send out for herbs and roots. Den one of de slaves who knew how to cook and mix 'em up for medicine use would give de doses. All de men and women wore charms, something like beads, and if dey was any good or not I don't know, but we didn't have no bad diseases like after dey set us free.

I was at Pine Bluff when de Yankees was shooting all over de place. De fighting got so hot we all had to leave; dat's the way it was all de time for us during de War—running away to some place or de next place, and we was all glad when it stopped and we could settle down in a place.

We was back at Waco when de peace come, but Master Frank was away from home when dat happen. It was on a Sunday when he got back and called all de slaves up in de yard and counted all of dem, young and old.

The first thing he said was, "You men and women is all free! I'm going back to my own mammy in old Virginia, but I ain't going back until all de old people is settled in cabins and de young folks fix up wid tents!"

Den he kinder stopped talking. Seem now like he was too excited to talk, or maybe he was feeling bad and worried 'bout what he going to do wid all of us. Pretty soon he said, "You men and women, can't none of you tell anybody I ain't always been a good master. Old folks, have I ever treated you mean?" He asked. Everybody shout, "No, sir!" And Master Frank smiled; den he told us he was going 'round and find places for us to live.

He went to see Jim Tinsley, who owned some slaves, about keeping us. Tinsley said he had cabins and could fix up tents for extra ones, if his own Negroes was willing to share up with us. Dat was the way it worked out. We stayed on dere for a while, but times was so hard we finally get dirty and ragged like all de Tinsley Negroes. But Master Frank figure he done the best he could for us.

After he go back to Virginia we never hear no more of him, but every day I still pray if he has any folks in Richmond dey will find me someway before I die. Is dere someway I could find dem, you s'pose?

¹ WPA field worker Ethel Wolfe Garrison interviewed Mrs. Liza Smith at her home in Muskogee, Oklahoma, probably sometime in the winter of 1937–38. On 18 January 1938 project employee Craig Vollmer edited and typed her notes into a rough draft entitled "Interview with Liza Smith, Slave Born, Age 91, 1705 Pickens Street, Muskogee, Oklahoma," available in the OHS Slave Narratives. Later that year the rough draft was revised and retyped into an intermediate version, "Liza Smith, Age 91, Muskogee, Oklahoma," available in ribbon-copy typescript and carbon copy in the OHS Slave

Narratives. That intermediate draft was further polished on 19 October 1938 into a final draft with the same title, which is published here and which was forwarded to Washington and is available in ribbon-copy typescript in the LC Slave Narratives and in carbon copy as item 350078 in the LC Slave Narratives Carbon Copies. About the time of this interview the informant was listed in the Muskogee city directory as Mrs. Eliza Smith, widow of George Smith, residing at 1705 Pickens Avenue in the city. *Polk's Muskogee City Directory, 1932,* 176, 259.

LOU SMITH[1]

Age 83 Yrs.   *Platter, Okla.*

Sho,' I remembers de slavery days![2] I was a little gal but I can tell you lots of things about dem days. My job was nussing de younguns. I took keer of them from daylight to dark. I'd have to sing them to sleep too. I'd sing:

> By-lo Baby Bunting
> Daddy's gone a-hunting
> To get a rabbit skin
> To wrap Baby Bunting in.

Sometimes I'd sing:

> Rock-a-bye baby, in a tree top
> When de wind blows your cradle'll rock.
> When de bough breaks de crad'll fall
> Down comes baby cradle'n all.

My father was Jackson Longacre and he was born in Mississippi. My mother, Caroline, was born in South Carolina. Both of them was born slaves. My father belonged to Huriah Longacre. He had a big plantation and lots of niggers. He put up a lot of his slaves as security on a debt and he took sick and died so they put them all on de block and sold them. My father and his mother (my grandma) was sold together. My old Mistress[3] bought my grandmother and old Mistress' sister bought my grandma's sister. These white women agreed that they would never go off so far that the two slave women couldn't see each other. They allus kept this promise. A Mr. Covington offered old Master[4] $700 for me when I was about ten years old, but he wouldn't sell me. He didn't need to for he was rich as cream and my, how good he was to us.

Young Master married Miss Jo Arnold and old Master sent me and my mother over to live with them. I was small when I was took out from old man McWilliams' yard. It was his wife that bought my grandmother and my father. My mother's folks always belonged to his family. They all moved to Texas and we all lived there until after the surrender.

Miss Jo wasn't a good Mistress and mother and me wasn't happy. When young Master was there he made her treat us good but when he was gone she made our lives a misery to us. She was what we called a "low-brow." She never had been used to slaves and she treated us like dogs. She said us kids didn't need to wear any clothes and one day she told us we could jest take 'em off as it cost too much to clothe us. I was jest a little child but I knowed I oughten to go without any clothes. We wore little enough as it was. In summer we just wore one garment, a sort of slip without any sleeves. Well, anyway, she made me take off my clothes and I just crept off and cried. Purty soon young Master come home.

He wanted to know what on earth I was doing without my dress on. I told him, and my goodness, but he raised the roof. He told her if she didn't treat us better he was going to take us back to old Master. I never did have any more good times 'cepting when I'd get to go to visit at old Master's. None of our family could be sold and that was why old Master just loaned us to young Master. When old Master died, dey put all our names in a hat and all the chilluns draw out a name. This was done to 'vide us niggers satisfactory. Young Master drawed my mother's name and they all agreed that I should go with her, so back we went to Miss Jo. She wouldn't feed us niggers. She'd make me set in a corner like a little dog. I got so hungry and howled so loud they had to feed me. When the surrender come, I was eleven years old, and they told us we was free. I ran off and hid in the plum orchard and I said over'n over, "I'se free, I'se free; I ain't never going back to Miss Jo." My mother come out and got me and in a few days my father came and lived with us. He worked for young Master and the crops was divided with him. Miss Jo died and we lived on there. My mother took over the charge of the house and the chillun for young Master and we was all purty happy after that. They was a white man come into our settlement and bought a plantation and some slaves. My, but he treated them bad. He owned a boy about fifteen years old. One day he sent him on a errand. On the way home he got off his mule and set down in the shade of a tree to rest. He fell asleep and the mule went home. When he woke up he was scared to go home and he stayed out in de woods for several days. Finally they caught him and took him home and his master beat him nearly to death. He then dug a hole and put him in it and piled corn shucks all around him. This nearly killed him 'cause his body was cut up so with the whip. One of the niggers slipped off and went to the jining plantation and told about the way the boy was being treated and a bunch of white men came over and made him take the child out and doctor his wounds. This man lived there about ten years and he was so mean to his slaves 'til all the white men round who owned niggers finally went to him and told him they would just give him so long to sell out and leave. They made him sell his slaves to people there in the community, and he went back north.

My mother told me that he owned a woman who was the mother of several chillun and when her babies would get about a year or two of age he'd sell them and it would break her heart. She never got to keep them. When her fourth baby was born and was about two months old she just studied all the time about how she would have to give it up and one day she said, "I just decided I'm not going to let old Master sell this baby; he just ain't going to do it." She got up and give it something out of a bottle and purty soon it was dead. 'Course didn't nobody tell on her or he'd of beat her nearly to death. There wasn't many folks that was mean to their slaves.

Old Master's boys played with the nigger boys all the time. They'd go swimming, fishing and hunting together. One of his boys' name was Robert but everybody called him Bud. They all would catch rabbits and mark them and turn them loose. One day a boy come along with a rabbit he had caught in a trap. Old Master's boy noticed that it had Bud's mark on it and they made him turn it loose.

Old Master was his own overseer, but my daddy was the overlooker.[5] He was purty hard on them too, as they had to work just like they never got tired. The women had to do housework, spinning, sewing and work in the fields too. My mother was a housewoman and she could keep herself looking nice. My, she went around with her hair and clothes all Jenny-Lynned-up all the time until we went to live with Miss Jo. She took all the spirit out of poor mother and me too.

I remember she allus kept our cabin as clean and neat as a pin. When other niggers come to visit her they would say, "My you are Buckry Niggers" (meaning we tried to live like white folks).

I love to think of when we lived with old Master. We had a good time. Our cabin was nice and had a chimbley in it. Mother would cook and serve our breakfast at home every morning and dinner and supper on Sundays. We'd have biscuit every Sunday morning for our breakfast. That was something to look forward to.

We all went to church every Sunday. We would go the white folks' church in the morning and to our church in the evening. Bill McWilliams, old Master's oldest boy, didn't take much stock in church. He owned a nigger named Bird, who preached for us. Bill said, "Bird, you can't preach, you can't read, how on earth can you get a text out of the Bible when you can't even read? How'n hell can a man preach that don't know nothing?" Bird told him the Lord had called him to preach and he'd put the things in his mouth that he ought to say. One night Bill went to church and Bird preached the hair-raisingest sermon you ever heard. Bill told him all right to go and preach, and he gave Bird a horse and set him free to go anywhere he wanted to and preach.

Old Master and old Mistress lived in grand style. Bob was the driver of their carriage. My, but he was always slick and shiny. He'd set up in front with his white shirt and black clothes. He looked like a black martin (bird) with a white breast. The nurse set in the back with the chillun. Old Master and Mistress set together in the front seat.

Old Master and Mistress would come down to the quarters to eat Christmas dinners sometimes and also birthday dinners. It was sho' a big day when they done that. They eat first, and the niggers would sing and dance to entertain them. Old Master would walk 'round through the quarters talking to the ones that was sick or too old to work. He was awful kind. I never knowed him to whip much. Once he whipped a woman for stealing. She and mother had to spin and weave. She couldn't or didn't work as fast as Ma and wouldn't have as much to show for her day's work. She'd steal hanks of ma's thread so she couldn't do more work than she did. She'd also steal old Master's tobacco. He caught up with her and whipped her.

I never saw any niggers on the block but I remember once they had a sale in town and I seen them pass our house in gangs, the little ones in wagons and others walking. I've seen slaves who run away from their masters and they'd have to work in the field with a big ball and chain on their leg. They'd hoe out to the end of the chain and then drag it up a piece and hoe on to the end of the row.

Times was awful hard during the War. We actually suffered for some salt. We'd go to the smoke house where meat had been salted down for years, dig a hole in the ground and fill it with water. After it would stand for a while we'd dip the water up carefully and strain it and cook our food in it. We parched corn and meal for coffee. We used syrup for sugar. Some folks parched okra for coffee. When the War was over you'd see men, women and chillun walk out of their cabins with a bundle under their arm.[6] All going by in droves, just going nowhere in particular. My mother and father didn't join them; we stayed on at the plantation. I run off and got married when I was twenty. Ma never did want me to get married. My husband died five years ago. I never had no chillun.

I reckon I'm a mite superstitious. If a man comes to your house first on New Year's you will have good luck; if a woman is your first visitor you'll have bad luck. When I was a young woman I knowed I'd be left alone in my old age. I seen it in my sleep. I dreamed I spit every tooth in my head right out in my hand and something tell me I would be a widow. That's a bad thing to dream about, losing your teeth.

Once my sister was at my house. She had a little baby and we was setting on the porch. They was a big pine tree in front of the house, and we seen something that looked like a big bird light in the tree. She begun to cry and say that's a sign my baby is going to die. Sho' nuff it just lived two weeks. Another time a big owl lit in a tree near a house and we heard it holler. The baby died that night. It was already sick, we's setting up with it.

I don't know where they's hants or not but I'se sho heard things I couldn't see.

We allus has made our own medicines. We used herbs and roots. If you'll take poke root and cut it in small pieces and string it and put it 'round a baby's neck it will cut teeth easy. A tea made out of dog fennel or corn shucks will cure chills and malaria. It'll make 'em throw up. We used to take button snake root, black snake root, chips or anvil iron and whiskey and make a tonic to cure consumption. It would cure it too.

[1] Mrs. Lou Smith was interviewed by WPA field worker Mrs. Jessie R. Ervin at Platter, Oklahoma, probably sometime in spring or summer 1937. From Ervin's notes, a preliminary typescript was prepared entitled "Interview with Lou Smith (Ex-Slave, Aged 83, Platter, Oklahoma)," available in the OHS Slave Narratives. From this version, project employees prepared an edited final draft, "Lou Smith, Age 83 Yrs., Platter, Okla.," which was sent to Washington on 16 August 1937. This final draft, published here, is available in ribbon-copy typescript in the LC Slave Narratives and in carbon copy as item 350090 in the LC Slave Narratives Carbon Copies and in the OHS Slave Narratives. Benjamin A. Botkin, folklore editor for the Federal Writers' Project, appraised Lou Smith's narrative as "outstanding for its significance and interest," noting that in her expression Smith had "a sense of the right word," and he used three extracts from her remembrances in his 1945 book, *Lay My Burden Down* (39, 50, 154, 274–75, 278). B. A. B[otkin], LC Slave Narratives Appraisal Sheets, Accession no. 350090, 5 December 1940; Stephens to Cronyn, 16 August 1937, WPA Notes on Interviews.

² In the preliminary draft this sentence begins with the direct address "My good lack-a-day lady."

³ The preliminary draft consistently renders "mistress" as "mistis."

⁴ The preliminary draft consistently renders "master" as "massa."

⁵ In the preliminary draft the following sentence appears at this point: "He had to see that everybody worked."

⁶ At this point in the preliminary draft this sentence has the following additional clause struck out by a WPA editor: "the chillun would have a cup."

MOSE SMITH[1]

Age 85   *Muskogee, Oklahoma*

I was born in New Orleans, but don't remember anything about that place for I was sold to Master Jack Dunn when a little boy and moved to Paris, Texas. Master Jack and his wife, Suda, owned four pretty big farms around Paris and he was kept busy all the time going around to each of them, with me going along sometimes on a horse beside him. He'd be gone for a week at a time, come home and get some home cooking, clean up and be gone again.

There was twelve slave families on the farm where I lived and the overseers was three. More families on the other places, how many I don't know, but the old master was well fixed with slaves and money, too.

My father was Isom Smith. He lived on a different farm than mother and us children. Her name was Laura and my brother's name was Max; my sister was Rochelle. We lived in a log cabin just like all the other houses on the farm. It was two rooms, one a kitchen, but they both had fireplaces made of mud, grass and sticks, and the biggest piece of furniture was the wooden bed put together with wooden pegs.

Father worked out for extra money and every Saturday night he come over and give each of us children a nickel. That went for the old fashioned kind of horehound candy what we could get in town, or if the sweet tooth wasn't craving for it, we'd get a little can of sardines.

Before I got big enough to work in the fields the mistress would say for me to stay about the big house with her, but Master Jack say, "No, wife, get his sister. Swiger (that was my pet name in them long days), he's going with me." But lots of times they would let me sleep on the floor at the foot of Miss Julie's (Dunn's daughter) bed.

Sometimes I would do pranks around the big house and when the mistress chase me I'd run home and crawl under the bed, telling my mother not to let Mistress Suda get me. Pretty soon the mistress come to the door. "Where is Swiger?" She'd ask my mother. "He's there under the bed!"

Then I'd answer from under the bed: "If you whip me one lick I won't stay with you no more." But I knew all the time she wasn't going to whip, because both the mistress and master was good to all the colored folks. The mistress laughed and say, "Come on out from under the bed and I'll give you a gun." She did, too, a wooden gun that I played with for a long time. She was always giving me things when I was little.

When I growed up a little more they give me so many rows of cotton to hoe or pick. I work my own rows and they timed me so I had to hurry and get the work done, and when they send me off the farm to do a chore they time me on that. Sometimes I would take the axe and split rails for fence-making. There was always something to do around the place.

I even have helped with the spinning and weaving. Mother spin her colored thread and make caps and cotton clothes for us. She sewed the pants by hand and maybe make a coat to go with the pants; that made a pretty nice suit.

One time the master go away on a trip and left me behind. I'd been hearing about slaves running away and it seemed like a mighty good time for me to get away. I just walked off like I was going someplace to cut wood. Didn't cut no wood—just kept on going and going and hiding out until I [got] to Louisiana, whereabout I don't know, but long before I got safe away I was wishing to be back with the master and get full of them good baked sweet potatoes!

And then I got to thinking about how mean Maw was, how hard she'd whip me and I just kept a-going. One time she put a sack over my head, tying it with my arms inside and whipped to the hollow. God, she did whip! She was so mean the master would send her away on other farms for awhile, but she always come back, promising to do good.

That was what I was running away from more than the master. Down there in Louisiana I hid out until after the war was over and then went to work for old Doctor Thomas. Just sort of cleaned up his office and around his home. He was a good man.

I never been married like folks do nowadays. There was an Egyptian woman who had a pretty young girl and she give me the girl to live with. The girl was named Lula and we had three children.

About the war I know nothing, except I heard the folks talking about, but never seen any fighting or battles. We was too far from the ruckus, I reckon.

¹ Mose Smith was interviewed in Muskogee, Oklahoma, by Ethel Wolfe Garrison probably sometime in winter or early spring of 1938, for on 2 March of that year project employee Craig Vollmer edited and typed her now lost rough draft from the interview into the narrative "Interview with Mose Smith, Slave Born, Age 85, 2202 No. Euclid Ave., Muskogee, Oklahoma," available in the OHS Slave Narratives. At some later date the interview was slightly revised and retyped into final form as the typescript "Mose Smith, Age 85, Muskogee, Oklahoma," published here and likewise available in the OHS Slave Narratives. For reasons not known, this narrative was never forwarded to Washington.

R. C. SMITH¹

Age 96   *Alderson, Oklahoma*

One morning in May
I heard a poor rebel say;
"The federal's a home guard
Dat called me from home. . . ."

I wish I was a merchant
And I could write a fine hand,
I'd write a love letter
So she would understand.

I wish I had a drink of brandy,
And a drink of wine,
To drink wid dat sweet gal
How I wish dat she was mine.

If I had a drink of brandy
No longer would I roam,
I'd drink it wid dat gal of mine
Dat wishes me back home.

I've heard the soldiers sing that song a heap of times. They sung it kind of lonesome like and I guess it sort of made them home sick to sing it. Us niggers learned to sing it and it is about the only one I can sing yet. I remembers the words to another one we used to sing but I've forgot the tune but the words go like this:

Old man, old man,
Your hair is getting gray,
I'd foller you ten thousand miles
To hear your banjo play.

I never was much at singing though. I guess my voice is just about wore out just like my body.

I've always had good health and I never had a doctor in my life. In the last three or four years I've had some pains from rheumatism. I think all our sickness is brought on by the kidneys and I made my own kidney medicine and allus stayed well.

I used to get a weed called hoarhound, it grows everywhere wild. I'd make a tea and drink it and it would cure the worst kind of kidney ailment. Peach tree leaves tea and sumac seed tea also were good kidney medicines. These were old Indian remedies.

My father was half Cherokee Indian. His father was bought by an Indian woman and she took him for her husband. She died and my grandfather, father and Auntie were bought by John Ross.[2] He later bought up a lot of land claims from some Indian people named Tibets and he paid for the claims with slaves. My father was in this trade. Ross kept my grandfather till he died and he gave my auntie to one of his sisters. All of her offspring live up around Tahlequah now. My father played with Cornelius Boudinot when he was a child.[3] Cherokee Bill was my second cousin.[4]

My auntie hated being a slave. She had to take care of the babies on the farm while their mothers worked in the field. Sometimes she would git cranky and wouldn't speak to anybody for a week. This only made it harder for her but I guess she just couldn't help it.

My father was a big man, he weighed around 225 lbs. He had never been treated bad and it was purty hard for him to git used to being a slave. His master ordered him to be whupped and he wouldn't stand for it and he put up such a fight that they had him took to Fayettesville, Arkansas, and put in jail and held them there for sale. Didn't anybody want a big unruly ox of a nigger so he stayed in jail a long time.

Presley R. Smith was the jailer and he was kind to Pappy. They was two outlaws in jail at the same time pappy was and one day he overheard them plotting to git out. They planned that when the jailer brought their meal to them that they would overpower him and take his keys and git out.

Sure enough when he come in that evening one of them knocked him down. No sooner than he done it my pappy waded in and took them by surprise and laid them both out. He kept them both from escaping and killing the jailer. Smith went right out and hunted up pappy's owner and give him $600 for him.

Pappy's owner was more than glad to sell him as he considered him a bad old darky. Smith took him home and never from that day on did he have a bit of trouble with him. He never allowed his grown slaves to be whupped and when they went away from home he didn't write them no passes either. The patrollers didn't pay them no mind for they knowed Smith took care of his own niggers. We was all known as "Smith's free niggers."

My mother was give to Smith by his father when he married.

Our family didn't live in no quarters but we lived in one open room of the big house. The house was built in the shape of an "L." A big white house, three rooms across the front and three in the "L." We lived in the back one of the "L." A big gallery ran clean across the front and one went down the "L." The kitchen was away from the house but was joined to it by a plank walk. All around the house was big trees what we called "Heavenly trees" but the right name for them was Paradise trees. They made a heavy shade. Old Mistress had lots of purty flowers and they was a row of cedars from the gate to the house. The house was built in a rocky place and up above the house pappy built a stone wall and we had a garden on the level place along side of the wall. We called it the high place. There was enough level ground for a nice size garden. We also had a peach and apple orchard. We raised figs, too.

Master Smith always remembered about my father saving his life and he was good to him. Pappy learned the stone mason's trade and old Master let him hire out and he let him keep the money that he made.

Old Master's children went to school and they would come home and try to learn us everything they learned at school. I couldn't be still long enough to learn anything but my pappy and mammy both learned to read and write.

Old Master Smith was elected County Clerk and he held the office till the War broke out and for a while after. There wasn't much work for my pappy to do as he just looked after the garden and yard so old Master let him work at his trade as stone mason all over the country. Old Master was reasonably wealthy and very prominent. He owned a big farm but it wasn't all in cultivation. He had nine slaves besides our family and they worked the farm. Pappy took care of the yard, garden and barn and mammy done the cooking. Us children run errands, minded the flies off the table at meal-time and also minded them off Old Mistress when she took her nap. We also brought the cows or calves and as soon as we got big enough we helped mammy with the milking. None of us worked very hard except mother. I think back and I don't hardly remember ever seeing her setting down unless she was sewing or weaving. Poor thing, hard work was all she ever knowed.

My master refugeed me to Texas at the outbreak of the War. We went down in the winter and it was awful cold. We crossed the Indian Territory and the snow was two foot deep. We went out in west Texas on a ranch. The Kiowa and Comanche Indians give them a lot of trouble. They was always slipping into the country and stealing horses and cattle.

The owner of the ranch had a boy named Charley. He and I would ride, rope calves, and play around. We had good times together. His father would let us go with the boys sometimes when they went on round-ups.

One day the men started out to round up and brand the young stock and we wanted to go. Charley's father, for some reason, did not want us to go and he told us to stay at home. After they left he saddled his horse and started after them. He said that his father would let him stay with the outfit if he just caught up with them. I wouldn't go with him so he went without me. I can still see him as he turned and waved to me just before he rode out of sight. I couldn't help wishing that I could go with him but I dassent disobey the Master.

Nobody ever saw Charley again. They tracked his horse for several miles. That was easy as his horse had shoes on it. His horse was running and there was other tracks along with his that we supposed belong to a band of Kiowas or Cheyennes. They were hidden and the cowboys passed them but when Charley come by they surprised him and finally captured him. I'm sure they killed him for he would a come back if he could have. I always wished I'd gone with him for they wouldn't bother a nigger but they sure had it in for white folks. I missed my friend so I could hardly stay on at the ranch. I never had no good times any more.

My Master went to Clarksville, Texas and bought a herd of cattle and I went over there and we took them to the Indian Territory around Webbers Falls in the Cherokee Nation and herded them there. I was there till the close of the war. My father and a lot more of the slaves of the neighbors around Fayettesville had slipped away and joined the northern army in Kansas. They belonged to the first and second Kansas regiment.[5] They heard that if they would join up with the Yankees they would be set free so that's what they done.

Father died in Lawrence, Kansas at the close of the War. He and Mother never saw each other again after he enlisted. He died with pneumonia. Never got to enjoy his freedom after he fought so hard for it.

I was 17 or 18 years old when Abe Lincoln declared us free but I never got my freedom till August 4, 1866. Slaves in Texas never got their freedom till June 19, 1867 [*sic*].

We had an awful hard time after the War. My brother and I got a job in the Indian Territory as cowboys and we sent our money to mother when we could. She was an extra good cook and she managed to make a living for herself and my two sisters. Brother and I had a few head of stock that we sold and we bought her a house in Fayettesville and after that we got along purty well. We had a home to go to when we wanted to. I was a purty bad boy. I knowed a lot of outlaws. Knowed Belle Starr well.[6] I never got mixed up in any of their shady dealings though. It's a wonder that I didn't though as there was plenty of it going on and I was a regular little dare-devil.

I was always so pert that it seemed like everybody wanted me to work for them. I never did have no trouble getting a job. I never had nobody that I ever worked for to turn me off.

There was an old man in Fayettesville, old Judge West, that we always sort of shunned. He and my father had a little trouble once and we supposed he would hold it agin us boys. My father's master took the job of putting a fence around the court house and grounds and he had my pappy out doing the job. Old Judge West come out and found fault with the way he was setting the posts. A nigger wasn't supposed to talk back but Pappy got back at the Judge. The old Judge got mad and said that he was going to have him whupped and he went to pappy's master and told him that he had to have him whupped publicly. Old Master wouldn't do it and for a while there was a sight of hard feelings over it.

One day after the surrender I met up with old Judge West. He asked me who my master was and I told him Presley R. Smith. He said, "Oh yes, you are one of Dave's boys." I told him that I was and he said, "He had a heap more sense than that master of his."

Jest before the War they had a heap of trouble with the Underground Railroaders. Nearly everybody lost one or two slaves. Old Judge West had a sight of vexation about that time. I remember he lost one of his men who got clean away to the north and he couldn't git him back. Another one decided he would try his hand at gitting away so he stole a horse and a suit of clothes and away he went. He got away to free territory and if the fool had had sense enough sense to a sold the horse they never would a done nothing about it but he strutted around with a fine horse and a fine broadcloth suit and his master told them that he'd stole the horse so they had to let him go back with his master. Judge West was purty hard on his slaves.

As I said I was a cousin to Cherokee Bill. He was a good feller when he was sober but he was hard to git along with when he was drinking. He always carried a pistol and he was a perfect shot so he was dangerous and everybody was scared to death of him. I could always handle him and git him to go home with me but I wasn't always with him.

Bill's trouble come about through ignorance. They was at a dance and several federal officers come there looking for a man. They finally got into a battle and one of the laws was killed. There was about thirty men in the battle and all was shooting to kill but Bill was known as a good shot and everybody said that ever time he shot somebody fell and they accused Bill of murder. He started scouting around first one place and then another. I still say they wouldn't a done nothing to him if he hadn't a shot that blacksmith. He went into town to have his horse shod and he didn't have the money to pay for it and the blacksmith wanted to hold the horse and Bill shot and killed him.

Bill's sweetheart lived in the neighborhood and he'd slip back once in a while to see her. Clint Scales, a colored deputy, said he would arrest him. Clint come to the girl's house and found Bill there. He never said anything to Bill about going to arrest him and they was setting there talking. Bill stooped over to get a coal of fire to light a cigarette and Clint hit him over the head with a fire stick and knocked him out and took him to jail in Fort Smith.

He might of got out of this if he hadn't shot the jailer at Fort Smith. After he had been in jail about a month his sister managed to slip a gun in to him. If he had waited till the jailer brought his supper to him and of taken the keys away from him he might of got away but he took the gun and tried to make the jailer open the door and let him out but the jailer wouldn't do it so he shot and killed him.

They hung Bill at Fort Smith and when they asked him if he had anything to say he said, "I didn't come out here to talk, I come out here to die." He was plucky to the last.

We had a lot of trouble gitting things settled after the War. I remember some excitement that we had in Arkansas over a governor's election. It caused what we called State War. I was about nineteen at the time and I was eager to enlist but they didn't need me. Baxter, a Democrat, and Brooks, Republican, was both running for governor.

When the election was held there was so much fraud that you couldn't tell who was elected. Sides was drawn and they built up breastworks there on the State house grounds at Little Rock. They actually had war. The state house is right on the river and a steam boat, the Hallis, belonging to a man named Houston went to Fort Smith and come back loaded with Baxter men. Brooks' men cracked down on the boat with infantry rifles—these rifles shot a ball as big as the end of your finger and there was so many holes shot in the boat that it sunk and Houston was killed. Finally the United States militia was sent down and after about two months they settled it peaceably. Baxter was declared governor and Brooks was appointed postmaster.[7]

I went back and forth from the Cherokee Nation to Fayettesville until my mother died. Then I married and settled there till I decided to go to Lehigh, Indian Territory and dig coal. My wife died there in 1900 and I've been batching ever since.

After my wife died I couldn't hardly do my work. I would go down into the pit and try to load coal and I'd have a room full but I couldn't load one car. I was so dissatisfied that I decided to go down in the mountains by myself for a while. I went down into the McGee Mountains the other side of Atoka.

I am a prophet, yessum, the kind you read about in the Bible. I was born one. I can see and talk with hosts of people. AmHouf, a famous prophet in London, say that I was born to be a prophet but I had a poor chance. I wrote to AmHouf and kept up a correspondence with him till his death.

I wandered around in them mountains for days. I never seen a varmit, not even a wolf. One night I took a notion I'd go home. When I come to Boggy, just below Atoka, I started to walk across on a footlog. Just as I started to step on it I heard somebody say, "Look out, you'll fall." I looked around and I couldn't see nobody. I started two or three times to cross and every time I'd hear them say, "Look out, you'll fall." I turned and went to the bridge about a quarter of a mile down the stream. I crossed and come back up to the footlog. I could still hear people talking but I couldn't see nobody.

By this time I done got hungry so I went up to a house to try to buy something to eat. The man told me where there was a store and I went there and bought some sardines and crackers. The storekeeper told me if I could course my way through the wood that it would be a lot nearer. I went on about a mile and built a fire and camped for the night.

Next morning I started on and all of a sudden I heard a Wham. It sounded like somebody loading cross ties. Purty soon I seen about twenty-five or thirty people. One real old man and a woman in a wagon with wood on it. I walked on to meet them and the man hailed me with the Odd Fellows sign. The woman had on a gray coat and the man snatched it off her and put it on his shoulders and the woman disappeared. I walked up and tried to touch him but couldn't. Just then I realized that I had seen Father Abraham—Yessum, the one we read about in the Bible. I looked around and recognized my father and a lot more people. Some of them had just been buried but my father had been dead ever since the War. I didn't talk to them as they all disappeared.

When I got home I had a letter from AmHouf saying that he needed me. I answered his letter but another prophet answered me and told me AmHouf was dead.

I see things all the time. I'm in what they calls "firey trivets." I can foresee and foretell. Moses and the old prophets was in the firey trivets. I'm a natural born treasure hunter. I don't need no instruments to find treasure. I can walk over it at night and tell where it is located. I'm trying to raise one-hundred dollars right now to try to finance a trip for me on a treasure hunt. I know just where it is located but it will take a hundred dollars to git it out.

I ain't been able to do nothing for a month on account of the hosts that surround me. Their presence is so powerful over me that they weaken me.

Prayer and faith can overcome everything. Remember Jesus Christ was called Bellzebub but that didn't make it true.

---

[1] Mrs. Jessie R. Ervin interviewed R. C. Smith in Alderson, Oklahoma, on 8 December 1937, as part of the Federal Writers' Project in Oklahoma. In 1977 George P. Rawick published the narrative produced as a result of the interview, citing it as preserved in the Oklahoma Historical Society. Rawick apparently secured it from Dr. Norman R. Yetman, who with his children and research assistants reproduced some of the Oklahoma slave narratives used by Rawick for the supplement series to his multivolume compilation of American slave narratives. The original typescript of that narrative, however, apparently was lost sometime between Yetman's work at the Oklahoma Historical Society in the 1970s and the initiation of the present editorial project in 1990. Rawick, *The American Slave,* supplement series I, 12:xiii-xiv, xliii, 280–92; William D. Welge, [Director, Archives and Manuscripts Division], Oklahoma Historical Society, Oklahoma City, Oklahoma, to T. Lindsay Baker, 13 January 1994, telefacsimile letter in Baker's possession.

[2] For the life of the Cherokee chief John Ross, see Rachel Caroline Eaton, *John Ross and the Cherokee Indians;* Gary E. Moulton, *John Ross, Cherokee Chief.*

[3] Elias Cornelius Boudinot, brigadier general in the Confederate States Army, became

one of the most prominent attorneys in the Cherokee Nation. Muriel H. Wright, "Notes on Colonel Elias C. Boudinot," *Chronicles of Oklahoma* 41 (Winter 1963–64): 382–407.

[4] For other remembrances and information about Cherokee Bill (Crawford Goldsby), see the narrative of Joe Bean, above, as well as additional material farther into this narrative.

[5] The Kansas First and Second Colored Volunteer Infantry served through much of the Civil War, part of the time in the Indian Territory. For an overview of Civil War black military service in present-day Oklahoma, see Lary C. Rampp, "Negro Troop Activity in Indian Territory, 1863–1865," *Chronicles of Oklahoma* 47 (Spring 1969): 531–59.

[6] For remembrances of Belle Starr, see the narrative of Milton Starr, below.

[7] For background on the 1873 election between Elisha Baxter and Joseph Brooks, see Florene Pauline Edwards, "Civil War and Reconstruction in Arkansas" (M.A. thesis, University of Oklahoma, 1930), 111–23; Jimmy Hefley, "The Brooks-Baxter War," *Arkansas Historical Quarterly* 14 (Summer 1955): 188–92.

JAMES SOUTHALL[1]

Age 82 Years   *Alderson, Oklahoma*

I was born in Clarksville, Tenn. My father was Wesley and my mother was Hagar Southall. Our owner was Dr. John Southall, an old man. Father always belonged to him but he bought my mother when she was a young girl and raised her. She never knew anything 'bout her people but my father's mother lived with us in de quarters at Master Southall's.[2] Master John never sold any of his slaves.

We was known as "Free Niggers." Master said he didn't believe it was right to own human beings just because dey was black, and he freed all his slaves long before de War. He give 'em all freedom papers and told dem dat dey was free as he was and could go anywhere dey wanted. Dey didn't have nowhere to go so we all stayed on wid him. It was nice though to know we could go where we pleased 'thout having to get a pass and could come back when we pleased even if we didn't take advantage of it.

He told his slaves dat dey could stay on at his farm but dey would have to work and make a living for deyselves and families. Old Master managed de farm and bought all de food and clothes for us all. Everybody had to work, but dey had a good time.

We had good clothes, plenty of food and good cabins. We had what was known as Georgia bedsteads. Dey was wooden bedsteads wid holes bored in de side pieces and in de foot and head-boards. Ropes was laced back and forth across and this took de place of both slats and springs. De ropes would git loose and we had what was called a "following-pin" to tighten 'em wid. We'd take a block of wood wid a notch in it and catch de rope and hold it till de following-pin could be driven in and den we'd twist de ropes tight again. We had grass or cotton beds and we slept good, too.

We had tin plates but no knives or forks so we et with our fingers. Old Master was a doctor and we had good attention when we was sick. We had no wish to take advantage of our freedom for we was a lot better off even than we is now and we knowed it. We never had to worry about anything.

De quarters was about a half mile from de "Big House" as we called Master John's house. It really wasn't such a big house as it had only four or five rooms in it. It was a common boxed house, painted white and wid a long gallery across de front. Maybe it was de gallery dat made it look so big to us. We liked to set on de steps at night and listen to Master John talk and to hear old Mistress and de girls sing. Sometimes we'd join in wid dem and fairly make de woods ring. Everybody thought dey was crazy to let us have so much freedom but dey wasn't nothing any of us black folks wouldn't a-done for that family.

He never employed any overseers as he done his own overseeing. He'd tell de older hands what he wanted done and dey would see it was done. We was never punished. Jest iffen dey didn't work dey didn't have nothing to eat and wear and de hands what did work wouldn't divide wid 'em iffen dey didn't work. Old Master sho' was wise fer he knowed iffen we was ever set free dat we would have to work and he sure didn't bide no laziness in his hands. Dey got up 'bout four o'clock in de morning and was at work as soon as dey could see. Dey would work and sing as happy as you please.

We used to hear stories 'bout how slaves was punished but we never saw any of it. Dey would punish 'em by whupping 'em or by making 'em stand on one foot for a long time, tie 'em up by de thumbs as high as dey could reach and by making 'em do hard tasks and by going without food for two–three days.

Niggers was very religious and dey had church often. Dey would annoy de white folks wid shouting and singing and praying and dey would take cooking pots and put over dey mouths so de white folks couldn't hear 'em. Dey would dig holes in de ground too, and lie down when dey prayed.

Old Master let us have church in de homes. We had prayer-meeting every Wednesday night. All our cullud preachers could read de Bible. He let dem teach us how to read iffen we wanted to learn.

In de evening when we was through wid our work dey would

gather at one of de cabins and visit and sing or dance. We'd pop corn, eat walnuts, peanuts, hickory nuts, and tell ghost stories. We didn't have any music instruments so de music we danced by wasn't so very good. Everybody sang and one or two would beat on tin pans or beat bones together.

Us boys played marbles. I got to be a professional. I could hit de middler ever time. We made a square and put a marble in each corner and one in de middle and got off several feet from de ring and shot at de marbles. Iffen you hit de middler you got de game. I could beat 'em all.

Old Master kept us through de War. We saw Yankee soldiers come through in droves lak Coxey's Army. We wasn't afraid for ourselves but we was afraid dey would catch old Master or one of de boys when dey would come home on a furlough. We'd hep 'em git away and just swear dat dey hadn't been home a-tall.

After de war we stayed until old Master died. It broke us all up for we knowed we had lost de best friend dat we ever had or ever would have. He was a sort of father to all of us. Old Mistress went to live with her daughter and we started wandering 'round. Some folks from de North came down and made de cullud folks move on. I guess dey was afraid dat we'd hep our masters rebuild dey homes again. We lived in a sort of bondage for a long time.

De white folks in de South as well as de cullud folks lost de best friend dey had when Abe Lincoln was killed. He was God's man[3] and it was a great loss when he died.

God created us all free and equal. Somewhere along de road we lost out.

Cullud folks would have been better off iffen dey had been left alone in Africa. We'd a-had better opportunities. We should have some compensation for what we have suffered. Yes, we could be sent back and we'd like it if dey would help us to get started out again. Dat's where our forefathers come from.

I learned a long time ago dat dey was nothing to charms. How could a rabbit's foot bring me good luck? De Bible teaches me better'n dat. I believes in dreams though. I've seen de end of time in my dreams. Saw de great trouble we going through right now, years ago in a dream. It's clear in my mind how de world is coming to a end.

I believe all Christians should all join up together as dat makes 'em stronger. I believe in praying for what we want and need. I'm a licensed preacher in de Baptist church. I've been a member for forty years but have just been a licensed preacher about ten years.

[1] WPA field worker Mrs. Jessie R. Ervin interviewed James Southall in Alderson, Oklahoma, on 5 October 1937. A preliminary draft of Southall's interview is available as the typescript "Interview with James Southall (Ex-Slave, Aged 82, Alderson, Oklahoma)" in the OHS Slave Narratives. This version was edited and retyped into a final draft, "James Southall, Age 82 Years, Oklahoma City [*sic*], Oklahoma," published here and available in ribbon copy in the LC Slave Narratives and in carbon copy as item 350027 in the LC Slave Narratives Carbon Copies and in the OHS Slave Narratives. The final draft was sent to Washington on 2 November 1937 and rubber-stamped "received" there three days later. Stephens to Cronyn, 2 November 1937, WPA Notes on Intreviews.

[2] The preliminary draft renders "master" as "marse" or "massa."

[3] The preliminary draft states "emissary" rather than "man."

MILTON STARR[1]

Age 80   *Gibson Station, Oklahoma*

I was born a slave, but was not treated like other slaves and my folks never told me anything about slavery. So there is very little I can tell of those days. My birthplace was in the old Flint District of the Cherokee Nation; the nearest town was Russellville, Arkansas, and the farm was owned by Jerry Starr, half-breed Cherokee, who was my master and father. They told me I was born February 24, 1858, right in my master's house, and when I was a baby had the care of the average white child.

My mother was Jane Coursey of Tennessee, a slave girl picked up by the Starrs when they left that country with the rest of the Cherokee Indians. My mother wasn't bought, but was stole by the Indians, and when she was freed she went back to Tennessee; I stayed with Starr family and was raised by Millie and Jerry Starr.

Jerry Starr said when the Cherokees come to this country they crossed Barron Fork Creek east of Proctor (Okla.); they were riding in a Government wagon and they crossed Barron Fork on ice so thick the mules and wagons didn't break through.

My master had a brother named Tom Starr, and he came to this country with some earlier Cherokees than did Jerry. Tom settled at Walking-Stick Spring east of Tahlequah, where he had 20 slaves working on a 40-acre patch of rocks and sand, or at least that's the way Jerry Starr always talked about Tom's place. He said all the slaves did was fish and hunt.

The Starrs got mixed up with some pretty bad folks, too, after the war. I heard about it when I was a young man; about how Tom Starr had a son named Sam who married a white woman the folks called Belle Star.[2] She was the baddest woman in the whole country before she got killed down on her farm near Briartown, about 1888, I think it was. Shot from her horse, but they never found out who killed her.

Old Tom was a kind of outlaw too, but not like his son's wife. He never went around robbing trains and banks, his troubles was all account of Indian doings long before the war, so they say. Seem like they said he killed a man name Buffington and run away to Texas for a long time, but he come back when the Cherokee Government send word for Tom to come back home and behave himself.

Jerry Starr was close kin to another mixed-blood Cherokee who was a bad man that most of the folks nowadays remember pretty well. He was Henry Starr[3] and it ain't been long ago that he robbed a bank over in Arkansas and got hisself shot in the back before he could get away with the money. (Henry was killed at Harrison, Arkansas, in 1921, during an attempted bank robbery, but the old Negro couldn't remember the date.) The Starr boys always seem to be in pecks of trouble most of the time.

Jerry Starr was known best around the place of Tahlequah where we all moved to after the war. I saw a hanging there; Lizzie Redbird was hanged for selling dope of some kind. The hanging tree was an old oak that stood near the little creek that runs on the edge of town. Don't know if it's still there or not.

There's one Indian law I remember Jerry Starr told me about, and it was the death law. If an Indian found any silver, or gold, or any kind of mineral that was rich, he was to hide it and never tell anybody about it or where it was. If anybody went against that law he was bound to die.

My mistress and stepmother had three girls; Mamie, Ella and Tiger. They had some slave girls and one of them, Jessie, I married long after the war, in 1883. We went to Tyler, Texas, for awhile, but she died and years later I married Jenona Alberty. We had two girls, Irena and Esther, but they're both dead.

But, like I said, my folks never told me about slavery; they never whipped me, always treated like I was one of the family, because I was, so I can't tell anything about them days.

---

[1] Milton Starr was interviewed at Gibson Station, Oklahoma, by WPA field worker Ethel Wolfe Garrison probably sometime in the early winter of 1937–38. Her initial transcript of the interview, no longer surviving, was edited and typed by project employee Craig Vollmer on 11 January 1938 as the text "Interview with Milton Starr, Slave Born, Age 80, Gibson Station, Oklahoma" in the OHS Slave Narratives. This transcript then was further polished into a final form on 19 October 1938. Published here, that typescript is available as "Milton Starr, Age 80, Gibson Station, Oklahoma"

in the OHS Slave Narratives. This interview was never forwarded to project headquarters in Washington.

[2] For a book-length biography of Belle Star, see Glenn Shirley, *Belle Starr and Her Times: The Literature, the Facts, and the Legends.*

[3] For background on Henry Starr, see Mary Scott Gordon, interview by Jennie Selfridge [at unidentified location], 31 March 1937, Indian-Pioneer Papers, 4:101–11; "Henry Starr's Career as Bandit Ends with Death in Cell: Bullet Wound in His Spine Proves Fatal," *Daily Oklahoman,* 23 February 1921, 2; Wellman, *Dynasty of Western Outlaws,* 253–57, 286–91; "Wound Proves Fatal to Old Time Bad Man," *Indian Journal* (Eufala, Okla.), 24 February 1921, 1.

INTERVIEW WITH J. W. STINNETT[1]

Slave Born, Age 75   *Route 1, Box 139, Muskogee, Oklahoma*

What with raising nine grandchildren whose mammy is dead, this old head of mine has too many troubles to remember much about them slave days, but anyways I was born in 1863, at a place in Grayson County, Texas, name of Prairie Grove.

My mammy come from Virginia, where pappy come from I don't know, and where he went I don't know, because he take off to the north during the war and never come back. His name was George Stinnett and mammy's name was Mary Stinnett. They belonged to a big and fat Creek Indian name of Frank Stinnett who one time lived right around Muskogee here. That was before the War I guess, for mammy told me when the fighting begun the old master bundled up a tent with some food stuffs and moved down to Texas, taking mammy and pappy with him. They was his only slaves and they said he treated them good and fed them good.

That old Indian live in a tent during the summer and cook everything on the open fire, but in the winter he go into his log cabin, coming out once in a while for to hunt squirrels and rabbits for the stew. Mammy said he didn't have much of a farm, just a little patch of garden ground. After they moved to Texas my mammy said she broke the planting ground with oxen, then when pappy run off she had all the work to do in the house and in the field.

[1] WPA field worker Ethel Wolfe Garrison interviewed J. W. Stinnett in Muskogee, Oklahoma, probably sometime in the winter of 1937–38. On 3 February 1938 her coworker Craig Vollmer edited and typed her now nonexistent rough draft into an intermediate draft of Stinnett's remembrances. This narrative, never forwarded to Washington, is available in ribbon-copy typescript as "Interview with J. W. Stinnett, Slave Born, Age 75, Route 1, Box 139, Muskogee, Oklahoma" in the OHS Slave Narratives and is published here.

EVA STRAYHORN[1]

Age 79   *McAlester, Oklahoma*

When I was a child in Arkansas we used to go to camp-meetings with the white folks. We went right along by they side till we got to church and we set down on the back seat. We took part in all services. When they wasn't any church our old Master would call us in on Sunday morning and read the Bible to us and we would sing some good old songs and den go 'bout our ways. Some of the songs that we sung still ring in my ears and I still remember the words to some of them:

> "Must Jesus bear the cross alone
> And all the world go free . . .
> No, there's a cross for everyone
> And there's a cross for me."

Another one was:

> "Oh, Jesus is a rock in a weary land,
> A weary land, a weary land;
> Jesus is a rock in a weary land
> A shelter in the time of storm."

We sung a lot of others such as: "I am Bound for the Promised Land," "The Old Time Religion," and "When I Can Read My Title Clear, To Mansions In The Skies." My favorites was the ones I just give you and they are still my favorite songs.

I was born in Johnson County, Clarksville, Arkansas. My father was Henry and my mother was Cindy Newton. Master Bill Newton owned them both.

Father was owned by a man named Perry when he first married my mother and he had to have a pass every time he come to visit her. The Patrollers give him so much trouble dat Old Man Bill Newton just put a stop to it by buying father from his master.

Master Newton let my father build a nice little two-room log house just outside the regular quarters and he went with him to the Turners[2] and had two nice bedsteads made, the kind that had ropes laced across for springs. Father then made some white-oak chairs with split bottoms. Mother made some rag rugs and they settled down to keeping house. We had a nice big fireplace and we had a cozy little home and was as happy as the day was long.

Our old Master was a really good man. He was kind to us and provided well for us. He never allowed his slaves to be whipped and if any of them was sick he saw to it that they was well cared for and had a doctor if dey needed one.

Mother was the cook for the white folks and all the food for everybody was cooked in the kitchen at the big house. The white folks' food was carried to the dining room and our food was carried to our homes. I reckon we had the same food that dey had for I know we always had plenty of good food.

We had a nigger overseer. Some folks called colored overseers "nigger drivers" or "nigger overlookers." This overseer had complete charge of the plantation and the hands, for old Master was hardly ever at home. He was a Legislator at Little Rock.

The overseer's name was Solomon and he had the right name for he sure was a smart man. When he was a young boy he used to take his young mistress, Miss Liza, to school. She was jest a little girl and if the road was muddy he would carry her on his shoulder. She was his special charge and he would a died for her. Dey would sit down to rest by de roadside and she would learn him out of her books. Dey would do this every day and soon he could read as good as she could. As she growed up she kept learning more and Solomon had married and Miss Liza would go down to his cabin every night and teach him some more. His wife learned to read a little.

Miss Liza finally married and went away and nobody knowed Solomon could read, as Miss Liza never had said anything about teaching him for she was afraid her pappy wouldn't like it. One night old Master went down to his house to give him orders for the next day and there set Sol with the Bible on his lap. Old Master said, "Sol, what are you doing with that Book?" Sol say, "I'ze reading it, Marse Bill. I ain't going to tell you no lie about it." Master Bill say, "How on earth did you learn to read?" Sol told him that Miss Liza learnt him when he used to tote her to school. Master Bill set there a minute and he said, "I want you to read it to me." Sol read it to him jest like he was talking it off. This sure did tickle Master Bill and he told him that he wanted him to practice up good, that he was going to have his head examined on Sunday. This sort of scared old Sol but he went ahead and sure enough on Sunday they was several men come out from town and old Master had Sol read for dem. A Dr. Weems was in the crowd. He had Sol set down in a chair and he felt all over his head and talked all de time he was examining them. He told old Master that Sol was an on-commonly smart man.

I never did have no regular job. There was two other children that lived with us, one a girl about my age and size. Her name was Ann.

Me and her had to run errands for our old Miss and my mother. We swept and dusted the white folks' house, swept the yards, carried water from the spring and drove the calves to the pasture and any other little job dat we was big enough to do. Sometimes mother would let us help her cook and we liked that best of all.

The country began to be all torn up and everybody was talking about war. Dey commenced recruiting soldiers and all de young men went off to de army.

Old Master had two sons, Robert and William. Dey had been to California to the gold fields for two or three year. When they come home old Master hoped dey would settle down and stay at home so he give dem some slaves. He gave my old grandmother and two of her children to Master William and he gave Hannah and her brother to Master Robert. Dey kept dem for awhile and den dey said de war was coming on and dey would be likely to lose dem anyway so dey was going to sell dem and realize something from dem. Old Master tried to get dem to keep dem but dey wouldn't do it. My grandmother and her children sold together for $1,100. The other poor woman, Hannah, was sold away from her children. Ann was about seven year old and Frank was five. When she left she said to my mother, "Cindy, be a mother to my children, will you? I hate to leave dem, poor little things, but I can't help myself. Dere poor father is dead and only God knows what will become of dem," and dey took her away to Texas.[3]

Mother kept her promise and took de two children into our house and looked after dem jest like dey was hers. Old Miss Tessie and Master Bill loved dem and was awful good to dem, too.

Both of Master Bill's boys went to de army. Dere wasn't no men or boys at home during de war. The white men dat was not too old was in de army and de colored men and boys had been refugeed to Texas. Dere owners thought dat if dey could get dem to Texas dey wouldn't have to free dem. De women had to do all de work. Mother had to work mighty hard as she had to cut wood and haul it in with a team of oxen. Us children helped her all we could.

Master Bill and Miss Tessie talked things over and dey decided that Master Bill would slip away after night with his colored men and boys and keep dem in Texas for awhile and maybe dey could save dem dat way. He thought dat Miss Tessie would be safe at home with mother and us children. One night about midnight he took father and Jim and Sol and all the boys over ten year old and dey left for Texas and we never saw dem anymore for a long time.

Young Master William was shot in the war and dey brought him home. He lived about a week after dey brought him back. Master Robert found out dat his brother was about to die and he and a squad of men slipped back home to see him. Dey dassent stay at home but scouted 'round in the woods nearby.

One morning 'bout daylight my mother called me and Ann and told us to go to the big house, dat Miss Tessie had something to tell us. She told us that she wanted us to go on up on de hill and for me to stand at de corner of the field and for Ann to go a little further on and for us to watch for the blue-coated soldiers. She had heard dat dere was a squad scouting around in de neighborhood trying to catch Master Robert and his friends. Well, me and Ann went to our posts and set down to watch. I was too young and sleepy to bother much about soldiers or anything else so I put my head down on my knees and went fast asleep. The next thing I knew I heard guns popping all 'round me right over my head. I jumped up and looked down de road and saw my mother with her hands full of food and coffee. She was on her way to take food to Master Robert and de soldiers had seen her and were shooting at her. I jumped up and ran to her jest as fast as I could and de soldiers quit shootin' when dey saw me. Mother stood right still and de soldiers rode right by us jest like we wasn't dere. Dey rode in the direction dat mother was going and found de boys and Master Robert. Dey started runnin' but most of dem was captured but none of dem was killed. Dey shot a fine black horse down from under one man and it fell on him and of course dey got him. Master Robert and one of de boys jumped in a creek and hid under a big drift and dey didn't catch dem.

Mother was wearing a white sunbonnet and it had three holes shot in it, one in the tail and two in the crown. Dey put out poor spies when dey put me and Ann out to watch.

All the colored people in de country, men, women and children, 'cept mother and her children and de two little children dat Hannah left in her care, had gone wid de soldiers to de north where dey would be set free. Mother wouldn't leave for she told de officers, "Henry is in de South and I'll never see him again if I leave de old home place for he won't know where to find me." De officer told her dat he was coming back de next day after us and for her to be ready to go. Mother told Miss Tessie dat she was going to town and take the oath of peace and dey couldn't make her leave. Old Miss told her to go on, so that night she hitched up the oxen and took her children and set out to Dover, Arkansas, twelve miles away, to see the bureau man[4] and take the oath.

We traveled till 'bout midnight and come to a man's house that we knew. He let us stay all night and we was up by good daylight and on our way again. We come to a creek and it was up. It was runnin' wild and mother was afraid to try to cross it. A man come along and he tied de wagon bed down with hickory withes so we could cross. Mother drove in and de oxen swum and drug de wagon along behind dem. We crossed safely and drove till we come to a narrow pass in de mountains. Blue coat soldiers began to pass us, walking two and two. Mother stopped de wagon and when dey would come up to it dey would separate and one would go on one side of de wagon and one on de other, but dey didn't say anything to us. It seemed like dey was in a great hurry. We set dere in de wagon till late dat evening before de soldiers quit passing us and den it was too late for us to go on. We went about a mile and come to a house and dey let us stay all night and de next morning we drove on into town. It was de first time any of us ever had been to town and I know mother was scared but she was determined to take de oath so she could stay on wid old Miss Tessie. She left us children in de wagon while she went in to talk to de bureau man.

Mother was awfully light, had gray eyes and straight hair and when she got to see de bureau man he said, "What are you coming here for, you ain't no nigger, you are a darned Sesesh white and I ain't got no time to fool wid you." Mother done everything she could to convince him dat she was a colored woman but she couldn't do it. She had an aunt 'bout ten miles from town and she decided to go dere and if she hadn't gone away she would get her to come back wid her and swear dat she was a colored woman. She took us and away we went again to try to find her aunt Susan. We got dere about dark and sure enough aunt Susan was still dere and her master let her go back wid us. Aunt Susan was dark and she swore that mother was her sister's child and dey finally let her sign the oath.

The oath of peace was dat you would obey de law and wouldn't harbor no Rebel soldiers nor no bushwhackers or do nothing dat was wrong or would hinder de cause of de North.

When we got back home we didn't have no home. De very night dat we left, de bushwhackers, or toe-burners as dey was called, come to our house and told Miss Tessie dat dey wanted her money. She told dem dat she didn't have any but dey didn't believe her and told her dat dey would burn her if she didn't give dem her money. She kept

tellin' dem dat she didn' have any money and dey took everything
dey wanted and den jerked the curtains off de windows and piled
dem in de middle of de room and de furniture on top of dem and set
dem afire and burned everything 'cept the nigger quarters. It was a
pity to burn dat big pretty two-story house, but dey done it.

Mother and us children went to live on the side of de mountain
in a little cabin by ourselves and Miss Tessie went to live wid Miss
Liza, her daughter. Mother had to keep her oath and she was afraid
dat if she went wid Miss Tessie dat Master Robert might come
home and dey would say she had broke her oath and make her leave.
One night mother was spinnin' and I was cardin' and everything
was jest as quiet and we heard somebody tap in de door. We set real
quiet and den we heard it again. You dassent speak above a whisper
so mother went to de door and say real low, "Who's dere?" "It's your
old Master Bill Newton." Mother forgot and said louder, "Is that really you Master Bill, and how did you know where I was?" He told
her to open de door and let him in and he would tell her. She opened
de door and sure enough it was Master Bill. He had come back to
see how we was all gettin' along and found his house burnt. Somebody told him dat his wife was at Miss Liza's so he went dere and
she told him where we was. He told mother dat he wanted her to go
to his brother Nazor's and wait for him dere and he would take us
to where father was. She hitched up de oxen and we went down to
Uncle Nazor's and one night Old Master and Miss Tessie slipped in
dere and got us and took us to Texas. We found father and we was
all happy again.

I never had seen slaves punished before we went to Texas but I saw
a woman tied down and whipped one day. Old Master was jest as
good to us as he always had been and never punished any of us. Dey
say dat de people in Texas was a lot harder on dere slaves during de
war dan dey ever had been before.

Old Miss Tessie had kept de two little children wid her after de
house was burned and took dem wid her when we went South. After
peace was made and we started back home she heard from somebody
dat my grandmother was down dere pretty close to where dey were
so dey went by dere and found grandmother and Hannah, too. She
almost died she was so happy to see her little children again. She
thanked mother and Miss Tessie over and over for taking care of her
children for her.

After peace was made old Master called us all to him and told us
dat we was free now, jest as free as he was, and dat he had some things

dat he wanted to tell us. He talked to us jest like we was his own children wid tears running down his cheeks. He said, "Cindy, I've raised you from a baby and you, Henry, since you was a young man. I've tried to be good to you and take good care of you in return for de good work you have always done for me. I want you to go out in de worl' now and make good citizens. Be honest and respectable and don't turn against the good raisin' you have had and remember dat me and my wife loves you all."

We all went back wid dem to de old home place in Arkansas, and father went on 'bout 50 miles and got a job and come back after mother and us children. Young Master Robert bought a plantation 'bout fifteen miles from where we lived and old Master and Miss Tessie lived wid him. She got down low sick and begged and begged mother to come take care of her. Master Robert come and told mother and father hitched up the oxen and dey left dat night. Old Master said de very sight of Lucindy cured Miss Tessie. She got well and lived 'bout ten year after dat. When she took sick again mother went back and took care of her as long as she lived. Old Master lived several year after Miss Tessie died.

I married when I was fifteen. I remembered what a fine wedding Miss Liza had and I said I was going to git Old Master to let me have one jest like hers. I married in my mother and father's home and I had my wedding jest as near like Miss Liza's as I could. I had a long white dress and a long veil and a big bouquet of flowers. I didn't have things as fine as she did but I done my best. She had roses and I had jest common paper flowers. Her dress was satin and mine was cotton, my veil was cotton, too, but I thought it was fine and so did everybody else. We married on Christmas night and we had a big supper. Dey was as many white folks dere as colored and we had a grand time. De next day we went to housekeepin' and we lived together till nineteen year ago when my husband died. I had fifteen children but dere is only three living today.

---

[1] WPA field worker Mrs. Jessie R. Ervin interviewed Mrs. Eva Strayhorn at McAlester, Oklahoma, on 14 January 1937. The transcript of the interview was prepared as the narrative "Interview with Eva Strayhorn, Age 79, 1016 E. Grand Ave., McAlester, Oklahoma," from which the first four typewritten pages survive in the OHS Slave Narratives. At some later date the narrative was lightly edited (still containing inconsistent dialect usage) and retyped into an intermediate draft, available in the OHS Slave Narratives in ribbon copy as "Eva Strayhorn, Age 79, McAlester, Oklahoma" and published here. This interview was never sent to Federal Writers' Project headquarters in Washington.

2 The earlier draft lower-cases this word, suggesting that the individuals who made the bed may have been woodworkers who used a turning lathe in furniture making.

3 This sentence in the earlier draft reads: "'Their poor father is dead and only God knows what will become of them when Master Bill and Miss Tessie dies.' She just hugged and hugged them both and they took her away to Texas."

4 A reference to a representative of the Bureau of Refugees, Freedmen, and Abandoned Lands, commonly termed the Freedmen's Bureau.

BEAUREGARD TENNEYSON[1]

Age 87 Yrs.   *West Tulsa, Okla.*

My mother and father just about stocked Jess Tenneyson's plantation with slaves. That's a fact. The old folks had one big family—twenty-three children was the number. With the old folks that make twenty-five (there were only five more slaves), so I reckon they done mighty well by Master Jess.

The Master done well by them, too. Master Jess and Mistress Lula was Christian peoples. They raised their two sons, Henry and George, the same way.

There was so many of us children I don't remember all the names. Three of the boys was named after good southern gentlemen who soldiered in the War. Price, Lee and Beaugard. Beaugard is me. Proud of that name just like I'm proud of the Master's name.

My folks named Patrick and Harriett. Mother worked round the house and father was the field boss. They was close by the Master all the time.

The plantation was down in Craig County, Texas.[2] Nine hundred acre it was. They raise everything, but mostly corn and cotton. Big times when come the harvest. Master fix up a cotton gin right on the place. It was an old-fashioned press. Six horses run it with two boys tromping down the cotton with their feets.

In the fall time was the best of all. Come cotton picking time, all the master[s] from miles around send in their best pickers—and how they'd work. Sometimes pick the whole crop in one day! The one who picked the most win a prize. Then come noon and the big feast, and at night come the dancing.

Something like that when the corn was ready. All the folks have the biggest time. Log rollings. Clearing the new ground for planting. Cutting the trees, burning the bresh, making ready for the plow. The best worker wins hisself a prize at these log rollings, too.

Them kind of good times makes me think of Christmas. Didn't have no Christmas tree, but they set up a long pine table in the house and that plank table was covered with presents and none of the Negroes was ever forgot on that day.

Master Jess didn't work his slaves like other white folks done. Wasn't no four o'clock wake-up horns and the field work started at seven o'clock. Quitting time was five o'clock—just about union hours nowadays. The Master believed in plenty of rest for the slaves and they work better that way, too.

One of my brother took care of the Master's horse while on the plantation. When the Master join in with rebels that horse went along. So did brother. Master need them both and my brother mighty pleased when he get to go.

When Master come back from the War and tell us that brother is dead, he said brother was the best boy in all the army.

The Tenneyson slaves wasn't bothered with patrollers, neither the Klan. The Master said we was all good Negroes—nobody going to bother a good Negro.

We was taught to work and have good manners. And to be honest. Just doing them three things will keep anybody out of trouble.

¹ L. P. Livingston interviewed Beauregard Tenneyson in West Tulsa, Oklahoma, probably sometime in the summer of 1937. On 11 August of that year his coworker Craig Vollmer edited and typed a now lost rough draft into a preliminary draft entitled "Interview with Beaugard Tenneyson, West Tulsa, Oklahoma," preserved in the OHS Slave Narratives. Later that summer the text was further polished and retyped into its final form, "Beauregard Tenneyson, Age 87 Yrs., West Tulsa, Okla.," which was forwarded to Washington on 14 September 1937 and is published here. The ribbon copy is available in the LC Slave Narratives, while carbon copies are available as item 350060 in the LC Slave Narratives Carbon Copies and in the OHS Slave Narratives. In his 1970s compilation of American slave narratives, George P. Rawick erroneously stated that the preliminary version of the Tenneyson narrative in the OHS Slave Narratives was a later draft, for the dates document conclusively that it is an earlier version. Rawick, *The American Slave,* supplement series I, 12:lix; Stephens to Cronyn, 14 September 1937, WPA Notes on Interviews.

Above "Beaugard" in the title of the preliminary draft of the narrative, L. P. Livingston printed in pencil the standard spelling, "Beauregard." Typewritten below the title is: "Note: This ex-slave was born in 1845—age 87. Correct spelling is probably 'Beauregard.'"

Roughly contemporary Tulsa city directories provide more details on where the informant resided, noting that he had no formal street address but lived on the west side of the Frisco Railway tracks south of West Twenty-first Street. *Polk's Tulsa City Directory, 1934,* 475; *Polk's Tulsa City Directory, 1935,* 532.

² This may be phonetic spelling for Gregg County.

JOHNSON THOMPSON[1]

Age 84						*Fort Gibson, Oklahoma*

Just about two weeks before the coming of Christmas Day in 1853, I was born on a plantation somewheres eight miles east of Bellview, Rusk County, Texas. One year later my sister Phyllis was born on the same place and we been together pretty much of the time ever since, and I reckon dere's only one thing that could separate us slave born children.

Mammy and pappy belong to W. P. Thompson, mixed-blood Cherokee Indian, but before that pappy had been owned by three different masters; one was the rich Joe Vann who lived down at Webber Falls and another was Chief Lowery of the Cherokees. I had a brother named Harry who belonged to the Vann family at Tahlequah. Dere was a sister named Patsy; she died at Wagoner, Oklahoma. My mother was born 'way back in the hills of the old Flint District of the Cherokee Nation; just about where Scraper, Okla., is now.

My parents are both dead now—seems like fifty, maybe sixty year ago. Mammy died in Texas, and when we left Rusk County after the Civil War, pappy took us children to the graveyard. We patted her grave and kissed the ground . . . telling her goodbye. Pappy is buried in the church yard on Four Mile Branch.

I don't remember much about my pappy's mother; but I remember she would milk for a man named Columbus Balredge, and she went to prayer meeting every Wednesday night. Sometimes us children would try to follow her, but she'd turn us around pretty quick and chase us back with: "Go on back to the house or the wolves'll get you."

Master Thompson brought us from Texas when I was too little to remember about it, and I don't know how long it was before we was all sold to John Harnage; "Marse John" was his pet name and he liked to be called that-a-way. He took us back to Texas, right down near where I was born at Bellview.

The master's house was a big log building setting east and west, with a porch on the north side of the house. The slave cabins was in a row, and we lived in one of them. It had no windows, but it had a wood floor that was kept clean with plenty of brushings, and a fireplace where mammy'd cook the turnip greens and peas and corn— I still likes the cornbread with fingerprints baked on it, like in the old days when it was cooked in a skillet over the hot wood ashes. I eat from a big pan set on the floor—there was no chairs—and I slept in a trundle bed that was pushed under the big bed in the daytime.

I spent happy days on the Harnage plantation; going squirrel hunting with the master—he always riding, while I run along and throw rocks in the trees to scare the squirrels so's Marse John could get the aim on them; pick a little cotton and put it in somebody's hamper (basket), and run races with other colored boys to see who would get to saddle the master's horse, while the master would stand laughing by the gate to see which boy won the race.

Our clothes was home-made—cotton in the summer, mostly just a long-tailed shirt and no shoes, and wool goods in the winter. Mammy was the house girl and she weaved the cloth and my Aunt 'Tilda dyed the cloth with wild indigo, leaving her hands blue looking most of the time. Mammy work late in the night, and I hear the loom making noises while I try to sleep in the cabin. Pappy was the shoe-maker and he used wooden pegs of maple to fashion the shoes.

The master had a bell to ring every morning at four o'clock for the folks to turn out. Sometimes the sleep was too deep and somebody would be late, but the master never punish anybody, and I never see anybody whipped and only one slave sold.

Pappy wanted to go back to his mother when the War was over and the slaves was freed. He made a deal with Dave Mounts, a white man, who was moving into the Indian country, to drive for him. A four-mule team was hitched to the wagon, and for five weeks we was on the road from Texas, finally getting to grandmaw Brewer's at Fort Gibson. Pappy worked around the farms and fiddled for the Cherokee dances.

Den I went to a subscription school for a little while, but didn't get much learning. Lots of the slave children didn't ever learn to read or write. And we learned something about religion from an old colored preacher named Tom Vann. He would sing for us, and I'd like to hear them old songs again!

The first time I married was to Clara Nevens, and I wore checked wool pants and a blue striped cotton shirt. Dere come six children: Charley, Alec, Laura, Harry, Richard and Jeffy, who was named after Jefferson Davis. The second time I married a cousin, Rela Brewer.

Jefferson Davis was a great man, but I think Roosevelt is greater than Davis or Abraham Lincoln.

1. Johnson Thompson was interviewed at Fort Gibson, Oklahoma, by WPA field worker Ethel Wolfe Garrison probably sometime in the early winter of 1937–38. On

3 January 1938 project employee Craig Vollmer prepared a revised preliminary typescript based on her notes which is available as "Interview with Johnson Thompson, Ex-
Slave, Age 84, Living with a Sister, Phyllis Petite, 4 Miles East of Fort Gibson, Oklahoma" in the OHS Slave Narratives. This narrative later was revised into a final draft,
"Johnson Thompson, Age 84, Fort Gibson, Oklahoma," also available in the OHS Slave
Narratives and published here. For the remembrances of Thompson's sister, many of
them relating to the subject matter in this interview, see the narrative of Phyllis Petite,
above. For reasons not documented, the Johnson Thompson narrative was never sent to
Washington.

For another, contemporary interview with this informant, see Johnson Thompson,
interview by Breand Adams [probably at Fort Gibson, Oklahoma, ca. 1937], Indian-
Pioneer Papers, 10:472–75.

VICTORIA TAYLOR THOMPSON[1]

Age 80   *Muskogee, Oklahoma*

My mother, Judy Taylor, named for her mistress, told me that I was
born 'bout three year before the war; that make me about 80 year old,
so they say down at the Indian Agency where my name is on the
Cherokee rolls since all the land was give to the Indian families a
long time ago.

Father kept the name of "Doc" Hayes, and my brother Coose was
a Hayes too, but mother, Jude, Patsy, Bonaparte (Boney, we always
called him), Lewis and me was always Taylors. Daddy was bought by
the Taylors (Cherokee Indians); dey made a trade for him with some
hilly land, but he kept the name of Hayes even den.

Like my mother, I was born on the Taylor place. Dey lived in Flint
District, around the Caney settlement on Caney Creek. Lots of the
Arkansas Cherokees settled around dere long times before the Chero-
kees come here from the east, my mother said.

The farm wasn't very big, we was the only slaves on the place, and
it was just a little ways from a hill everybody called Sugar Mountain,
because it was covered with maple sugar trees, and an old Indian lived
on the hillside, making maple sugar candy to sell and trade.

Master Taylor's house had three big rooms and a room for the
loom, all made of logs, with a long front porch high off the ground.
The spring house set to the east, in the corner like. Spring water
boiled up all the time, and the water run down the branch which we
crossed on a log bridge.

On the north side of the front porch, under a window in the mistress' room, was the grave of her little boy who was found drowned
in the spring. The mistress set a heap of store by dat child; said she

wanted him buried right where she could always see his grave. She was mighty good.

So was the master good, too. None of us was ever beat or whipped like I hear about other slaves. Dey fix up a log cabin for us close by the big house. The yard fenced high with five or six rails, and dere was an apple orchard that set off the place with its blooming in the spring days.

Mother worked in the fields and in the house. She would hoe and plow, milk and do the cooking. She was a good cook and made the best corn bread I ever eat. Cook it in a skillet in the fireplace—I likes a piece of it right now! Grub dese days don't taste the same. Sometime after the war she cook for the prisoners in the jail at Tahlequah.

Dat was the first jail I ever saw; they had hangings there. Always on a Friday, but I never see one, for it scare me and I run and hide.

Well, mother leave us children in the cabin while she gets breakfast for the master. We'd be nearly starved before she get back to tend us. And we slept on the floor, but the big house had wood beds, with high boards on the head and foot.

Mother took me with her to weaving room, and the mistress learn me how to weave in the stripes and colors so's I could make up one hundred kind of colors and shades. She ask me the color and I never miss telling her. Dat's one thing my sister Patsy can't learn when she was a little girl. I try the knitting, but I drop the stitches and lay it down.

Some of the things mother made was cloth socks and fringe for the hunting shirt that daddy always wore. The mistress made long tail shirts for the boys; we wore cotton all the year, and the first shoes I ever see was brass toed brogans.

For sickness daddy give us tea and herbs. He was a herb doctor, dat's how come he have the name "Doc." He made us wear charms, made out of shiny buttons and Indian rock beads. Dey cured lots of things and the misery too.

I hear mother tell about the slaves running away from mean masters, and how she help hide them at night from the dogs that come trailing them. The high fence keep out the dogs from the yard, and soon's they leave the runoffs would break for the river (Illinois [River]), cross over and get away from the dogs.

The master had a mill run by oxen, the same oxen used in the fields. Dey stepped on the pedals and turn the rollers, dat how it was done.

Dere was another mill in the hills run by a white man name of

Uncle Mosie. One day he stole me to live in a cabin with him. He branded a circle on my cheek, but in two days I got away and run back to the Taylors where I was safe.

When the war broke out my daddy went on the side of the South with Master Taylor. Dey was gone a long time and when they come back he told of fighting the Federals north of Fort Gibson (it may have been the battle of Locust Grove), and how the Federals drove dem off like dogs. He said most of the time the soldiers starved and suffered, some of them freezing to death.

After the war I was stole again. I was hired to Judge Wolfe, and his wife Mary took good care of me and I helped her around the big two-story house. She didn't like my father and kept him off the place. One day an Indian, John Prichett, told me my daddy wanted to see me down by the old barn, to follow him. He grabbed me when we got back of the barn and took me away to his place where my daddy was waiting for me. We worked for dat Indian to pay for him getting me away from Judge Wolfe. Dat was around Fort Gibson.

Dat's where I married William Thompson, an uncle of Johnson Thompson, who was born a slave and lives now on Four Mile Branch (near Hulbert, Okla.). Dere was seven boys; where dey is I don't know, except for my boy George Lewis Thompson, who lives in this four-room house he builds for us, and stays unmarried so's he can take care of his old mammy.[2]

I been belonging to church ever since there was a colored church, and I thinks everybody should obey the Master. He died, and I wants to go where Jesus lives. Like the poor Indian I saw one time waiting to be hung. Dere he was, setting on his own coffin box, singing over and over the words I just said: "I wants to go where Jesus lives!"

Dere's one thing I wants to do before I go. My time is short and I wants to go back to the Taylor place, to my old mistress' place, and just see the ground where she use to walk—dat's what I most want, but time is short.

[1] Victoria Taylor Thompson was interviewed in Muskogee, Oklahoma, by WPA field worker Ethel Wolfe Garrison probably sometime in the early winter of 1937–38. On 4 January 1938 project employee Craig Vollmer revised her notes and typed them into a preliminary draft entitled "Interview with Victoria Taylor Thompson, Ex-Slave, Age 80, 1613 Spruce Addition, Muskogee, Oklahoma," available in the OHS Slave Narratives. At a later date this transcript was slightly polished and a final draft was prepared as the typescript "Victoria Taylor Thompson, Age 80, Muskogee, Oklahoma," available in the OHS Slave Narratives and published here. For reasons not known, the Victoria Taylor Thompson narrative was never sent to Washington.

INTERVIEW WITH JIM THREAT¹

Age 86   *West Harrison Ave., McAlester, Okla.*

"I went down to Dad's old corn field.
Black snake bit me on my heel.
I turn around and run my best,
Stuck my head in a hornet's nest.

Run nigger, run,
De Patteroll'll git you!
Run nigger, run,
De Patteroll come!
Run Nigger, run,
De Patteroll'll git you!
Run nigger, run,
You better make it home!

We all sung dat song and had a lot of fun singing it but it was true jest the same. Dat was one of the things dat the niggers dreaded most, was a patteroller.

Slaves would have a little party; all the niggers would gather at one of the cabins and lock the door so the patterollers couldn't git in. When the party was over and they started home, the patterollers would stop them and demand their passes. Woe to the nigger that didn't have one!

I guess they was all right in some cases but they over-done it I can tell you.

I recollects that down in the neighborhood jest below us we was all the time hearing about the patterollers beating some nigger. Finally the slaves got tired of it and decided to do something about it. One night they got some grape vines and twisted them together and stretched them across the road. They went down the road and waited and finally four or five patterollers come along. The nigger boys started running back up the road and by this time the Patterollers was running their horses full speed after them. Just before they got to the vines the niggers ducked out of the road and the horses run full tilt into the vines. You never saw such a spill. The horses turned "summer-sets" and one man was killed, two had their legs broke and one got a arm broke. Course these boys had to take to de woods and finally made their way to the north. Several colored folks lost their lives over it, too, but Patterollers was sorter scarce in them parts from then on.

I was born in September 1851. My old Master kept a record of his slaves' ages and we all knowed how old we was. I was one of twenty-two children. All of us lived to be grown 'cept Tommy, Ivory and a little girl. Now there's jest two of us left, [me and] my brother, who was born the first year after the surrender. He's a preacher and lives in Parsons, Kansas. His name is Bill Threat.

My mother, her brother, grandmother and auntie belonged to old man Johnnie Bowman, an Indian. He got in a tight and had to sell 'em. He sold them to Russell Allen and he made him promise not to sell them one by one but in pairs or all together. He sold grandmother and Auntie to old man Hollis Montgomery but kept mother and her brother till freedom.

Russell Allen wasn't mean to his niggers but he shore expected them to stay on the plantation and do their work. After he sold my grandmother and aunt, mother and Uncle Jack got awful lonesome to see them. One day Jack decided he would run off and go to see them. It was forty some-odd miles to where they lived but that didn't seem far to him for he kept thinking about him seeing his mother. His master sent a man after him. He tied a rope around Jack's waist and led him behind his horse all the way home. He rode so fast dat Uncle Jack had to run to keep up. When they got home they give him a whupping but he didn't mind it so much as he was too tired.

I knowed another man who was purty hard for his master to handle. He was always doing something and getting whupped and he'd run away. His master was always slick enough to catch him. One day he run off and he made up his mind he was not gonna be as smart as the best of 'em. He saw a big hollow stump about eight or ten feet high and they was a small hole at the bottom. The stump was large enough around for him to git inside and set down. He wasn't thinking of any thing else 'cepting hiding from his master so he clum up and dropped down inside. Jest imagine how he felt when he dropped down and found four little bear cubs inside. Man, was he scared!

He tried and tried to git out but couldn't. The hole was so small and he couldn't climb back up. There he set expecting the old bear back any minute and realizing that iffen the bear didn't eat him he'd starve to death.

Along about dark he heard the old bear coming, he looked up and she was coming down hind part first. All on a sudden he got desprit and he reach up and grab onto her and she started climbing back out. He hung on for dear life and as soon as he could he grabbed holt of the stump and he fell off on one side and the bear the other, 'twas hard to tell which was the worse scared. He ran home and took his whupping and he never did give his master no more trouble.

I was born and raised near Talidiga, Alabama in Talidiga County, on the Coosa river. This river is called the Tallapoosa river now. We lived right on the line between Talidiga and Sinclair Counties.[2]

My father, Jim Threat, belonged to Gum Threat, and my mother, Hannah Allen, was owned by Russell Allen.

My grandmother's name was Mary Swine. Old man Swine got overstocked with children and sold her along with a passel of kids to Johnnie Bowman. He sold her to Russell Allen. Dan Threat bought my father in Maryland, Va. when he was seven and brought him to Alabama. He never saw his parents again. Dan Threat kept him till his son Gum Threat was grown and married and he gave him and three other slaves to Gum for a wedding present.

Iffen they ever was a devil on this earth it was Gum Threat. He jest didn't have any regard for his slaves. He made 'em work from daylight to dark and didn't give them any more food and clothes than they could possibly git along with. He beat them for everything they done and a lot they didn't do so you may know they all hated him. He had one man, Charles Posey, that would take and take till he couldn't stand it no longer and he'd run off. He run off once and Gum sent three white men to hunt him and he told them he would kill 'em iffen they didn't catch him. Course they did all in they power and finally caught him. They brought him home.

Gum Threat's house was built on a high foundation and the gallery was high off the ground. Charles was standing by the edge of the gallery and Gum come walking out and walked up close to him and drawed back his foot with a heavy boot on it and kicked Charles under the chin. You could hear his neck pop. He fell to the ground and kicked around like he was dying. They brought him to and then Gum Threat stripped him to the waist and took him into an old building, stretched him out and fastened his feet and hands wide apart, then he took a live coal of fire as big as your hand and laid it in the middle of his bare back. I remember seeing the scar there and it was about 1/8 of an inch deep.

He always seemed to have it in for Charles after that and beat him for everything. When the war started he run off and joined the northern soldiers and was made a guard in the army. The soldiers protected him and he never did have to go back any more.

My father married my mother while he was living with Dan Threat and he would git to come home every Saturday night. Gum let him keep on coming till the war started. Everbody was harder on their slaves then and Gum wouldn't let father come home any more. One night he slipped off and come home and spent the night. He overslept the next morning and ran all the way so he would git there in time to go to work. The hands were jest starting to the field when he got there but the overseer started in to give him a whupping anyway and father bit his thumb so he called for help and strapped him down and gave him thirty lashes.

To punish him they put him under a hard taskmaster. He couldn't do all the work they set for him to do so he run away. He'd slip in to us at night and hide out in the daytime. All of Russell Allen's niggers knowed he stayed with us for a good while. I now think old Master knowed he was staying there but he didn't let on.

Father finally decided to try to slip off to the northern soldiers and he left one night about three o'clock. He met up with Sterl Beavers, a white man. Sterl pretended that he was sorry for father and told him that if he would go home with him he would hide him till he could git away to the north. They had to cross a big creek on a footlog. Father was afraid to trust Sterl and about half-way across the creek he jumped in and stayed under water jest as long as he could. He jest let himself drift with the current of the water. When he come to the top Sterl shot at him but didn't hit him. Father stayed out for a few days longer and he came back and give himself up and took his whupping. When they whupped a slave they made him say, "Oh, pray Master" to show that he had to be humble.

Gum Threat had a brother-in-law named Alex Jordan and they was all the time gitting drunk and fighting. Once they had a fight and Gum knocked Alex down and stomped him in the face with his heavy boots. Alex never got over it but he decided that Gum was the best man so he jest bided his time.

As the war come on, food and clothes got powerful scarce. Gum and Alex decided they would kill off their old niggers so they wouldn't have to take care of them any longer as they couldn't sell them and nobody wanted old niggers. I remember one man they had in the bunch that they was going to kill was Uncle Pinkley Clinkenscales. They was all on the way to the woods where they had planned to do the killing when Alex Jordan's gun went off and blowed the top of Gum's head off. This broke up the killing game.

I went back to my old home about seventeen years ago and I went to the spot where Gum was killed. The print of his body is still there, the place where his head struck and in fact the print of his whole body is there, no grass will grow there. He fell on a sloping place and his blood run down about two or three feet and now when it is damp and cloudy that blood will come up on the ground just like sweat.

Alex Jordan died six years later. He was buried in the same graveyard that Gum Threat was buried. The graveyard was near Jordan's house and the third night after Alex was buried two big balls of fire rose out of that graveyard and went up clean out of sight, it done this four, five times and then come down and bust on Alex Jordan's chimney. Everybody said it was Gum and Alex fighting. I guess they're still at it.

Yassum, I've seen lots of spooks. Back where I was raised they hung so many deserters and spies from the army that ghosts was a common thing.

Once I went to a place to dig for money. The place was guarded by two men who buried it and was killed there. Everbody was afraid to go there to dig but an old conjure woman told me to go there and iffen they come for me to say, "What in the name of the Father, Son and the Holy Ghost do you want back in this old sinful world?" and they would go away.

Well, I got there and was onloading my tools to go to digging and here come the two men. They was average size and there wasn't the color of blood in their faces. I was so scared that I forgot what I was supposed to say and I jest said, "What do you want?" They looked at me a minute and jest gradually disappeared. I loaded my tools in my wagon and cleared out. I never went back there either. I am not afraid of spirits now.

I've known some witches or conjure women, too. When I was first married I was working for a colored man helping him gather corn. His wife didn't like me and she didn't want me to help him. On Sunday evening she walked up to me and tapped me on the breast twice. I went to the field the next day and I had to go back home for I had the hardest chill I ever had in my life. Late that evening I had another one and it was so bad I shook the whole bed. I had one of those chills every day for a week and I knowed in my mind that she had conjured me.

On Saturday I noticed an old hen feeding around my door. I

picked up a piece of iron and took after her. She run around the house two or three times and then stopped and stood with her wings drooping and looked up at the top of the chimney. I hit her and knocked her about ten feet. I beat her till I was sure she was dead and I got the axe and chopped her up. To break the evil spell you have to bury a piece of de flesh, burn a piece and throw a piece into running water. I done all this.

The next morning the woman come down and set awhile and made mention that sometimes a stray chicken comes to your house. I speak right up and I say, "Yes Ma'am, a old hen come here yesterday and I killed her and chopped her up and burned a piece, buried a piece and throwed a piece in some running water." She say, "Oh, my goodness, what made you kill my hen?" Then she asked for a cup of coffee and my wife told her she couldn't git nothing there and she keep begging and say, "Please give me something." My wife handed her a little old piece of cloth and she grabbed it and away she went home. I took a piece of pure silver and chipped or ground off some of it and put it in some whiskey and drank it. I sure broke her charm over me.

I knowed another woman a few years ago that had power of conjuring a body, and one time one of her grandsons got in jail and she give her son-in-law some dried roots and told him to go up to the jail and chew these roots and to spit all around the jail and to give some to his son so he could spit it all around inside and the jailer would let him out. They done as she told them and sure enough the jailer turned him out and he went back home with his Pa.

My mother's master, Russell Allen, was a purty good man and was good to his slaves as a general rule. He expected them to stay on the plantation and to do their work. My mother's daily task was to milk seven cows twice a day, cook all the meals for the family and weave seven yards of cloth a day.

The kitchen was some distance from the house and mother and us children lived in the kitchen. Mother done all the cooking and my sisters carried the food to the dining room and waited on the table. My brother Sam had to swing the fly brush over the table to mind the flies off the food.

Mother and us smaller children slept in the kitchen. The bed we slept in was called a Coosa-filley. A hole was bored in the wall and a pole run in it, a forked stake was fastened to the floor near the center of the room and the end of the pole rested in it. Another pole was placed across for the foot and one end rested in this fork and the other in a hole on the other side of the house. Split puncheons were used for slats with the flat side up. Mother wove coarse ducking for the grass or leaves to be placed in. We had a layer of cotton on the top and this made the bed softer. Some of these beds were made solid and shucks, straw, or leaves were put on this and blankets spread over it. We had a good bed, warm clothes and good food. Mother made us children help her spin and weave our own clothes.

I didn't work any as my old master kind of petted me. He always called me Sharp Head. I'd go up to the big house and he would split open a biscuit and spread it with butter and give it to me. That was a treat for we didn't get biscuits very often.

The big house was a frame house, painted slate gray, and had five rooms in it. The quarters was back of the house about three hundred yards. The overseer lived close to the quarters. It was a good thing that mother belonged to Russell Allen instead of Gum Threat for he never would have let her keep her big batch of children. Master Allen always kept all the children and he had the old decrepit women to take care of the babies and small children while their mothers worked.

When slave owners got in a tight and couldn't pay their debts or wanted to raise money for something they would put [up] one or two of their slaves and on the first Tuesday in the month they would cry them off to the highest bidder. Buyers from all over the country would be there. Some of them was just speculators who just bought and sold. Niggers sure hated to be sold and especially to speculators. They lived in constant fear that they would be sold away from their families. The block was about three feet high and had two steps leading up to it. I've seen old men and women, young men and women and even little children sold there. The slave would stand up and turn slowly round while the buyers inspected them. They'd even look at their teeth. The owners would tell what kind of disposition they had and the kind of work they was best at. Some times a husky young man or woman brought $1000 to $1100.

During the war slave owners was mighty hard on their slaves. Bill Allen refugeed Elsie, Clarissy, Hester and sister Phoebe to Texas and we never saw or heard of them any more.

Bob Allen went to the war and as he was so used to having somebody to wait on him he took my mother's brother with him to be his special servant. Uncle took smallpox and died and was buried at the camp.

We could hear the cannons at Talidiga. Miss 'Lizabeth walked the floor all day with her arms folded. Her face was so sad it made you want to cry. After the battle the Yankees commenced to cross the river and we could see them and everyone got just as solemn as death. They camped close to our house and the captain come up and began asking all sorts of questions. Old Master was sitting out in the yard in the shade of a big tree and the Cap'n say to him, "Are you a rebel?"

Old master say, "I am a know-nothing."

"You have some sons in the Sesesh army, haven't you?"

"Yes, but they're all twenty-one years old."

The captain and some of his men went in the house and got all the guns and took them out and broke them over a tree, then they hunted all through the house and took all the jewelry they could find. Old Master had buried a big sack full of money and they didn't git very much money. I remember the guns they broke was a musket and an old human rifle.[3]

They then went to the barn. We had a row of six or seven cribs and they was all full of corn. The men pried up the logs and took out about three close to the bottom and then they got in and stomped the corn out till it fell all 'round on the ground. They turned three-hundred horses in and they et corn all night.

We had a neighbor named Kelso who was terrible mean to his niggers. He had about seventy-five and all he fed them was cotton seed boiled and thickened with corn meal. This was poured into long troughs and the people ate it with wooden spoons. Most any night you could see a light in his gin house till nine o'clock and you could hear them beating someone and hear them crying, "Oh, pray Master." Everybody knowed how mean he was and several times the white men in the country went to him and tried to git him to treat them better but he kept it up.

The next morning after the Yankees camped at our house the captain put me and my brother on a horse and told us to go show him where old man Kelso lived. When we got there the old man was setting in the yard in the shade and the cap'n ordered his men to go to the smokehouse and bust it open. You never saw the like of fine meat. He divided it out among the slaves. There must have been at least a thousand pounds of flour; they busted the ends out of the barrels and just scattered it all over the place. Next they emptied three hogsheads of lard. There was about twenty barrels of New Orleans molasses, they split the barrels and let the syrup all spill. You never saw such a mess of flour, lard and syrup. They got on their horses and went on their way and old man Kelso didn't say a word.

Soon after this the war ended and some more Yankee soldiers came to our place and tole Russell Allen, "Your colored folks are as free as you are now so turn them loose and let them go where they please and do as they please." About nine o'clock my father come and old man Allen called to him and he told him, "You niggers is free now and I want you to take your family and git away from here jest as quick as you can."

Father was stumped for he didn't know what on earth he was going to do with that big family. We had no home, no food and mighty few clothes.

Old man Ramsey told father that he had an old house down in the field that needed a floor and a chimney that he could have if he would fix it up. Pappy and the older boys set in and built a chimbley and we moved in on the dirt floor. We stayed there about a month when Ramsey said he needed the house so we had to move out. Our old doctor moved from the bend of the river and he let us have his house till we could find some place to live and we stayed there for three weeks. Old lady Drummonds let us build a house on her place and we lived there a long time. Pappy built a double log house and it seemed like a mansion to us.

We would work for folks and take our pay in meat scraps, corn-meal, shorts and anything they was a mind to give us. Nobody had much to eat or wear and it was nearly out of the question to ever git any money.

We got along better when spring came, for berries were plentiful and we would go to a pine tree and peel the outside bark off and scrape the body of the tree and get these scrapings. I don't know how much good was in this but it was good and sweet and we liked it. I've seen men plow for about two hours and stop their teams and go to the berry patch and eat berries. This was their breakfast; then they would go back and plow until about half-past ten and turn their teams on the grass and they would go back to the berry patch to get their dinner. We had almost no clothes, just sacks with holes cut for our heads and arms.

Old man Buchannan lost all his slaves and the Yankees took all his horses, so he got two boys, Luther and John, to help him. He hitched them to a double plow and turned all of his ground and planted cotton. When it got big enough he put John to hoeing and Luther to pulling a single plow. He made four bales of cotton and sold it for a dollar a pound. All the boys got was what they et and a suit of clothes. I guess at that they done pretty well considering the way the rest of us got along.

After the war we had the Ku Kluxers to take the place of the Patterollers. They was mighty hard on the colored folks. If a white man wanted a colored man or woman to work for him and they didn't go, the Ku Kluxers would come at night and take them out and whup them. They would ride right up in the yard to your door and have horses head inside the door. If you asked him please not trample up your yard he'd say, "Dam your yard."

After dark all colored people went into their house and they'd talk in low whispers. Ku Kluxers was always snooping around to see if you was talking about them. Colored folks didn't dare do that.

I'll tell you some of the songs we used to sing:

"Jest anything it is my song,
Through the globe we march along.
Marching on we sweet-like sing,
Sound the praise of anything"

"Now ladies and gentlemens you needn't think wrong,
You asked me sing you a little song—
I asked you what must I sing
And you said jest anything."

"As I went down to Logan's stream,
Purty, fair maiden I chanced for to meet,
She looked so near, she looked so sweet,
Purtier than anything."

"Now my song is almost complete,
Think you gentlemens ought to treat,
You can treat the ginger sling,
But I'll put up with anything."

* * * *

"Ha! Ha! white folks going for to see,
Ha! Ha! White folks going for to see,
Going for to tell you this, that and 'tother,
Fell in love with a great waterfall."

"Fell in love with Dinah Crow,
Teeth was shining like banks of snow,
Eyes as bright as rings of the moon,
Teeth as sharp as a 'possum or a coon."

(Dat nigger's teeth was plenty sharp—
Great consolation between us niggers.)

"Ask Miss Dinah to be my bride,
She bit my arm, she tore my coat,
Give such a rash-tash—
She mashed her d— nose."
(Dat nigger's temper was plenty rash—
Great consolation between us niggers.)

[1] Jim Threat was interviewed in McAlester, Oklahoma, by WPA field worker Mrs. Jessie R. Ervin on 4 November 1937. Only one typescript of Threat's remembrances has been located, and it is published here. The typescript, entitled "Interview with Jim Threat, Age 86, West Harrison Ave., McAlester, Okla.," is available in the OHS Slave Narratives. This interview was never forwarded to Washington.

[2] The counties referred to here are Talladega and St. Clair and the town is Talladega. The Coosa River is actually a number of miles to the east of the Tallapoosa River.

[3] Possibly a misunderstood reference to a Hawken rifle.

LUCINDA VANN[1]

Life on an Old Cherokee Plantation

Yes, Sa. My name's Lucinda *Vann,* I've been married twice, but that don't make no difference. Indians wouldn't allow their slaves to take their husband's name. Oh, Lord, *no.* I don't know how old I is; some folks say I'se ninety-two and some say I must be a hundred.

I'se born across the river in the plantation of old Jim Vann in Webbers Falls, I'se born right in my marster and missus' bed. *Yes I was.* You see, I'se one of them sudden cases. My mother, Betsy Vann, worked in the big house for the missus. She was weavin' when the case came up so quick, missus Jennie put her in her own bed and took care of her. Master Jim and Missus Jennie was good to their slaves. *Yes, Lord, yes.*

My missus' name was Doublehead before she married Jim Vann. They was Cherokee Indians. They had a big, big plantation down by the river and they was rich. Had sacks and sacks of money. There was five hundred slaves on that plantation and nobody ever lacked for nothin'. Everybody had fine clothes, everybody had plenty to eat. Lord, yes, *su—er.* Now I'se just old forgotten woman. Sometimes I eat my bread this mornin', none this evenin'.

Seneca Chism was my father. He was a slave on the Chism plantation, but came to Vann's all the time on account of the horses. He had charge of all Marster Chism's and Marster Vann's race horses. He and Marster took race horses down the river, away off, and they'd come back with sacks of money that them horses won in the races.

My mother died when I'se small and my father married Delia Vann. Because I'se so little, Missus Jennie too me into the Big House and raised me. Somehow or other they all took a liking to me, all through the family. I slept on a slidin' bed. Didn't you never see one of them slidin' beds? Well, I'll tell you; you pull it out from the wall something like a shelf.

Marster had a little race horse called "Black Hock." She was all jet black, exceptin' three white feet and her stump of a tail. Black Hock was awful attached to the kitchen. She'd come up and put her nose on you just like this—nibble, nibble, nibble. Sometimes she pull my hair. That meant she want a biscuit with a little butter on it.

One day Missus Jennie say to Marster Jim, she says, "*Mr. Vann, you come here.* Do you know what I am going to do? I'm goin' give Lucy this black mare. Every dollar she make on the track, I give it to Lucy." She won me lots of money, Black Hock did, and I kept it in the Savings Bank at Tahlequah. My mother, grandmother, aunt Maria and cousin Clara, all worked in the big house. My mother was seamstress. She bossed all the other colored women and see that they sew it right. They spun the cotton, and wool, weaved it and made cloth. After it was wove they dyed it all colors, blue, brown, purple, red, yellow. It took lots of clothes for all them slaves.

My grandmother, Clarinda Vann, bossed the kitchen and the washin' and turned the key to the big bank. That was sort of vault, where the family valuables was kept. Exceptin' master and mistress, couldn't nobody put things in there but her. When they wanted something put away they say, "Clarinda, come put this in the vault." She turned the key to the commissary too. That was where all the food was kept.

All the slaves lived in a log house. The married folks lived in little houses and there was big long houses for all the single men. The young, single girls lived with the old folks in another big long house.

The slaves who worked in the big house was the first class. Next came the carpenters, yard men, blacksmiths, race-horse men, steamboat men and like that. The low class work in the fields.

Marster Jim and Missus Jennie wouldn't let his house slaves go with no common dress out. They never sent us anywhere with a cotton dress. They wanted everybody know we was Marster Vann's slaves.

He wanted people to know he was able to dress his slaves in fine clothes. We had fine satin dresses, great big combs for our hair, great big gold locket, double ear-rings, we never wore cotton except when we worked. We had bonnets that had long silk tassels for ties. When we wanted to go anywhere we always got a horse, we never walked. Everything was fine, Lord, have mercy on me, *yes*.

The big house was made of log and stone and had big, mud fire-places. They had fine furniture that Marster Vann had brought home in a steamboat from far away. And dishes, they had rows and rows of china dishes; big blue platters that would hold a whole turkey.

Everybody had plenty to eat and plenty to throw away. The com-missary was full of everything good to eat. Brown sugar, molasses, flour, corn-meal, dried beans, peas, fruits, butter, lard, was all kept in big wooden hogsheads; look something like a tub. There was lots of preserves. Everything was kept covered and every hogshead had a lock.

Every morning the slaves would run to the commissary and get what they wanted for that day. They could have anything they wanted. When they get it they take it back to their cabin. Clarinda Vann and my aunt Maria turned the keys to the vault and commissary. Couldn't nobody go there, less they turn the key.

We had a smoke-house full of hams and bacon. Oh, they was good. Lord, have mercy, I'll say they was. And we had corn bread and cakes baked every day. Single girls waited on the tables in the big house. There was a big dinner bell in the yard. When meal-time come, someone ring that bell, and all the slaves know it's time to eat and stop their work.

In summer when it was hot, the slaves would sit in the shade evenin's and make wooden spoons out of maple. They'd sell 'em to folks at picnics and barbecues.

Everybody had a good time on old Jim Vann's plantation. After supper the colored folks would get together and talk, and sing, and dance. Someone maybe would be playin' a fiddle or a banjo. Every-body was happy. Marster never whipped no one. No fusses, no bad words, no nuthin' like that.

We had our time to go to bed and our time to get up in the morn-ing. We had to get up early and comb our hair first thing. All the col-ored folks lined up and the overseer he tell them what they must do that day.

There was big parties and dances. In winter white folks danced in the parlor of the big house; in summer they danced on a platform under a great big brush arbor. There was seats all around for folks to watch them dance. Sometimes just white folks danced; sometimes just the black folks.

There was music, fine music. The colored folks did most of the fiddlin'. Someone rattled the bones. There was a bugler and someone called the dances. When marster Jim and missus Jennie went away the slaves would have a big dance in the arbor. When the white folks danced, the slaves would all sit or stand around and watch. They'd clap their hands and holler. Everybody have a good time. *Lord yes, su—er.*

When they gave a party in the big house, everything was fine. Women came in satin dresses, all dressed up, big combs in their hair, lots of rings and bracelets. The cooks would bake hams, turkey, cakes and pies and there'd be lots to eat and lots of whiskey for the men folks.

I'd like to go where we used to have picnics down below Webbers Falls. Everybody went—white folks, colored folks. There'd be races and people would have things what they was sellin', like moccasins and beads. They'd bring whole wagon loads of hams, chickens, cake and pie. The cooks would bring big iron pots and cook things right there. There was great big wooden scaffolds. They put white cloths on the shelves and laid the food on it. People just go and help themselves, till they couldn't eat no mo'! Everybody goin' on, races, gamblin', drinkin', eatin', dancin', but it as all behavior, everything all right. Yes, Lord, it was, have mercy on me, yes.

I remember when the steamboats went up and down the river. *Yes, Lord, yes.* Sometimes there was high waters that spoiled the current and the steamboats couldn't run. Sometimes we got a ride on one, cause we belonged to old Jim Vann. He'd take us and enjoy us, you know. He wouldn't take us way off, but just for a ride. He tell us for [before] we start, what we must say and what to do. He used to take us to where Hyde Park is and we'd all go fishin'. We take a big pot to fry fish in and we'd all eat till we nearly bust. *Lord, Yes.*

Christmas lasted whole month. After we got our presents we go way anywhere and visit colored folks on other plantations. In one month you have to get back. You know just what day you have to be back too.

Marster had a big Christmas tree, oh, great big tree, put on the porch. There'd be a whole wagon-load of things come and be put on the tree. Hams, cakes, pies, dresses, beads, everything. Christmas morning marster and missus come out on the porch and all the colored folks gather around. Someone call our names and everybody get a present. They get something they need too. Everybody laugh and was happy. Then we all have big dinner, white folks in the big house, colored folks in their cabins. People all a visitin'. I go to this house, you come to my house. Everybody, white folks and colored folks, havin' good time. *Yes, my dear Lord, yes.*

I've heard 'em tell of rich Joe Vann.[2] Don't know much about him. He was a traveler, didn't stay home much. Used to go up and down the river in his steamboat. He was a multi-millionaire and handsome. All the Vann marsters was good looking.

Joe had two wives, one was named Missus Jennie. I dunno her other name. Missus Jennie lived in a big house in Webbers Falls. Don't know where the other one lived. Sometimes Joe bring other wife to visit Missus Jennie. He would tell 'em plain before hand, "Now, no trouble." He didn't want 'em to imagine he give one more than he give the other.

The most terrible thing that ever happen was when the Lucy Walker busted and Joe got blew up. The engineer's name was Jim Vann. How did they hear about it at home? Oh, the news traveled up and down the river. It was bad, oh, it was bad. Everybody a hollerin' and a cryin'. After the explosion someone found an arm up in a tree on the bank of the river. They brought it home and my grandmother knew it was Joe's. She done his washing and knew the cuff of his sleeve. Everybody pretty near to crazy when they bring that arm home. A doctor put it in alcohol and they kept it a long time. Different friends would come and they'd show that arm. My mother saw it but the colored chillun couldn't. Marster and missus never allowed chillun to meddle in the big folks' business. Don't know what they ever did with that arm. Lord, it was terrible. *Yes, Lord, yes.*

I went to the missionary Baptist church where Marster and Missus went. There was a big church. The white folks go first and after they come out, the colored folks go in. I joined the Catholic church after the war. Lots of bad things have come to me, but the good Father, high up, he take care of me.

We went down to the river for baptizings. The women dressed in white, if they had a white dress to wear. The preacher took his candidate into the water. Pretty soon everybody commenced a singin' and a prayin'. Then the preacher put you under water three times. There was a house yonder where was dry clothes, blankets, everything. Soon as you come out of the water you go over there and change clothes. My uncle used to baptize 'em.

When anybody die, someone sit up with them day and night till they put them in the ground. Everybody cry, everybody'd pretty nearly die. *Lord have mercy on us, yes.*

When the war broke out, lots of Indians mustered up and went out of the territory. They taken some of their slaves with them. My marster and missus buried their money and valuables everywhere. They didn't go away, they stayed, but they tell us colored folks to go if we wanted to.

A bunch of us who was part Indian and part colored, we got our bed clothes together, some hams and a lot of coffee and flour and started to Mexico.³ We had seven horses and a little buffalo we'd raised from when it's little. We'd say, "Come on buffalo," and it would come to us. We put all the bed clothes on its back. When night came we cut grass and put the bed clothes on top for a bed. In the morning we got up early, made a fire, and made a big pot of coffee. We didn't suffer, we had plenty to eat. Some of us had money. I had the money Black Hock had won on the track.

We got letters all the time from Indians back in the territory. They tell us what was happening and what to do. One and a half years after the war we all come back to the old plantation. There wasn't nothing left. Marster and Missus was dead.

Our marshal made us all sign up like this; who are you, where you come from, where you go to. We stayed here till everything got fixed up, then we went back to Mexico. My father was a carpenter and blacksmith as well as race-horse man and he wanted to make money. He worked in the gold mines. We made money and kept it in a sack.

After everything quiet down and everything was just right, we come back to territory second time. Had to sign up all over again and tell who we was. It's on record somewhere; old Seneca Chism and his family.

I remember Chief John Ross. He courted a girl named Sally. He was married, but that didn't make no difference, he courted her anyhow. Some of the old chiefs' names was Gopher John, John Hawk and Wild Cat. This was before the war.

After the war I married Paul Alexander, but I never took his name. Indians made us keep our master's name. I'se proud anyway of my Vann name. My husband didn't give me nothing. Lord, no, he didn't. I got all my money and fine clothes from the marster and the missus.

Everything was cheap. One time we sold one hundred hogs on the foot. Two pounds of hog meat sold for a nickel. A whole half of ribs

sold for twenty-five cents. Little hog, big hog, didn't make no difference.

After the old time rich folks die, them that had their money
buried, they come back and haunt the places where it is. They'd come
to the door like this, "sh. . . . . . ," and go out quick again. I've seen
'em. My father he say, "Now chillun, don't get smart; you just be still
and listen, rich folks tryin' tell us something." They come and call
you, say so much money buried, tell you where it is, say, it's yours,
you come and get it. If someone they didn't want to have it try to dig
it up, money sink down, down deep in the ground where they couldn't
get it.

[1] Mrs. Lucinda Vann was interviewed in Muskogee, Oklahoma, by Federal Theater
Project reporter Annie L. Faulton in the period of about 1937–39. In 1977 George P.
Rawick published the narrative produced as a result of the interview. He apparently secured it from Dr. Norman R. Yetman, who with his children and research assistants reproduced some of the Oklahoma slave narratives from the collection at the Oklahoma
Historical Society used by Rawick in the supplement series to his multivolume compilation of American slave narratives. The original typescript for Lucinda Vann's narrative, however, apparently was lost sometime between Yetman's work at the Oklahoma Historical Society in the 1970s and the initiation of the present editorial project
in 1990. Rawick, *The American Slave,* supplement series I, 12:xiii–xiv, xliii, 342–53;
Welge to Baker, 13 January 1994, telefacsimile letter in Baker's possession.

The heading on this interview transcript contains substantial information on the informant and the interview: "Vann, Lucinda[;] Oklahoma Research Department[;] Federal Theatre Project 765 3–4 S 203[;] Classification: Indian[;] Title: Life on an Old
Cherokee Plantation[;] Source: Interview, Lucinda (Aunt Lucy) Vann, Muskogee. Sub-
mitted by: Annie L. Faulton, reporter." Faulton is the same Oklahoma Federal Theater
Project field worker who prepared the narrative of Chaney McNair, reproduced elsewhere in this book.

[2] For another remembrance of and background on "Rich Joe" Vann and his steamboats, see the narrative of Betty Robertson, above.

[3] In his study of the Cherokee freedmen, Daniel F. Littlefield, Jr., reports that some
Cherokee slaves apparently were taken to Mexico during the Civil War, with some of
them not returning for several years. Littlefield, *Cherokee Freedmen,* 29.

SWEETIE IVERY WAGONER[1]

Age 73   *Muskogee, Oklahoma*

If I was born the year of freedom or the year before my mammy didn't
know. Her name was Bitty Ivery and pappy's name was Louis Ivery,
belonging to old Newt Tittsworth who had a big plantation somewheres in Arkansas, but I don't know what the name of the town.
Only thing I know that man had a big place—as far as the eye could

see that man owned it. He had seven or eight slave families on the place; my mother was the house girl, done the spinning, the cooking, the cleaning and all such. The old master was good to the slaves my mammy always said; never whipped them, but if they got mean and worthless he would sell them.

My father was a slave, but he wasn't a Negro. He was a Creek Indian whom the Cherokee Indians stole long years ago and put in slavery just like he was a Negro, and he married with a slave woman (her mother, Betty) and raised a big family. There was King, Louis, Mary, Cindy, Lucy, Jane, Fannie, Martha, Emma, Adeline and myself. I don't know where any is now, we all get separated after the war and never find each other.

Master Titsworth's house was a pretty good frame place; the slave families sleep in their own cabins, but all their eating was done together in a long house made of rough brick, and the eatings was plentiful with fresh killed beef or pork, plenty of corn pone made of meal ground by the old rock mills, with potatoes and vegetables seasoned high with the meats.

The eatings wasn't so good after the war when the slaves have to reach out for themselves; mostly it was corn grits, then maybe it wouldn't be nothing like it is now when I gets hardly enough to live on, hungry most of the time and in the misery so deep I can do no work (she is an invalid and seems likely to die within a short time).

There was a white overseer on the plantation and he blowed the whistle which sent everybody to their work. Mammy said he was a good man.

The slave owners was always wanting more young slaves and if there was a woman on the place that didn't have no man the old masters would send to another plantation and borrow a big husky slave man for the woman and when the woman was done with child they would send the man back to this own place.

Everybody get scared when the war come along; the master was afraid somebody steal his slaves so he ups and takes us to Texas and then we come back to Arkansas after a while and stay there until freedom.

We stay for a while with the old master after the war, then my pappy go to farming and making things like wooden tubs, oat straw hats, horse collars and most anything he could sell or trade to the neighbors.

My folks was part Indian alright; they wore blankets and breeches with fur around the bottoms. My father's own daddy was Randolph Get-a-bout, and when the Indian lands given out by the allotments I got me 160 acres right here in Muskogee just north of where I live now. I use to own all that, but no more.

Lots of the slaves never learn to read or write, but the mistress teach my own mammy after the day's work was done. They set in the house long after dark and the mistress teach her, and then on Sunday, every Sunday too, they would go to a little church for the preaching. My mammy would set back over on one side of the seat rows; never did she miss the Sabbath meeting.

I belong to the Methodist Church, but since it been eight year that I been unable to get out, I just do all my praying at home. There's nothing else like religion for folks to enjoy.

[1] Sweetie Ivery Wagoner was interviewed by WPA field worker Ethel Wolfe Garrison in Muskogee, Oklahoma, probably sometime in the winter of 1937–38. On 19 January 1938 project employee Craig Vollmer revised and typed Garrison's notes into a preliminary draft entitled "Interview with Sweetie Ivery Wagoner, Slave Born, Age 73, 1602 N. 3rd Street, Muskogee, Oklahoma," available in the OHS Slave Narratives. At a later date this preliminary draft was slightly polished and retyped into a final draft, published here and available as "Sweetie Ivery Wagoner, Age 73, Muskogee, Oklahoma" in the OHS Slave Narratives. This interview was never forwarded to Washington.

WILLIAM WALTERS[1]

Age 85 Yrs.   *Tulsa, Oklahoma*

Mammy Ann (that was my mother) was owned by Mistress Betsy, and lived on the Bradford plantation in Relsford County, Tennessee,[2] when I was born in 1852.

My daddy, Jim Walters, then lived in Nashville, where my mammy carried me when she ran away from the Mistress after the Rebs and Yanks started to fight. My daddy died in Nashville in 1875.

We were runaway slaves. The slipper-offers were often captured, but Mammy Ann and her little boy William (that's me) escaped the sharp eyes of the patrollers and found refuge with a family of northern sympathizers living in Nashville.

Nashville was a fort town, filled with trenches and barricades. Right across the road from where we stayed was a vacant block used by the Rebs as an emergency place for treating the wounded.[3]

I remember the boom of cannons one whole day, and I heard the rumble of army wagons as they crossed through the town. But there was nothing to see as the fog of powder smoke became thicker with every blast of Sesesh cannon.

When the smoke fog cleared away I watched the wounded being carried to the clearing across the road—fighting men with arms shot off, legs gone, faces blood smeared—some of them just laying there cussing God and Man with their dying breath!

Those were awful times. Yet I have heard many of the older Negroes say the old days were better.

Such talk always seemed to be but an expression of sentiment for some good old master, or else the older Negroes were just too handicapped with ignorance to recognize the benefits of liberty or the opportunities of freedom.

But I've always been proud of my freedom, and proud of my old mother who faced death for her freedom and mine when she escaped from the Bradford plantation a long time before freedom came to the Negro race as a whole.

[1] WPA field worker L. P. Livingston interviewed William Walters in Tulsa, Oklahoma, probably in summer 1937, for on 15 July of that year project employee Craig Vollmer revised Livingston's notes into a preliminary draft of the Walters narrative. This text, available as the typescript "Interview with William Walters (Age 85) (Slave Born—December 27, 1852)" in the OHS Slave Narratives, was revised later that summer into a final form, "William Walters, Age 85 Yrs., Tulsa, Oklahoma." The latter version, published here, is available in ribbon copy in the LC Slave Narratives and in carbon copy as item 350068 in the LC Slave Narratives Carbon Copies and in the OHS Slave Narratives. Because of the brevity of the narrative, on 10 August 1937 Ron Stephens at the state headquarters asked Robert Vinson Lackey in the Tulsa office if Walters could be reinterviewed. Two weeks later, Craig Vollmer responded that he had been unable to speak further with Walters, who was out of town. On 2 September, perhaps to meet quotas for interviews forwarded, the existing final draft of the Walters narrative was sent on to Washington, and Walters apparently was never interviewed further. After the text arrived in Washington, Federal Writers' Project folklore editor Benjamin A. Botkin noted that the narrative was "relatively unimportant in itself" but "valuable as one of the few runaway slave narratives." B. A. B[otkin], LC Slave Narratives Appraisal Sheets, Accession no. 350068, 6 December 1940; Stephens to Lackey, 10 August 1937; Vollmer to DeWitt, 24 August 1937; Stephens to Cronyn, 2 September 1937; all three letters in WPA Notes on Interviews.

[2] This may be a reference to Rutherford County, Tennessee, just southeast of Nashville.

[3] The fighting remembered by William Walters apparently was that associated with the capture of the city by Union forces in late February 1862. The wounded soldiers observed may have been Confederate troops passing through the city after the fall of Forts Henry and Donelson several days earlier. Two years later additional fighting took place on the outskirts of Nashville when in December 1864 federal forces overwhelmingly defeated an ill-fated attempt by the Confederate general John B. Hood to

take the city. Stanley F. Horn, "Nashville during the Civil War," *Tennessee Historical Quarterly* 4 (March 1945): 3–22; Stanley F. Horn, ed., *Tennessee's War, 1861–1865, Described by Participants,* 60–72, 320–52; Peter Maslowski, *Treason Must Be Made Odious: Military Occupation and Wartime Reconstruction in Nashville, Tennessee, 1862–65,* 3–152.

INTERVIEW WITH ROCHELLE ALLRED WARD[1]

Slave Born, Age 91   *Route 2, Box 9, Fort Gibson, Okla.*

My mother, Lottie Beck, was belonging to old master Joe Beck when I was born about 1847, on the Beck farm in Flint District of the old Cherokee Nation. That a mighty long time ago and lots of things my old mind won't remember, but I never forgot the old Beck mill place because I done many a cooking there and watch the mill grind up the corn and wheat for the Indians' meal and flour.

Before I tell about the mill I want to tell about paw; Jim he was named, and belong to Sarah Eaton, who must have stole him when he about eight or nine year old from his folks in Georgia and brought him out here, maybe to Fort Gibson near as he could tell. That make paw born about 1827 because he was a young man grown to full grown when he met my maw.

He come to the mill place for his mistress, that the way he always tell about it, and the only girl he see right off was Lottie, one of the Beck slave girls, but they was lots more on the place, only he could see no one but Lottie and fall in love with her. She feel the same way about him; she asked old Master Joe to buy Jim Eaton so's they can marry, build a cabin.

Master Joe want to know if the young slave a good worker, and when Jim Eaton say, "I is the best cane stripper and field man in the whole country," the master offer Sarah Eaton $500 for her slave boy and that done bought him. So he come to the Becks, change his name to Jim Beck and keep it ever since.

My paw always told me he was part Indian account of his mamma was a Cherokee Indian girl name Downing; that make my paw some kin to Chief Downing who was a big man among the Cherokees after the Civil War when the Indians stop fighting amongst themselves.[2]

Two of my sisters, Sabra and Celia, was both real light in color, but my brothers was all dark. They was named Milton, Louie, Sam, Nelson and Dennis.

Well, the old mill had done been built by some of the Becks when they first come out to this country a long time before I was born. Some of Master Joe's kin they was; all over this country was Beck families, but other folks come in here too, one of them new settlers run the old mill for awhile until he died. I hear his name when I was a young girl, seem like it was Hildebrand; different from all them Indian names anyways.

We all done move away from the mill place during the war, but bad things happen around the old place after the war and I hear about it the way folks tell it then.

When the old miller die his wife marry one of the men who work in the mill, but an Indian name Proctor (Zeke) work up a grudge for the woman's husband and fix up to kill him. When the Indian come to the mill and start a ruckus with the man, his wife mix in and get shot. Seem like she jump in front of the Indian when he try to shoot and get the bullet herself. She died; that cause lots more trouble and it was a long time before it was settled and folks stop killing each other.[3]

After my paw come with the Becks they make him a kind of overseer. There was several families living in the little log cabins on the farm, and all these slave families look to my paw for the way to do things. The mistress say, "Whatever Jim do is alright." She trusted him and she saw he was a good worker and would do the right thing.

None of the Beck slaves was sold, but paw said he seen slaves sold off. He told us children, that was after the war, "We was all good negroes, that's why the Becks keep us. And we ought to be glad, because I see sorrow at the auctions, and crying, when the mother sold off from her child, or when the child is took away from her."

The mistress always get us anything we need; even after the war, and she come down to where we live around Fort Gibson, and bring cloth for our dresses and help make them, and one time she said she was going to bring her old Bible down for paw to get all the children's ages, but she died before she could get back the next spring.

Some of the slaves work around and get money and pay this money to their master for freedom, so there was some freed before the close of the war. Some others try to run away after the war start, and maybe they get caught, like the one man who hide in a house around the old mill. Some said he was a freedman, too, but anyways some of the Confederates find him in the old house, take him off to Texas and sell him. They got a big price for him, $5,000 they said, but it was Confederate money and that kind of money got worthless as a cotton patch without no hoeing.

But the patrollers didn't bother nobody with a pass and when anybody leave the Beck place it was with a pass. But lots of slaves was stole and the masters fix up to get their slaves out of the hills and take them to Fort Gibson for safety. The Confederate soldiers was there then (1862).

The mistress was getting old and she cried terrible when all the slaves leave in the night for the fort. Everybody loaded in the ox wagons, hating to leave the mistress, but they all have to go.

We camped around the garrison place at Fort Gibson and there was no buildings there like there is now. The soldiers was all camped there in tents. They was all Confederate soldiers and I mean there was lots of soldiers camped in the tents.

The negroes piled in there from everywheres, and I mean there was lots of them, too. Cooking in the open, sleeping most anywhere, making shelter places out of cloth scraps and brush, digging caves along the river bank to live in. There was no way to keep the place clean for there was too many folks living all in one place, and if you walk around in the nighttime most likely you stumble over some negro rolled up in a dirty blanket and sleeping under a bush.

I never was where the fighting went on, but I heard the cannon go "Bum! Bum!" and the little guns go "Bang!" in all directions. I seen the soldiers come in after the fights; they be all shot up with blood soaking through the clothes, trying to help each other tie on a bandage (she calls it "bannage")—the awfulest sights I ever see.

The generals have some young boys, I guess they was soldiers, herding the horses a little way south of the fort. Then one day a scout come riding in and yell, "The Federals is coming!" All the soldiers run for the horses and gallop out for the mountain south from the fort. I hear that fighting, guns speaking in the hills, and the Federals was whipped. Lots of them killed and some of them captured and brought back to the fort, and some got away.

Some folks say that while the war is on the Federals take charge of the old Beck mill. Guess they stole the grain, too, for to make meal, anyway they kept the soldiers in food when the other folks was starving. They captured one of the Confederate boys and made him run the mill.

Master Joe Beck died during the war by a horse kick, and after the war everything so upsettled that folks don't know what to do. For a while we lived on Carroll Branch near Fort Gibson and I nursed around first one family and another.

Then come a time of cholera; people die all that season, and the dead—seem like they pass and pass all the time—was carried on little two wheel wagons pulled by a mule to a burying place out near the National Cemetery. Lots of soldiers die, and some time after the cholera die out, their bodies was moved to the National Cemetery, and the slaves was buried back in the woods to the north.

The Federals tried to catch the cholera germs. They kill beefs, hung the pieces high up in the air, leave the meat for days and days out in the open—say it catch the germs, but I don't know.

Mostly in my coming up time we didn't know what doctoring was. Some of the older men and women use to dig roots and get different herbs for medicine; them medicines cure the chill fever and such.

When I married Amos Allred, a State man from Freeport, Texas, more than seventy year ago, we had to get signers before old Judge Walker at Fort Gibson could say the words. I get seven signers, all of them Cherokee Indians who know I was a good slave woman. We divorced a long time later and I married a State man from Mississippi, Nelson Ward. There was thirteen children, but I done forget all the names: some was, Amos, Susie, Jess, Will, Frank, Lottie, Cora.

[1] A woman identified as Rochelle Allred Ward was interviewed at Fort Gibson, Oklahoma, by field worker Ethel Wolfe Garrison probably sometime in the winter of 1937–38. On 14 January 1938 project employee Craig Vollmer in the Tulsa office of the project revised and typed her initial notes into the typescript "Interview with Rochelle Allred Ward, Slave Born, Age 91, Route 2, Box 9, Fort Gibson, Okla.," which is available in the OHS Slave Narratives. The interview text was apparently forwarded to the state headquarters of the project, for supervisor Ned DeWitt initialed a note appended to the typescript stating "To Typist 10–19–38." Apparently no clerk was ever assigned to retype the narrative, however, for it is known to exist in only the one ribbon-copy typescript in the OHS Slave Narratives. This interview was never forwarded to Washington.

The name of the informant was undoubtedly garbled at the time of the interview. She actually was Rachel Aldrich Ward, former slave of Joe Beck, and was enrolled by the Dawes Commission as a Cherokee freedwoman together with her children. Cherokee Freedmen Census Cards, no. 294 (Rachel and Cora Ward; William, Jesse, and Lewis Aldrich; and Dan Vann); Cherokee Freedmen Enrollment Application Testimony, file 294 (Rachel and Cora Ward; William, Jesse, and Lewis Aldrich). For another, contemporary interview with this informant, see Rachel Ward, interview by Breland Adams [probably at Fort Gibson, Oklahoma], 2 March 1937, Indian-Pioneer Papers, 11:206–8.

[2] A leader of the Unionist Cherokees during the Civil War, Lewis Downing served as principal chief of the Cherokee Nation in 1866 and in 1867–72. Gaston L. Litton, "The Principal Chiefs of the Cherokee Nation," *Chronicles of Oklahoma* 15 (September 1937): 264–66; John Bartlett Meserve, "Chief Lewis Downing and Chief Charles Thompson (Oochalata)," *Chronicles of Oklahoma* 16 (September 1938): 315–25.

[3] For accounts of the shooting at the Beck (Hildebrand) Mill and the feud that it

began, see, among other sources, Kelley Agnew, "Tragedy of the Goingsnake District: The Shoot-out at Zeke Proctor's Trial," *Chronicles of Oklahoma* 64 (Fall 1986): 90–99; Stanley A. Clark, interview by Ja[me]s S. Buchanan at Muskogee, Oklahoma, 30 October 1937, Indian-Pioneer Papers, 65:147–53; Henry Downing, interview by Alfred E. Hicks at Nowata, Oklahoma, [ca. 1937], Indian-Pioneer Papers, 3:224; Martha Horn Mitchell, interview by James R. Carselowey at Vinita, Oklahoma, 13 April 1938, Indian-Pioneer Papers, 81:59–60; Daniel F. Littlefield, Jr., and Lonnie E. Underhill, "Hildebrand's Mill near Flint, Cherokee Nation," *Chronicles of Oklahoma* 58 (Spring 1970): 83–94; E. H. Whitmire, interview by W.J.B. Bigby [at unidentified location], 26 February 1937, Indian-Pioneer Papers, 11:371–76.

INTERVIEW WITH MOLLIE WATSON[1]

Ex-Slave, Aged 83   *Colbert, Oklahoma*

"Yes Ma'am, Lincoln was a good man. He took us niggers out from under de bull-whup and de patterollers and give us freedom. I think he was de bes' man dat was ever bawn on dis green earth. He was nex' to God I think."

"Well, effen what I'ze heard about Jeff Davis is true he wasn't no good. I don't think he was much punkin."

I remember hearin' a story about how de confederates was about to git whupped and dey was a cullud man dat advised him what to do and jest how he could win de battle. Jeff Davis told dis man dat he was goin' to do jest as he say and do an' effen he win de battle he was goin' to set all the cullud folks free. Well, dey fit de battle and won it. Did he do lak he promised? No siree. He jest wasn't a man of his word.

I sho' can remember dem old times befo' de war and endurin' of de war, too. I had a good time as I was jest a little chile and Old Miss sort o' petted me I reckon.

We lived in Centerville, Leon County, Texas. My mother was Patience Garner and my father was Wesley Garner. Our owner was Squire Garner and our young Massa was Sebastian Stroud.

Ole Miss was a widow wid three chillen, Sebastian, Linnie, and Betty Stroud, when she married Square Garner. We was all her slaves, ceptin my father and one or two more he had when they married.

Ole Miss and Squire Garner decided to move into town and run de tavern and livery stable. She didn't need very many slaves so she give 'em all out to her children and her brother. She give my mother and my brother and Aunt Harriet's daughter, Dinah, to Miss Linnie. She told my mother dat she'd keep me cause somebody might run over me. I stayed right in de house wid her so long dat

I thought ever thing in it belonged to me. I sho' was a spiled youngun.

My main job was to fill and light Ole Miss's pipe and to keep her room tidy. Ole Massa kept my father and several of de men to do de work around de yard and stables and to take keer o' de horses and de kerriges [carriages].

Our house sho' was a nice one. It was a big white house with a long gallery clean across de front of it and it had twenty-four rooms in it. De bedrooms all had a fireplace in 'em and de kitchen set away from de house about twenty feet. Dey was a board walk dat jined it to de house and dis walk was kivered wid a grape arbor.

De furniture was bought in New Orleans. Dey was sofas, lounges and chairs dat was kivered wid red plush wid blue flowers. De carpets was hand woven and kivered de whole flo'.

In de bedrooms was nice furniture, too. Corded beds and chairs and bureaus wid beveled glasses and marble tops, wash-stands wid purty wash-bowls and pitchers to match. They wasn't no springs on de beds. Dey used rope slats and de biggest feather beds you ever seen. Sheets and pillow-cases, pillow shams and coverlids was all hand made.

Dey cooked in pots dat hung on racks in de fireplace. Dey had racks out in de yard where dey cooked sometimes. When dey cooked in dese big pots dey would take a big middlin' o' meat and cut it in about four pieces and dey would boil it wid greens, collards, peas, turnips or beans. Dey cooked corn-bread in a big oven dat was built in de yard.

We allus had a lot o' good things to eat as Ole Miss set a good table for de travelers. I got to eat jest what de white folks et and we had pie or cake or somethin' sweet to eat ever day.

De coffee was made outen rye or corn meal or sweet potatoes that was dried and parched.

When dey made it from sweet potatoes dey would slice 'em and put 'em in de sun to dry lak dey did fruit or corn. When it was plum dry it was put in de oven and parched and den dey would grind it in a little hand mill. It made purty good coffee but Ole Miss and Squire Garner had Lincoln coffee to drink. Dey called it Lincoln coffee because it was real coffee. Dey couldn't afford to serve it on de table as it was too 'spensive.

She had a coffee pot that held four cups o' coffee. Every mornin' I'd git up and make a pot o' coffee then I'd get a tray and put two cups on it. I'd put de cream, sugar bowl and the spoon holder and two napkins. I'd take it to de bed and pour out a cup fer Ole Miss and Squire Garner to drink befo' dey got up. Squire Garner allus drank two cups but de other one was fer me when dey got through with drinkin' theirs. Effen dey went away from home I'd take de Lincoln coffee and de pot and hide 'em. I'd hide 'em under de house on de flo' sills.

Ole Miss's brother married a po' gal and she didn't like it a bit. She say he could a done better'n dat effen he tried. I didn't like her either cause Old Miss didn't. I thought she was po' white trash. Her name was Miss Jane. I played with all de white chillen and I called 'em all by name. Miss Jane didn't like dat but Old Miss say effen I call dem Miss an' Massa it would make 'em vain.

I sho' loved Marse Bastian's chillen, Billy and Sue. We played together all de time and we got along good. Sometimes we'd git into a fight and we'd all git spanked. Lots o' white folks wouldn't whup dey chillen fer fightin' nigger chillen but Ole Miss an' Marse Bastian sho' would.

Miss Jane told Ole Miss dat she didn't think it was right to whup her chillen when we had a fight an' Ole Miss say, "I done give you folks some niggers and you all de time whuppin' 'em. I kept dis chile fer myself an' I ain't gonna have her run over, I can tell you." So effen us chillen got in a scrap we knowed we'd ever one git spanked good an' proper so we allus managed to have a purty good fight befo' we got kotched up wid.

De town we lived in had a town square. Our house was on de south side an' de jail an' de court house was right across de square in front of us.

Speclators uster buy up niggers jest lak dey was animals and dey would travel around over de country an' sell 'em. I've seen 'em come through there in droves lak cattle. De owners would ride in wagons or buggies. Dey would come into town an' camp over night an' nex' mornin' dey would parade 'em round town an' den take 'em to de town square an' put 'em on de block an' sell 'em. I've seen men, wives an' little chillen sold away from each other.

When de sales would be goin' on me an' Billy an' Sue would ride our stick horses up purty close an' watch 'em. I wasn't scared cause I knowed Ole Miss an' Square Garner was settin' on de gallery a watchin' it jest lak we was an' I knowed she would keep me safe.

Marse Bastian lived on at de farm after Ole Miss moved into town. His house was a big two-story white house. Right behind it was de first quarters where de workin' slaves lived. Next was de quarters where de nigger drivers lived. Nigger drivers was de cullud overseers. Dey sho' was mean. Dey was so biggety an' such smart-alexs an' dey worked de niggers so hard dat all de hands hated 'em. Dey was a lot harder'n de white overseers.

In de lower quarters was de white overseers' homes. Dey had very nice boxed houses. Dey was right kind to de niggers but dey give 'em to understand dat dey had so much work to do and dey usually managed to do it.

Once Marse Bastian had a cullud overseer dat was allus beatin' on some one and one day all de hands ganged up on him an' beat him till he died.

De cabins where de slaves lived were not very big an' didn't have much furniture in 'em. Dey had jest one room and dirt flo's. Dey would spread ashes over de flo's an' dampen 'em and pack 'em down so it would be white and smooth.

For bedsteads dey would stick a puncheon in a crack in de wall an' would drive a forked pole in de middle of de flo' to rest de other end o' de pole on. Den dey would put another puncheon in de crack o' de wall on de other side an' rest de end in de fork o' de post. Dey would string ropes across dese an' put de beds on dem. Some had cotton beds an' others jest had straw beds. Dey would be one o' dese beds in all four corners o' de room, each bed had only one leg. Dere was a fireplace an' dey used benches fer chairs.

I recollect that my mother's house had one room an' dey was four beds in it. Ma, Aunt Cindy, Margaret, Dinah, an' seven chillen slept in dis room.

Aunt Luce lived by herself an' had more room den de rest and Marse Bastian would let de niggers dance at her house. All de women wore hoop skirts dat come down to de ground. They'd dance an' stir up de dirt an' ashes on de flo' till de dust git in de chillen's eyes an' make 'em cry an' dey'd have to take 'em home an' dis would break up de dance.

We made our own candles. Ole Miss had some tall brass candle sticks. We would polish 'em wid ashes till dey would shine lak gold. She used dese tall ones in de parlor. De ones she used in de bedrooms was short ones.

De black folks used "huzzies." Dat was a saucer like thing wid a lip to it. We'd fill dis wid grease an' take a wick dat was made outen homespun an' plaited. We wet de wick in de grease an' lit it. It made a po' light, too. Old Miss got some little brass kerosene lamps about de beginnin' o' de war.

Didn't none o' de slaves know de A.B.C.'s. Squire Garner bought a man dat had his right fore finger cut off. He say he learned to write an' when his master found it out he had his finger cut off.

We all wore red russet shoes. De leather was tanned at home. Dey'd dig a pit lak a barbecue pit in a swampy place an' take red-oak bark an' beat it till ooze come out. Den they'd take a layer o' bark an' a layer o' leather an' pack in de pit. When de leather became supple it was already tanned. It was den made into shoes. I went barefooted in summer an' winter as I'd ruther do dat dan wear shoes.

De women had two work dresses a year an' two changes o' underwear. De white ladies give 'em dey old dresses to dress up in. When de everday clo's nearly wore out dey took 'em an' made baby clo's outen 'em. I guess babies wasn't as tender as dey are now fer dey has to have de finest o' cloth now to make baby clo's outen.

Dey was a big cane-brake close to Marse Bastian's farm an' de niggers uster slip down in dere an have church an' parties. Dey would git happy an' shout an' somebody would hold a pot over dey mouth so de white folks couldn't hear 'em. De Patterollers was afraid to follow 'em into de cane-brake. Effen he did de men would hide an' knock him in de head an drag him out an' say they found him near de cane-brake an' no one would a knowed who done it. De niggers sho' hated dem patterollers cause dey was so mean to 'em. Effen dey caught a nigger off o' his master's plantation dey would beat him lak he had stole a horse.

All de women an' girls could spin an' weave an' nearly all of 'em could sew. We spun blankets durin' de war. We could keep de nappy blankets but had to send de good ones to de army. I was small an' didn't hurt myself at any kind o' work.

Sometimes when Ole Miss was gone Ole Margaret, the cook, would give me lumps o' brown sugar to wash an' dry de dishes fer her. She was good to me an' I liked to do things fer her. It would take me all evenin' as dey was so many an' I'd have to climb up in de shelves to put 'em away. Lucy was a kitchen woman, too. She'd try to make me help her an' she'd tell me she'd whup me effen I didn't. I was afraid o' her an' I'd go in de kitchen an' wash de dishes. I wouldn't do 'em good an' I'd always break somethin' so Ole Miss would ask about it an' I could tell her than Luce made me wash de dishes an' I couldn't reach de shelves an' I jest dropped it an' [it] broke. Old Miss git right in after Luce an' she be afraid to make me wash 'em any more fer a long time.

I never knew much about music but I sho' did like to hear Miss Betty play de piano. I never knew what she'd play unless she sung it.

I recollect how she played an' sung, "Shoo Fly, Don't You Bother Me," "Granny Will Yo' Dog Bite?" "Dixie," and "Darling Black Mustache." She uster sing good songs too, sech as "Rock Of Ages," "De Lord's A Rock," "Swing Low Sweet Chariot," an' lots o' others.

My father was sold away from us an' his master wouldn't let him come back to see us any more so he married again. He married a woman from de piney woods. My mother never did git married any more.

Ole Squire Garner died durin' de war an' after de war my father come back an' took me to live with some cullud folks close to him. I hated to leave Old Miss an' I couldn't git along with de folks I was livin' with so I run away an' went back to Ole Miss. I had a hard time gettin' back but I made it an' I stayed about six month before he come an' got me again. I run off ever chance I got till finally he took me so far away dat I couldn't come back. I never saw Old Miss any more but I'll see her when I git to Heaven. I never saw my mother any more either.

When I growed up I sho' did like to dance. I'd ruther dance den eat an' I'd go to dances an' dance all night. Father would say, "Git back by daylight an' cook breakfast." I allus did an' den I'd go to de field and chop or pick cotton all day. I could plow or chop wood or do any kind o' work dat a man could do. I don't reckon it hurt me none as I allus felt good.

We'd have log-rollin' an' railsplittin's, house-raisin's, corn-shuckin's an' quiltin's. De old women would cook, de young women would burn brush an' de men would roll logs or build de house. After supper we'd dance all night.

The old folks uster scare us wid "Raw Head an' Bloody Bones." I never did see him but it sounded scary enuff to make me want to be good an' quit whatever I was doin'. Lots o' folks carry lucky pieces. It can be a rabbit's foot, a buckeye, coin or even a button. It all depends on how much faith you have in it. For my part I'd ruther trust in de good Lord to keep me safe from harm den in all the lucky pieces in de world. He can take care o' you an' keep yo' safe both here an' in de nex' world whar we will be de same color an' on equal grounds.

[1] WPA field worker Mrs. Jessie R. Ervin interviewed Mrs. Mollie Watson at Colbert, Oklahoma, probably sometime in autumn 1937. From her interview notes a preliminary draft of Watson's narrative was prepared as the typescript "Interview with Mollie Watson (Ex-Slave, Aged 83, Colbert, Oklahoma)," available in the OHS Slave Narratives. On 4 November 1937 Ron Stephens, at the Federal Writers' Project office in Oklahoma City, asked Ervin if she could reinterview Watson, but there is no evi-

dence that a second interview was ever undertaken. Approximately a year passed with no further work on this narrative. Then Ned DeWitt at the Oklahoma City office of the Federal Writers' Project jotted a note on 19 October 1938 and clipped it to the edited preliminary typescript, sending it to be typed into a final draft, but apparently the final typing was never done. Only the preliminary draft in Oklahoma City is known to survive, and the Mollie Watson narrative was never sent to Washington. Ron Stephens, [Oklahoma City, Oklahoma], to Jessie Ervin, McAlester, Oklahoma, 4 November 1937, WPA Notes on Interviews.

INTERVIEW WITH WILLIAM W. WATSON[1]

Exslave, Age About 85 Years Old   *R. 3, Box 151,*
Being with Wife Betsy Ann Davis
Three Miles North of Muskogee, Oklahoma

Do I remember slavery? Who could forget these lash prints on my back. Some time I set here and look at my wife and think Lord help me look what I bin through. Me and my wife had a car wreck early last year, that made her lose her mind so she just sings all the time, can't think. Raises chickens and talks like a baby. She is two years older than me, and too she is the mother of thirteen children, had lots of trouble. I am still able to feed the cows and horses that belong to my son.

My wife has the prettiest name, Betsy Ann Davis, then she was sold to Doninan, he called her Annie, but I still say Betsy Ann. My wife just weigh 120 pounds, use to weigh one hundred. My mother belonged to the same master that my wife did, old man Davis, Master Tom we calls him.

My mother was Eliza Davis, and my paw was Boler Watson. Father was brought from some place to W. Virginia and sold. I never learned the place. When they was bought they come to Tenn. I do not know the place. Henry Watson owned my father, and Tom Davis owned my mother. Davis lived in Tenn. Watson's plantation joined Davis some place about ten miles below Palaksa.[2] They lived in the deep country. Master Davis' children was named Simon, Susie, George, Minnie. Their house I was born in was a one room mud log room in white folks, Davis, yard. Boy I was born at Master Davis. Master Watson had a big slave house made like a barn, had one room stables, like you put horses in for the slave families. Our beds was made on the wall, each room had a mud fireplace. Master had nice beds, made of cherry, ash, walnut, high tops.

I don't know any thing about any my old grand parents; guess they was left across the water.

During of the war and before it I plowed, handled rock, to make a building out of, cut logs, cleaned up new ground, thrashed, cut hay, fenced, worked in black smith shops, shoe horses. Done every thing a farmer could do and be alive now. I pressed and loaded and toted cotton a bale at the time on my back. I weighed 280 pounds when I was about grown.

Me and my wife raised our children out of a iron pot and a three leg skillet. I made buckeye wood trays, made bread up in these, didn't have no dishes. We had wood home made bowls. We wasn't fed like we eat now, we eat then like a hog, better not ask Master Watson for no lean meat either. After the first year we was free we had lean hams. Do I remember the bull whip and cat of nine lashed with a hole in each leather lash to draw blood; my back sure did blead.

If you didn't do the work or be a little slow, Master Watson tell you once, but better mind him. Next time the cat of nine tails was salted and boy it hurt. I didn't know what a shoe was until I was grown. Come up all my growing years barefooted.

Henry Watson whipped all the niggers. Old man Davis was a father to me but I was took away from him.

Master Davis had sons named George, Jim, Ben, Billie, Isom, the daughters was Ann, Susie. Master Davis' old lady was named Margarite. Margarite made me tote water and make fires. Henry Watson got me and was gone, then I had to do all the churning for his slaves. He had pappy first, guess he bought me but Master Davis didn't say I sold you. My paw come and said come go with me so I went.

I am the father of thirteen children. Old Watson had 250 acres in his plantation. I heard him tell the overseer, say white man ride the 250 today and watch for any strayed niggers, if so bring them in my house. Master Davis had 600 acres in his plantation, he owned my mother, Martha, Benner, Harret, Bennett, John, that's a few the slave names I remember. My mother was on the Davis plantation when my paw took me away to Watson's place. My mother and paw married the old way first, then after the war they sure got married, that's the way me and my wife done. After the war we got together, all hired out to plantation owners, got our start at farming but it was hard go.

We got up by a bell and went to bed by a horn. You better get up when you hear that bell. Watson's overseer come to the door to see, little kids and all come out of bed so they could get that ash cake.

At dinner when we come from the field we eat at Watson's back porch for a table. In winter we eat in our own house.

At Davis dinner time we eat in his kitchen summer and winter.

After I left Davis he moved down to the little village of Bunker

Hill, Tenn. Me and my wife bin married old way before slave time don't know how meny years. I got children way over 60 years old. Got one gets the old age pension. My living children names are Matilda, Blanch, Thomas, Ebnezer, some of the dead ones' names are Mamie, Anne, Baxter, & for the two sets of twins' names, maybe they wasn't named. My wife don't remember.

In slave days after Master Davis brought my wife to me, we set up all night, spin, knit, weave. I done this too, same as she did. Was I always a good boy, never cursed, gambled, or drank. Was always at church. My wife could sew good. I used to get after her. But she hasn't any mind any more since that car from Porter hit our wagon [and] the mules run away.

I went to sunday school after the War with domestic breeches on. My wife dye them with milk persely; it make them purple; she used copperas to dye yellow, walnut bark to dye brown, smart weed for dark purple. I bin married just one time in my days, don't never want another woman, couldn't be like my Anna. When I had my wagon wreck I was unconscious for two days. My wife was knocked out too.

That is all I can remember. I was treated mean in slave times, glad to the Lord I am free and serving the Lord and Abe Lincoln's spirit, that's how much I love that man. I got his picture here too.

Lincoln lived in a log house, and I live in a one room cellar under the ground. My son lives in a house close but [I] can't listen to his children; they got about two dozen. One dozen grandchildren, two great grandchildren; you got them in your picture with us. Master Davis was an irish man. Watson was white trash.

When peace was declared I was on the auction block with my mother.

I don't know when, but my mother died and I went to Paw, after the war.

Master Davis when I was free give me a spotted horse and saddle; this was directly after the war, 1865. I have belonged to the church all my life, was when I was a slave boy. I prayed; I was ten years old first time. I know I prayed.

I come from Bunker Hill to Gipson Station,[3] then Muskogee; bin here ever since for years. Jehovah No 1 first church I belonged to at Gipson Station, then to St John Baptiste, Muskogee, at agency hill. These great grandchildren are named Phyllys and Joe.

[1] William W. Watson was interviewed by WPA field worker Ethel Wolfe Garrison on his farm near Muskogee, Oklahoma, on 11 March 1938. Garrison's handwritten

interview notes on Oklahoma Federal Writers' Project letterhead stationery are available as "Interview with William W. Watson, Exslave Age about 85 Years Old, R. 3, Box 151, Being with Wife Betsy Ann Davis Three Miles North of Muskogee, Oklahoma" in the OHS Slave Narratives. Garrison's coworker Craig Vollmer in the Tulsa office of the Federal Writers' Project edited and very substantially shortened Watson's narrative on 24 May 1938 into the typescript "Interview with William W. Watson, Ex-Slave, About 85 Years Old, Route 3, Box 151, Muskogee, Oklahoma," also in the OHS Slave Narratives (in the WPA Notes on Interviews file). Because the handwritten transcription of the interview is considerably more comprehensive than and includes all the data in the later, edited typescript, the former is published here. For reasons not known, the William Watson narrative was never forwarded to Washington.

2 An apparent reference to Pulaski, Tennessee.

3 An apparent reference to Gibson Station, Oklahoma.

MARY FRANCES WEBB[1]

Grand Daughter of Sarah Vest, Aged 92 (Deceased)   *McAlester, Okla.*

I've heard my grandmother tell a lot of her experiences during slavery. She remembered things well as she was a grown woman at the time of the War of the Rebellion.

Her home was at Sedalia, Mo., and her owner was Baxter West [*sic*], a prominent farmer and politician. He was very kind and good to his slaves. He provided them with plenty of food and good clothes. He would go to town and buy six or eight bolts of cloth at a time and the women could pick out two dresses apiece off it. These would be their dresses for dressing up. They wove the cloth for their everyday clothes.

The men wore jeans suits in winter. He bought shoes for all his slaves, young and old. He had about twenty slaves counting the children.

My grandmother was a field hand. She plowed and hoed the crops in the summer and spring, and in the winter she sawed and cut cord wood just like a man. She said it didn't hurt her as she was as strong as an ox.

She could spin and weave and sew. She helped make all the cloth for their clothes and in the spring one of the jobs for the women was to weave hats for the men. They used oat-straw, grass, and cane which had been split and dried and soaked in hot water until it was pliant, and they wove it into hats. The women wore a cloth tied around their head.

They didn't have many matches so they always kept a log heap burning to keep a fire. It was a common thing for a neighbor to come in to borrow a coal of fire as their fire had died out.

On wash days all the neighbors would send several of their women to the creek to do the family wash. They all had a regular picnic of it as they would wash and spread the clothes on the bushes and low branches of the trees to dry. They would get to spend the day together.

They had no tubs or wash boards. They had a large flat block of wood and a wooden paddle. They'd spread the wet garment on the block, spread soap on it and paddle the garment till it was clean. They would rinse the clothes in the creek. Their soap was made from lye, dripped from ashes, and meat scraps.

The slaves had no lamps in their cabins. In winter they would pile wood on the fire in their fireplace and have the light from the fire.

The colored men went with their master to the army. They made regular soldiers and endured the same hardships that the white soldiers did. They told of one battle when so many men were killed that a little stream seemed to be running pure blood as the water was so bloody.

After the war the slaves returned home with their masters and some of the older ones stayed on with them and helped them to rebuild their farms. None of them seemed to think it strange that they had been fighting on the wrong side in the army as they were following their white folks.

Those who stayed with their old master were taught to read and write and were taught to handle their own business and to help themselves in every way possible to take their place in life.

---

[1] WPA field worker Mrs. Jessie R. Ervin interviewed Mrs. Mary Frances Webb, the granddaughter of former slave Sarah Vest, at McAlester, Oklahoma, on 7 October 1937. She prepared a preliminary draft of the interview as the typescript "Interview with Mary Frances Webb, Grand Daughter of Sarah Vest, Ex-Slave Aged 92, (Deceased), McAlester, Oklahoma" in the OHS Slave Narratives. On receiving the typescript, Ned P. DeWitt at the project office in Oklahoma City wrote Mrs. Ervin to ask if further information might be secured from Webb, to which the field worker replied that she "could have made it longer perhaps" if she had known whether interviews with descendants of slaves were acceptable. (In reality the interviews were indeed supposed to be with individuals actually born in servitude.) Apparently Mrs. Ervin was unable to secure further information from Mrs. Webb, for in time the narrative was retyped and sent on to Washington. The final draft, published here, is available as "Mary Frances Webb, Grand Daughter of Sarah Vest, Aged 92 (Deceased), McAlester, Okla." in ribbon copy in the LC Slave Narratives and in carbon copy in the "Non-Slave Narratives" file, box A906, LC Slave Narratives, and in the OHS Slave Narratives. [Mrs. Jessie R. Ervin, McAlester, Oklahoma], to Ned P. DeWitt, Oklahoma City, Oklahoma, [October or November 1937], WPA Notes on Interviews.

EASTER WELLS[1]

Age 83   *Colbert, Okla.*

I was born in Arkansas, in 1854, but we moved to Texas in 1855. I've
heard 'em tell about de trip to Texas. De grown folks rode in wagons
and carts but de chaps all walked dat was big enuff. De men walked
and toted their guns and hunted all de way. Dey had plenty of fresh
game to eat.

My mother's name was Nellie Bell. I had one sister, Liza. I never
saw my father; in fact, I never heard my mammy say anything about
him and I don't guess I ever asked her anything about him for I never
thought anything about not having a father. I guess he belonged to
another family and when we moved away he was left behind and he
didn't try to find us after de War.

My mammy and my sister and me belonged to young Master Jason
Bell.[2] We was his onliest slaves and as he wasn't married and lived at
home wid his parents; we was worked and bossed by his father, Cap'n
William Bell and his wife, Miss Mary.

After we moved to Texas, old Master built a big double log house,
weather-boarded on de inside and out. It was painted white. Dey was
a long gallery clean across de front of de house and a big open hall
between de two front rooms. Dey was three rooms on each side of de
hall and a wide gallery across de back. De kitchen set back from de
house and dey was a board walk leading to it. Vines was planted
'round de gallery and on each side of de walk in de summer time. De
house was on a hill and set back from de big road about a quarter of
a mile and dey was big oak and pine trees all 'round de yard. We had
purty flowers, too.

We had good quarters. Dey was log cabins, but de logs was peeled
and square-adzed and put together with white plaster and had shut-
tered windows and pine floors. Our furniture was home made but it
was good and made our cabins comfortable.

Old Master give us our allowance of staple food and it had to run
us, too. We could raise our own gardens and in dat way we had purty
plenty to eat. Dey took good care of us sick or well and old Mistress[3]
was awful good to us.

My mammy was de cook. I remember old Master had some purty
strict rules and one of 'em was iffen you burnt de bread you had to
eat it. One day mammy burnt de bread. She was awful busy and forgot it and it burnt purty bad. She knowed dat old Master would be
mad and she'd be punished so she got some grub and her bonnet and

she lit out. She hid in de woods and cane brakes for two weeks and dey couldn't find her either. One of de women slipped food out to her. Finally she come home and old Master give her a whipping but he didn't hurt her none. He was glad to git her back. She told us dat she could'a clipped off to de North but she didn't want to leave us children. She was afraid young Master would be mad and sell us and we'd a-had a hard time so she come back. I don't know whether she ever burnt de bread any more or not.

Once one of de men got his 'lowance and he decided he'd have de meat all cooked at once so he come to our cabin and got mammy to cook it for him. She cooked it and he took it home. One day he was at work and a dog got in and et de meat all up. He didn't have much food for de rest of de week. He had to make out wid parched corn.

We all kept parched corn all de time and went 'round eating it. It was good to fill you up iffen you was hungry and was nourishing, too.

When de niggers cooked in dere own cabins dey put de food in a sort of tray or trough and everybody et together. Dey didn't have no dishes. We allus ate at de Big House as mammy had to do de cooking for de family.

I never had to work hard as old Master wanted us to grow up strong. He'd have mammy boil Jerusalem Oak and make a tea for us to drink to cure us of worms and we'd run races and get exercise so we would be healthy.

Old Mistress and old Master had three children. Dey was two children dead between Master Jason and Miss Jane. Dey was a little girl 'bout my age, named Arline. We played together all de time. We used to set on de steps at night and old Mistress would tell us about de stars. She'd tell us and show us de Big Dipper, Little Dipper, Milky Way, Ellen's Yard, Job's Coffin, and de Seven Sisters. I can show 'em to you and tell you all about 'em yet.

I scared Arline and made her fall and break her leg twice. One time we was on de porch after dark one night and I told her dat I heard something and I made like I could see it and she couldn't so she got scared and run and hung her toe in a crack and fell off de high porch and broke her leg. Another time while de War was going on we was dressed up in long dresses playing grown-ups. We had a playhouse under some big castor-bean bushes. We climbed up on de fence and jest for fun I told her dat I seen some Yankees coming. She started to run and got tangled up in her long dress and fell and broke her leg again. It nigh broke my heart for I loved her and she loved me and she didn't tell on me either time. I used to visit her after she was married and we'd sure have a good visit talking 'bout de things we used to do. We was separated when we was about fifteen and didn't see each other any more till we was both married and had children. I went to visit her at Bryant, Brazos County, Texas[4] and I ain't seen her since. I don't know whether she is still living or not.

I 'members hearing a man say dat once he was a nigger trader. He'd buy and trade or sell 'em like they was stock. He become a Christian and never sold any more.

Our young Master went to de War and got wounded and come home and died. Old Master den took full charge of us and when de War ended he kept us because he said we didn't have no folks and he said as our owner was dead we wasn't free. Mother died about a year after de War, and some white folks took my sister but I was afraid to go. Old Master told me iffen I left him he would cut my ears off and I'd starve and I don't know what all he did tell me he'd do. I must a-been a fool but I was afraid to try it.

I had so much work to do and I never did git to go anywhere. I reckon he was afraid to let me go off de place for fear someone would tell me what a fool I was, so I never did git to go anywhere but had to work all de time. I was de only one to work and old Mistress and de girls never had done no work and didn't know much about it. I had a harder time dan when we was slaves.

I got to wanting to see my sister so I made up my mind to run off. One of old Master's motherless nephews lived with him and I got him to go with me one night to the potato bank and I got me a lap full of potatoes to eat so I wouldn't starve like old Master said I would. Dis white boy went nearly to a house where some white folks lived. I went to de house and told 'em I wanted to go to where my sister was and dey let me stay fer a few days and sent me on to my sister.

I saw old Master lots of times after I run away but he wasn't mad at me. I heard him tell de white folks dat I lived wid dat he raised me and I sure wouldn't steal nor tell a lie. I used to steal brown sugar lumps when mammy would be cooking but he didn't know 'bout dat.

On holidays we used to allus have big dinners, 'specially on Christmas, and we allus had egg-nog.

We allus had hog-jowel and peas on New Years Day 'cause iffen you'd have dat on New Years Day you'd have good luck all de year.

Iffen you have money on New Years Day you will have money all de year.

My husband, Lewis Wells, lived to be one-hundred and seven years old. He died five years ago. He could see witches, spirits and ghosts but I never could. Dere are a few things dat I've noticed and dey never fail.

Dogs howling and scritch owls hollering is allus a warning. My mother was sick and we didn't think she was much sick. A dog howled and howled right outside de house. Old Master say, "Nellie gonna die." Sure nuff she died dat night.

Another time a gentle old mule we had got after de children and run 'em to de house and den he lay down and wallow and wallow. One of our children was dead 'fore a week.

One of our neighbors say his dog been gone 'bout a week. He was walking and met de dog and it lay down and stretch out on de ground and measure a grave wid his body. He made him git up and he went home jest as fast as he could. When he got dere one of his children was dead.

Iffen my left eye quiver I know I'm gwineter cry and iffen both my eyes quiver I know I gwinter laugh till I cry. I don't like for my eyes to quiver.

We has allus made our own medicine. Iffen we hadn't we never could astood de chills and fevers. We made a tea out'n bitter weeds and bathed in it to cure malaria. We also made bread pills and soaked 'em in dis tea and swallowed 'em. After bathing in dis tea we'd go to bed and kiver up and sweat de malaria out.

Horse mint and palm of crystal (Castor-bean) and bullnettle root boiled together will make a cure for swelling. Jest bathe de swollen part in dis hot tea.

Anvil dust and apple vinegar will cure dropsy. One tea cup of anvil dust to a quart of vinegar. Shake up well and bathe in it. It sure will cure de worse kind of a case.

God worked through Abraham Lincoln and he answered de prayers of dem dat was wearing de burden of slavery. We cullud folks all love and honor Abraham Lincoln's memory and don't you think we ought to?

I love to hear good singing. My favorite songs are: "Am I A Soldier Of The Cross," an "How Can I Live In Sin and Doubt My Savior's Love." I belongs to de Baptist church.

[1] Mrs. Easter Wells was interviewed by WPA field worker Mrs. Jessie R. Ervin at McAlester, Oklahoma, on 21 September 1937. Ervin's preliminary draft of the interview transcription is available as the typescript "Interview with Easter Wells (Ex-Slave, Aged 83, Colbert, Oklahoma.)" in the OHS Slave Narratives. The narrative was edited

and retyped at the Oklahoma City project headquarters on 14 October 1937 as "Easter Wells, Age 83, Colbert, Okla.," published here. This final draft, forwarded to Washington on 2 November 1937, is available in ribbon copy in the LC Slave Narratives and in carbon copy as item 350025 in the LC Slave Narratives Carbon Copies and in the OHS Slave Narratives. Stephens to Cronyn, 2 November 1937, WPA Notes on Interviews.

² The preliminary draft consistently renders "master" as "massa."

³ The preliminary draft consistently renders "mistress" as "miss."

⁴ This clearly is a reference to Bryan, the seat of Brazos County, Texas.

CHARLOTTE JOHNSON WHITE[1]

Age 88   *Fort Gibson, Oklahoma*

Near as I ever know, I was born in de year of 1850, away back in dem hills east of Tahlequah; the Cherokee folks called it de Flint District and old master Ben Johnson lived somewheres about ten miles east of the big Indian town, Tahlequah. Never did know jest where his farm was, and when de new towns of dis country spring up it make it dat much harder for me to figure out jest where he lived and where at I was born.

Don't know much about own folks either, 'ceptin' that my mother's name was Elasey Johnson and my pappy's name was Banjo Lastley, who one time lived 'round where Lenapah now is. Dere was one brother name of Turner Whitmire Johnson, and a half sister name of Jennie Miller Lastley, who is still living down in Muskogee, but brother Turner been dead most 40 year ago I guess. Pappy was belonging to another master, that's how come my folks' name was different, but I kept the old Johnson name, even though the old master was the meanest kind of a man.

His wife, Mistress Anna, died when one of their children was born; maybe dat's why he was so mean, jest worried all de time. De master lived in a double log house, with a double fireplace in de middle of two rooms, and I was one of de girls who stayed in de house to take care of dere children. How many children dey had I never remember and I don't remember dere names, but dey was all pretty mean, like de master and de overseer dat drive the folks who work in de field.

The cabin where I live wid my mother was a two-room log house havin' two doors dat open right into de yard. Dere was no gallery on the slave cabins and no windows, so the corners of the rooms get dark early and sometime I get pretty scared before mother got in from the fields in de evenin'. She be gone all de day and always leave me a big baked sweet potato on de board above the fireplace and dat I eat about noon for my dinner.

Dat was before I got big enough to work in de master's house and take care of de children. She always work in de fields; she was sick all de time, but dat didn't keep her out of de fields or the garden work. Sometimes she be so sick she could barely get out of the old wood bunk when de morning work call sound on de farm.

One day my mother couldn't get up and de old master come around to see about it, and he yelled, "Get out of dere and get yourself in de fields." She tried to go but was too sick to work. She got to de door alright; couldn't hurry fast enough for de old master though, so he pushed her in a little ditch dat was by the cabin and whipped her back wid the lash, den he reached down and rolled her over so's he could beat her face and neck. She didn't live long after dat and I guess de whippin's helped to kill her, but she better off dead than jest livin' for the whip.

Time I was twelve year old I was tendin' the master's children like what dey tell me to do, and den one day somehow I drop one of dem right by where de old master was burning some brush in de yard. "What you do that for?" he yelled, and while I was stoopin' to pick up de baby he grabbed me and shoved me into de fire! I sent into dat fire head first, but I never know how I got out. See this old drawn, scarred face? Dat's what I got from de fire, and inside my lips is burned off, and my back is scarred wid lashings dat'll be wid me when I meet my Jesus!

Dem things help me remember about de slave days and how once when I got sick of being treated mean by everybody after mother died, I slipped off in de woods to get away and wandered 'round 'til I come to a place folks said was Scullyville. On de way I eat berries and chew bark from de trees, and one feed I got from some colored people on de way.

But de old master track me down and dere I is back at de ol' farm for more whippin's. Den I was give away to my Aunt Easter Johnson, but she was a mean woman—mean to everybody. She had a boy six year ol'. Dat boy got to cryin' one day and she grabbed up a big club and beat her own chil' to death. Den she laughed about it! Like she was crazy, I guess. And the only thing was done to her was a lockin' up in de chicken house, endin' up wid a salt and pepper whippin'.

All de slaves wore cotton clo's in summer, wool jackets in de winter and brass-toed shoes made from de hide of some old cow dat wasn't no good milker anymore. I lost de first pair of shoes dey give me and had to go barefoot all dat winter. Out in a thicket I had seen a rabbit so I started after it, but took off my shoes and set dem down so's I could sneak up wid out making noise. Den I miss de rabbit and go back for de shoes but dey was nowhere I could find dem. When Master Johnson find out de shoes was lost I got another whippin'.

I hear about de slaves being free when maybe a hundred soldiers come to de house. Dey was a pretty sight settin' on dey horses, and de men had on blue uniforms wid little caps. "All de slaves is free" one of de men said, and after dat I jest told everybody, "I is a free Negro now and I ain't goin' to work for nobody!"

A long time after de war is over and everybody is free of dey masters, I get down to Muldrow, (Okla.) and dat's whar I join de church. For 58 year I belong to the colored Baptists and I learn dat everybody ought to be good while dey is livin' so's dey will have a better restin' place when dey die.

In 1891, I met a good man, Randolph White, and we got married. I still got some of the pieces or scraps of my weddin' dress, a cotton dress it was, wid lots of colors printed on it—wild colors like the Indians use to wear.

---

[1] WPA field worker Ethel Wolfe Garrison interviewed Mrs. Charlotte Johnson White at Fort Gibson, Oklahoma, probably sometime in the winter of 1937–38. On 1 February 1938 her fellow employee Craig Vollmer revised and typed her notes into a preliminary draft, "Interview with Charlotte Johnson White, Slave Born, Age 88, Rt. 1, Box 107, Fort Gibson, Oklahoma," available in the OHS Slave Narratives. At some later date the narrative was superficially edited and retyped into an intermediate draft, "Charlotte Johnson White, Age 88, Fort Gibson, Oklahoma," also available in the OHS Slave Narratives and published here. The Charlotte Johnson White narrative was never forwarded to Washington and has never before been published.

JOHN WHITE[1]

Age 121 Years   *Sand Springs, Okla.*

Of all my Mammy's children I am the first born and the longest living. The others all gone to join Mammy. She was named Mary White, the same name as her Mistress, the wife of my first master, James White.

About my pappy. I never hear his name and I never see him, not even when I was the least child around the old Master's place 'way back there in Georgia more'n one-hundred twenty years ago!

Mammy try to make it clear to me about my daddy. She married like the most of the slaves in them days.

He was a slave on another plantation. One day he come for to borrow something from Master White. He sees a likely looking gal, and the way it work out that gal was to be my Mammy. After that he got a paper saying it was all right for him to be off his plantation. He come a'courting over to Master White's. After a while he talks with the Master. Says he wants to marry the gal, Mary. The Master says it's all right if it's all right with Mary and the other white folks. He finds out it is and they makes ready for the wedding.

Mary says a preacher wedding is the best but Master say he can marry them just as good. There wasn't no Bible, just an old Almanac. Master White read something out of that. That's all and they was married. The wedding was over!

Every night he gets a leave paper from his Master and come over to be with his wife, Mary. The next morning he leaves her to work in the fields. Then one night Mammy says he don't come home. The next night is the same, and the next. From then on Mammy don't see him no more—never find out what happen to my pappy.

When I was born Mammy named me John, John White. She tells me I was the blackest "white" boy she ever see! I stays with her till I was eleven year old. The Master wrote down in the book when I was born, April 10, 1816, and I know it's right. Mammy told me so, and Master told me when I was eleven and he sold me to Sarah Davenport.

Mistress Sarah lived in Texas. Master White always selling and trading to folks all over the country. I hates to leave on account of Mammy and the good way Master White fared the slaves—they was good people. Mammy cry but I has to go just the same. The tears are on my face a long time after the leaving. I was hoping all the time to see Mammy again, but that's the last time.

We travels and travels on the stage coach. Once we cross the Big River (Mississippi) on the boat and pick up with the horses on the other side. A new outfit and we rides some more. Seems like we going to wear out all the horses before we gets to the place.

The Davenport plantation was way north of Linden, Texas, up in the Red River country. That's where I stayed for thirty-eight year. There I was drug through the hackles by the meanest master that ever lived. The mistress was the best white woman I ever knew but Master Presley used his whip all the time, reason or no reason, and I got scars to remember by!

I remembers the house. A heavy log house with a gallery clear across the front. The kitchen was back of the house. I work in there and I live in there. It wasn't built so good as the Master's house. The cold winds in the winter go through the cracks between the logs like the walls was somewheres else, and I shivers with the misery all the time.

The cooking get to be my job. The washing too. Washday come around and I fills the tub with clothes. Puts the tub on my head and walks half a mile to the spring where I washes the clothes. Sometimes I run out of soap. Then I make ash soap right by the spring. I learns to be careful about streaks in the clothes. I learns by the bull whip. One day the Master finds a soapy streak in his shirt. Then he finds me.

The Military Road goes by the place and the Master drives me down the road and ties me to a tree. First he tears off the old shirt and then he throws the bull whip to me. When he is tired of beating me more torture is a-coming. The salt water cure. It don't cure nothing but that's what the white folks called it. "Here's at you," the Master say, and slap the salt water into the bleeding cuts. "Here's at you!" The blisters burst every time he slap me with the brine.

Then I was loosened to stagger back into the kitchen. The Mistress couldn't do nothing about it 'cept to lay on the grease thick, with a kind word to help stop the misery.

Ration time was Saturday night. Every slave get enough fat pork, corn meal and such to last out the week. I reckon the Master figure it to the last bite because they was no leavings over. Most likely the shortage catch them!

Sometimes they'd borrow, sometimes I'd slip somethings from out the kitchen. The single women folks was bad that way. I favors them with something extra from the kitchen. Then they favors me—at night when the overseer thinks everybody asleep in they own places!

I was always back to my kitchen bed long before the overseer give the get-up-knock. I hear the knock, he hear me answer. Then he blew the horn and shout the loud call, ARE YOU UP, and everybody know it was four o'clock and pour out of the cabins ready for the chores.

Sometimes the white folks go around the slave quarters for the night. Not on the Davenport plantation, but some others close around. The slaves talked about it amongst themselves.

After a while they'd be a new baby. Yellow. When the child got old enough for chore work the master would sell him (or her). No difference was it his own flesh and blood—if the price was right!

I traffic with lots of the women, but never marries. Not even when I was free after the War. I sees too many married troubles to mess up with such doings!

Sometimes the master sent me along to the grinding mill. Load in the yellow corn, hitch in the oxen, I was ready to go. I gets me fixed up with a pass and takes to the road.

That was the trip I like best. On the way was a still. Off in the bresh. If the still was lonely I stop, not on the way to but on the way back. Mighty good whiskey, too! Maybe I drinks too much, then I was sorry.

Not that I swipe the whiskey, just sorry because I gets sick! Then I figures a woods camp meeting will steady me up and I goes.

The preacher meet me and want to know how is my feelings. I says I is low with the misery and he say to join up with the Lord.

I never join because he don't talk about the Lord.[2] Just about the Master and Mistress. How the slaves must obey around the plantation—how the white folks know what is good for the slaves. Nothing about obeying the Lord and working for him.

I reckon the old preacher was worrying more about the bull whip than he was the Bible, else he say something about the Lord! But I always obeys the Lord—that's why I is still living!

The slaves would pray for to get out of bondage.[3] Some of them say the Lord told them to run away. Get to the North. Cross the Red River. Over there would be folks to guide them to the Free State (Kansas).

The Lord never tell me to run away. I never tried it, maybe, because mostly they was caught by patrollers and fetched back for a flogging—and I had whippings enough already!

Before the Civil War was the fighting with Mexico. Some of the troops on they way south passed on the Military Road.[4] Wasn't any fighting around Linden or Jefferson during the time.

They was lots of traveling on the Military Road. Most of the time you could see covered wagons pulled by mules and horses, and sometimes a crawling string of wagons with oxen on the pulling end.

From up in Arkansas come the stage coach along the road. To San Antonio. The drivers bring news the Mexicans just about all killed off and the white folks say Texas was going to join the Union.[5] The country's going to be run different they say, but I never see no difference. Maybe, because I ain't white folks.

Wasn't many Mexicans around the old plantation. Come and go. Lots of Indians. Cherokees and Choctaws. Living in mud huts and cabin shacks. I never see them bother the whites, it was the other way around.

During the Civil War, when the Red River was bank high with

muddy water, the Yankees made a target of Jefferson. That was a small town down south of Linden.[6]

Down the river come a flat barge with cannon fastened to the deck. The Yankee soldiers stopped across the river from Jefferson and the shooting started.

When the cannon went to popping the folks went a running—hard to tell who run the fastest, the whites or the blacks! Almost the town was wiped out. Buildings was smashed and big trees cut through with the cannon balls.

And all the time the Yankee drums was a-beating and the soldiers singing:

> We'll hang Jeff Davis on a sour apple tree,
> As we go marching on!

Before the Civil War everybody had money. The white folks, not the negroes. Sometimes the master take me to the town stores. They was full of money. Cigar boxes on the counter, boxes on the shelf, all filled with money. Not the crinkley paper kind, but hard, jingley gold and silver! Not like these scarce times!

After the War I stay on the plantation 'til a soldier man tells me of the freedom. The master never tell us—negroes working just like before the War.

That's when I leave the first time. Slip off, saying nothing, to Jefferson. There I found some good white folks going to New Orleans. First place we go is Shreveport, by wagon. They took me because I fix up with them to do the cooking.

On the Big River (Mississippi) and boards a river steamboat for New Orleans. Lots of negroes going down there—to work on the canal.

The whole town was built on logs covered with dirt. Trying to raise itself right out of the swamp. Sometimes the water get high and folks run for the hills. When I got there almost was I ready to leave.

I like Texas the best. Back to Jefferson is where I go. Fifteen—twenty mile below Linden. Almost the first person I see was Master Davenport.

He says, "Black rascal, you is coming with me." And I do. He tried to keep his slaves and just laugh when I tell him about the freedom. I worked for food and quarters 'til his meanness come cropping out again.

That wasn't long and he threatened me with the whip and the buck and gag. The buck and gag was maybe worse. I got to feeling that iron stick in my mouth, fastened around my head with chains, pressing hard on my tongue. No drinking, no eating, to talking!

So I slip off again. That night I goes through Linden. Crawling on my hands and knees! Keeping in the dark spots, hiding from the whites, 'til I pass the last house, then my feets hurries me to Jefferson, where I gets a ride to Arkansas.

In Russellville is where I stop. There I worked around in the yards, cutting the grass, fancying the flower beds, and earned a little money for clothes and eats, with some of it spent for good whiskey.

That was the reason I left Arkansas. Whiskey. The law got after me to tell where was a man's whiskey still. I just leave so's I won't have to tell.

But while I was making a little money in Russellville, I lose out on some big money, account some white folks beat me to it.

I was out in the hills west of town, walking along the banks of a little creek, when I heard a voice. Queer like. I called out who is that talking and I hears it again.

"Go to the white oak tree and you will find Ninety Thousand Dollars!" That's what I hear. I look around, nobody in sight, but I see the tree. A big white oak tree standing taller than all the rest 'round about.

Under the tree was a grave. An old grave. I scratch around but finds no money and thinks of getting some help.

I done some work for a white man in town and told him about the voice. He promised to go with me, but the next day he took two white mens and dug around the tree. Then he says they was nothing to find.

To this day I know better. I know wherever they's a ghost, money is around someplace! That's what the ghost comes back for.

Somebody dies and leaves buried money. The ghost watches over it 'til it sees somebody it likes. Then ghost shows himself—lets know he's around. Sometimes the ghost tells where is the money buried, like that time at Russellville

That ain't the only ghost I've seen or heard. I see one around the yard where I is living now. A woman. Some of these times she'll tell me where the buried money is.

Maybe the ghost woman thinks I is too old to dig. But I been a-digging all these long years. For a bite to eat and a sleep-under cover.

I reckon pretty soon she's going to tell where to dig. When she does, then old Uncle John won't have to dig for the eats no more!

[1] John White was interviewed by WPA field worker L. P. Livingston at Sand Springs, Oklahoma, probably in summer 1937. On 9 August 1937 project employee Craig Vollmer prepared a preliminary draft of White's remembrances based on Livingston's notes; it is available as the typescript "Interview with John White, 131 Oak St., Sand Springs" in the OHS Slave Narratives. The next day Ron Stephens, state administrator for the Oklahoma Writers' Project, wrote to the Tulsa office asking that the "best reporter" from the office return to reinterview White *"word for word."* In the meantime back in Oklahoma City, a final draft of the narrative was being prepared by other project employees, who may have been unaware that further interviewing of White had been requested. That initial final draft, "John White, Age 121 Years, Sand Springs, Okla.," was forwarded to Washington on 13 August 1937. It is available in ribbon-copy typescript filed with item 350016 in the LC Slave Narratives Carbon Copies and in the OHS Slave Narratives. Back in Tulsa, John White was revisited by a field worker, who indeed obtained more information with which to expand his narrative. Subsequently a second final draft of White's narrative was prepared and on 18 November 1937 sent to Washington project headquarters. This second final draft, published here, is available as "Revision of Story Sent in 8–13–37. John White, Age 121 Years, Sand Springs, Okla." in ribbon copy in the LC Slave Narratives and in carbon copy as item 350016 in the LC Slave Narratives Carbon Copies. Stephens to Lackey, 10 August 1937; Stephens to Cronyn, 13 August 1937; Craig Vollmer, Tulsa, Oklahoma, to Miss Churchill, [Oklahoma City, Oklahoma], 16 August 1937; Stephens to Alsberg, 18 November 1937; all in WPA Notes on Interviews.

The preliminary draft of the John White narrative contains below its title data the following information: *"Note:* This ex-slave was born April 10, 1816 (121 years ago), at Augusta, Georgia, on the plantation owned by James White, trader and planter."

[2] This sentence in the preliminary and first final drafts reads: "But he don't talk about the Lord."

[3] The preliminary and first final drafts at this point add the words "all during of the War."

[4] At this point the preliminary and first final drafts add the following three sentences: "Once I see the soldiers riding and marching on the road, going south. The white folks say they was going to fight the Mexicans. The battles was a long way off 'cause I never hear the fighting."

[5] At this point in the preliminary and first final drafts, this sentence reads: "Then folks say the Mexicans just about all killed off and the white folks was going to run the country."

[6] The general index to the 130-volume *The War of Rebellion: A Compilation of the Union and Confederate Armies* lists no fighting at Jefferson, Texas, suggesting that the informant confused Jefferson with another location in which there were hostilities. U.S., Department of War, *War of Rebellion.*

CHARLEY WILLIAMS[1]

Age 94 Yrs.   *Tulsa, Okla.*

Iffen I could see better out'n my old eyes, and I had me something to work with and de feebleness in my back and head would let me 'lone,

I would have me plenty to eat in de kitchen all de time, and plenty tobaccy in my pipe, too, bless God!

And dey wouldn't be no rain trickling through de holes in de roof and no planks all fell out'n de flo' on de gallery neither, 'cause dis one old nigger knows everything about making all he need to git along! Old Master done showed him how to git along in dis world, jest as long as he live on a plantation, but living in de town is a different way of living, and all you got to have is a silver dime to lay down for everything you want, and I don't git de dime very often.

But I ain't give up! Nothing like dat! On de days when I don't feel so feeble and trembly I jest keep patching 'round de place. I got to keep patching so as to keep it whar it will hold de winter out, in case I git to see another winter.

Iffen I don't, it don't grieve me none, 'cause I wants to see old Master again anyways. I reckon maybe I'll jest go up and ask him what he want me to do, and he'll tell me, and iffen I don't know how he'll show me how, and I'll try to do it to please him. And when I git it done I wants to hear him grumble like he used to and say, "Charley, you ain't got no sense but you is a good boy. Dis here ain't very good but it'll do, I reckon. Git yourself a little piece o' dat brown sugar, but don't let no niggers see you eating it—if you do I'll whup your black behind!"

Dat ain't de way it going be in Heaven, I reckon, but I can't set here on dis old rottendy gallery and think of no way I better like to have it!

I was a great big hulking buck of a boy when de War come along and bust up everything, and I can 'member back when everybody was living peaceful and happy, and nobody never had no notion about no war.

I was borned on the 'leventh of January, in 1843, and was old enough to vote when I got my freedom, but I didn't take no stock in all dat politics and goings on at dat time, and I didn't vote till a long time after old Master passed away, but I was big enough before de War to remember everything pretty plain.

Old Master was John Williams, and old Mistress' name was Miss Betty, and she was a Campbell before she married. Young Missy was named Betty after her mommy, and Young Master was named Frank, but I don't know who after. Our overseer was Mr. Simmons, and he was mighty smart and had a lot of patience, but he wouldn't take no talk nor foolishness. He didn't whup nobody very often, but he only had to whup 'em jest one time! He never did whup a nigger at de time the nigger done something, but he would wait till evening and have old Master come and watch him do it. He never whupped very hard 'cept when he had told a nigger about something and promised a whupping next time and the nigger done it again. Den that nigger got what he had been hearing 'bout!

De plantation was about as big as any. I think it had about three hundred acres, and it was about two miles northwest of Monroe, Louisiana. Then he had another one not so big, two–three miles north of the big one, kind of down in the woodsy part along the White river bottoms. He had another overseer on that place and a big passel of niggers, but I never did go down to that one. That was where he raised most of his corn and shoats, and lots of sorghum cane.

Our plantation was up on higher ground, and it was more open country, but still they was lots of woods all around and lots of the plantations had been whacked right out of de new ground and was full of stumps. Master's place was more open, though, and all in the fields was good plowing.

The big road runned right along past our plantation, and it come from Shreveport and run into Monroe. There wasn't any town at Monroe in them days jest a little cross roads place with a general store and a big hide house. I think there was about two big hide houses, and you could smell that place a mile before you got into it. Old Master had a part in de store, I think.

De hide houses was jest long sheds, all open along de sides and kivered over wid cypress clapboards.

Down below de hide houses and de store was jest a little settlement of one or two houses, but they was a school for white boys. Somebody said there was a place where they had been an old fort, but I never did see it.

Everything boughten we got come from Shreveport, and was brung in by the stage and the freighters, and that was only a little coffee or gunpowder, or some needles for the sewing, or some strap iron for the blacksmith, or something like dat. We made and raised everything else we needed right on the place.

I never did even see any quinine till after I was free. My mammy knowed jest what root to go out and pull up to knock de chills right out'n me. And de bellyache and de running off de same way, too.

Our plantation was a lot different from some I seen other places, like way east of there, around Vicksburg. Some of them was fixed up fancier but dey didn't have no more comforts than we had.

Old Master come out into that country when he was a young man, and they didn't have even so much then as they had when I was a boy. I think he come from Alabama or Tennessee, and way back his people had come from Virginia, or maybe North Carolina, 'cause he knowed all about tobacco on the place. Cotton and tobacco was de long crops on his big place, and of course lots of horses and cattle and mules.

De big house was made out'n square hewed logs, and chinked wid little rocks and daubed wid white clay, and kivered wid cypress clapboards. I remember one time we put on a new roof, and de niggers hauled up de cypress logs and sawed dem and frowed out de clapboards by hand.

De house had two setting rooms on one side and a big kitchen room on de other, wid a wide passage in between, and den about was de sleeping rooms. They wasn't no stairways 'cepting on de outside. Steps run up to de sleeping rooms on one side from the passageway and on de other side from clean outside de house. Jest one big chimbley was all he had, and it was on de kitchen end, and we done all de cooking in a fireplace dat was purty nigh as wide as de whole room.

In de sleeping rooms dey wasn't no fires 'cepting in braziers made out of clay, and we toted up charcoal to burn in 'em when it was cold mornings in de winter. Dey kept warm wid de bed clothes and de knitten clothes dey had.

Master never did make a big gallery on de house, but our white folks would set out in de yard under de big trees in de shade. They was long benches made out'n hewed logs and all padded wid gray moss and corn shuck padding, and dey set pretty soft. All de furniture in de house was home-made, too. De beds had square posts as big around as my shank and de frame was mortised into 'em, and holes bored in de frame and home-made rope laced in to make it springy. Den a great big mattress full of goose feathers and two—three comforts as thick as my foot wid carded wool inside! Dey didn't need no fireplaces!

De quarters was a little piece from de big house, and dey run along both sides of de road dat go to de fields. All one-room cabins, but dey was good and warm, and every one had a little open shed at de side whar we sleep in de summer to keep cool.

They was two or three wells at de quarters for water, and some good springs in de branch at de back of de fields. You could ketch a fish now and den in dat branch, but Young Master used to do his fishing in White River, and take a nigger or two along to do de work at his camp.

It wasn't very fancy at de Big House, but it was mighty pretty jest de same, wid de gray moss hanging from de big trees, and de cool green grass all over de yard, and I can shet my old eyes and see it jest like it was before de War come along and bust it up.

I can see old Master setting out under a big tree smoking one of his long cheroots his tobacco nigger made by hand, and fanning hisself wid his big wide hat another nigger platted [plaited] out'n young inside corn shucks for him, and I can hear him holler at a big bunch of white geese what's gitting in his flower beds and see 'em string off behind de old gander towards de big road.

When de day begin to crack de whole plantation break out wid all kinds of noises, and you could tell what going on by de kind of noise you hear.

Come de daybreak you hear de guinea fowls start potracking down at de edge of de woods lot, and den de roosters all start up 'round de barn and de ducks finally wake up and jine in. You can smell de sow belly frying down at the cabins in de "row," to go wid de hoecake and de buttermilk.

Den purty soon de wind rise a little, and you can hear a old bell donging 'way on some plantation a mile or two off and den more bells at other places and maybe a horn, and purty soon younder go old Master's old ram horn wid a long toot and den some short toots, and here come de overseer down de row of cabins, hollering right and left, and picking de ham out'n his teeth wid a long shiny goose quill pick.

Bells and horns! Bells for dis and horns for dat! All we knowed was go and come by de bells and horns!

Old ram horn blow to send us all to de field. We all line up, about seventy-five field niggers, and go by de tool shed and git our hoes, or maybe go hitch up de mules to de plows and lay de plows out on de side so de overseer can see iffen de points is sharp. Any plow gits broke or de point gits bunged up on de rocks it goes to de blacksmith nigger, den we all git on down in de field.

Den de anvil start dangling in de blacksmith shop: "Tank! Deling-ding! Tank! Deling-ding!" and dat old bull tongue gitting straightened out!

Course you can't hear de shoemaker awling and pegging, and de card spinners, and de old mammy sewing by hand, but maybe you can hear de old loom going "frump, frump," and you know it all right iffen your clothes do be wearing out, 'cause you gwine git new britches purty soon!

We had about a hundred niggers on dat place, young and old, and about twenty on de little place down below. We could make about every kind of thing but coffee and gunpowder dat our whitefolks and us needed.

When we needs a hat we gits inside cornshucks and weave one out, and makes horse collars de same way. Jest tie two little soft shucks together and begin plaiting.

All de cloth 'cepting de Mistress' Sunday dresses come from de sheep to de carders and de spinners and de weaver, den we dye it wid "butternut" and hickory bark and indigo and other things and set it wid copperas. Leather tanned on de place made de shoes, and I never see a store boughten wagon wheel 'cepting among de stages and de freighters along de big road.

We made purty, long back-combs out'n cow horn, and knitting needles out'n second hickory. Split a young hickory and put in a big wedge to prize it open, then cut it down and let it season, and you got good bent grain for wagon hames and chair rockers and such.

It was jest like dat until I was grown, and den one day come a neighbor man and say we in de war.

Little while young Master Frank ride over to Vicksburg and jine de Sesesh army, but old Master jest go on lak nothing happen, and we all don't hear nothing more until long come some Sesesh soldiers and take most old Master's hosses and all his wagons.

I bin working on de tobacco, and when I come back to de barns everything was gone. I would go into de woods and git good hickory and burn it till it was all coals and put it out wid water to make hickory charcoal for curing de tobacco. I had me some charcoal in de fire trenches under de curing houses, all full of new tobacco, and overseer come and say bundle all de tobacco up and he going take it to Shreveport and sell it befo' de soldiers take it too.

After de hosses all gone and most de cattle and de cotton and de tobacco gone, here come de Yankees and spread out all over de whole country. Dey had a big camp down below our plantation.

One evening a big bunch of Yankee officers come up to de Big House and old Master set out de brandy in de yard and dey act purty nice. Next day de whole bunch leave on out of dat part.

When de hosses and stuff all go old Master sold all de slaves but about four, but he kept my pappy and mammy and my brother Jimmie and my sister Betty. She was named after old Mistress. Pappy's name was Charley and mammmy's was Sally. De niggers he kept didn't have much work without any hosses and wagons, but de blacksmith started in fixing up more wagons and he kept them hid in de woods till they was all fixed.

Den along come some more Yankees, and dey tore everything we had up, and old Master was afeared to shoot at them on account his womenfolks, so he tried to sneak the fambly out but they kotched him and brung him back to de plantation.

We niggers didn't know dat he was gone until we seen de Yankees bringing dem back. De Yankees had done took charge of everything and was camping in de big yard, and us was all down at de quarters scared to death, but dey was jest letting us alone.

It was night when de white folks tried to go away, and still night when de Yankees brung dem back, and a house nigger come down to de quarters wid three—four mens in blue clothes and told us to come up to de Big House.

De Yankees didn't seem to be mad wid old Master, but jest laughed and talked wid him, but he didn't take de jokes any too good.

Den dey asked him could he dance and he said no, and dey told him to dance or make us dance. Dar he stood inside a big ring of dem mens in blue clothes, wid dey brass buttons shining in de light from de fire dey had in front of de tents, and he jest stood and said nothing, and it look lak he wasn't wanting to tell us to dance.

So some of us young bucks jest step up and say we was good dancers, and we start shuffling while de rest of de niggers pat.

Some nigger women go back to de quarters and git de gourd fiddles and de clapping bones made out'n beef ribs, and bring dem back so we could have some music. We git all warmed up and dance lak we never did dance befo'! I speck we invent some new steps dat night!

We act lak we dancing for de Yankees, but we trying to please Master and old Mistress more than anything, and purty soon he begin to smile a little and we all feel a lot better.

Next day de Yankees move on away from our place, and old Master start gitting ready to move out. We git de wagons we hid, and de whole passel of us leaves out for Shreveport. Jest left de old place standing like it was.

In Shreveport old Master git his cotton and tobacco money what he been afraid to have sent back to de plantation when he sell his stuff, and we strike out north through Arkansas.

Dat was de awfullest trip any man ever make! We had to hide from everybody until we find out if dey Yankees or Sesesh, and we go along little old back roads and up one mountain and down another, through de woods all de way.

After a long time we git to the Missouri line, and kind of cut off through de corner of dat state into Kansas. I don't know how we ever git across some of dem rivers but we did. Dey nearly always would be some soldiers around de fords, and dey would help us find de best crossing. Sometimes we had to unload de wagons and dry out de stuff what all got wet, and camp a day or two to fix up again.

Purty soon we git to Fort Scott, and that was whar de roads forked ever whichaways. One went on north and one east and one went down into de Indian country. It was full of soldiers coming and going back and forth to Arkansas and Fort Gibson.

We took de road on west through Kansas, and made for Colorado Springs.

Fort Scott was all run down, and the old places whar dey used to have de soldiers was all fell in in most places. Jest old rackety walls and leaky roofs, and a big pole fence made out'n poles sot in de ground all tied together, but it was falling down too.

They was lots of wagons all around what belong to de army, hauling stuff for de soldiers, and some folks told old Master he couldn't make us niggers go wid him, but we said we wanted to anyways, so we jest went on west across Kansas.

When we got away on west we come to a fork, and de best road went kinda south into Mexico, and we come to a little place called Clayton, Mexico whar we camped a while and then went north.

Dat place is in New Mexico now, but old Master jest called it Mexico. Somebody showed me whar it is on de map, and it look lak it a long ways off 'n our road to Colorado Springs, but I guess de road jest wind off down dat ways at de time we went over it. It was jest two or three houses made out'n mud at dat time, and a store whar de soldiers and de Indians come and done trading.

About dat time old Master sell off some of de stuff he been taking along, 'cause de wagons loaded too heavy for de mountains and he figger he better have de money than some of de stuff, I reckon.

On de way north it was a funny country. We jest climb all day long gitting up one side of one bunch of mountains, and all de nigger men have to push on de wheels while de mules pull and den scotch de wheels while de mules rest. Everybody but de whitefolks has to walk most de time.

Down in de valleys it was warm like in Louisiana, but it seem lak de sun ain't so hot on de head, but it look lak every time night come it ketch us up on top of one of dem mountains, and it almost as cold as in de winter time!

All de niggers had shoes and plenty warm clothes and we wrop up at night in everything we can git.[2]

[When we git to Colorado Springs we didn't know we was at de place, it was so little. I been thinkin' we gwine to a big place about like Shreveport, but it was little bitsy. Shreveport wasn't so big, but it was awful busy, with de boats and de tan yards and hide houses and de cotton barges and de traders, but Colorado Springs jest set there in de woods and dey wa'n't nothin' goin' on it seem like. . . .

We niggers pitch in an' build Ole Massa a good log cabin and us some cabins, too, wid de axes and froes we bring along, and den we fix a lot of traps all out in de woods and ketch varmints and dress de hides.

It too late in de yar to raise anythin' and pretty soon de winter come on and I never seen it so cold. Jes' de varmit hides and de money Old Massa had was all dat got us through de winter.

He put us out two three times to help people git dey crops in, and later on we helped some more clear up some new ground an' burn bresh, and den we done some wood choppin' dat he got paid for, and de rest de time we jest trapped and tried to keep warm.

He decide after dat winter dat he didn't want to put in no crop, an' we jest pull up and start back for Louisiana.

We went back jest about de same way we went out, and when we git to Kansas de Yankee soldiers was all over de place. Dey allus stop Ole Massa and squabble aroun' bout us niggers bein' wid him, an' bimeby he get some Yankee officers to sign up a paper sayin' we ain't his niggers but dat he jest takin' us back to Louisiana whar we come from. . . .

Well we git along right well] we git to Fort Scott again, and den de Yankee officers come and ask all us niggers iffen we want to leave old Master and stay dar and work, 'cause we all free now. Old Master say we can do what we please about it.

A few of de niggers stay dar in Fort Scott, but most of us say we gwine stay wid old Master, and we don't care iffen we is free or not.

When we git back to Monroe to de old place us niggers git a big surprise. We didn't hear about it, but some old Master's kinfolks back in Virginia done come out dar an fix de place up and kept it for him while he in Colorado, and it look 'bout as good as when we left it.

He cut it up in chunks and put us niggers out on it on de halves, but he had to sell part of it to git de money to git us mules and tools and found [sic] to run on. Den after while he had to sell some more, and he seem lak he git old mighty fast.

Young Master bin in de big battles in Virginia, and he git hit, and den he git sick, and when he come home he jest lak a old man he was so feeble.

About dat time they was a lot of people coming into dat country from de North, and dey kept telling de niggers dat de thing for dem to do was to be free, and come and go whar dey please.

Dey try to git de darkeys to go and vote but none us folks took much stock by what dey say. Old Master tell us plenty time to mix in de politics when de younguns git educated and know what to do.

Jest de same he never mind iffen we go to de dances and de singing and sech. He allus lent us a wagon iffen we want to borry one to go in, too.

Some de niggers what work for de white folks from de North act purty uppity and big, and come pestering 'round de dance places and try to talk up ructions among us, but it don't last long.

De Ku Kluckers start riding 'round at night, and dey pass de word dat de darkeys got to have a pass to go and come and to stay at de dances. Dey have to git de pass from de white folks dey work for, and passes writ from de Northern people wouldn't do no good. Dat de way de Kluckers keep the darkeys in line.

De Kluckers jest ride up to de dance ground and look at everybody's passes, and iffen some darkey dar widout a pass or got a pass from de wrong man dey run him home, and iffen he talk big and won't go home dey whop him and make him go.

Any nigger out on de road after dark liable to run across de Kluckers, and he better have a good pass! All de dances got to bust up at about 'leven o'clock, too.

One time I seen three—four Kluckers on hosses, all wrapped up in white, and dey was making a black boy git home. Dey was riding hosses and he was trotting down de road ahead of 'em. Ever time he stop and start talking dey pop de whip at his heels and he start trotting on. He was so mad he was crying, but he was gitting on down de road jest de same.

I seen 'em coming and I gits out my pass young Master writ so I could show it, but when dey ride by one in front jest turns in his saddle and looks back at tother men and nod his head, and they jest ride on by widout stopping to see my pass. Dat man knowed me, I reckon. I looks to see iffen I knowed de hoss, but de Kluckers sometime swapped dey hosses 'round amongst 'em, so de hoss maybe wasn't hisn.

Dey wasn't very bad 'cause de niggers 'round dar wasn't bad, but I hear plenty of darkeys git whopped in other places 'cause dey act up and say dey don't have to take off dey hats in de white stores and such.

Any nigger dat behave hisself and don't go running 'round late at night and drinking never had no trouble wid de Kluckers.

Young Mistress go off and git married, but I don't remember de name 'cause she live off somewhar else, and de next year, I think it was, my pappy and mammy go on a place about five miles away owned by a man named Mr. Bumpus, and I go 'long wid my sister Betty and brother Jimmie to help 'em.

I live around dat place and never marry till old mammy and pappy both gone, and Jimmie and Betty both married and I was gitting about forty year old myself, and den I go up in Kansas and work around till I git married at last.

I was in Fort Scott, and I married Mathilda Black in 1900, and she is 73 years old now and was born in Tennessee. We went to Pittsburg, Kansas, and lived from 1907 to 1913 when we come to Tulsa.[3]

Young Master's children writ to me once in a while and told me how dey gitting 'long up to about twenty year ago, and den I never heard no more about 'em. I never had no children, and it look lak my wife going outlive me, so my mainest hope when I goes on is seeing Mammy and Pappy and old Master. Old overseer, I speck, was too devilish mean to be thar!

'Course I loves my Lord Jesus same as anybody, but you see I never hear much about Him until I was grown, and it seem lak you got to hear about religion when you little to soak it up and put much by it. Nobody could read de Bible when I was a boy, and dey wasn't no white preachers talked to de niggers. We had meeting sometimes, but de nigger preacher jest talk about bein a good nigger and "doing to please de Master," and I allus thought he meant to please old Master, and I allus wanted to do dat anyways.

So dat de reason I allus remember de time old Master pass on.

It was about two years after de War, and old Master been mighty poorly all de time. One day we was working in de Bumpus field and a nigger come on a mule and say old Mistress like to have us go over to de old place 'cause old Master mighty low and calling mine and Pappy's and Mammy's name. Old man Bumpus say go right ahead.

When we git to de Big House old Master setting propped up in de bed and you can see he mighty low and out'n his head.

He been talking about gitting de oats stacked, 'cause it seems to him lak it gitting gloomy-dark, and it gwine to rain, and hail gwine to ketch de oats in de shocks. Some nigger come running up to de back door wid an old horn old Mistress sent him out to hunt up, and he blowed it so old Master could hear it.

Den purty soon de doctor come to de door and say old Master wants de bell rung 'cause de slaves should ought to be in from de fields, 'cause it gitting too dark to work. Somebody git a wagon tire and beat on it like a bell ringing, right outside old Master's window, and den we all go up on de porch and peep in. Everybody was snuffling kind of quiet, 'cause we can't help it.

We hear old Master say, "Dat's all right, Simmons. I don't want my niggers working in de rain. Go down to de quarters and see dey all dried off good. Dey ain't got no sense but dey all good niggers." Everybody around de bed was crying, and we all was crying too.

Den old Mistress come to de door and say we can go in and look at him if we want to. He was still setting propped up, but he was gone.

I stayed in Louisiana a long time after dat, but I didn't care nothing about it, and it look lak I'm staying a long time past my time in dis world, 'cause I don't care much about staying no longer only I hates to leave Mathilda.

But any time de Lord want me I'm ready, and I likes to think when He ready He going tell old Master to ring de bell for me to come on in.

[1] Charley Williams was interviewed by an unidentified WPA field worker in Tulsa, Oklahoma, probably sometime in summer 1937. His remembrances were prepared in typewritten form, with only the final version surviving today. This typescript, "Charley Williams, Age 94 Yrs., Tulsa, Okla.," published here, is available in ribbon copy in the LC Slave Narratives and in carbon copy in the LC Slave Narratives Carbon Copies and in the OHS Slave Narratives. In all of the known typescripts of this narrative, page 11 is missing. The final draft was forwarded to project headquarters in Washington on 13 August 1937. Benjamin A. Botkin, folklore editor for the Federal Writers' Project, was so impressed with the text of the Charley Williams interview that he published it in 1945 in *Lay My Burden Down* (109–18, 276). Stephens to Lackey, 10 August 1937; Stephens to Cronyn, 13 August 1937; both letters in WPA Notes on Interviews.

The Charley Williams narrative is one of the few from the WPA Oklaham Slave Narrative Project to have been published in Oklahoma. Writers' Project employee Robert Vinson Lackey passed a copy of the interview text together with a photograph of Williams and his granddaughter to journalist Ruth Sheldon, who edited the narrative for publication in the *Tulsa Tribune*. It appeared in that paper on 22 July 1937 under the title "Vivid Story of Slavery Told by Tulsa Negro, from Plantation Days to Passing of Ole Massa."

[2] At this point in the three surviving typescripts the missing page 11 begins. The following material presented in brackets is reprinted from Charley Williams, "Vivid Story of Slavery," 12.

[3] The interviewee is listed as the Reverend Charles H. Williams, residing with his wife, Matilda, at 1425 North Kenosha Avenue in the contemporary Tulsa city directories. *Polk's Tulsa City Directory, 1934,* 517, 598; *Polk's Tulsa City Directory, 1935,* 577, 664; *Polk's Tulsa City Directory, 1940,* 634, 737.

HULDA WILLIAMS[1]

Age 81   *Tulsa, Oklahoma*

My mammy use to belong to the Burns plantation back in old Mississippi; that was before I was born, but the white overseer, a man named Kelly, was my father, so my mammy always said. She stayed with the Burns' until her Master's daughter married a man named Bond and moved to Jefferson County, Arkansas, about 25 miles south of Little Rock. The Old Master give mammy and two other slaves to the girl when she married—that's how come mammy to be in Arkansas when I was born, in 1857. The record says July 18. Mammy was named Emmaline[2] and after she got to Arkansas she married one of the Bond slaves, George Washington Bond.

My step-father told me one time that Master Bond tell him to get some slippery-elm bark, but step-paw forget it. And it seem like the Master done forgot it too, but on the next Sunday morning he called out for step-pappy. "Come here," he said. "I'm going to give you a little piece of remembrance!" That was a good flogging, and some of the white neighbors look on and laugh.

But there was one slave, Boyl Green, who lived on a plantation nearby that my husband told me about after we was married. That Negro said he never would let nobody whip him. One day the Master got killing mad about something and told his overseer to bring in Boyl from the field. When he come in there was his Master waiting with a whip and gun. He handed the gun to the overseer and spoke to the slave, "Boyl, you're going to get a good whipping or a shooting—which you going have!"

Boyl he just look straight at his Master and said, "You never going whip me! Nobody going whip me!" The Master motion and the overseer raise the gun and shoot Boyl right through the heart—that's the way some Masters done.

My husband, Nason Bond, told me about his Uncle Cal, a man whose face was all mashed in, one-sided like, like maybe his jaw was done broken by the kick of a mule.

It seemed like Uncle Cal hated his Mistress, even after she died. She was buried by a willow tree 'longside of a road, and everytime

Cal would ride by the tree he would stop and swear at the grave some-thing awful. One day he sitting on his mule, cussing the woman buried by the tree, when some-thing smack him side of the head and he roll off the mule, nearly dead. Whatever hit him change his face—he went through life marked by the Spirits! . . . everybody said.

After my husband's brother buried his wife, the man was so sad and lonely he would go to her grave every evening and pray. One time in the middle of his prayer he heard a voice: "What are you doing here? This is a place for the dead! The living folks has no busi-ness here!" He jumped up and looked around, but there was nobody to see. He run from the grave and never went back no more for prayers.

During War times there was a concentration camp for the Slaves at Pine Bluff. We was in the camp; there was lots of guns and soldiers. The soldiers give each family one piece of wood every day for the camp fire, and just enough food stuff to keep the Negroes from starving. I remember my mammy would slip out at night and steal wood and scraps from the soldiers' kitchen. That's all I remember about the War—if I saw any battles I done forgot.

The young darkies these days says they are modern; sass their mammy, too. When I was raising up, the children mind their folks—my mammy was the boss, and she whip me for something when I was 27-year old! The girls nowadays strip their shoulders and bare their legs so's they can catch a man. That's the wrong way to live, and I'm glad I'm a Christian. It makes your heart soft and kind, makes you do good things, and it's the sacrificing of personal pleasure and time that please the Lord!

[1] Mrs. Hulda Williams was interviewed by WPA field worker L. P. Livingston in Tulsa, Oklahoma, probably sometime in the winter of 1937–38. Livingston's notes were revised into an intermediate draft by Craig Vollmer in the Tulsa office on 14 January 1938. This typescript, "Interview with Hulda Williams, Slave Born, Age 81, 1155 No. Lansing St., Tulsa, Oklahoma," is available in the OHS Slave Narratives. The Williams narrative apparently sat for several months until a final draft was prepared on 20 October 1938, but for reasons unknown that polished version was never sent on to project headquarters in Washington. The final draft, published here, is available only as the typescript carbon copy, "Hulda Williams, Age 81, Tulsa, Oklahoma," in the OHS Slave Narratives. It should be noted that the roughly contemporary Tulsa city di-rectories list the informant as Mrs. Hulda A. Williams, widow of Lewis (1934 edition) or Louis (1935 edition) Williams, residing at 1148 North Lansing Avenue in the city. *Polk's Tulsa City Directory, 1934,* 518, 600; *Polk's Tulsa City Directory, 1935,* 579, 666.
[2] The preliminary draft spells the name "Emaline."

INTERVIEW WITH ROBERT WILLIAMS[1]

Age About 87 Years   *Lives with Granddaughter, Auston Williams*
                              2500 Topeka Street, Muskogee, Oklahoma

I lay here in bed with the heart trouble and don't see no body but case workers. I get a pension from uncle Sam to keep my medicine. I got just a few more days on this earth the way I feel.

I was a great big boy when the Civil War was going on, so I remember some thing, but children didn't know like they do now. We wait and let the young folks talk, but in slave times they didn't. Cause I know they took me out of a town, but I dont know the name of it now, bin so long. Near as I can think, it was Pontoc, Mississippi.[2] I don't know where I was born; they didn't tell us children; then I remember when the war ceased, and when they was going marching to the war. But done forgot all the names.

My pappy was called Auston Williams and my maw was named Nancy. I was a little bit of a fellow when they took me away from them. I never did learn where they come from. The slave buyers carried my mother away from, we will call [it] Pontoc, my pappy stayed in that town some long time. I had one sister named Martha; the way I remember her, I was a bad boy [and] threw a rock and hit her in the face. They scared me about it; that's how I know. Master told me I had others but don't know no names.

I know old man John Myers was my master, and I was sold to Robert Williams, a white man. Master Williams told me one time I was sold several times; that's the reason I moved so much; I didn't know why I was moving around. He told me, Sanders and Dowel had bin my masters. I never did know what year I was born in but master said when I was a little baby my ears were froze off, so guess it was winter time.

In that Civil War I heard the pop pop of the guns at Cupalo;[3] don't know what state we was running in. The Yankees passed by on the way to Cupalo master said. They passed by a big elm tree, a cannon ball come from some where and hit that tree.

I remember when young Master Andrew Myers, and his coz. Joe Eddington went to town horse back one morning to war to fight the Yankees, they didn't come back.

I don't think Master had many slaves, just hired them to work. Me and a cook was all I remember. I stayed in a little room with the cook in master's three room house. He had three chimneys, called stack chimneys. Master Williams had home made beds of plank. Guess he was kinder poor. Master owned two small 40 acre farms, and had a slave family on one but I didn't see them. Master's house was made of square logs, had a hall in the middle and a long porch; on one end of the porch was boxed up; that's where I slept.

After we was free Master built a new house of weather boards. Even after freedom he owned a darky or two; I was one. He had three women darkeys, them Josephine, Ellen, Birt.

Master's girl was named Josephine, Ellen and Birt. Ellen was married during of the war, her man hid in a cellar in the day time to keep from going to the war. Frank Skinner, Josephine['s husband] went to the war and didn't come back, was killed she didn't know where. I didn't know if I had any grand parents or not. In slavery I chopped wood, cut logs, hewed them, made boards, chopped cotton and all the time as a child I picked up chips. Lord a mercy, child, I never earned a dime in slave time, but you could buy as much for a dime as now for fifty cents. My master didn't have no stove, cooked on the fire place using a skillet and lid and pot hung down from the top of the fire place to boil in.

I remember my mother one time cooking bread on the ground, called them biscuits ash cakes. She would rake out fire and ashes, brush the ground clean, then cover the dough up with ashes and fire and let it cook; saw her wipe it off with her dress tail.

In slave times I hunted down many coon and fox to eat and save the hides [to] make clothes out of them, caps and jackets. Master and all eat the rabbits. When my mother was carried away Pappy married again. My step maw had a cake made, the first one I ever saw; it was in a box. I ate that cake. My pappy whipped me hard for that. My father raised a large garden for my master. Seems like old master lived years after the war. In slave time Negro and white children went in their shirt tails because I saw white boys.

When I was coming up I spun my four cuts of cloth every day I worked. I wore home spun cloth pants made by my mistress and the slave women. We had different colors of striped and solid color cloth. One time I had a pair of yellow pants; these was dyed with dock root because I got the weed. We had colors, gray, blue, and so on. Most of our clothes was white. I bin married since I was about twenty years old but not to the same woman, that's a long time. My first wife was Rilla; my boy is Robert, the girls was Anna, Irena, Sofa. Then my wife Manda's child was named Irene. I forgot the other wife's name, but the last one is name Sofa; she is here in Muskogee now some where. We didn't have no children. Any way I got two living some

where. My master didn't have no overseer, just a white man on the
other farm looked after the work. Some one told me I was sold with
a girl one time, said they stood us up in a row and had men looking
at us, then bid us off. Got a big price for a fat woman; said she could
bring in good children. When we wasn't free, we started out; one old
Negro gentleman went in front walking, singing, praying, there was
wagons going from place to place like lost cattle. The white people
was ahead of us. I guess they knew but we didn't, some said they had
started to town to sell us. We would camp out, then master go to
town, get a buyer, he pick out the one he wanted then we start back.
I don't know the town name but think Pontoc. I know they got $500
for my head; they sold by the head them days. I heard of them being
chained together. Master said it was the run aways chained to keep
them. Colored people didn't have no school. White folks brought us
to their house. We didn't have no church; we met at different houses,
and turned over a pot to deaden the sound so master couldn't hear it;
he wanted us to sleep so we could work. In slave days we didn't know
nothing but work. My main preacher was named Jack Dent, a white
man. I bin here at Spalding bridge 13 years before a year ago I moved
to Muskogee; we lived right at the north end of the bridge and
farmed. I was a Deacon in my church as long as I had my health but
now I just pray and sing, God be with you till we meet again. I heard
slaves run away to the North because masters and mistress was mean
to them, but when they brought them back was tighter and tighter
on them. All the slaves played on Saturday nights that didn't have to
set up and work, like washing the children's clothes. Maybe some
Negro friend got a pass and come over. On Christmas we had a big
dinner.

So meny of the masters hired the slaves back after freedom. Some
left and worked for 25¢ and 50¢ a day; got more then for that than
we do now for $1.50. Old Master Williams sowed a wheat patch, so
when we was free we done like he did, we had a big horse that walked
on the wheat and thrashed it, the horse went around like when you
make sorghum. He trampled that wheat on a big sheet, then he wind
it, carry it to the mill. Made shorts, middlings, and flour, had a wood
barrel. When we wasn't raising hogs, buy enough grease to last many
days for a quarter. To make us be saving Pappy would bore a hole in
the barrel; then we got the flour out with a paddle. When we would
get flour for baking biscuits was Wednesday and Sunday morning.
The white folks sure learned us how to save. We saved all biscuit
crusts in slave days. Mistress did and when she got a big stack she call

all the niggers, give them the crusts; we was proud of them as we are cookies now. Mistress didn't have no teeth. When I wanted to get on the old pension roll I had my granddaughter write back to Martha Baker, a granddaughter of old Master at Shreveport, Louisiana, for my age. I write for my age by the size of Young Mistress the third girl. Baker was stroked with paralysis. My Master's Grandson was living, named Jud Williams of Louisiana, he made a affidavit saying I bin knowing him for 75 or 80 years.

My father was stroked for 10 years before he died at Spalding bridge; that's where we come to from Shreveport, Louisiana, town.

When I heard the white people say you are free to dig for your self, I didnt know what he meant.

When I got married first time, a white preacher married me; just went like you go to eat a meal and go to work.

Me and my wife rolled logs, split rails. The white people around give log rolling[s] them days. My wife roll them white men down. We toted logs; my wife done this; she was a stout woman. We make cat tail chimneys. We got 50¢ a hundred for chestnut rails, and they were 8 foot long. This was the years after the war.

When I was a child we walked the rail fences for playing. My Pappy had oxen and jenny, pappy whipped me for making the jenny try to go fast. The first train we saw was in Aklama; we drew in a ox wagon. We stopped in the woods and camped; the train was late and all we had time to see was the wooden rails; it took day and night to get home but we thought that great. I was nearly grown but I was scared. I heard minks barking like dogs. I heard Master talking about Abe Lincoln. He freed us, and I feel proud because he freed us. As a Deacon in the Rose Baptist Church I saw The Lord is above all of us.[4] He left it all plain so a fool can enter heaven if he can say in earnest "forgive me." We could be better than we is but disaster coming up makes us do wrong. I don't read or write but you can't fool me out of any thing, but I am going to write my name in the big book on high. Miss Grant, a W.P.A. teacher, comes here to teach me from her school. I know my a.b.c. That is about all I feel like talking; my breath is getting short but I thank you for coming to see me.

[1] WPA field worker Ethel Wolfe Garrison interviewed Robert Williams in Muskogee, Oklahoma, on 9 April 1938. On Federal Writers' Project letterhead stationery she prepared a handwritten rough draft of the interview, which is available as "Interview with Robert Williams, Exslave, Age About 87 Years, Lives with Granddaughter, Auston Williams, 2500 Topeka Street, Muskogee, Oklahoma" in the OHS Slave Narratives. On 6 June 1938 Garrison's coworker Craig Vollmer revised her notes into a very

considerably abridged typescript, "Interview with Robert Williams, Ex-Slave, Age About 87 Years, 2500 Topeka Street, Muskogee," also in the OHS Slave Narratives. Although the manuscript version of the narrative is unpolished, it is much fuller than the typescript and for that reason is published here, with extensive spelling and punctuation corrections. This narrative was never forwarded to Washington.

Robert Williams is listed in a roughly contemporary Muskogee city directory as a farmer living with his wife, Sophie, at 2425 Topeka Avenue. His is the only household listed on either side of this block of Topeka Avenue in the semirural setting. *Polk's Muskogee City Directory, 1932*, 200, 273.

2 This is most likely phonetic spelling for Pontotoc, the seat of Pontotoc County, Mississippi.

3 An apparent reference to Tupelo, Mississippi, a few miles east of Pontotoc and the scene of fighting in mid-July 1864.

4 The church referred to here was the Little Rose Baptist Church, 706 North 26th in Muskogee. *Polk's Muskogee City Directory, 1932*, 126, 286.

CHARLES WILLIS, EX-SLAVE[1]
Oklahoma City, Oklahoma

I found Mr. Willis seated on the front porch eating lemon drops out of a bag. He consumed the whole bag during the interview which lasted about 3 hours. He talked slowly and between his sucks on the lemon drops. He is hard of hearing and is losing his eyesight. He possesses a good sense of humor. Talked incessantly about matrimony and pretty gals.

June 7, 1937

I was born in Lawrence County, Mississippi[2] on the Sharp Plantation. My missus' name was Sang Sharp and my mastah was name John Sharp.

My mastah had 10 or 12 slaves and we done very well. Jining our place, the folks owned hundreds of slaves and jest beat them nearly to death. Even beat blood outta their back. I was whipped once by the white folks. That one time was by my mistress and don't fergit she whipped me.

I never remembah having shoes on only in winter time. Ever body wore them jest in winter time less they was able to buy some.

We diden' work Sadday afternoon and Sundays and doing of dis time off and in evenin's off we would make money.

My mother was a right yeller woman. She worked in the fields jest like I done. When she stood up, her hair fell on the floor. I tuck hair after her. My mother died 28 years ago at 92 years of age. My father was sold befo' I could remember him.

I never got no learning cause I jest diden have no chance. My mastah and mistress was old folks and diden have no chillun young 'nuf to go to school.

I was 15 years old when the war started. I remember ever thing 'bout that war. In fact I remembers ever thing 'bout all slavery. Grant and Lee met in Richmond, Virginia. Grant was over the Union army an' Lee over the Yankees.

When the war was over, all mastah could say was the Yankees done freed you'all so you kin go where you wants. We stayed on 5 or 6 years and was paid 5 to 10 dollars per month and got room and board.

There wasn't a God's thing to old Jefferson Davis.[3] They wasn't nuthin' to him. He was s'posed to be president of the Rebels. He sho hid a lot to keep the niggers and soldiers from gittin' him. I think Booker T. Washington did the cullud folks a lotta good. He was a principal down in Alabama. I think Mr. Lincoln was all right. Nothing short about him. He said ever race should be free as far as the 'Merican flag rech [reach], and when he signed that proclamation, it was the bes' thing he ever done. He done more for us than any man done since Jesus lef'.

I was a mill boy. Had to ride a horse 5 or 6 miles. No steam mill lak today. Gins run all night ginning cotton.

Gals lak you was sold for seven or eight hundred dollars. The woman I married was sold for $800.

Mastah and mistress was our only bosses and over seers. We had to ask them to go to church doing of the week. They sildom whipped us and diden't 'low nobody else to whip us.

We went to the white folks' church and stayed on the church porch or out under the trees right by so we could hear. We sing old hymns we don't sing now. I am a Baptist and member of Tabernacle Baptist Church. I never seen no other 'nomination I cared anything 'bout.

We was let off Sadday at noon and could go to the fiddlin's and dance all night. You could hear the niggers dancin' a mile away. The same man called for us that called fer the white folks. He could sure call 'em too. We did the Back Step and Shuffle. The tunes was Egg Nog, Sugar and Beer and Natcha Under the Hill. I don't recollect none of the words of the tunes.

I married in February 1867. We moved to Oklahoma in 1891. My wife died in 1933. She was a good wife. My chillun is well read.

How old are you? Would you marry a man 90 years old? I would like to marry a nice gal wid a job, cause I had to quit even odd jobs 10 years ago. If you say so, we'll have a big dinner July 4th and be married. Come back and see me. Is this Monday? Come back Thursday and I'll tell all my other gals to stay 'way. Good bye, I gotta go in. Daughter, come give me a drink and take me in off the front porch.[4]

[1] Charles Willis was interviewed by WPA field worker Ida Belle Hunter in Oklahoma City probably in autumn 1938. From Hunter's interview notes a preliminary draft of Willis's narrative was prepared as the typescript "Interview with Charles Willis, Ex-Slave, 714 N.E. 4, Oklahoma City, Oklahoma" in the OHS Slave Narratives. On 4 November 1938 a slightly revised final draft was prepared, "Interview with Charles Willis, Ex-Slave, Oklahoma City, Oklahoma"; it is published here and also is available in the OHS Slave Narratives. The principal difference between these two drafts is that the latter includes at its beginning a note by Ida Belle Hunter from a slip of paper appended to the earlier draft. Neither version of the Willis narrative was sent to Washington.

[2] At this point in the preliminary draft Ida Belle Hunter added in handwriting "in 1844."

[3] The preliminary draft at this point has the following somewhat cryptic interlinear addition in Ida Belle Hunter's handwriting: "He just lived 117 miles north of me down in New Orleans. Did you ever hear of New Orleans? Well he lived there."

[4] The contemporary Oklahoma City directory lists Charles Willis as residing with Mrs. Leanna Combs, widow of Ernest Combs, at 714 Northeast Fourth. *Polk's Oklahoma City Directory, 1937,* 162, 801, 929.

SARAH WILSON[1]

Age 87 Yrs.							*Fort Gibson, Okla.*

I was a Cherokee slave and now I am a Cherokee freedwoman, and besides that I am a quarter Cherokee my own self. And this is the way it is.

I was born in 1850 along the Arkansas river about half way between Fort Smith and old Fort Coffee and the Skullyville boat landing on the river. The farm place was on the north side of the river on the old wagon road what run from Fort Smith out to Fort Gibson, and that old road was like you couldn't hardly call a road when I first remember seeing it. The ox teams bog down to they bellies in some places, and the wagon wheel mighty nigh bust on the big rocks in some places.

I remember seeing soldiers coming along that old road lots of times, and freighting wagons, and wagons what we all know carry mostly whiskey, and that was breaking the law, too! Them soldiers catch the man with that whiskey they sure put him up for a long tim, less'n he put some silver in they hands. That's what my Uncle Nick say. That Uncle Nick a mean Negro, and he ought to know about that.

Like I tell you, I am quarter Cherokee. My mammy was named

Adeline and she belong to old Master Ben Johnson. Old Master Ben bring my grandmammy out to that Sequoyah district way back when they call it Arkansas, mammy tell me, and God only know who my mammy's pa is, but mine was old Master Ben's boy, Ned Johnson.

Old Master Ben come from Tennessee when he was still a young man, and he bring a whole passel of slaves and my mammy say they all was kin to one another, all the slaves I mean. He was a white man that married a Cherokee woman, and he was a devil on this earth. I don't want to talk about him none.

White folks was mean to us like the devil, and so I jest let them pass. When I say my brothers and sisters I mean my half brothers and sisters, you know, but maybe some of them was my whole kin anyways, I don't know. They was Lottie that was sold off to a Starr because she wouldn't have a baby, and Ed, Dave, Ben, Jim and Ned.

My name is Sarah now but it was Annie until I was eight years old. My old Mistress' name was Annie and she name me that, and Mammy was afraid to change it until old Mistress died, then she change it. She hate old Mistress and that name too.

Lottie's name was Annie, too, but Mammy changed it in her own mind but she was afraid to say it out loud, a-feared she would get a whipping. When sister was sold off Mammy tell her to call herself Annie when she was leaving but call herself Lottie when she git over to the Starrs. And she done it too. I seen her after that and she was called Lottie all right.

The Negroes lived all huddled up in a bunch in little one-room log cabins with stick and mud chimneys. We lived in one, and it had beds for us children like shelves in the wall. Mammy used to help us up into them.

Grandmammy was mighty old and Mistress was old too. Grandmammy set on the Master's porch and minded the baby mostly. I think it was Young Master's. He was married to a Cherokee girl. They was several of the boys but only one girl, Nicie. The old Master's boys were Aaron, John, Ned, Cy and Nathan. They lived in a double log house made out of square hewed logs, and with a double fireplace out of rock where they warmed theirselves on one side and cooked on the other. They had a long front porch where they set most of the time in the summer, and slept on it too.

There was over a hundred acres in the Master's farm, and it was all bottom land too, and maybe you think he let them slaves off easy! Work from daylight to dark! They all hated him and the overseer too, and before slavery ended my grandmammy was dead and old Mistress was dead and old Master was mighty feeble and Uncle Nick had run away to the North soldiers and they never got him back. He run away once before, about ten years before I was born, Mammy say, but the Cherokees went over in the Creek Nation and got him back that time.

The way he made the Negroes work so hard, old Master must have been trying to get rich. When they wouldn't stand for a whipping he would sell them.

I saw him sell a old woman and her son. Must have been my aunt. She was always pestering around trying to get something for herself, and one day she was cleaning the yard he seen her pick up something and put it inside her apron. He flew at her and cussed her, and started like he was going to hit her but she just stood right up to him and never budged, and when he come close she just screamed out loud and run at him with her fingers stuck straight and jabbed him in the belly. He had a big soft belly, too, and it hurt him. He seen she wasn't going to be afraid, and he set out to sell her. He went off on his horse to get some men to come and bid on her and her boy, and all us children was mighty scared about it.

They would have hangings in Fort Smith courthouse, and old Master would take a slave there sometimes to see the hanging, and that slave would come back and tell us all scary stories about the hanging.

One time he whipped a whole bunch of the men on account of a fight in the quarters, and then he took them all to Fort Smith to see a hanging. He tied them all in the wagon, and when they had seen the hanging he asked them if they was scared of them dead men hanging up there. They all said yes, of course, but my old uncle Nick was a bad Negro and he said, "No, I ain't a-feared of them nor nothing else in this world," and old Master jumped on him while he was tied and beat him with a rope, and then when they got home he tied old Nick to a tree and took his shirt off and poured the cat-o-nine-tails to him until he fainted away and fell over like he was dead.

I never forget seeing all that blood all over my uncle, and if I could hate that old Indian any more I guess I would, but I hated him all I could already I reckon.

Old Master wasn't the only hellion neither. Old Mistress just as bad, and she took most of her wrath out hitting us children all the time. She was afraid of the grown Negroes. Afraid of what they might do while old Master was away, but she beat us children all the time.

She would call me, "Come here Annie!" and I wouldn't know what to do. If I went when she called "Annie" my mammy would beat me for answering to that name, and if I didn't go old Mistress would beat me for that. That made me hate both of them, and I got the devil in me and I wouldn't come to either one. My grandmammy minded the Master's yard, and she set on the front porch all the time, and when I was called I would run to her and she wouldn't let anybody touch me.

When I was eight years old, old Mistress died, and Grandmammy told me why old Mistress picked on me so. She told me about me being half Mister Ned's blood. Then I knowed why Mister Ned would say, "Let her alone, she got big blood in her," and then laugh. Young Mister Ned was a devil, too. When his mammy died he went out and "blanket married." I mean he brung in a half white and half Indian woman and just lived with her.

The slaves would get rations every Monday morning to do them all week. The overseer would weigh and measure according to how many in the family, and if you run out you just starve till you get some more. We all know the overseer steal some of it for his own self but we can't do anything, so we get it from the old Master some other way.

One day I was carrying water from the spring and I run up on Grandmammy and Uncle Nick skinning a cow. "What yo-all doing?" I say, and they say keep my mouth shut or they kill me. They was stealing from the Master to piece out down at the quarters with. Old Master had so many cows he never did count the difference.

I guess I wasn't any worse than any the rest of the Negroes, but I was bad to tell little lies. I carry scars on my legs to this day where Old Master whip me for lying, with a rawhide quirt he carry all the time for his horse. When I lie to him he just jump down off'n his horse and whip me good right there.

In slavery days we all ate sweet potatoes all the time. When they didn't measure out enough of the tame kind we would go out in the woods and get the wild kind. They growed along the river sand between where we lived and Wilson's Rock, out west of our place.

Then we had boiled sheep and goat, mostly goat, and milk and wild greens and corn pone. I think the goat meat was the best, but I ain't had no teeth for forty years now, and a chunk of meat hurts my stomach. So I just eats grits mostly. Besides hoeing in the field, chopping sprouts, shearing sheep, carrying water, cutting firewood, picking cotton and sewing I was the one they picked to work Mistress' little garden where she raised things from seed they got in Fort Smith. Green peas and beans and radishes and things like that. If we raised a good garden she give me a little of it, and if we had a poor one I got a little anyhow even when she didn't give it.

For clothes we had homespun cotton all the year round, but in winter we had sheep skin jacket with the wool left on the inside. Sometimes sheep skin shoes with the wool on the inside and sometimes real cow leather shoes with wood peggings for winter, but always barefooted in summer, all the men and women too.

Lord, I never earned a dime of money in slave days for myself but plenty for the old Master. He would send us out to work the neighbor's field and he got paid for it, but we never did see any money.

I remember the first money I ever did see. It was a little while after we was free, and I found a greenback in the road at Fort Gibson and I didn't know what it was. Mammy said it was money and grabbed for it, but I was still a hell cat and I run with it. I went to the little sutler store and laid it down and pointed to a pitcher I been wanting. The man took the money and give me the pitcher, but I don't know to this day how much money it was and how much was the pitcher, but I still got that pitcher put away. It's all blue and white stripedy.

Most of the work I done off the plantation was sewing. I learned from my Granny and I loved to sew. That was about the only thing I was industrious in. When I was just a little bitsy girl I found a steel needle in the yard that belong to old Mistress. My mammy took it and I cried. She put it in her dress and started for the field. I cried so old Mistress found out why and made Mammy give me the needle for my own.

We had some neighbor Indians named Starr, and Mrs. Starr used me sometimes to sew. She had nine boys and one girl, and she would sew up all they clothes at once to do for a year. She would cut out the cloth for about a week, and then send the word around to all the neighbors, and old Mistress would send me because she couldn't see good to sew. They would have stacks of drawers, shirts, pants and some dresses all cut out to sew up.

I was the only Negro that would set there and sew in that bunch of women, and they always talked to me nice and when they eat I get part of it too, out in the kitchen.

One Negro girl, Eula Davis, had a mistress sent her too, one time, but she wouldn't sew. She didn't like me because she said I was too white and she played off to spite the white people. She got sent home, too.

When old Mistress die I done all the sewing for the family almost. I could sew good enough to go out before I was eight years old, and when I got to be about ten I was better than any other girl on the place for sewing.

I can still quilt without my glasses, and I have sewed all night long many a time while I was watching Young Master's baby after old Mistress died.

They was over a hundred acres in the plantation, and I don't know how many slaves, but before the War ended lots of the men had run away. Uncle Nick went to the North and never come home, and Grandmammy died about that time.

We was way down across the Red river in Texas at that time, close to Shawneetown of the Choctaw Nation but just across the river on the other side in Texas bottoms. Old Master took us there in covered wagons when the Yankee soldiers got too close by in the first part of the War. He hired the slaves out to Texas people because he didn't make any crops down there, and we all lived in kind of camps. That's how some of the men and my uncle Nick got to slip off to the north that way.

Old Master just rant and rave all the time we was in Texas. That's the first time I ever saw a doctor. Before that when a slave sick the old women give them herbs, but down there one day old Master whip a Negro girl and she fall in the fire, and he had a doctor come out to fix her up where she was burnt. I remember Granny giving me clabber milk when I was sick, and when I was grown I found out it had had medicine in it.

Before freedom we didn't have no church, but slipped around to the other cabins and had a little singing sometimes. Couldn't have anybody show us the letters either, and you better not let them catch you pick up a book even to look at the pictures, for it was against a Cherokee law to have a Negro read and write or to teach a Negro.

Some Negroes believed in buckeyes and charms but I never did. Old Master had some good boys, named Aaron, John, Ned, Cy and Nat, and they told me the charms was no good. Their sister Nicie told me too, and said when I was sick just come and tell her.

They didn't tell us anything about Christmas and New Year though, and all we done was work.

When the War was ended we was still in Texas, and when old Master got a letter from Fort Smith telling him the slaves was free he couldn't read, and Young Miss read it to him. He went wild and jumped on her and beat the devil out of her. Said she was lying to him. It near about killed him to let us loose, but he cooled down after awhile and said he would help us all get back home if we wanted to come.

Mammy told him she could bear her own expenses. I remember I didn't know what "expenses" was, and I thought it was something I was going to have to help carry all the way back.

It was a long time after he knew we was free before he told us. He tried to keep us, I reckon, but had to let us go. He died pretty soon after he told us, and some said his heart just broke and some said some Negroes poisoned him. I didn't know which.

Anyways we had to straggle back the best way we could, and me and mammy just got along one way and another till we got to a ferry over the Red River and into Arkansas. Then we got some rides and walked some until we got to Fort Smith. They was a lot of Negro camps there and we stayed awhile and then started out to Fort Gibson because we heard they was giving rations out there. Mammy knew we was Cherokee anyway, I guess.

That trip was hell on earth. Nobody let us ride and it took us nearly two weeks to walk all that ways, and we nearly starved all the time. We was skin and bones and feet all bloody when we got to the Fort.

We come here to Four Mile Branch to where the Negroes was all setting down, and pretty soon Mammy died.

I married Oliver Wilson on January second, 1878. He used to belong to Mr. DeWitt Wilson of Tahlequah, and I think the old people used to live down at Wilson Rock because my husband used to know all about that place and the place where I was borned. Old Mister DeWitt Wilson give me a pear tree the next year after I was married, and it is still out in my yard and bears every year.

I was married in a white and black checkedy calico apron that I washed for Mr. Tim Walker's mother Lizzie all day for, over close to Ft. Gibson, and I was sure a happy woman when I married that day. Him and me both got our land on our Cherokee freedman blood and I have lived to bury my husband and see two great grandchildren so far.[2]

I bless God about Abraham Lincoln. I remember when my mammy sold pictures of him in Fort Smith for a Jew. If he give me my freedom I know he is in Heaven now.

I heard a lot about Jefferson Davis in my life. During the War we hear the Negroes singing the soldier song about hang Jeff Davis to a apple tree, and old Master tell about the time we know Jeff Davis. Old Master say Jeff Davis was just a dragoon soldier out of Fort Gibson when he bring his family out here from Tennessee, and while they was on the road from Fort Smith to where they settled young Jeff Davis and some more dragoon soldiers rid up and talked to him a long time. He say my grandmammy had a bundle on her head, and Jeff Davis say, "Where you going Aunty?" and she was tired and mad and she said, "I don't know, to Hell I reckon," and all the white soldiers laughed at her and made her that much madder.[3]

I joined the Four Mile Branch church in 1879 and Sam Solomon was a Creek Negro and the first preacher I ever heard preach. Everybody ought to be in the church and ready for that better home on the other side.

All the old slaves I know are dead excepting two, and I will be going pretty soon I reckon, but I'm glad I lived to see the day the Negroes get the right treatment if they work good and behave themselves right. They don't have to have no pass to walk abroad no more, and they can all read and write now, but it's a tarnation shame some of them go and read the wrong kind of things anyways.

¹ Mrs. Sarah Wilson was interviewed by WPA field worker Ethel Wolfe Garrison at Fort Gibson, Oklahoma, probably sometime in summer or autumn 1937. Her notes were revised and typed by Robert Vinson Lackey into an intermediate draft, "Interview with Sarah Wilson, Ex-Slave, Age 87 Years, Lives Four Miles East of Ft. Gibson, Okla., Route No. 1," available in the OHS Slave Narratives. This narrative was lightly edited and retyped into a final draft, "Sarah Wilson, Age 87 Yrs., Fort Gibson, Okla.," sent to Washington project headquarters on 18 November 1937 and published here. Typescripts of the final draft are available in ribbon copy in the LC Slave Narratives and in carbon copy as item 350017 in the LC Slave Narratives Carbon Copies and in the OHS Slave Narratives. Stephens to Alsberg, 18 November 1937, WPA Notes on Interviews.

For another, contemporary interview with this informant, see Sarah Wison, interview by H. L. Rummage at Fort Gibson, Oklahoma, 22 February 1937, Indian-Pioneer Papers, 11:492–93.

² Sarah Wilson and five of her children were enrolled by the Dawes Commission as freedmen members of the Cherokee Nation in the early 1900s, entitling them to land allotments. Cherokee Freedmen Census Cards, no. 60 (Sarah, Lelia, Thomas, Bertha, Allie, and Robert Wilson); Cherokee Freedmen Enrollment Application Testimony, file 60 (Sarah, Lelia, Thomas, Bertha, Allie, and Robert Wilson).

³ Jefferson Davis served as a young dragoon officer in the U.S. Army at Fort Gibson from 1833 to 1835. James Frederick Morgan, "Jefferson Davis: The Military Man and the Politician" (Master's thesis, California State University, Fullerton, 1974), 27–32; William Allen Shelton, "The Young Jefferson Davis, 1808–1846" (Ph.D. diss., University of Kentucky, 1977), 89–97.

INTERVIEW WITH ACEMY WOFFORD[1]

1713 Tamaroy St., Muskogee, Oklahoma

The folks say I'm about 100 years old but there's no way of me telling about that. I remember the master told me I was born on June 13, but I don't know what was the year. Maybe I know once, but not now, for the only things I remember now is about the master.

I mean my second master who brought me from somewhere in Mississippi to Texas. He was Doctor Hayes; the mistress was Malissa. She was mean, not like the master himself.

When the mistress got mad, and that was likely to happen most any time, the slaves got pretty rough handling. She would pick up anything close and let it fly. Buckets or stone jars, sticks or boards, didn't make no difference, just so's it was loose.

I didn't get around during the slave days. Just worked in the fields like a man and toted water to the master's house. It was a big log house and it seemed like somebody was always wanting water; I wear myself out keeping water in the house.

The night peace was told me, I prayed to the Lord. I was thankful. And then after the freed negroes got to leaving their old homes my husband left Mississippi and come to Texas for me. We stayed in Texas on a farm about four miles in the country from Midway.

My first son died during the last year of the war. About three years after the surrender my second son was born and I live with him now. His name is Enlow, same as his father who died December, 1925, in Muskogee.

That's all I know about slave times and when I tries to think more it brings a hurting in my head.

[1] Mrs. Acemy Wofford was interviewed in Muskogee, Oklahoma, by WPA field worker Ethel Wolfe Garrison probably in spring 1938. On 23 May 1938 her coworker Craig Vollmer edited her notes into a preliminary typescript entitled "Interview with Acemy Wofford, 1713 Tamaroy St., Muskogee, Oklahoma," available in the OHS Slave Narratives and published here. The Wofford interview remained in this stage of preparation and was never forwarded to Washington. Ethel Wolfe Garrison apparently misinterpreted the name of the street on which Mrs. Wofford lived, for she resided at 1713 Tamaroa Street in the home of Joseph, Henry S., and Anna Wofford. *Polk's Muskogee City Directory, 1932,* 202, 267.

TOM W. WOODS[1]

Age 83   *Alderson, Okla.*

Lady, if de nigger hadn't been set free dis country wouldn't ever been what it is now! Poor white folks wouldn't never had a chance. De slave holders had most of de money and de land and dey wouldn't let de poor white folks have a chance to own any land or anything else to speak of. Dese white folks wasn't much better off dan we was. Dey had to work hard and dey had to worry 'bout food, clothes and shelter and we didn't. Lots of slave owners wouldn't allow dem on deir farms among deir slaves without orders from de overseer. I don't know why, unless he was afraid dey would stir up discontent among de niggers. Dere was lots of "underground railroading" and I reckon dat was what Old Master and others was afraid of.

Us darkies was taught dat poor white folks didn't amount to much. Course we knowed dey was white and we was black and dey was to be respected for dat, but dat was about all.

White folks as well as niggers profited by emancipation. Lincoln was a friend to all poor white folks as well as black ones and if he could a'lived things would a'been different for ever'body.

Dis has been a good world to live in. I always been able to make a purty good living and de only trouble I ever had has been sickness and death. I've had a sight of dat kind of trouble. I've outlived two wives and eight children. I had 13 brothers and sisters and I was de oldest, and I'm de only one left.

I sits here at night by myself and gits to wondering what de good Lord is sparing me for. I reckon it's for some good reason, and I'd like to live to be a hundred if He wants me to. I'm not tired of living yet!

I was born in Florence, Alabama. My father's name was Thomas Woods and my mammy was Frances Foster. Mammy belonged to Wash Foster and father was owned by Moses Woods, who lived on an adjoining plantation. He worked for his Master ever' day but spent each night wid us. He walked 'bout a mile to his work ever' day.

Master Wash was a poor man when he married Miss Sarah Watkins of Richmond, Virginia. Her father was as rich as cream, he owned 7 plantations and 200 slaves to each plantation. When Master Wash and Miss Sarah got married her father give her 50 slaves. Ever'body said Miss Mary [*sic*] jest married Master Wash because he was a purty boy, and he sure was a fine looking man.

He was good and kind to all his slaves when he was sober, but he was awful crabbed and cross when he was drunk, and he was drunk most of de time. He was hard to please and sometimes he would whip de slaves. I remember seeing Master Wash whup two men once. He give 'em 200 lashes.

Miss Sarah was de best woman in de world. It takes a good woman to live wid a drunkard.

Two of the men ran away one time and was gone till dey got tired of staying away. Master Wash wouldn't let anyone hunt 'em. When dey finally come home he had dem strapped in stocks and den deir bodies bared to de waist and he sure did ply de lash. I guess he whupped 'em harder dan he would if he hadn't been so full of whisky.

He never did sell any of his slaves. He kept the 50 dat Miss Sarah's father give 'em and deir increase. He bought some ever' time dey had a sale. He owned two plantations and dey was about a hundred slaves on each one. Him and his family lived in town.

Me and a boy named John was sized and put to work when we was about nine or ten years old. We was so bad dey had to put us to work as dey couldn't do any thing else with us. We'd chase de pigs and ride de calves and to punish us dey made us tote water to de hands. Dey was so many hands to water dat it kept us busy running back and forth with de water. De next year dey put me to plowing and him to hoeing. We made regular hands from den on.

If we had behaved ourselves we wouldn't a' had to go to work till we was fourteen or fifteen anyway. Slave owners was awful good to deir nigger chaps for dey wanted 'em to grow up to be strong men and women.

Dey was about thirty children on our plantation. Two women looked after us and took care of us till our parents come in from de field. Dey cooked for us and always gave us our supper and sent us home to our parents for de night.

Our food was placed on a long table in a trough. Each child had a spoon and four of us eat out of one trough. Our food at night was mostly milk and bread. At noon we had vegetables, bread, meat and milk. He gave us more and better food than he did his field hands. He said he didn't want none of us to be stunted in our growing.

He bought our shoes for us but cloth for our clothes was spun and wove right there on de farm. In summer us boys wore long tailed shirts and no pants. I've plowed dat way many a day. We was glad to see it git warm in de spring so we could go barefooted and go wid out our pants.

Our overseers lived near de quarters and every morning about four o'clock dey'd blow a horn to wake us up. We knowed it meant to git up and start de day. We was in de field by de time we could see. We always fed our teams at night. We'd give 'em enough to keep 'em eating all night so we wouldn't have to feed 'em in de morning.

Master Wash Foster and his family lived in de finest house in Florence, Ala. It was a fine, large two-story house, painted white as nearly all de houses was in dem days. Dere was big gallery in front and back and a fine lawn wid big cedar and chestnut trees all 'round de house.

He had a fine carriage and a pair of spanking bays dat cost him $500 apiece. Old Monroe was his coachman and dey made a grand sight. Monroe kept de nickel plated harness and carriage trimmings shining and de team was brushed slick and clean and dey sure stepped out.

We lived on de plantation about eight miles from town and we liked for de family to come out to de farm. Dey was four children, Wash, Jack, Sarah and Sally, and dey always played with us. When dey come we always had a regular feast as dey children would eat wid us children. Dey had dishes though to eat out of. After dinner we would run and play Peep Squirrel. I think dey call it hide-and-seek now.

My mother was a regular field hand till Miss Sarah decided to take her into town to take care of her children. Dey all called her Frank instead of Frances. I used to get to go to town to visit my mother and we'd have glorious times I tell you.

We'd go out and gather hickory nuts, hazel nuts, pig nuts, and walnuts. We'd all set around de fire and eat nuts and tell ghost tales ever' night. Master Wash raised lots of apples too, and we had all that we wanted of dem to eat.

I saw lots of Yankee soldiers. Sherman and Grant's armies marched by our house and camped at Decatur, Ala. It took dem three days to pass. We wasn't afraid of dem.

In the second year of de war some Yankee soldiers come through and gathered up all de slaves and took us to Athens, Ala., and put us on a Government farm. We stayed dere till de end of de War. My father died jest before dey took us away.

My mother and us children were on de farm together and dey treated us all mighty good. We had plenty of good food and clothes.

Master Wash came to see us while we was on de Government farm. He was left in a bad shape and we was all sorry for him. A lot of his hands went back to him after de Surrender but we never did. Mother married another man named Goodloe and we all went to Arkansas, near Little Rock. Dis was his former home. I was about nineteen or twenty years old at this time.

I never went to school. My wife taught me how to read de Bible but I never learned to write. I have good eyesight. I guess dat is cause I never put dem out reading and going to moving picture shows.

When any of my family was sick I always sent for de doctor. We had a few of our own home remedies dat we used also. We boiled poke root and bathed in it for a cure for rheumatism.

A tea made from may apples was used for a physic.

[1] Tom W. Woods was interviewed by Mrs. Jessie Ervin at Alderson, Oklahoma, probably in the summer or autumn of 1938. From her field notes she prepared a preliminary draft of the Woods narrative entitled "Interview with Tom W. Woods, Ex-Slave, 83, Alderson, Okla.," available in the OHS Slave Narratives. This transcript was revised by project editors into the typescript "Tom W. Woods, Age 83, Alderson, Okla.," published here. Forwarded to Washington, this final draft is available in ribbon copy in the LC Slave Narratives and in carbon copy as item 350077 in the LC Slave Narratives Carbon Copies.

ANNIE YOUNG[1]

Age 86   *Oklahoma City, Okla.*

I was born in 1851, makes me 86 years old. I was born in Middle Tennessee, Summers County.[2] My mother was put on a block and sold from me when I was a child. I don't remember my father real good. Sister Martha, Sister Sallie, nor Sister Jane wasn't sold. But my brother John was. My mother's name is Rachel Donnahue. We lived in a log hut. The white folks lived in a frame white building sitting in a big grove yard. Old master owned a big farm.

We ate molasses, bread and butter and milk in wooden bowls and crumbled our bread up in it. Old master had big smokehouses of meat. Dey ate chickens, possums and coons, and my old auntie would barbecue rabbits for de white folks. We ate ash cakes too.

I washed dishes, swept de yard, and kept de yard clean wid weed brush brooms. I never earned no money. All de slaves had gardens, and chickens too. My auntie, dey let her have chickens of her own and she raised chickens, and had a chicken house and a garden down in de woods.

I remember in time of de War dey'd send me down in de woods to pick up chips and git wood. All de men had gone to de army. One morning and t'was cold dey sent me down in de woods and my hands got frostbitten. All de skin come off and dey had to tie my hands up in roasted turnips. Sallie she had gloves, and didn't get frostbitten. After my old master died, Master Donnahue was his name, his old son-in-law come to take over de plantation. He was mean, but my sister whipped him.

We had no nigger driver or overseer. We raised wheat, corn and vegetables, not much cotton, jest enough to spun de clothes out of.

At night when we'd go to our cabins we'd pick cotton from de seeds to make our clothes. Boys and girls alike wore dem long shirts slit up de side nearly to your necks. They'd have cornshuckings sometimes all night long. You see I didn't have no mother, no father, nobody to lead me, teach me or tell me, and so jest lived with anybody was good enough to let me stay and done what they did. They'd have log rollings, with all de whiskey dey could drink.

I remember going to church, de Methodist Church dey call it. We used to sing dis song and I sho did like it too:

> "I went down in de valley to pray,
> Studying dat good old way."

I been a Christian long before most of dese young niggers was born. My other favorites are:

> "Must Jesus Bear This Cross Alone."

and

> "The Consecrated Cross I'll Bear 'til
> Death Shall Set Me Free,
> Yea, There's a Crown for Everyone,
> And There's a Crown for Me."

Yes Lawd, there sho is.

One day a nigger killed one of his master's shoats and he catch him and when he'd ask him, "What's that you got there?" the nigger said, "A possum." De master said, "Let me see." He looked and seen it was a shoat. De nigger said, "Master it may be a shoat now, but it sho was a possum while ago when I put 'im in dis sack."

Dey didn't whip our folks much but one day I saw a overseer on another place. He staked a man down with two forked sticks 'cross his wrist nailed in de ground and beat him half to death with a hand saw 'til it drawed blisters. Den he mopped his back wid vinegar, salt and pepper. Sometimes dey'd drop dat hot rosin from pine knots on dose blisters.

When de Yanks come, business took place. I remember white folks was running and hiding, gitting everything dey could from de Yanks. Dey hid dey jewelry and fine dishes and such. Dose Yanks had on big boots. Dey'd drive up, feed dey hosses from old Master's corn, catch dey chickens, and tell old Master's cook to cook 'em, and they'd shoot down old Master's hogs and skin 'em.

De Yanks used to make my nephew drunk, and have him sing (dis is kind of bad):

> "I'll be God O'Mighty
> God Damned if I don't
> Kill a nigger,
> Oh Whooey boys! Oh Whooey!
> Oh Whooey Boys! Oh Whooey!"

I don't remember never seeing no funerals. Jest took 'em off and buried 'em. I remember dat old Master's son-in-law dat my sister whipped, he called hisself a doctor and he killed Aunt Clo. Give her some medicine but he didn't know what he was doing and killed her.

I married William Young and we had a pretty good wedding.

Married in Crittington County, Arkansas.[3] When I left Tennessee and went to Arkansas I followed some hands. You know after de War dey immigrated niggers from one place to another. I owned a good farm in Arkansas. I came out here some 42 years ago.

I have three daughters. Mattie Brockins runs a rooming house in Kansas City. Jessie Cotton lives right up de street here. Osie Olla Anderson is working out in North town.[4]

Well I think Abraham Lincoln is more than a type a man than Moses. I believe he is a square man, believe in union that every man has a right to be a free man regardless to color. He was a republican man. Don't know much 'bout Jeff Davis but I think Booker T. Washington was a pretty good man. He's a right good man I guess, but he is dead ain't he?

I can remember once my auntie's old Master tried to have her and she run off out in de woods and when he put those blood hounds or nigger hounds on her trail he catched her and hit her in de head wid something like de stick de police carry, and he knocked a hole in her head and she bled like a hog, and he made her have him. She told her mistress, and mistress told her to go ahead and be wid him 'cause he's gonna kill you. And he had dem two women and she had some chillun nearly white, and master and dey all worked in de fields side by side.

[1] Annie Young was interviewed by an unidentified WPA field worker in Oklahoma City probably sometime in summer or autumn 1937. From the interview notes a preliminary draft of her narrative was prepared as the typescript "Annie Young, Age 86 Yrs., Oklahoma City, Okla.," available in the OHS Slave Narratives. From this draft a final typescript was prepared and sent on 14 September 1937 to project headquarters in Washington. This final version, "Annie Young, Age 86, Oklahoma City, Okla.," is published here and is available in ribbon-copy typescript in the LC Slave Narratives and in carbon copy as item 350055 in the LC Slave Narratives Carbon Copies and in the OHS Slave Narratives. Stephens to Cronyn, 14 September 1937, WPA Notes on Interviews.

[2] Apparently a reference to Sumner County, Tennessee.

[3] Apparently a reference to Crittenden County, Arkansas.

[4] The contemporary Oklahoma City directory lists Mrs. Annie Young, the widow of William Young, as residing at 1304 Northeast Sixth, also the home of James and Elizabeth Gray. Jessie Cotton and her husband, Eli H. Cotton, a barber, lived at 1224 Northeast Sixth, only a block away, while Mrs. Ossie Anderson worked as a maid for Robert E. Garnett, a certified public accountant, and his wife and resided in servant's quarters behind their home at 2131 Northwest Sixteenth. *Polk's Oklahoma City Directory, 1937,* 35, 172, 271, 292, 821, 937, 982.

BIBLIOGRAPHY

Books, Articles, Theses, and Dissertations

Abel, Annie Heloise. *The American Indian as Participant in the Civil War.* Cleveland: Arthur H. Clark Co., 1919.

———. *The American Indian as Slaveholder and Secessionist: An Omitted Chapter in the Diplomatic History of the Southern Confederacy.* Cleveland: Arthur H. Clark Co., 1915.

———. *The American Indian under Reconstruction.* Cleveland: Arthur H. Clark Co., 1925.

Abernethy, Francis Edward. *Singin' Texas.* Dallas: E-Heart Press, 1983.

AF Encyclopedia of Textiles. 2d ed. Englewood Cliffs, N.J.: Prentice-Hall, 1972.

Agnew, Kelley. "Tragedy of the Goingsnake District: The Shoot-out at Zeke Proctor's Trial." *Chronicles of Oklahoma* 64 (Fall 1986): 90–99.

Aldrich, Gene. *Black Heritage of Oklahoma.* Edmond, Okla.: Thompson Book and Supply Co., 1973.

———. "A History of the Coal Industry in Oklahoma to 1907." Ph.D. diss., University of Oklahoma, 1952.

Allen, Virginia R. "Medical Practices and Health in the Choctaw Nation, 1831–1885." *Chronicles of Oklahoma* 48 (Spring 1970): 60–73.

Allen, William Francis, Charles Pickard Ware, and Lucy McKim Garrison. *Slave Songs of the United States.* Rpt. ed. New York: Peter Smith, 1929.

Andrews, Thomas F. "Freedmen in Indian Territory: A Post–Civil War Dilemma." *Journal of the West* 4 (July 1965): 367–76.

Bailey, M. Thomas. *Reconstruction in Indian Territory: A Story of Avarice, Discrimination, and Opportunism.* Port Washington, N.Y.: National University Publications Kennikat Press, 1972.

Ballard, Michael B. *A Long Shadow: Jefferson Davis and the Final Days of the Confederacy.* Jackson: University Press of Mississippi, 1986.

Banks, Dean. "Civil War Refugees from Indian Territory in the North." *Chronicles of Oklahoma* 41 (Autumn 1963): 286–98.

Bartholomew, Ed. *The Encyclopedia of Texas Ghost Towns.* Fort Davis, Tex.: privately printed, 1982.

Bass, Althea. *The Story of Tullahassee.* Oklahoma City: Semco Color Press, 1960.

Bearss, Edwin C. "The Civil War Comes to Indian Territory, 1861: The Flight of Opothleyohola." *Journal of the West* 11 (January 1972): 9–42.

Billington, Monroe. "Black Slavery in Indian Territory: The Ex-Slave Narratives." *Chronicles of Oklahoma* 60 (Spring 1982): 56–65.

Blassingame, John W. *The Slave Community: Plantation Life in the Antebellum South.* Rev. and enl. ed. New York: Oxford University Press, 1979.

———. *Slave Testimony: Two Centuries of Letters, Speeches, and Autobiographies.* Baton Rouge: Louisiana State University Press, 1977.

————. "Using the Testimony of Ex-Slaves: Approaches and Problems." *Journal of Southern History* 41 (November 1975): 473–92.

————, and John R. McKivigan, eds. *The Frederick Douglass Papers.* 5 vols. New Haven: Yale University Press, 1979–92.

Boatner, Mark Mayo, III. *The Civil War Dictionary.* New York: David McKay Co., 1959.

Botkin, B. A. *Lay My Burden Down: A Folk History of Slavery.* Chicago: University of Chicago Press, 1945.

————. "The Slave as His Own Interpreter." *Library of Congress Quarterly Journal of Current Accessions* 2 (July/September 1944): 37–63.

Brooks, Marian Stuart. "The History of the Indian Territory during the Civil War." Master's thesis, University of Oklahoma, 1917.

Brown, Sterling A. "On Dialect Usage." In *The Slave's Narrative,* by Charles T. Davis and Henry Louis Gates, Jr. New York: Oxford University Press, 1985.

Buice, Sammy David. "The Civil War and the Five Civilized Tribes: A Study in Federal-Indian Relations." Ph.D. diss., University of Oklahoma, 1970.

Burke, Francis Dominic. "A Survey of the Negro Community of Tulsa." Master's thesis, University of Oklahoma, 1936.

Campbell, Randolph B. *An Empire for Slavery: The Peculiar Institution in Texas, 1821–1865.* Baton Rouge: Louisiana State University Press, 1989.

Campbell, T. N. "Choctaw Subsistence: Ethnographic Notes from the Lincecum Manuscript." *Florida Anthropologist* 12 (March 1959): 9–24.

"Captain David L. Payne." *Chronicles of Oklahoma* 13 (December 1935): 438–56.

Carter, Dan T. *Scottsboro: A Tragedy of the American South.* Baton Rouge: Louisiana State University Press, 1979.

Chapman, Berlin B. "Freedmen and the Oklahoma Lands." *Southwestern Social Science Quarterly* 29 (September 1948): 150–59.

Clark, Carter Blue. "Opothleyahola and the Creeks during the Civil War." In *Indian Leaders: Oklahoma's First Statesmen,* edited by H. Glenn Jordan and Thomas M. Holm. Oklahoma City: Oklahoma Historical Society, 1979.

Cole, George S. *A Complete Dictionary of Dry Goods and History of Silk, Cotton, Linen, Wool and Other Fibrous Substances.* Rev. ed. Chicago: W. B. Conkey Co., 1892.

Coleman, Kenneth, and Charles Stephen Gurr. *Dictionary of Georgia Biography.* 2 vols. Athens: University of Georgia Press, 1983.

Cooper, W. M. *The Sacred Harp Revised and Improved.* Dothan, Ala.: W. M. Cooper & Co., 1909.

Crellin, John K., and Jane Philpott. *Herbal Medicine Past and Present.* Vol. 2, *A Reference Guide to Medicinal Plants.* Durham, N.C.: Duke University Press, 1990.

Crockett, Norman L. *The Black Towns.* Lawrence, Kans.: Regents Press of Kansas, 1979.

Crossley, Mildred McCraken. "A History of the Negro Schools of Oklahoma City." Master's thesis, University of Oklahoma, 1939.

Dagley, Asa Wallace. "The Negro in Oklahoma." Master's thesis, University of Oklahoma, 1926.

Dance, Daryl. "Wit and Humor in the Slave Narratives." *Journal of Afro-American Issues* 5 (Spring 1977): 125–34.

Danziger, Edmund J. "The Office of Indian Affairs and the Problem of Civil War Indian Refugees in Kansas." *Kansas Historical Quarterly* 35 (Autumn 1969): 257–75.

Davis, Charles T., and Henry Louis Gates, Jr. *The Slave's Narrative.* New York: Oxford University Press, 1985.

Davis, J. B. "Slavery in the Cherokee Nation." *Chronicles of Oklahoma* 11 (December 1933): 1056–72.

Davis, Lucinda. "Tulsa Negro Woman Who Was Slave to Creek Indian Family Relates Some of Experiences." [Edited by Ruth Sheldon.] *Tulsa Tribune,* 18 August 1937, 18.

Davis, William C. *Jefferson Davis: The Man and His Hour.* New York: Harper-Collins, 1991.

Dawson, Anthony. "'Niggers Wasn't Free Then and They Ain't Now,' Says 105-Year-Old Ex-Slave in Tulsa." [Edited by Ruth Sheldon.] *Tulsa Tribune,* 12 August 1937, 12.

Debo, Angie. *The Rise and Fall of the Choctaw Republic.* Norman: University of Oklahoma Press, 1934.

———. *The Road to Disappearance: A History of the Creek Indians.* Norman: University of Oklahoma Press, 1941.

———. *And Still the Waters Run.* Princeton, N.J.: Princeton University Press, 1940.

Douglass, Frederick. *Life and Times of Frederick Douglass Written by Himself.* New rev. ed. Boston: DeWolfe, Fiske & Co., 1892.

Dyer, Brainerd. "The Treatment of Colored Union Troops by the Confederates, 1861–1865." *Journal of Negro History* 20 (July 1935): 273–86.

Dyer, Frederick H. *A Compendium of the War of the Rebellion.* Des Moines, Ia.: Dyer Publishing Co., 1908.

Eaton, Rachel Caroline. *John Ross and the Cherokee Indians.* Chicago: University of Chicago Libraries, 1921.

Edwards, Florene Pauline. "Civil War and Reconstruction in Arkansas." Master's thesis, University of Oklahoma, 1930.

Ellsworth, Scott. *Death in a Promised Land: The Tulsa Race Riot of 1921.* Baton Rouge: Louisiana State University Press, 1982.

Escott, Paul D. "The Art and Science of Reading WPA Slave Narratives." In *The Slave's Narrative,* by Charles T. Davis and Henry Louis Gates, Jr. New York: Oxford University Press, 1985.

———. *Slavery Remembered: A Record of Twentieth-Century Slave Narratives.* Chapel Hill: University of North Carolina Press, 1979.

Fischer, LeRoy H. "The Honey Springs National Battlefield Movement." *Chronicles of Oklahoma* 47 (Spring 1969): 515–30.

Foreman, Carolyn Thomas. "Early History of Webbers Falls." *Chronicles of Oklahoma* 29 (Winter 1951–52): 444–83.

Foreman, Grant. "The California Overland Mail Route through Oklahoma." *Chronicles of Oklahoma* 9 (September 1931): 300–317.

————. *Down the Texas Road: Historic Places along Highway 69 through Oklahoma.* Historic Oklahoma Series, no. 2. Norman: University of Oklahoma Press, 1936.

————. *The Five Civilized Tribes.* Norman: University of Oklahoma Press, 1935.

Fort Pillow Massacre. U.S., 38th Cong., 1st sess., House Report no. 65 (serial set 1206). Washington, D.C.: Government Printing Office, 1864.

Franklin, Jimmie Lewis. *The Blacks in Oklahoma.* Norman: University of Oklahoma Press, 1980.

————. *Born Sober: Prohibition in Oklahoma, 1907–1959.* Norman: University of Oklahoma Press, 1971.

————. *Journey toward Hope: A History of Blacks in Oklahoma.* Norman: University of Oklahoma Press, 1982.

————. "That Noble Experiment: A Note on Prohibition in Oklahoma." *Chronicles of Oklahoma* 43 (Spring 1965): 19–34.

Freeman, Charles R. "The Battle of Honey Springs." *Chronicles of Oklahoma* 13 (June 1935): 154–68.

Fulkerson, Fred Grover. "Community Forces in a Negro District in Oklahoma City, Oklahoma." Master's thesis, University of Oklahoma, 1946.

Gaskin, J. M. *Black Baptists in Oklahoma.* Oklahoma City: Messenger Press, 1992.

Genovese, Eugene D. *Roll, Jordan, Roll: The World the Slaves Made.* New York: Pantheon Books, 1974.

George, Preston, and Sylvan R. Wood. *The Railroads of Oklahoma.* Railway and Locomotive Historical Society Bulletin no. 60. Boston: Railway and Locomotive Historical Society, 1943.

Halliburton, Janet. "Black Slavery in the Creek Nation." *Chronicles of Oklahoma* 56 (Fall 1978): 298–314.

Halliburton, R., Jr. "Origins of Black Slavery among the Cherokees." *Chronicles of Oklahoma* 52 (Winter 1974–75): 483–96.

————. *Red over Black: Black Slavery among the Cherokee Indians.* Westport, Conn.: Greenwood Press, 1977.

————. *The Tulsa Race War of 1921.* San Francisco: R and E Research Associates, 1975.

Harlan, Louis R. *Booker T. Washington in Perspective: Essays of Louis R. Harlan.* Edited by Raymond W. Smock. Jackson: University Press of Mississippi, 1988.

————. *Booker T. Washington: The Wizard of Tuskegee, 1901–1915.* New York: Oxford University Press, 1983.

Hedin, Raymond. "Muffled Voices: The American Slave Narrative." *Clio* 10 (Winter 1981): 129–42.

Hefley, Jimmy. "The Brooks-Baxter War." *Arkansas Historical Review* 14 (Summer 1955): 188–92.

Heitman, Francis R. *Historical Register and Dictionary of the United States Army from Its Organization, September 29, 1789, to March 2, 1903.* 2 vols. Washington, D.C.: Government Printing Office, 1903.

"Henry Starr's Career as Bandit Ends with Death in Cell: Bullet Wound in His Spine Proves Fatal." *Daily Oklahoman* (Oklahoma City), 23 February 1921, 2.

Hill, Mozell C. "The All-Negro Communities of Oklahoma: The Natural History of a Social Movement." *Journal of Negro History* 31 (July 1946): 254–68.

Holley, Mary Austin. *Texas.* Baltimore: Armstrong Plaskitt, 1833.

Horn, Stanley F. "Nashville during the Civil War." *Tennessee Historical Quarterly* 4 (March 1945): 3–22.

———, ed. *Tennessee's War, 1861–1865, Described by Participants.* Nashville: Tennessee Civil War Centennial Commission, 1965.

Hudson, Peter J. "Choctaw Indian Dishes." *Chronicles of Oklahoma* 17 (September 1939): 333–35.

Jackson, Neeley Belle. "Political and Economic History of the Negro in Indian Territory." Master's thesis, University of Oklahoma, 1960.

James, Parthena Louise. "Reconstruction in the Chickasaw Nation: The Freedmen Problem." *Chronicles of Oklahoma* 45 (Spring 1967): 44–57.

Jeltz, Wyatt F. "The Relations of Negroes and Choctaw and Chickasaw Indians." *Journal of Negro History* 33 (January 1948): 24–37.

Johnson, J. H. "Documentary Evidence of the Relations of Negroes and Indians." *Journal of Negro History* 14 (January 1929): 21–43.

Kensell, Lewis Anthony. "Phases of Reconstruction in the Choctaw Nation, 1865–1870." *Chronicles of Oklahoma* 47 (Summer 1969): 138–53.

Lackey, Vinson. *The Chouteaus and the Founding of Salina, Oklahoma's First White Settlement, 1796.* Tulsa: C. F. Neerman Co., 1939.

———. "New Springplace." *Chronicles of Oklahoma* 17 (June 1939): 178–83.

———. "Northeast Oklahoma's 'Mystery House' May Be Sam Houston's 'Wigwam on the Neosho.'" *Tulsa Tribune,* 18 August 1937, 24.

Lauderdale, Virginia E. "Tullahassee Mission." *Chronicles of Oklahoma* 26 (Autumn 1948): 285–300.

"Leads Them All: Oklahoma Cotton Captures First Prize at Paris." *Daily Oklahoman* (Oklahoma City), 2 February 1901, 1.

Lefler, Hugh Talmage, and Albert Ray Newsome. *The History of a Southern State: North Carolina.* 3d ed. Chapel Hill: University of North Carolina Press, 1973.

Lincoln University College and Theological Seminary Biographical Catalogue, 1918. Lancaster, Penn.: Press of the New Era Printing Co., 1918.

Littlefield, Daniel F., Jr. *Africans and Creeks: From the Colonial Period to the Civil War.* Westport, Conn.: Greenwood Press, 1979.

———. *Africans and Seminoles from Removal to Emancipation.* Westport, Conn.: Greenwood Press, 1977.

———. *The Cherokee Freedmen from Emancipation to American Citizenship.* Westport, Conn.: Greenwood Press, 1978.

———. *The Chickasaw Freedmen: A People without a Country.* Westport, Conn.: Greenwood Press, 1980.

———, and Lonnie E. Underhill. "Black Dreams and 'Free' Homes: The Oklahoma Territory, 1891–1894." *Phylon* (Atlanta) 34 (December 1973): 342–57.

———, and Lonnie E. Underhill. "Hildebrand's Mill near Flint, Cherokee Nation." *Chronicles of Oklahoma* 48 (Spring 1970): 83–94.

Litton, Gaston L. "The Principal Chiefs of the Cherokee Nation." *Chronicles of Oklahoma* 15 (September 1937): 253–70.

Loughridge, Robert McGill. "History of Mission Work among the Creek Indians from 1832 to 1888 under the Direction of the Board of Foreign Missions, Presbyterian Church in the U.S.A." N.d. Typescript, Library Division, Oklahoma Historical Society, Oklahoma City, Oklahoma.

———, and David M. Hodge. *English and Muskogee Dictionary Collected from Various Sources and Revised.* Philadelphia: Westminster Press, 1914.

McFadden, Marguerite. "The Saga of 'Rich Joe' Van." *Chronicles of Oklahoma* 61 (Spring 1983): 68–79.

McFeely, William S. *Frederick Douglass.* New York: W. W. Norton & Co., 1991.

McLoughlin, William G. "Red Indians, Black Slavery and White Racism: America's Slaveholding Indians." *American Quarterly* 26 (October 1974): 367–85.

McPherson, James M. *The Negro's Civil War: How American Negroes Felt and Acted during the War for the Union.* New York: Vintage Books, 1965.

Malcolm, John. "Colbert Ferry on Red River, Chickasaw Nation, Indian Territory." Edited by W. B. Morrison. *Chronicles of Oklahoma* 16 (September 1938): 302–14.

Mangione, Jerre. *The Dream and the Deal: The Federal Writers' Project, 1935–1943.* Boston: Little, Brown and Co., 1972.

Martindale, James Stanley. "The Bootlegger in Oklahoma City." Master's thesis, University of Oklahoma, 1950.

Maslowski, Peter. *Treason Must Be Made Odious: Military Occupation and Wartime Reconstruction in Nashville, Tennessee, 1862–65.* Millwood, N.Y.: KTO Press, 1978.

Mellon, James, ed. *Bullwhip Days: The Slaves Remember.* New York: Weidenfeld & Nicholson, 1988.

Meserve, John Bartlett. "Chief Allen Wright." *Chronicles of Oklahoma* 19 (December 1941): 314–21.

———. "Chief Lewis Downing and Chief Charles Thompson (Oochalata)." *Chronicles of Oklahoma* 16 (September 1938): 315–25.

———. "Chief Opothleyahola." *Chronicles of Oklahoma* 9 (December 1931): 439–53.

———. "The MacIntoshes." *Chronicles of Oklahoma* 10 (September 1932): 310–25.

———. "The Perrymans." *Chronicles of Oklahoma* 15 (June 1937): 166–84.

Miles, Mark Fisher. *Negro Slave Songs in the United States.* Ithaca, N.Y.: Cornell University Press for the American Historical Association, 1953.

"Minutes of the Meeting of the Board of Directors of the Oklahoma Historical Society." *Chronicles of Oklahoma* 18 (March 1940): 87–91.

Minutes of the Synod of Canadian of the Presbyterian Church in the United States of America. N.p., 1912.

Mitchell, Irene E. "Bloomfield Academy." Master's thesis, University of Oklahoma, 1953.

———, and Ida Belle Renken. "The Golden Age of Bloomfield Academy in the Chickasaw Nation." *Chronicles of Oklahoma* 49 (Winter 1971–72): 412–26.

Moore, Cherrie Adair. "William Penn Adair." *Chronicles of Oklahoma* 29 (Spring 1951): 32–41.

Morgan, James Frederick. "Jefferson Davis: The Military Man and the Politician." Master's thesis, California State University, Fullerton, 1974.

Morris, A. Suman. "Captain David L. Payne: The Cimarron Scout." *Chronicles of Oklahoma* 42 (Spring 1964): 7–25.

Morrison, W. B. "The Saga of Skullyville." *Chronicles of Oklahoma* 16 (June 1938): 234–40.

Moulton, Gary E. *John Ross, Cherokee Chief.* Athens: University of Georgia Press, 1978.

National Urban League. *A Studg {sic} of the Social and Economic Conditions of the Negro Population of Tulsa, Oklahoma.* [New York]: National Urban League, [ca. 1941].

———. *A Study of the Social and Economic Conditions of the Negro Population of Oklahoma City, Oklahoma.* New York: National Urban League, 1945.

Neal, John Randolph. *Disunion and Restoration in Tennessee.* Freeport, N.Y.: Books for Libraries Press, 1971.

Neilson, John C. "Indian Masters, Black Slaves: An Oral History of the Civil War in Indian Territory." *Panhandle-Plains Historical Review* 65 (1922): 42–54.

Nichols, Charles H. "Who Read the Slave Narratives?" *Phylon* 20 (Summer 1959): 149–62.

Nichols, Charles H., Jr. "Slave Narratives and the Plantation Legend." *Phylon* 10 (Fall 1949): 201–10.

Nichols, William W. "Slave Narratives: Dismissed Evidence in the Writing of Southern History." *Phylon* 32 (Winter 1971): 403–9.

O'Beirne, H. F., and E. S. O'Beirne. *The Indian Territory: Its Chiefs, Legislators and Leading Men.* St. Louis: C. B. Woodward Co., 1892.

Oklahoma City, Oklahoma, Negro City Directory, 1941–1942. Oklahoma City: Oklahoma City Negro Chamber of Commerce, 1941.

Overbeck, Ruth Ann. "Colbert's Ferry." *Chronicles of Oklahoma* 57 (Summer 1979): 212–23.

Patton, James Welch. *Unionism and Reconstruction in Tennessee, 1860–1869.* Chapel Hill: University of North Carolina Press, 1934.

Penkower, Monty Noam. *The Federal Writers' Project: A Study in Government Patronage of the Arts.* Urbana: University of Illinois Press, 1977.

Perdue, Charles L., Jr., Thomas E. Barden, and Robert K. Phillips, eds. *Weevils in the Wheat: Interviews with Virginia Ex-Slaves.* Charlottesville: University Press of Virginia, 1976.

Perdue, Theda. "Cherokee Planters, Black Slaves, and African Colonization." *Chronicles of Oklahoma* 60 (Fall 1982): 322–31.

———. *Nations Remembered: An Oral History of the Five Civilized Tribes, 1865–1907.* Westport, Conn.: Greenwood Press, 1980.

———. *Slavery and the Evolution of Cherokee Society, 1540–1866.* Knoxville: University of Tennessee Press, 1979.

Phoenix Directory of Muskogee and Muskogee County, 1921. Muskogee, Okla.: Phoenix Directory Co., 1921.

Polk's Muskogee (Oklahoma) City Directory, 1932. Kansas, City, Mo.: R. L. Polk & Co., 1932.

Polk's Oklahoma City Directory, 1923. Dallas, Tex.: R. L. Polk & Co., 1923.

Polk's Oklahoma City (Oklahoma County, Okla.) Directory, 1937. Kansas City, Mo.: R. L. Polk & Co., 1937.

Polk's Oklahoma City (Oklahoma County, Okla.) Directory, 1938. Kansas City, Mo.: R. L. Polk & Co., 1938.

Polk's Oklahoma City (Oklahoma County, Okla.) Directory, 1939. Kansas City, Mo.: R. L. Polk & Co., 1939.

Polk's Oklahoma City (Oklahoma County, Okla.) Directory, 1940. Kansas City, Mo.: R. L. Polk & Co., 1940.

Polk's Tulsa (Oklahoma) City Directory, 1929. Kansas City, Mo.: R. L. Polk & Co., 1929.

Polk's Tulsa (Tulsa County, Okla.) City Directory, 1934. Kansas City, Mo.: R. L. Polk & Co., 1934.

Polk's Tulsa (Tulsa County, Okla.) City Directory, 1935. Kansas City, Mo.: R. L. Polk & Co., 1935.

Polk's Tulsa (Tulsa County, Okla.) City Directory, 1940. Kansas City, Mo.: R. L. Polk & Co., 1940.

Polk's Tulsa (Tulsa County, Okla.) City Directory, 1944. Kansas City, Mo.: R. L. Polk & Co., 1944.

Polk's Tulsa (Tulsa County, Okla.) City Directory, 1947. Dallas, Tex.: R. L. Polk & Co., 1947.

Polk's Tulsa (Tulsa County, Okla.) City Directory, 1954. Dallas, Tex.: R. L. Polk & Co., 1954.

Porter, Kenneth Wiggins. *The Negro on the American Frontier.* New York: Arno Press and the New York Times, 1971.

Powell, William S. *The North Carolina Gazetteer.* Chapel Hill: University of North Carolina Press, 1968.

Pyles, Henry F. "Hoodoo 'Hand' Didn't Win Him His Gal, Just Got Him into Trouble, Ex-Slave Here Relates." [Edited by Ruth Sheldon.] *Tulsa Tribune,* 23 August 1937, 5.

Rampp, Lary C. "Negro Troop Activity in Indian Territory, 1863–1865." *Chronicles of Oklahoma* 47 (Spring 1969): 531–59.

———, and Donald L. Rampp. *The Civil War in the Indian Territory.* Austin, Tex.: Presidial Press, 1975.

Rawick, George P., ed. *The American Slave: A Composite Autobiography.* 41 vols. Westport, Conn.: Greenwood Press, 1972–79.

Redkey, Edwin S. *Black Exodus: Black Nationalist and Back-to-Africa Movements, 1890–1910.* New Haven: Yale University Press, 1969.

Richards, Eugene S. "Trends of Negro Life in Oklahoma as Reflected by Census Reports." *Journal of Negro History* 33 (January 1948): 38–52.

Rister, Carl Coke. *Land Hunger: David L. Payne and the Oklahoma Boomers.* Norman: University of Oklahoma Press, 1942.

Robinson, Edgar Sutton, ed. *The Ministerial Directory of the Ministers in "The Presbyterian Church in the United States" (Southern), and in "The Presbyterian Church in the United States of America" (Northern).* Oxford, Ohio: Ministerial Directory Co., 1898.

Roller, David C., and Robert W. Twyman, eds. *The Encyclopedia of Southern History*. Baton Rouge: Louisiana State University Press, 1979.

Rowe, Katie. "'I Seen Chillun Sold Off an' de Mammy Not Sold,' Former 'Slave Gel' Reminisces Here." [Edited by Ruth Sheldon.] *Tulsa Tribune*, 30 July 1937, 12.

Sameth, Sigmund. "Creek Negroes: A Study in Race Relations." Master's thesis, University of Oklahoma, 1940.

Savage, W. Sherman. "The Role of Negro Soldiers in Protecting the Indian Territory from Intruders." *Journal of Negro History* 36 (January 1951): 25–34.

Sekora, John, and Darwin T. Turner, eds. *The Art of Slave Narrative: Original Essays in Criticism and Theory*. [Macomb, Ill.]: Western Illinois University, 1982.

Sewell, Steve. "Amongst the Damp: The Dangerous Profession of Coal Mining in Oklahoma, 1870–1935." *Chronicles of Oklahoma* 70 (Spring 1992): 66–83.

Shannon, C. W. *Coal in Oklahoma*. Edited by C. L. Cooper. Oklahoma Geological Survey Bulletin no. 4. Norman, Okla.: Oklahoma Geological Survey, 1926.

Shelton, William Allen. "The Young Jefferson Davis, 1808–1846." Ph.D. diss., University of Kentucky, 1977.

Shirk, George H. *Oklahoma Place Names*. 2d ed, rev. and enl. Norman: University of Oklahoma Press, 1974.

Shirley, Glenn. *Belle Starr and Her Times: The Literature, the Facts, and the Legends*. Norman: University of Oklahoma Press, 1982.

Slater, Mary Ann. "Politics and Art: The Controversial Birth of the Oklahoma Writers' Project." *Chronicles of Oklahoma* 68 (Spring 1990): 72–89.

Slave Narratives: A Folk History of Slavery in the United States, from Interviews with Former Slaves. 17 vols. St. Clair Shores, Mich.: Scholarly Press, 1976.

Smallwood, James M. *Crossroads Oklahoma: The Black Experience in Oklahoma*. Stillwater, Okla.: Crossroads Oklahoma Project, Oklahoma State University, 1981.

Speck, Frank G. "The Creek Indians of Taskigi Town." *American Anthropological Association Memoirs* 2, part 2 (1907): 101–64.

Starling, Marion Wilson. *The Slave Narrative: Its Place in American History*. Boston: G. K. Hall and Co., 1981.

Swanton, John R. *The Indians of the Southeastern United States*. Bureau of American Ethnology Bulletin 137. Washington, D.C.: Government Printing Office, 1946.

———. "Religious Beliefs and Medical Practices of the Creek Indians." In *Forty-second Annual Report of the Bureau of American Ethnology to the Secretary of the Smithsonian Institution, 1924–1925*. Washington, D.C.: Government Printing Office, 1928.

———. "Social Organization and Social Usages of the Indians of the Creek Confederacy." In *Forty-second Annual Report of the Bureau of American Ethnology to the Secretary of the Smithsonian Institution, 1924–1925*. Washington, D.C.: Government Printing Office, 1928.

———, ed. "The Green Corn Dance." *Chronicles of Oklahoma* 10 (June 1932):170–95.

"Swing Low: Federal Theater of Oklahoma, Works Progress Administration." [Oklahoma City: Federal Theater Project, ca. 1940.] Mimeographed. "Fed. Theatre" vertical file, box 9. Federal Writers' Project Collection, Archives and Manuscripts Division, Oklahoma Historical Society, Oklahoma City, Oklahoma.

Teall, Kaye M. *Black History in Oklahoma: A Resource Book.* Oklahoma City: Oklahoma City Public Schools, 1971.

Thompson, Lawrence. "Works Office Aid Goes East as Reds Rally: Writers' Project Secretary Takes a 'Vacation.'" *Daily Oklahoman* (Oklahoma City), 27 May 1938, 12.

Tolson, Arthur L. *The Black Oklahomans: A History, 1541–1972.* New Orleans: Edwards Printing Co., 1974.

———. "The Negro in Oklahoma Territory, 1889–1907: A Study in Racial Discrimination." Ph.D. diss., University of Oklahoma, 1966.

U.S. Commissioner-General to the International Universal Exposition, Paris, 1900. *Report of the Commissioner-General for the United States to the International Universal Exposition, Paris, 1900.* 6 vols. U.S., 56th Cong., 2d sess., Sen. Doc. no. 232 (serial set 4055–4060). Washington, D.C.: Government Printing Office, 1901.

———. *The War of Rebellion: A Compilation of the Official Records of the Union and Confederate Armies.* 130 vols. Washington, D.C.: Government Printing Office, 1880–1901.

Vann, R. P. "Reminiscences of Mr. R. P. Vann, East of Webbers Falls, Oklahoma, September 28, 1932." Edited by Grant Foreman. *Chronicles of Oklahoma* 11 (June 1933): 838–44.

Vlach, John Michael. "The Shotgun House: An African Architectural Legacy." In *Common Places: Readings in American Vernacular Architecture,* edited by Dell Upton and John Michael Vlach. Athens: University of Georgia Press, 1986.

Walton-Raji, Angela Y. *Black Indian Genealogy Research: African American Ancestors among the Five Civilized Tribes.* Bowie, Md.: Heritage Books, 1993.

Wardell, Morris L. *A Political History of the Cherokee Nation, 1838–1907.* Norman: University of Oklahoma Press, 1938.

Warden's Oklahoma City Directory, 1913–1914. Oklahoma City: Warden Printing Co., Publishers, [ca. 1913].

Warren, Hanna R. "Reconstruction in the Cherokee Nation." *Chronicles of Oklahoma* 45 (Summer 1967): 180–89.

Washington, Nathaniel Jason. *Historical Development of the Negro in Oklahoma.* Tulsa: Dexter Publishing Co., 1948.

Watson, Mrs. Irwin A. "Creek Indian Burial Customs Today." *Chronicles of Oklahoma* 28 (Spring 1950): 95–102.

Webb, Walter Prescott, ed. *The Handbook of Texas.* 2 vols. Austin, Tex.: Texas State Historical Association, 1952.

Wellman, Paul I. *A Dynasty of Western Outlaws.* Garden City, N.Y.: Doubleday & Co., 1961.

Wideman, John Edgar. "Charles Chesnutt and the WPA Narratives: The Oral and Literate Roots of Afro-American Literature." In *The Slave's Narrative,* by Charles T. Davis and Henry Louis Gates, Jr. New York: Oxford University Press, 1985.

Williams, Charley. "Vivid Story of Slavery Told by Tulsa Negro, from Plantation Days to Passing of Ole Massa." Edited by Ruth Sheldon. *Tulsa Tribune,* 22 July 1937, 12.

Williams, Lee E., and Lee E. Williams II. *Anatomy of Four Race Riots: Racial Conflict in Knoxville, Elaine (Arkansas), Tulsa and Chicago, 1919–1921.* Jackson: University and College Press of Mississippi, 1972.

Willis, William S. "Divide and Rule: Red, White, and Black in the Southeast." *Journal of Negro History* 48 (July 1963): 157–76.

Wilson, Walt. "Freedmen in Indian Territory during Reconstruction." *Chronicles of Oklahoma* 49 (Summer 1971): 230–44.

Wingate, Isabel B., ed. *Fairchild's Dictionary of Textiles.* New York: Fairchild Publications, 1967.

Woodward, C. Vann. "History from Slave Sources." *American Historical Review* 79 (April 1974): 470–81.

"Wound Proves Fatal to Old Time Bad Man." *Indian Journal* (Eufala, Okla.), 24 February 1921, 1.

Wright, J. Leitch, Jr. *Creeks and Seminoles: The Destruction and Regeneration of the Muscogulge People.* Lincoln: University of Nebraska Press, 1986.

Wright, Mildred S. *Hardin County, Texas, Cemeteries.* Beaumont, Tex.: Southeast Texas Genealogical and Historical Society, 1976.

Wright, Muriel H. "American Indian Corn Dishes." *Chronicles of Oklahoma* 36 (Summer 1958): 155–66.

———. "Early Navigation and Commerce along the Arkansas and Red Rivers in Oklahoma." *Chronicles of Oklahoma* 8 (March 1930): 65–88.

———. "General Douglas H. Cooper, C.S.A." *Chronicles of Oklahoma* 32 (Summer 1954): 142–84.

———. "Historic Places on the Old Stage Line from Fort Smith to Red River." *Chronicles of Oklahoma* 11 (June 1933): 798–822.

———. "Notes on Colonel Elias C. Boudinot." *Chronicles of Oklahoma* 41 (Winter 1963–64): 382–407.

———. "Old Boggy Depot." *Chronicles of Oklahoma* 5 (March 1927): 3–17.

Wright, Peter Melton. "Fort Reno, Indian Territory, 1874–1885." Master's thesis, University of Oklahoma, 1965.

Yetman, Norman R. "The Background of the Slave Narrative Collection." *American Quarterly* 19 (Fall 1967): 534–53.

———. "Ex-Slave Interviews and the Historiography of Slavery." *American Quarterly* 36 (Summer 1984): 181–210.

———. *Voices from Slavery: Selections from the Slave Narrative Collection of the Library of Congress.* New York: Holt, Rinehart and Winston, 1970. Paperback edition available as *Life under the "Peculiar Institution": Selections from the Slave Narrative Collection.* New York: Holt, Rinehart and Winston, 1970.

Archival Sources

Library of Congress, Washington, D.C. Manuscript Division. U.S. Works Progress Administration. Federal Writers' Project. Slave Narratives.
Alabama. Vol. 1. Box A917.
Oklahoma. Vol. 13. Box A927.
Oklahoma. "Appraisal Sheets, A–Y" file. Box A905.

Oklahoma. Carbon Copies. Boxes A905–A906.

Oklahoma. "Non-Slave Narratives" file. Box A906.

National Archives and Records Administration, Fort Worth, Texas. U.S. Department of the Interior. Office of Indian Affairs. Dawes Commission.

Cherokee, Chickasaw, Choctaw, and Creek Freedmen Census Cards. Microcopy M1186.

Cherokee, Chickasaw, and Choctaw Freedmen Enrollment Application Testimony. Microcopy M1301.

National Archives and Records Administration, Washington, D.C.

U.S. Census of 1860. Texas. Manuscript Population Schedules. Microcopy M653.

U.S. Department of War. Army. Compiled Military Service Records for the 1st Kansas Colored Volunteer Infantry (79th U.S. Colored Infantry), 9th U.S. Cavalry, and 100th U.S. Colored Infantry.

Oklahoma Historical Society, Oklahoma City, Oklahoma. Archives and Manuscripts Division.

Federal Writers' Project Collection.

Indian-Pioneer Papers. 16 vols.

Slave Narrative Collection.

Oklahoma State Archives, Oklahoma City, Oklahoma. Oklahoma Department of Agriculture Biennial, Annual, Semiannual, Quarterly, and Financial Reports, box 1. Annual Reports for the Years Ended 30 June 1912, 1919, 1920, 1922, 1923, 1924, 1925, 1926, 1927.

INDEX

ACJ 7092